Publication Number 26

Duke University Commonwealth-Studies Center

Research on the Bureaucracy
of Pakistan

Volume One in the publication series of the
Program in Comparative Studies on Southern Asia

Duke University Commonwealth-Studies Center Publications

1. *The British Commonwealth: An Experiment in Co-operation among Nations,* by Frank H. Underhill   2. *South Africa: Economic and Political Aspects,* by Hector Menteith Robertson   3. *Some Comparative Aspects of Irish Law,* by Alfred Gaston Donaldson   4. *Economic Analysis and Policy in Underdeveloped Countries,* by P. T. Bauer   5. *The Higher Public Service of the Commonwealth of Australia,* by Howard A. Scarrow   6. *Economic Opinion and Policy in Ceylon,* by Henry M. Oliver, Jr.   7. *Problems of the New Commonwealth,* by Sir Ivor Jennings   8. *Commonwealth Perspectives,* by Nicholas Mansergh, *et al.*   9. *Evolving Canadian Federalism,* by A. R. M. Lower, F. R. Scott, *et al.*   10. *The Commonwealth Economy in Southeast Asia,* by T. H. Silcock   11. *Public Expenditures in Australia,* by B. U. Ratchford   12. *The American Economic Impact on Canada,* by Hugh G. J. Aitken, John J. Deutsch, W. A. Mackintosh, *et al.*   13. *Tradition, Values, and Socio-Economic Development,* edited by Ralph Braibanti and Joseph J. Spengler   14. *The Growth of Canadian Policies in External Affairs,* by Hugh L. Keenleyside, *et al.*   15. *Canadian Economic Thought: The Political Economy of a Developing Nation 1814–1914,* by Craufurd D. W. Goodwin   16. *Economic Systems of the Commonwealth,* edited by Calvin B. Hoover   17. *The Nigerian Political Scene,* edited by Robert O. Tilman and Taylor Cole   18. *Administration and Economic Development in India,* edited by Ralph Braibanti and Joseph J. Spengler   19. *Canada-United States Treaty Relations,* edited by David R. Deener   20. *Post-primary Education and Political and Economic Development,* edited by Don C. Piper and Taylor Cole   21. *Bureaucratic Transition in Malaya,* by Robert O. Tilman   22. *The West African Commonwealth,* by C. W. Newbury   23. *The Transfer of Institutions,* edited by William B. Hamilton   24. *Economic Enquiry in Australia,* by Craufurd D. W. Goodwin   25. *A Decade of the Commonwealth, 1955–1964,* edited by W. B. Hamilton, Kenneth Robinson, and C. D. W. Goodwin

Research on the Bureaucracy of Pakistan

*A critique of sources, conditions, and issues,
with appended documents*

Ralph Braibanti

Published for
The Program in Comparative Studies on Southern Asia
of the
Duke University Commonwealth-Studies Center
Duke University Press, Durham, N. C.
1966

© 1966, Duke University Press

Library of Congress Catalogue Card number 66–14888

Printed in the United States of America
by Kingsport Press, Inc., Kingsport, Tenn.

To
Officials of the Government of Pakistan
who, in the face of adversity, created a legal and
administrative order deserving of wider recognition.

Preface

The purpose of this essay is to identify, classify, and evaluate source materials for the study of the bureaucracy of Pakistan and to assess conditions for research there. To accomplish this, documents and other sources are fitted into a narrative dealing with the substantive problems of government. In the course of developing this narrative, the feasibility of subjects and directions for research are suggested as encouragement to further study of the political development of a major nation which heretofore has received little research attention. While the textual analysis sometimes becomes rather extended, the primary object of the essay remains that of ordering the public record issuance of Pakistan during the period from 1947 to 1965.

The study of bureaucracy and other aspects of government in some developing states is impeded by absence of established habits of official written exposition of governmental problems and by paucity or inaccessibility of ordered empirical data. Much social science investigation, accepting the face value of this generalization, fails to probe for documentary sources or, finding them, minimizes their relevance to the dynamics of political growth. In such circumstances, the primary means of research is contemporary observation and interview. These approaches, which reflect the contemporary social science propensity for immediacy of experience, are sometimes presumed to have greater validity than documentary materials. In fact, the first part of this generalization regarding absence of written sources is inapplicable to the group of developing states which share the traditions of the Indian Civil Service, i.e., India, Pakistan, Malaya, Burma, and Ceylon. For these states documentary and secondary sources for the study of the civil public bureaucracy, while perhaps not as voluminous as those found in mature constitutional systems, are fairly extensive.[1]

The second aspect of the generalization relating to relevance of written materials cannot be dismissed with quite as much certainty as can the question of volume of sources. The historiographic importance of such documentation needs no justification. Too much, however, cannot be expected of the written record which is no more than it appears, namely, a source of ideological aspiration rather than necessarily a record of accomplishment. When one searches primarily for *accomplishment* in a developing state like Pakistan, it is easy and perhaps justifiable to dismiss documentation as irrelevant. Yet recorded aspiration is a crucial source of ideology. This is especially so in the absence of both a legislative and a political process from whose performance and platforms contemporary thought may be distilled. In Pakistan, judicial judgments, episodic reports on various aspects of policy, ordinary government reports, and statutory instruments have been the primary, if not the exclusive, sources for ascertaining national aspiration. The documentary record is disenchanting only when there is expectation that aspiration is identical to reality. While not identical, the record is nonetheless relevant to reality because of both its divergence and congruence with it. Integration of the written record with other means of understanding governmental behavior may, then, provide a basis for ascertaining a further relevance which might not be discovered if the record were rejected out of hand. A system of ordering, describing, locating, and preserving the records of seventeen years of governmental tribulation, therefore, may be a useful first step in evaluating the bureaucratic system of Pakistan.

Despite the traumatic administrative and political conditions in Pakistan consequent to partition, the condition of public record

[1] For Malaya see documentation cited in Robert O. Tilman, *Bureaucratic Transition in Malaya* (Durham, N. C., 1964). On India, see Bernard S. Cohn, *The Development and Impact of British Administration in India* (New Delhi: Indian Institute of Public Administration, 1961). Indeed, the propensity for public record keeping seems to have followed British imperial rule along with a system of government in areas other than the subcontinent. For a suggestion of this with respect to an African state, for example, see documentation cited in Taylor Cole, "Bureaucracy in Transition: Independent Nigeria," *Public Administration*, XXXVIII (1960), 321–337.

issuance is of a high order when compared to that of other nations recently emerged from colonial status. There are indications that the research situation has stabilized and will probably further improve. On June 8, 1962, martial law, which had been declared on October 7, 1958, was ended and constitutional government restored. While it is obvious that this records the beginning of a new and significant chapter in the history of Pakistan, this date is also of importance for research. It marks the end of a period of nearly four years during which relative stability in government prevailed, albeit under the uneasy compulsion of martial law. During this period there was extensive publication of documentary materials and a relatively liberal policy regarding their accessibility and use. Paradoxically, the chief reasons for this somewhat felicitous state of affairs were direct consequences of martial law. First, because of their stringency and fear of their application, the latent power of martial law regulations compelled an attitude of caution and responsibility on the part of the public. This climate of moderation was enhanced by the absence of political parties and legislatures and by pre-censorship of the press. The consequent stability and outward calm relieved the bureaucracy of the burden of irresponsible, carping criticism and enabled administration to operate somewhat more publicly without fear of vicious political attack. Finally, the attitude of President Ayub was an important determinant of this new atmosphere. Although cloaked with the absolute powers of martial law, his influence in the direction of reason and common sense was able to suppress the seething animosities and destructive, irresponsible attacks which had clouded the atmosphere before 1958 and had led the nation to the brink of chaos. The relative calm began to deteriorate during the first few months of 1962 and it is not yet clear whether a political order can be continued under the new constitutional government, or whether the very existence of legislatures and openly operating political factions will re-create the conditions prevailing before martial law. Either way, the ultimate effect on research possibilities will be crucial.

For several reasons 1965 is a strategic juncture at which review and assessment of documentary materials issued since 1947 can be

made. Most of the seventeen years since independence have been
marked by such uncertainty that government has not been able
to restore completely to its pre-partition state of bibliographical
order the system of public record issuance which prevailed under
British imperial rule. Disarray in documentary classification and
accessibility which characterized the period from 1947 to 1958
has begun to be replaced by some regularity and consistency in
publication. It is likely that further stabilization and refinement
will follow, for the period of large-scale inquiry and exploration of
basic policy under martial law is over, and a period of consolidation and implementation has begun. The polity of the nation and
the structure of its government have been determined, put into
operation, and have successfully survived the national presidential
election of 1965 in which both polity and form were challenged.
Secondly, a systematic effort to procure documents and channel
them into the main currents of American scholarship has been
begun under provisions of the 1958 amendment to Public Law 480
(Section 104n of Public Law 85–931, An Act to Extend and Amend
the Agricultural Trade Development and Assistance Act of 1954).
Under terms of this program the Library of Congress and eighteen
university libraries receive virtually all government as well as
commercial publications printed in Pakistan, and three hundred
college libraries receive a few serial publications and books. This
development in itself marks the beginning of a new period of
rationalization of Pakistani source materials for which a record
of the past is vital. Thirdly, systematic research effort partly under
American guidance has begun in the Civil Service Academy, the
Administrative Staff College, the three institutes of public administration in Dacca, Karachi, and Lahore, and in the University
of the Panjab and will augment the pioneering work initiated as
early as 1954 by the Pakistan Planning Board and later by the two
academies for rural development at Peshawar and Comilla. This
research effort (except for that of the present Planning Commission) has been co-ordinated by the Establishment Division of the
President's Secretariat through a national council for research on
administration. Perhaps the stability, continuity, and efficiency of
this effort can be enhanced in a small way by a survey and classi-

fication of the documentation of the first decade and a half of Pakistan's history. The research interest and energy available in Pakistan probably will be adequate to record systematically research developments for the period beyond 1965. The present study is designed merely to fill the seventeen-year gap left untended by the pressure of other work. Thereby the superb, unbroken historiographic tradition developed under British rule may be carried across, however feebly and inadequately, from the trauma of independence in 1947 to the more hopeful years starting in 1964.

Some of the data and charts compiled for this study may appear to be inconsequential to anyone who has not done research on the government of a developing nation. It may be thought that such data are accessible in convenient form in government sources and hence can be easily transferred into a study of this kind. If that were the case in Pakistan, there would indeed be little need for this study. Unfortunately, however, the simplest and most elementary kind of information is not easily available and must be searched for sometimes over a period of several years. Two examples will illustrate this. The various efforts to reorganize the administration of government which are tabulated in Table 2 have not been listed either in government sources or elsewhere. Since many of the efforts were not published in the official *Gazette* and are not even mentioned in secretariat files, they can be learned about only by extensive interview, cross-checking, and in some cases by eventual discovery of documentary reference in an unsuspected source. Thus, the mere listing of a committee and the accurate citation of its establishment, which in the United States would entail merely a few minutes' reference to the *Federal Register, Congressional Digest*, or a query addressed to a member of Congress, involves in Pakistan relentless searching, a year or two of time and patience, and a measure of good luck. The same observations apply to data on government statutory corporations compiled in Table 4; it might be assumed that such data as the law creating them, the membership of their boards of directors, and the reports they submit would easily be found in some one location, perhaps in the Ministry of Finance. But such, in fact, is not the case. While there are partial lists, there is no complete source giving all pertinent data. With respect to the public service generally, even such basic data as the number of employees in government service are not available in figures which have a margin of error of less than 30 per cent.

The reasons for this state of affairs are not hard to find. The tradition of systematic publication of government documents was a legacy of British rule in 1947, but administrative conditions were not stable enough to permit purposeful continuance of the tradition, which necessarily gave way to more urgent tasks. Secondly, only a small group of officers (not more than two hundred) with high-level experience in government joined the government in Pakistan. Their values and standards of competence were not able sufficiently to penetrate the total bureaucracy. Hence, the initiative for documentary publication rested entirely with a small group which had neither the stamina nor the time to generate impetus in an infinite number of bureaucratic endeavors. A correlative reason was the level of competence and familiarity in the use of English which diminished sharply within the bureaucracy below the level of a few hundred officers at the top. Such technical and linguistic deficiency is not conducive to writing for publication. Finally, the trauma of partition was severe. Records were destroyed or lost in transit from India, or were never sent. For at least a year, administration was conducted like a military operation in the field, with few records even of major decisions.

In Chapter I of this analysis there is a discussion of research conditions in Pakistan and commentary on types, utility, and accessibility of sources. In Chapters II through VIII an effort is made to bring documentary and secondary sources which bear on the study of the civil public bureaucracy into an orderly system of manageable dimensions. The range of materials thus included may exceed the narrow limits often assigned to technical administrative problems. The regnant assumption is that knowledge of the political and social context in which bureaucracy functions is not necessarily alien to administration. Where appropriate, even literary materials which illuminate administrative problems are included. On the other hand, there are practical limits, and a large body of materials on Pakistan is omitted from this survey when such materials have been dealt with bibliographically and otherwise in other places.[2] Therefore, such issues as constitutional development, Islamic political theory, and the development of the Pakistan freedom movement, while bearing to some extent on bureaucracy, have been omitted. On the other hand, the theory, organization, and recruitment of the bureaucracy as well as technical aspects of administrative organization and procedure come within the scope of this essay. Sources in community development, administrative reform, constitutional law, and martial law, all crucially bearing on the subject of bureaucracy, are also included. No attempt is made to make an exhaustive list of government publications, partial compilations of which can be found in catalogues of the central and provincial government presses and in other compilations which are referred to throughout the essay. The purpose here is really to classify selected sources and arrange them in an order which may be helpful for the systematic study of government in Pakistan.

Since several sources discussed in this essay appear to relate to India rather than to Pakistan, some explanation is warranted. In reality, the India dealt with in most of these studies is Imperial India before partition in 1947, whose history refers as much to Pakistan as it does to post-partition India. This fact of historical continuity is implicit in the legal presumption of the unchanged status of government documents. Whatever status the document had before partition, it continues to have after partition unless this status has been specifically modified or abrogated by law.[3] Thus, for example, the Douie manuals on settlement and land administration for the Punjab, first issued in 1899 and 1908,

[2] For surveys of research in the social sciences in Pakistan, see John E. Owen, "Sociology in Pakistan," *The Journal of Asian Studies,* XX (1960), 139–144; Wolfram Eberhard, "Social Research at Pakistani Universities," *The Asia Foundation Program Bulletin No. 5* (December, 1957); Ralph Braibanti, "Note on Social Science Research Relating to Pakistan," mimeographed for the Committee on South Asia of the Association for Asian Studies (1959).

[3] See Indian Independence Act, 1947, as adopted in Pakistan by Provisional Constitution Order, 1947, par. 18 (3). This provision was incorporated in the Constitution of 1956 in Article 224 and after the abrogation of the Constitution by martial law was further incorporated in the law of the land by President's Order (Post-Proclamation) No. 1 of 1958, Laws (Continuance in Force Order, 1958), October 10, 1958, Sec. 2(1) 4(1). Continuity of legal validity from martial law to constitutional government is provided by Article 225 of the new Constitution, which became effective June 8, 1962, and by President's Order No. 30 of 1962 (Removal of Difficulties) Adaptation Order, dated June 8, 1962.

respectively, are valid in contemporary Pakistan.[4] In the ideological realm this continuity is suggested by such claims as that the Civil Service of Pakistan is the lineal descendant of the Indian Civil Service. Finally, partition of the subcontinent has not drastically altered social and economic problems in the two countries, and many Indian studies of administration and village problems (even some of those published after partition) have relevance to problems in Pakistan. The common nature of problems faced by India and Pakistan after partition is suggested by the fact that over a period of years after 1947 both countries appointed several commissions for the study of almost identical national problems. Both countries, for example, created commissions for the study of company law, reorganization of states (in Pakistan, the analogous issue was the integration of West Pakistan), film industry, taxation, law, the press, administrative reform, and finance. Each country also established two pay commissions (1947 and 1957 in India; 1949 and 1959 in Pakistan) to study conditions of the public service. To be sure, each nation also has its separate problems reflected in other published inquiries unique to each country, but the commonality of the two nations' troubles during the first decade and a half was almost as important as the differences which are now becoming more pronounced and more obvious. Certainly in Pakistan, martial law, a presidential form of government, indirect elections, an extensive network of economic, military, and intellectual ties with the United States, and a commitment to a capitalist economy are factors which are moving the nation along quite a different path of development from that of India. Nevertheless, problems during the early post-independence years were analogous, hence some mention of selected Indian studies seems not inappropriate.

Most of the pre-partition studies included in this essay are those which are common to Indo-Pakistani tradition. Regional studies relating to the Deccan or South India are omitted since these areas are in many respects quite different from the areas which now comprise Pakistan. The fairly numerous pre-partition studies on Bengal and the Punjab have peculiarly direct relevance since

[4] See pp. 165–171 below for a description of these manuals.

the major parts of these provinces are now in Pakistan. Baluchistan, Sind, and the Northwest Frontier Province, also in Pakistan, have not been the subject of as much written attention as Bengal and the Punjab. Contemporary Indian studies are included only when they appear to be dealing with problems equally relevant to Pakistan. A more comprehensive analysis of works relating to Indian administration can be found in Bernard Cohn's essay, *The Development and Impact of British Administration in India.*[5]

The study of bureaucracy in Pakistan is almost coterminous with the study of government. This is true of many developing states in which the political process is either not as advanced as the bureaucratic process or where it has been in temporary abeyance, as it was in Pakistan for forty-four months. One consequence of the abolition of legislatures and political parties with the declaration of martial law in October, 1958, was a moratorium on legislative publishing. While legislative public records before that time were quantitatively eclipsed by administrative publications, they were of a high order. The publication of legislative public records was resumed in June, 1962, but has been limited thus far to debates of the national and provincial assemblies. Publication within the administrative branch of government continues to be of greater volume and constitutes the main emphasis here.

Some explanation of the format and style of this essay seems warranted. The first chapter dealing with the environment of research is an analytical narrative rather than a bibliographical survey, hence references are placed in footnotes in the conventional manner. Succeeding chapters, however, are essentially a running commentary on source materials, hence citations of these sources are included in the text itself, following the style of bibliographical essays. In the bibliographical chapters, I have tried to use footnotes only when referring to matters not discussed fully at that point in the text. This distinction has not always been easy to make, and I must beg the indulgence of the reader for inconsistencies which I am certain can be found. Somewhat different styles have been used for citing books and government publications. For books published in the United States or England or

[5] Cited above in n. 1.

which can be easily found in standard bibliographic references, only the place and date of publication are given. For books published in Pakistan or which are not likely to be listed in standard Western sources, the name of the publisher is usually included with place and date of publication. The latter practice is also followed for government publications. Finally, there is the perennial problem of inconsistency in Roman transliteration of names from the Urdu and other scripts. I have tried to use the same rendering used in the publication or document itself. This practice results in curious inconsistencies. For example, a High Court case may use the rendering "Fazlul"; the same case, reviewed by the Supreme Court may use the rendering "Fazle." Despite the inconvenience which may be caused the reader by not making the spellings consistent within the essay, I have retained the spellings as they are in the original. This policy is dictated by the bibliographic nature of the work. This will explain the spelling of "Punjab" which appears also as "Panjab" in various documents because of different systems of transliteration in vogue at various times. The University of the Panjab was founded when *a* was used, and most literature written in the nineteenth century follows this spelling. Currently the sound is transliterated as *u* except in most publications of the university which retain the *a*. Difficulties are presented, however, by the fact that not all government documents use the *a* spelling in referring to the university and by the fact that laws referring to the former province and now to the geographic area of the Punjab use the *u* rendition. In this essay, the *u* spelling is used except when citing a title using the *a* spelling.

   This study has been made possible by the help of many persons and organizations. The materials described—scattered in Pakistan, India, and England—were collected and studied in the course of visits to these countries in 1957, 1958, and 1959 under sponsorship of the Social Science Research Council and the Duke University Commonwealth-Studies Center. The Asia Foundation made possible the purchase of several publicly released government publications, including court decisions. Further progress on the study was made during 1960–1962 while on leave from Duke University to serve as chief adviser to the Civil Service

Academy of Pakistan under terms of a United States Agency for International Development contract administered by the University of Southern California. A revision of the study was made consequent to return visits to Pakistan in the summer of 1963 and in December, 1964, and January, 1965.

The generous co-operation of the Government of Pakistan must also be mentioned with deep appreciation. While it is hardly possible to list the hundreds of officers of the Government of Pakistan who have been helpful, my indebtedness to those government officials who have shown uncommon appreciation of research problems generally and of source materials particularly is hereby recorded. Among these are *Government of Pakistan:* A. R. Cornelius, chief justice, Pakistan Supreme Court; Zakir Husain, minister of home affairs until 1962; N. A. Faruqui, cabinet secretary; G. Mueenuddin, establishment secretary until 1964; Riazuddin Ahmed, commissioner, Co-operative Societies; Q. U. Shahab, secretary to the president until 1962; A. A. Mirza, registrar, Pakistan Supreme Court; Nasim Hasan Shah, editor, *Pakistan Supreme Courts Reports;* M. M. Ahmed, secretary, Commerce; Central Public Service Commission: A. S. B. Shah, chairman, 1958–1963, Q. A. Huque, chairman, 1963 to 1965; Agha A. Hamid, chairman, 1965 to the present, and Agha Iftikhar Hosain, assistant secretary; L. A. Sherwani, joint secretary, Pakistan Institute of International Affairs; Aslam Siddiqi, principal information officer, Ministry of Reconstruction and Information; Abid Husain, deputy secretary, Establishment Division; Zain-ul-Abedin and M. Masihuzzaman, deputy secretaries, Ministry of Information and Broadcasting; S. Z. Mahdi, manager, Government Publications; *Government of West Pakistan:* Malik Amir Mohammad Khan, governor, 1960 to the present; M. R. Kayani, late retired chief justice, High Court of West Pakistan; Rashid Ahmed, joint secretary, Organization and Methods; Inayatullah, West Pakistan Academy for Rural Development; *Government of East Pakistan:* Lt. Gen. M. Azam Khan, governor until 1962; Syed M. Murshed, chief justice, East Pakistan High Court; Hamid Shafi-ul-Islam, assistant accountant-general; Abdul Latif Biswas, section officer, secretariat library.

I am indebted also to various officials of the Government of Pakistan for permission to discuss certain issues and to reproduce statements and extracts of publications. Permission to publish a statement on the contempt of courts jurisdiction by Chief Justice A. R. Cornelius of the Supreme Court of Pakistan was given in a letter of June 21, 1962. The entire chapter on legal research was read by Chief Justice Cornelius and I am appreciative of many valuable suggestions made by him. Permission to reproduce six addresses by Chief Justice Cornelius (Appendices 10 through 15) was granted in letters of February 8 and May 7, 1965. Permission to reproduce a statement on contempt of court and to analyze judgments of the High Court of West Pakistan was given by the late Chief Justice M. R. Kayani of the West Pakistan High Court in a letter of June 21, 1962. Permission to analyze judgments of the East Pakistan High Court was given by Chief Justice Syed M. Murshed of that court in a letter of February 3, 1965. Authority to reprint, extract, and discuss the *Memorandum on Training Policy* of October 31, 1961, was given by M. Azfar, establishment secretary, President's Secretariat, in a letter of November 14, 1964. Reproduction of an extract from the report of the National Assembly's Second Economy Committee of 1957–1958 and of scattered extracts from the *Debates* of the National Assembly was authorized by G. Ahmed, Pakistan ambassador to the United States, in a letter of February 24, 1965. Permission to reproduce excerpts from speeches by Maulvi Farid Ahmad and other assembly members and to quote generally from the National Assembly *Debates* was given by A. K. M. Fazlul Quader Chowdhury, speaker of the National Assembly, in letters of January 9 and April 6, 1965. Extracts from government reports in Appendices 7, 8, and 9 are derived exclusively from official press handouts, the reproduction of which is authorized. Other authorizations are mentioned in appropriate places throughout the volume.

The editorial assistance of my colleague, Dr. Robert N. Kearney, and of several of my graduate students, Willard Berry, Harry W. Blair, II, S. M. Haider, and Asrar Husain, is gratefully acknowledged. Mrs. Mary Ellen Earp typed several revisions of the manuscript with patience and care. I am also indebted to Mrs. Glenn Negley who compiled the index in a painstaking and efficient manner.

Finally, I am grateful to my colleagues on the Commonwealth-Studies Committee of Duke University, whose constant encouragement and wise counsel made this brief study possible. Three trips to Pakistan in 1957, 1958, and 1959 were financed in part by that portion of the Commonwealth-Studies Center's activities supported by the Carnegie Corporation. Preparation of the manuscript and publication of the volume were financed in part by Ford Foundation funds supporting the Center's Program in Comparative Studies on Southern Asia. I am also appreciative of the encouragement of my colleagues on the subcommittee administering this program. I am indebted to both the Carnegie Foundation and the Ford Foundation as well as to the Social Science Research Council and the Asia Foundation for making this study possible. Neither facts nor analysis presented in this volume can be attributed to any of these organizations or to the Commonwealth-Studies Center. Similarly, none of the persons mentioned above or in the essay bears any responsibility for the facts and views herein expressed, which are solely those of the author.

RALPH BRAIBANTI

Durham, North Carolina
October, 1965

Contents

Tables

Tables

Research on the Bureaucracy
of Pakistan

Environment of Research

Volume of Documentation

Neither scarcity nor irrelevancy of documents is an impediment to research on bureaucracy in Pakistan. Even pre-partition documents of Imperial India are of value as much because of their pertinence to contemporary problems as because of historical interest. This relevance of pre-independence sources derives from the fact that, despite vigorous reform activity, the bureaucracy of Pakistan has undergone surprisingly little fundamental change since independence in 1947. Such crucial problems as structure, spatial distribution of power, and locus of impetus for social innovation are much the same as those discussed in reports issued under British rule a half-century earlier. Rejection of British imperial control has not necessarily resulted in an emotional or even intellectual severance from British bureaucratic norms. Pakistani officialdom particularly is not without pride in its imperial bureaucratic heritage. There is recognition that the colonial system must change to meet the demands of popular sovereignty, but it is, in fact, an uncommon preoccupation with the presumed piety of the British system which gives the bureaucracy much of its strength of resistance to radical reform. This does not mean that the contemporary scene can be effectively studied through exclusive reliance on documentary sources of the past, but it does suggest that no analysis of bureaucracy in Pakistan will be adequate in depth and in historical perspective without some immersion in sources antedating independence.

Since 1947 the propensity to publish government documents has only slightly diminished, and with respect to issues of administration it can be said that acceleration rather than diminution of publication has occurred. During the fifty-nine years from 1887 to 1946, some fourteen major reports prepared under the British Raj were either exclusively or predominantly concerned with administration in the area which is now Pakistan. From partition in 1947 through the end of martial law in 1962 (a fifteen-year period) some twenty-eight significant reports on bureaucracy or closely related administrative problems have been issued in Pakistan.[1] This suggests a seven-fold increase in the incidence of relevant public reports. The twenty-eight administrative reports total about 3,621 pages. These administrative reports are but one segment of government documents of relevance to the study of bureaucracy. From 1957 through 1964, thirty-three major commissions of inquiry were appointed to advise on crucial aspects of government policy.[2] Excluding five commissions on administrative reform whose reports (totaling 1,415 pages) have been included in the 3,621 pages mentioned above, the Commission on Taxation and Tariff whose report has not yet been submitted, and the Federal Capital Commission whose several technical reports have not been released, these twenty-six reports confront us with an additional 5,370 pages. Assuming the two unsubmitted or unavailable reports will be at least one hundred pages, the total is raised to 5,570. The total for administrative reports and reports of commissions of inquiry thus approximates 9,191 pages or about thirty volumes of three hundred pages each.

It is noteworthy that of the 3,621 pages of reports on administration, about 1,809 pages of the material were completed (and, in most cases, published) during the forty-four months of martial law extending from October 7, 1958 to June 8, 1962. To put it another way, half of this public issuance of reports on administration appeared within one-quarter of Pakistan's sixteen-year existence. Or, of the total of 9,191 pages of reports on administration and of inquiry commission reports (both published and scheduled for publication), 80 per cent appeared during the forty-four months of martial law. This computation includes only a small portion of the total documentary production. It does not, for

---

[1] These reports are listed in Table 2, following p. 214.
[2] These commissions are listed in Table 9, following p. 312.

example, include periodic or annual reports such as those of the three public service commissions, or of the thirty-six government corporations, or the annual reports of government departments which are too numerous to reduce to anything resembling precise quantification. Also excluded are episodic reports on subjects not directly affecting administration. Finally, a significant omission is research studies emanating from the three national institutes of public administration at Dacca, Karachi, and Lahore and from the Administrative Staff College, the Civil Service Academy, and the two academies for rural development at Comilla and Peshawar. With extensive financial and advisory help from the United States Agency for International Development and from the Ford Foundation, these seven institutions since 1960 have published an impressive corpus of material directly relevant to the study of bureaucracy. Other institutions, such as the Institute for Development Economics, and the Social Sciences Research Centre, supported by the Ford Foundation and the Asia Foundation, respectively, are also the source of research studies and reports.

The order of magnitude of publication of documentary materials on administration may have some meaning when compared to that of other developing countries and to other activities within Pakistan.[3] In India, fourteen major central government reports on administration, totaling 1,723 pages, have been issued. Excluding those reports in Pakistan which are analogous to state reports in India, Pakistan issued seventeen comparable reports of 2,496 pages. If state reports are included, seventy-three more reports would have to be added for India, and eleven more for Pakistan. In Ceylon, eight reports totaling 3,565 pages have been published; in Malaya, eleven reports totaling 828 pages have been issued; in Nepal, fourteen reports of 710 pages have been written since 1947; and in Burma, seven reports totaling 547 pages have appeared. These six countries have issued seventy-eight reports on administration totaling 10,173 pages. Of this bulk, Pakistan has issued 21

[3] For a list of reports (excluding state government reports in India) on administrative reform in India, Pakistan, Ceylon, Malaya, Burma, and Nepal, see the concluding chapter in Ralph Braibanti and associates, *Asian Bureaucratic Systems Emergent from the British Imperial Tradition,* publication scheduled for 1966 by Duke University Press. A list of reports issued by the states in India can be found in *The Indian Journal of Public Administration,* IX (1963), 583–586.

per cent of the number of reports and 24 per cent of the number of pages. Of greater significance than sheer volume is a qualitative comparison. Of these countries, Pakistan is the only one whose reports on administration have probed deeply and systematically into every major problem of bureaucracy, and some of whose reports (those prepared under martial law) are integrated into a comprehensive program of reform.

Another indication of the magnitude of public reporting is by reference to another government publishing activity within Pakistan. For example, the printed judgments of the Supreme Court of Pakistan average about seven hundred pages a year. Thus, in terms of volume alone, the written work of administrative inquiries over a sixteen-year period is equal to about five years of printed judgments of the Supreme Court, and the written work of the twenty-eight administrative reports and thirty additional martial law commissions of inquiry is equal to about thirteen years of printed judgments of the Supreme Court.[4]

Finally, the fourteen reports issued under British rule from 1887 to 1946, if the voluminous appendices of questionnaires and answers are excluded,[5] total about half the number of pages of the fifty-eight reports issued by administrative reform groups and martial law commissions of inquiry in Pakistan from 1947 through 1964.

In Pakistan, a decade of recession in candor, vigor, intellectu-

---

[4] This is useful merely as a point of reference rather than as a comparison, for there is no qualitative significance which can be related to the two efforts. Published judgments constitute only part of the written judgments of the court. Moreover, they are decided and written by five judges, whereas the deliberations of the administrative inquiries and martial law commissions involved the participation of some four hundred officials.

[5] Since complete citations and commentary are given elsewhere in this essay (pp. 101–112 ff.), identification is here abbreviated to the name of the commission chairman by which the report is commonly known. Reports during British rule: Aitchison, 1887; Hobhouse, 1909; Levinges, 1915; Islington, 1917; Montagu-Chelmsford, 1918; Llewellyn-Smith, 1919; Lee, 1924; Simon, 1930; Wheeler, 1937, Maxwell, 1937; Chapman, 1938; Rowlands, 1945; Ahmad, 1946; Tottenham, 1946. The arbitrary exclusion of appendices of reports prepared under British rule and their inclusion in computing the volume of Pakistani reporting requires explanation. Appendices of British reports consisted largely of answers to questionnaires and hence are not essential to the report proper. Shorter appendices to Pakistani reports are usually tables, charts, or notifications and are much more crucial for understanding the text of the reports. When appendices to Pakistani reports consist of answers to questionnaires they have also been excluded from the page count.

ality, and quantity of documents has been superseded since 1958 by a wave of published national self-analysis which should be satisfying to the most captious bibliographic enthusiast. The termination in 1958 of an eleven-year partial moratorium on public record issuance created the not unpleasant anomaly of a martial law regime which relied on the rudiments of an empirical methodology to achieve a kind of consultative, research-oriented consensus. This in itself fomented appreciation for and activity in research. More importantly, the validity of the stereotype of martial law as essentially repressive and secretive has been seriously challenged by Pakistan's public record issuance during this period.

Language Medium

Any appraisal of the potential for scientific research on bureaucracy and allied problems must consider first the language in which written and oral government business is conducted. At least through 1965 scholars using English were confronted by no serious linguistic barrier to research on the bureaucracy of Pakistan. The language used in government and higher education in both provinces is English, although Urdu and Bengali are proclaimed by Article 215 of the 1962 Constitution (as they were by Article 214 in the 1956 Constitution) as state languages. The 1962 Constitution specifies that English may also be used as the official language until 1972, at which time the president shall constitute a commission to examine the question of the replacement of English for official purposes. This principle has been in force since 1956 without interruption, for the language provision of the 1956 Constitution was never abrogated by martial law. All government reports are in English. These include legislative debates; decisions of the Supreme Court, high courts, sessions and district courts; budgets; and civil lists. Even staff memoranda, drafts, notes, and minutes are written in English within the executive and judicial branches and, to a lesser extent, in the legislatures. The study of bureaucracy, therefore, entails only the use of English unless research is done at the village or *tehsil* (group of villages) level. There records, such as the record of land rights and the *lal kitab* (literally, red book: a book of village records), are kept in one of the vernaculars.

While research based on written materials can be done exclusively in English, knowledge of the vernaculars is nevertheless important for interviewing of villagers, for developing the sensibility to understand village problems, and for reading the vernacular press, whose news coverage and point of view may be quite different from the English language press.

Notwithstanding these circumstances of the present, there is slow but perceptible movement toward the use of the vernaculars in government business at lower levels. Increasingly, union, *tehsil*, and district councils are voting to conduct their deliberations and to record their proceedings in the vernaculars. Research on these units of Basic Democracies can no longer rely exclusively on English. Even for such studies, however, knowledge of the vernaculars is not essential since the collation of village and *tehsil* records for all government activities is done in English at the district headquarters, which is organized into two separate establishments: the English office and the vernacular office. In the latter, documents are translated into English. Since the creation of Basic Democracies, the records of union council and *tehsil* council meetings are also translated at the district offices. The Official Language Committee of the West Pakistan government, which has already completed translation of 63,660 official terms and phrases into Urdu, is about to embark on the translation of documents, reports, acts, and regulations. The immediate effect of this will not obstruct research in English, for even when such translations have been completed the documents will still be printed in English as well. There are other forces pushing toward use of the vernaculars. Muslim groups such as the Anjuman-i-Himat-i-Islam strongly advocate the development of Urdu in education in West Pakistan. This point of view is espoused also (although for different reasons) by such officials as Masihuzzaman [6] and High Court Justice Mohammad Sharif, who are not otherwise closely identified with fundamentalist Muslim groups.

[6] See Masihuzzaman, "English—An Impediment to Economic Growth," *Pakistan Times*, April 30, 1962, p. 4.

The rationale of such a view is a search for cultural identity and an allied effort to resist foreign ideas and manners by completing "the revolution against the domination of western powers." Urdu, moreover, is gradually gaining ground in all levels of education. For example, in 1962, the Lahore Board of Intermediate and Secondary Education approved the use of Urdu for examination in science subjects; formerly examinations in these subjects were conducted exclusively in English.

Among politicians, the vernaculars are not much more widely used than among high-ranking administrators. In the first few sessions after the reopening of the national and provincial legislatures in June, 1962, there was a temporary surge in the use of vernaculars. The 156 members of the National Assembly which convened on June 8, 1962, took their oaths in Bengali, Urdu, and English in almost equal numbers. When the provincial assemblies of East and West Pakistan met under the new Constitution on June 9, 1962, of the three hundred members who took the oath of office, ninety-three used English, ninety-five Bengali, eighty-two Urdu, twenty-one Sindhi, eight Pashtu, and one Baluchi. These figures are a rough index not so much of ability to use the language in which the oath was taken as of a desire to demonstrate sentiment for the use of a particular regional language. Urdu was used almost entirely in the deliberations of the West Pakistan Provincial Assembly after the opening ceremonies, although the rules allow the use of English as well. The budget message was presented in Urdu, and even on June 21, 1962, nearly two weeks after the opening of the Provincial Assembly, the request of Begum Shahnawaz that she be allowed to speak in English so that her speech would be adequately reported in the English press was rejected by the assembly and she was compelled to speak in Urdu.

This transitory popularity of the vernaculars has given way somewhat to the use of English in debates. Section 155 of the *Rules of Procedure, National Assembly of Pakistan* (Karachi, 1963) declares that "Members shall address the Assembly in English, Bengali, or Urdu, unless the Speaker permits a Member, who cannot adequately express himself in any of those languages, to address the Assembly in any other language." Although Ayub

Hall in Rawalpindi, where the National Assembly meets until it is shifted to its "principal seat" in Dacca, is equipped with a simultaneous translation system for English, Urdu, and Bengali, English is almost exclusively used. In the printed *Debates* of the National Assembly, all speeches appear in English. If a speech was actually given in a vernacular, a footnote to that effect appears in the *Debates*. This practice of recording the proceedings in English is in accordance with Section 155(2) of the *Rules of Procedure*.

In the East Pakistan Provincial Assembly, about 34 per cent of the speeches are made in Bengali; the remainder are given in English. The debates are printed in the language in which they are delivered. In the West Pakistan Provincial Assembly, about 65 per cent of the debates are printed in Urdu; the remainder appear in English. The debates are printed in the language of delivery, except for the case of speeches in Sindhi, Pashtu, or Punjabi which are translated into Urdu and so indicated by a footnote.

Deliberations of the Council of Ministers of the central government are almost entirely in English and minutes are kept in English. Deliberations of both provincial cabinets are similarly in English, although English is somewhat more often punctuated with one of the vernaculars. Provincial cabinet minutes are also kept in English.

It may be that there is an irreversible trend toward eventual displacement of English by the vernaculars. This probability is increased by deterioration of English teaching in lower schools and in some universities. On the other hand, the emergence of universities, institutes, and departments within universities staffed entirely by Americans or by faculty trained through the doctorate in the United States is giving further impetus to English. Any trend toward displacement which may exist is further deflected by the physical separation of the two provinces and the cultural diversity and competition implicit in the two main linguistic blocs, Bengali and Urdu. Since English is one of the few links between the provinces, it may well continue as the official national language even after 1972. There may be gradual vernacularization in the provincial legislative assemblies (although this is not yet clearly evident) and in politics generally, while the use of English in both provincial and central administration will continue. But if the assemblies eventually function as they do in other presidential systems, legislative oversight through questioning of the executive branch and scrutiny of its reports is likely not to discourage and perhaps even to accelerate vernacularization in administration (especially at the provincial level) as well.

The concomitant oral use of at least two languages in government and one language, English, for all written business above the village level creates problems in administration which bear on research. In every governmental activity there is a point at which linguistic and cultural mediation occurs. In judicial practice, for example, hearings in the Supreme Court, high courts, and sessions courts are conducted entirely in English. Even when an occasional witness uses a vernacular, the testimony is repeated by the counsel in English. In the district courts, oral testimony is invariably in the vernacular, but the magistrate translates orally almost simultaneously, and the court reporter records the testimony in English from the magistrate's English dictation. Since translation is a difficult technical skill not usually possessed by those who are merely multilingual, the possibility of serious error in shades of meaning is very great in such court cases. In the secretariats and other large government offices the descending scale of English competence, which parallels the rank structure, is broken somewhere below the middle by superintendents and assistants who function as linguistic and cultural mediators, communicating upward in English and downward in one of the vernaculars. This phenomenon of linguistic-cultural mediation is even more pronounced in local administration because the differences in society at these levels are much more sharply drawn. There is a positive correlation between skill in spoken English and status in the eyes of the vernacular-speaking public. A similar correlation exists with respect to Western dress. The same official speaking English and dressed in Western clothes is shown greater deference and privilege than when he wears Pakistani-style clothes or speaks a vernacular. One of the consequences of this linguistic duality is what might appear to be over-staffing. In the districts particularly, translation occupies the time of significant numbers of people.

This unfamiliarity with rapid use of English by the vast majority of government servants creates delay, confusion, and even error in completing forms and writing notes. This is true even at higher levels where major written production is involved. For example, the chief justice of the High Court of West Pakistan must draft and write his own judgments and correct the syntax and spelling of research notes presented to him by his staff. Even final editing of proofs of published judgments must be done by the chief justice. The delay and frustration caused by such an added burden on the chief justice of a large judicial system are obvious. The same predicament confronts most senior officials on the executive level. At the cutting edge of administration where the humble citizen must seek government action, this linguistic confusion gives rise to extensive use of unofficial "brokers" who commercially exploit the citizen's total ignorance of English and exaggerate their own marginal English competence—thereby making themselves indispensable middlemen in dealing with the English-functioning bureaucracy. Another consequence of this dilemma for administration is the incapacity to delegate authority within the bureaucracy, for effective delegation cannot occur where there is neither common experience nor a common sense of values and where there is disparate linguistic competence. This linguistic differential, combined with other attributes of class structure analyzed later in this essay,[7] makes it mandatory for the researcher to deal with much higher-ranking officials in government than would be the case, for example, in the United States. This can be either an advantage or an impediment, depending on the accessibility of the official and the personal relationship which the researcher is able to establish.

Perhaps the best indication of future developments in language usage can be derived from recommendations of the Commission on National Education.[8] The commission's report has been approved by the cabinet and was being implemented under the direction of S. M. Sharif, who until May, 1965, had been secretary

[7] See below, pp. 131–140.
[8] Government of Pakistan, Ministry of Education, Report of the Commission on National Education (Karachi, 1960), pp. 281–289.

of the Ministry of Education for more than a decade and who served as chairman of the commission. The commission recommended that the two national languages—Urdu and Bengali—"gradually and progressively replace English as the media of instruction at all levels." It further suggested that both languages be enriched by assimilating new words and terms essential to cope with modern issues and that common elements of the two languages be identified and a common scientific terminology developed. In East Pakistan the problem of regional vernaculars does not arise since Bengali is universally spoken. In West Pakistan the problems created by such vernaculars as Sindhi, Baluchi, Punjabi, and Pashtu were dealt with by the proposal that the vernacular of the region be used as the medium of instruction for the first five years of school. Urdu is introduced as a second language during the third year and becomes the exclusive medium of instruction starting with the sixth year. The commission envisaged a transitional period of fifteen years (1960–1975), during which Urdu and Bengali will be taught and will gradually replace English as the language of higher education. Even so, the complete abandonment of English is not recommended. On the contrary, after extolling the merits of English as an international language of diplomacy, commerce, and learning, the commission recommends that English be a compulsory language from the sixth to the twelfth years of school and in colleges and universities. Presumably, English would be a second language in higher education, for the commission had earlier suggested that the national language be the instructional medium at the university level. The need for intellectual comity between the universities of the two provinces will almost certainly mitigate against the use of Urdu and Bengali at the higher levels and will influence the continuance of English. The fifteen-year transitional period contemplated by the commission may be somewhat optimistic. There will probably be delay caused by the fact that members of university and college faculties have received their own educations in English. It is likely that such delay will be aggravated by the continuing practice of sending prospective scholars to British and American universities for their doctorates. Even in new universities of agriculture and technology, established under auspices of the United States Agency for International Development, the original members of the faculty were Americans and their replacements are Pakistanis trained in the United States exclusively in English and in the use of English-language teachings aids.

It would be folly to hazard a prediction as to the future development of English usage. It can be said with certainty only that vernacularization is increasing, and the decade of 1970, when the Constitution requires a further recommendation and the transitional period envisaged by the commission comes to an end, will probably be crucial.

Status of Scholarship as a Profession

While, as the preceding pages have attempted to suggest, quantity, relevance, and language are not impediments to documentary research in Pakistan, there nevertheless are certain adverse conditions which should be noted. By far the most serious deterrents to efficient research in Pakistan have been the low status of scholarship as a profession and widespread lack of comprehension of the role of intellectual activity as a prerequisite for a modernized social order. The evidences of this state of affairs are manifold and cannot be explored exhaustively here. They have been presented in fairly systematic fashion in the reports of the Scientific Commission and the Commission on National Education and have been analyzed in more forthright terms by such well-known scholars as Abdus Salam and I. H. Usmani.[9]

There are, however, certain elements of the climate of scholarship which have been neglected by the commission reports on education and science and therefore merit further exploration. Research efficiency depends to a large degree on public and bureaucratic attitudes toward scholarship. Within the bureaucracy, respect for scholarship outside bureaucratic circles is minimal. The reasons for this are varied, and the fault cannot be assigned to any one institution—certainly not to the bureaucracy

[9] The latter's views are set forth in his "Presidential Address," CENTO Scientific Symposium, Lahore, January 8, 1962, and his "Convocation Address" at Dyal Singh College, April 30, 1962.

itself. Inherently and necessarily, all bureaucracies are oriented to action rather than reflection. Even in the American bureaucracy the elaborate apparatus for collating data, programming, and forecasting (all presumably devices facilitating reflection) is a rather recent development. The struggle to implement a concept of general staff and of planning in the American system, and to gain acceptance for active, effective intellectual activity on a large scale in government, is little more than a quarter of a century old (if an exception is made for the classical era of Jefferson and Hamilton). Throughout the past three decades, too, this concept has met constant resistance, as exemplified by the epithets "brain trust" in the New Deal years, "egghead" in a later period, and "schoolboy government" in the sixties. Even now, the status of research in the United States is not without ambivalence, for in times of budgetary stringency some of the first activites to be curtailed have been research and long-range planning.

The orientation toward action of Pakistan's bureaucracy is not undergirded by the deep residual respect for extra-bureaucratic intellectual endeavor which is found in the Chinese, Japanese, British, German, and American systems, to name but a few. While there is a tradition of intellectuality in the bureaucracy, its strength is derived more from the disposition of the Indian Civil Service created by the British than from indigenous Muslim culture. Hence, its roots are not deep and its manifestations fluctuate in strength with whatever status the legacy of British imperial administration may have.

The reason for this is probably the separation of Muslim intellectual life from secular bureaucratic life. At least three important elites can be identified in Pakistan.[10] They are (1) a religious elite which holds Islamic tradition above other values, (2) the secular-oriented military and civil public bureaucracy, and (3) a non-bureaucratic intelligentsia. The latter comprises the professions (of which the most articulate is law), the business community, and those politicians who are secularly oriented. In Pakistan, there

[10] This analysis of convergence of elites is essentially a recapitulation and elaboration of pp. 19–22 of the author's "Reflections on Bureaucratic Reform in India," in Ralph Braibanti and J. J. Spengler (eds.), *Administration and Economic Development in India* (Durham, N. C., 1963).

is very little effective interaction among these three elites; membership in one does not confer membership in another and may even preclude it. The sphere of influence of each of the three elites is detached from the others. Therefore, the disposition toward intellectuality and respect for learning which may prevail in any one or two of these elites will have minimal influence on the others. The venerable and sophisticated intellectual tradition of Islam became, on the subcontinent, oriented exclusively to Qur'anic and Persian scholarship.[11] It sought to preserve its identity by isolating itself from Western learning which the Hindus eagerly accepted. The Aligarh movement of Sir Syed Ahmed Khan, which sought to provide a Western dimension to the Muslim intellectual heritage, was started in the 1860's—too late to permit the same harmonious confluence of elites which had developed in other societies. The penetration by Muslims into the bureaucracy, particularly in the higher reaches of the Indian Civil Service, was minimal. By 1947 only 9 per cent of the total cadre of 1,157 officers was Muslim as contrasted with 39 per cent Hindu and others and 52 per cent British. But the significant fact is that the Muslims who entered service were not themselves the religious elite, as were the Hindu Brahmins. The *maulana* or *maulvi* of traditionalistic Qur'anic culture was not part of the same elite which wielded bureaucratic power.[12] Hence, the intellectuality which characterizes the Muslim component of the ICS and the present bureaucracy of Pakistan derives its strength from more recent British influence unsustained by the Islamic tradition of learning which continues to flow in a separate stream.[13] Only in the lower clerical reaches or among superintendents and assistants are *maulana* or

[11] For further analysis see Ishtiaq Husain Qureshi, "The Background of Some Trends in Islamic Political Thought," in Ralph Braibanti and J. J. Spengler (eds.), *Tradition, Values, and Socio-Economic Development* (Durham, N. C., 1961), pp. 181–212.

[12] Even such highly influential Qur'anic-oriented Muslims as India's minister of education, Maulana Abul Kalam Azad, and Pakistan's unanimously elected speaker of the new National Assembly, Maulvi Tamizuddin Khan, reached public eminence through the freedom movement and politics rather than administration.

[13] This isolation of the higher bureaucracy from the mainstream of what the traditional Muslims insist is true Islamic culture is a common criticism made by the traditionalists against the Civil Service of Pakistan. See especially the trenchant criticism by Maulvi Farid Ahmad, National Assembly of Pakistan, *Debates,* February 15, 1957, pp. 434–435. See also below, p. 134, n. 16; p. 135; appendix 4.

maulvi types to be found. The designations *maulana* and *maulvi*, while highly regarded as symbols of a traditional way of life, seldom command the same eminence of respectability among the Western-oriented elites as does the term *sensei* among Japanese. Indeed the term *maulvi* in some contexts has about the same degree of esteem as *babu;* in fact, both terms are used as equivalents in the printed character rolls of the government of Bengal. The titles *babu* and *maulvi* are, of course, respected by the larger society but are held in somewhat lesser regard by the higher reaches of the Western-oriented bureaucracy. If a Japanese official were to be mistakenly addressed as *sensei,* he would feel flattered. But if a Muslim official of high rank were to be mistakenly addressed as *maulvi sahib* or *maulana sahib,* he might feel offended and would wonder what he had done to create an impression that he was old-fashioned and obscurantist rather than modern, enlightened, and practical.[14] The term *Allama,* meaning "Great Learned," is analogous to *sensei.* It connotes a congruence of secular and religious learning according to the highest values of Muslim scholarship. This is the title accorded such distinguished scholars as Allama Iqbal, Allama Mashriki, and Allama Ala-ud-Din-Siddiqi. The fact that it is so seldom used in modern Pakistan suggests the separation of Qur'anic and secular values.

However valid for the period under discussion, the foregoing description may be made obsolete in a decade or so by significant social changes now taking place. The need for Islam to withdraw and look inward and backward to the real and imagined glories of caliphates of the Middle East disappeared with partition in 1947. Insulation and retrospection as means of preserving Islamic culture in the face of an overwhelming Hindu majority are no longer necessary. The re-entry of Qur'anic learning into the main currents of secular intellectual life is a natural consequence of the confi-

[14] The following episode is illustrative. A foreigner in Pakistan was befriended by an uncommonly helpful and generous librarian of gentle demeanor and "old world" manners, who wore full beard, *sherwani,* and *karakuli topi.* Thinking the librarian was probably a *maulvi* or *maulana,* he addressed a note to him using *maulvi sahib* as the mode of address. The librarian was offended by this term of address and let it be known that he should be called *chaudhry.* It is revealing that he preferred the title *chaudhry* (which implies simply that he was himself or came from the family of a minor village landholder) to the title *maulvi.*

dence and security of collective experience in a nearly totally Islamic social order. This natural development is stimulated vigorously by government policy. Orthodox, iconoclastic organizations like the Jamaat-e-Islami have been discouraged at every turn. Total suppression of the Jamaat-e-Islami has been prevented only by a resilient judiciary, bent on preserving the spirit of public freedom by libertarian interpretation of the fundamental rights of the amended 1962 Constitution. Since 1958, the attitude of government has been to modify the attitudes of iconoclastic *mullahs*. Muslim religious properties (*waqf* or *auqaf*) are administered by provincial governments, but this is primarily to insure regularity in administration of finances. Such properties continue to have religious functions which are not under governmental control. Forced modernization by abolition of *purdah*, or the fez, or by secularization of mosques (as was done in Turkey and to some extent in Iran, for example) has not been part of this policy. Except for minor revisions in marriage and family laws, no Muslim custom or tradition, however "unmodern," has been modified. The policy has been one of bringing Muslim religious leaders face to face with the problems of modern life and of letting adaptation take place at a gradual pace within a religious rather than a secular context.

Several institutional forms have emerged within which interaction of secular and Qur'anic learning may be expected to occur. The Advisory Council of Islamic Ideology, provided for by Article 199 of the 1962 Constitution, and under the chairmanship of Allama Siddiqi, seeks to reinvigorate Islamic learning with secular knowledge primarily by re-examination of the roots of Islam. The Central Institute of Islamic Research, charged by Article 207 of the Constitution to do research to assist in the "reconstruction of Muslim society on a truly Islamic basis," has attempted to utilize natural science and social science learning in its work. Under the direction of Fazlur Rahman, the institute, located in Karachi, has established a significant library of Islamic materials in Persian, Arabic, and other languages, and publishes a journal, *Islamic Studies*, which has won international recognition. The institute offers courses of study in Islam leading to the master's and doctor's degrees. Such reinvigoration of Islam has been encouraged at another level by the recent reorganization of the West Pakistan Jamia Islamia at Bahawalpur. The chairman of the board of governors is S. M. Ikram, CSP, a Western-oriented career civil servant who serves also as a member of the provincial board of revenue and as commissioner of mosque properties (*auqaf*). Ikram once taught at Columbia University and has written extensively in the field of Muslim history. The Jamia's aim is to supervise courses of training in Muslim pre-collegiate schools (*madrasas*), train local religious leaders and keepers of mosques (*mullahs, imams*) to degree level, and train government employees engaged in the administration of *auqaf*.[15]

This post-1958 cultural thrust and the new institutions emerging from it may ultimately restore the convergence of secular and Qur'anic intellectual traditions which has long characterized Islamic thought, even though the Pakistani social order remained bifurcated. Until such convergence plays a greater role in the intellectual realm, the contrast between the present bipolarized society and other societies, such as that of Japan, is marked. In Japan, Buddhist and Confucian scholarship has not only penetrated the civil bureaucracy but has influenced the military bureaucracy as well. Interpenetration of religious and military values can be found in the emergence of the highly disciplined, paramilitary austerity of Zen Buddhism. Application of the Japanese title *sensei* to both teachers and those government officers deemed to have scholarly qualities is a manifestation of a convergence of scholarly and bureaucratic values seldom found in other modern societies. In Hindu society such convergence also occurred. The ancient tradition of Sanskritic scholarship molded the Brahmin mind, permeated the civil bureaucracy, and was an important cultural impulse of the non-bureaucratic, secular intelligentsia as well. The extent of Brahmin participation in the bureaucracy is indicated by the fact that in 1913, 40 per cent of the posts held by non-British officials carrying salaries of Rs. 200 a month and above were filled by Brahmins.[16] Even today it is not uncommon to find an officer of

[15] See West Pakistan Jamia Islamia (Bahawalpur), Ordinance XVII of 1964, in *Gazette of West Pakistan, Extraordinary,* September 30, 1964.
[16] *Report of the Royal Commission on Public Services,* August 14, 1915, Cmd. 8382 (1917) (*Islington Report*), I, 31.

the Indian Civil Service, learned in or at least respectful of Sanskritic intellectual tradition and Brahmin by caste, wielding bureaucratic power and acknowledged as a leader among the non-bureaucratic intelligentsia. Some of Pakistan's political leaders, such as the Quaid-i-Azam and Chaudhury Mohamad Ali, have been men of spectacular brilliance. But few were known for bookish or scholarly qualities, except for some members of the judiciary such as A. R. Cornelius, M. R. Kayani, S. M. Murshed, and M. Munir, who stand among the most distinguished jurists in their time. A pronounced administrative or political skill unsullied by excessive intellectuality has characterized Pakistan's leadership from the beginning. Even more important is the fact that it is a source of pride rather than an occasion for regret. When President Ayub once humorously commented in answering a criticism concerning the new Constitution that the intelligentsia read too many books, he may have unwittingly reflected a widely held value in Pakistani society. Since systematic, voracious reading as an important means of acquiring secular knowledge is less regarded than experience, the intelligentsia may have been surprised to learn of their bookish proclivities. Some members of the Supreme Court and high courts and of the bar itself complain that lawyers do not prepare their cases adequately and do not read the relevant case law. And, of course, this is clearly the dominant disposition in university life.

Another reason for the state of scholarship is the unstable (from the point of view of ordered intellectual activity) conditions of the universities, which have perpetuated the less desirable features of the British system without the sociological preconditions prevailing in Britain. The condition of higher education has been decried by reports of the Central Public Service Commission and the Commission on National Education, and by other agencies and individuals.[17] Certainly the less than adequate condition of its

[17] A conference of educational leaders held in 1951 agreed in a report of 502 pages, *Proceedings of the Educational Conference Held at Karachi on the 4th and 5th December, 1951* (Karachi: Manager of Publications, 1956), on the need to overhaul the whole educational structure. The oldest university in Pakistan surveyed its own standing and in *Report of the Panjab University Enquiry Commis-*

universities is not peculiar to Pakistan. Similar situations can be found in most ex-colonial societies of Asia.[18] Nor are the reasons easily found; the causes are diverse and deeply rooted in the nature of colonial rule and bifurcated culture. Many of the causes are common to educational systems in Latin America, Africa, and other Asian states. Of these, perhaps the most important is the student's self-image as the vanguard of modernity for his society. Students absorb Western educational norms which they do not fully comprehend. Integration of competing norms rarely occurs; rather an uncomfortable separation and consequent frustration is the typical result. A second cause is the galvanic attraction which politics has for students, in part as a result of deliberate exploitation by politicians who find students a large, conveniently cohesive group which can be easily reached. But more important, much of the students' Western-oriented education has given attention to political ideas which lead inevitably to the practice of politics as a laboratory demonstration of considerable novelty and fascination.

---

sion, 1951–52 (Lahore: Superintendent, Government Printing, 1955) concluded that it was "not what a modern university ought to be." In East Pakistan, the first publication of the Pakistan Institute of Human Relations related to education, Ghulam Jilani and B. M. Omar, *An Inquiry into the Factors Influencing the Academic Atmosphere of the Dacca University* (Dacca: University of Dacca, 1956), concludes that conditions of the University of Dacca are far from satisfactory. A comprehensive survey of education in East Pakistan was published in *Report of the Educational Reforms Commission—East Pakistan 1957* (2 vols.; Dacca: East Pakistan Government Press, 1957) and concludes that the quality and content of higher education are "almost incomparably inferior to some of the advanced countries." The *Report of the Commission on National Education January–August 1959* (Karachi: Manager of Publications, 1960) is an over-all appraisal on which subsequent educational reform will be based. Some insight into the direction in which Pakistan's universities are developing may be gained from the "Third Five Year Plan 1965–1970" of the University of the Panjab, a mimeographed document labeled "Tentative" published by the university in Lahore in July, 1963. Concern over educational standards is corroborated by M. Bashir, "The Scholar and Society in Pakistan," in *The Scholar and Society,* Bulletin No. 13 of the Committee on Science and Freedom (Manchester, England, November, 1959) pp. 59–64. See also Alex Page, "Asyntasia; or, Learning Attitudes in Pakistan," *The Educational Record,* XLIII (1962), 269–271; Robert J. Kibbee, "Higher Education in Pakistan," *Journal of Higher Education,* XXXIII (1962), 179–189.

[18] *Minerva,* a British "review of science, learning and policy," is a particularly valuable source of analysis and documentation on higher education in the new states. Its regular feature, "Politics in the World of Science and Learning," reveals situations in other states almost identical to those described for Pakistan in this essay. See especially, Ralph Pieris, "Universities, Politics and Public Opinion in Ceylon," *Minerva,* II (1964), 434–454, and a synopsis of the *Report of the* [Ceylon] *Universities Commission 1962, ibid.,* pp. 492–518.

Since the political process is regarded as essentially Western, both in its institutional forms and behavior, there is a natural affinity for it. Finally, most students upon graduation enter government employment and are thereby prohibited from political activity; their student life presents the only opportunity for political activity and they seek to make the most of it.

It is relevant to examine cursorily some of the specific reasons for this inadequate condition of universities in Pakistan which have been neglected or inadequately analyzed by government reports and other commentaries. First, there has been excessively rapid expansion of higher education during traumatic times. Four new universities, Karachi, Peshawar, Sind, and Rajshahi, were established after independence, and the number of colleges, technical and professional schools nearly doubled. In 1950, the total number of bachelor's degrees granted was 2,287; in 1961, 10,297 persons were awarded bachelor's degrees. It would have been difficult to staff two universities even at the level of their pre-partition size; adequately staffing six universities with five times the 1947 enrolment was impossible. Even before 1947 learning and scholarship of a Western, secular type in the Muslim areas were dominated by Hindus and British. Some academic vacancies created by their departure in 1947 were often enough filled by unqualified Muslim scholars who enjoyed little respect in their own society or by Europeans hired on contract. Not all the appointees were inadequate, but appointments which were less than desirable seemed numerous enough to affect the status of the total academic community. Thus, the already low estate of secular scholarship was reduced to an even lower range of respectability. University teachers engaged to fill the gaps rarely had advanced degrees and often found themselves teaching classes composed of persons who only a few days before had been their student colleagues. This fact, more than any other, has probably been responsible for the lack of student discipline. Even now, the university teacher enjoys very little esteem. Young graduates who engage in teaching for a few years merely wait out their time until they pass the civil service examination for entrance into the public bureaucracy. Universally, the civil servant, particularly if he is a member of the Civil Service of Pakistan, is, irrespective of rank, accorded greater deference than the university teacher. This position is enhanced by the knowledge that the best students in university classes rarely remain in teaching for more than a year or two.

A second factor behind the low estate of the universities is the subordinate status of the university to government. This subordination is quite clear not only in terms of prestige but in most aspects of administrative control. The operating head of the university, the vice-chancellor, is appointed for merely a four-year term. Although the university is, in theory, "semi-autonomous" and the vice-chancellor is legally responsible only to the chancellor, who is the governor of the province, in reality there are five supervising entities: (1) the Ministry of Education of the central government, whose secretary is one of the most powerful officials in government, and who ultimately determines much educational policy, (2) the provincial department of education, whose secretary is a member of the governor's staff, (3) a university commission, which allocates funds, (4) the chancellor, who is legally responsible for the university, (5) the university syndicate, eight of whose eleven members are appointed by the chancellor. By virtue of the political power of some of its members and because of the statutory ambiguity on the question of its relationship with the vice-chancellor, the syndicate often contributes to rather than reduces administrative disarticulation. The basic ordinance regulating the affairs of the university in considerable detail is promulgated by the provincial governor functioning as chancellor.[19] A typical ordinance prescribes the hours to be spent by each rank of the faculty on lectures, tutorials, student guidance, research, and administration. University vice-chancellors are regarded as subordinate to both the central government secretary of education and the provincial government secretary of the education department. This subordination is reflected in the Warrant of Precedence, which places vice-chancellors four ranks below the central government education secretary, and, although in the same rank as

[19] For more detailed discussion and citations to university ordinances, see below p. 34, n. 39; p. 41, nn. 59, 60, 61.

provincial government secretaries, two positions lower within that rank.[20]

The higher social and official status of the government official is further suggested by the behavior surrounding important scholarly lectures. The customs of public speaking require that a government official preside at a seminar or special lecture. Even if the lecture is given by a distinguished scholar, the lecture itself becomes ancillary to the presence of the government official and to his summary of the lecture at its conclusion. The audience appears to be less concerned with what the lecturer says than with its impact on the presiding officer. This state of affairs is perpetuated by the universities themselves and by the press, which often fails to mention the lecture proper but may devote its entire comment to the remarks of the presiding government official. The reasons for this practice can be found embedded in the legacy of British imperial rule. High-ranking government officers were invariably British, hence there was considerable prestige value in having the occasion graced by their presence as members of the ruling caste and as representatives of the viceroy. But there was still another motive. Most meetings and seminars invariably touched on volatile political issues related to independence, especially during the quarter-century before partition. The conveners avoided the risk of becoming suspect and even arrested for anti-state activities by the presence of a government officer under whose protection harsh things might be said against the government with impunity. Finally, the presence of a government officer gave the conveners a seldom achieved opportunity to present grievances which would make them appear heroic before the assembly and would acquaint

[20] In the Warrant of Precedence in effect at partition and until 1955, vice-chancellors of universities were ranked "30," one rank below major generals, joint secretaries to the central government, and members of the Federal Public Service Commission. See Royal Warrant of Precedence published in *Combined Civil List for India, Pakistan and Burma No. 160*, October–December, 1947 (Lahore, 1948), pp. 643–652. In the new Warrant of Precedence now in effect, vice-chancellors are ranked "24" on a par with major generals and joint secretaries to the central government. Rank "24," however, is four ranks below full secretaries to the central government. See Ministry of Home and Kashmir Affairs, Notification No. 21/2/61 Public, Warrant of Precedence, published in the *Gazette of Pakistan, Extraordinary*, March 9, 1963, pp. 233a–233h.

the government with the needs of the particular assembled group. It may be the latter reason which prompts continuance of the ritual in modern Pakistan, almost without exception whatever the occasion.[21] This may have been a satisfying ritualistic performance in the days of British rule—a ritual in reality serving as a device for airing grievances—but there appears to be little utility in perpetuating the practice. The fact that it endures suggests that the profession of scholarship has not risen to a position of parity of esteem with the bureaucracy. It continues to act as supplicant and is regarded as no more than that by the bureaucracy as well as by other sectors of society. The responsibility for the perpetuation of this distortion of the role of intellectual activities rests partly with the intellectual community itself, for it is no longer under compulsion to subvert the integrity of an intellectual performance to the purposes of politics. On the other hand, the continued unease with which academic scholars confront government results from a variety of measures, such as provisions of university ordinances for removal of university employees for "misconduct" and restrictions on discussion of "integration" problems. Until the climate of free, responsible discussion becomes more certain, the supplicant attitude of the university is not likely to change greatly.

Low salaries, poor libraries, and difficult teaching conditions contribute to unrest and even turbulence among the faculty. Relations within the faculty are sometimes characterized by disruptive attitudes.[22] The remarks of I. H. Usmani, an officer in the

[21] A typical pattern of custom followed at academic lectures is this: Professor X is invited to speak at a meeting at a university or college. A secretary to government is asked to preside. The college principal opens the assembly by giving an address of welcome to the "guest of honor" who is the government officer presiding, not the lecturer. The address of welcome may include only a sentence or two of welcome and will then elaborate on the need of the college for more money, promotions, buildings, and other matters. Professor X speaks, after which the presiding officer briefly comments on his lecture and then launches into a full-scale rebuttal of the principal's grievances, ending by enumerating the faults of the law college and scolding the assembly.

[22] One example which can be taken from many is a long-standing feud between the head of a department at one of the universities and the department's senior reader. This dispute on one occasion resulted in physical struggle (a not uncommon form of conflict resolution); students aligned themselves with the two men and work in the department is said to have been virtually paralyzed. Ultimately, the university syndicate authorized an inquiry by a judge of the High Court. See report in *Pakistan Times*, June 24, 1962, p. 7.

Civil Service of Pakistan who took a foreign doctorate in physics and is now chairman of the Pakistan Atomic Energy Commission, although referring to science faculty, are equally relevant to other university faculties.

Libraries are starved of scientific journals and technical books. Workshops are practically non-existent. Science teachers draw less pay than stenographers of Secretaries and Ministers to the Central Government. The budget of the universities is nominal which does not admit of planning in advance because of annual vagaries of financial grants. The total budget of all the science departments of all the six universities of Pakistan is less than 40% of the budget of the Council of Scientific and Industrial Research, when most of the basic work of the Council could well be done in the universities, except when a process reaches the pilot plant stage. Under such conditions no wonder that the best of our talented scientists emigrate and settle in countries abroad. If this state of affairs continues, we will produce a generation of angry young men with consequences too horrible to imagine.

The few scientists that we have can be divided into four categories. The first is that of the completely dried up and fossilized men who by virtue of their age and seniority sit in positions of authority without doing an iota of scientific work. They are busy intriguing or planning to obtain extensions in their term of service. Quite a few in this category unfortunately occupy Chairs and Readerships in the universities. This is tragic indeed as they ruin the chances of brilliant young men getting into their places. Such men had better be removed to some inactive posts or retired. The second category is of those scientists who are what I might call "careerists" and who do a routine job of work but are jealous of their promotions and prospects in service. Such men should go to government departments and never be put in charge of teaching or research.

The third category of our scientists is that of talented young men who are completely divorced from the realities of life in Pakistan and either grumble all the time blaming others for their inability to work or take on problems of research which are neither too fundamental to be of importance to science for its own sake nor too practical from the point of view of application of results. Such men need guidance and advice. In the conditions prevailing in the country which is beset with problems after problems our talented scientists in this class should select problems carefully in the applied field. In their attempt to solve such problems they may come up against some fundamental aspects in which case their hunger for basic research can be satisfied. Finally there are talented and brilliant young men who have their feet on the ground and who realize that the cause of science in Pakistan will suffer if they did not solve some of these problems whose solution will make a positive dent on the economy of Pakistan.[23]

The collective power of the students who have traditionally been easily incited by politicians to riot and strike is still feared. Nor is this predicament improved by government officials who have sometimes given the impression of siding with students against faculty members. For example, in April, 1962, the West Pakistan secretary of education declared at Government College, Sargodha, that the "entire responsibility for the mass failure of students rested on teachers." He further declared that henceforth teachers' promotions and even retention in service would depend on the results they achieved.[24] This statement suggests that the senior government official responsible for education in the province may hold views regarding relative responsibilities of scholar and student markedly different from those prevailing in the best academic systems of Western nations.

Strikes, riots, disturbances, and boycotting of classes are especially endemic when examinations are scheduled. Since periodic internal examinations are not given and class attendance is not compulsory, the student's standing depends entirely on the final examination, which, until 1962, was given at the end of two years, usually in May. The professor has no means of compelling the students to work during the interim, hence students waste their time in coffeehouses, bemoaning the poor quality of the faculty and deploring how little time students have to study. As examinations approach the students become frantic, accuse the professor of not covering the material adequately, strike for postponement, and more often than not force the administration to accede to their demands. The generic rubric under which blame is assessed is well-known in developing states, namely, that fault lies with the unscrupulous scheming of politicians who use student demonstrations as a vehicle for increasing their own power. This may not

[23] I. H. Usmani, "Presidential Address," CENTO Scientific Symposium, Lahore, January 8, 1962. See also *Report of the Scientific Commission of Pakistan* (Karachi, 1960) which lists trained scientists who have left Pakistan because of poor opportunities in scholarship.

[24] As reported in *Pakistan Times,* April 29, 1962, p. 7.

be the primary reason for student indiscipline, for demonstrations (although admittedly less frequent and less violent) continued under martial law in the total absence of politicians and of political parties. In the first two months of 1962, disturbances occurred in several colleges and universities in Pakistan. Official and unofficial comment tended to blame this on "enemies of Pakistan taking undue advantage of impetuosity and exuberance of . . . young students and . . . [exploiting] them in the name of Islam and the country." [25]

These external causes may be present and each disturbance was precipitated by its own peculiar set of local extenuating circumstances, but essentially the common, fundamental cause relates to the absence of a settled intellectual tradition embracing: (1) the role of the scholar in society, (2) the relative roles of student and teacher in the academic community, (3) the necessity for independence and insulation of the university from society, (4) the concept that education must be earned by hard work and earnestness, (5) the need for discipline and order, (6) the necessity of day-to-day hard work and study, (7) the necessity of failing and suspending students who cannot successfully do the prescribed work. The distortions of these essential characteristics which undergird the settled university systems of the United States, England, and Germany are so many that the higher educational system in Pakistan is almost chaotic.

A brief review of disturbances, most of which took place even under martial law in February, 1962, will illustrate the misconstruction of the roles of university and scholarship in society. At Emerson College in Multan there was a demonstration against the principal who allegedly slapped a student. The principal claimed he merely reprimanded the student who later apologized; he further claimed that the demonstration was "exploited by rowdy elements." [26] Students at Dow Medical College in Karachi struck because eight of their number were fined Rs. 50 each and placed under surveillance for allegedly throwing rotten eggs onto the

[25] Vice-Chancellor S. M. Sharif of the Panjab University, as reported in *ibid.*, April 23, 1962, p. 7.
[26] *Ibid.*, February 20, 1962, p. 12.

stage during a play. The students insisted that the dramatic club itself threw the eggs to start the disturbance as a distraction because they were embarrassed by the poor quality of their own performance. They demanded a long list of conditions to "restore their honour." [27] At the Lahore College of Animal Husbandry twenty-four allegations against the principal were made by striking students. Among them were mismanagement of mess funds by a mess committee of students and elimination of an Urdu section in the college magazine.[28] Subsequently, they demanded resignation of the principal. One disturbance which reveals the nature of university disarticulation is that of the West Pakistan Engineering and Technical University which has had such troubles in the past as the murder of its British principal immediately after partition.[29] Three professors publicly protested the appointment of a vice-chancellor in 1962 and were consequently removed from their positions. The students supported the professors, struck for eight demands, only two of which related directly to the removal of the teachers. Among the demands were three which suggest the underlying cause of most such disturbances, namely, examination panic. One demand was that examinations be held after the courses had been completed to the satisfaction of the students. Since students expect professors to lecture in detail on every point and since they are disinclined to study themselves, such a demand would force the professor to answer examination questions in advance. Portions of courses not lectured on (as determined by the students) were to be excluded from the examinations. These demands reflect the refusal of the students to work independently. Paradoxically, while criticizing the faculty as incompetent, they rely exclusively on the same faculty to drill them for the examinations. The third provision demanded postponement of the date of the examinations. The governor of the province refused to accept the demands, closed the university, and ordered students to vacate the hostels. But eventually he capitulated in part by reopening the university after discharging the vice-chancellor.

[27] *Ibid.*, February 18, 1962, p. 14.
[28] *Ibid.*, February 20, 1962, p. 12.
[29] *Civil and Military Gazette*, December 27, 1961, p. 4.

What is especially revealing is the attitude of the public and some of the press toward the governor's action. One Urdu paper, for example, instead of applauding his initial stand defying such student indiscipline, deplored his decision to close the university. Pakistan, it said, belongs to the people and "one thousand vice-chancellors should be sacrificed in deference to their wishes." [30] Another incident reveals the attitude toward examinations. In June, 1962, 150 students of King Edward Medical College, a distinguished school which observed its centenary in 1960, walked out of the examination hall in protest against the examination in surgery which they deemed too difficult. They then forced their way through barred doors into the Fatima Jinnah Medical College for Women and persuaded the women students to join them in the walkout.[31] Prospective physicians were not the only professional students to walk out of examinations. Two years earlier, in May, 1960, more than three hundred students of the Law College of Panjab University turned back their examination papers protesting that the questions were too difficult and were not included in the course. Several of the students who seemed to start the agitation were found guilty of misconduct but allowed to take the examination the next month upon payment of a fine. One student sought a writ compelling the university to allow him to take the examination without paying the fine. The High Court upheld the writ on the ground that he had not been heard by an inquiry committee before being fined.[32]

The earlier practice of politicians addressing students, which diminished somewhat under martial law, seemed to have been resumed when Z. A. Bhutto, then minister of industries and natural resources, spoke to students of the University of the Panjab in February, 1962. In the course of his address, he was interrupted by loud shouting and by a student fist fight in which the president

---

[30] *Hilal-i-Pakistan*, May 23, 1962, p. 1.

[31] As reported in *Pakistan Times*, June 21, 1962, p. 3. Medical students in Calcutta earlier in May were more aggressive. When the university called the police to control a demonstration demanding postponement of examinations, they stayed away from ward duty in the university hospital, locked the vice-chancellor in his rooms, and demanded his resignation and that of the dean of the medical faculty. The examinations, scheduled for May 29, 1962, were postponed (*The Statesman*, May 25, 1962, p. 1).

[32] *Muzaffar Ali v. Vice-Chancellor, Panjab University*, PLD 1961 Lah. 130.

of the student union was manhandled.[33] The Panjab student union accused its president of not keeping order during Bhutto's address, although the vice-chancellor was presiding. The student union president resigned "under duress" and filed a civil action against the vice-chancellor which was rejected by the court. This incident reveals the role of student unions and provocative speeches as elements contributing to the atmosphere of the university. Here the disturbance was probably due to student union politics. By far the most serious disturbance was the Dacca riots which started when students boycotted classes on February 1, 1962, and two days later demonstrated against a cabinet minister. On February 6 and 7, 1962, some four hundred students clashed with police. Subsequently, more than a hundred students were arrested and eleven were convicted by a military court and subsequently pardoned. The Dacca disturbances, however, were due primarily to Bengali discontent precipitated by the arrest of the Bengali politician, H. S. Suhrawardy. Nevertheless, this resurgence of student disorders which have been endemic at Dacca amply attests to the contorted values concerning scholarship which are regnant in the society. Nor has raising the banner of Islam been neglected as a reason for disturbing academic discipline. At Forman Christian College in Lahore students struck and asked for the principal's resignation on the ground that they were being required to take courses in Christianity. In fact, they were not so required, but the impression of Christian missionaries converting Muslims, created during a period of anti-Christian, anti-American feeling, appeared to be an effective cover for a plea to postpone examinations. In the Forman College disturbances, a new element was added, namely, the leadership of a small group of African students who were more volatile than their Pakistani colleagues. A different sort of disturbance is suggested by a case which was pending in June, 1962, in which it was alleged that three men conspired in the murder in Sialkot of the headmaster of Pasrur Government High School because he failed to promote one of the suspects.[34]

[33] *Pakistan Times,* February 25, 1962, p. 6.
[34] As reported in *ibid.,* June 11, 1962, p. 10.

Student unions play an increasingly prominent role in university disturbances, perhaps manipulated by "anti-state elements" or perhaps used as a vehicle for student frustration, and probably strengthened by both. It is especially interesting that American assistance strengthened the most important student union: that at Panjab University. Under auspices of a philanthropic foundation grant administered by an American university, a constructive program to remedy student unrest involved a strengthened student union with diversified social activities. The expectation, based on American experience, was that this would provide a healthy outlet for adolescent turmoil. But the union, once its status was thus enhanced by American money and organizational zeal, became a more powerful political agency through which the student body could negotiate with the vice-chancellor and others.[35] The student union president became a figure often rivalling the vice-chancellor in importance, and the press sometimes gave more prominence to his statements, walkouts, resignations, and threats than to any words or actions of the vice-chancellor. The student union became an outlet, but not for the anticipated release of tension through "healthy" social and physical activity. It became, rather, an agency for tough trade-union bargaining between a powerful adolescent president and a harried university administration.[36] Allegations of police interference in university student affairs are not uncommon. East Pakistani members of the National Assembly complained about an alleged police *lathi* charge on students in Chittagong in 1962. In March, 1963, Qamarul Ahsan complained of a "province-wide strike of students" which allegedly occurred on March 13, 1963, and of the "unprecedented" situation which "has left no institution unaffected." In April, Syed Abdus Sultan complained of "unprecedented official

---

[35] See editorial in *ibid.*, January 18, 1962, p. 4, for sympathetic comment on a memorandum submitted to the vice-chancellor outlining grievances.

[36] This is one of many instances of the problem of unpredictability of the direction which externally introduced reforms may take when there is only marginal understanding of the indigenous social forces at work. This example is reminiscent of the introduction in Japan during the American occupation of parent-teachers' associations which became powerful political groups, initially dominated by leftist elements. For further analysis see the author's "The Relevance of Political Science to the Study of Underdeveloped Areas," in Braibanti and Spengler, (eds.), *Tradition, Values and Socio-Economic Development*, pp. 152 ff.

interference . . . [which] has surpassed all British colonial ways." In East Pakistan, the 1963 convocation had to be cancelled at Rajshahi University because students objected to participation by the president.[37] Since the 1962 Constitution went into effect, discussion of the problem appears to have been affected by ambiguity as to responsibility for education. Education is now regarded as a provincial subject because it is not enumerated in the central list, hence extensive debate on student unrest has not been permitted in the National Assembly.

Political and educational leaders, cabinet ministers, the provincial governors, and President Ayub have repeatedly implored the students to attend to their studies and to eschew political activities. But the fundamental problem remains untouched by such hortatory declamations. One root of the problem is the absence of a system of discipline embracing rigorous daily routine which keeps students busy studying. Others are the absence of frequently evaluated requirements and the means of releasing students who do not meet these standards. The British system of higher education, of which the Pakistani system is a clouded reflection, assumes a high degree of student responsibility, careful pre-university preparation under conditions of rigid discipline, faculty responsibility and devotion to scholarship, and a widely diffused appreciation in society (at least among "The Establishment") of the proper role of the university. None of these preconditions exists in Pakistan, as the episodes described above suggest. The Pakistani system, revolving around the paramountcy of the final examination, makes possible months of leisure and dilettantish coffeehouse carousing, capped by a month of frantic cramming from outline books written by professors who thus supplement their meager teaching salaries. Chief Justice Kayani of the West Pakistan High Court summed up the problem in his deceptively simple style when he said in an address to the Panjab University students' union on December 7, 1959:

They [women] might devote some time to the correct bringing up of children so that when you come to the college or to the university you

[37] For these allegations see National Assembly of Pakistan, *Debates*, July 15, 1962, p. 1579; March 14, 1963, p. 386; April 11, 1963, pp. 1674 ff.

don't organize your fellow students to make a demonstration in front of the principal's house to close the college for a holiday or force the vice-chancellor to postpone an examination because you are fasting or because you have not prepared your courses. . . . You will never prepare them if you have not prepared them in two years. During these two years, you have digressed from the main purpose of your college life. Either it was aimless wandering or too much play and too little reading or too many love letters.[38]

The Commission on National Education considered the examination system but suggested only a minor change when it recommended that 25 per cent of the final total grade be based on periodic internal examinations given by the professor. This recommendation was only vaguely implemented by the ultimate university statute which said simply that teachers should give assignments and periodic tests and maintain a record of student performance on such assignments and tests.[39] But the number of such tests and their value in determining the students' ultimate standing was not clearly defined. This is insufficient to give the teacher the disciplinary control over his students which he must have. Indeed, the system of external examiners on whose judgments 75 (and before 1962, 100) per cent of the grade is based creates many of these problems. In the case of professional schools, students are not entirely unjustified in their complaints against examination papers which are usually prepared by non-teaching lawyers, physicians, or others. Presumably, those who set the papers have been apprised of the material covered in the course, but rarely is the co-ordination very satisfactory. As a consequence, the examiner often sets questions which have not been covered in the syllabus and often places questions pertaining to one part of the course into a separate paper. For example, a course may be divided into four papers, with certain parts of the course assigned to each paper. The student studies for each paper separately and is examined on each paper on separate days. If a question announced for the third paper is incorporated into the first paper, he

38 Full text in M. R. Kayani, *Not the Whole Truth* (Lahore, 1963), pp. 94–109. Quotation at p. 99.
39 Ordinance XXII of 1961, West Pakistan (University of the Punjab) Ordinance, 1961, in *Gazette of West Pakistan, Extraordinary*, September 18, 1961, pp. 2203–2234.

is justifiably disconcerted, since he did not study for that question. All students, professional and undergraduate alike, are confronted by the likelihood that, since the brief syllabus will not adequately guide the external examiner, questions will be written on the examiner's notions of what might be or should have been included in the instruction. This uncertainty combined with the substantial disparity in knowledge and method between the older examiner and the young teacher presents a frustrating situation. Further, since the older examiners are far more skilled in the use of English than the post-independence students, confusion results from linguistic misunderstanding. A related difficulty is that the student feels that a question based on a lecture is "out of the course" when it is not covered in the written text. This is his excuse for not having attended the lecture.

The system of higher education is almost as much to blame as the student. Nothing short of wholesale change in the direction of professional autonomy and strict discipline is likely to solve the situation. Discipline under any circumstances is hard enough to achieve. Even when a peaceful situation prevails, the conduct of classes is hardly conducive to careful, systematic learning under conditions of intellectual detachment and rationality. Within the classroom the psychology of the advocate dominates; the lecturer defends his point of view, while student inquisitors by use of sophistry, rhetoric, and sheer confusion aim to demolish it. The class divides into factions; the professor does not remain detached from them and is thought to recriminate against factions not in his "favor." The academic atmosphere created by the various conditions here described does not elevate the position of the scholar in the community, and the respect accorded to research is reduced as well.

The final means of seeking redress of grievances within the academic community is by filing a suit with the High Court in the writ jurisdiction, usually on the ground of denial of natural justice.[40] While the High Court rejects more writ applications

[40] On the writ jurisdiction, see Ralph Braibanti, "Public Bureaucracy and Judiciary in Pakistan," in Joseph LaPalombara (ed.), *Bureaucracy and Political Development* (Princeton, 1963), pp. 360–441.

relating to universities than it accepts, it acts in a sufficient number of instances so that students are not discouraged by the possibilities of the writ's failure. In any event, the pending litigation delays the final outcome of whatever university action the student protests and gives him time to seek the application of political pressure on the syndicate or some other entity in the university. From 1954 through March, 1965, nineteen decisions involving educational matters were published by the judiciary. Sixteen of these were cases in the High Court of West Pakistan. Only one was tried in the High Court of East Pakistan and two by the Supreme Court. Seventeen of the cases focused on issues in higher education; two cases involved lower schools. The incidence of substantive issues dealt with is as follows: examinations, nine; election, one; rank, two; admission, three; rustication (suspension), two; miscellaneous, one; student indiscipline, one. Seven of the cases involved the University of Karachi, six arose from conflict at the University of the Panjab, Dacca National Medical Institute, Dow Medical College, Hailey College of Commerce, Government College (Lahore), and Dacca University. Two cases involved secondary schools. The High Court of West Pakistan had asserted its jurisdiction over educational matters as early as 1954 [41] when it noted that nothing in the Karachi University Act barred its jurisdiction and that a civil court may review a university action if university authorities act *ultra vires* (in disregard of their own statutes, rules, and regulations). The court showed some restraint in this decision by ruling that it would not review a university action if the university acted *intra vires* (in consonance with its own regulations). It continued to manifest this restraint in its second relevant decision,[42] in which M. R. Kayani upheld the power of the university to review credentials of degree candidates and refused to substitute the judgment of the court for that of the university in such a review *intra vires*. In the third case [43] Kayani departed from the posture of restraint and, by distinguishing between the civil action of the earlier Siddiq case and the writ of

[41] *Shafqatullah Qadri v. University of Karachi,* PLD 1954 Sind 107.
[42] *Muhammad Siddiq v. University of the Panjab,* PLD 1954 Lah. 5.
[43] *Fazal Karim Chaudhri v. Panjab University,* PLD 1955 Lah. 404.

mandamus of the present case, he directed by mandamus that a university regulation be interpreted as the court interpreted it. This expansionist view of the court was upheld in all subsequent cases until 1961 and was ultimately given further support by invoking the doctrine of "natural justice." This doctrine assumes the paramountcy of the right of any individual to be heard before being condemned. Thus, the court upheld the right of a student to be heard before being rusticated [44] and of professors to be heard before the results of a faculty election could be set aside by the vice-chancellor.[45] In a subsequent case, that of a vice-chancellor who declared certain students to be "mischief-mongers" and imposed a fine on them, the court struck down his action on the same ground that the "condemned" students were not given a hearing.[46] The judiciary consistently struck down any effort on the part of the executive branch to interfere with internal university matters when such interference was challenged by the university. Thus, the Ministry of Education could not order a college principal to cancel the admission of a student [47] and the Ministry of Health could not order a college to admit students by a quota system.[48] Nor did the court allow a provincial government to order the closing of a medical college which it regarded as substandard. This, said the court, was an invasion of the right of freedom of association.[49]

In 1961, there was some indication of a return to a doctrine of judicial self-restraint in a case decided by the High Court of West Pakistan. A number of employees of the West Pakistan University of Engineering and Technology were displeased with the appointment of a new vice-chancellor, and several subordinate employees made public statements urging his removal. The vice-chancellor, regarding a group of professors as being particularly antagonistic,

[44] *Muhammad Munir Shahid* v. *Principal, Government College, Sargodha,* PLD 1958 Lah. 466.
[45] *S. M. Saleem* v. *Vice-Chancellor, University of Karachi,* PLD 1958 Kar. 297.
[46] *Muzaffer Ali Shah* v. *Vice-Chancellor, University of the Punjab,* PLD 1961 Lah. 130.
[47] *A. Rehman Kureshi* v. *Principal, Dow Medical College and others,* PLD 1957 Kar. 534.
[48] *Syed Abdul Wadood* v. *Pakistan and others,* PLD 1957 Kar. 740.
[49] *The Dacca National Medical Institute* v. *Province of East Pakistan,* PLD 1958 Dacca 560.

allegedly ordered four of them to go to Karachi, Dacca, and Lahore to prepare lists of books and journals.[50] Allegedly, this was done for the purpose of removing them from the site of conflict. The High Court considered the application but refused to grant the writ.[51] Again in 1962 there was some indication of restraint. Students entered a university in 1958 when the requirement was that the final examination count for 40 per cent of the total grade.[52] Two years later the requirement was changed to 45 per cent. The students' qualification for graduation was based on the new requirements and they failed to meet them. They sought a writ of mandamus to compel the university to use the 1958 requirement as a basis for qualification. The High Court dismissed the writ and the Supreme Court upheld the dismissal.

The "natural justice" formulary was the basis of the most significant judgment by the Supreme Court involving educational institutions.[53] The case arose as a consequence of action taken by the University of Dacca against certain students who allegedly were guilty of indiscipline, misconduct, and rowdyism during the university convocation of March, 1964. A group of students, opposed to the chancellor's presiding over the convocation, clashed with a group favoring his participation. Disturbances occurred during the ceremony and later in the same evening riots by some five hundred persons were brought under police control. The university closed for an indefinite period to prevent the situation from becoming worse. In response to a request from the university registrar, faculty members submitted written reports naming students believed to have been responsible for the disturbances. The university board of discipline expelled for two years several students named in the reports. One of the students, Zakir Ahmad, sought a writ under Article 98 of the Constitution prohibiting the university from expelling him because he was not served with notice nor was he given an opportunity to refute the

[50] For various accounts see *Civil and Military Gazette*, December 27, 1961, p. 4.
[51] Mumtaz Husain Qureshi and three others *v.* Vice-Chancellor of West Pakistan University of Engineering and Technology, Writ No. 832, High Court of West Pakistan, December 27, 1961 (unpublished).
[52] *Sultana Khokar* v. *University of the Punjab*, PLD 1962, SC 35.
[53] *University of Dacca* v. *Zakir Ahmad*, PLD 1965, SC 90.

charges against him. The case was argued before a division bench of the East Pakistan High Court and was again heard by a special bench of five judges of that court. The High Court unanimously ruled that the university had violated the rule of natural justice embodied in the maxim *audi alteram partem*. An appeal was made to the Supreme Court by the University of Dacca which engaged Manzur Qadir, former chief justice of the West Pakistan High Court and said to be the draftsman of the 1962 Constitution, as its counsel. In a unanimous decision by five judges, the Supreme Court upheld the High Court. Manzur Qadir argued that the rule of natural justice cannot apply to government institutions which must maintain internal discipline. The Supreme Court conceded the necessity for maintaining discipline in universities but concluded that they must observe "certain formalities which have been designed to assure the minimum essential principles of justice and fairness." Such principles include "at least telling the persons sought to be punished or condemned what are the allegations against him and . . . giving him a fair opportunity to correct or contradict any relevant statement to his prejudice." Thus, in the Dacca case, the Supreme Court clearly established the duty of the judiciary to assure observance of "natural justice" in university treatment of students.

The nineteen published cases [54] are revealing as descriptions of factious and traumatic problems that commonly arise in university life. Such conflict within universities emerges not only for the reasons alluded to in the earlier analysis of education, but also because there is highly uneven diffusion of standards of justice derived from Western jurisprudence and great likelihood that these standards are not understood or, if understood, not observed. Hence, the judiciary enters a vacuum created by absence

[54] In addition to those cited in notes 41–53 above, the other judgments are: *Warisali Khan Khattack* v. *University of Karachi*, PLD 1956 Kar. 156; *Iftikar Ahmad and another* v. *University of Karachi and another*, PLD 1957 Kar. 635; *Ismail* v. *Principal, Dow Medical College and others*, PLD 1957 Kar. 493; *Lt. Col. Aziz K. M. Khan* v. *A. B. A. Haleem, Vice-Chancellor, University of Karachi*, PLD 1957 Kar. 496; *University of Punjab* v. *Mohsan Tirmizey*, PLD 1958 Lah. 943; *Begum Wasim Intizar* v. *Punjab Province*, PLD 1958 Lah. 319; *Hassan Imam* v. *Principal, Hailey College of Commerce*, PLD 1959 Lah. 872; *Muzaffar Ali Shah and others* v. *Vice-Chancellor, University of Punjab*, PLD 1961 Lah. 130; *Muhammad Nawaz* v. *Chairman, District Council etc.*, PLD 1961 Pesh. 152.

or erosion of norms. While the effect of such juridical action may be the attainment of justice in the immediate instance, the chronic fear that a writ may be sought does little in the long run to enhance the requirement of disciplined, hierarchical relations within the university community.

The incidence of student disturbances seems to have increased in 1964 partly because of excitement over the presidential elections on January 2, 1965. The only major institution where no student disturbances had occurred, the University of Peshawar, became the scene of disturbances late in 1964. All universities were closed for several weeks late in 1964 and early 1965 to forestall further disturbances.

Despite this rise in incidence of disturbances, the government has taken several moves to improve conditions. Most plans are long-range and the results will not be discernible for several years. Nevertheless, the situation is actually improving. Some of the measures are designed to correct immediate problems, yet resistance to them by the academic community has made the situation somewhat more difficult. Immediate measures have focused on maintenance of order and discipline. In December, 1961, the governor of West Pakistan promulgated ordinances regulating the conduct of employees of Sind, Peshawar, and Panjab universities,[55] and in January, 1962, the vice-chancellor of the University of the Panjab issued instructions prohibiting teachers from visiting the university's administrative offices during working hours.[56] The latter were designed to prevent gossip, plotting, reading of office correspondence, eliciting information from clerks and typists, and similar practices which are endemic to university as well as to other administrative systems. The need for issuing such regulations bespeaks conditions in the universities. The President in June, 1962, amended the Penal Code by issuing an ordinance which makes it a crime to incite students to political activity.[57] The

[55] University of Panjab (Sind, Peshawar) Employees (Efficiency and Discipline) University Ordinances, 1961, in *Gazette of West Pakistan, Extraordinary,* November 30, 1961, pp. 2825–2853.
[56] *Pakistan Times,* January 22, 1962, p. 2.
[57] Pakistan Penal Code (Second Amendment) Ordinance, 1962, June 8, 1962, in *Gazette of Pakistan, Extraordinary,* June 7, 1962.

most sweeping and most controversial of the government's actions are embodied in the "University Ordinances" which became an issue in the presidential election of 1965. The manifesto of the Combined Opposition party listed the University Ordinances as one of eight "authoritarian enactments" which it pledged to repeal.[58] The University Ordinances, which have been the subject of much contention among students, professors, politicians, and the legal community are, in fact, a group of enactments and amendments put into effect in 1961 and 1962 before the end of martial law.[59] The 1962 amendment, promulgated the day before the end of martial law, is a particular irritant to these groups. Although each university is governed by a separate ordinance, the enactments are virtually identical. Ordinances for the University of the Panjab are cited below and are discussed here as typical, but analogous provisions apply to the other universities as well. Although the basic ordinance is the least objectionable of the three, critics point out that the chancellor's (provincial governor's) power to withdraw degrees granted to any person subsequently convicted of an offense involving moral turpitude is a provision not found in other countries.[60] Critics also find objectionable an amendment to the basic ordinance which gives universities the power to supervise "extra-curricular activities and discipline of students . . . and to ensure that undesirable persons do not take advantage of or otherwise exploit any association of students for extracurricular or other activities." [61] But the sharpest criticism is leveled against the efficiency and discipline ordinances

[58] *Nine-Point Manifesto and Joint Declaration of the Combined Opposition Party* (Dacca, July 14, 1964), Point 3.

[59] The basic enactment is West Pakistan (University of the Punjab) Ordinance XXII of 1961, published in *Gazette of West Pakistan, Extraordinary,* September 18, 1961. Ancillary to this is University of the Punjab Employees (Efficiency and Discipline) University Ordinances, 1961, published in the *Gazette of West Pakistan, Extraordinary,* February 2, 1962, and West Pakistan (Universities) Removal of Undesirable Government Servants Ordinance XX of 1962, published in *Gazette of West Pakistan, Extraordinary,* May 25, 1962. The basic ordinance for all West Pakistan universities and the ancillary ordinances on efficiency and discipline for the same universities were subsequently amended by a single enactment, West Pakistan Universities (Amendment) Ordinance XL of 1962 published in *Gazette of West Pakistan, Extraordinary,* June 7, 1962.

[60] West Pakistan (University of the Punjab) Ordinance XXII of 1961, Chapter III, Section 9, par. (4).

[61] West Pakistan Universities (Amendment) Ordinance XL of 1962, 3, (a) (xiii).

as amended in 1962. These ordinances transfer disciplinary authority from the university syndicate or vice-chancellor to the chancellor, who is the provincial governor. There is also an enlargement of the grounds for penalty which make it possible for the governor to suspend any employee whom he deems to be "engaged, or is reasonably suspected of being engaged, in subversive activities or activities detrimental to the interest of the University or national security, or is reasonably suspected of being associated with others in such activities, and whose retention is considered prejudicial to the interest of the University or national security." Such suspension is not the final penalty; it is merely preparatory to final determination of guilt by an inquiry committee to be convened by the chancellor. The ambiguity of this ground, and transfer of the suspension power out of the hands of the university syndicate into the ambit of non-academic bureaucracy, is disturbing to the academic community. The government response is that the syndicate is itself subject to political pressures, hence cannot deal with "subversion" as effectively as the governor, who is appointed by and responsible only to the president of Pakistan. A particular source of irritation is the apparent failure of the amending Ordinance XL of 1962 either to amend or rescind Ordinance XX of 1962, which empowers the provincial governor to remove any university employee whom he deems "undesirable" and whose removal he deems "expedient in the public interest." The only legal safeguard in this removal is notification to show cause against the proposed action.

The potential of the amended enactments for political use is obvious. The intention of the government was to control university disorder by strengthening the hand of the governor. But the antagonism of the university community was increased rather than lessened and large numbers appeared to support the Combined Opposition party in part because of its pledge to rescind the University Ordinances. The government was sufficiently impressed by the seriousness of the situation to appoint a Commission on Students' Problems and Welfare in December, 1964.[62] The

[62] See notification and terms of reference in *Gazette of Pakistan, Extraordinary,* December 15, 1964, p. 5960.

commission consisted of Supreme Court Justice Hamood-ur-Rahman, chairman, West Pakistan High Court Justice S. A. Mahmood, Qazi Anwar-ul-Haq, chairman of the Central Public Service Commission, and Nasir Ahmad, chairman of the West Pakistan Public Service Commission. That the problems have affected both provinces is indicated by the fact that Justice Hamood-ur-Rahman and Mr. Anwar-ul-Haq are East Pakistani and the other two members West Pakistani. The first term of reference is "to examine the provisions of the University Ordinances and suggest modifications wherever necessary." The commission is also empowered to examine programs of study, welfare facilities, and any other matter affecting student life.

The major changes made in universities will probably not be felt for some years. The most important of these is the steady improvement of teaching staff at all universities. Younger scholars now have American and sometimes British doctorates. This training will probably bring about the social and intellectual distance between professor and student which is a necessity in Pakistani, indeed in any, society. The quality of teaching is bound to improve and the work assigned students will be more rigorous. Secondly, the creation of departments *de novo* based on the American pattern of compulsory attendance at lectures and regular examinations is already widely respected by students and will probably influence the total structure. Thirdly, the creation of two agricultural universities and two engineering and technology universities, based entirely on the American pattern, will subject a large segment of the student population to the American system of rigorous discipline. Gradually, university campuses are being shifted out of cities or are being made entirely residential. Karachi and Panjab universities have new suburban locations, and it is expected that the removal of students from the urban centers of unrest and the regulation over conduct implicit in campus residence will eliminate some causes of disturbance.

The effect of the resumption of political activity by organized parties cannot yet be assessed. If parties resume their old habits of exploiting student groups, despite the Penal Code, the politicization of the university environment will increase and ordered intellectual activity will be in greater jeopardy. It is conceivable, on the other hand, that the existence of parties may mitigate the frustrations now felt by students with respect to political affairs.

Implications of National Integration

Pakistan is by no means a homogeneous cultural, linguistic, or ethnic entity. Even Islam, the religion of nearly all of West Pakistan, and of about 80 per cent of East Pakistan, has internal cleavages: Sunni, Shias, Qadiani, Ismaili. These have sometimes caused serious upheavals, such as the Punjab disturbances of 1953 which resulted from the belief of certain orthodox groups that the Qadiani were heretics rather than true Muslims. Within West Pakistan, Sindhi, Baluchi, Pathans, and Punjabis constitute the major cultural groups, each with its own language. Until 1955, each group had its own province within which an active political process provided an outlet for regional political forces. Since the integration of the four provinces into the one province of West Pakistan, some regional animosities persist, particularly among Pathans. Such feelings are manifested principally in concern for parity of representation in the public services.[63]

While the various political and social dimensions of cleavages within West Pakistan are important subjects for research, they are not as significant in affecting research generally as are the differences between the two provinces of East and West Pakistan. Research must take into account two major risks related to the cultural-linguistic and political differences of the two provinces. The first is that generalizations for the whole of Pakistan based on experience in only one province are of questionable validity and should be avoided. Yet the formulation of nationwide generalizations is an easy error for foreign students to make even if they have experience in both provinces. This is acerbated by the fact that the researcher derives his impressions from government officials and others who, although invariably parochically oriented to their own province, tend unwittingly to make nationwide

[63] See, for example, discussion relating to selection of Sindhis in the 1962 recruitment to the CSP in National Assembly of Pakistan, *Debates*, June 4, 1963, pp. 449–451.

generalizations. Such impressions tend to reinforce the foreign researcher's parochial view and thus is distortion compounded. The second risk is that the question of relations between the two wings is an uncommonly sensitive issue, the rational, objective discussion of which is improbable among Pakistani. Yet, while it should be approached with finesse and scholarly detachment by the foreign student, it should not, merely because of its delicacy, be altogether avoided. Such avoidance would make any national analysis of issues totally unrealistic and would place out of the realm of research one of the most challenging and difficult problems of political development in modern times. It is, therefore, worthwhile in an essay on research to suggest the dimensions of and dangers implicit in the problem and at the same time to suggest some of the aspects which make this a significant subject for research.

The problem (commonly denominated "national integration" or "East-West integration") is accentuated by the fact that Bengalis are inevitably competitively cast with the Punjabis, the group in West Pakistan which dominates administration and whose influence is greater than that of other groups. Of the major groups in West Pakistan (Pathans, Sindhis, Baluchi), the Punjabis by temperament and history are probably the least similar to Bengalis. Pathans, while ethnically more dissimilar, are popular among Bengalis, in part because of their directness of manner and because they offered continuing resistance to British rule. The Punjab was in many ways the most favored province of India and came under sustained, concentrated British influence. From this area, the "martial races" came and there is scarcely a village which does not have one or more military pensioners with some knowledge of English, nostalgia for the army, and great respect for the British. In the Punjab were the great *zamindar* families with huge landholdings, whose sons were educated in England from an early age (often living with the family of a rural vicar) and in many instances were knighted by the Crown. The general headquarters of the Indian Army was located in Rawalpindi, and in Lahore was the largest and most attractive military cantonment in the whole of India. In Lahore, center of Punjabi society, was Aitchison College (commonly called Chiefs' College), an elite school of British pattern for the education of sons of tribal chiefs and other leaders. The presence in Lahore of the political resident to the Punjab states meant much coming and going of the princely rulers and a consequent quickening of the social pulse. The outward symptoms of this concentration of British and local social influence of landed wealth are obvious: one of the largest and most elaborate *gymkhanas* in India and a cosmopolitan, leisured society devoted to British customs and immodest enough to regard itself as the most "advanced" and "modernized" society in Pakistan. The prosperous surplus farm lands of the canal colonies gave the Punjab a hardworking, sturdy peasant group, usually Jats, and Arains, both Muslim and Sikh. The values of Punjabi society were essentially pragmatic rather than poetic or philosophical. A respect for military precision, administrative talent, agricultural pursuits, and Western social practices was dominant.

Probably no region in India (certainly none in North India) could be more opposite to the Punjab in externals and in spirit than East Bengal which was joined together with West Pakistan with no more common bond than Islam. The Bengalis are by ethnic origin more closely related to Southeast Asia than to Persia and Afghanistan, the twin fountainheads of Punjabi and Pathan culture. More importantly, Bengalis have a remarkably homogeneous culture, rich in art, music, dance, language, poetry, and philosophy epitomized in Rabindranath Tagore. A highly developed aesthetic sensitivity makes them more akin to the culture of Southeast Asia than to the practical earthiness of the Aryan Punjabi. Their temperament, molded by the lush, riverine, tropical lands in which they live, combines a quick, volatile, sensitive independence with a keen love of political activity and of intellectual disputation. Although their intellectual proclivity [64] naturally

[64] The very first Indians to pass the difficult examinations for the Indian Civil Service were Bengali Hindus. In 1864, Satyendranath Tagore, brother of the Nobel prize winner, Rabindranath Tagore, passed the examination but did not enter the service. In 1869, Behari Lal Gupta, Surendranath Banerjea, and Romesh Chandra Dutt passed and entered the service. Chandra Dutt had a remarkably distinguished career as both an administrator and an economic historian. Although mastering Western intellectual values, these and other Bengali intellectuals did not turn away from Bengali culture.

impelled the Bengalis to learn English, the profoundity and homogeneity of their culture enabled them to reject successfully the influence of British social mores. Moreover, they actively resisted rather than acquiesced in British rule. They were neither interested in nor allowed to serve in the combat military forces, hence no web of allegiance to the British was spun by military experience. The spirit of Bengali independence compelled the development of vigorous local self-government and the early demise of large landholdings, while in the Punjab feudal conditions of serfdom prevailed and the *zamindari* were not challenged until martial law land reforms in 1958. Such factors as these have given Bengali administration a different quality from that of the Punjab. It is more egalitarian in demeanor, more democratic in outlook, more informal, closer to the people in mood and attitude, and less haughty. At the same time, administration and politics are less stable, highly charged with turbulent emotion, and exceedingly fractious. So pervasive is the quality of Bengali culture that it has developed a very strong corporate sense. Bengalis, more aware of their Bengali culture than are Punjabis of their own heritage, are more likely to cling together and support each other simply because they are Bengalis. The Bengali communities in Karachi, Lahore, and Rawalpindi are in many ways more isolated and self-contained than the Parsi communities. Moreover, Bengalis in East Pakistan, living as they do with 20 per cent of their population Hindu, have greater understanding of Hinduism and Buddhism than do West Pakistani. In this respect, they are at once more tolerant of diversity of religious belief and more cosmopolitan in their cultural outlook. But the cosmopolitanism is within an Asian cultural ambit and does not extend quite as much to Britain. On the other hand, what cosmopolitanism is found in West Pakistan is limited to identification with Britain and Iran. The pervading force of Bengali culture somewhat reduces the importance of whether the Bengali is Hindu or Muslim. In contrast, the almost total absence of Hindus in West Pakistan (the few hundred Hindus are concentrated almost entirely in certain villages in the Sind) gives Punjabis and others no contact with Hindus. This reinforces attitudes of animosity, and, conjoined with grave distrust of India, conjures up images of what is regarded as Hindu villainy. The consequent closer identity of the Muslim of East Pakistan with the Hindu Bengali has given rise to a misconception in West Pakistan, namely, that East Pakistan is too friendly to India and therefore "anti-Pakistan." This is not a fair interpretation of a problem which is essentially one of culture rather than of politics.

The sensitivity of relations between the two provinces derives essentially from these differentials and from the feeling of the Bengali that East Pakistan, which has 54 per cent of the nation's total population, has not been given adequate attention in the past. Above all, the Bengali finds exasperating the typical Punjabi attitude of condescension which seems to assume that East Pakistan is a backward area culturally as well as economically.

To examine all the causes of tension between the two wings is not possible within the scope of this essay on research. It may be helpful, however, to survey briefly some of the feelings of the Bengalis. One issue has been inadequate representation in government services. For various historical reasons, Muslim Bengalis had always been underrepresented in government service, especially in the ICS. The problem of parity of Bengali representation had many dimensions, all delicate to resolve and potentially fissive. Administration after partition was affected in at least two ways. There arose the need, first, to secure greater Bengali representation in the total administrative system (both central and provincial), and second, to provide Bengali administrators for high-level positions of an ICS character in East Pakistan. Neither problem was ever completely solved to the satisfaction of East Pakistan, although by 1958 the situation was greatly improved. Some idea of the intensity of Bengali feeling on the issue of parity can be gained from debates in the National Assembly before its dissolution in 1958. As late as April, 1956, a detailed statement of assignments in diplomatic missions made by the foreign minister in response to close questioning by a member from East Pakistan revealed that parity had not been achieved. It was said that of 129 gazetted officers, fifty-three (or 41 per cent) came from East Pakistan; of 976 non-gazetted officers, 176 (or 18 per cent) were

East Pakistani.[65] Some 36 per cent of chiefs of missions were from East Pakistan. In the same year, Sheikh Mujibur Rahman of East Pakistan, complaining bitterly of disparity in the government's industrial development policy, cited that no director of the Pakistan Industrial Development Corporation was a Bengali and that only one of ninety officers and twelve of seven hundred subordinate staff members were Bengalis.[66] Again in 1957, in a long speech describing the relations of the two wings of Pakistan, Maulvi Farid Ahmad, reminding the assembly "that East Pakistan had to make tremendous sacrifices as regards the numerical superiority over West Pakistan" warned that the government was not moving quickly enough toward parity of representation in the Civil Service of Pakistan.[67] When the new National Assembly convened on June 8, 1962, the subject of parity in the public services was again brought up within the first week of debates and continued to be discussed almost daily. The *Pakistan Times* commented that parity between the two wings seemed to be the only topic discussed in the assembly, much to the boredom of the reporters. But the administrative dimensions of the problem of regional parity confronting the nation in 1947 were formidable. Only one Bengali was among the total 133 ICS-IPS officers available to Pakistan at partition. To have achieved parity immediately would have required a moratorium on recruitment from West Pakistan. Perhaps this might have been possible, and most Bengalis would argue that it was. But it is doubtful if so large a number of qualified candidates for the CSP cadre could have been found in any single year. It has also been argued that a larger number of older officers from other services could have been brought in by lateral entry, and it is true that when in 1952 fifteen members of the provincial civil services were integrated into the CSP cadre, only four were Bengalis.

Whatever the reasons may have been, rapid attainment of parity was not the policy followed by the government. That policy

[65] National Assembly of Pakistan, *Debates*, April 5, 1956, pp. 431 ff.

[66] *Ibid.*, March 21, 1956, pp. 311 ff. The same issue was repeated after martial law. See, for example, *ibid.*, July 3, 1962, pp. 938 ff.

[67] *Ibid.*, February 15, 1957, pp. 427 ff. See extract from this speech in Appendix 4.

was gradually to bring about parity in the CSP cadre using a formula which would permit entrance both on merit and on a regional quota basis. Given the assumptions that an elite cadre was necessary and that its mystique would be destroyed by too great an infusion of neophytes irrespective of regional origin, the government's policy of gradualism was consistent. Even in 1964, parity had not been achieved, for the percentage of Bengalis in the CSP cadre of 432 was 30 per cent.[68] It is of crucial importance in understanding the reasons for this to remember that the initial regional composition of the ICS-IPS group that transferred from India was very much imbalanced: one to 133. To have achieved greater balance without completely destroying the merit basis of entrance is a statistical improbability.

Representation in the services was but one facet of the vexing problem of national integration. Brief reference to some of the other issues will enhance understanding of the acuteness of feeling on the problem of integration. During the first decade of Pakistan's existence, the issue of a national language was the most serious source of antagonism between the two provinces. The Quaid-i-Azam had declared in 1949 that Urdu would be the national language and this was provided for in the interim report of the Basic Principles Committee. Violent demonstrations took place at the University of Dacca as a protest against this provision. The final report made no mention of a national language and the Constitution of 1956 gave equal status to Urdu and Bengali as two state languages. The 1962 Constitution continues this policy, hence the language problem is no longer the burning issue it once was. Nevertheless, sensitivity to this question has not entirely disappeared, and Bengalis continue to criticize the central government for failure to use Bengali script on signs, currency, and in public notifications whenever Urdu is officially used. The exclusive use of Urdu on currency notes issued in 1948–49 acerbated

[68] Debates in the National Assembly are the most valuable source of information on parity generally and parity in the services particularly. For example, for parity in the central government, see *ibid.*, June 18, 1962, pp. 111–113; on appointment of section officers and CSP officer, see *ibid.*, March 11, 1963, pp. 146–148 and 156–157.

Bengali feelings.[69] The President's address to the assembly in 1956 was sharply criticized for its failure to deal with problems of East Pakistan, and especially for not presenting an effective plan for bringing about parity in the service.[70] Many of these problems have since been resolved; certainly there is a better balance of representation in the services than in the early days of independence. Yet the problems of national integration have by no means been surmounted. In recent years they have been focused more in the economic than in the political realm.

The unrest of Bengal is not always concealed beneath a surface of outer calm. Immediately before martial law, a riot broke out in the Provincial Assembly in Dacca, resulting in the death of the speaker.[71] This disturbance was specifically mentioned by President Iskander Mirza in his proclamation of October 7, 1958, presumably as evidence of political deterioration serious enough to warrant his action. Under martial law the situation in East Pakistan stabilized somewhat. The appointment of Lt. Gen. M. Azam Khan, a Pathan, as governor was a popular move which was probably more responsible than any single factor for the Bengalis' outward acceptance of the fact of martial law. But even Azam Khan's popularity as governor did not completely allay the dissatisfactions and suspicions of the Bengalis toward West Pakistan. Usually firebrands in politics, suspension of the National Assembly and provincial assemblies now deprived them of their principal means of political participation. Since their representation in the civil services was small and in the military services was almost nil, they felt this aspect of martial law all the more acutely. Open discussion of provincial grievances was reduced but not eliminated entirely by the provisions of Martial Law Regulation No. 34,[72] which declared: "Whoever by word of mouth or in writing or

[69] *Ibid.*, April 9, 1956, p. 669. The issue of use of Bengali script whenever Urdu is used in all central government printing was again raised when the National Assembly was reconstituted in June, 1962. The fact that Bengali has been omitted more often than not illustrates the government attitude toward these matters of which the Bengalis have bitterly complained. See *ibid.*, July 3, 1962, pp. 924 ff.; *ibid.*, July 6, 1962, p. 1093.

[70] *Ibid.*, March 29, 1956, pp. 197 ff.

[71] See Asir Report mentioned below, p. 212.

[72] Published in *Gazette of Pakistan, Extraordinary*, October 15, 1958, p. 1964.

otherwise spread news, rumours, or reports on provincial, sectarian and linguistic basis calculated towards territorial or administrative dismemberment of Pakistan shall be punished with rigorous imprisonment which may extend to 14 years." Certainly few, if any, Bengalis favored "dismembering" the nation, but talk of provincial grievances, which necessarily included the linguistic problem of Bengali, might easily be construed as coming within the prohibition of this inclusive regulation. As a consequence, the provincial issue was smothered. In the meantime, affirmative measures were taken by the central government to allay the fears of East Pakistan. Larger portions of the budget for economic development were allocated to the east wing, and the quota system for entrance into the Civil Service of Pakistan was enforced, thus increasing the ratio of Bengalis in the CSP. The Bureau of National Reconstruction took positive steps to probe a theoretical basis for "integration" of the two wings. The five-day seminar held in Lahore in September, 1961, revealed, however, the depth of feeling in East Pakistan. Rehman Sobhan, an economist of the University of Dacca, advocated two separate "functional economies" with each province having full control over its foreign and domestic resources. This touched on a sensitive issue, for it was thought that the jute of East Pakistan was the principal means in all Pakistan of earning foreign exchange. There were sharp repudiations of Sobhan's thesis by West Pakistani economists,[73] and in November, 1961, East Pakistan held its own seminar on "Pakistan Nationhood" in which the Bengali point of view was given wider expression.

For some months prior to promulgation in June of the 1962 Constitution, the martial law government was moving with vigor toward decentralization of policy-making and administrative activities. The nationalized railways were divided into two separate provincial railway systems, the Pakistan Industrial Development Corporation was divided into two separate provincial corporations, and when it was decided to tackle agricultural problems with the corporate device, two separate provincial corporations

[73] See accounts in *Pakistan Times,* September 23, 1961, p. 1; November 10, 1961, p. 9; and editorial, September 25, 1961, p. 6.

were created. As the announced time for the end of martial law
neared, East Pakistan became more restive, and when H. S.
Suhrawardy, the chief minister of Bengal during partition and
later prime minister of Pakistan, was arrested for "anti-state activities" and imprisoned in Karachi without trial, serious disturbances
took place. A student strike on February 1, 1962, at the University
of Dacca spread to other colleges and areas. The incidents were
first reported by the Indian newspaper, *The Statesman,* and its
Dacca correspondent was given forty-eight hours to leave. Subsequently, the governor issued statements describing the riots. The
central government held the view that these disturbances were
caused primarily by Communist agitators based in Calcutta. For
undisclosed reasons, Lt. Gen. Azam Khan was allowed to retire as
governor, and the East Pakistani, who regarded him as their
spokesman and protector, were once again displeased. But the
appointment of Ghulam Faruque, a distinguished initiator of
development projects, who was chairman of the Pakistan Industrial Development Corporation and later chairman of the West
Pakistan Power and Development Authority, seemed to offer
hope that economic development would be accelerated in the
province. For whatever reasons, there were no disturbances over
Azam Khan's resignation. Whatever the causes of the agitation
may have been, when the new Constitution was announced and
the new government formed, the attention given to the problems
of East Pakistan was greater than ever before. The doctrine of
parity in all spheres was included as a principle of policy in the
1962 Constitution. When the National Assembly added the first
amendment which enumerated ten fundamental rights and made
them justiciable, the eighth right prohibited discrimination in
services, but to permit attainment of parity, posts might be reserved for a fifteen-year period to secure adequate representation
of "persons belonging to any class or area." The Constitution
(Article 211 [5]) designated Dacca to be the "principal seat of the
National Assembly" and further declare that Dacca would be a
"second Capital of the Republic" (Article 211 [3]). When the
cabinet was formed, five of the nine members were Bengalis, including Mohammad Ali Bogra, a former prime minister of Paki-

stan and a leading Bengali politician, who was made foreign minister. Maulvi Tamizuddin Khan, another Bengali politician, was elected speaker. The conciliatory gesture of the chief election commissioner, Akhter Husain, a Punjabi, who read the oath of office in Bengali to Bengali members of the National Assembly, was received with warm praise. The inclusion of so many seasoned politicians in important positions of the national government prompted the *Pakistan Times* to comment editorially that East Pakistan now had unfair political advantage over West Pakistan, whose cabinet representatives were not experienced politicians.[74] After years of similar comments by Bengalis, this was a curious turnabout.

The campaign preceding the presidential election of January 2, 1965, revealed some of the feeling against West Pakistan. The popularity in East Pakistan of the Combined Opposition party which campaigned against President Ayub was due to the affiliation of the Bengalis' former provincial governor, Lt. General Azam Khan, who had become a hero. There was widespread sentiment that Azam Khan would be a powerful influence behind the presidency of Fatima Jinnah, and that this would compel Miss Jinnah's Government to pay proper attention to the needs of East Pakistan. This hope probably accounted for the slim majority of 2,578 votes by which President Ayub carried East Pakistan as compared with his majority of 10,257 votes in West Pakistan and for the fact that the only districts in the whole country in which Miss Jinnah obtained a majority of votes were Dacca, Comilla, Syhlet, and Noakhali—all in East Pakistan.

Though the election campaign may have been an index of regional animosity, the results may actually improve relations between the two provinces. The feelings of East Pakistan have been unmistakably registered, and the central government has apparently been impressed and is likely to be more sensitive in its handling of regional issues. In any event, there is now cause for reasonable hope that, if east-west problems can be adequately protected from foreign interference, relations between the two provinces will be improved. If this occurs, research may be able

[74] *Ibid.*, June 24, 1962, p. 6.

candidly to probe into all aspects of provincial relations with less fear of provoking regional animosities and central government disapproval.

Absence of Clinical Disinterest as an Attitude

There are other attitudinal deterrents to research which have origins in the culture and which are rarely satisfactorily eliminated by university education. One of the most serious problems lies in the disposition to personalize research attitudes by a web of involvement in non-objective considerations. There is only vague understanding of research as an autonomous process devoid of considerations other than rigorous scientific detachment. The insecurity of life and the pervasive influence of feudal and caste patterns of society have enforced a highly personalized set of relations which permeates politics, commerce, education, and bureaucracy. Under this rigid framework, it is necessary for one to feel that he is a protégé ("favorite" is the term used) of a higher-ranking person, who is thereby a benefactor, in a reciprocal relationship of blind loyalty and benevolent obligation. This transfer of feudal relations to bureaucracy and to scholarship profoundly affects social science research, particularly when sensitive issues are studied. The volatility of issues varies in time and space, but Islam, Kashmir, India, foreign aid, and the Civil Service of Pakistan have often been subjects of some delicacy. There is an inclination to label scholars as friend or foe and to prejudge their conclusions from an a priori assessment of loyalty. This predicament is especially difficult for comparative studies, when Pakistani developments are compared with those of other nations. Such comparison leads to difficulties, particularly if the comparison made appears to be adverse to Pakistan. The typical reaction in Pakistan is that a scholar making such a comparison cannot be a friend of Pakistan. The implication is that "good things" cannot be said both of Pakistan and of such countries as India. Since the intellectual tradition is oral rather than bibliophilic, the danger of partial comprehension of written scholarship is unusually great and the extraction of ideas out of context is a common daily risk.

In sum, sentiment, nationalism, and felt needs of personal security have not yet been sieved out from scientific objectivity and clinical disinterest. This is not surprising, for it is a condition found in virtually all developing nations and in many older states as well. This disposition, however, should not be confused with the intellectual environment of most totalitarian societies in which there is an official government view, deviations from which are harshly punished. There was no such climate of intellectual rigidity and suppression in Pakistan during the forty-four months of martial law. On the other hand, it is not here suggested that there was complete freedom, for martial law did prohibit discussion on several important issues. But on balance, the climate of moderation, even though forced by martial law, somewhat counterbalanced the prohibitions on free speech and resulted in a net gain for the exercise of responsible discussion of certain (though not all) issues. The Bureau of National Reconstruction, created after declaration of martial law as a source for a new ideology, has actually stimulated empirical research on bureaucracy and other sensitive issues. The emotional involvement described here appears to be a natural concomitant of newly achieved independence and is the product of an involuntary state of mind within society, unsupported and in many ways even discouraged by government policy and action. It is a condition rapidly eroding but likely to persist as a problem in research for some years to come.

Reliance on Orally Transmitted Knowledge

The conduct of research is impeded by the propensity to accord vague generality the same status as meticulously documented fact, and to cloak such generality with verbiage so persuasive that the most disciplined scholar is at least temporarily dislodged from his moorings. Another is the almost exclusive reliance on oral rather than written communication as a means of acquiring knowledge. Reading serious scholarship with copious documentation or carefully developed reasoning is often looked upon as inferior because it is "dull." The reading preferred is the provocative essay (preferably satirical) of the type found in popular periodicals. This attitude conduces to little respect for the written or spoken exposition if it is qualified by scholarly caution and circumspection. There being great admiration for verbal cleverness, sharp repartee, and sophistry, the intellectual hero is usually someone who has spectacularly confused with words rather than one who has modestly elucidated with care. The truism which is accepted in the best academic traditions of the West—namely that glib, ready, oratorical prowess may bear inverse correlation to cautious scholarship—seems not to be widely accepted in intellectual circles in Pakistan.

Yet there is a powerful countervailing influence, namely, the Islamic emphasis on record-keeping necessitated by interpretation of Muslim law based on precedent. It is probable that relatively stable conditions since 1958 have created a climate conducive to the re-emergence of such legal precision. Still it is not at all clear that the same respect for the written word in Islamic matters pervades the secular realm as well. This reliance on oral credibility is immediately beneath the surface of a thinly veneered allegiance to empirical, scientific norms and appears to be the more powerful influence on the minds of men. Yet it can certainly be said that the values implicit in reliance on orally transmitted knowledge are being supplanted by an empirical disposition which places value on doubt and uncertainty. Ultimately this change may affect research conditions generally.

Public Access to Data

In all countries, developed and developing, a basic impediment to research on bureaucracy is the attitude held by government that statecraft is essentially a private matter to be shielded from public scrutiny. This factor is somewhat more important in Pakistan than in older constitutional systems. Under conditions of political government prior to 1958, means of controlling bureaucracy existed through political channels, but this control was usually so irresponsible that the bureaucracy retreated all the more behind a protective wall, sometimes genuinely to preserve its dignity and the integrity of state business, sometimes to conceal deficiency, and sometimes in fear of quixotic political behavior. Under martial law, such political interference disappeared, but the protective instinct remains; the research use of government materials now depends largely on an appeal to good will or friendship. Every government must, of course, protect certain of its affairs from untimely public interference, although in a mature constitutional system the sector of such non-public action must necessarily be kept small and the burden of proof must rest on the desire to conceal rather than on the right to reveal. In Pakistan, as in most former colonial possessions, the sector of concealed or withdrawn information is understandably large simply because bureaucracy was, less than two decades ago, operated by British officials who were compelled to prevent Indian agitation for independence from obstructing state business. In this respect the public was the natural enemy of government, and in many ways this relationship has not greatly changed since then. It is sustained ideologically if not in practice by provisions of the statute known as the Official Secrets Act first imposed under the British Raj in 1911 [75] and revised in 1923. This act was designed to prevent information concerning government from being transmitted from the increasing number of Indian officials to their compatriots who were agitating against the government in the independence movement. Theoretically, its provisions can be used for lesser matters involving ordinary knowledge of government affairs. Fortunately, the awareness that popular sovereignty requires a totally different relationship between government and people mitigates against the stringent, minatory application of the Official Secrets Act in Pakistan. Nevertheless, it does exist as a valid statute and as recently as 1961 it was thought by two High Court judges to have been used as a threat to the High Court itself.

The issue was the case of Sir Edward Snelson, law secretary, who was being tried for contempt of High Court for statements he made on the writ jurisdiction of that court. [76] In defending the law

[75] The Official Secrets Act, Act No. XIX of 1923, April 2, 1923. For background of this enactment see *Gazette of India*, 1922, Part V, p. 210; and *ibid.*, 1923, Part V, p. 61. The Official Secrets Act is in force in the whole of Pakistan. It was recently extended to the tribal areas in the Northwest Frontier, presumably as a measure against covert activities relating to agitation among Pathans and neighboring countries. See Regulation I of 1963, Tribal Areas (Official Secrets) Regulation, 1963. Text is given in *Gazette of Pakistan, Extraordinary*, December 30, 1963.

[76] *The State* v. *Sir Edward Snelson*, PLD 1961 Lah. 78; *Sir Edward Snelson* v. *Judges of High Court of West Pakistan*, PLD 1961 SC 237. The contempt issue and the Snelson case are examined below, pp. 263–268.

secretary, the attorney-general stated that since Snelson's talk was meant only for a group of government officials its circulation among the public at large would naturally have been prevented by the Official Secrets Act. It came to public attention, the attorney-general argued, only after the speech appeared in the press as an enclosure to the notice for contempt issued to Snelson. Justices Shabir Ahmed and M. Yaqub Ali construed this statement as being "nothing but a hint that the sword of Damocles in the shape of appropriate action for contravention of the *Official Secrets Act, 1923,* hung over the heads of the Judges." In the subsequent judgment by the Supreme Court, Chief Justice Cornelius did not agree that the attorney-general's comment constituted a threat. The fact that Cornelius disagreed and that other observers felt Shabir Ahmad may have been too sensitive on this issue are of some comfort. Nevertheless, the attorney-general, whatever his intention may have been, did cite the existence of the Official Secrets Act as a presumably effective means of preventing Snelson's speech from reaching the general public. Yet the very fact that the speech was circulated to government offices both in Pakistan and abroad and reached the non-official public in this way, as well as by publication with the contempt charge, shows that the Official Secrets Act is not always interpreted strictly by government officials with respect to the lowest classification.[77] There seems to be a tacit understanding that its strict construction is not only irrelevant to circumstances of sovereignty and constitutional government but may be actually detrimental.

Certainly there is strict control over matters classified as "confidential" and higher. The "official use only" category has been used almost entirely for publications relating to administrative reform. Publications of the judiciary, government corporations, and rural development program do not use this classification. Only a few of the reports of the martial law commissions of inquiry have been so classified. In many instances, such classification is temporary, in force while the cabinet or legislature has a

[77] The Press Commission dismissed the argument of some journalists who thought that the Official Secrets Act should be amended. The commission saw no need for amendment since "no instance [had] been cited . . . of the Act having ever been used against the press in an unreasonable manner," Government of Pakistan, *Report of the Press Commission* (Karachi, 1959), p. 20.

report or related issue under consideration. After a decision is taken, the report is sometimes released without classification, as was the report of the G. Ahmed Committee, which studied administrative reorganization. At other times a full summary or the full text is released to the press, thus removing, in effect, the classification. In recent years, especially during the forty-four months of martial law, classification practices do not appear to be due to a calculated effort to suppress governmental data so much as to the momentum of earlier practice and custom. Classification practices have not been given systematic study by any committee, commission, or other agency either of the executive branch or of the legislature. In the apparent absence of new high-level policy, the earlier classification scheme appears to have been adjusted to post-independence needs by official press summaries and by non-classification of a major portion of publications.

The usual categories of top secret, confidential, and restricted, provided for by secretariat rules of business, are customarily found in all large public bureaucratic systems and these are necessary and desirable classifications. There are two additional categories of publications, namely, (1) official and (2) open documents. "Official" publications, bearing the legend "for official use only," may be distributed only to government offices, and the information contained in the document may not be communicated directly or indirectly to the press or to any person not authorized to receive it. "Open" publications are those which may be placed on sale by the manager of publications of the central or provincial governments for a stated price. These are listed in periodical catalogues and while the supply lasts are easily obtained. The impediment to research lies in the "official use only" category and in an *ad hoc* refinement of the "open" category which has emerged, perhaps unintentionally, as fairly common practice. Within the "open" category many ministries and attached departments publish documents for their own internal use. These are known informally as "unpriced" publications. Since they are not classified "for official use only," however, they are available to persons outside of the department and government offices.

This category of publications presents two difficulties. First, few persons beyond officials of the department concerned know of the existence of such publications, for they are not listed in the official periodical catalogues of the government printing offices. Issuance is controlled entirely by the separate ministries which only rarely keep up-to-date lists of such publications, and even then such lists are for their own internal use. Finally, since the documents are not for sale, they can be procured only through the relevant department on loan or as a gift. In the past the "official use only" category has made inaccessible several reports, even though in scope and substance they were similar to the widely distributed Hoover Commission reports in the United States or the two Appleby reports and the Gorwala Report in India, all of which have been extensively distributed and often reprinted. The Egger and Gladieux reports [78] in Pakistan, which are counterparts of the Appleby and Gorwala reports in India, remained classified until 1960 and hence were unavailable to non-official persons. It is true that both of these were reports which were submitted to the prime minister and the Planning Board, respectively, to be used as bases for action. But, of course, all reports are submitted to some agency of government; certainly reports and inquiries, unless they are instruments of the legislature, are not submitted initially to the public. In a viable constitutional system which lays claim to the doctrine of bureaucratic stewardship of popular sovereignty and is aware of the strategic advantages in utilizing public energy to implement reforms thus suggested, such submission is a common and desirable practice. On the other hand, suppression of such reports might easily be construed as absence of desire on the part of the bureaucracy to implement the suggested reforms.

The rationale for this secretiveness in Pakistan cannot have been the degree of critical candor in the reports, for other Pakistani reports published and released to the public, especially since martial law, are more critical of certain aspects of government than many not so classified. For example, parts of the Food and Agriculture Commission Report, and of the First Five Year Plan, which were two of the most widely distributed unclassified documents, may be more critical of administration than many of the

[78] Cited and discussed below, pp. 218–220; 221–222.

documents which have not been made available. The Egger and Gladieux reports were no less complimentary to Pakistani administration than the Appleby and Gorwala reports were to Indian administration. The reason for such classification in Pakistan seems to be the justifiably greater sensitivity of bureaucracy (as contrasted with law, education, and the public service commissions) to criticism consequent to the acute instability of the early years of the nation's development. A correlative reason may be that the unusually high degree of interest which the public has in every activity of government results in impassioned discussion of government reports and statements. Any government, even when free from colonial rule, might prefer not to face the irresponsible distortions which such discussion engenders among poorly educated but articulate persons. Government must balance the ultimate ill-effect of badly distorted comment based on "official" leaks, rumor, and gossip that follows when reports are not released with the probable lesser distortion consequent to official publication. Properly handled, the advantages of the latter policy are probably greater than the former. Whatever the reasons, the exclusion of such documents from the main channels of information and research tends to engender suspicion and hostility and to conjure up images of bureaucratic evils which may, in reality, be nonexistent. This has been precisely the effect of both the Egger and the Gladieux papers. Pakistani critics of the nation's administrative system, and particularly critics of the Civil Service of Pakistan, imagine these reports as being hostile and destructively critical when, in fact, they are not. Indeed, if government were to conduct a public relations campaign to demonstrate the extent to which foreign observers have admired (though not uncritically) the work of bureaucracy, it could do no better than to publicize widely these documents which for so long remained classified.

The quality of government documents in Pakistan is generally of a high order. Some of the reports on administration rank with the best analytical literature in the field. Curiously, many of the documents published during periods of greatest stress and governmental instability are of the highest quality; some are unexcelled in candor, depth of analysis, and thoroughness of workmanship. It is unfortunate that because of classification and small printings these reports cannot take their rightful places in the international literature of government and administration. It is even more tragic that because copies of many documents are no longer extant and hence will not be in archives, there will be serious lacunae when future historians write on the development of government in the first crucial decades of Pakistan's history.

The propensity to overclassify in Pakistan is probably a legacy of British rule. It also stems from the climate of mutual suspicion and vindictive, irresponsible politics often erupting in violence which was generated by unstable government in the years 1952 to 1958. These conditions were much less apparent under martial law, during which period government manifested few paranoiac characteristics or little disposition toward secretiveness. On the contrary, the propensity was clearly one of vigor, confidence, and sincere concern for public participation in the work of government, although that public participation did not accord with the ideals of constitutionalism espoused by the intelligentsia. It seems not unreasonable to expect, therefore, that the accessibility of public records will eventually become greater and that research will thereby be made more efficient. But there is an imponderable which can upset this expectation. The re-emergence of national and provincial legislatures, the end of martial law, and the emergence of political parties may produce in the bureaucracy the pre-1958 attitude of withdrawal and secretiveness. If the political process is as irresponsible and as destructively critical as it was before martial law, such a consequence appears inevitable. If, however, under the new presidential system, a vigilant yet constructive form of legislative supervision emerges, bureaucratic activity may be more public and better documented than before.

Compartmentalization and Research

There is one minor problem which confronts the foreign researcher. The tradition of the scholar doing his own searching, extracting, and reading is absent in the bureaucracy just as it is relatively absent in the universities of Pakistan. Caste division of labor and a rigid hierarchy of status symbolism require the mediation of several persons standing between the frustrated scholar and the documents he has long sought. He can browse in the stacks only at the risk of losing his own dignity and embarrassing his hosts. Moreover, an immense social and attitudinal chasm divides classes of bureaucrats. The chasm is difficult to bridge. The identification of type of work with special status is rigid and unyielding, and absence of vertical mobility between classes of ranks within the bureaucracy precludes the probability of each class really understanding the detailed problems of classes above and below it or even being interested in them. Those who possess adequate discretionary power and sympathetic understanding of research problems are unlikely to be acquainted with details as to location, availability, and contents of documents. Conversely, those acquainted with details are usually powerless to take any decision as to accessibility. Their attitude is likely to be that of the petty functionary who has no intellectual comprehension of research and who feels greater security in negative rather than in affirmative decisions.

Dispersion of Materials

Another impediment to research is wide dispersion of materials over two continents and in three countries, and the correlative disruption in progressive, systematic archival activity created by the disabilities of partition. In this respect, research facilities differ from those in India, Ceylon, and Malaya, where substantial collections have rested undisturbed since the days of British rule and have been systematically augmented since then. The partition of the subcontinent in 1947 badly affected libraries and archives in Pakistan. Although an "equitable" division of assets was to be made between the two countries,[79] it is said by Pakistani officials that Pakistan's rightful share has not been given by India. The physical division of library resources is always a tragedy for scholarship. Such a solution as the proposal to microfilm documents of the India Office Library and thus make copies available in London, India, and Pakistan was not suggested in the chaos of

---

[79] Reports of the partition proceedings of which assets were one issue are discussed below, pp. 113–115.

1947 as a means of dividing libraries. For many historical materials the India Office Library in London and libraries of Delhi, Calcutta, and Bombay remain indispensable for research on Pakistan. As a result of the administrative disabilities of partition in both East and West Pakistan, only two libraries of significance for research maintained an uninterrupted flow of acquisitions. The secretariat library of the provincial government of West Pakistan in Lahore inherited the secretariat facilities of the Punjab—one of the most developed and best-administered provinces of British India. After the integration of West Pakistan in 1955, the secretariat libraries of the former Sind and Northwest Frontier provinces were merged with the renamed West Pakistan secretariat library in Lahore, and by 1962 most of the new materials were classified and integrated for effective use. The value of the old Punjab secretariat library was greatly enhanced by these acquisitions, many of which remedied deficiencies in the Punjab collections.

Valuable as this integrated library is for pre-1947 documents, it still has serious gaps for the post-independence period. The East Pakistan provincial secretariat library, created in 1947 by transferring the secretariat library from Darjeeling (the summer capital of Bengal) to Dacca, is also excellent for old materials. The main Bengal secretariat library remains in Calcutta as the secretariat library of West Bengal, India. The central government secretariat library in Rawalpindi, started in 1947, has few pre-partition materials and cannot be classed with the provincial secretariat collections in Lahore and Dacca. Even with their inadequacies the two provincial secretariat libraries are useful collections of documents on bureaucracy in Pakistan. Yet, curiously, they are probably the least-known and least-used libraries in the nation. The physical accommodations for these libraries are not adequate enough to prevent rapid deterioration of documents because of humidity, floods, and inadequate space. Nevertheless, for reasons already mentioned, they remain the two best collections in Pakistan.

As good as the secretariat libraries are they do not solve the problem of accessibility of documents. Secretariat libraries, by definition, are not intended for public use or for non-official scholarship, and access to them is a matter of official privilege rather than public right. This is a justifiable state of affairs found in all bureaucracies which require record keeping and research facilities for their own internal operation. Certainly the libraries of the United States Bureau of the Budget or of the British Treasury are not, and cannot be, open at random to private researchers. In developed states, however, secretariat libraries or their equivalents are of limited utility and are surpassed in most particulars by the highly developed and immense research facilities of universities, research foundations, and business corporations, and by those of major government units. The contrary is true in Pakistan where secretariat libraries overshadow all others for the study of government. The almost total absence of such alternative facilities in Pakistan poses a difficult role for the government secretariat library which cannot easily be assigned a public research responsibility. So far as the foreign scholar is concerned, this problem exists largely in the abstract, for the foreigner's externality to the value and power system and the amenity of traditional courtesy to the visitor seem to outweigh the instinct of exclusivity. Hence, facilities of secretariat libraries are sometimes extended to foreigners as a courtesy; but their availability to the very few Pakistani who have tried to use them is another matter.

The libraries of the former National Assembly in Karachi and provincial assemblies in Lahore and Dacca have collections of predominantly secondary materials and good collections of documents issued under British rule. In the assembly libraries the impetus for rehabilitating the collections disappeared with the dissolution of the legislative bodies in 1958. The reopening of the assemblies in June, 1962, reactivated the libraries, but effective rehabilitation of the National Assembly library will be delayed by the fact that it has been located in Karachi, was relocated in Rawalpindi in 1962, and will be moved to Dacca, which the new Constitution proclaims as the principal seat of the National Assembly. But until the move to Dacca is made (probably not until 1966) the assembly will continue to meet in Rawalpindi. In any case, none of the assembly libraries has made a systematic effort to collect government documents issued since 1947. Consequently, they resemble more an English gentleman's personal library than a working center for organized, efficient, scientific research. One of the best research libraries, the West Pakistan Archives (housed in Anarkali's Tomb in Lahore), has a superb collection of documents on Sikh and British rule in the Punjab. Before partition an excellent tradition of service to scholarship developed in the archives, and many masters' theses and doctoral dissertations in the history of this period were written from research done there. Since 1947, the library is visited only by an occasional foreign scholar, a random tourist who has lost his way, or the curious who wish to see the tomb of Jahangir's beloved. The libraries of the two high courts in Dacca and Lahore are quite adequate for legal research in Indian and British precedent, but they are not designed to concentrate on documentary collections. The Supreme Court uses the library of the High Court of West Pakistan since it is temporarily located in the High Court building. In addition, it has its own library, which is about the same size as the High Court library, in the same building. In recent years, the Supreme Court library has been improved and enlarged. The National Archives in Karachi, started in 1947, remains very small, and the Liaquat National Library in the same city is in reality a community public library with no research bias.

A few other libraries are worthy of mention.[80] The Administrative Staff College in Lahore, established in 1960 and supported by Syracuse University under a Ford Foundation contract, has made a systematic effort to collect documents, and a fragmentary collection is now available under relatively attractive circumstances for research. An index to its acquisitions of government publications is the most complete and valuable compilation available.[81] Similar efforts have been made by the three national institutes of public administration in Lahore, Dacca, and Karachi, and by the Civil Service Academy supported by the University of

---

[80] A brief description of all libraries in Pakistan with data on size of collections is given in a publication of the Pakistan Bibliographical Working Group, *A Guide to Pakistan Libraries, Learned and Scientific Societies and Educational Institutions, Biographies of Librarians in Pakistan* (rev. ed.; Karachi, 1960).
[81] Administrative Staff College, "Alphabetico-Classed Catalogue" (Lahore, 1961). This 99-page mimeographed catalogue is corrected up to April 30, 1961.

Southern California under terms of a contract with the United States Agency for International Development activated in 1960. These four efforts hold promise for the future, particularly since they have had the full-time services of an American librarian and another American advising on research, and are slowly emerging as significant research centers. An earlier enterprise, also supported by the United States Agency for International Development, known as the Institute of Public and Business Administration, located in Karachi, assembled somewhat more than ten thousand volumes, largely secondary sources but including many government publications as well. Here the materials are well classified, a catalogue has been published,[82] and a nucleus of a modern research library exists. Most of the acquisitions of this library were transferred to the Graduate School of Business Administration opened in 1961 at the University of Karachi by the University of Southern California under a USAID contract. The libraries of the Social Sciences Research Centre at the University of the Panjab and of the academies for rural development in Peshawar and Comilla are significant first steps toward the emergence of adequate research collections. Both academies are fortunate in having had the full-time library services of a United States Peace Corps volunteer. At present these institutions are effectively generating an appreciation for empirical research which unavoidably exceeds the magnitude of the documentary collections available to sustain the new attitude.

Other miscellaneous libraries throughout the country are of little value for research on contemporary bureaucracy of Pakistan. Public and university libraries, and foreign libraries such as those of the British Council and United States Information Service, are intended for purposes other than research. Such government agencies as the State Bank of Pakistan and the Planning Commission are developing useful libraries, but they necessarily concentrate on foreign materials rather than on indigenous documents.

The three government press establishments, that of the central

[82] George Moreland and Akhtar H. Siddiqi, *Publications of the Government of Pakistan, 1947–57* (Karachi, 1958). The title is misleading since this is a list of publications collected in the Institute of Business and Public Administration library rather than a list of all government publications issued during the period shown.

government in Karachi, the West Pakistan (formerly Punjab) Press in Lahore, and the new East Pakistan Press in Dacca, have impressive technical printing facilities, but their sales organizations and cataloging systems are not aggressively aimed at wide distribution of public records. All three government presses have arrangements with private bookdealers to act as their agents, but with a few exceptions this is not as convenient as it appears, and it is usually more satisfactory to deal with the sales depot of the press directly. Each of the provincial government press establishments serves as a distributing point for central government publications as well. Printed catalogues are issued roughly in five-year intervals, and all three government presses release mimeographed supplements in the interim. The latest printed catalogues are *Catalogue of the Government of Pakistan Publications* (Karachi: Manager of Publications, 1962); *West Pakistan Government Publications General Catalogue* (corrected up to March 31, 1961) (Lahore: Superintendent, Government Printing, West Pakistan, 1961); and *Catalogue of Publications, Government of East Pakistan, 1st September 1959* (Tejgaon, Dacca: East Pakistan Government Press, 1960). The utility of the catalogues is affected in all three instances because of the classifications used and because they continue to list items no longer in stock. The central government's catalogue is largely a collection of annual lists with duplication, inconsistencies, and confusing arrangement. The press establishments in Karachi and Dacca are new, hence they have no supply of documents published before partition and virtually none published in the first few years of independence. The West Pakistan government printing office, on the other hand, inherited intact the well-developed printing facilities of the Punjab, and in its stockrooms can still be found a dwindling supply of many pre-partition publications, especially historical monographs, settlement reports, and district gazetteers. Similarly, pre-partition reports still relevant to Pakistan can be found in the Bengal government printing office in Alipore, outside of Calcutta, India, but here too the stock is rapidly diminishing.

The variety of imprints under which government publications appear calls for explanation. What is now East Pakistan was known as the province of Bengal before partition. In 1905 the province was divided into East Bengal and West Bengal, the former being virtually coterminous with what is now East Pakistan. The partition of Bengal ended in 1911 and the province became reunited. The part of Bengal remaining in India since independence in 1947 is officially designated as West Bengal; East Pakistan is still sometimes popularly referred to as East Bengal. Confusion is compounded by the fact that from partition in 1947 until 1955 many documents of East Pakistan appeared under the imprint of "East Bengal Government Press." Government publications for that province thus appear under all three imprints: Bengal, East Bengal, or East Pakistan. Laws enacted before partition when East Bengal and Bengal were provinces are often amended, but such amendments still carry the designation "East Bengal" or "Bengal" instead of "East Pakistan." In West Pakistan, the situation is also less than clear. At independence, the province of the Punjab was divided into East Punjab in India and West Punjab in Pakistan. In Pakistan, "Punjab" immediately became the name of the province, although the term "West Punjab" was sometimes used. With the abolishment of the provinces of Sind, Baluchistan, Northwest Frontier, and Punjab and their merger into the one province of West Pakistan in 1955, the term "West Pakistan" replaced the old term, "Punjab." Currently, the names of these former provinces are commonly but not officially used, but they refer to cultural areas rather than to legal divisions.

The problem of building collections of documents issued in the early days of independence is made difficult if not impossible by the fact that such documents were issued in relatively small printings and are now unavailable. The *Parliamentary Debates* of the National Assembly of Pakistan and its antecedent *Debates* of the Constituent Assembly of Pakistan were printed in only 770 copies until 1952 and in 340 copies after that year. This stock is insufficient for the eighty members, three hundred key government officials, two hundred libraries in Pakistan and abroad, hundreds of researchers, and a reserve for several years. The West Pakistan Assembly had somewhat larger printings of one thousand copies of its debates, and the East Pakistan Assembly printed 850 copies of its proceedings. Sets of the debates are now almost impossible to obtain. The important *Report of the Pakistan Pay Commission* was issued in 1949 in only 1,250 copies and only three thousand copies of the (*Munir*) *Report on the Punjab Disturbances of 1953* were printed. Three more recent examples are the *Report of the Economy Committee of 1957* which was released in one thousand copies, the *Law Reform Commission Report* printed in 1959 in two thousand copies, and the *Report of the Constitution Commission* released in 1962 in only a thousand copies.[83] No doubt small printings are thought to be dictated by the stringent economy of the nation, but such policy imposes an almost insuperable obstacle in the subsequent development of research facilities in Pakistan and in the inclusion of crucial documents in foreign libraries. These needs can best be met by maintenance of a substantial reserve stock of government publications and by subsequent rationing to the public and to research agencies on the basis of a carefully devised formula.

The single most important material hindrance to research efficiency is the fact that there is no single site in the whole of Pakistan at which comprehensive collections of government documents issued since 1947, together with a complete collection of publications issued under British rule, are to be found. This is aggravated by the physical separation of the two provinces, which for research purposes are almost completely cut off from each other. Complete files, for example, of the *Dacca Gazette,* the official document of notices of the East Pakistan government, cannot be found anywhere in West Pakistan. Files of provincial documents both retrospective and current are not available in the other province. In one province it is difficult to get newspapers published in the other. Newspapers do not have extensive coverage of matters relating to the province other than their own. Neither of the secretariat libraries, since each is designed to serve only its own provincial government, makes an effort to keep documents of the other provincial government. Nor is it possible to find provincial documents in the secretariat library of the central government in Rawalpindi. This provincial insulation of research

[83] These reports are cited and discussed below, pp. 178, 216, 222–224, 318, 327.

facilities not only is inconvenient, it also contributes to east-west misunderstanding which has been discussed elsewhere in this essay.

No government agency or affiliated research organization has made an aggressive, deliberate effort to collect documents of the three (central and two provincial) units of government. The reasons for this situation are not hard to ascertain and can be easily appreciated. Foremost is the fact of partition and the urgent priority given to creating an apparatus of government. No nation's founders are so little occupied with affairs of immediate urgency that they can afford the luxury of projecting plans for posterity's documentary research facilities. Perhaps a systematic survey of documents and a project for selected reprinting might now be planned by developing states whose important written record of transition to mature independence can more easily be preserved by modern technical means. If it is true, as has been suggested, that a strong tradition of esteem for secular scholarship is not one of the assets inherited by Pakistan, it may take some time to generate the attitudes necessary to demand an efficient research apparatus and to make use of it when it is developed. Dispersion and accessibility, then, are serious impediments to research efficiency, and, while this condition may have its appeal for the itinerant scholar, it poses problems of time and cost.

Statistical Organization

Advances made in organization of statistical data are one of the most promising of research developments. The results of a program of advisory services and help in procuring equipment, started by the United States Agency for International Development in 1952, are now becoming evident. Two fundamental problems, however, remain to be solved. The first is the disinclination of administrators to regard raw data as autonomous facts; the second is their reluctance to analyze with clinical disinterest. In the use of statistical data, this problem is acerbated by placing statistical organizations under jurisdiction of substantive units of government, thus making factual material more liable to distortion for such ends as public relations or internal power. There has been an effort to detach the statistical function from the operating units, but it has not met with success. Hence, co-ordination of existing activities seems to be the trend in structural organization. Lt. Col. Nazir Ahmed, director-general of the Central Statistical Office, in an unpublished address has characterized the statistical situation in Pakistan as failing to provide a "worthwhile understanding of (1) the working of the economy as a whole, (2) the social structure of the nation, (3) the nature of the forces and their mutual relationships. There are few [statistical] series that deserve the description good and all too many that are worse than useless."

The statistics system is highly decentralized and loosely integrated. The Central Statistical Office of the central government, established in 1950, has no structural relationship with corresponding statistical units of the two provincial governments. Whatever co-ordination and co-operation exist among these three units of necessity must result from personal rather than official relations. The major activities of the Central Statistical Office include the preparation of national income estimates and estimates of crop production and agricultural income.[84] In 1962 a National Statistical Council was established, with representatives from both provinces. The chairman is the secretary of the Ministry of Commerce. The council has appointed a general advisory commission made up of statistical experts to advise on technical aspects of statistics. Within the advisory commission are several panels of specialists in such substantive fields as agriculture and manpower distribution.

Responsibility of the National Assembly to legislate in statistical matters is assigned by Article 131 and the Third Schedule of the 1962 Constitution. The latter lists the census (par. 32) and "inquiries and statistics for the purposes of any of the matters enumerated in [the Third] Schedule" (par. 45) as powers of the central legislature. Efforts have been made to draft a general statistical law. Early in 1965, such a law had been drafted and was being circulated to various ministries for approval. When such a

---

[84] For an appraisal of methods used in these estimates, see Government of Pakistan, *Interim Report of the National Income Commission, September, 1964* (Karachi, 1964), pp. 16–38.

law is passed it will supersede the statistics provisions of other
laws such as the factory act and labor acts which allocate responsibilities for statistical activity. There are at least four installations
of electronic statistical equipment, including those of Pakistan
International Airlines and the West Pakistan Water and Power
Development Authority. Both of these are used for highly specialized processing activities and are not likely to be available for
general social science research. The third installation is that of the
Central Statistical Office.

In both the central and provincial governments, every department has a statistical cell. Each provincial government has a
statistical bureau located in the provincial planning unit. The
Bureau of Statistics of the West Pakistan government has an
installation which includes two complete IBM 420 systems, including two reproducing summary punches, two sorters, and
several IBM 024 alpha numeric punches. In 1965 there were plans
to replace the two 420's with an IBM 407 tabulator, which will be
the first such equipment in Pakistan. There were also plans to add
a 101 electronic statistics machine, an alpha-numerical interpreter,
additional 024 punches, and an alpha-verifier. This will be the
most extensive unit record installation in Pakistan and will be
purchased entirely from Pakistan government funds rather than
from monies forwarded by the United States Agency for International Development.

Probably the most significant statistical development affecting
research on bureaucracy is the census of government employees
advocated by Muzaffer Ahmed, then additional chief secretary of
the Government of West Pakistan. The project was undertaken by
the Bureau of Statistics. This is an instance of American technical
assistance operating effectively. No accurate classificatory census
of government employees including low-ranking employees in the
districts had been made since 1947. The need was seen and
statistical advice sought from the provincial office of USAID in
Lahore. The result was a carefully devised questionnaire, the
answers to which were electronically tabulated. The census,
completed and published in 1962, is the first scientific census of

government employment made in Pakistan.[85] A similar census of the central and East Pakistan provincial governments is being compiled. In West Pakistan another census of government employees to include all categories through class IV was expected to be completed late in 1965. This census will include employees of government corporations and similar semi-autonomous bodies as well as employees of line agencies. It is expected that civil lists, now laboriously compiled from various sources, will ultimately be derived from these censuses.

While fairly adequate electronic computing facilities exist, the question which arises is that of their availability for research which is not an official part of governmental activities. For several years to come this equipment probably will not be used to its maximum capacity for projects undertaken directly by the parent organization. This fact, combined with the uncommon zeal and professional pride of the statisticians, may militate in favor of using the computing equipment for research projects not directly related to government activity. This is conjecture, however, and the circumstances may not remain the same.

The Press

Newspapers are more important for research in Pakistan than in developed countries precisely because there are few alternative sources of printed contemporary information and opinion. Consequently, some newspapers fill the roles of quarterly journals, court reporters, and administrative gazettes as well as the more common function of purveying current events. The press of the subcontinent has had a distinguished history of vigorous political action on behalf of independence.[86]

The Muslim press became strong somewhat later than the Hindu and British presses, but from the founding in 1910 of *Comrade* and *Al-Hilal* by Maulana Mohammad Ali and Maulana Abul Kalam Azad it was marked by stimulating political commen-

[85] This census is cited and discussed below, pp. 131–132.
[86] For a survey, see Government of India, *Report of the Press Commission* (New Delhi, 1954). See also *Report of the Press Commission* cited in n. 77 and discussed below p. 316.

tary. The intense public interest in politics and administration is
reflected in all papers, both vernacular and English language. But
the *Pakistan Times* of Lahore, the *Pakistan Observer* of Dacca,
and *Dawn* of Karachi, somewhat more than other papers, devote
an unusually large part of their space to verbatim publication of
entire High Court and Supreme Court judgments, speeches of
officials, and legislative assembly debates. It is not at all uncommon for some papers, especially the *Pakistan Times*, to devote as
many as five full pages to a court judgment. Most of these
materials appear later in conventional official printed sources, but
this unusual practice of the press is a boon for research in terms of
immediate, full, and convenient access to certain types of materials. This early availability of materials is quite crucial for research
because of the average lapse of twelve months between an actual
court decision handed down and its official publication. Even the
commercial reporting system (Pakistan Legal Decisions) is not
much faster in publishing; its lapse is usually three months from
the judgment date.[87] Thus, for research on legal issues, newspapers
are indispensable for judgments handed down within a year.
During the first few weeks after the legislative assemblies re-
opened in June, 1962, the debates were reported almost verbatim
for the National Assembly and the provincial assembly of the
paper's province. In this case such extensive documentary coverage was due to the long period of political inaction under martial
law, and after a few weeks it was reduced to brief summaries and
commentary; but even these were more extensive than usually
found in Western newspapers. Another somewhat different characteristic of Pakistani newspapers is the frequent use of
special supplements, often as many as fifteen a year, for occasions
such as Republic Day, openings of major buildings, and birthdays
of Iqbal. The frequent appearance of supplements is due to their
profit-making potential from advertising. There is very little advertising in the daily press, but commercial firms which have no
real incentive for advertising are induced to place large advertisements in supplements, presumably for reasons of patriotism or

[87] See below pp. 275–280 for discussion of legal reporting.

allied non-commercial motives. Supplements contain fairly long articles written by scholars, government officials, and other well-known figures, and thereby serve as literary outlets for analytical writing. Some of the best writing in Pakistan has appeared in supplements.

The principal English language newspapers with their circulations as of 1960 [88] are *Dawn* (Karachi), 32,000; *Pakistan Times* (Lahore and Rawalpindi), 33,000; *Morning News* (Dacca and Karachi), 16,000; *Pakistan Observer* (Dacca), 12,000; *Civil and Military Gazette* (Lahore), 6,000. The *Civil and Military Gazette*, incidentally, ceased publication in 1963.

The vernacular press is strong and widely read. The principal vernacular dailies with their circulations as of 1960 are *Jang*, (Karachi and Rawalpindi), 70,000; *Anjam* (Karachi), 32,000; *Nawa-i-Waqt* (Lahore, Multan, and Rawalpindi), 18,000; *Imroz* (Lahore, Multan, and Karachi), 18,000; *Azad* (Dacca), unknown; *Hilal-i-Pakistan* (Lahore), 400; *Kohistan* (Lahore, Rawalpindi, and Multan), 22,000. All of the vernacular newspapers listed here are published in Urdu, except for *Azad* which is in Bengali.

The press as a whole has been criticized for taking partisan stands on many issues, and the vernacular press especially finds it difficult to separate objective news reporting from editorial opinion. Inflammatory language, personal denunciation, and extravagant description seem to come easily in all journalism. It is commonly said, especially in government circles, that most newspapers will publish anything for which they are paid and will the

[88] Circulation data for 1960 supplied by Maqbul A. Shariff, former secretary, Journalists Wage Board. Current circulation figures, kept by the Audit Bureau of Circulation, Ministry of Information and Broadcasting, Government of Pakistan, are not released. It is likely that 1965 circulation figures differ considerably. It was reported, for example, that *Nawa-i-Waqt* increased its circulation during the election campaign of 1964–1965 from 12,000 to about 80,000 (*The Economist*, February 13, 1965, p. 653). *The Economist* did not disclose its source of information. A more comprehensive list of 176 English language and vernacular newspapers in which government placed its classified advertisements is given in National Assembly of Pakistan, *Debates*, March 28, 1963, pp. 830–836. This tabulation for December, 1962, lists six English and sixteen Bengali papers in East Pakistan and twenty-five English and 119 vernacular papers in West Pakistan. This tabulation, however, differs from the oral statement made by Malik Allah Yar Khan, parliamentary secretary, that there are 290 newspapers in West Pakistan on the "approved list as against 33 . . . in East Pakistan" (*ibid.*, p. 837).

next day publish a retraction. These criticisms are probably an exaggeration by those who do not understand the importance of a free press, but they point up one of the weaknesses of the press, i.e., it too often shows intense partisan feeling and occasionally is used as a means of recriminating against the opposition by various means. Yet the press may not be entirely to blame for this condition, for it often reflects rather than creates the extreme political feelings of the nation. The politics of Pakistan and of most developing states are often characterized by personalization of issues and use of somewhat extravagant language. A recent example was the reference by the newly appointed foreign minister, Mohammad Ali Bogra, on the floor of the National Assembly on June 11, 1962, to a "political upstart." The person was an "upstart" presumably because of his alleged role in formulating the 1962 Constitution under which Mohammad Ali was serving in office. The press made certain assumptions concerning the person thus characterized, but it reported the incident without gross distortion. Here the extravagance complained of was merely extravagance made in comments originating in the legislature rather than the press.[89]

A classic instance of embroilment of the press in politics through behavior of questionable integrity was that which resulted in the Gurmani defamation case of 1958.[90] On September 3, 1957, the *Times of Karachi* published on the first page of its evening edition what was purported to be a photostatic copy of a letter from M. A. Gurmani, prime minister of the state of Bahawalpur in 1947, to

---

[89] Although Mohammad Ali did not mention Manzur Qadir by name, the implication was clear. The statement is recorded in the National Assembly *Debates* as follows: "Md. Ali Bogra: 'Knowing the President so well as I do, Sir, I am confident that, had he been left to himself, many of the objectionable features, including the omission of the fundamental rights being justiciable to the people, would have been removed. . . .' (Interruptions.) Mr. Mohammed Ali: '. . . but for the influence of a political upstart who was the Pakistani prototype of Russia's Rasputin who is trying to cool his conscience in the clouds of Natiagali Hills.' Some Members: 'This is unfair. This is unfair. . . .' Mr. Mohammed Ali: 'We are fortunate that the evil influence has disappeared'" (*ibid.*, June 11, 1962, p. 19). The *Pakistan Times* mentioned Manzur Qadir as the object of Muhammad Ali's "frontal attack" in a report of the incident in the issue of June 12, 1962, p. 1. A version of the Bogra statement is accessible in *ibid.*, p. 6. Mohammad Ali apologized later for exceeding "parliamentary conventions in attacking a person who was not there to answer it" (*ibid.*, June 14, 1962, p. 1). In the same issue the *Pakistan Times* editorialized that Muhammad Ali had been "unreasonable."

[90] *Mushtaq Ahmad Gurmani v. Z. A. Suleri*, PLD 1958 Lah. 747.

Sardar Patel, Indian minister for states.[91] In this supposed letter, written in 1947, Gurmani was negotiating with Patel for the accession of the state to India rather than to Pakistan. After publication of this document, Gurmani notified Z. A. Suleri, the paper's editor-in-chief, that the letter was a forgery and that he would sue for defamation of character unless an apology were published within twenty-four hours. The *Times* published Gurmani's notice, protesting that the original letter was authentic, and that its publication was a "national service." The High Court found the letter to be a forgery, sentenced Suleri to two years' imprisonment, and imposed a fine of Rs. 6,000. Gurmani was embroiled in political conflict when the *Times of Karachi* published the forged letter. He had resigned as governor of West Pakistan the day before the letter was published, and before that he had been under heavy attack by the *Times of Karachi*. Although the Gurmani case is the most spectacular instance of press irresponsibility in Pakistan's history, it must not be regarded as typical of newspaper behavior.[92] But it indicates in the extreme the difficulty which the press has had in keeping itself from being enmeshed in the volatile, recriminatory politics of the nation.

A group of papers owned by Progressive Papers, Ltd., are generally regarded as being the best-edited in Pakistan. Progressive Papers, Ltd., was incorporated in 1946 by several well-known politicians and landholders. The largest stockholder and the company's first managing director was Mian Iftikhar-ud-Din. Other directors were the Khan of Mamdot, Mian Mumtaz Daultana, Sardar Shaukat Hayat Khan, and Amir Hussain Shah. This was a group of unusually able, educated Punjabi leaders. Three served at various times as ministers in the Punjab cabinet; two, Daultana and the Khan of Mamdot, having been chief ministers.

[91] For background on Bahawalpur and M. A. Gurmani, see Penderel Moon, *Divide and Quit* (London, 1961). Moon, as finance minister of Bahawalpur, worked closely with Gurmani at the time of partition.

[92] The Gurmani case is important for another reason unrelated to the present discussion of Pakistan's press. In the course of the proceeding, Justice Shabir Ahmed, who tried the case, made certain remarks against Prime Minister Feroze Khan Noon who later sued in the Supreme Court for their expunction. The Supreme Court expressed regret over the "extraneous" comments of the High Court judge and ordered expunction of his remarks. See *Feroze Khan Noon v. The State* (1958) 2 P.S.C.R. 1.

The company purchased modern printing presses from the United States, constructed one of the most efficient printing plants and office buildings in Pakistan, and secured expert advice from foreign journalists on lay-out and business policies. The results of these efforts were several excellent papers, the three leading ones being the *Pakistan Times,* an English daily; *Imroz,* an Urdu daily; and the Urdu weekly, *Lail-o-Nahar.*

Most of the directors were leading figures in the Muslim League, and Iftikhar-ud-Din especially played a leading role in the Punjab Provincial Muslim League's civil disobedience movement for the achievement of Pakistan. The papers were thus involved from the beginning in both ideological and practical Punjabi politics. The *Pakistan Times* reached its heights of excellence under the editorship of Faiz Ahmed Faiz, Pakistan's most distinguished Urdu poet and literary figure. While the technical excellence of the paper was acknowledged in Pakistan and abroad, its editorial policies were disliked by many groups, who regarded the paper as leftist and anti-American. The *Pakistan Times* opposed Pakistan's participation in regional pacts such as SEATO, took strong editorial stands against government policy, both foreign and domestic, and appeared sympathetic toward the Soviet Union. This "leftist" impression was enhanced by the fact that Faiz Ahmed Faiz had been involved in a minor way in the Rawalpindi conspiracy case of 1951 in which an effort to overthrow the government by force was aborted. He was convicted and served a jail sentence. Subsequently, he was made chairman of the Pakistan Arts Council, an organization subsidized by government.

The *Pakistan Times* continued its policies after Faiz left the editorship. On April 16, 1959, the President promulgated an ordinance amending section 11 of the Security of Pakistan Act and, on April 17, 1959, passed an order seizing control and management of Progressive Papers, Ltd.[93] The government allegation was that its three papers contained, "news, reports or information likely to endanger the security of Pakistan and that the . . . [pa-

[93] Security of Pakistan (Amendment) Ordinance, 1959 (XIII of 1959), *Gazette of Pakistan, Extraordinary,* April 16, 1959.

pers were] printed and published with the aid of foreign sources."
In a writ petition before the Supreme Court, Mian Iftikar-ud-Din
sought to disprove this allegation, maintaining that all three
papers had submitted to martial law censorship and that the purchase of newsprint from the Soviet Union and coal from the Peo-
ples' Republic of China was done with government approval. In
any event, Iftikhar-ud-Din maintained, the papers were not under
foreign control in any way. A brief prepared by A. K. Brohi and
Mahmud Ali Qasuri, two of Pakistan's most distinguished lawyers,
arrayed evidence showing that the paper was merely independent
in its political views, successful journalistically but victimized by
government and by its own competitors. The issue as to whether or
not the paper was under foreign control was never decided by the
courts and remains an unsolved mystery of Pakistan's political life.
The martial law order was put into effect, shares in Progressive
Papers, Ltd., were sold by auction to approved buyers,[94] and
Muhammad Sarfraz was appointed administrator of the newly
reorganized company. For undisclosed reasons but at the request
of Ahmad Dawood, the government later ordered cancellation of
the sale of Iftikhar-ud-Din's shares to Dawood. Iftikhar-ud-Din's
writ to the High Court and subsequent appeal to the Supreme
Court were decided on jurisdictional grounds, i.e., that the validity of the President's action under the Security of Pakistan Ordinance could not be judicially questioned unless *mala fides* were
proved.[95] Hence, the important substantive issue as to whether
Progressive Papers, Ltd., was actually under foreign influence
remained still undetermined. The view of the martial law government was that it was under such control; the view of many of the
intelligentsia, including government officials, was to the contrary.
Whatever the truth, the papers were reorganized by new ownership approved by government and its editorial policy became less
hostile to official policy. Paradoxically, the appointment of Z. A.
Suleri (whose sentence in the Gurmani defamation case had been
commuted) as chief editor in 1962 brought another change in

[94] See full-page advertisement for sale of shares in *Pakistan Times*, August 7,
1959, p. 8.
[95] *Iftikhar-ud-Din* v. *Muhammad Sarfraz,* **PLD** 1961 Lah. 842; *Iftikhar-ud-Din*
v. *Muhammad Sarfraz,* PLD 1961 **SC 585.**

editorial policy, again one which opposed the government's pro-
Western foreign policy. Despite what many Pakistani regard as a
deterioration in the *Pakistan Times* in the first part of 1962,[96] it
continues to occupy a dominant, controversial position in the press
world.

The *Civil and Military Gazette,* founded in 1870, has had a
distinguished history. Widely known as the paper for which
Rudyard Kipling worked as a reporter, it has research significance
as well, for its press published documents which enjoyed virtually
semi-official status. Its *Combined Civil List,* for example, was a
more convenient (though sometimes less accurate) document
than the official civil lists. After partition, the *Gazette* diminished
in quality and importance and in 1960 it was thought that it would
have to cease publication. Under new editorship, and with a
totally new format, it regained much of its earlier reputation for
excellence and was becoming increasingly popular among educated people. More moderate and balanced in tone than the
Pakistan Times, it was distinguished also by series of analytical
articles and political commentary. Unable to compete successfully, it ceased publication in 1963 and the publishing firm went
out of existence.

The *Pakistan Observer* of Dacca is a well-edited paper, whose
quality of analytical reporting is often superior to that of other
papers. It is an especially important source for scholars because it
reflects the point of view of East Pakistan and is more critical of
government policies than any other newspaper in Pakistan.

During the martial law period all newspapers were subject to
control. A few days after the proclamation of martial law,
censorship was lifted but a press adviser was appointed and
voluntary pre-censorship was arranged. Since all controversial
items were submitted to the press adviser for approval, there was
no overt criticism of government in the press during this period.
With the lifting of martial law in June, 1962, the press has assumed

[96] See editorial in *Pakistan Observer,* May 17, 1962, p. 4, which viewed Suleri's
appointment as chief editor as the "tragedy of a great newspaper." This comment
resulted from an editorial in the *Pakistan Times* on the resignation of Lt. Gen.
M. Azam Khan as governor of East Pakistan, which the *Pakistan Observer* construed as being detrimental to east-west relations.

a moderate tone of criticism. Whether it resumes its intemperance of earlier years depends on the general climate of reason in the larger Pakistani society. It is evident that government continues to be apprehensive about press irresponsibility. In June, 1962, the speaker of the West Pakistan Provincial Assembly, irritated by what he regarded as false reporting of its proceedings, moved to warn the press that it could not sit in "judgment on the house, its proceedings and the rulings given by its speaker." The speaker was objecting to a report which appeared in the *Pakistan Times* criticizing "unconventional proceedings in the Assembly." [97] The provincial law minister, Sheikh Khurshid, made a vigorous defense of freedom of the press and the speaker, mollified, merely issued a warning to the press. But the notion that the press can be punished for contempt of legislature, even when it comments moderately (as did the *Pakistan Times*) but critically on legislative proceedings, reveals differing interpretations of the doctrine of legislative immunity and of the crucial importance of a free critical press. Unless such views as those of Sheikh Khurshid, the provincial law minister, are allowed to prevail, relations between press and government are likely to become as strained as before martial law.

The government's effort to make the press responsible (the press would say to control it) culminated in promulgation of press and publications ordinances.[98] Critics of the basic ordinance point out that, like other crucial policies, it was promulgated under the ordinance-making powers of the executive (Article 79[1], Constitution of Pakistan), enabling the executive to make policy when the legislative assembly is not in session. This ordinance prohibits publication of accounts of legislative and judicial proceedings which were not, in fact, part of the proceedings or which were ordered expunged, or publication of which was forbidden by the

---

[97] *Pakistan Times,* June 28, 1962, p. 1. See warning issued by the assembly speaker and statement of the law minister, *ibid.,* June 30, 1962, p. 4.

[98] The controlling enactment is now West Pakistan Press and Publications Ordinance XXX of 1963 published in *Gazette of West Pakistan, Extraordinary,* October 10, 1963. Ordinance XXX repealed and replaced Press and Publications Ordinance XV of 1960, published in *Gazette of Pakistan, Extraordinary,* April 26, 1960, and Press and Publications (West Pakistan) (Amendment) Ordinance, 1963, published in *Gazette of West Pakistan, Extraordinary,* September 3, 1963.

legislatures or courts. It further prohibits publication of matter which tends to incite interference with law and order or to excite disaffection toward the government. The object of government apparently has been to prevent distortions resulting from extravagant interpretations or publication of partial proceedings of courts and legislative bodies. (The 1963 amendment to the Press Ordinance in West Pakistan went so far as to require the press to publish official press releases in their entirety or not at all. This was subsequently rescinded in 1964.) The central government prohibition is qualified by a statutory explanation which allows adverse comments about government actions when the comments are designed to achieve alterations by lawful means without exciting hatred or disaffection. The ordinance further provides for an appeal from actions of government against the press to a tribunal of three persons, one of whom must have been a High Court or Supreme Court judge. The order of the tribunal is deemed to be final and cannot be called into question by any court. The distinction between adverse comments without excitation and those deemed to have unlawful effect is a difficult one. The difficulty is suggested by the fate of a Karachi weekly newsmagazine, *Outlook*, with a circulation of 2,200 which in February, 1964, was ordered by the West Pakistan Department of Information to post a bond of Rs. 10,000 or show cause, under terms of the press ordinance, why it should not be suspended. The government objection focused on an article in the January issue entitled "Rationed News." The August, 1964, issue included an article which criticized local press reports of the enthusiastic receptions for President Ayub on his return from London and accused the government of promoting a personality cult. The magazine stopped publication in September, 1964, allegedly because the government brought pressure on the printshops which refused to print it.[99]

The Contempt of Courts law is also an important means of seeking to achieve press responsibility. There exists not only the customary prohibition against adverse criticism of any litigation pending before the court, but also a lack of understanding con-

[99] As reported in *New York Times*, September 13, 1964, p. 27.

cerning the appropriateness of printing various court documents other than the authorized judgments. The most celebrated recent case which illustrates this lack of understanding is *Attorney-General of Pakistan* v. *Abdul Hamid and others*, PLD 1963 SC 170. Several newspapers printed the text of a petition filed with the Supreme Court for expunction of certain remarks made by a special bench of the West Pakistan High Court in the case of *Syed Ali Nawaz Gardezi* v. *Lt. Col. Md. Yusuf Khan*, PLD 1962 Lah. 558. The Supreme Court found all the newspapers in the case guilty of contempt on the ground that publication of the petition prejudiced the administration of justice. The judgment stated that both parties to a cause must be heard at "the same time in the presence of each other by an unprejudiced tribunal. This object will be entirely frustrated if newspapers are permitted to print extracts of pleadings in advance, for it would constitute a serious interference with what is the Court's duty, namely, the decision of the pending case."

The Press Ordinance, contempt power, and legislative sensitivity are significant restraints on absolute press freedom. Such restraints are consistent with a point of view which has been expressed many times by President Ayub. Addressing the Ninth Commonwealth Press Union Conference in Rawalpindi on October 29, 1961, he explained that in nations "where most of the people are strangers to the written word, anything that is printed acquires authority merely by getting printed. . . . In order to protect the freedom of thought of all, therefore, it can become imperative in such circumstances to insist by legal provision of certain standard requirements to ensure responsibility among those who have the mighty instrument of a printing press under their control." [100] Judged by press freedom in older constitutional systems, this combination of restraints stringently interpreted and applied is likely to curtail liberty of the press. Whether it will compel the press to be responsibly critical rather than captious and extravagant remains to be seen. The consequence for research in Pakistan is likely to be a less spectacular press and a press which, unable to master the subleties of difference between criti-

[100] Full text in *Pakistan Times*, October 29, 1961, p. 9.

cism and excitation of disaffection, may be acquiescent and uncritical of crucial issues. The researcher will then have to rely on other sources for non-official views of government and politics.

For some time President Ayub has challenged the press to establish its own system of self-regulation. He promised to reconsider the Press Ordinances when he was satisfied with the effectiveness of such a system. In 1964 the National Press Trust was formed as a holding company owning most of the newspapers in Pakistan. Little is known about the nature of the trust; its first chairman, Akhter Husain, was succeeded upon retirement by Major General M. Hayauddin who, along with a group of journalists, was killed in the fateful crash of a Pakistan International Airlines flight in Egypt. In 1965 the Council of Pakistan Newspaper Editors worked out a code of ethics and established a court of honor to regulate press conduct. The President suspended the application of the Press Ordinances for a year, effective July 29, 1965, promising that if the court of honor, a "unique experiment in self restraint," operates well, in the course of time the press laws "would wither away." [101] Congratulating the editors for evolving the code of ethics, the President reiterated that he had no objection to responsible press criticism of government but that the press was obligated to be constructive and to assist in the diffusion of new ideas necessary for national development. If this experiment is successful, a new pattern of press responsibility may characterize Pakistan's development.

Research Leadership

The fundamental question for the future of research on bureaucracy in Pakistan is the locus from which impetus, direction, order, clinical disinterest, and actual productivity will emerge. There are three possibilities: (a) private research foundations or institutes, (b) the universities, (c) the public bureaucracy. The first of these can be dismissed almost at once as a probable source of research initiative and action. There is no concept of private philanthropic foundational activity which is highly developed in Pakistan. Only two financiers, Zakaria Adamjee and Ahmad Da-

[101] Embassy of Pakistan, *Press Release No. 22* (Washington, D. C., July 30, 1965).

wood, have done anything remotely approaching foundational research activity found in the United States. Even if such activity were to be generated, so much of a social welfare nature demands priority that research for its own sake can hardly be expected to receive attention for decades. There is neither the tradition, the disposition, the resources, nor the felt need to indicate anything to the contrary.

The universities present a somewhat more hopeful prospect, for change is occurring in the system of higher education which ultimately will be encouraging to research grounded on scientific objectivity. Even so, the pace of change in universities is slower than that of government proper, although not because of lack of attention to the problems or because of lack of effort. Universities are faced with the awesome task of developing effective teaching; this is so difficult an endeavor that research tends to be subordinated. Change in the attitude and organization of intellectual activity depends solely on highly trained, mature scholars who cannot, under any circumstances, be developed in less than a generation. Slowly the universities are moving away from the dilettantish facsimile of Oxbridge which has been their legacy. At Lahore, Dacca, and Karachi, totally new physical plants in spacious suburban locations have been constructed. Foreign teaching assistance from varied sources has bolstered the entire system and some co-ordinated master direction for change has been provided by the report of the Commission on National Education. The training of young scholars through the doctor of philosophy degree at universities of high standard in the United States will be felt in the course of a generation. Already the political science departments at Karachi and Dacca and the economics department at Dacca are staffed largely by young American-trained scholars. As they rise to positions of authority within the university, respect for a research tradition may be quickened. The establishment in both wings of separate agricultural and engineering universities, modeled after American land-grant institutions and substantially assisted by the United States Agency for International Development in both financial resources and personnel, may serve as somewhat of a model, although this may not directly affect other universities or the status of the scholar in other fields for many years if not decades. Within each of the major universities, research units of varying degrees of competence have been established. At the University of the Panjab, for example, the Social Sciences Research Centre, initially under Asia Foundation auspices and under a foreign director, has made research possible without relying on the insecure foundations of the traditional university structure. Theoretically, respectability of scholarship should be thereby enhanced, but actually permeation of this new attitude into the university proper is limited by the quasi-autonomy of these institutes. Such status is necessary, yet it does insulate their effectiveness. The creation of a department of public administration at the Panjab University, staffed by Americans under terms of a USAID program, may eventually help to change the image of the scholar and the role of research in society. But the effectiveness of this enterprise depends on whatever conception will emerge of scholarship implicit in American public administration as a university discipline. There is strong possibility that the impact has been favorable. The greatest handicap of the university is that it does not command the respect of the bureaucracy. Hence, it will not be taken into the bureaucracy's confidence. Even in 1962, when a proposal was made for training government officers and university graduate students in administration, government insisted that classes for the two groups not be held together, and that while they might share library facilities, there must be separate commons rooms for the two groups. To some extent this attitude is justified, for university scholarship has not been able to exercise that degree of responsibility and detachment which inspires collaboration. The first requirement then, is that the universities become detached completely from political turmoil, a condition which will result only when students can be effectively controlled. When this is done, universities may be looked upon by government as a collaborator in the search for a political system of developing viability.

Under these circumstances it is likely that the most immediate hope for attitudes and conditions favorable to research on bureaucracy will emerge from within the bureaucracy and its affiliated research institutes rather than from the universities. The utility and respectability of research was first diffused in Pakistani administrative thought via the planning function. Supported by the Ford Foundation, the Government of Pakistan concluded an agreement in 1954 with Harvard University to recruit an advisory group to assist the Pakistan Planning Commission, which was then known as the Planning Board. Over a decade, a total of fifty-six advisers and twenty-six consultants were recruited by Harvard University to work with the Planning Commission. The preparation of two Five Year Plans during this period generated extensive research activities and stimulated the establishment of statistical units throughout the central and provincial governments. In 1964, the Planning Commission and the planning departments of the provincial governments had about 160 officers assigned. A significant consequence in terms of diffusion of research doctrine and technique was the establishment of the Institute of Development Economics in Karachi which since 1960 has published the *Pakistan Development Review,* a sophisticated learned journal. In 1962 the institute started work-study courses for officers concerned with development planning. The generation of research activities, particularly those utilizing statistics, has warranted the characterization of "[t]he documentary basis of Pakistan's development plans . . . [as being] considerably above that of most emerging countries." [102] The research orientation of the planning apparatus is matched by developments in administrative training and reform.

The beginnings of a new attitude toward research had been generated by the Institute of Public and Business Administration under University of Pennsylvania–USAID auspices in Karachi as early as 1955. Several men trained in the United States under this program subsequently held important posts in the accelerated research program which started in 1960 under a new University of Southern California–USAID contract. Faqir Mohammad Chaodhri became director of research for the National Institutes of

---

[102] Ford Foundation, *Design for Pakistan: A Report on Assistance to the Pakistan Planning Commission by the Ford Foundation and Harvard University* (New York, 1965), p. 21.

Public Administration; M. Afzal became head of the department of public administration at the Panjab University; Anwar Syed became senior lecturer in political science at the Panjab University; Mohammad Iqbal became director of research at the Administrative Staff College; and Zahid Shariff became research associate at the Civil Service Academy. The second development was the establishment of the academies for rural development at Comilla and Peshawar under Ford Foundation auspices and administered by Michigan State University. The work of these academies is one of the most influential factors in Pakistan in inducing new attitudes toward research. A carefully picked staff was trained at Michigan State University in community development before the academies were started. The academies then became the natural vehicle for the expression of research interests which had been generated in the United States. While the Peshawar and Comilla academies may have been less successful in actual training activities due to the 1959 change in government policy toward community development, they remain as eminently respectable influences in fomenting research in the social sciences. The work of the Peshawar Academy is particularly relevant, for it has focused its interest on administration and local government. Among other accomplishments the academy published the second book on administration in Pakistan.[103]

The curriculum of the Administrative Staff College since 1962 has been modified in the direction of what is called "operations research." The term is used somewhat differently than in the United States where it refers to research oriented toward a specific, predetermined end designed to improve a strategic or administrative operation. At the Administrative Staff College the aim of "operations research" is primarily that of changing the attitude of participants toward an empirical methodology, although a concomitant result may be the improvement of a particular operation. The operation attempts to acquaint senior officers with research and analysis of a particular problem in the field. The

[103] Inayatullah (ed.), *Bureaucracy and Development in Pakistan* (Peshawar, 1963). This 453-page volume is the result of a symposium on administration held at the Academy for Rural Development in Peshawar in April, 1962. Considering the state of research and publication in Pakistan, it is an impressive achievement.

reports are then written by groups, discussed widely, and ultimately constitute the rudimentary beginnings of administrative
case studies. If this experience succeeds in demonstrating the
importance of empirical research, further improvements in the
attitude of government toward research may be justifiably expected in the long run.

The largest new undertaking is the public administration contract of the United States Agency for International Development
administered by the University of Southern California. This program, started in October, 1960, includes institutes of public administration at Dacca, Lahore and Karachi, a department of
public administration at the University of the Panjab, and advisory services at the Civil Service Academy. The initial emphasis of
the program was on training for management of middle-level
government officials, but in 1962 attention was also given to the
organization of research and a public administration research
center was established in Lahore with an American adviser. An
effort has been made to stimulate research by a staff of some
fifteen research associates assigned to the three institutes. Results
have been slower than in the case of the rural development
academies, but the total resources of the public administration
program (approaching seven million dollars for three years) are
greater and will ultimately have profound effect. Stimulated by
this program, publication of various materials has begun. At the
Civil Service Academy, a volume of essays on administration,
made up largely of lectures given at the academy, was the first
book on administration to appear in Pakistan.[104] The research
activities of the three national institutes are impressive. Each
publishes a journal of public administration and each has
launched a series of reprints of important reports on administration.[105]

Of at least equal significance is the response in terms of organizational structure of the Government of Pakistan to the research
fomentation created under American aegis. The Establishment

---

[104] M. R. Inayat (ed.), *Perspectives in Public Administration* (Lahore, 1962).
[105] The activities of the institutes are described below, pp. 148–149, and their
publications are cited in appropriate places throughout this essay.

Division of the President's Secretariat, under the leadership of G. Mueenuddin, has sought to give form and direction to the various efforts of research in administration. It has consolidated its control over the rural academies, the Administrative Staff College, and Civil Service Academy, the three public administration institutes, and its own organization and methods wing. It has also appointed a joint secretary to co-ordinate the activities of these organizations. Co-ordination is enhanced by a committee on research and training with the principal of the Administrative Staff College as chairman. The libraries, records, staff facilities, and foreign contacts thus placed within the ambit of the Establishment Division are virtually unmatched in Pakistan. Nor is the interest of the Establishment Division limited to administrative problems. On the contrary, its control over the Administrative Staff College necessarily extends its interest to all aspects of economic development. Its control over the two rural development academies further extends its interest to sociological problems implicit in rural change and to allied problems of local government, regionalism, agriculture, public works, and education. The total planning function is controlled by the Planning Division also located in the President's Secretariat. There is thus concentrated in the central government some five hundred generalists and two hundred planning and rural development specialists more or less committed to research as a crucial aspect of their work. Most of the data for research are also under the control of one of these divisions. In sum, the planning and administrative functions have extended the range of substantive interest of these divisions almost without limit. Virtually every problem of social science research can easily be conceived as falling within this ambit. This development is in consonance with the pattern of governmental power in Pakistan which emphasizes relatively tight controls by a small, cohesive group at the highest governmental level.

While all of these programs and trends have their advantages, the disadvantages should not be overlooked. The organizational changes described are certainly in the right direction, but comprehension of the meaning and requirements of research may not yet equal the enthusiasm shown for its virtues. The term "research" has entered the language of bureaucracy, and after 1962 rarely did an important government officer give an address without paying tribute to research and to the need for humility in its pursuit. But the research alluded to carries with it assumptions of operational investigation sponsored and controlled by government and conducted by officials functioning within the bureaucracy. The directors of the various institutes find it difficult to accommodate organizationally to the need for complete independence in research, and it is not uncommon for research staff to be regarded as subordinates who must respond to orders as do other personnel. Freedom to keep the findings of administrative research from being changed to suit personal political ambitions is always difficult to preserve in all bureaucratic systems. In the environment of insecurity which has characterized Pakistani government, the release of a research study which is true and objective rather than dissembling and flattering may provoke animosities. The responsible administrative official, who is subject to frequent transfer and may later be assigned to a line organization, may sense the threat inherent in this situation and may feel less than free in permitting completely detached research from being conducted or released.

Yet there are forces operating within the bureaucracy which mitigate these risks somewhat. There is some potential within the system for the generation of effective self-criticism. There is much truth in the notion that in Pakistan "bureaucrats are the severest critics of government." What is meant by this somewhat extravagant assertion is that government includes within its ranks large numbers of persons who do not have the uncreative turn of mind commonly associated with bureaucracy, and who would have pursued other professions had there been parity of prestige, salary, and opportunities. Such persons sometimes constitute an important nucleus of internal criticism and dissatisfaction which is a significant source of innovation within the system. Moreover, their dissenting views and innovations are somewhat protected from vindictiveness and punishment by conditions of tenure and the more or less automatic promotion pattern which has long been the ICS tradition. It is supported by the ICS traditions of independence, courage, and forthrightness in expressing views. The ICS officer in the field (where he spent perhaps twenty years of his career) was typically critical of secretariat headquarters and wrote uncommonly critical reports. This spirit has been somewhat tamed by the diminished security implicit in frequent arbitrary transfer in recent years, but it is still characteristic of the senior members of the CSP who belonged to the Indian Civil Service before partition. If they can generate sufficient impetus for a critical attitude, an important source of strength in historical precedent can thus be tapped. Such distinguished CSP officers as M. M. Ahmad, Dr. I. H. Usmani, A. A. Hamid, G. Mueenuddin, S. M. Q. Rizavi, and several of their colleagues have been constructive critics of some aspects of the existing bureaucratic system and some have been decorated for their work.

Of more importance than this latent critical sense is the attitude of objectivity found occasionally at high policy levels. G. Mueenuddin, the establishment secretary from 1961–1964 and the most senior CSP officer in the administration, approached this problem with considerable courage as well as finesse. The issue first arose as a result of a study of village development by Inayatullah of the Rural Development Academy in Peshawar. The study disclosed deficiencies in administration which adversely reflected on various departments of government. By research standards in the United States, the report was very mild, the deficiencies it disclosed were rather normal disarticulations, and their publication would have raised no objection. But the fact that its critical tone was raised as an issue at all is indicative of the sensitivity that exists in Pakistan. Even the fact that the report was written by a government entity was not a sufficient guarantee of its acceptability, for the report was in reality a scholarly monograph designed for wide public distribution. A decision was made to publish the report with fictitious village and personal names, and in the foreword G. Mueenuddin set a tone for research which, if followed and accepted, will do much to alleviate the problem discussed above. Its value, he said, "lies in giving an empirical base to vague conjectures, in substituting facts for guesses and supplying pre-

mises on which objective decision-making ought to be based."
While such a point of view is certainly not unusual in most Western nations, it represents a major landmark in the acceptance of
empirical research in Pakistan. As to the natural inclination of
bureaucracy to resent criticism, the establishment secretary en-
joined government thus:

Care must, however, be taken to ensure that this study does not
unnecessarily antagonize the departments—a criticism of whose conduct is implicit in this study. For, if they withdrew their cooperation,
valuable studies like these would become difficult and may do more
harm than good. It would be equally tragic, if the members of the
Academy are identified as inspectors or spies. For this reason, I would
feel unhappy if this study leads to any censures of defaulting employees. For I am sure that the experiences recounted in this study are
not unique. They are symptomatic of conditions elsewhere. To single
out these employees for punishment, because they have been "caught"
may suppress but will not cure the disease. General action on the study
is essential but no action in particular cases.[106]

Although the attitude of government toward internal criticism
can be more or less molded by such policy as is implicit in the
Mueenuddin statement, the more basic problem is not so amenable to control. The crucial element is the atmosphere of moderation, objectivity, tolerance, and responsibility in society at large. If
this atmosphere prevails, research can flourish without fear that
criticism in a published report will be used for mischievous
political ends. If the irresponsibility, name-calling, and vicious
recrimination of the pre-1958 period recur, the bureaucracy will
inevitably retreat behind a wall of secrecy and scientific research
as it is known in a relatively open society will be unknown in
Pakistan.

Whatever the development of attitudes toward research within
the bureaucracy, it cannot be relied upon exclusively for continuing to generate and to sustain critical scientific research. The
situation described above is but a transitory phenomenon. Ultimately, leadership in research must rest with groups outside the

[106] G. Mueenuddin in the Foreword to Inayatullah, *An Experiment in Village
Development: First Quarterly Report* (Peshawar, 1961).

bureaucracy with maximum access to information. Universities can best perform this function, and it may be that a drift on the part of bureaucracy to classification and secrecy may be counter-balanced by a growing strength of university research and a spreading appreciation for the autonomy, dignity, and utility of professional scholarship.

2

History and Organization of the Bureaucracy

Administrative Concepts and Training of Administrators

The term "public services" in Pakistan embraces the totality of public bureaucratic employment, approximating a million persons.[1] The term "civil service," unlike its usage in the United States, Britain, and elsewhere, refers to a small group within the public services, numbering between four hundred and five hundred men, designated the Civil Service of Pakistan (CSP). During the period following independence in 1947 until November, 1950, this cadre (the "premier administrative service") was designated the Pakistan Administrative Service, but this term has not been used since then either officially or unofficially. The Civil Service of Pakistan, like the Indian Administrative Service, the Burma Civil Service, the Malay Civil Service, and (until 1963) the Ceylon Civil Service, is derivative in structure and ethos from the Indian Civil Service (ICS). The physical manifestation of this derivation is the fact that it was formed by 157 officers of the ICS (thirty-six of whom were British) who migrated to Pakistan at partition. Some eighty (all but four of whom were Pakistani) of these same officers remained in the service in 1964, occupying the senior positions at all levels of government and all the crucial positions in training, establishment, and administrative reform. While it is easy to overemphasize the importance of the CSP in a dynamic bureaucratic system which is undergoing rapid change, it must also be said that the CSP cadre hold crucial positions in all government activities, central, provincial, and local, and wield an influence far disproportionate to their numbers.

[1] This figure is further analyzed below, pp. 131–132.

Throughout its history members of the Indian Civil Service have been maligned as the "heaven-born" and the "kept class" and praised as the "steel frame" of the government of India. Certainly it was one of the most carefully organized civil service systems in history, and the pride which it generated is not easily contained. An institutional relationship between the examination system of China and Western civil service systems, including the ICS, has often been inferred. First suggested by Ssü-Yu Têng in "Chinese Influence on the Western Examination System," *Harvard Journal of Asiatic Studies*, VII (1943), 267–312, further historical work on this subject is in progress. H. G. Creel in "The Beginnings of Bureaucracy in China: The Origin of the Hsien," *Journal of Asian Studies*, XXIII (1964), 155–185, characterizes Têng's paper as "classic" and refers to further research under way by Donald F. Lach and others. Rupert Wilkinson, in a senior honors thesis written at Harvard University, subsequently published as *Gentlemanly Power* (London, 1964), deals with relationships between English public school values, concepts of leadership, and the Confucian system.

The "greatest civil service in the world," as the ICS has often been called, recruited young Englishmen (and later small numbers of Indians) and trained them carefully in a literary-generalist tradition which was presumed to impart the virtues of Platonic guardianship. It is from this concept that the retired ICS officer, Philip Mason (whose pseudonym is Woodruff), has taken the title for the second of his two-volume study, *The Men Who Ruled India* (New York, 1954). Volume I is called *The Founders of Modern India;* volume II, *The Guardians.* These sympathetic, somewhat sentimental, and nostalgic descriptions of ICS officers at work are a necessary as well as agreeable juncture from which a study of the bureaucracy of Pakistan may be started. Woodruff has combined astute analysis with interesting biographical studies of ICS officers at work in the field and in the secretariats. He does not deny his partiality to the ICS, and his study must be read with this in mind.

The philosophy of education of ICS and CSP officers was determined more than a century and a half ago by a statement of the Marquis Wellesley in establishing the College of Fort William at Calcutta for the training of East India Company officials. Known as Wellesley's "Minute in Council," the text and commentary thereon can be found in at least three documentary collections: *The College of Fort William in Bengal* (London, 1805); *Letters of the Marquis Wellesley Respecting the College of Fort William* (London, 1812); and *The Despatches, Minutes and Correspondence of the Marquess Wellesley, K. G. During His Administration in India* (London, 1837). Fort William College was gradually superseded by Haileybury College (whose formal name was East India College—Herts) in England. Haileybury, which operated from 1806 to 1857, had a reputation for the vigorous intellectual quality of its teaching. The distinguished demographer, T. R. Malthus, spent much of his career at Haileybury and, when the college was under attack, wrote a learned 105-page pamphlet elucidating the philosophy by which the young ICS probationers were trained: *Statements Respecting the East-India College with an Appeal to Facts in Refutation of the Charges Lately Brought against it in the Court of Proprietors* (London, 1817). The immense influence of Haileybury as a source of ICS *élan* is developed by Woodruff and also by G. O. Trevelyan in his series of letters on administrative life in India, *The Competition Wallah* (London, 1864). Trevelyan deplored the closing of Haileybury and with it the passing of the days when a young officer "came out in company with a score of men who had passed the last two years of their English life in the same quadrangle as himself." Haileybury, he maintained, formed a tie which the "vicissitudes of official life could never break." Careful studies of the influence of Haileybury are now being undertaken by several researchers, but these are only in the preliminary stages. Bernard Cohn has completed a study of the background of 426 writers appointed by the Court of Directors to Haileybury College from 1809 to 1860, in the course of which he analyzes the two-year course of study at Haileybury. This research appears in "Recruitment and Training of the East India Company's Civil Service in India, 1600–1860," a chapter in Ralph Braibanti and associates, *Asian Bureaucratic Systems Emergent from the British Imperial Tradition*, to be published by Duke University Press in 1966.

Of the five nations jointly inheriting the ICS tradition, Pakistan, more than the others, seems to have preserved the cohesive, strong corporate sense which was the hallmark of Haileybury. In India, this characteristic was almost completely lost by rapid expansion of the IAS cadre, by bringing in older officers by emergency and state recruitment, and, finally, by merging the training of IAS officers with that of other cadres in a large academy of more than two hundred probationers. In Burma, the training system has collapsed and in Malaya and Ceylon there were no academies for training. In the latter country, the elite cadre was abolished in 1963 and merged with a larger group of officers to become the Unified Administrative Service. In Pakistan, the cadre was kept small, and entrance into the service (with the exception of fifteen officers from the provincial services and fifteen from the army) was limited to university graduates between twenty-one and twenty-four years of age. These were admitted in small batches (the term used in Haileybury) of not more than thirty probationers a year and were trained as a group for one year in a residential academy, rightly described by one American observer as "baronial," very much like Haileybury. Subsequent training in England gave the group an even greater corporate sense. It would be difficult if not impossible to understand the bureaucracy of modern Pakistan without knowledge of the sources of tradition which elucidate the elitist philosophy undergirding the system. Training at the Civil Service Academy in Lahore is unchanged in its essentials from the education imparted at Haileybury College. Much of the criticism directed against the CSP cadre derives from the belief that this training continues to be too British and has not been sufficiently adapted to the needs of a democratic, underdeveloped state.

The education of the higher civil service was further affected by what has been called one of the most momentous decisions made under British rule: Thomas Babington Macaulay's establishment of English as the language of government and higher education in India. Macaulay's "Minute on Education" written in 1835 was a provocative, haughty defense of English by one who had no knowledge of Oriental languages. It is included in H. Woodrow (ed.), *Macaulay's Minutes on Education in India in the Years 1835, 1836, and 1837* (Calcutta, 1862). Macaulay's arrogance was resented by Indians and one of the best refutations of his view was made by Banerjea in a speech available in Ram Chandra Palit (ed.), *Speeches by Babu Surendra Nath Banerjea, 1876–80* (Calcutta, 1894). Nor were his views acceptable to all Englishmen, as is made clear by H. R. James, *Education and Statesmanship in India, 1797 to 1910* (London, 1911). Macaulay elaborated further on the need for a classical emphasis in the civil service in his *Report* of November, 1854, which later appeared as Appendix F (pp. 35–43) to the Aitchison Commission Report. Some of his speeches in the House of Commons (e.g., *Parliamentary Debates,* 3rd series, Vol. CXXVII, June 24, 1853, cols. 739–759) are expositions of the education and work of the Indian Civil Service.

Pre-Partition Official Reports on Indian Bureaucracy of Relevance to Pakistan

From 1812 through 1946, there appeared some forty-four reports on administration in India. A convenient listing of these may be found in the special issue of the *Indian Journal of Public Administration,* IX (1963), 581–582, devoted to administrative reforms since independence. While all of these reports are to some degree relevant to modern problems of administration, at least fourteen may be regarded as directly pertinent to administrative problems of contemporary Pakistan.

From 1887 to 1930 there appeared under British rule a distinguished group of six reports which dealt in whole or in part with the Indian public bureaucracy. These reports were not planned as an organized, integrated series; on the contrary, they arose as responses to the need for re-evaluation of the apparatus of British rule. But examined in retrospect they can be regarded as a collection of related surveys, each attempting to integrate the reasoning of the previous one and to reinterpret former premises rather than depart from them. In total some fifty published volumes [2] comprise

[2] Including three separate but related volumes connected with the Simon Commission Report: *Report of the Indian Central Committee,* Cmd. 3451 (1929); *Supplementary Note by Dr. A. Suhrawardy, M.L.A.,* Cmd. 3525 (1930); and *Review of Growth of Education in British India,* Cmd. 3407 (1929).

these six reports. They are similar in format, the first volume of each being the substance of the findings and the remaining volumes consisting of appendices and annexures of questionnaires, interviews, and statistics. Most of the reports are linked to the preceding reports, in some cases by fairly elaborate summaries and explanations of preceding reports and in all cases by frequent reference to them.

The first major comprehensive analysis of the civil service was the *Report of the Public Service Commission, 1886–87*, Cmd. 5327 (8 vols.; Calcutta: Superintendent of Government Printing, India, 1888). More commonly known by the name of its chairman, Sir Charles U. Aitchison, the first volume gives an excellent history of the civil service from the beginning of the East India Company. The significance of the report is that it establishes the basic structure and conceptual premises of the services which exist even now in Pakistan. The Aitchison recommendations were essentially a pragmatic response to indigenous demands for Indianization of the services. Provincial services were created, and the term "covenanted service" was changed to Indian Civil Service (the recommended term "Imperial Civil Service" was not accepted). Candidates for the ICS were to be recruited only in London. Indians were admitted into the service, but mostly into the provincial services, which were local and inferior in power, responsibility, and prestige. Indians were also admitted to the new ICS, but since the examination had to be taken in London, few were eligible. Thus, the locus of power continued to rest with the British. Much of the feeling which now exists between the provincial services in Pakistan and the Civil Service of Pakistan can be traced to the Aitchison scheme which even then noted, to no avail, that the ICS and provincial services "should be put on a footing of social equality." The crucial issue of spatial distribution of power as between district, division, province, and center was the concern of the Hobhouse Commission, whose *Report of the Royal Commission upon Decentralisation in India*, Cmd. 4360 (10 vols.; 1909), is a comprehensive study of orthodox district administration and local government. The bureaucracy developed in the Aitchison pattern until the next major reassessment headed by Lord Islington in 1915: *Report of the Royal Commission on Public Services, August 14, 1915,* Cmd. 8382 (20 vols.; 1917). The Islington Commission found it necessary to abandon exclusive reliance on the distinction between ICS and the provincial services as a formula for equalizing opportunity between Indians and British in the services. It recommended division of services by levels of work. This resulted eventually in the present-day divisions into classes I, II, III, and IV. The concept of remuneration of civil servants enunciated by the Islington Commission has continued as the basis for salaries of Pakistan's service. Islington asserted that:

The only safe criterion is that Government should pay so much and so much only to their employees as is necessary to obtain recruits of the right stamp, and to maintain them in such a degree of comfort and dignity as will shield them from temptation and keep them efficient for the term of their service. Whilst, therefore, we have noted the rise in prices which has taken place, we have not based on this any general recommendation. Where we have advised changes of salary it has been to meet inequalities of remuneration prejudicial to efficiency, to fulfil expectations reasonably founded on formal announcements made by Government, and to improve recruitment, where the existing terms have been shown to be insufficient to obtain a satisfactory personnel.

A 95-page minute of dissent by the Muslim member of the Islington Commission, Sir Abdur Rahim, is one of the most useful parts of the report for Pakistan not only because Rahim was a Muslim but also because it includes a cogent advocacy of separation of judicial and executive functions, a problem which continues to be vexing in Pakistan. The Rahim dissent is primarily a refutation of the British argument that the services must be Indianized slowly. Rahim argues that Indianization had not occurred in accordance with plan and that Indians were more prepared to assume administrative responsibility than the British would admit. The Islington suggestions in general irritated rather than satisfied Indian opinion. The Servants of India Society published a criticism by an eminent Brahmin statesman, Hirday Nath Kunzru, *The Public Services in India* (Allahabad, 1917), in which the dissent by Abdur Rahim is praised.

In 1918 "the most momentous utterance ever made in India's chequered history" (Mr. Montagu to the House of Commons,

August 20, 1917), the Montagu-Chelmsford Reforms, was published: *Report on Indian Constitutional Reforms,* Cmd. 9109
(1918). These reforms sought gradually to introduce local self-
government in India and were the basis for the first Government
of India Act (1919), and hence ultimately for the second Government of India Act (1935) and the Indian Independence Act
(1947). The latter, with modifications, was the paramount legal
instrument in Pakistan until 1956, when it was succeeded by the
first Constitution. Government authority was divided into central
and provincial subjects and, within the province, certain subjects
were controlled by elected Indian ministers rather than by professional British and Indian civil servants. This system, which came
to be called dyarchy, profoundly affected the ICS and the role of
the district officer. It changed the mode of power of the civil
servant in several spheres from autocratic rule to consultation,
persuasion, and co-ordination, a relationship described by
Woodruff as one in which "one partner had the wheel and the
other the accelerator and the brake" (*The Guardians,* p. 211).
Dyarchy remained the pattern of government from 1919 to 1937.
The effort to create a partnership between elected local officials
and permanent members of the bureaucracy continues as one of
the crucial problems in Pakistan, where the concepts of community development and Basic Democracies meet with resistance
from the traditional bureaucracy of district administration. A
caveat of the Montagu-Chelmsford Report has direct contemporary relevance: "Our aim throughout must be to make the change
not needlessly difficult for the services, to enlist their cooperation
with the popular element in the government, and to induce on
both sides the habit of goodwill and mutual toleration, which is
essential if India is to pass peaceably through the trying transitional period in front of her" (par. 126). Many of the documents
which relate to constitutional development during this period are
reprinted in Panchanadas Mukerji (ed.), *Indian Constitutional
Documents,* Vol. I, *1600–1918;* Vol. II, *1915–1916* (Calcutta,
1918).

Demands for Indianization and worsening of relations between
classes of the services made the solutions proposed by the Aitchi-

son, Islington, and Montagu-Chelmsford reports inadequate. In 1924, a new analysis of these problems was made by the Lee Commission: *Report of the Royal Commission on the Superior Civil Services in India,* Cmd. 2128 (1924). While this report did not substantially modify the bureaucratic structure created by the preceding commissions, it increased the proportion of Indians, changed the pay structure, and urged the creation of the public service commissions which had been contemplated by section 96o of the Government of India Act (1919). The Lee Report includes a cogent rationale and detailed plan for public service commissions which eventually were created in India and on which the central and provincial commissions of Pakistan are patterned. The Lee Commission also espoused a policy of remuneration which continues to be a perennial source of disputation in Pakistan:

A great rise in prices has taken place since the scales of pay were fixed on the recommendation of the Islington Commission, and that while the Government was not in a position to treat its own employees in as generous a fashion as commercial houses of the better class were treating their superior employees, the disparity of remuneration as between a commercial and an official career had become so conspicuous and so discouraging to civil servants that something had to be done without delay to restore contentment and make service career attractive.

The last massive effort to reassess the conditions of British rule in India came in 1930 with the Simon Commission whose report, *Report of the Indian Statutory Commission,* Cmd. 3568 (17 vols.; 1930), is the most comprehensive of the series. The first volume includes a 400-page survey of Indian history and government and is one of the most valuable documents issued under British rule. A long chapter describing the administrative system includes a comprehensive analysis of the work of the district officer. The Simon Report departs in some respects from the views elaborated in the Aitchison and Islington reports and confirmed by the Lee Report. It reflects the increase in communal disorders and the nationalist movement which now had become extremist and often violent. It reasserts the importance of vast authority for the district officer, minimizes the immediate need for local self-government, and justifies continued use of British officers who alone can bring an impartiality to administration and "in whom the practice of British democracy is instinctive." The report met with widespread criticism, summarized in C. F. Andrews, *India and the Simon Report* (London, 1930). A document allied with the Simon Report which is of particular relevance to Pakistan is *Review of Growth of Education in British India* by the auxiliary committee appointed by the Simon Commission, issued as Cmd. 3407 (1929). This includes a 29-page chapter (Chapter IX) on the education of Muslims in undivided India and useful statistical tables which assist in explaining the early disadvantages which Pakistan suffered in creating an independent nation. These six documents, the Aitchison, Hobhouse, Islington, Montagu-Chelmsford, Lee, and Simon reports, are the ideological roots of the Indian administrative system. Read together in chronological sequence, they are a noteworthy intellectual achievement in the construction of a bureaucratic apparatus. They were an impressive effort to assess the surrounding tissue of Indian culture, to adjust to emerging independence sentiments, and to introduce certain imperatives of constitutionalism without relinquishing ultimate control. Above all, they established and gave ideological support to a public bureaucracy whose structure and internal distribution of power shifted with the times but whose generating concepts were constant. The shadow of this edifice is seen and felt in the contemporary bureaucracy of Pakistan; some critics would say that the shadow looms larger than the edifice which casts it.

There are eight other reports issued before independence which are of significance to administration. The reports of this second group are concerned primarily with technical aspects of internal administration rather than with broader problems of bureaucratic structure and power. Like the six major reports, they deal with many problems which remain unsolved in modern Pakistani administration and which continue to be discussed. Among these problems is the perennial question of reform of administrative procedure to increase efficiency, dealt with both by the central and provincial secretariats at various intervals. Pre-partition reports on this subject are of some utility in determining the contours of administrative reform for contemporary Pakistan. One of the issues in planning such reform has been the difficulty of empirical determination of administrative deficiency and, consequently, of constructing a program of positive remedial measures. Foreign consultants who may be expert in another cultural context find it difficult to understand the Pakistani situation without lengthy contact with it; Pakistani officials may have been catapulted into positions of responsibility only recently and, in any case, may find it difficult to take a broad and analytical view of their own needs. Hence, the collation of past experience in Indian administrative reform may be of value in identification of equivalent contemporary problems, especially since pre-partition reforms were undertaken under circumstances allowing more careful, lengthy, and detailed study than is now thought possible. Moreover, the comparative study of all such administrative reports may indicate a pattern of recurrence of issues that may enable current reformers to separate imperative and persistent administrative problems from those which are ephemeral and transitory.

The earliest of these eight reports, one of the best studies on district administration in part of the area which is now East Pakistan, is the *Bengal District Administration Committee Report, 1913–14* (Calcutta, 1915). This 191-page analysis was prepared under the direction of E. V. Levinges, ICS, who was then a member of the Governor-General's Executive Council. The earliest study dealing with secretariat aspects of administrative reform was that undertaken under the chairmanship of H. Llewellyn-Smith, *Report of the Government of India Secretariat Procedure Committee* (New Delhi, 1919). This report was prepared before the first Government of India Act was put into effect, and since it dealt exclusively with allocation of work among departments, forms to be used, and technical efficiency, it was not a report which excited controversy. Moreover, it was premised on the dyarchy which prevailed in India from the reforms of 1919 to the implementation of the Government of India Act of 1935. The prospect of replacing the dyarchical system with provincial autonomy prescribed by the 1935 Government of India Act required a new assessment of the responsibilities of the central secretariat.

This was undertaken by a committee headed by Sir Henry Wheeler, *Report of the Government of India Secretariat Committee* (New Delhi, 1937). The Wheeler Report went beyond the question of procedure and dealt with the selection of officers for superior posts in the central secretariat. It envisaged enlarging the ICS cadre and assigning competent provincial service officers to the central secretariat (though not necessarily to the ICS). In the same year a group headed by R. M. Maxwell published a *Report on Secretariat Organization and Procedure—1937* (New Delhi: Government of India, 1937). The Maxwell recommendations were intended to reorganize the secretariat in accordance with the 1935 Government of India Act. Since this act served, with modifications made by the Indian Independence Act of 1947, as the basic polity of Pakistan until 1956, the structure recommended by the Maxwell committee was essentially that found in Pakistan at independence and until 1956. All three reports (Llewellyn-Smith, Wheeler, and Maxwell) have been reprinted in Pakistan by the National Institute of Public Administration in Karachi as part of its reprint series.

Two useful reports on Indian administration concerned the provincial government of Bengal. Since East Bengal is now East Pakistan, with a revenue system quite different from that of West Pakistan and a somewhat different administrative system generally, these reports are of considerable utility. The first of these, by L. A. Chapman, ICS, *Report Regarding the Establishment of the Secretariat Departments* (Alipore: Superintendent, Government Printing, Bengal Government Press, 1938), was prepared for the Finance Department of the Government of Bengal. The Chapman Report was reprinted in 1963 by the National Institute of Public Administration in Dacca and is now available throughout Pakistan. A short document of some fifty pages, it deals with practical details of office work such as work load, staffing patterns, and procedure. It includes no historical survey of the secretariat nor does it expound a concept of administration. It is, indeed, one of the most pragmatic reports of these here considered.

In a quite different genre is the Rowlands Report: Sir Archibald Rowlands, *Report of the Bengal Administration Enquiry Commit-*

tee, 1944–45 (Alipore: Superintendent, Government Printing, Bengal Government Press, 1945). This 206-page report recommends the abolishment of commissioners' divisions (the major unit of government after the province) and points to the need for provincial and district development plans. Since 1960 the role of the commissioner in Pakistan has increased rather than diminished in importance, and few officials would now agree with Rowlands that the posts should be abolished. The suggestions for planning have current relevance, for there is opinion in Pakistan that more planning should devolve not necessarily upon local bodies of Basic Democracies but on orthodox district administration, and, in fact, such devolution is implicit in the rural works program started in 1960 in East Pakistan and now extended to West Pakistan. The Rowlands Report is the best empirical analysis of district administration in print, for it avoids the usual nostalgia and sentimentality of an approach which dwells on the district as a microcosmic empire ruled by a "young Socrates." It includes an excellent history of the differences in administrative practices in East and West Bengal and warns that "district offices [are] on [the] verge of breakdown." Rowlands' candor is illustrated by this observation (p. 27, par. 66):

The independent and disconnected activities of Government in the mufassal have reached such a point of confusion that District Officers are unanimous that something must be done. In our view also, the situation, if left to itself, can only deteriorate further because the activities of Government in the mufassal will increase and practically every department is thinking in terms of a "Provincialised Service" and makes little attempt to disguise its determination to go ahead with its own plans without reference to any other part of Government.

Rowlands, citing such American administrators as David Lilienthal and Luther Gulick, urged a strong unified administration under a district officer with power to compel co-ordination. This plea for invigoration of district administration is noteworthy because it was made as early as 1938 by the British about their own system. While Pakistan has not deviated significantly from a pattern of strong district administration, there is a sentimental disposition to regard the district apparatus as an immutable mechanism designed by British genius and perfected by the refining passage of time. As a consequence, it has undergone less critical analysis than any other aspect of government. A careful study of the Rowlands Report would do much to dispel the fantasy of the idyllic and would bring to the subject of district administrative reform the sense of reality and candor which is needed. The Rowlands Report has also been reprinted by the National Institute of Public Administration in Dacca and is readily available. The Chapman and Rowlands reports have an unanticipated internal relatedness as well as a relevance to current problems. This is suggested by the likelihood that devolution of planning responsibility to the district will probably require substantial overhauling of the dominant attitude, structure, and workways of orthodox district administration and of organization of the provincial secretariats.

A forerunner of five-year plans was the 447-page document, *Post-War Reconstruction: Bengal Government's Plan* (Alipore: Superintendent, Government Printing, 1945), prepared by a group under the chairmanship of A. Ahmad. This includes a preliminary draft and first instalment of a twenty-year plan which is interesting to compare with Pakistan's two Five Year Plans. The Bengal plan aims primarily at agricultural development and includes schemes for strengthening police and jail administration because it deems law and order to be a matter of special importance in Bengal.

Finally, the study by Sir Richard O. Tottenham, *Report on the Reorganisation of the Central Government, 1945–46* (New Delhi: Government of India Press, 1946), deserves a significant place in administrative literature on several counts. First, it demonstrates that the British Raj was not indifferent to problems of economic development. Sir Richard, quoting approvingly another source, assumes the desirability of renouncing "the old conception of Government as a regulatory, policing and taxing mechanism" and of openly adopting "the conception of Government as the nation's common instrument for expanding its social and economic welfare in all those spheres where individuals or private associations cannot achieve equally effective results." Finally, it shows how secretariat efficiency has been hampered by the importation into secretariat work of the district officers' values and attitudes of personal rule and influence. One historical curiosity revealed by this report is Tottenham's advocacy of what amounts to a "section officer scheme" which was introduced in Pakistan government first in the Punjab in 1958 and in the secretariat of the Government of Pakistan in 1959. This significant advance in administrative efficiency was often referred to by the press as an "American scheme," but it is, in fact, found in all highly developed bureaucracies and was suggested by Tottenham in this report. A second curiosity is Tottenham's recommendation against creating an administrative staff college, which both India and Pakistan have now established. The Tottenham Report has been reprinted in Pakistan by the National Institute of Public Administration in Karachi as the first in its reprint series.

Two additional reports (on the periphery of the group of eight described above) deserve passing mention. The kind of fiscal reasoning which undergirds the need to contract the size of bureaucracy is illustrated by the report of the Inchcape Committee: *Report of the Indian Retrenchment Committee, 1922–23* (Delhi: Superintendent of Government Printing, 1923). A second pertinent document concerns the establishment of a military college in India: *Report of the Indian Sandhurst* [Skeen] *Committee*, November 14, 1926 (London, 1927). There is now in Pakistan an institutional relationship between the CSP and military training. Starting in 1960, five army officers were admitted into the CSP each year. In addition, in 1962 probationers were to be trained for six months at the Pakistan Military Academy in Kakul prior to nine months of training at the Civil Service Academy. The Kakul program was abandoned a few weeks after it started. Since these changes give a military slant to administrative training, the report of the Skeen Committee is important for understanding the concepts underlying training at the Kakul Academy, which is Pakistan's counterpart of the Indian Military Academy established consequent to the Skeen Committee recommendations. Further, since Pakistan was under martial law for forty-four months, no document which may shed light on the ethos of the military should be neglected.

Disabilities Consequent to Partition

No comprehensive study has been made of the administrative problems encountered and solved by Pakistan in creating the machinery for a new state immediately after partition. The fact of this creation was a notable achievement, since there were no records, few other physical assets, and very little executive talent transferred from India. It is a matter of regret that no research has been started on the formation of the government in Pakistan in 1947 and the following years. Certainly, interviews with the few remaining men who played a major role in establishing the administrative system should form a significant aspect of such research. Thus far, only Chaudhury Mohammad Ali, formerly secretary-general and prime minister, has put his memoirs in writing. These are now being edited and will be published by Columbia University Press. One section of his memoirs deals with organization of administration immediately after partition. Such men as S. Ikramullah, Aziz Ahmed, G. Ahmed, and G. Mueenuddin were also among the architects of the bureaucratic system. Their memoirs are not being written nor are their valuable experiences being recorded. This is an unfortunate lacuna which will make it difficult to write a subsequent administrative history of the early development of Pakistan.

The inadequate supply of Muslim executive talent described below was in part due to a tradition of Muslim reluctance to be educated in the British tradition, an educational problem described cogently in an essay by the present vice-chancellor of the University of Karachi, I. H. Qureshi, "Islamic Elements in the Political Thought of Pakistan," Chapter VII in Ralph Braibanti and J. J. Spengler (eds.), *Tradition, Values, and Socio-Economic Development* (Durham, N. C., 1961), and in Mufti Intizamullah Shikabi, "Muslim System of Education Under the Later Moghuls," and A. R. Malick, "British Educational Policy," Chapters VIII and IX of *A History of the Freedom Movement*, Vol. II (Karachi,

1960). Volume II of the *Freedom Movement* series is bound in two parts. Part II includes two chapters relevant to Muslim education in India: S. Moinul Haq, "The Aligarh Movement: Educational" (Chapter XIX), and A. Hamid, "The Aligarh Movement: Social and Political" (Chapter XX). All the essays in the *Freedom Movement* series are well done, although always sympathetic to the Muslim point of view, and several are relevant to administration. The 95-page dissent of Abdur Rahim in the Islington Report [3] is a particularly good analysis of the causes of this condition among Muslims. Statistical tables in text and appendices of the Islington Report are valuable sources showing the number of degrees conferred on members of the Muslim and other communities. Other tables show the small number of Muslims in government service.

The condition of Muslims generally in India is discussed in W. W. Hunter, *The Indian Musalmans* (London: Trübner, 1871); S. S. Thorburn, *Mussalmans and Moneylenders in the Punjab* (London, 1886); W. H. Moreland, *The Agrarian System of Moslem India* (Cambridge, 1929); and Ram Gopal, *Indian Muslims, A Political History (1858–1947)* (Bombay: Asia Publishing House, 1959). Probably the best and most comprehensive analysis of Muslims on the subcontinent is Ishtiaq Husain Qureshi, *The Muslim Community of the Indo-Pakistan Subcontinent (610–1947)* (The Hague, 1962), published as part of a series in the Near and Middle East studies program at Columbia University.

Some understanding of the magnitude and complexity of the administrative problems of partition is gained through study of documents known as *Partition Proceedings,* comprising six volumes totaling nearly a thousand pages. Prior to partition, these affairs were handled by a special cabinet committee of the Government of India. After August 15, 1947, this committee was replaced by the Partition Council for India and Pakistan composed of three Hindus, Sardar Patel, Rajendra Prasad, C. Rajagopalachari, and three Muslims, M. A. Jinnah, Liaquat Ali Khan, and Sardar Abdur Rab Nishtar. The chairman was Lord Mountbatten

[3] See above, pp. 102–103.

who remained as governor-general of India for several months after independence. Disagreements which could not be resolved by the expert committees, the steering committee, or the Partition Council, were to be decided by an arbitral tribunal. The Partition Council worked through a steering committee which guided ten expert committees, each composed of Hindu and Muslim (and in a few instances, Sikh) members. The expert committees were (1) organization, records, and personnel, (2) assets and liabilities, (3) central revenue, (4) contracts, (5) currency, coinage, and exchange, (6) economic relations (controls), (7) economic relations (trade), (8) domicile, (9) foreign relations, and (10) armed forces reconstitution. There are very few copies of the *Partition Proceedings* extant, and there appears to be no complete set anywhere in Pakistan, though one fairly complete set is in the East Pakistan provincial secretariat library in Dacca and another is in the personal library of William Spengler who, in 1965, was United States Consul in Peshawar. Volume I, *Report of Expert Committee No. 1* (New Delhi: Manager, Government of India Press, 1949), consists of 258 pages and includes a chapter on division of personnel which describes special arrangements for training Muslim officers in the work of government departments in which they had no experience. Volume II is *Assets and Liabilities* (Simla: Manager, Government of India Press, 1948). It is only 108 pages. There is also a separately published *Appendix 1 to Volume II— Assets and Liabilities* (Simla: Manager of Publications, 1948), which is 278 pages. Volume III, *Report of Expert Committee III— IX* (New Delhi: Manager, Government of India Press, 1948), deals with the remaining eight topics in 298 pages. Volumes IV and V presumably were not published, and Volume VI is *Reports of the Members and Awards of the Chairman of the Boundary Commissions* (Alipore: Superintendent, West Bengal Government Press, 1950) in 322 pages.

On the same level with the Partition Council three groups were to decide on the boundaries of areas which were to be divided between India and Pakistan: The Bengal Separation Council, the Punjab Partition Committee, and the Assam Separation Council. The Bengal and Punjab groups were each made up of two Muslim and two Hindu High Court judges. The Assam council consisted of two members from East Bengal (belonging to Pakistan) and two from Assam. The chairman of these groups, Sir Cyril Radcliffe, had authority to make final decisions in the event of stalemate in the committees. The boundary reports show not only the complexity of the task of demarcation but also the intensity of Hindu and Muslim feeling which eventuated in a stalemate in both commissions and a final decision given by Radcliffe. The magnitude of the task facing Pakistan after partition is suggested by the extent of migration of Muslims and non-Muslims. Although no accurate figures are available, it is estimated that five and a half million Muslims moved into West Pakistan from India and an equal number of non-Muslims moved from West Pakistan into India. About one and a quarter million Hindus moved from East Pakistan into India. Thus, the nation was confronted with the immediate problem of law and order in the face of widespread disturbances, with the subsequent problem of rehabilitating the refugees, and with the later legal problems of allocating property left behind by non-Muslim evacuees to the new refugees from India. Two journalistic accounts which depict the trauma of partition are of some interest. Leonard Mosely's *The Last Days of the British Raj* (New York, 1962) is especially provocative and purports to describe the manner in which Sir Cyril Radcliffe decided on the boundaries. The authenticity of Mosely's observations, however, would be open to question by serious students. Penderel Moon's *Divide and Quit* (London, 1961) is a more reliable account of problems of partition, although it is limited to his own experience in Bahawalpur (now in Pakistan) where he was minister of finance. Moon was an ICS officer of considerable perception and the book merits study. Khushwant Singh's novel, *Mano Majra* (New York, 1956), depicts the atrocities accompanying partition, and while it does not pretend to be historically valid it probably is not an unfair description of actual events. It was released in Pakistan under the title *Train to Pakistan*.

The acute shortage of managerial talent experienced in the complexity of decision-making at a high level of government is not generally appreciated. So severe was the lack and so great the problems of creating a nation from two separate parts of the subcontinent, that it is remarkable Pakistan was able to exist at all. An analysis of managerial talent available to Pakistan can be found in Ralph Braibanti, "Public Bureaucracy and Judiciary in Pakistan," an essay in Joseph LaPalombara (ed.), *Bureaucracy and Political Development* (Princeton, 1963). In a series of six tables of statistics, part of this study analyzes the quantitative and qualitative experience of officers joining the Government of Pakistan at partition in 1947. There is also included a survey of the influence of British officers who remained in Pakistan after independence. During the first quarter of 1947 the cadres of the Indian Civil Service and Indian Political Service had a strength of 1,157 officers (excluding those assigned to Burma). Of these, 101, or 9 per cent, were Muslim. Ninety-five of these opted for Pakistan. They were joined by one Christian officer, fifty British officers, and eleven Muslim army officers. Of these 157 officers, only 136 were actually available for administrative work, the remainder being posted to judicial or diplomatic assignments. Of these 136, fewer than twenty had more than fifteen years' experience, and half had less than a decade of service. Qualitatively, only eight of these officers held positions in the secretariat of the Indian government and only three attained the rank of joint secretary to the central government. About ten other officers in services other than the ICS and IPS can be added, thus making a total of 146 officers of administrative experience available for creating the new state of Pakistan. It is doubtful if any other nation of Pakistan's size faced independence with such a shortage of talent. This predicament explains much in Pakistan's administrative history.

Muslim Antecedents of Administration

It is not unexpected that in Pakistan, which was founded initially on the ideological impetus of Islam, there should be considerable feeling for Muslim origins of the present administrative pattern. Indeed, the pattern of administration in North India was adapted by the British largely from Mughal administration. This is reflected both in territorial divisions and the Persian nomenclature of officials, such as *kanungo* and *patwari*. A bibliographical account of Mughal administration is given in Bernard S. Cohn's *The Development and Impact of British Administration in India* (New Delhi: Indian Institute of Public Administration, 1961). Cohn also reveals Mughal influence in his case study of the Benares region, "The Initial British Impact on India," *Journal of Asian Studies*, XX (1960), 418–431. Much of the research on Mughal administration is in Arabic or Persian, but several works have appeared in English. One of the best is I. H. Qureshi, *The Administration of the Sultanate of Delhi* (Karachi, 1958). Others are Sri Ram Sharma, *Muslim Government and Administration* (Bombay, 1951), and R. S. Tripathi, *Some Aspects of Muslim Administration* (Allahabad, 1936). Tripathi's work is especially valuable because it traces from Persian sources the development of the Sultanate and the Vizarat chronologically from the Ghaznavides to the end of the reign of Akbar. It shows, among other things, the Persian origin of many terms of government still in use in Pakistan. The Bureau of National Reconstruction contributed to the effort to resurrect Muslim origins of administration by publication in 1960 of a small pamphlet, *Epistles of Hazrat Ali*. Surendranath Sen's *Administrative System of the Marathas* (Calcutta, 1925) shows the extent to which the Marathas absorbed Mughal administrative patterns. One of the most interesting accounts of judicial administration, based on actual cases decided between A.D. 1206 and 1750, is M. B. Ahmad, *The Administration of Justice in Mediaeval India* (Karachi: Manager of Publications, 1951). Since there is now a strong movement to base criminal law in Pakistan on pre-British norms,[4] Ahmad's study is important because it elucidates concepts of justice regnant before the diffusion of English juridical values.

General, Secondary Materials

Secondary works on bureaucracy and administration are not as numerous as the specialist might hope. A view of the Indian Civil Service almost universally shared by the generation of Indians who fought for independence can be found in Jawaharlal Nehru's writings. In his autobiography, *Toward Freedom* (Boston, 1958),

[4] See below, pp. 187–198.

he deprecates the ostentation and pomp of government and, although acknowledging the good qualities of the ICS, refers to its officers as "kept classes" and as an expensive luxury. In his later book, *The Discovery of India* (Calcutta, 1946), he deplores the absolute power of the ICS which he describes as a "close and well-knit corporation," to which the Indian members, even though they wore the insignia and conformed to its rules, did not really belong. The views on this subject of Mohammed Ali Jinnah, the founder of Pakistan, have not been recorded. The only relevant statement known to be extant is reprinted in the appendix of this volume.[5] A standard, general study is L. S. S. O'Malley, *The Indian Civil Service, 1601–1930* (London, 1931). A similar study is Edward A. H. Blunt, *The Indian Civil Service* (London, 1937). Professor Akshoy Kumar Ghosal's doctoral dissertation, *Civil Service in India Under the East India Company* (Calcutta, 1944), is a fairly thorough account of the period ending with the mutiny of 1857 and includes the texts of some useful documents in the appendices. *The Civil Service in India* by Naresh Chandra Roy (Calcutta, 1958) covers the same period less thoroughly and extends the account to the post-independence period. Roy's study is topical and somewhat more analytical, though much less detailed, than Ghosal's work. R. Dwarkadas' *Role of the Higher Civil Service in India* (Bombay, 1958) is a doctoral dissertation, less well organized and less free from error than might be hoped for. One of the best analytical works on administration, Asok Chanda, *Indian Administration* (London, 1958), includes an excellent chapter on historical background which is of value in understanding the Pakistani system. A study by an Indian which asserts that the British administrative system in India is one of the "noblest structures whose records illuminate the annals of the art of administration" is M. Ruthnaswamy, *Some Influences That Made the British Administrative System in India* (London, 1939).

General, secondary studies of the Pakistani bureaucracy are few. Muzaffer Ahmed Chaudhuri's "The Growth of the Civil Service in British India and Pakistan," *Journal of the Asiatic Society of Pakistan* (Dacca), V (1960), 72–127, is a survey of

[5] See below, Appendix 1.

reports on the civil service under British rule. Part of Chaudhuri's doctoral dissertation at the University of London appeared as "The Organization and Composition of the Central Civil Services in Pakistan," *International Review of Administrative Science,* XXVI (1960), 280–292. The entire dissertation was published in 1963 by the National Institute of Public Administration in Dacca and appears under the title, *The Civil Service of Pakistan.* Another doctoral dissertation is that of Henry Goodnow, published by Yale University Press under the title *The Civil Service of Pakistan* (New Haven, 1964). Ralph Braibanti's "The Civil Service of Pakistan, A Theoretical Analysis" appeared in the *South Atlantic Quarterly,* VIII (1959), 258–304, and was reprinted by the Duke University Commonwealth-Studies Center and the United States Operations Mission in Pakistan. A useful general description can be found in Faqir Mohammad Choudhri, "Administrative Structure in Pakistan," in S. M. Z. Rizvi (ed.), *A Reader in Basic Democracies* (Peshawar: Academy for Rural Development, 1961). An unusually perceptive article is Khalid Bin Sayeed, "The Political Role of the Civil Service of Pakistan," *Pacific Affairs,* XXXI (1958), 131–146. In the same author's *Pakistan, The Formative Phase* (Karachi, 1960), there is a chapter of twenty-two pages on the civil service. Keith Callard, *Pakistan: A Political Study* (New York, 1957), includes a chapter on the public services. Brief chapters on the services also appear in Mushtaq Ahmad, *Government and Politics in Pakistan* (Karachi, 1959), and Nasim Zakaria, *Parliamentary Government in Pakistan* (Lahore, 1958).

Recruitment

Selection of civil servants in Pakistan is a function carried on by the Central Public Service Commission and two provincial public service commissions. The former was known as the Pakistan Public Service Commission but when the first Constitution came into force on March 2, 1956, its designation was changed to Federal Public Service Commission, a name retained under martial law as well. The second Constitution, made effective June 8, 1962, designated this commission as the Central Public Service

Commission. The concept of public service commissions for India was analyzed in the Lee Commission Report of 1924.[6] One of the characteristics of such commissions in India and Pakistan has been their constitutional rather than statutory basis. The Government of India Act (1935) provided for commissions in Chapter III (sec. 264–284), and the 1956 Constitution of Pakistan included equivalent provisions in Articles 184–190. These constitutional provisions governed all three commissions, hence their powers are identical although the sphere of their authority differs. The second (1962) Constitution, like its predecessor, defines the powers of the commissions in a fairly long chapter (2 of Part VIII) of ten articles. Members of the commissions are appointed by the president or provincial governors for three-year terms. The number of members is not constitutionally specified. It has usually been fixed by president's and governors' orders at five for each commission, although as few as three members have sometimes been in office at the same time. There are no special qualifications for appointment except the requirement that not less than half the members shall be persons who were in the service of the Government of Pakistan before appointment. The 1962 Constitution defines the functions of the central commission as: conducting tests for selection of persons for appointment to the services, advising the president, and other activities defined by law. The president is obligated to consult the commission on methods of recruitment, principles of appointment and promotion, principles of transfer, matters affecting terms and conditions of service, and matters of discipline. In practice, this authority is not as extensive as it may appear, for the president may, by order made after consulting the commission, remove any of these matters from the commission's jurisdiction. Moreover, while he is otherwise obliged to consult the commission, there is no obligation to accept the commission's advice. The same provisions apply *mutatis mutandis* to the provincial governors and the provincial commissions.

Although it was the intention of the Lee Commission to give the public service commissions extensive powers so that recruitment and other service matters could be insulated from partisan consid-

[6] See above, p. 105, for summary of the report of the Lee Commission.

erations, the commissions in Pakistan have, in fact, little policy-making power. The reasons for this are manifold. Unstable political conditions resulted in a deliberate circumvention of much of the commissions' authority by such rules as the Federal Public Service Commission (Consultation by the Governor-General) Regulations, 1953, and the Public Service Commission (Limitation of Function) Regulations, 1957. Equivalent orders were issued by provincial governors for each of the provincial commissions. Subsequent amendments to these regulations have progressively excluded important categories of employment from the jurisdiction of the commissions. The rank of chairmen of public service commissions in the Warrant of Precedence is an index of their status in relation to officials of the executive government. The Royal Warrant of Precedence in effect in 1947 ranked the chairman of the Federal Public Service Commission as number "25," which was one rank above a full secretary to the central government. Chairmen of provincial commissions were ranked with provincial chief secretaries.[7] In the most recent revision of the Warrant of Precedence of 1963 [8] the chairman of the Central Public Service Commission ranks with the secretaries to central government (number "20"), and the chairmen of the provincial commissions rank with secretaries to the provincial governments (number "24"). The real distinction in status rests on the prestige of the cadre to which the establishment secretary and the commission chairman belong. The former has always been a member of the CSP, which is the premier cadre, while the latter has never been a CSP officer. A situation approaching parity of rank between the two positions was almost achieved from 1958 to 1963, during

---

[7] The Warrant of Precedence in effect in 1947 ranked positions as follows: chairman, Federal Public Service Commission, "25"; secretary, Government of India, "26"; chairmen, provincial public service commissions of Madras, Bombay, Sind, and Bengal, "28" (equal to chief secretary of those provinces); chairmen of all other provincial public service commissions, "34" (equal to chief secretary of those provinces); members of all provincial public service commissions, "45" (equal to additional deputy secretary, Government of India). Since additional and joint secretaries to local governments ranked "38," provincial public service commission members were seven places below these officers. Text of Royal Warrant of Precedence is available in *The Combined Civil List for India, Pakistan and Burma,* No. 160, October–December, 1947 (Lahore, 1947), pp. 643–652.

[8] Warrant of Precedence for Pakistan, *Gazette of Pakistan, Extraordinary,* March 9, 1963, pp. 233a–233h.

which period Lt. Col. A. S. B. Shah, a senior officer of the pre-
partition Indian Political Service and holding rank number "10" [9]
in the CSP at the time of his retirement, was chairman of the
commission. During part of this period, the establishment secretary was G. Mueenuddin, who was one rank below Col. Shah. But
this rank differential was mitigated by the fact that Col. Shah had
been retired from the CSP cadre when he became commission
chairman and G. Mueenuddin was still on active duty.

In fact, the Public Service Commission has been subordinated
to the Establishment Division of the President's Secretariat to
which it is related as an attached department. In testimony
presented before the Administrative Reorganisation Committee,
the chairman of the Federal Public Service Commission deplored
this state of affairs, but the establishment secretary felt there was
nothing basically wrong in the relationship. The committee felt
that the position of the Public Service Commission should not be
changed and that a decision as to its status as an attached
department of the Establishment Division should be deferred
until the question of relations of all attached departments to
ministries is considered. The President's cabinet concurred in the
Reorganisation Committee's views, and further decided that the
secretary of the Public Service Commission should be given the
ex-officio status of joint secretary in the Establishment Division.[10]
This latter decision attaches the commission all the more firmly to
the establishment agency.

Another reason for the weakness of the public service commissions generally is the inadequate size and competence of administrative staff at their disposal. The Central Public Service Commission in 1963 had sixteen gazetted officers, 138 assistants and clerks,
and some forty class IV employees: a total staff of 199 persons.
Each of the provincial commissions has a total staff of about fifty
persons. The manner in which commission members construe their
responsibilities has actually served to reduce whatever authority
they might have acquired as a central personnel agency. Members

[9] Government of Pakistan, *Gradation List of the Civil Service of Pakistan* (Karachi, 1957), p. 1. This list is corrected up to January 1, 1957.
[10] Government of Pakistan, *Report of the Administrative Reorganisation Committee* (Karachi, 1960), pp. 242–245.

of the commissions personally interview and examine candidates for positions, and although assisted by other government officers on interview boards, the interviews consume most of the time of the commission members. The consequence is that very little time is available for the formulation of basic public service policy. The commissions' role in maintaining the probity of the services, setting pay scales, and determining promotions is virtually nil. They are, in effect, largely examining bodies rather than agencies of control over public employment. A candid statement of the inadequate powers of the commissions can be found in the *Annual Report of the Working of the West Pakistan Public Service Commission for the Period 14 October 1955 to 31 Dec. 1956* and in the subsequent annual report for 1957. In these reports the West Pakistan commission deplores the restrictions placed on its authority and cites with favor the broad scope of duties given the Public Service Board in Canada. The report calls attention to the fact that the commission's power can be enlarged within the terms of the Constitution if the government wishes to consult it on service matters. The commission cites the selection of candidates for overseas training, in which it has not participated, as an instance of government's bypassing its jurisdiction.

The inadequate powers of the commissions were more forcefully criticized in Government of Pakistan, *The First Five Year Plan, 1955–60* (Karachi: Government of Pakistan Press, December, 1957), which asserted that the commissions "do not occupy a position of effective command over the field of public service management." Even within their limited jurisdiction they are victims of conflicting policies covering the services. The plan proposed that the commissions deal with training, redress of grievances, morale, and salary determination, all of which functions are now handled by other agencies. Membership, the plan urged, should be expanded with staggered terms of officers. Direct access to the prime minister or chief minister should be provided. The plan also suggested that the commissions delayed unduly in selecting candidates for posts and that the mechanics of recruitment had to be greatly improved. Increased technical staff would be needed by the commissions and the plan suggested that technical aid agencies might provide consultants. None of the suggestions made in the plan for the improvement of the commissions was implemented by the end of 1964. The views of the former chairman (1958–1963) of the commission, Col. A. S. B. Shah, are given in an article, "Public Service Commission: Its Function and Responsibilities," *Pakistan Times*, August 14, 1961, p. 6. A former chairman, Mian Afzal Husain, in an article, "Public Service Commissions: The Way to a Clean Administration," *Pakistan Times Supplement*, October 27, 1960, p. 17, tells how the commission submitted to political pressures to the extent that publication of its annual reports was deliberately curtailed by the government. Both of these articles dwell excessively on the work of commissions in other countries. No lengthy or detailed study of the commissions in Pakistan has yet appeared, nor has there been detailed analysis of the progressive debilitation of the commission by political pressures of government. The brief description in the *Pakistan Times Supplement* by Mian Afzal Husain, whose chairmanship from 1948 through September, 1952, was marked by uncommon courage and independence, is the only account available and therefore merits inclusion here:

If a research is conducted into the working of, let us say, the Central Public Service Commission, it will become apparent that the Commission had to engage in a constant struggle to maintain their position as independent and effective advisers to Government. Such a study will also reveal that Government's disregard of Commission's advice and irregular use of its own powers in dealing with services led to the evils from which the country has suffered. It is one of the duties of a P.S.C., to publish its reports to place before the country the situation of the civil service. The Government of the day did not permit the Commission to publish their reports from 1948 to 1952, apparently for fear of exposure. It was only in 1954, when a new Government had come in three of the Reports were published. Violations of statutory rules, irregular appointments and promotions made, non-acceptance of the advice of the Commission are mentioned in these reports. Progressively irregularities increased, privileges were misused, fair and open selection for positions became difficult, promotions on merit became rare, and miscreants did not suffer for their sins. Secretaries and Head of Departments had favourites whom they pushed. Unqualified persons were appointed to technical posts in preference to qualified men.

Favouritism and nepotism increased. There were a few who maintained old standards. They became unpopular with their bosses, as well as their subordinates. Subterfuges employed were many and varied. For instance, a minister enjoys the privilege of appointing his own private secretary. A person would be appointed as such and then pushed into a better, more remunerative permanent appointment. This process would be repeated without remorse. A person would be appointed to a post, without advertisement and without any competition, retained in the post for months or even years and his name sent up to the Commission, with a strong recommendation, for approval. If the Commission were obdurate and insisted on advertisement the qualifications demanded by the department concerned would be woven round the favoured one, including age and length of experience. Thus a person with accrued merit and the support of the departmental adviser, would score over a candidate with higher basic qualifications and superior potentialities. An ingenious *modus operandi* was to demand exceptionally high technical qualifications and when men with such merit could not be found, one from the office, having none of the original qualifications would be appointed, perhaps on temporary basis to start with, on the plea that a suitably qualified person was not available. Sometimes rejected candidates were sent abroad for special training and through some scholarship scheme, the post kept in abeyance, awaiting the privileged man's return. There were some interesting cases where persons rejected by the Commission repeatedly went from one temporary post to another for years. Several appointments of high status were given to men not recommended by the Commission and in some cases in preference to the Commission's nominees. There were cases where officers recommended for dismissal for serious offences were retained in service. In one case even a Commission did not honour the findings of their predecessors in office.

Some insight into the efforts of the commissions to assert what little authority they now possess can be found in three court judgments. The first is *Abdul Latif Sethi and others* v. *Pakistan,* PLD 1961 Kar. 457. The case arose from a ruling which allegedly exempted a group of several hundred civil servants appointed in 1959 as section officers from control by the Federal Public Service Commission. The commission held an examination for those promoted as section officers. A group of officers sought a mandamus preventing the commission from examining them on the ground that the requirement of consultation with the commission was ousted by office memoranda issued under Pakistan Public Service

Commission (Consultation by Governor-General) Regulations, 1953. Clause 4(c) of the Section Officer Scheme provided, however, that a certain percentage of posts were to be filled by appointments made by the government subject to the approval of the Federal Public Service Commission. The High Court of West Pakistan ruled that the examination given by the commission was not competitive to determine who would be appointed but was merely a device for enabling the commission to determine the suitability of appointed officers so that it could advise the president accordingly. In the case of S. I. Mahbub v. *Province of West Pakistan* (1959) P.L.R. 2 Lah. 1274, Chief Justice M. R. Kayani criticized the failure of the Punjab government to follow the advice of the Federal Public Service Commission. Kayani maintained that the convention established by the Government of India was adopted by the Government of Pakistan on June 13, 1950. That convention was that in disciplinary matters "the advice of the Commission will be accepted, save in exceptional circumstances." But, in fact, the failure of government to accept the advice of the commissions is a major problem in public administration, as the annual reports of all three commissions amply attest. In a later decision in *Province of East Pakistan* v. *K. A. Mansur*, PLD 1963 Dacca 211, the Dacca High Court, while agreeing that under the 1956 Constitution the government can legally refuse to accept the recommendation of the Public Service Commission regarding recruitment, reaffirmed Kayani's view by stating that "in practice . . . occasions for overriding the Commission's advice by the Government will arise rarely, for the Government is normally expected to accept the Commission's advice in all cases except in exceptional cases warranting special considerations."

The publication of documents and annual reports by the three public service commissions has been irregular and delayed, although the situation since 1960 has been much improved. Despite absence under the Government of India Act (1935) of a constitutional requirement that the commissions publish accounts of their work, the Federal Public Service Commission started publishing retrospective annual reports in 1955. A decision was made in 1954 to publish reports retrospectively except for the first year covering the period August 14, 1947, to December 31, 1948, a period too traumatic to have made accurate reporting possible. The Constitution of 1956 departed from the Government of India Act by requiring in Article 190 that the central and provincial public service commissions submit reports annually to the president and governors, respectively. The same provision was incorporated in Article 189 of the 1962 Constitution. The first published report of the central commission was *Second Report of the Pakistan Public Service Commission for the Period 1st January to 31st December, 1949* (Karachi: Manager of Publications, 1955). The reports continue under this title until the *Seventh Annual Report* for 1955. With the next report, the title changes to *Eighth Report of the Federal Public Service Commission for the Period 1st January to 31st December, 1956* (Karachi: Manager of Publications, 1958). The latest report released is the *Central Public Service Commission Annual Report* for the year 1963. If the title of this report followed the same sequential numbering as the others, it would be the fourteenth annual report. In August, 1964, reports for 1958, 1959, 1960, and 1961 had not yet been approved for publication and there appeared to be no estimate as to the date of their release. The annual reports have gradually increased in length; the report for 1963 was 124 pages. The reports vary in quality. The earlier reports were largely descriptive; except for the regular reporting of cases in which the commission's advice had not been accepted, very little insight into the actual problems of the commission could be gleaned from them. Starting with the *Report for the Year 1962*, however, the amount and quality of statistical data have improved. Prior to the 1962 report, a publication more valuable in terms of analysis of the qualifications of candidates for public office was the series known as *Pamphlet of the Central Superior Services Examination Held at Karachi, Lahore and Dacca in February, 1950* (Karachi: Manager of Publications, 1957). These pamphlets are uncommonly valuable because of detailed analysis of the results of the examination, questions asked, and candid evaluation of the educational system of Pakistan and problems of the public service. Published annually under the designation *Pamphlet . . .* for 1950, 1951, and 1952, the title of the series was changed in following years to *Report on the Central Superior Services Examination Held at Karachi, Lahore, Dacca, London and Washington in January–February, 1953* (Karachi: Manager of Publications, 1957). After the 1953 report, the commission ceased publication of its commentary and analysis and released in their place the question papers used in examinations. These papers had been included with other analytical data in the earlier series of pamphlets and reports. For the first of these published question papers, *Report* was used as the initial word of the title, although it is not actually a report: *Report on the Central Superior Services Examination Held at Karachi . . . in January, 1954* (Karachi: Manager of Publications, 1954). Thereafter, the series continues simply as *Central Superior Services Examination Held at Karachi*. These have been printed through 1955.

An important part of this series of pamphlets (reports) is the "Table of the Combined Competitive Examination Results, . . ." printed on several sheets at the end of the report. This table lists the name of each of the candidates (an average of 480 each year) who took the examination and the score which he obtained in each of the papers. The tables are important raw data for determining the preferences and hence the academic preparation of those who competed for examinations. Unfortunately, the tables do not exist for an unbroken period of time since partition. The table for 1949, when examinations were first given, was not compiled. For 1950, 1951, and 1952, the tables are included with the *Pamphlet . . .* and in 1953 with its successor, the *Report. . . .* Data for 1954, 1956, and 1957 were printed in tables but were no longer included with the *Report*. This is unfortunate, because although the tables after 1953 are on file in the Central Public Service Commission, few persons know about them and they are not in effective circulation for research. No tables were published for 1955 when the work load of the commission was excessive. Tables for 1958 and 1959 have not been printed and those for 1960 are in press. In any case, tables have not been included in the more comprehensive publication (*Pamphlet . . .* or *Report . . .*) since 1952. The new series of annual reports starting with the *Report . . . for 1962* incorporates within one volume most of the material formerly included in the pamphlets and tables. Although this new format is a convenience, the loss is in the candor and trenchant quality of analysis which had characterized the pamphlets. This sort of analysis is no longer found in publications of the Central Public Service Commission.

Another series of informative reports is the *Quinquennial Report on the Ministerial Services Examinations Held at Karachi.* . . . The first of these covered the years 1945 through 1953, during which period some six thousand applicants were examined for positions as assistants and upper division and lower division clerks. This report, published in 1957, includes, like the reports on the Central Superior Services Examinations published before 1953, an illuminating analysis of educational deficiencies of the applicants. It also includes the names and marks on each paper of all six thousand applicants who took the examination. Such compilation of raw data makes these reports of the Central Public Service Commission extremely valuable for further research.

The two provincial public service commissions for East and West Pakistan function within the framework of Part VIII, Chapter II, of the 1962 Constitution. The powers of the provincial commissions are similar to those of the Central Public Service Commission except that they are limited to the provincial public services. The powers of the provincial bodies are restricted somewhat by governor's orders and the Limitation of Functions Regulations which are the provincial equivalent of the regulation limiting powers of the Central Public Commission. Before the functioning of the West Pakistan Public Service Commission in 1955, there were two public service commissions in the province: the Sind Commission which was appointed in 1947 and the Punjab and Northwest-Frontier Province Joint Public Service Commission organized in 1952. Prior to 1947 Sind recruitment was managed by the Bombay-Sind Public Service Commission. The Bahawalpur State Commission issued no reports or pamphlets. The Sind Commission published annual reports for each year from 1947 through 1953. One report appeared for the Punjab-NWFP Commission: *Report of the Working of the Punjab and NWFP Joint Public Service Commission for the Period 15th*

August, 1947 to 31st March, 1949 (Lahore: Superintendent, Government Printing, 1950). It also published *Pamphlet for the Competitive Examination for Recruitment to the Punjab Civil Service for Nov.–Dec. 1948* (Lahore: Superintendent, Government Printing, 1950). Subsequent pamphlets appeared for 1949, 1950, and 1951. They were followed by *Pamphlet for the Combined Competitive Examination for Recruitment to the Punjab Civil Service, Punjab Tahsildars' Service, Northwest F. P. Provincial Civil Service for 1952 and 1953.* Annual reports are now regularly published under the title *Annual Report on the Working of the West Pakistan Public Service Commission for the Year. . . .* The first report was for the period October 14, 1955, to December 31, 1956, but subsequent issues cover the regular calendar year; the last report published is for 1963. The annual reports of the West Pakistan commission are unusually well written and organized and reveal a critical understanding of the functions of a public service commission. The commission has also issued two sets of *Old Question Papers* and has several more in the process of publication.

The Public Service Commission of East Pakistan was created in 1947 from the Bengal commission which had been functioning since 1937. The first report is *Report on the Working of the Public Service Commission, East Pakistan for the Period from 15th August, 1947 to 14th August, 1949* (Dacca: East Bengal Government Press, 1955). The second report covers a three-year period ending March 31, 1952. For reasons which have not been disclosed by the commission, no annual reports were published from 1952 until 1962. At that time publication was resumed in a somewhat different format under the title, *Report on the Activities of the East Pakistan Public Service Commission During the Year Ending on the 31st December, 1962* (Dacca, 1963). The East Pakistan commission also issues *Old Question Papers* of departmental and provincial civil service examinations which they conduct semi-annually.

Probably the best-known activity of the Central Public Service Commission is the recruitment of officers for the central superior services. To pass the central superior services examination is the highest aspiration of the best university graduates each year. From 1950 through 1964, 13,817 persons applied to take this annual examination. This was 10.2 per cent of the total number of 109,252 persons who received B.A., B.Sc., and B. Com. degrees during the same period. During this period 11,511 of the applicants actually took the examination and some three thousand were interviewed by the commission. Recruitment rules for this examination are published annually in leaflet form by the commission as a notice, such as *Central Public Service Commission Notice, Karachi, the 23rd June 1962 No. F2/1/62–E–II.* One of the most valuable parts of this notice is the official statement of recruitment policy in Appendix V. This is the policy designed to establish parity in the central superior services.

Composition (Establishment) of the Public Services

The term "establishment" is used in Pakistan as in other countries formerly under British imperial rule to refer to composition or structural organization of the bureaucracy. The order of magnitude of the total public bureaucracy is more difficult to estimate for Pakistan than for many other developing states. Sources of data are uneven in their reliability; extrapolation and estimates must be combined with statistical data to produce a meaningful figure. No census of government employment or sufficiently detailed manpower surveys exist for the whole of Pakistan. There is an excellent census for the Government of West Pakistan: [11] Government of West Pakistan Planning and Development Department, Bureau of Statistics, *Census of West Pakistan Government Employees, 1962* (Lahore, 1963), but there is nothing comparable for the central government or for East Pakistan. Notwithstanding this lacuna, total employment in government is probably about a million persons. It is important to indicate how this figure was obtained, so that adjustments in the total can be made when additional data for certain sectors of employment are released. The West Pakistan *Census* enumerates total government employment, all classes, as 376,521. This figure includes teachers and railway employees but not post and telegraph employees who are stationed in the prov-

[11] See above, pp. 74–75.

ince but are employed by the central government. Unpublished
data of the Establishment Division of the President's Secretariat
list 122,000 central government employees in 1963, including post
and telegraph employees. This figure, added to the West Pakistan
figure, totals 498,521. It is assumed that provincial employment in
East Pakistan approximates that of West Pakistan, hence 376,521
may again be added to 498,521, thus making 875,042. To this
should be added an estimated fifty thousand employees of government corporations and thirty-seven thousand local government
employees. The latter figure is calculated on the basis of an
estimated five hundred local employees for each of seventy-four
districts. This makes a total of 962,042. These figures do not
include an estimated annual growth rate from 1962 to 1964.
Allowing for a 4 per cent underestimation and for rounding off, the
total would be 1,000,000. This includes police, teachers, railway,
postal and telegraph employees, and government corporation and
local government employees.[12] This is approximately 1 per cent of
the total population of nearly ninety-nine million. In West Pakistan, nearly 33 per cent of the total employment works in the
railways, 17 per cent in education, and 20 per cent in local
government. It is likely that this distribution is nearly the same in
East Pakistan. Distribution on a national scale, however, may be
somewhat less in these three categories, since a larger percentage
of central government employees are in post and telegraph and
central secretariat positions.

The structural organization of the public services of Pakistan is
one of the most complicated of any bureaucratic system in existence. It is the product of a series of pragmatic responses to
political necessity under British rule as developed in the Aitchison
and Islington reports, which have been previously discussed. The
structure has remained essentially unchanged; indeed, its rigidity
has enabled it to defy the winds of reform more than any single
institution in Pakistan. The division of services into almost
completely autonomous cadres subject to no over-all, unifying

[12] This estimate has been prepared with the assistance of Leon Margosian and
J. Maslowski, public administration and statistical advisers, respectively, in the
Pakistan Mission of the United States Agency for International Development.

central control is its most prominent characteristic. In addition to functional cadre divisions, there are class divisions of rank (I, II, III, IV) and spatial divisions (central and provincial) which now have little practical rationale. Yet proposals to change the structure of the system have been vigorously resisted, especially by the "premier cadre"—the Civil Service of Pakistan. It is not without significance that despite major martial law reforms in virtually every aspect of Pakistan's institutional life, the structure of public services was the only major institution which remained unreconstructed, as late as 1964. Even such tenacious institutions as the *zamindari* and Muslim family laws were modified. The report of the second Pay and Services Commission, submitted in June 1962, was nearly three years (exactly one thousand days) in preparation. This is twice the length of time spent in the preparation of fifty-one major reports on administration and other matters.[13] To be sure, the Pay and Service Commission was concerned with minute details of rationalizing hundreds of salary patterns as well as establishing broad public service policy. But the time it took to complete its task suggests the complexity of the structure out of which it sought order.

Study of the structure of Pakistan's bureaucracy must start with the group of six reports issued in Imperial India and described elsewhere in this essay.[14] Analysis of these reports should then be followed by study of a more recent sequence of pay commission inquiries. Since immediately before partition in both India and Pakistan, the pay commission has been the reporting device for inquiring into the structure and conditions of the public services. In this respect the pay commissions are lineal bibliographic descendents of the Aitchison, Islington, and Lee reports. The first of the pay commission inquiries in India was the *Report of the Central Pay Commission, 1946–47* (New Delhi: Government of India, 1947), more commonly known as the Varadachariar Commission after the name of its chairman. This 486-page document includes an excellent survey of the reasons for the classifications of the services and the terminology used. The first such commission

[13] See Tables 2 and 8 for data on commissions of inquiry referred to here.
[14] See above, pp. 102–107.

appointed in Pakistan was under the chairmanship of the then chief justice of the Supreme Court, Muhammad Munir. Its findings, called *The Report of the Pakistan Pay Commission* (2 vols.; Karachi: Governor-General's Press, 1949), attracted wide attention in the nation and considerable adverse criticism within the bureaucracy by its comment that government service need not necessarily require the best talent.[15]

Those who find this passage of the Pay Commission's report objectionable often assert that it was the opinion of Chief Justice Munir alone. In fact, the report was subscribed to by all four members of the commission. The first part of this controversial paragraph raises the fundamental issue of the immense cultural gulf that exists in Pakistan between the Anglo-oriented bureaucratic elite on the one hand, and the tradition-directed masses and lower-ranking civil servants on the other. The commission's comment touched a sensitive chord, for perhaps no aspect of Pakistan's administrative system has been subjected to as much criticism and has aroused more concern within government service than the social distance between members of the CSP and other government employees. The remarks of Farid Ahmad, Bengali member of the Constituent Assembly, are an accurate reflection of such sentiments: [16]

Our Civil Service has been formed and drawn up by the best talent in the country, yet what is the training that is imparted? . . . They are being taught the same tradition as in the British days to live in the Punjab and D.M.'s bungalow on the hilltop in East Pakistan. They are inaccessible people. . . . Is it that you are going to train your own people to hate your own system, to hate your own civilization and culture? Are you going to give to the country out of this manufacturing laboratory of the Civil Service Academy at Lahore some more Anglicized officers? If you are really keen that a person should be taught to

[15] This section is reproduced as part of a longer extract in Appendix 5.

[16] National Assembly of Pakistan, *Debates*, February 15, 1957, pp. 434–435. A note on p. 435 of Farid Ahmad's speech indicates that the speech was printed without being corrected by him. See Appendix 4. The same opinions were stated by Maulvi Akhtar Ali of West Pakistan who said CSP officers are not "sympathetic to the rural population and become members of an association which I would liken to the Freemasons Society. Even . . . Ayub does not enjoy the powers that these people possess. All the hatred in the hearts of the people against any Government is due mainly to the self-conceited and haughty behaviour of these functionaries" (*ibid.*, June 20, 1962, p. 221–222).

become an adapt [*sic*] in what dresses should be worn on what particular occasions and if you want to convert the youth of our country into connoisseurs of drinks and cocktails, then what the training should lead to? [*sic*] . . . So, if you really want to bring up a band of old ICS people stiff necked with a bow-tie and who know how to bow and say "How do you do?," then bring some from England. They will be better people, with better integrity.

The second issue raised by this section of the report is that of creating an incentive system that will facilitate rational allocation of scarce entrepreneurial skills between public and private sectors. When public bureaucracy, because of historic images of status, high salary, or concentration of power, is able to monopolize a developing state's talent, a serious imbalance results. Such monopoly may be at the expense of entrepreneurs available to the private sector [17] and, more importantly, may perpetuate unilateral control of the nation's destiny in the hands of an elite which, assuming that it possesses a monopoly of virtue, prevents the emergence of a pluralistic society of competing interests. Viewed in this context, not only do these two controversial proposals of the Pay Commission appear not unreasonable, but, indeed, they touch on a fundamental problem of political development as yet unresolved in Pakistan.

In determining a principle for remuneration of public servants, the Munir Commission rejected the Indian Pay Commission's reliance on sliding pay articulated to cost of living. Instead, the rule used by the Islington Commission providing remuneration adequate to attract able persons, maintain their dignity, and shield them from temptation of corruption was adopted. The report includes a long analysis of the economic position of the nation and a cogent summary of the development of the public services. Most of the report deals with specific recommendations of pay for the thousands of categories of positions in the public service.

The second Pay Commission report was prepared under the chairmanship of Supreme Court Chief Justice A. R. Cornelius: *Report of the Pay and Service Commission* (Karachi: Government of Pakistan Press, June, 1962). It is said to be a major effort to

[17] See analysis of this point in Joseph J. Spengler, "Public Bureaucracy, Resource Structure and Economic Development: A Note," *Kyklos*, XI (1958), 459–489.

alter the structure of the services. The Cornelius Report, however, has not been released by the government and hence its substance cannot be discussed.

The first principal structural division of the bureaucracy is the existence of separate cadres of the central superior services. Seventeen of these services existed in 1962. Shown with their cadre strengths they are: [18]

1.	Civil Service of Pakistan	357
2.	Pakistan Foreign Service	140
3.	Police Service of Pakistan (West Pakistan)	92
4.	Police Service of Pakistan (East Pakistan)	71
5.	Pakistan Audit and Accounts Service	69
6.	Pakistan Railway Accounts Service	37
7.	Pakistan Military Accounts Service	51
8.	Pakistan Taxation Service	137
9.	Pakistan Customs and Excise Service	35
10.	Telegraph Engineering Service, Class I	23
11.	Post and Telegraph Traffic Service, Class I	14
12.	Telegraph Traffic Service, Class I	2
13.	Pakistan Postal Service, Class I	23
14.	Pakistan Railway Service of Engineers	214
15.	Pakistan Railway Transportation (Traffic and Commercial Service)	76
16.	Central Engineering Service, Class I	54
17.	Pakistan Military Lands and Cantonments Service	35

This division into seventeen cadres is relatively clear-cut. Each is a separate cadre, recruited by the Central Public Service Commission by means of a common examination. After recruitment each cadre is separately administered, and posts are reserved specifically for members of particular cadres. There is virtually no interchange of personnel; indeed, the functions of each cadre are compartmentalized and there is only rarely any working contact between members of different cadres. Questions of personnel policy are determined for the Civil Service of Pakistan by the

[18] Computed from *Civil List of Class I Officers Serving Under Government of Pakistan, 1st January, 1961* (Karachi, Government of Pakistan Press, 1961), pp. 345–487. Strengths shown are for 1961, the latest year for which data were made available. The same cadres existed in 1964 although with strengths increased by about 15 per cent.

Establishment Division of the President's Secretariat, by the Ministry of External Affairs for the Foreign Service, by the Ministry of Home Affairs and the provincial home departments for the police services, and by the provincial railway boards, the Post and Telegraphs Department, and the Ministry of Finance for the other services. In addition, there exists a small cadre known as the General Administrative Reserve, recruited in the early days following partition to augment the small group of ICS officers available to Pakistan. It was generally thought that GAR officers would ultimately be integrated into the CSP cadre since they usually held CSP posts, but such integration has not occurred. A Finance and Commerce Pool was created in 1950 but did not function until 1959 when it was reconstituted as the Economic Pool. The concept of an economic pool derives from pre-partition policy in the central secretariat of the Government of India. The Economic Pool is a device for modifying the rigid exclusivity of cadres by drawing financial talent from various services into a common cadre. Certain younger officers of at least six years' service, but more than thirty-five years of age, who are deemed to have unusual training and ability in economic affairs are selected for the Economic Pool. One hundred and thirty positions have been designated as reserved for the Economic Pool; 60 per cent of the positions are reserved for CSP officers.[19] These positions have been classified into classes A, B, and C, based on rank. Class A posts have the rank of secretary or its equivalent; class B, deputy secretary; class C, section officers. Posts are reserved in the ministries of economics, commerce, and industries, provincial finance departments, and boards of revenue. Certain positions as economic counselor, trade commissioner, and commercial attaché in diplomatic missions are also reserved for the Economic Pool. Such a device as the Economic Pool is needed only because of the inflexibility of the cadre system with its reserved posts. The consequence is a more rational allocation of scarce expertise in economic and financial administration throughout the total bureaucracy. Although the Economic Pool has high prestige, it has

[19] In 1963, ninety-five positions in the Economic Pool were filled, twenty-nine incumbents were from East Pakistan and forty-nine were from West Pakistan. See National Assembly of Pakistan, *Debates,* April 9, 1963, pp. 1484–1489.

not yet developed into a truly corporate entity with its own *élan* and traditions.

Beyond the seventeen cadres of the central superior services, the structure of administration becomes more confused. An attempt by the first (Munir) Pay Commission to simplify the organizational pattern was never completely implemented. The consequence is a structure no longer like that of either pre-partition or post-partition India and only partially resembling the projection of the Munir Commission. There are central gazetted services divided into classes I and II and non-gazetted services including classes III and IV. The class designation is based on functional hierarchy. The central gazetted services are also divided into cadres such as the central secretariat service, public information service, and education service, but these are not designated as "superior" cadres. Similarly, the provincial governments have cadres, services, and classes. The principal cadre is the provincial civil service, divided into executive and judicial branches. There is also a secretariat service, education service, other technical services, and four classes of employees. The disposition to proliferate the number of specialist cadres is strong; indeed, until the second Pay Commission proposals of June, 1962, there was no serious thought given to eliminating cadre distinctions. The pattern of reform has usually been that of creating new, distinctive cadres, emulating the elite CSP corps. Thus, the Law Commission proposed a separate judicial service, the Scientific Commission recommended a distinctive scientific service, and a separate medical service suggested by the Medical Reforms Commission [20] was created in 1962 and abolished in 1963. A new Taxation Service has been created, and several other separate

---

[20] Further discussion of these proposals can be found below, pp. 318, 321, 326. The Medical Service of Pakistan Order of 1962 was said by a member of the National Assembly to have "lifted [doctors] from the status of scheduled cast[e]s to the class of Brahmins—in the class of Brahmins like C.S.P. officers or P.S.P. and P.F.S. officers" (*ibid.*, March 30, 1963, p. 1051). The order, however, was not implemented because under the 1962 Constitution, public health was thought to be a provincial rather than a central subject (*ibid.*, May 29, 1963, pp. 58–62). For pertinent legislation creating and abolishing the medical service, see President's Order No. 15 of 1962, *Gazette of Pakistan, Extraordinary*, May 12, 1962, and Act XX, Medical Service of Pakistan Order (Repeal) Act, 1963, *ibid.*, September 14, 1963.

cadres are being considered.[21] The elaborate and complex division into cadres is the result of the imposition of a colonial structure on the ancient, functional caste system which characterized Indian society. While it has been deplored and criticized by American observers, its premises have only rarely been questioned within the higher bureaucracy.

There are three major agencies of government concerned primarily with establishment matters. The first is the Establishment Division in the President's Secretariat of the central government, which exclusively handles all personnel matters relating to the Civil Service of Pakistan, General Administrative Reserve, and the Central Secretariat Service. Since 1960 the Establishment Division has added to its responsibilities and begins to approximate a central personnel agency of considerable power. It is now responsible for co-ordinating and directing the training program of not only the Civil Service of Pakistan but of the two rural development academies, three institutes of public administration, the Secretariat Training Institute, Administrative Staff College, and Civil Service Academy. It has also expanded its organization and methods wing, added a statistical unit, and seeks to co-ordinate research on administration, which is being generated in the various training institutions. It continues its older function of administering all awards and decorations for all services. Each of the provinces has a unit in the secretariat which operates as a provincial establishment office. In East Pakistan this responsibility is carried on by the General Administration (Appointments and Establishments) units of the Home Department. In West Pakistan the Services and General Administration Department is the equivalent unit. All three agencies are concerned, however, only with service problems of higher ranks of some services. It is the Finance Ministry of the central government and the finance departments at the provincial level which have the widest power over organiza-

[21] The Taxation Service began with the 1961 issue of the *Pakistan Taxation Service Magazine,* an annual publication of some three hundred pages printed in Karachi in English and Urdu. Designed to promote *esprit de corps* in the newly created Taxation Service, it is what would be called in the United States a "house organ." Half the articles are serious short commentaries on tax problems, the remainder are literary pieces. More than half the total number of pages consist of commercial advertisement. No other cadre has a separate journal like this.

tion of the bureaucracy. They oversee their own cadres of finance service officials, control the strength of other cadres, perform some functions of personnel management for many other services, publish service rules affecting all the services, and determine salary policy. In addition to these agencies, each ministry and attached department of the central government and each department and attached directorate of the provincial governments keep personnel records and control subordinate employees who constitute the bulk of public employment. The public service commissions are not the central personnel agencies which they commonly are in other countries, hence information regarding establishments is not available from them.

The major portion of the important documentation regarding establishment matters is unpublished and scattered. Each ministry and department which controls various cadres and sets policies reserving certain posts for particular cadres has statements regarding such assignments and composition. Although usually not classified, they are nevertheless not easily available simply because they are unlisted and often mimeographed rather than printed.

One of the most carefully compiled annual documents is the *Gradation List of the Civil Service of Pakistan* prepared by the Establishment Division of the central government. This lists by rank the 432 (in 1964) members of the CSP, states their dates of birth, entry into service, and present assignment. The first *Gradation List* appeared in 1951 in Establishment Branch, Cabinet Secretariat, *No. 3(1)/48-SEIII*, June 6, 1951. The second appeared on January 1, 1952, and issuance of subsequent lists has remained on a calendar-year basis except that no issue appeared for 1956. Information on the Civil Service of Pakistan is the most complete and up-to-date available in the bureaucracy. The *Gradation List* is an indispensable research document, and, in this respect, ranks with the central and provincial gazettes and reports of the three public service commissions.

The composition of the Civil Service of Pakistan and the formula for the reservation of CSP posts is set forth in a series of *Resolutions* of the Establishment Branch, *No. F.25/450 Ests.*

(*SEI*), November 8, 1950, *No. F.25/12/51—SEI*, June 1, 1954, *No. 25/12/51—SEI*, November 3, 1954, *No. 25/47/49—SEI*, June 15, 1954, *No. 25/12/51—SEI*, June 21, 1954.

Perhaps the single most important category of documents on the bureaucracy is the series known as civil lists. Under British rule, civil lists were meticulously compiled and regularly issued four times a year. Since partition there has been a lapse in this regularity, but since 1960 efforts to restore the earlier situation have been partly successful. Before partition, the official civil lists issued by the government were supplemented by a highly useful publication issued by the press of the *Civil and Military Gazette* in Lahore: the *Combined Civil List of India*. It was convenient because it put together in one volume the ICS cadres of all the provinces of India and, in addition, listed all the major incumbents of posts of the central and provincial governments. In this respect it served as an effective directory and organization chart of all units of government in India. Since it was published quarterly, it was not very much out of date. Even though unofficial, its reliability was of a high order. A complete set of the *Combined Civil Lists* is available in the West Pakistan secretariat library in Lahore but cannot be found elsewhere in Pakistan. *The Civil and Military Gazette* continued publication of this excellent document for both India and Pakistan for a few months after partition, but publication was then discontinued. In June, 1961, the first printed official civil list published by the central government since 1947 made its appearance: *Civil List of Class I Officers Serving Under Government of Pakistan, 1st January, 1961* (Karachi: Government of Pakistan Press, 1961). This 487-page document was compiled by the newly established statistical section of the Establishment Division. It is a useful document in several respects. It includes the gradation lists of the seventeen central superior services and lists of officers assigned to the ministries, secretariat, and attached departments of the central government. The lists include date of birth, province of domicile, date of appointment to class I service, date of present appointment, tenure in continuous appointment at present grade, and monthly salary (including special pay).

Equally indispensable are the official civil lists published annually by each of the provincial governments. These have been published for a somewhat longer time than the central government's civil list; the East Pakistan civil list first appeared in 1954 and that for West Pakistan in 1950. *The West Pakistan Civil List, 1st January 1963* (Karachi: West Pakistan Government Press, 1963) and *The East Pakistan Civil List, 1961–62* (*No. 8*) (Dacca: East Pakistan Government Press, 1962) are the latest issues. They are almost identical in organization and format, although the length varies. The West Pakistan *Civil List* is an unpriced publication, hence is more difficult to obtain than that of East Pakistan, which is priced and listed in the catalogue of government publications. The West Pakistan *Civil List* for 1963 was 811 pages; the East Pakistan list for 1961–1962 was 1,067 pages. The provincial civil lists, arranged by department of government, list all class I and class II officers in the provincial government except railway service employees. Rank, date of birth, and salary are shown. Both provincial civil lists include an alphabetical index of names of all officers listed elsewhere in the volume. The three civil lists taken together, however, still do not make a comprehensive tabulation of government service in Pakistan. Since all three include the same gradation lists of cadres, there is duplication of names. Moreover, none of the civil lists show employment in government corporations, nor do they include class III and IV employees and low-ranking employees such as *tehsildars* and *patwaris* operating out of district offices. Hence, computation of the size of the total bureaucracy from civil lists is extremely difficult if not impossible. To make an approximation of the numbers of such employees, an annual central government publication related to the annual budget is useful: *Details of Demands and Appropriations*. This is a document of some six hundred pages listing the numbers of employees by class and the amount of money needed for each class. The demands are listed by ministries. Also of some utility are the *Quarterly Gradation Lists* for provincial civil service published by the provincial governments. These are printed separately for executive branch and judicial branch officers and are accurate and up-to-date. The gradation and civil lists make possible a fairly accurate count and classification of class I and II officers and a virtually accurate count of officers of separate cadres.

The official publication in which public service appointments, postings, and administrative orders are announced is the *Gazette of Pakistan*, published each Friday by the central government. From the title of this publication comes the term "gazetted officer," indicating an officer of certain rank whose appointments are announced in the gazette. In addition to routine administrative announcements much like those found in the *Federal Register* of the United States, the gazette often contains service rules published by various ministries. The central government also publishes occasional supplementary issues known as the *Gazette of Pakistan, Extraordinary*, which are valuable because they often contain reports of various inquiries which have not been separately published. The "extraordinary" gazettes are not indexed or catalogued and often cannot be learned about without careful perusal of complete files of the gazette. Several examples of reports published in the "extraordinary" gazettes will suggest the importance of this source. The *Report of the Commission on Marriage and Family Laws*, a 152-page document published in the June 20, 1956, and the August 30, 1956, issues of the *Gazette of Pakistan, Extraordinary*, has been discussed elsewhere in this essay.[22] The little-known but important report on the disturbances in the East Pakistan Legislative Assembly which were cited in the Proclamation of Martial Law in 1958 as being a precipitating factor in suspending representative government is found only in the *Dacca Gazette, Extraordinary*, May 9, 1959 (pp. 597–672).[23] Often decisions in labor disputes are thus published, e.g., the decision in the case of *Petroleum Workers Federation* v. *Six Oil Companies*, announced in the *Gazette of Pakistan, Extraordinary*, July 23, 1958. Occasionally, annual reports of government agencies are published in the gazette as was the 1958 *Report of the State Bank* in the October 4, 1958, issue of *Gazette of Pakistan*,

[22] See below, p. 315.
[23] This report is further discussed below, p. 212.

Extraordinary. Another example of an important item affecting bureaucracy which would be found in no other accessible source is the controversial government order prohibiting a civil servant from marrying a foreign (except Indian) national. This rule is found in *Gazette of Pakistan,* Part I, May 10, 1963. More recently, the important report of the Franchise Commission, which traced the development of voting in the subcontinent, analyzed concepts of elections, and prescribed the election system under the 1962 Constitution, appeared in the *Gazette of Pakistan, Extraordinary,* August 23, 1963. Each provincial government also publishes a weekly gazette and extraordinary issues. In East Pakistan the *Dacca Gazette* is published each Thursday; in West Pakistan the *Gazette of West Pakistan* appears on Friday. It is common for the two provincial gazettes to reprint orders and notifications issued by the central government and published first in the *Gazette of Pakistan.* All three gazettes, published only in English, are indispensable documents for research in administration. With the gazette there sometimes appears a supplement which lists statistical data such as crop reports and meteorological information. The unexpected use of the gazettes as a medium for a variety of significant reports makes regular reading of all issues imperative for the researcher.

Another publication, *History of Services of Officers Holding Gazetted Appointments in . . . Ministries,* has been published irregularly by the central government. The *History* lists officers who are in middle management, that is, who do not belong to the central superior services, yet who are gazetted officers. Two of these presently exist for the central government: *History of Services of Officers Holding Gazetted Appointments in Constituent Assembly, Cabinet Secretariat . . . , Ministries of . . . Industries and Defence, etc.* (corrected up to July 1, 1952) (Karachi: Manager of Publications, 1957); *History of Services . . . Gazetted Appointments in CSP, Ministry of States and Frontier Regions, etc.* (corrected up to July, 1952) (Karachi: Manager of Publications, 1957). These histories are of limited utility, for there is a gap of several years between the validity of the data and date of publication. Moreover, the information given is incomplete.

Civil service rules are well compiled and easily accessible. For West Pakistan there was a 1958 reprint of the old Punjab rules in two volumes, *Civil Service Rules (Punjab)* (2 vols.; Lahore, 1958). In East Pakistan, the equivalent is *The East Bengal Service Rules* (2 parts; Dacca: East Bengal Government Press, 1953). Also useful are *Compilation of Provident Fund Rules* (Karachi: Government of Pakistan Press, 1954) and *Superior Civil Services (Extraordinary Pension Rules, 1936)* (Karachi: Government of Pakistan, 1951), which give the details of public service retirement schemes.

The mechanics of administrative procedure in the secretariat of the central government are governed by *Rules of Business* which were reformulated in 1962 and by detailed *Secretariat Instructions* amplifying the rules. Provincial administration is controlled by similar rules of business.

An important aspect of the work of the Establishment Division is that of the Efficiency and Organization and Management Wing (E, O & M Wing), first organized in 1953 but strengthened and enlarged in 1958 after the proclamation of martial law. This wing is empowered to inspect the procedures of government agencies, investigate complaints against government offices, make surveys of staff assignments, compile statistics on government employment, simplify procedures and forms, and handle staff welfare activities. In sum, it is designed to be a powerful central personnel agency and administrative control center. Apart from a booklet, *Development of O & M in Pakistan,* which it issued in 1962, the major publication of the E, O & M Wing has been Volume I of the *Establishment Manual* (Karachi: Efficiency, O & M Wing, Establishment Division, January, 1963), a 402-page compilation of rules, regulations, and instructions on establishment matters issued from 1947 to 1962. This is an important document for the study of administration and is to secretariat work what the Douie manuals and the *District Office Manual* are to district operations. The *Establishment Manual* includes policy on such matters as the role of the secretariat and attached departments, rules of conduct and discipline, directions for the preparation of efficiency reports, and descriptions of civil awards and decorations.

Training in Administration

Since most of the programs in administrative training were established after 1960, there is not yet a corpus of documentation to sustain extensive research on training matters. A brief survey of training institutions can be found in Virgil H. Stevens, *Public Administration in Pakistan,* a mimeographed publication of the Institute of Public and Business Administration in Karachi, issued in July, 1960. A recent and somewhat more analytical survey of the major training programs is included in a volume edited by Inaya-tullah, entitled *Bureaucracy and Development in Pakistan,* published by the Academy for Rural Development in Peshawar in 1963. This compilation, resulting from a symposium held in March, 1962, includes essays by the directors of each training establishment on the scope of their activities. Still more recently, a paper by Richard Niehoff, "Technical Assistance in the In-Service Training of Pakistani Civil Servants since 1958," was prepared for a conference on Pakistan held at McGill University in June, 1964. Except for these there are virtually no secondary materials on training; hence, reliance must be placed on the files and reports of each training establishment, on the reports of American contract-ing groups (Michigan State University, the University of Southern California, and Syracuse University) advising these institutions, and on the agencies providing the ultimate fiscal support of these operations, namely the United States Agency for International Development and the Ford Foundation.

The oldest and best-established training institution is the Civil Service Academy in Lahore, a residential postgraduate institution which has been in operation since 1948, exclusively for training of the CSP cadre. This is the lineal descendant of Haileybury College to which some thirty university graduates are admitted annually for one year of training. Except for an article by the then deputy director, Mirza Rafiq Inayat, in the volume edited by Inayatullah described above, no analysis of this important training institution has appeared in print. Since the academy was not created under auspices of the United States Agency for International Development but merely had advisory services of one American from USAID for a two-year period (1960–1962), there are no pertinent reports in the files of USAID or contracting agencies.

In 1955, the Institute of Public and Business Administration was established in Karachi with the advisory assistance of the University of Pennsylvania under contract with what was then the United States International Cooperation Administration. The institute ceased to exist in 1960. Its mimeographed semi-annual reports are important documents which candidly reveal the immense problems of achieving administrative reform in Pakistan. These reports, issued under the title *Semi-Annual Progress Report on the Institute of Public and Business Administration,* are available at the University of Pennsylvania and the United States Agency for International Development in Washington.

The Secretariat Training Institute established in Karachi in 1957 similarly has released no analysis of its own operations. It publishes descriptive leaflets somewhat in the nature of abbreviated college catalogues, but this is quite different from analytical surveys. The Secretariat Training Institute received advisory services from the University of Southern California contract with the United States Agency for International Development from 1961 to 1962, but it was essentially a Pakistani institution and little mention of it is made in USAID or USC reports.

The Administrative Staff College, which had been recommended in the report of Rowland Egger in 1953, was established in Lahore in 1960, financed by the Ford Foundation with the advisory assistance of Syracuse University and the Administrative Staff College, Henley-on-Thames, England. Some publications have emerged from the staff college program, and, since it has had at least one resident staff member from Syracuse University from its inception, reports are available at the Maxwell Graduate School of Citizenship and Public Affairs, Syracuse University, and at the Ford Foundation. The latest of these reports is *Pakistan Administrative Staff College Interim Report on Activities* (Syracuse, June 30, 1963). The Administrative Staff College is also the source of important substantive studies on various aspects of government. The syndicate and staff studies prepared by participants and directing staff are often of a high quality. These papers, covering hundreds of subjects, are on file in the library of the college, usually in typed or mimeographed form.

By far the most prolific in the production of documentary materials are the two academies for rural development at Comilla and Peshawar. These academies emerged as the result of recommendations of a survey team from Michigan State University which visited Pakistan in 1956. The Ford Foundation agreed to underwrite continuing advisory services for the two academies, and the Government of Pakistan agreed in 1957 to create the two institutions. Directors and faculty spent the 1958–1959 academic year at Michigan State University, the contracting institution, and the academies opened in May, 1959. The academies have been unusually productive in published materials relating to their internal administrative operations, curricula, special programs, self-evaluation surveys, and monthly and annual reports. The candor as well as the volume of such documentary publication is refreshing and represents a new awareness of public responsibility somewhat in advance of the nation's general state of development as a constitutional democracy. The totally different attitude of these academies in dealing with the public, disseminating information, and subjecting their own operations to rigorous self-criticism stands as one of the most impressive and hopeful achievements in Pakistan. The official reports of the academies, approximately one hundred pages long, are issued annually in mimeographed form. The Pakistan Academy for Rural Development in Comilla issued its *Fifth Annual Report, June 1963–May 1964* in July, 1964. The West Pakistan academy's *Fifth Annual Report, 1963–1964* appeared in November, 1964. These reports are lively narrative, self-critical, and reflect the ethos of the community development concept. The academy in Peshawar is oriented more toward administrative problems; at Comilla the emphasis is somewhat more on agriculture. The annual reports reflect that emphasis. The West Pakistan academy issues a series of short reports under the title,

The Academy in Operation, which includes reports of research activities, faculty council meetings, and seminars. Announcements of various training programs and the annual reports show the scope of the academies' activities. The East Pakistan academy issues monthly reports which give the details of its operations. The *Journal of the East Pakistan Academy for Village Development* started in April, 1960, and a similar journal, *The Academy Quarterly,* began publication with a September, 1961, issue in Peshawar. The Peshawar journal was renamed the *Journal of Rural Development and Administration* starting with the September, 1964, issue. These two publications are learned journals dealing with rural development. Speeches and papers of Raja Muhammad Afzal Khan, director of the West Pakistan academy, have been compiled by Muhammad S. Sajid in *Images and Goals: The Director Speaks* (Peshawar: West Pakistan Academy for Village Development, 1960).

All of these publications as well as substantive publications which are described in the section of this chapter on rural development are available in the well-maintained and efficient libraries of the two academies as well as at Michigan State University. Secondary sources describing the work of the academies include several publications in the South Asia Series (Pakistan) of the reports of the American Universities Field Staff. In this series, Louis Dupree has written "The Comilla Experiment" (Vol. XIII, No. 2, January, 1964) and "The West Pakistan Academy for Village Development: Peshawar: An Experiment in Bureaucratic Education" (Vol. IV, No. 2, January, 1960). A systematic survey of the whole rural development program in Pakistan is *Dynamics of Community Development* (New York, 1963) by Jack D. Mezirow, who served as a village AID adviser in Pakistan.

The largest administrative training effort in terms of manpower and expenditure is the USAID-sponsored program operated by the University of Southern California. This is concentrated principally in Contract No. AIDc-1690 for activities amounting to $2,104,560, not including counterpart support funds. The contract began in 1960 and was extended to October 31, 1965. It was preceded by a $25,000 contract with the University of Southern California for the training of government officers of middle-management rank. As a result of this activity, three institutes of public administration were established, a department of public administration was established at the University of the Panjab, an adviser to the Civil Service Academy was furnished for two years, and a number of Pakistanis were trained in public administration in the United States. The institutes by 1963 had thus far trained sixty-seven CSP officers, 230 officers of the provincial services, and 240 other officers (a total of 537 officers) in various courses such as management development, conference leadership, and administrative systems; the courses lasted from eight days to three months. The present basic plan is for the three institutes to train approximately 180 additional officers each year.

The same contract has provided for training in public administration through the doctorate in the United States. Those so trained will staff the institutes upon their return. In 1964, two students who received the doctor of public administration degree, one who received the master's degree, and one librarian had returned to the institutes. There are presently seventeen candidates for the doctor of public administration degree studying in the United States: twelve at the University of Southern California, two at Syracuse, and one each at George Washington, Pittsburgh, and New York universities. It was planned that all but one of these students would have returned to Pakistan by September, 1965.

The complete details of this extensive operation are officially chronicled in a mimeographed series of reports, averaging about 150 pages each. The latest is "Eighth Semi-Annual Report (April 1964–September 1964), Public Administration Program in Pakistan." These reports are available at the University of Southern California and the United States Agency for International Development in Washington. Other important sources are the elaborate and detailed syllabi and subjects of study for each of the many training courses conducted in this program. These are available at the national institutes of public administration in Dacca, Karachi, and Lahore. This program in public administration training has generated a significant amount of research activity, not the least of which is the reprinting of the Wheeler, Llewellyn-Smith, Totten-ham, Chapman, Maxwell, and Rowlands reports.[24] Each of the institutes has established a research library, and a systematic program for accession of research materials is under way. The institute in Lahore publishes the *NIPA Public Administration Review,* the first issue of which appeared late in 1962. The Karachi institute publishes *NIPA Reporter,* which first appeared in December, 1961. Intended initially as a small "news and notes" publication, its format was changed in June, 1962, and it became a journal. Neither journal has yet featured much empirical research or analysis relating to governmental problems of Pakistan.

The establishment of eight administrative training organiza-tions, all controlled by the Establishment Division of the Presi-dent's Secretariat, has created problems of co-ordination and allo-cation of scarce manpower for training. This problem has been met in principle by a policy document issued by the Establishment Division, which marks a clear departure from policies of the past: Government of Pakistan, President's Secretariat, Establishment Division, *Letter No. 2/17/61-A-IV,* dated October 31, 1961, from the establishment secretary to the chief secretaries, govern-ments of East and West Pakistan, subject "Public Administration Training Policy" (3 pp., mimeographed). The new policy implic-itly recognizes the need for continuous in-service training for all levels of public employment (except custodial and related groups). It explicitly relates such training to promotion policy; it distinguishes the responsibilities of six of the eight training organi-zations, and it designates the ranks of civil servants who will be the clientele for such institutions. The document on training policy does not mention the Civil Service Academy since, although this is the oldest and the premier training institution, it is not confronted by problems of overlapping coverage or competition for clientele. For the same reasons, there is no mention of the Secretariat Training Institute which is designed to train clerks, stenographers, and assistants. The training policy document clearly states that certain one-year fellowships for study in England at the Imperial Defense College and in the United States, under an Eisenhower

---

[24] Cited and described above, p. 107.

fellowship (usually at Harvard), are for "carefully selected officers who are earmarked for Secretaryship to the Central Government in course of time." This program of foreign training therefore
commands the highest prestige. Final selections for these fellowships are made by the President upon recommendation of the
establishment committee of the cabinet. This document on co-
ordinated training policy is one of the most important in the study
of contemporary bureaucracy.

The fact that most of the administrative training in Pakistan has
been initiated or supported by technical assistance from either the
Ford Foundation or the United States Agency for International
Development suggests possibilities for research. The manifold
problems of gauging the effectiveness of training institutions as
media for the diffusion of new managerial ideologies is one such
subject. Problems related to this are explored in David S. Brown,
"Concepts and Strategies of Public Administration Technical
Assistance," and Ralph Braibanti, "Transnational Inducement of
Administrative Reform: A Survey of Scope and Critique of
Issues," in John D. Montgomery and William D. Siffin (eds.),
Politics, Administration and Change: Approaches to Development
(New York, 1966). Both of these essays draw extensively on
experience in Pakistan. An inter-university consortium on
institution-building, composed of the University of Pittsburgh and
Syracuse, Indiana, and Michigan State universities, is planning a
series of studies, some of which will analyze the effectiveness of
administrative training institutions in various developing states.
One of the institutions which will be studied in this project is the
Administrative Staff College at Lahore.

Public Employee Associations

In Pakistan there are no strong employees' unions or civil
service associations as are found in many Western nations and in
such Asian states as Ceylon. Almost every cadre and class of
service does have an informal organization, however, which meets
infrequently, usually to voice a grievance on some special issue.
The Civil Service of Pakistan Association is more or less the model
for other such groups. It elected Chief Justice M. R. Kayani of the

West Pakistan High Court as its president for seven consecutive years since 1955. In Pakistan's early years, its annual dinner exclusively for its members at the Civil Service Academy capped a series of social events during "CSP Week." As public feeling against the alleged "social snobbery" of the CSP mounted, these activities were gradually reduced to the annual dinner. The CSP Association has been an important mechanism for mobilizing the strength of the CSP cadre in behalf of various service matters. When it was thought that the second (Cornelius) Pay Commission was to make recommendations detrimental to the separate identity of the CSP as a cadre, the association was active in drafting briefs which presented its views before the commission.

Other service associations perform similar functions in safeguarding their interests. Usually inactive, they rise in importance when they deem the welfare of their particular service jeopardized or see a possibility of promoting their interests. As rumors of the second Pay Commission's point of view reached the services from 1960 until the report was released in June, 1962, the service organizations rose to the occasion by demanding that they be heard. All the associations except the CSP Association favored implementation of the second Pay Commission Report since they presumed it recommended higher remuneration generally, a diminution of the favored position of the CSP, and a corresponding increase in the status of other cadres.

Service associations in Pakistan have no buildings, offices, or other physical facilities, nor do they keep any but the most elementary records of dues payment. Files of their correspondence and special-interest briefs usually do not exist. None of the associations publishes materials of any kind. Their informal organization is derived from the strong tradition under British rule prohibiting formal collective action on the part of civil servants. Yet the British officers, by virtue of their race and position and their exclusive membership in *gymkhanas* and regional clubs like those at Dacca, Peshawar, Sind, or Punjab, did form powerful and cohesive interest groups outside the formal structure of bureaucracy. Their physical entity was obscured by anonymity and informality, but their presence was felt. The associations which have emerged in Pakistan unwittingly reflect this pre-partition British pattern. The fact that the CSP Association emphasized social events was a reflection of the exclusiveness of earlier British ICS society with its morning riding, afternoon tennis, evening whiskey, and nightly bridge. It was so certain of its legal and actual bureaucratic power that no formal association was needed. After independence it was not surprising that an effort to preserve the *élan* of the ICS took the form of an annual reminder that the ICS were the elite of the bureaucracy. The "headquarters" of the various associations is merely the desk and telephone of its secretary in whatever government office he works. Its meetings are usually small groups of officers planning a lobbying strategy in a coffeehouse or at a member's home. The number of such associations is unknown. Often they appear to spring up overnight when they feel that some issue affects them. In addition to the CSP Association, there are associations of the provincial civil services, financial services, engineering services, secretariat assistants, stenographers, typists, clerks, and various other groups including the irrigation research assistants' association.

The role of service organizations or trade unions in openly seeking redress of alleged grievances through such actions as strikes or walkouts had been virtually unheard of in Pakistan until the early sixties. Government Servants' (Conduct) Rules (1964) prohibit government employees from membership in any association representing government employees unless the membership is confined to "a distinct class" of government servants. Such associations cannot engage in political activity, and they cannot be members of any federation of associations unless the federation is also confined to a distinct class of government servants. The United Council of Associations of Central Government Employees of Pakistan (UCACEP) represents primarily class III and class IV employees of some thirty-two unions, such as the Post and Telegraph Workers' Union, Land Customs Union, and Sea Customs Union. An impending strike by UCACEP was averted by the passing of an ordinance in East Pakistan early in 1963 declaring strikes by government employees to be illegal. This action was discussed in the National Assembly, some of whose members regarded the government's action as a violation of the convention of the International Labour Organization of which Pakistan is a member.[25] The issue also became tangled in the ambiguity surrounding central-provincial powers and subsequently in matters of civil liberties resulting from action by the provincial government prohibiting publication of news of the impending strike.[26]

[25] National Assembly of Pakistan, *Debates*, March 13, 1963, pp. 328–341; April 3, 1963, pp. 1238–1254; April 4, 1963, pp. 1287–1291.
[26] *Ibid.*, March 29, 1963, pp. 962–967.

3

Local Government

The title of this chapter is not the term customarily used to describe district and division administration in Pakistan. It has been advisedly selected because it more accurately describes the several kinds of government activity below the central and provincial secretariats. Historically, there are four strands of thought identifiable in local government. The first and oldest is orthodox district administration in which the power of the provincial and central governments is extended to the district in the person of the district officer. The district officer is legally responsible to the provincial and central governments which appoint him, train him, and control his actions. Essentially, district administration has been autocratic rule with a strong touch of paternalism, but its autocratic quality has been modified by the varying success of three other movements which have had impact on local government. The first and the oldest of these was the co-operative societies movement, carried on under government supervision, originally broadly conceived but narrowing its scope through the years to the lending of money and equipment. The second was rural uplift (self-help, rural reconstruction, Village AID, community development), derived from Brayne's Village Guide system, which sought to generate an enthusiasm and an ideology which would sustain improvement in all aspects of village life. The ideology of this movement was that of participative democracy in which the impetus for total social amelioration was to come from village groups. It was an ideology based on the mobilization of zeal, rather than on the formal use of bureaucratic or legal power. The third was local self-government, started by the Montagu-Chelmsford Reforms, legitimized by law and formal structure, and involving election of officials. These latter three historic strands were merged into a system known as Basic Democracies, which seeks to conjoin them into a unified system sustained by a common zeal and ideology and buttressed by formal political power. The administrative structure for this is still being built, and the pattern of local government which will emerge is not yet clear.

Orthodox District Administration

The district in Pakistan is the principal unit of government and the main influence in shaping administrative attitudes of the higher civil service. All members of the Civil Service of Pakistan start their careers as district officers, as did ICS officers before partition, and remain in districts during the most impressionable years of their lives. Only after seven or eight years' assignment in districts are some of the officers posted to provincial secretariats or to the central secretariat, and after about fifteen years' service many return to the districts to become division commissioners. This means that virtually every CSP officer spends the years between his twenty-fourth and thirtieth years of life as a district officer, and many after forty spend a period of years either as division commissioners or dealing in some capacity with district affairs.

The basic administrative units of the country are much the same as they were at the time of partition and even before. The principal difference lies in the integration of the former provinces of Sind, Punjab, Baluchistan States Union, and the Northwest Frontier Province, together with several princely states (such as Khairpur and Bahawalpur) into the single province of West Pakistan. This was accomplished in 1955 by the Establishment of West Pakistan Act, 1955 (October 3, 1955), published in the *Gazette of Pakistan, Extraordinary,* October 3, 1955. An analysis of the reasons for unification of the province can be found in the same issue of the *Gazette,* pp. 1453–1455. The two provinces, each with its own governor appointed by the president and with an elected legislative assembly, are further divided for administration into sixteen divisions and seventy-four districts (including eight political agencies in West Pakistan). In 1964, as Table 1 below shows, only seventy districts had actually been established, but seventy-four were approved by the cabinet. Districts are further divided into subdivisions. In West Pakistan, subdivisions are divided into *tehsils* (called *taluqa* in some areas) which are groups of villages. In East Pakistan, fifty-nine subdivisions are divided into some 413 circles, or *thana*. Prior to 1962, circles and *thanas* were not necessarily coterminous, but since reforms of that date, the two entities are identical, and *thana* has come to refer to the police function, just one element of the administration which is the responsibility of the circle. In West Pakistan, the eight political agencies are at the same level as districts, and the officer in charge is known as political agent. The difference lies in the fact that agencies are inhabited by tribal Pathans, whose criminal law is quite different and who are loosely administered in accordance with long-established tribal customs. Although the Provincial Administration Commission in its report of 1960 recommended certain minor changes in the grouping of districts, and most of these changes were approved by the cabinet of the central government on June 23, 1960, not all of the changes have yet been made. Because it is difficult to find an accurate list of districts and divisions, Table 1 which follows may be of convenience in research.

Nomenclature of the officers in charge of these administrative units is somewhat confusing. In both provinces a division is under the charge of a commissioner—a term which has not been changed for nearly a century. In both provinces since 1962 (when nomenclature in East Pakistan was made compatible) the district has been under the charge of a deputy commissioner. In East Pakistan, prior to 1962, that officer was known as district magistrate and collector. Political agencies on the Northwest Frontier are headed by political agents whose rank is equal to that of deputy commissioners. Subdivisions in both provinces are headed by subdivisional officers, who are sometimes also called assistant commissioners. Additional commissioners are sometimes assigned to assist in a division as "extra commissioners," having rank almost equal to that of commissioners and above that of deputy commissioners.

Table 1. *Names of Authorized Divisions, Districts, and Agencies, 1964*

Province of West Pakistan

(12 divisions, 54 districts and agencies)

I. Peshawar Division *

Districts
1. Peshawar *
2. Mardan *
3. Hazara
4. Kohat *

Agencies
5. Malakand
6. Mohmand *
7. Khyber
8. Kurram *
9. Chitral
10. Dir

II. Dera Ismael Khan Division

Districts
11. Dera Ismael Khan
12. Bannu

Agencies
13. North Waziristan *
14. South Waziristan

III. Multan Division *

Districts
15. Multan *
16. Dera Ghazi Khan *
17. Muzaffergarh *
18. Montgomery
19. (Vehari)

IV. Bahawalpur Division *

Districts
20. Bahawalpur *
21. Bahawalnagar
22. Rahimyarkhan

V. Rawalpindi Division *

Districts
23. Rawalpindi *
24. Campbellpur *
25. Gujrat
26. Jhelum

VI. Sargodha Division *

Districts
27. Sargodha *
28. Mianwali
29. Lyallpur *
30. Jhang

VII. Khairpur Division *

Districts
31. Khairpur
32. Jacobabad *
33. Sukkur *
34. Larkhana *
35. Nawabsha *

VIII. Hyderabad Division *

Districts
36. Hyderabad *
37. Tharparkar *
38. Sanghar
39. Thatta *
40. Dadu

IX. Quetta Division *

Districts
41. Quetta-Pishin *
42. Zhob #
43. Loralai # *
44. Sibi # *

X. Kalat Division

Districts
45. Kalat
46. Mekran
47. Kharan *
48. Chagai

Table 1. *Names of Authorized Divisions, Districts, and Agencies, 1964 (cont.)*

Province of West Pakistan (*cont.*)

XI. Karachi Division *

    Districts

    49. Karachi *

    50. Lasbella

XII. Lahore Division *

    Districts

    51. Lahore

    52. Sialkot

    53. Gujranwala *

    54. Sheikhupura *

Province of East Pakistan
(*4 divisions, 20 districts*)

XIII. Dacca Division

    Districts

    55. Dacca *

    56. Mymensingh *

    57. Faridpur

    58. (Nasirabad)

    59. (Quaidabad)

XIV. Chittagong Division *

    Districts

    60. Chittagong *

    61. Chittagong Hill Tracts *

    62. Comilla *

    63. Noakhali

    64. Sylhet *

XV. Khulna Division *

    Districts

    65. Khulna *

    66. Khustia

    67. Bakarganj *

    68. Jessore *

    69. (Patuakhali)

XVI. Rajshahi Division

    Districts

    70. Rajshahi *

    71. Rangpur *

    72. Dinajpur

    73. Bogra

    74. Pabna *

* Officer in charge (as of 1964) is member of CSP cadre. Thus, twelve of sixteen division commissioners and forty of seventy (four districts not yet established) deputy commissioners (or political agents) are CSP officers.

Officially designated as districts, but officer in charge is known as political agent.

( ) Recommended by Provincial Administration Commission and approved by cabinet, but district not yet established in 1964.

Sources: This list is derived from interviews, correspondence, and the *Gradation List of 1964* and *West Pakistan Civil List for 1963.*

One aspect of local government administration is clear in Pakistan, namely, that district and division administration has been made more powerful and somewhat more autocratic, especially since 1958. The declaration of martial law in that year resulted in a moratorium on the political process which had detracted from the autonomy of the district officer. Even after martial law, the Basic Democracies Scheme and consequent politicization of the social order have not been able to dislodge bureaucratic paramountcy of the district and divisional apparatus, especially in West Pakistan. In East Pakistan, district administration is also strong, but its style is leavened by the more egalitarian social structure of Bengal and the vigor of the Rural Works Programme and Basic Democracies.

Any study of bureaucracy must encompass an understanding of district administration which involves the collection of land revenues, the maintenance of law and order, the co-ordination of all government activities within the district, the stimulation of economic development, and the encouragement of local initiative. The personalized rule of powerful district officers was an efficient and economical means by which a small handful of colonial officials could control large numbers of peasants. Moreover, the system was thought to correspond to traditional methods of control. Hence, although usually associated with the subcontinent, district officer rule was also found in the British colonies of Africa. The British journal *Local Government Administration Overseas* often includes studies of district administration in African states which are of interest to Pakistan studies as well.

The adventure and fascination of district work in the subcontinent has captured the imagination of novelists whose accounts are one means of re-creating the spirit of district rule which generally eludes statutes and manuals. They should be read for color and feeling rather than for precision of analysis. Novels purporting to describe administrative situations have not been uncommon in the Western world as the work of C. P. Snow, Franz Kafka, and George Orwell suggests. But the authenticity of such "administrative literature" has not been systematically studied.[1] Caution is more important for this genre in the non-Western milieu, since the cultural setting is usually less familiar to the Westerner. The importance of local customs and the effectiveness of an understanding district officer in dealing with them in India is the theme of Aubrey Menon's *The Prevalence of Witches* (London, 1947). George Orwell's *Burmese Days* (London, 1949) is a perceptive

---

[1] See Rowland Egger, "The Administrative Novel," *The American Political Science Review*, LIII (1959), 448–455; Morton Kroll, "Administrative Fiction and Credibility," *Public Administration Review*, XXV (1965), 80–84.

account of officialdom in Burma which was institutionally related to the higher civil service structure established in India. But the distinction for recording with accuracy, feeling, and insight the problems of district administration goes to Philip Woodruff, not only for his two-volume *The Men Who Ruled India,* but for his two lesser-known novels, *The Wild Sweet Witch* (London, 1947) and *Call the Next Witness* (London, 1945). The latter is an account of the dilemmas and complexities of applying English law to indigenous custom and is as illuminating as many a technical treatise on the interaction of legal systems. The problems may be found today in Pakistan in any number of criminal cases and in the phenomenon of expansion of jurisdiction of the Frontier Crimes Regulation. John Masters, perhaps the most powerful of Western historical novelists on India, touches on aspects of district administration in several of his seven novels, but most particularly in *Far, Far the Mountain Peak* (New York, 1957) and *The Lotus and the Wind* (New York, 1953). The others are useful for general color of Indian life touched by administration: *Nightrunners of Bengal* (New York, 1951), a novel about the mutiny of 1857; *Coromandel!* (New York, 1955) deals with the arrival of the English in South India in the seventeenth century; *The Deceivers* (New York, 1952) is an exotic, vivid account of the successful British effort to eliminate *thugee* (a peculiar Indian form of banditry); *Bugles and a Tiger* (New York, 1956) is an autobiographical account of Indian army life; *Bhowani Junction* (New York, 1954) deals with the Anglo-Indian community and the period through independence in 1947. Colonel Jim Corbett's classics of adventure in India are disarmingly simple accounts of the adventures of a remarkable hunter. At first glance, they would appear to have no place in a specialized bibliography. But it is now generally acknowledged that, as Geoffrey Cumberlege has said, "many felt his saintly quality and none would deny that he was a great man." Corbett's stories are full of profound insight into the life and problems of the villager and, indirectly, into the work of the district officials. All six of Corbett's books on India, published in London by Oxford University Press, deserve a high place in the literature of the subcontinent: *My India* (1952); *Man-Eaters of Kumaon* (1944); *Temple Tiger* (1954); *More Man-Eaters of Kumaon* (1954); *The Man-Eating Leopard of Rudraprayag* (1947); and *Jungle Lore* (1953).

A number of British and Indian officials wrote commentaries on district administration. G. O. Trevelyan's *The Competition Wallah* (London, 1864) is an appealing series of letters commenting on the civil service and life in the districts. A detailed description of the organization of a district office and a listing of the duties performed can be found in C. W. Whish, *A District Office in Northern India* (Calcutta, 1892). C. H. Buck's *The Assistant Commissioner's Notebook* (London, 1906) is a similar description of duties and a compilation of suggestions for district officers. A candid account of the work of district judicial officers is given in C. A. Kincaid, *Forty-four Years a Public Servant* (London, 1934). An anecdotal and nostalgic account of an ICS career spent largely in Madras can be found in S. K. Chettur's *The Steel Frame and I* (New York, 1962). One of the best descriptions of district administration is that of R. D. Macleod, *Impressions of an Indian Civil Servant* (London, 1938). It makes an interesting comparison with the sentimental though not uncritical account in Bernard Houghton, *Bureaucratic Government* (London, 1913). Literature on social life of the British rulers in the district is an important source for understanding district administration, although it is too voluminous to mention except in passing. It would be a serious omission not to note George Francklin Atkinson, *Curry and Rice* (*on Forty Plates*); or, *The Ingredients of Social Life at Our Station in India* (London, n. d. [probably *ca.* 1870–1900]) and Hilton Brown (ed.), *The Sahibs* (London, 1948). Neither is a serious, scholarly work, but there is much sheer enjoyment, considerable wisdom and self-revelation in these accounts of life among the rulers of India. Atkinson, who was a captain in the Bengal Engineers, has depicted life in a district somewhere in north India, humorously called Kabob "in the plains of Dekchy, in the province of Babarchy." Each of his forty essays is accompanied by lithograph plates. His incisive characterizations of "our judge," "our colonel," "our collector," "our German missionary," and others are fine satirical pieces which will be familiar to anyone who has lived on the subcontinent. *The Sahibs* is in a different genre. It is a collection of extracts from letters written from India by wives of British officials. Arranged by topics, such as "health," "servants," and "climate," chronologically under each topic, Brown's compilation reveals how little the fundamental problems of life on the subcontinent have changed. Two historical essays both appearing in the same issue of the journal, *Comparative Studies in Society and History*, IV (1962), 169–199, 200–208, are of particular value. The first is Bernard Cohn's "The British in Benares," and the second, Robert Eric Frykenberg's "British Society in Guntur in the early Nineteenth Century."

Land Revenue and Settlement Literature

Unlike activities in the maintenance of law and order in which the district officer relied on the superintendent of police, the collection of revenue and the maintenance of land records received the district officer's close attention and demanded his active participation. The questions of revenue and settlement of land revenue rates are a crucial part of district administration. A concise review of land revenue in both provinces of Pakistan is a 23-page section of the *Report of the Taxation Enquiry Committee*, Vol. I (Karachi: Government of Pakistan Press, 1960).

The earliest compilation of rules for the collection of land revenue was prepared under the direction of James Thomason, who was lieutenant-governor of the Northwest Frontier Province from 1843 to 1853: *Directions for Collectors of Land Revenue.* The first edition of this was printed in two parts, Part I in 1846 at Agra and Part II in 1848. Part II was *Directions for Settlement Officers.* Copies of Thomason's *Directions* are rare; the India Office Library has only Part I, and the Northwest Frontier Province secretariat library, the office most crucially concerned with the *Directions,* apparently has none. A second edition of Thomason's *Directions* appeared in 1850 under the editorship of D. G. Barkley, and both parts were included in one volume entitled *Directions for Revenue Officers in the Northwestern Frontier Provinces of the*

Bengal Presidency Regarding the Settlement and Collection of the Land Revenue and the Other Duties Connected Therewith (*promulgated under authority of the Honourable the Lieutenant-Governor, Agra, November 1, 1849*) (Calcutta: Baptist Mission Press, 1850). Although Thomason's *Directions* was intended primarily for the Northwest Frontier Province, it was an authoritative text in the Punjab as well. The title is appropriately modest; Thomason's work is a masterly, authoritative textbook on district administration. It is difficult to improve on his description (in Part I, par. 26 of the 1850 edition) of the work of the district officer.

Nothing can pass in the district of which it is not the duty of the collector to keep himself informed and to watch the operation. The vicissitudes of trade, the administration of civil justice, the progress of the public works, must all affect materially the interests of the classes of whom he is the constituted guardian. Officious interference in matters beyond his immediate control must be avoided, but temperate and intelligent remonstrance against anything which he sees to be wrong is one of his most important duties.

Thomason's *Directions* was replaced in 1908 by an equally indispensable guide in Sir James M. Douie's *Punjab Land Administration Manual* (3rd ed.; Lahore: Superintendent, Government Printing, West Pakistan, 1960). Parts of the *Manual* are almost chatty in tone and contain homely advice to young district officers. There is an excellent glossary of vernacular terms and careful descriptions of the work of *patwaris* and *kanungos*. Although the Douie *Manual*, first issued in 1908 and revised in 1931, had been a rare item, it was reissued by the Government of West Pakistan in 1960 and is now available. Douie continued the comprehensiveness and lucidity of Thomason, whom he often quoted with admiration, and in many ways he excelled Thomason in the shrewdness of his insight. An example (p. 110) is his comment on training new district officers which follows the same quotation from Thomason reproduced above.

It is a mistake to give newly joined officers routine executive work during their first six months of service. The average assistant commissioner arrives without any experience of essentials. He hopes and expects to be given work at once, and is only too pleased to take over a "subject" such as passports or the licensing of motor vehicles. His request for work is sometimes difficult to resist, but if it is acceded to, he is almost certain to be deceived by his clerks and may learn habits of irresponsibility which he will later regret.

It may be obvious to anyone who has studied modern district administration that these injunctions of Thomason and Douie are not always honored. This default is, indeed, symptomatic of one of the most serious administrative problems of Pakistan, namely, that preoccupation with irrelevant "modern" notions of "scientific" administration may be eroding the tested elementary wisdom so lucidly recorded by Thomason and Douie.

The land revenue systems of the Punjab and Bengal are different, the former having periodic settlement and the latter permanent settlement. The best general description of the two systems is B. H. Baden-Powell, *Land-Systems of British India* (3 vols.; Oxford, 1892). The section on the Punjab was extracted from Volume II and reprinted under the title *Extract from Volume II of the Land Systems of British India* by the Punjab Government Press in 1908. A comprehensive and cogent review of land revenue is *The Report of the Land Revenue Committee* (Lahore: Superintendent, Government Printing, Punjab, 1938). This is commonly known as the Darling Report after the name of its chairman, Sir Malcolm Darling, author of the classic study, *The Punjab Peasant in Prosperity and Debt,* which is cited later in this essay on page 179. The pattern of ownership and tenancy of land was changed in 1959 by the land reforms recommended in the *Report of the Land Reforms Commission for West Pakistan* (Lahore: West Pakistan Government Printing, 1959) and enacted into law by the West Pakistan Land Reforms Regulation (Martial Law Regulation No. 64, February 7, 1959). The implementation of these reforms, which limit individual holdings to five hundred acres of irrigated or one thousand acres of unirrigated land, is controlled by the West Pakistan Land Commission. The commission has brought together various regulations and orders on land reform in its *Report on the Working of the West Pakistan Land Commission* (Lahore: Punjab Educational Press, April, 1959).

For land revenue in East Pakistan, the standard historical

survey is Radha Kumud Mookerji, *Indian Land Systems, Ancient, Mediaeval and Modern* (Alipore: West Bengal Government Press, 1958). The modern period in Mookerji's work ends in 1793, and it remains valid as a historical survey for East Pakistan. A landmark in the development of land revenue in Bengal is *Report of the Land Revenue Commission, Bengal* (commonly known as Flood Commission) (Alipore: Bengal Government Press, 1940). It is essential to complement this historical background, however, with events in East Pakistan since independence. The major development was the abolition of permanent settlement *zamindari* soon after independence by the East Bengal State Acquisition and Tenancy Act, 1950 (published by the East Pakistan Government Press, Dacca, 1957). Subsequent developments are analyzed in *Report of the Land Revenue Commission, East Pakistan* (Dacca: East Pakistan Government Press, 1959). These changes in land revenue created a substantial administrative problem. Specific rules and directions for implementing the new system are given in the Board of Revenue's *Government Estates Manual, 1958* (Dacca: East Pakistan Government Press, 1958).

The fundamental document which determines the amount of land revenue to be collected is the district settlement report (sometimes referred to as assessment report). It is doubtful if many district documents are more important than these since they are essentially assessments on the value of land (in the Punjab) or on crops (in the Sind) which vitally affect the poverty or prosperity of most of the population. Settlement also involves preparation of maps (cadastral survey) which are used to determine land ownership as registered in the carefully maintained record of rights, which is kept up-to-date by settlement. Settlement reports, following a fixed form, cover a description of the resources, terrain, and people of the district, history of previous settlements, revision of land records, and revision of assessments. The settlement officer relies heavily on assessment reports prepared by the *tehsildar* (or *mukhtiarkar*) in charge of each *tehsil* or similar unit into which the district is divided. The *tehsildar*, his assistants, the *naib tehsildars*, and his staff of *kanungos, patwaris*, or *tapedars* have functions resembling those of the underclerks of Chinese bureaucracy who were the connecting link between the mandarin and the masses. These officials, whose titles are of Persian origin, are vernacular-speaking natives of the district, intimately acquainted with their area, and wielding immense power through their mediating role between the peasant and the English language government of the district level and above. The *tehsildar* was, and continues to be, one of the most important officials in the whole revenue structure. A careful historical study which includes comment on the *tehsildar's* work is Cohn's study of local Mughal government in the Benares region (located in India but applicable to Pakistan as well).[2] The settlement reports are carefully compiled economic analyses of the districts based on empirical data and prepared by officials who know the district as intimately as is possible. When such compilation of data is combined with imagination and deep insight, the result is microcosmic economic planning of high quality. Such, for example, was the settlement report for Karnal district in what is now East Punjab: Sir Denzil Ibbetson, *Settlement Report for Karnal, 1873–1879* (Lahore: Superintendent, Government Printing, Punjab, 1879). As was the case for many superior settlement reports, parts of the Ibbetson Report were reproduced in subsequent district gazetteers for Karnal.

Settlements are required by law in the Punjab for periods not exceeding forty years and not less than ten years for canal-irrigated land (Punjab Land Revenue Act, 1887 [Act XVII], Sec. 53-A[2][i]). Since no statutory period is fixed for the Sind and there is no settlement in Baluchistan, numerous settlement reports exist only for the Punjab, the Northwest Frontier, and East Pakistan. There are only two reports for the Sind. Districts became canal-irrigated at different times, hence there are no fixed, standard dates for the publication of all settlement reports. Since partition, settlements have been completed for Rawalpindi and Montgomery districts and are in progress now in Hazara and Mardan districts and in Kalat division in West Pakistan. In East Pakistan settlement reports for Faridpur and Bakerganj districts and Sunderbans portion of Khulna district have been published

[2] See above, p. 117.

since 1947, and settlement work is in progress under the 1960 Acquisition and Tenancy Act in all districts except Bakerganj and the Chittagong Hill Tracts.

An experienced officer was assigned the task of settlement work, which required an average of four years for its completion. Settlement reports are significant for contemporary Pakistan because they can be used as models for economic reporting and planning within the district. In recent years, the shortage of trained officials and pressure of other work has resulted in a deterioration of settlement reports, but the model with its traditions of precise research method remains. If the same skill, precision, and energy which characterized settlement reports could now be regenerated and channelled into district economic plans, a major advance in economic planning would be made. Settlement reports are published by the provincial revenue departments which have responsibility for settlement work. The reports average fifty pages in length and are somewhat technical treatises rather than literary narratives. Few copies of these settlement reports are now available in Pakistan. The 1961 *General Catalogue* of West Pakistan provincial government publications lists some fourteen as available, but in reality the stock of most of them is exhausted. Legally, settlement reports are recommendations for a revenue assessment rate which are submitted to division commissioners, then to the revenue commissioners (now called boards of revenue) of the province, and finally to the revenue department. Each of these authorities reviews the report, and the revenue department then issues the report as the official assessment. In many reports, the detail of the review and the disagreements expressed by the reviewing authorities suggest the expertness and thoroughness which has traditionally characterized settlement work. For this purpose, a good illustrative report is that of H. S. Williamson, *Final Report of the Fourth Regular Settlement of the Gujrat District, 1912–1916* (Lahore: Superintendent, Government Printing, Punjab, 1916). The report was sent by Williamson to the commissioner of Rawalpindi division in which Gujrat district was located. The commissioner approved the terms of settlement stating "that a difficult settlement has been completed with reason-

able expedition, with satisfactory results to Government, and with
scrupulous fairness to the people. Mr. Williamson's village inspections (so infinitely important a branch of settlement work) were
most thorough, and his distribution has, within limits of practi-
cality, been equitable." This review was sent with the settlement
report to the financial commissioners of the Punjab, who, while
agreeing with the basis of settlement and commending Williamson "whose assessment reports have already received the commen-
dation of Government," nevertheless took issue with some points.
In one instance the financial commissioners disagreed with part of
the commissioner's review which took "a much too gloomy view of
the efficiency of our district staff for the maintenance of land
records and of the constant efforts which are being made to
improve the machinery." The revenue secretary, to whom the
financial commissioner's review was addressed, concurred with
the basis of assessment. The final report, he said, "is in respect of
lucidity and consciseness hardly up to the high level of the
assessment reports. It shows signs of haste and incompleteness."
But this adverse criticism was tempered by the remark, "Sir
Michael O'Dwyer, however, recognizes that too much importance
need not be attached to minor blemishes in a report written under
the strain of several years arduous work in exacting conditions." In
the Williamson settlement report is an important lesson for all
research on bureaucracy in Pakistan; namely, the fact that the
report was carefully reviewed, and disagreements and adverse
criticism publicly revealed. It is significant also that no part of the
report was classified or its public accessibility limited in any
way.

It is again Sir James McC. Douie to whose careful scholarship
we must turn for authoritative directions in land settlement. His
Punjab Settlement Manual (5th ed.; Lahore: Superintendent of
Government Printing, West Pakistan, 1961) is as valuable as his
later work on land administration. Originally issued in 1899 and
reissued in 1909, 1914, and 1930, the *Settlement Manual* is somewhat more formal in tone than the *Land Administration Manual*
and includes a survey of the history of the Punjab, the historical
development of settlement policy, and careful analysis of the

Record of Rights, a basic document of land ownership. Douie's *Settlement Manual* replaces Part II of the earlier work by James Thomason: *Directions for Settlement Officers*. Although Douie adapts a few sections of Thomason's earlier text in his own volume, it is essentially an independent work.

Douie's *Settlement Manual* and *Land Administration* texts were intended to be quasi-official handbooks but soon became indispensable for district work. The official publication, *Punjab Land Administration Acts and Rules Having the Force of Law Thereunder* (Lahore: Superintendent of Government Printing, 1933) states in the Preface to Volume I that the two Douie manuals are official books of reference for revenue officers. The legal status of settlement reports and of the Douie *Settlement Manual* is illustrated by a major case decided by the Supreme Court, *Province of West Pakistan* v. *Khizar Hayat Khan Tiwana*, PLD 1963 SC 423. In this decision, reliance is placed on two settlement reports for areas in the Punjab and on Douie's *Settlement Manual*. While they are often cited in cases decided by the Board of Revenue, they are less commonly given this attention by the Supreme Court.

Technical directions for measuring land and making assessments for East Pakistan are given in *Technical Rules and Instructions of the Settlement Department, 1957* (Dacca: Directorate of Land Records and Surveys, East Pakistan, 1958). Annual land administration reports are published by each province; the latest available for West Pakistan is for 1951–1952.

Land revenue matters are directed by the provincial government, whose organization for this purpose has undergone several changes which may be confusing at the outset. In the Punjab under British rule, the controlling body was known as the financial commissioners. After the integration of West Pakistan in 1955, this was redesignated as the Board of Revenue, but there continued to exist a revenue department over which the board had no effective administrative control. In 1961, the Board of Revenue members became secretaries to government and exercised direct control over the functions of the revenue department. Members of the Board of Revenue continue to judge revenue cases as they did in the past. Assessment rates may be appealed to each of the provincial revenue boards. For the Punjab, cases decided on appeal were printed in an annual *Punjab Record of Reference Book for Revenue Officers Containing the Report of Revenue Cases Decided by the Financial Commissioners of the Punjab*. The last of these was published for 1932. Since partition, decisions of the Board of Revenue of West Pakistan are published monthly with judgments of the two high courts and the Supreme Court in *All-Pakistan Legal Decisions*. Some decisions of the East Pakistan Board of Revenue have, since 1960, been printed in *Dacca Law Reports*.

Gazetteer Literature [3]

Closely related to the settlement reports are the volumes on individual districts and princely states variously titled (according to period or part of the country) statistical memoir; historical, statistical, and geographical account; statistical report; manual; handbook; or gazetteer. In Maureen L. P. Patterson's projected study of this literature, these are considered part of the over-all local (district or princely state) "gazetteer literature" of the Indian subcontinent. The period of compilation ranges from at least as far back as 1849 (*Statistical Report of the District of Cawnpoor . . .*) to the present new series for districts in India and Pakistan.

While the early volumes were "efforts [that] were isolated, directed by no central organisation, and unsustained by any continuous plan of execution," [4] each in itself was of great value to administrators and is still valuable to historians and other scholars.

In 1869 the governor-general in council directed William Wilson Hunter to survey the descriptive work already done by the various provincial governments and "to submit a comprehensive scheme for utilising the information already collected, for prescribing the principles according to which all local gazetteers are in future to be prepared, and for the consolidation into one work of

---

[3] I am indebted to Maureen L. P. Patterson for a critical reading of this description of gazetteer literature and for comments on the role of W. W. Hunter in organizing this literature. The latter comments are incorporated in the first four paragraphs of this section.

[4] W. W. Hunter, preface to Vol. I of *Statistical Account of Bengal* (20 vols.; London; 1875–1877), p. vii.

the whole of the materials that may be available." [5] Thus, in 1869, taking the district as the chief administrative unit, Hunter prepared his "Plan for an Imperial Gazetteer of India." His plan involved eventual collation of the district and small princely state materials into a provincial gazetteer, and in like manner the collation of provincial and large princely state materials into the "Imperial Gazetteer."

Hunter's prescription of a standardized, simple outline and format was rejected by one province (Madras insisted on much greater detail than Hunter thought necessary), and certain policy obstacles prevented its acceptance by some of the native princely states. Nevertheless, the 1869 plan was to a very great extent implemented so quickly and so effectively that the first edition of the *Imperial Gazetteer of India* could be published in 1881 in nine volumes. Meanwhile, such provincial volumes as the *Gazetteer of the Province of Oudh* (3 vols.; 1877–1878) were published and were quickly followed by the *Panjab Gazetteer* (8 vols.; Calcutta, 1883) and the *Rajputana Gazetteer* (3 vols.; Calcutta, 1879). And further, in consequence of Hunter's plan, he himself published his own monumental works, *A Statistical Account of Bengal,* which deals with each of the fifty-nine districts and small states then within Bengal, and *A Statistical Account of Assam* (2 vols.; London, 1879).

District gazetteers are related to settlement reports in the respect that they were compiled at the time of revenue settlement, usually by the settlement officer. Even if the deputy commissioner in charge of a district did not compile the gazetteer himself, he was usually much more involved in its preparation than he was with the settlement report. The gazetteers are perhaps more widely known than settlement reports, probably because they make much more interesting reading. But they are really less important in terms of bureaucratic power since they do not have the legal standing of the settlement report, which is the official assessment on land or crops. District gazetteers are official to the extent that they are prepared by government, but they do not immediately activate specific policy. Twentieth-century district

[5] *Ibid.,* p. viii.

gazetteers, considerably longer than settlement reports, are usually divided into Part A, a long narrative of at least three hundred pages, and Part B, consisting of about two hundred pages of statistical tables. They were issued not only for districts which come directly under British rule, but also for semi-autonomous princely states which came under British influence but were not part of British India. The district gazetteer is an informative document describing the history and physical aspects of the district, its population, tribes, castes, customs, leading families, agriculture, irrigation, and district administration. In most of the district gazetteers, administration occupies about one-third of Part A. The gazetteer accounts of district administration are of importance to the study of bureaucracy, since they are the only careful, detailed descriptions of district administration available; no other such descriptions or analyses have appeared since partition. In the Punjab, district and princely state gazetteers were first issued in the 1880's and most of them have gone through two revisions of the text, one in the 1900's and the last in the 1930's. The statistical volumes have been revised more frequently. But there are many exceptions to this excessively broad generalization, for compilation of the gazetteer was tied to periodic settlement and this varied, as has been shown, from forty- to twenty-year intervals depending on the province and on irrigation status. Division of district gazetteers into Parts A and B was started in undivided India in 1902 (Government of India, Home Department, *Letter No. 3375*, dated October 1, 1902). The purpose of this format was to separate more or less permanent material, such as terrain and religion, from statistical data which are quickly outdated. Part B was to be compiled at the same time that the decennial census (started in 1881) was taken. The frequency for revising Part A was left to the discretion of provincial governments, with the provision that some kind of updating (by addenda if not by complete revision) be made with each settlement. Since partition, no new district gazetteers have been issued, but in at least one instance the deputy commissioner has had published brief notes and statistics which supplement the gazetteer. An example is *A*

Note on the Administration of Peshawar District (Peshawar: Manager, Government Printing, West Pakistan, 1960).

District gazetteers and related literature, of which more than 1,200 volumes were published, were used as source material for subsequent compilation of provincial gazetteers and for the *Imperial Gazetteer of India*. Provincial gazetteers were often printed locally by the provincial government, but the principal issue was *Imperial Gazetteer of India—Provincial Series* (25 vols.; Calcutta: Superintendent of Government Printing, 1908–1909). The *Imperial Gazetteer of India* was first published in 1881 in nine volumes; a second edition appeared between 1885 and 1887 in fourteen volumes and the third and final edition from 1907 to 1909 in twenty-six volumes (*The Imperial Gazetteer of India* [new ed.; 26 vols.; Oxford, 1907–1909]). The *Imperial Gazetteer* is a monumental work of careful scholarship, embracing not only immense encyclopedic knowledge of the subcontinent, but analysis and interpretation of a very high order. The settlement reports and gazetteers together constitute perhaps the most detailed and comprehensive description and analysis of government which has ever been prepared for any nation. All the twentieth-century volumes of the three series of gazetteers proper have been reproduced on microfiche cards by the International Documentation Centre, Tumba, Sweden, although not all important earlier books such as Hunter's *Statistical Account of Bengal* have been reproduced. An index with cross references and tables for various editions of the district gazetteers is being compiled by Maureen L. P. Patterson and its release in book form by the Centre is projected for 1967.

The details of district administrative procedure are governed by the *District Office Manual, Punjab* (3rd ed.; Lahore: Superintendent, Government Printing, Punjab, 1960) a document which should be found well-worn with use on the desk of every deputy commissioner and commissioner. This manual, in use in all the areas of West Pakistan, was first published in 1934, reprinted in 1960, and is now easily available. It is a consequence of the general disarray of documentary materials since 1947 and the disinclination to read these crucial writings of the British period that few CSP or other district officers who entered the service since 1947 are acquainted with the *Manual.* It is only rarely found in an accessible place in the district offices; nor was it used as a text in district administration at the Civil Service Academy even after its reprinting in 1960. Yet the *Manual* is indispensable both as a legal document on the conduct of district business and as a source of homely wisdom. A few sentences taken from Chapter IV will illustrate its style and content:

Obviously a deputy commissioner cannot manage with success the great estate committed to his care without an intimate personal knowledge of every part of it. Much of the work, moreover, that is carried on can only be effectively supervised by him on the spot. Above all it is impossible to keep in touch with the people unless he seeks frequent opportunities of that informal, frank intercourse with them which is only possible in camp. . . . Free access should be allowed to all classes without reference to immediate business; and the custom, universal on the first acquisition of the country, according to which, on the arrival of a district officer at the village, the headmen at once waited on him and paid their respects, should still be insisted upon. It is an important part of the district officer's duty to gain the acquaintance, and ascertain the sentiments, temper and circumstances of all sections of the population within his charge.

The *District Office Manual* includes a long list of documents and manuals which each district is required to keep in the district library. This list is of special utility for research. From it the researcher can apprehend the scope of district administration. A complete list of district records and minute directions for keeping them is also included. The detailed instructions in the *Manual* seem to lend credence to the quip that district administration succeeds by its own momentum irrespective of the competence of the incumbent district officer. Whether this is true or not, the *Manual* is a model of precision and clarity, and acquaintance with it is essential for an understanding of bureaucracy. In East Pakistan, the equivalent source consists of three publications: *Manual for the Inspection of Departments Under Magistrates* (Calcutta: Bengal Government Press, 1925); *The Manual of Rules and Questions for the Inspection of Revenue Offices in the Districts*

(Calcutta: Bengal Secretariat Book Depot, 1919); and *The Bengal Records Manual, 1928* (Calcutta: Bengal Secretariat Book Depot, 1928).

Many senior Pakistani officials trained in the pre-partition ICS tradition maintain that if the Douie *Land Administration Manual,* the Douie *Settlement Manual,* the *District Office Manual,* and equivalent manuals for Bengal were carefully studied and followed by officials, no reform in district administration would be needed. After careful study of these five publications—settlement reports, gazetteers, Douie's two manuals, and the *District Office Manual*—it is difficult to avoid the conclusion that this observation is appropriate.

The disarticulation consequent to partition and various reforms in government leading essentially to decentralization of power have made it difficult to analyze the precise legal responsibilities of district officers and divisional commissioners. Students of government are once again indebted to M. Muzaffer Ahmed, who has almost singlehandedly carried on the tradition of Thomason and Douie in his regard for documentary publication and classification of data. It was Ahmed who ordered the reprinting of Douie's manuals and the *District Office Manual,* which had become all but forgotten in the trauma of partition. Under his direction as additional chief secretary of the Government of West Pakistan in 1961, a two-volume manual classifying all powers and functions of local officers was prepared: Vol. I, *Manual of Powers and Functions of Commissioners and Deputy Commissioners Under Important Heads;* Vol. II, *Manual of Powers and Functions of Commissioners and Deputy Commissioners Under Various Central and Provincial Laws* (Lahore: Government of West Pakistan, 1961). The first volume is a 120-page tabulation arranged to show powers delegated to commissioners and deputy commissioners under various rules in force. The second volume is considerably longer, a 663-page compilation which tabulates chronologically all legal powers vested by the central and provincial governments in commissioners and deputy commissioners. Since the earliest statute cited is for 1861, the tabulation includes over a thousand entries. Both volumes extract from the pertinent legal instrument the nature and scope of power delegated to officers; consequently they are useful as a digest of law bearing on local government.

A report of a seminar, under auspices of the Social Sciences Research Centre, was published as *The Expanding Role of the Public Servant in Pakistan's Democratic Structure* (Lahore: Bureau of National Reconstruction, 1960). One of the earliest attempts at empirical political science research was a series of studies begun under the direction of Gerard Friters at the University of the Panjab. One of the publications, A. H. Aslam, *The Deputy Commissioner* (Lahore: Panjab University Press, 1957), represents a commendable effort to describe the statutory authority and scope of work of the district officer.

Various annual reports released by the provincial governments on such activities as police administration, public instruction, and the administration of jails are valuable sources. Each department is required to publish annual reports of its activities, but this requirement has, since 1947, not been universally met. One of the lacunae in studies of the bureaucracy of Pakistan is descriptions or case studies of district administration. The only document resembling a case study in the dynamics of district administration is the 386-page *Report of the Court of Inquiry Constituted under Punjab Act II of 1954 to Enquire into the Punjab Disturbances of 1953* (Lahore: Superintendent, Government Printing, 1954). More commonly known as the Munir Report, it was prepared by a two-man court consisting of the then chief justice of the Supreme Court, Md. Munir, and the former chief justice of the High Court of West Pakistan, M. R. Kayani. Although the major importance of the Munir Report lies in its analysis of politics and the nature of Islam and an Islamic state—considerations basic to the background of the riots in Lahore which necessitated the declaration of martial law—there is a revealing section (pp. 287–384) on the capacity of district administration to cope with the crisis and on the relations of the district officer, the police, and division and provincial officials. If a list of documents for required reading on Pakistani administration were to be prepared, certainly the Munir Report would rank high on the list.

The changing nature of district administration and the relationship of district, division, and provincial authority is one of the most challenging subjects for subsequent research. No careful, systematic, empirical studies have yet been made. A preliminary study by Richard W. Gable, *Introduction to District Administration,* was published by the newly created department of public administration at the University of the Punjab in 1964. Masihuzzaman, an experienced officer in the CSP cadre, has written a series of illuminating essays on district administration, but these remain in draft form, unpublished. One of the most sophisticated studies of local administration has been done in East Pakistan under auspices of the National Institute of Public Administration in Dacca. This is Md. Anisuzzaman, *The Circle Officer: A Study of His Role* (Dacca, 1963). Probably the best work thus far published is a symposium volume, Inayatullah (ed.), *District Administration in West Pakistan, Its Problems and Challenges* (Peshawar: Academy for Rural Development, 1964). Among the twenty-seven essays are some empirical and theoretical studies of high quality.

District administration cannot be understood without study of village life and agricultural and economic conditions. No such study can start without mention of one of the most perceptive and interesting books written on the subcontinent, Sir Malcolm Darling's *The Punjab Peasant in Prosperity and Debt* (4th ed.; London, 1947). The extent of economic development activities undertaken under British rule in the Punjab, as revealed in Darling's study, should soften the most convinced Anglophobe. The significance of canal irrigation and its impact on flourishing canal colonies such as Lyallpur and Montgomery show the agricultural potential of the Punjab. Because of Darling's unparalleled background, a subsequent report which he prepared after joining the International Labour Office is also informative: Sir Malcolm Darling, *Report on Labour Conditions in Agriculture in Pakistan* (Karachi: Government of Pakistan, Ministry of Labour, 1955). This study is not limited to the Punjab but covers both East and West Pakistan. More recent village studies have begun to appear, although no comprehensive treatments like those of Dube and Marriott for India have yet been done. The economic status of the villager is surveyed in the *First Five Year Plan* and in Chapter IV, *Report of the Food and Agriculture Commission* (Karachi: Government of Pakistan Press, 1960), which concludes that the outlook for the rural peasant is a somber one.

The Board of Economic Inquiry, Punjab, a quasi-governmental organization established in the early twenties under the aegis of British and Indian officers like Sir Malcolm Darling, is an important source for data. The research undertaken extended over the whole range of agricultural economics and, taken together, constitutes a school of economic thought for the Punjab which has been admired by economists in other parts of India and in the Western world as well. The board has published some seventeen Punjab village surveys written under the supervision of officers who had settlement experience. These are invariably competent studies, mainly economic rather than sociological in their bias, and differing from settlement reports and gazetteers in that they concentrate on one village instead of an entire district. An especially useful publication of the board (not a village survey, however) is Abdul Aziz Anwar, *Effects of Partition and Industries in the Border Districts of Lahore and Sialkot* (Lahore: West Pakistan Government Press, 1953). The board's tenth publication stands as a testament to bibliographic precision which characterized the British Raj. *A Guide to Punjab Government Reports and Statistics* by Cyril P. K. Fazal (Lahore: Punjab Government Press, 1939) is a 255-page survey of forty-six reports, classified and cross-indexed with more than ten thousand references. It is a singularly valuable compilation for research. Many of the reports described in Fazal's *Guide* are no longer issued, and no subsequent guide has appeared summarizing currently issued reports.

The Social Sciences Research Centre of the University of the Panjab has published two studies under the general title, *Village Life in Lahore District*. The first of these, *A Study of Selected Sociological Aspects* (of village life in Lahore district), was published in 1959, and the second, *A Study of Selected Political Aspects,* appeared in 1960. Both were published by the Panjab University Press. The Academy for Rural Development in Peshawar, West Pakistan, has also stimulated research on village life.

One of its faculty members, Inayatullah, has published "Weltans-
chauung of the Punjab Villager" in *Baessler-Archiv*, Neue Folge,
VII (1960), 165–180, and "Caste, Patti and Faction in the Life of a
Punjab Village," *Sociologus*, VIII (1958), 170–186. Inayatullah
and Q. M. Shafi have also written *Dynamics of Development in a
Pakistani Village* (Peshawar: Academy for Rural Development,
1963). Not a typical village study, the volume explores the progress of development activities in a village near Lahore at two
different times, a year apart.

The best literary account of life and culture of East Pakistan is
Nirad C. Chaudhuri, *Autobiography of an Unknown Indian* (London, 1951). The East Pakistan Academy for Village Development
in Comilla has initiated a series of reports called "Technical
Publications" mostly on agriculture but some bearing on village
life, e.g., S. A. Qadir, *Village Dhanishwar: Three Generations of
Man-Land Adjustment in an East Pakistan Village* (Comilla,
1960). Qadir's Dhanishwar study is a fairly sophisticated analysis
derived from rigorously compiled empirical data. The institution
of the *chaukidar,* or watchman, a particularly important local
government activity in East Pakistan, is comprehensively studied
in a pre-partition report which still has relevance, *Report of the
Chaukidari Enquiry Committee, 1938–40* (Alipore: Superintendent Government Printing, Bengal, 1940).

The Punjab, as one of the most developed areas of India, has
been the subject of a considerable amount of historical research,
much of it undertaken under auspices of the Punjab government
which, at the time of partition had published more than twenty
major historical monographs. Those specifically relevant to the
study of administration are: Ram Lal Handa, *A History of the
Development of the Judiciary in the Punjab (1846–1884)*
(Lahore: Punjab Government, 1927); Daya Krishna Kapur, *A
History of the Development of the Judiciary in the Punjab
(1884–1926)*, (Lahore: Punjab Government, 1928); Amar Nath,
*The Development of Local Self-Government in the Punjab,
1849–1900* (Lahore: Punjab Government, 1929); R. R. Sethi, *John
Lawrence as Commissioner of the Jullundur Doab (1846–1849)*
(Lahore: Punjab Government, 1930). The deeds of a hundred

European adventurers who served as officers and in other capacities in the kingdoms of the Punjab are recorded in C. Grey, *European Adventurers in Northern India, 1785 to 1849* (Lahore: Superintendent, Government Printing, Punjab, 1929). Of similar interest is J. Hutchison and J. Ph. Vogel, *History of the Panjab Hill States* (2 vols.; Lahore: Superintendent, Government Printing, Punjab, 1933), which deals with the quasi-independent states outside British India.

To some extent the extreme compartmentalization of the bureaucracy of Pakistan is a reflection of the caste structure of the Punjab, an analysis of which can be found in Sir Denzil Ibbetson, *Punjab Castes* (Lahore: Superintendent of Government Printing, Punjab, 1916). Ibbetson's work is a reprint of his chapter in the *Report of the Census of the Punjab* published in 1883 and was long regarded as one of the leading works on caste. Ibbetson and his critics are discussed in the 1907 edition of the *Imperial Gazetteer of India* (I, 336–348).

The creation of the canal colonies of Montgomery, Lyallpur, and Shahpur in the Punjab raised many problems of administration of land and water. Minute regulations for the solution of these problems are given in a series of colony manuals and supplements. The most recent revision of the manual proper, F. B. Wace, *Punjab Colony Manual* (Lahore: Superintendent, Government Printing, 1934), gives an excellent history of the colonies. There are six supplements.

The reports of the *Census of India,* started in 1891 and taken decennially thereafter, are of great importance. The first *Census of Pakistan* was taken in 1951; the second, taken early in 1961, is published in separate pamphlets for each district.

Several miscellaneous documents, which are still to be found in libraries and less often in the stock rooms of the government presses, reveal the pattern of official behavior under British rule and thus help explain some of the attitudes of modern bureaucracy of Pakistan. One such document is *Memorandum on the Subject of Social and Official Intercourse Between European Officers in the Punjab and Indians* (corrected up to October 31, 1922). An appendix includes the Minute of Sir John Malcolm, dated June 28, 1821, in which he decries arrogant official behavior and asserts that there is no superiority of one race over another.

In the Punjab, the raw data of provincial administration were formerly presented without extensive analysis or commentary in a series of annual reports called "Punjab Administration Reports." The last of these was published in 1936 for 1934–1935. A similar annual report was published in East Pakistan by the Revenue Department, *Report on Administration of Bengal, 1935–36* (Calcutta: Bengal Government Press, 1936) but no subsequent issues have appeared.

Administration of Special Areas

Government of tribal, semi-tribal, or unsettled areas is a neglected aspect of research on bureaucracy and one for which few documents are available. Some of these areas are in a transitional stage from tribal to settled society. Transition is being accelerated by the impact of developments such as the hydroelectric project at Warsak in the former Northwest Frontier Province and at Kaptai in East Pakistan, and by construction near Kashmir of the Indus link canals financed by an international consortium under auspices of the International Bank for Reconstruction and Development. The manner in which progression occurs from tribal organization and values to the acceptance of Western values and a bureaucratized social order is a significant subject for investigation. The Northwest Frontier in West Pakistan is one of the few remaining areas in the world where the process of bureaucratization as described for other societies in earlier periods by Franz Michael, Owen Lattimore, and Karl Wittfogel can be analyzed. Interaction of bureaucratic influences and frontier tribal norms has been a continual process. Analytically, areas undergoing this transition can be classified into three different groups, based on the degree of interaction of frontier norms with the bureaucratic apparatus. The two classes at each extreme—those where maximum and minimum absorption has taken place—should be mentioned first. The middle range group, which is the largest geographically and the most challenging to research, merits more extended analysis last.

The first group includes those areas where the transition to bureaucratic controls is nominally complete. In this group, local feudal ruling classes and judicial systems have been absorbed into the formal apparatus by which the whole of the nation is governed. Former princely states such as Khairpur and Bahawalpur, for example, now come under the regular bureaucratic administration of divisions and districts common throughout most of Pakistan.

A second group, at the other extreme, consists of several small princely states whose internal administration is entirely in the hands of ruling feudal chiefs. Although incorporated into West Pakistan by the Establishment of West Pakistan Act of 1955, and although the executive authority of the provincial governor may extend to these states, in reality their internal administration has remained outside the conventional district system. These are Amb, Chitral, Swat, and Hunza. Dir is in a somewhat different category since the governor in 1960 ordered the organization of an advisory council to assist the ruler. The most important of these, Swat, ruled by the *Wali*, is the site of important Buddhist religious institutions now being excavated. Since the promotion of tourism, Swat is the most accessible of the four states and can be reached in a four-hour drive in cars which meet air flights at the Peshawar airport. The pattern of government in Swat is the subject of an anthropological study by Frederik Barth, *Political Leadership Among Swat Pathans* (London, 1959). Some research has been carried on by John Honigmann, an anthropologist at the University of North Carolina, but has not been published. In a somewhat different category is the state of Hunza in the northernmost part of West Pakistan near Kashmir. It is the least accessible of all such tribal states. Although administratively part of the political agency of Gilgit, the authority of the ruling chief is paramount and is exercised personally by the *Mir*, whose government staff is familial rather than bureaucratic. Hunza is of particular importance not only because of its strategic location as a borderland of the Himalayas, but also because its population belongs almost entirely to the Ismaili sect of Islam whose spiritual head is Karim, the Agha Khan. The remoteness of Hunza has attracted seekers of

Shangri-La, and in recent years it has been an area of interest to Britons and Americans interested in natural methods of agriculture and their relation to health and longevity. Hunza is regarded as a model in these matters because of its agricultural and dietary practices and its almost complete isolation from the outside world. Several books, some privately printed, some eccentric, and all of dubious scientific validity but of interests nonetheless, have been written about Hunza. Among them are John T. Tobe, *Hunza: Adventures in a Land of Paradise* (Emmaus, Pa.: Rodale Books, 1960); John Clark, *Hunza, Lost Kingdom of the Himalayas* (New York: Funk & Wagnalls, 1956); Barbara Mans, *High Road to Hunza* (London: Faber & Faber, 1958); Jerome I. Rodale, *The Healthy Hunzas* (Emmaus, Pa.: Rodale Press, 1948); Allen Banik and Renee Taylor, *Hunza Land* (Long Beach, Calif., Whitehorn Publishing Co., 1960). Such books as these would not ordinarily appear in a survey of this kind, yet so little is known of the almost inaccessible state of Hunza that their inclusion here appears to be not totally without merit. In this group of states the authority of the feudal ruler (variously designated *Wali, Nawab, Mir, Khan, Nizam*) is paramount, although contact with the ruler and the bureaucracy of Pakistan is maintained through a political agent usually in residence in an adjacent area. Although these states are not entirely unaffected by social and bureaucratic forces of the outside world, such influences are minimal and have affected only the small ruling groups which insulates the population at large from contact with the few outsiders who may visit the areas.

The third group of areas in which maximum interplay of tribal and settled values is found are the Pathan and Baluchi tribal areas of the Northwest Frontier Province and Baluchistan and the three districts of Mirpur, Punch, and Muzafferabad in that part of Kashmir held by Pakistan. The latter area, whose government is officially known as the Azad (Free) Government of Jammu and Kashmir, is difficult to place in any category. Its inhabitants are Kashmiri and not really organized on a tribal basis like the Pathans. Its status is not quite clear because it is intertwined with the larger issue of the international dispute over the state of Jammu and Kashmir. The three districts are popularly known as

Azad Kashmir, which is organized much as a sovereign state with its own president and cabinet, flying its own flag. Unlike the states described above however, Azad Kashmir has integrated most of the political reforms of Pakistan into its own system. Its orthodox district administration is influenced by the fact that it has sent officers to be trained at the Civil Service Academy in Lahore. It has also adopted the Basic Democracies Scheme of Pakistan, both for rural development and for electoral purposes. This electoral base reveals an important connection between Pakistan proper and Azad Kashmir, namely, the presence of several thousand Kashmiri refugees living in Pakistan in areas adjacent to Kashmir. These refugees are organized into Basic Democracy electoral units and exercise franchise in Azad Kashmir elections. In the 1961 election for the presidency of Azad Kashmir, for example, half of the 2,400 basic democrats elected in Azad Kashmir were representatives of Kashmiri refugees actually resident in Pakistan. A constitutional relationship between Pakistan and Azad Jammu and Kashmir is suggested by Article 241 of the 1962 Constitution of Pakistan which provides that, for purposes of holding office in the service of Pakistan, persons deriving their nationality from the State of Azad Jammu and Kashmir are deemed to be citizens of Pakistan. Another link is the reporting of decisions of the High Court of Azad Jammu and Kashmir in the unofficial, commercial legal reporting services of Pakistan. This linkage extends somewhat to judicial review. Although the courts of Pakistan ordinarily have no jurisdiction over the High Court of Azad Jammu and Kashmir, death sentences issued by it are subject to final confirmation by the President of Pakistan.[6] The international question of the status of Jammu and Kashmir has received considerable attention in books and journals but the political, administrative, and social circumstances of Azad Jammu and Kashmir have not been studied. Few foreigners have been allowed to visit the area. Because of the delicate international implications of these areas, neither Hunza, Azad Jammu and Kashmir, nor certain tribal regions may be visited without prior approval of the Ministry of

[6] Letter to the author from the Chief Justice of Pakistan, October 20, 1964.

Kashmir Affairs which has in Peshawar a political resident for Northern Areas, whose territory includes Gilgit and Hunza.

It is on the Pathan and Baluchi tribal areas of the former Northwest Frontier Province and Baluchistan that the issue of interaction of tribal and bureaucratic norms is most clearly focused. The institutional matrix is criminal law, but the impact on bureaucratic norms is important as well. There is a jostling of three juridical normative spheres: (1) that of Western criminal law embodying such features as fixed rules of evidence and right to be defended by legally trained persons, (2) that of tribal law, based on usage and values of tribal honor and retribution, (3) an institutionalized blend of the other two spheres. The phenomenon is fairly well-documented, has been an important part of martial law ideology, and is a lively issue of discussion in contemporary constitutional law. For these reasons, the subject is more dynamic and more amenable to research than the other two categories in which minimum and maximum interaction has taken place. The area here considered adjoins Afghanistan and Iran and is occupied by Pushtu-speaking tribes ethnically and culturally related to the Afghans across the border. The tribesmen are independent, orthodox Muslims, with immense pride in their own culture and respected as fighters. They were not controlled by the British, but their affairs were administered loosely by political agents through a variety of systems ranging from those allowing complete autonomy to those in which various laws of the "settled" areas were applicable. Nomenclature for these areas has changed since British rule, and it appears best to use here the convenient generic term "tribal areas" which is in common use. The Establishment of West Pakistan Act, 1955, first introduced the term "special areas" and this was substantially followed in Article 218 of the 1956 Constitution. Article 223 of the 1962 Constitution, however, reverts to usage of the older term "tribal areas." [7] The transitional yet

---

[7] *The Report of the Provincial Administration Commission* (Lahore: Government Printing, West Pakistan, February, 1960) gives a technical classification of tribal areas, which is not used by the 1962 Constitution. In this essay, I have oversimplified a very complex system of classifying areas on the basis of tribal origins, customs, and extent of applicability of various laws by using the generic terms "tribal" and "settled." This is more a device of expediency than of accuracy.

distinctive character of these areas and their changing relationship with bureaucratic and legal values in the remainder of Pakistan are indicated by the provision that no central or provincial law shall apply to a tribal area unless the president or governor so directs. The president and governor may, within their respective competences, make regulations for the tribal areas and may declare that an area is no longer in the tribal category. A recent example of a presidential decision to extend the provisions of a central government law to the tribal areas is Tribal Areas (Official Secrets) Regulation, 1963, published in the *Gazette of Pakistan, Extraordinary,* December 30, 1963, extending the provisions of the Official Secrets Act to the tribal areas. This is merely one example illustrative of the expanding and contracting contours of two spheres of validity acting upon each other.

General, secondary works relating to the tribal areas of the Northwest Frontier are Khalid bin Sayeed, "Pathan Regionalism," *South Atlantic Quarterly,* LXII (1964), 478–506. Sayeed had access to unpublished papers of Sir George Cunningham, one of the last British governors of the Northwest Frontier Province. His study makes judicious use of these papers and includes an excellent two-page map showing distribution of the Pathans. Wayne Wilcox' book, *Pakistan: The Consolidation of a Nation* (New York, 1963), is an analysis of the integration of former princely states and certain tribal areas. James W. Spain's *The Way of the Pathans* (London, 1962) is an informative account of tribal lore and customs. Peter Mayne's *Journey to the Pathans* (New York, 1955) and Sir William Barton's *India's Northwest Frontier* (London, 1939) are also instructive for background reading. An illuminating study of behavior whose feudal qualities gave rise to the Frontier Crimes Regulation of 1901 can be found in G. R. Elsmie, *Notes on Some of the Characteristics of Crime and Criminals in the Peshawar Division of the Punjab* (Lahore, 1884). An account of other problems, especially of British control in the area, is Lt. Col. G. L. Mallam, "The N. W. Frontier Problem," *Journal of the United Service Institution of India,* LXXVI (1946), 387–392. For a history of the Pathans and an authoritative analysis of the problems of government in the tribal areas, Sir Olaf Caroe's *The*

Pathans (London, 1958) is a comprehensive work. The court decisions in the Dosso, Abdul Rauf, and Sumundar cases, discussed below, are indispensable analyses of the characteristics of tribal society which gave rise to the special laws governing the area. Sind, the last major region of India to come under British domination, and Baluchistan, which like Sind has many characteristics of tribal society, are the subjects of two well-written histories by a former ICS officer who was assigned to those areas: H. T. Lambrick, *Sir Charles Napier of Sind* (Oxford, 1952), and *John Jacob of Jacobabad* (London, 1960).

The specific problem of changing norms of criminal law derives from the statute known as the Frontier Crimes Regulation of 1901 with amendments. The text of the FCR, as it is known in common parlance, with all amendments and interpretations is included in R. N. Iyer and A. R. Khosla (eds.), *The Punjab and Northwest Frontier Province Acts*, Annotated, Vol. I (Madras: Madras Law Journal Office, 1934). Although the FCR is a mere seventeen pages in length, the case law interpreting it is voluminous. Background of the concept of tribal law in the Northwest Frontier Province can be found in the *Report of the Frontier Regulations Enquiry Committee* (New Delhi: Government Printing, 1931). This committee is commonly known, after the name of the chairman, as the Niamat Ullah Committee. Current problems in frontier law are discussed in Chapter XXIV of the *Report of the Law Reform Commission 1958–59* (Karachi: Manager, Government Publications, 1959) and in the well-known Dosso case discussed later in this essay. Neither the report nor the Dosso case, however, deals with the theoretical issues of diffusion of juridical norms. The FCR permitted the deputy commissioner to refer disputes likely to cause a blood feud, murder, breach of peace, and other named crimes for settlement to a *jirga,* or council of elders, to be appointed by him. While the action of the *jirga* was reviewable by the deputy commissioner and the commissioner, no appeal could be made to the regular civil courts. Legal practitioners were not allowed to take part in the *jirga* proceedings. The *jirga* was not obliged to follow evidence laws and decided cases in accordance with tribal values of retribution. Critics of the FCR most disliked

Section 40 which empowered the district officer to require a
person to execute a bond for good behavior when it was felt
necessary to "prevent dissemination of sedition." This made it
possible to suppress public liberties arbitrarily without due process of law. Critics also felt that the immense police powers
inherent in this provision were one of the reasons for government's
decision in 1962 to extend the FCR to the whole of West Pakistan.

Under the 1901 FCR, the governor of what since 1955 is West
Pakistan had authority to extend or withdraw its validity in areas
within the Northwest Frontier Province. This authority was seldom used. Hence, in 1960 the geographical area in which the FCR
was operative did not differ much from the original area mentioned in the 1901 enactment. This included the six political
agencies of Khyber, Malakand, Mohmand, Kurram, North and
South Waziristan, and certain strips of territory along the districts
of Hazara, Dera Ismail Khan, Kohat, Bannu, and Peshawar. It also
was operative (with some modifications in the *jirga*) in most of
Baluchistan, including Quetta.

In 1960, by two extensions ordered under authority of the 1901
enactment, Kalat, Kharan, Makran, Lasbela, and Mianwali were
included.[8] It was in 1962 that the conflict between Western and
tribal juridical norms was joined by enactment by the Central
Government of Frontier Crimes (Amendment) Ordinance VIII of
1962 permitting the West Pakistan governor to extend the FCR at
his discretion to the whole of West Pakistan. Under this new
authority, the governor extended the validity of the FCR to the
entire divisions of Peshawar, Kohat, Dera Ismail Khan, and
Quetta, to the districts of Mianwali, Dera Ghazi Khan, and Lasbela, and to the Nasirabad subdivision of Jacobabad district.[9] The
governor subsequently announced that he would be guided by
requests from district councils in any subsequent extension of the
FCR. The spatial validity was further extended to the districts of

[8] Frontier Crimes Regulation (West Pakistan Extension) Ordinance XXVII,
1960, *Gazette of West Pakistan, Extraordinary,* August 23, 1960; Frontier Crimes
Regulation (West Pakistan, Second Extension) Ordinance XXIII, 1960, *ibid.,*
December 13, 1960.
[9] Frontier Crimes Regulation (Amendment) Ordinance VIII, 1962, *Gazette of
Pakistan, Extraordinary,* February 15, 1962.

Sargodha and Sukkur and withdrawn from certain areas in Larkana and Sukkur.[10] These extensions had three significant effects. They increased the number of persons subject to the provisions of FCR from roughly four million to about seven million. More importantly, jurisdiction was extended to classes of people no longer classified as tribal in the sense intended by the original 1901 regulation. The spatial extensions drew into the FCR ambit parts of city, town, and "settled" populations who no longer observed tribal customs and who no longer lived in tribal organization. Moreover, the FCR was made applicable to residents of areas where it did not apply who committed offenses in an area where it did apply. It was not surprising, then, that the legal community and Western-oriented elites denounced the extension with vigor, asserting that it meant retrogression to "primitive" norms for persons who had long lived under Western criminal law. The third potential effect was the use of FCR jurisdiction as a means of deprivation of public liberties by avoiding due process of law and judicial review. While records are not available to substantiate what many of the critics of the FCR assert to be true, there are suggestions that the potential for such use may be a warranted cause for anxiety. In December, 1962, it was reported in the National Assembly that Maulana Qazi Abdul Karim was arrested under Section 40 presumably for publicly criticizing a statement made by Sir Zafrullah Khan concerning the founder of the Qadiani sect.[11] Presumably, if this arrest did occur under Section 40, it might have been to prevent "dissemination of sedition," since comparable criticism made by orthodox Muslims concerning the Qadiani provoked the Punjab disturbances of 1953. Another aspect of potentially oppressive use of the FCR was the broad discretion in which was imbedded the right of the deputy commissioner to assign a case to a *jirga* rather than leave it for trial by

[10] Frontier Crimes Regulation (West Pakistan Amendment) Ordinance XII, 1962, *Gazette of West Pakistan, Extraordinary*, April 19, 1962. A review of extensions and withdrawals of the FCR subsequent to the basic amendment of February, 1962, and citations to relevant administrative notifications may be found in *Masud Ahmad* v. *The State*, PLD 1962 Lah. 878.

[11] National Assembly of Pakistan, *Debates*, December 6, 1962, p. 514. Discussion in the assembly was curtailed by the fact that the case, having been referred to an ordinary court, was *sub judice*.

ordinary courts. Chief Justice A. R. Cornelius suggested that the jurisdiction of ordinary courts was being avoided to an increasing extent by assignment of cases to *jirgas* on the grounds of expediency.[12] Thus, in the Nawab Gul case he deplored the reference of accused persons to a *jirga* when there appeared to be no case against them.

The origins of the 1962 move to extend the concepts of the FCR throughout West Pakistan are not precisely known. President Ayub had often spoken of the need for simple justice quickly meted out. In an address before the West Pakistan High Court Bar Association on April 27, 1962, he defended the ordinance he had promulgated two months earlier allowing extension of the FCR. He referred to Penderel Moon's *Strangers in India* (London, 1944) as an "illuminating little book" which supported his view that the process of justice had to be based on the values paramount in society. Moon had been a British member of the Indian Civil Service who saw service both in the Frontier Province and served as finance minister in the princely state of Bahawalpur. Moon was not alone among Britons who respected the process of justice achieved by the tribal *jirga*. His conclusion that it was futile to apply British legal norms to litigation arising from totally different societal values was also dealt with in Philip Woodruff's novel, *Call the Next Witness* (London, 1947). Sir Olaf Caroe, last British governor of the Northwest Frontier Province before independence, writes in *The Pathans* that the *jirga* system is most suitable for the tribal areas because "the law of one civilization cannot be applied to a society with utterly different standards without the most dire results."

While the President's ground for extending the FCR concepts seems to be based on the achievement of a positive relationship between reigning norms and institutions, Chief Justice Cornelius, in agreement with the President, has somewhat broadened justification of the extension. Agreeing that there is a need for normative correlation, he suggests that there are also considerations of national pride in seeking indigenous norms, and implies the need for eliciting Islamic norms and blending them with a

[12] *The State* v. *Nawab Gul*, PLD 1963 SC 270.

reconstructed apparatus of justice. In an address to staff officers of the Pakistan Army at general headquarters in Rawalpindi July 11, 1962,[13] Cornelius maintained that the juridical order must be fully adapted to the understanding and sentiment of the people, and that the English legal system did not meet that requirement. He held that the primary task for a newly established independent government is that of "repairing the damage done to the national character in the years of subjection," that the first requisite for this purpose is finding the "nation's true roots," to be followed by restoration of local liberties and powers "as nearly as possible on traditional lines" operating under "age-old incentives and controls." Of all these powers, judicial power is the most important and must be exercised by local communities in accordance with their own values. Not all the maxims upon which British legal concepts are based are universally true; indeed, many are in opposition to basic concepts in vogue "for twenty centuries and more in the countries of the Middle East, to which [Pakistan] . . . by religion and culture [is] more closely allied." Cornelius answered the critics of the extension of the Frontier Crimes Regulations who insist that the British system is universally regarded as one of the best systems of justice. This, he insists, is merely a superficial answer to the problems coming from judges and lawyers, who as beneficiaries of the system, "can be relied upon to make something of a fight to maintain their livelihood."

A voluminous body of case law has interpreted the old Frontier Crimes Regulation. Principles evolved rested on the assumption that two juridical spheres existed concurrently, each based on different concepts, yet each influencing the other to some degree. In *Sumundar v. The Crown*, 1954 1 F.C.R. 235, the Supreme Court held that it could not accept an appeal from a commissioner on the ground of absence of due process in the *jirga* proceedings, since these proceedings were based on different concepts of justice. Cornelius in *Mohammad Akram v. The State*, PLD 1963 SC 373,

[13] A. R. Cornelius, "Restoration of Judicial Responsibility to the People" in PLD 1963 Journal, 1–13. Cornelius emphasized the need for codification of Muslim law to facilitate its penetration into the total legal order in an address before the Pakistan Legal Aid Society in Dacca in March, 1964. Text is available in *ibid.*, 1964 Journal, 125–132.

reaffirmed that the court cannot scrutinize the *jirga's* procedure. Yet the interaction of the two juridical norms is indicated by his comment in the same decision that the court must restrict its concern to the process by which a case is diverted into the ambit of the *jirga* system. Thus, the interaction here occurred specifically at the point of movement of an issue from one sphere to another. Once such transfer was made, no further application of norms outside tribal norms was allowed. When efforts were made to combine the two juridical systems by appointing legally trained magistrates as council instead of tribal chiefs in accordance with accepted Pathan, Baluch, or other usage, they were struck down by the Supreme Court (*The Crown* v. *Ghulam Muhammad Khan,* 1956 F.C.R. 90) on the ground that the provision allowing this was an *ultra vires* effort to amend the FCR.

Soon after the first (1956) Constitution had been promulgated with its specified fundamental rights made justiciable, the validity of two distinct juridical norms operating within a single national state whose constitution guaranteed equal rights for all its citizens was challenged. As early as 1956, the High Court of West Pakistan in *Khair Muhammad Khan* v. *Government of West Pakistan,* PLD 1956 Lah. 668, had asserted that the FCR's denial of the right to engage counsel was inconsistent with the article of the Constitution which must now be a part of all laws relating to trial for any offense. In *Abdul Rauf* v. *NWFP Government,* PLD 1958 Pesh. 73, the question of discrimination against classes of persons was argued. While the majority held that law need not be uniform throughout the country and that classification is not unconstitutional, Abdul Hamid dissented from the majority by reasoning that different laws may be made for geographical areas but not for classes of persons. A major assault against the constitutionality of the Frontier Crimes Regulation came in *The State* v. *Dosso* (1958 2 P.S.C.R. 180), in which the Supreme Court grouped together several appeals from the high courts which had ruled that the FCR was invalidated by the constitutional guarantee of equality before the law. The issue of the constitutionality of the FCR became lost in the larger issue of legitimacy of martial law, but Cornelius in a partially dissenting opinion defended the juridical concepts of the FCR. In a significant dictum he also defended the appointment of magistrates on the *jirga* as "a provision [which] may be one in aid of gradual modernisation of ideas of justice in the areas concerned." This dictum is probably not at variance with the 1956 Ghulam Muhammad Khan judgment, with which Cornelius concurred, since the substantive issue of the validity of using magistrates was not reached in that case.

Even as early as 1931 the Niamat Ullah Committee had attacked the *jirga* system. While not recommending complete abolition, the committee proposed that criminal cases be tried by a trained judge with the *jirga* sitting as jury, and that in civil cases the deputy commissioner be given extensive power to infuse Western norms into the total trial procedure. The most vigorous attack against the system came from a report submitted on August 14, 1958, one week after the proclamation of martial law, which went unnoticed in the excitement of the coup d'état. Until it was referred to a year later in the report of the Law Reform Commission, it was little known, and since only fifty copies were printed, its accessibility was limited. This document was the 44-page *Report—Quetta-Kalat Judicial System* by the Quetta-Kalat Laws Commission (Lahore: Superintendent, Government Printing, 1958). The commission, appointed by the Governor of West Pakistan, was composed of Justice Sheikh Abdul Hamid (chairman) and Kazi Ghazanfar Hussain. The two commissioners saw no merit in continuing the *jirga* system in Quetta and Kalat and urged its replacement by the civil and criminal codes derived from English law and in force in the settled areas of Pakistan. They reasoned that the structure of tribal responsibility had deteriorated, that tyranny by tribal chiefs was extolled as tribal justice by the British only because they were compelled to depend on tribal leadership patterns. Finally, they insisted that modern constitutionalism demanded uniformity in the application of laws throughout the nation. One of the most interesting elements in the well-written report on Quetta-Kalat laws is the inclusion of written opinion solicited from Sir Olaf Caroe, whose earlier favorable impressions of the *jirga* system had often been cited from his book, *The Pathans*. Although Caroe said that the *jirga* system should be

retained in some parts of Baluchistan, he concluded in his statement that British administration was "too static in the treatment of
these problems" and that acceptance of simple tribalism is not
enough. Accepting the implications in this remark of the need for a
changing system, Sheikh Abdul Hamid and Kazi Ghazanfar Hussain conclude that the government should complete what Caroe
said was left undone, i.e., the *jirga* system should be abolished
completely and replaced by the regular courts.

The Law Reform Commission of 1959 found opinion in Pakistan
sharply divided on the issue of retention of the *jirga* system. It
reported that the intelligentsia, business class, and lawyers were
against the system, while most witnesses in rural areas or having
tribal associations favored it with some modification. The commission concluded that replacement of the *jirga* system with regular
law should be the ideal, but conditions in some areas did not
justify such a change yet. The commissioners suggested retention
of the tribal system in most tribal areas but with certain controls
by the deputy commissioner over selection of *jirga* members and
the securing of evidence. They urged also that lawyers be allowed
to appear at least at the revisional procedure before the division
commissioner. Thus, the Law Reforms Commission identified
itself with the "transitionist" concept of the 1931 Niamat Ullah
Committee rather than with the "abolitionist" views of the Sheikh
Abdul Hamid Commission.

Subsequently, the Constitution Commission of 1962 found that
57 per cent of those questioned felt that the Frontier Crimes
Regulation should be abrogated. But the commission recommended that the FCR be kept in force in those areas where it
would be felt needed. It reconciled this with fundamental rights
by treating retention of the FCR as one of two exceptions to
fundamental rights, the other being land reforms in West Pakistan
introduced under martial law.

Criticism of the concepts underlying the FCR and of its extension had its effect. In 1963, a new law, the West Pakistan Criminal
Law (Amendment) Act VII of 1963 [14] modified both jurisdictional

---

[14] Text in *Gazette of West Pakistan, Extraordinary*, April 19, 1963; available
also in pamphlet form published by Law Book House, Lahore.

and substantive aspects of this phenomenon. The new criminal
law was made applicable to the whole of West Pakistan except the
tribal areas in which the FCR before the 1962 extension was
applicable. As in the 1901 FCR, only some crimes related to blood
feuds come within its scope. In its substantive provisions the new
law lies between the FCR and British-derived criminal law found
elsewhere in Pakistan. Neither the *jirga* as an institution, nor the
process, nor the scope of jurisdiction remain as under the 1901
regulation. The several changes made are a meaningful instance of
the manner in which norms permeate an indigenous structure and
may accelerate detribalization and bureaucratize tribal society.

The 1963 statute vests authority for transferring a case to its
jurisdiction in the division commissioner rather than the deputy
commissioner. Reasons for the transfer must be recorded in
writing. Both of these modifications will compel restraint in moving cases to the tribunal system and probably diminish the operative scope of the tribal judicial system. Cases involving government officials, and the crimes of adultery and abduction, have
been withdrawn from the sphere of indigenous law and transferred to "settled" criminal law. The composition of the tribunal
(formerly called *jirga*) has been drastically changed. The president must be a magistrate and the remaining four members must
be drawn from a panel of from thirty to fifty persons appointed by
the commissioner considering "integrity, education and social
status." The criterion of education, combined with a provision
allowing legal practitioners to appear in defense of the accused,
rather dramatically injects aspects of Western norms into the
process. Another difference is the requirement that a record of
proceedings be kept in English in cases in which a fine exceeding
Rs. 200 or a sentence of imprisonment has been made. Maintaining the record in English may have the effect of detaching the
process further from tribal values and invigorating its conceptual
base with Western values. Finally, the new law has no equivalent
of the controversial Section 40 of the FCR, hence cannot be easily
used arbitrarily to suppress free speech.

The 1963 West Pakistan Criminal Law (Amendment) Act does
not necessarily result in a retrogression to tribal justice, as some

critics continue to insist. The dynamics of interaction of legal norms are far more complicated. There are now three spheres of law operating concurrently: (1) The 1901 Frontier Crimes Regulation which is applicable to the same six agencies and strips of territory as it was before the 1962 extension. In these areas, the *jirga* system and other FCR provisions are in effect. (2) The 1963 West Pakistan Criminal Law (Amendment) Act, which is now applicable to all of West Pakistan except the six agencies and strips of territory. Certain crimes relating to blood feuds, but excluding abduction and adultery, can be tried under this law by a process which has aspects of both the FCR and British criminal law. (3) British-derived criminal law utilizing the regular court system and rules of evidence operative in East Pakistan for all offenses under the British-derived criminal code and in West Pakistan (except the tribal areas) for offenses under the criminal code except those related to blood feuds. It would be more accurate to say that the spatial validity of a blend of Western and tribal norms has expanded, but the normative content of that sphere has changed so that it resembles more the sphere of Western juridical norms.

Although in 1965 the three juridical spheres continued to operate concurrently, the FCR again received a serious setback, this time from the judiciary. Previously the constitutional validity of a different apparatus of justice had been upheld by the courts and even the Constitution Commission and the Commission on Law Reform had not disputed the regulation's constitutionality. But early in 1965 a division bench of five judges of the West Pakistan High Court held the major provisions of the FCR inconsistent with fundamental rights of the 1962 Constitution (*Malik Muhammad Usman* v. *The State*, PLD 1965 Lah. 229). The decision rested mainly on the provisions for assigning particular cases to *jirga* proceedings without the guidance of settled principles, an action which the courts consistently regarded as subject to their review. This procedure for the transfer of cases from one sphere to another was held to be repugnant to the due process of law and equal protection of the laws provisions (Fundamental Rights 1 and 15) of the Constitution. Whether this decision will be upheld by the Supreme Court remains to be seen.

Even less attention has been given to the quarter of a million hillmen of the Chittagong Hill Tracts in East Pakistan. Largely Buddhist in religion with a family structure similar to that of the Hindus, the hillmen of this area live in a separate district within the regular bureaucratic structure of the province. The deputy commissioner is a Bengali officer of the CSP. Although the superstructure of district administration has been established in the area, it blends with local custom as it approaches the level of *mouza* (group of villages) and the village. Detribalization is not occurring through the medium of law, for there is little crime and litigation among these people. On the other hand, the area is being industrialized rather rapidly by such projects as the Kaptai Dam on the Karnafuli River, plywood and paper mills, and construction of a highway into Chittagong. The infusion of values from the adjacent "settled" Muslim Bengali areas, then, will occur through economic influences. The radiation of this influence to social and bureaucratic organization and comparison of this mode of detribalization with the same process on the Northwest Frontier affords an opportunity for a study in culture change. Little research has been done on this area. There is a carefully written monograph by Pierre Bessaignet, *Tribesmen of the Chittagong Hill Tracts* (Dacca: Asiatic Society of Pakistan, 1958). It was the society's first publication.

Problems of the interaction of norms in the context of detribalization are not limited to Pakistan. But they do appear in sharp focus on the Northwest Frontier and in East Pakistan in a manner amenable to comparative analysis.

Rural Development

Rural development both as concept and as practice is of significance to the study of bureaucracy for several reasons. First, the administrative apparatus for rural development is itself a bureaucratic entity, even though its style, which elicits local initiative by persuasion and education, is presumed to be non-bureaucratic. Secondly, the existence of this apparatus, whose objectives of economic growth compete with and overlap those of the orthodox bureaucracy, poses issues of co-ordination which are crucial. Thirdly, rural development practice has undergone several major shifts in Pakistan as it has sought a mode of accommodating to the traditional power-oriented bureaucracy of district administration. The nature of this accommodation and experiments to achieve maximum developmental effectiveness are valid subjects for research. Fourthly, the rural development movement has its immediate derivation in the land-grant, extension service concepts of the United States, and its ideology and practice in Pakistan have continually been reinvigorated by American experience and by substantial financial and technical assistance and consultative services. The diffusional means are important issues for research. Lastly, the movement lends itself to instructive comparative analysis, since it has assumed different forms and achieved different results in the two provinces.

The historical and conceptual antecedents of the rural development movement can be traced to British rule in India. The reports of the three Indian famine commissions called attention to the need for a co-ordinated attack on the social milieu of crop yield: *Report of the Indian Famine Commission, 1880* (3 parts; London, 1880); *Report of the Indian Famine Commission, 1901* (Calcutta: Superintendent of Government Printing, India, 1901); *Report of the Indian Famine Commission, 1898* (Simla: Government Central Printing Office, 1898). The Cooperative Credit Societies Act of 1904 and the *Report of the Committee on Cooperation of 1914–15* (Maclagan Committee) also were highly pertinent to this subject.

As early as the 1890's Rabindranath Tagore urged reconstruction of the village, and his essays on this theme are eloquent philosophical justification of the virtues of rural life. His programs at Santiniketan and at Sriniketan were efforts in which he sought to practice what he had advocated. Tagore's essays, "A Poet's School," "City and Village," and "Cooperation," reprinted in a collection of his writings, *Towards Universal Man* (Bombay, 1961) are among the best expressions of his views on rural uplift.

His essay, "Society and State" read in 1904, and his program for the reorganization of rural Bengal stimulated by the 1905 partition of that province were further measures by which he sought to implement his views. While in Bengal the chief impetus for rural improvement came from rumination and poetic inspiration and from outside government initiative; in the Punjab the movement was from within government and was characterized by programs of action by energetic, practical British administrators. *The Report of the Royal Commission on Agriculture* by the Linlithgow Commission (Bombay: Central Government Press, 1928) emphasized the need for a many-sided attack on village problems and singled out the Village Guide system pioneered by F. L. Brayne in the Gurgaon district of the Punjab for special praise. Since then the nomenclature of the movement has changed with new words and concepts, such as rural uplift, rural development, Village AID, community development, village development, Basic Democracies, Rural Works Programme. While structure and nomenclature have altered, the problem has remained essentially that of moving the locus of impetus for change from the secretariat and district headquarters of the orthodox bureaucracy to the village, and of changing the mode of control from one of formal legal sanctions to one of informal consultation, collaboration, and persuasion.

In Imperial India the aspiration to transfer responsibility to local bodies was not always hailed with enthusiasm by the ICS and was foretold by the Montagu-Chelmsford Report as a problem; so the orthodox bureaucracy of Pakistan has not always appreciated the community-development idea. Tensions between the two approaches to government have developed, and the effort to converge the two concepts into one stream of administration constitutes one of Pakistan's major problems. Community development proponents regard the orthodox bureaucracy as their principal impediment to success; orthodox bureaucrats look down upon community development as a Utopian vision. The irony is that this antipathy did not always exist; indeed, the impetus for rural reconstruction emanated from orthodox district administration, and in the work of such deputy commissioners as F. L. Brayne, Malcolm Darling, and C. F. Strickland in the Punjab the two attitudes coverged. Darling's chapter on co-operatives in his *Punjab Peasant in Prosperity and Debt* shows the need of rural uplift, and Brayne's *Better Villages* (Calcutta: Oxford University Press, 1937) describes the success of the Village Guide idea. Brayne's *Socrates in an Indian Village*, first published by Oxford University Press in 1929, is in the form of conversations with Gurgaon villagers and is a lucid account of the whole gamut of rural problems. It is a remarkable book, disarming in its apparent simplicity, but wise in the insight into village life which it reflects.

The immediate source of a rural development movement in Pakistan was the report of a committee of five agricultural experts headed by M. H. Sufi, then deputy secretary of the Ministry of Food and Agriculture. In 1951, the committee spent four months, under auspices of the U. S. International Cooperation Administration, in the United States studying agricultural extension services. The committee's work was published by the Government of Pakistan as *Report on Agricultural Extension Work in the U.S.A. and Reorganization of Extension Service in Pakistan* (Karachi, 1952). For some time, it was almost impossible to obtain the text of this report. In 1960 the report was reprinted in a compilation, *Village AID: Some Articles and Reports,* released by the Village AID Administration of the Government of West Pakistan and printed in Lahore. Considering the importance of the Sufi Report in initiating so far-reaching a program, it is remarkably short. Since half of its sixty-four pages describe the agricultural extension system in the United States, it may be said that the rural development movement in Pakistan finds its ideological impetus, if not genesis, in a brief exposition of about thirty pages. As a result of the Sufi Report, the Village Agricultural and Industrial Development Program, which came to be known as Village AID, was established in 1952. Substantial help in the form of commodities and training of personnel was given by the International Cooperation Administration (now USAID). The Ford Foundation financed in part the establishment of the two academies for rural development at Comilla and Peshawar.

Abandonment of the Village AID structure was not entirely

unforeseen. As early as 1953 the Egger Report had noted fundamental difficulties of overlapping responsibilities and had suggested the abolition of Village AID as one of three viable solutions
to the problem. The Second Five Year Plan (1960) seemed am-
bivalent on the subject; on the one hand, it asserted that with the
creation of Basic Democracy institutions, Village AID would have
even greater opportunities for promoting rural advancement, while
on the other, it acknowledged that co-ordination had been a serious problem and that councils of Basic Democracies should be responsible for development in their areas. The Commission on Food
and Agriculture (1960) expressed doubts as to the effectiveness of
Village AID. In 1959 the Basic Democracies Scheme was put into
operation. Administrative control of Village AID and the new
scheme was vested in the National Development Organization.
The Basic Democracies Scheme was essentially the formal institu-
tionalization of rural development. It sought to combine the style
of persuasion which was the hallmark of Village AID with the
sanctional powers of a formal bureaucracy.

The organization of Basic Democracies is set forth in The Basic
Democracies Order, 1959, published in the *Gazette of Pakistan,
Extraordinary*, October 27, 1959, pp. 1759–1809. Basic Democracies, not an essentially new idea in the subcontinent, is the
formalization of a structure of local political power which had long
existed in the Punjab in the village council of five elders (*panchayat*) and in Bengal in the union boards. The convergence of
Bengali and Punjabi antecedents was symbolized by the first
announcement of Basic Democracies made by President Ayub on
September 2, 1959, in which a new term, "union panchayats," was
used. At the Governors' Conference in Dacca on the same day, this
was changed to "union council" and the new term was later used
in the Basic Democracies Law. The term "union" is derived from
the organization of union boards which had been highly developed in Bengal since the Bengal Village Self-Government Act of
1919 (Bengal Act No. V of 1919), and which are described in
detail in the *Union Board Manual* (2 vols.; Alipore: Bengal
Government Press, 1937).

Using the union councils and *panchayat* as a substructure, Basic

Democracies also incorporated the traditions of the local self-government which had been developed in India at levels of the village, district, and municipalities. The innovation in Basic Democracies is their use as an integrated electoral mechanism at all levels of government through the province, by which members at each level are selected from those at the lower level. Other characteristics such as fiscal power, defined authority, and nominated-elected membership are found in local bodies as they had developed on the subcontinent. There is no doubt that Basic Democracies occupy a key position at the center of governmental reform. Many other projected reforms in law, agricultural development, police, application of marriage law, and other areas of life are based on the delegation of powers to the union councils. Moreover, they constitute the mechanism by which legislators and the president are elected. In his announcement of the Basic Democracy Scheme on September 2, 1959, the President said that "all changes and reforms which have been introduced or contemplated in the agrarian, educational, local, and economic spheres are, in fact, designed to prepare the base on which an upward pyramid of a sound political system can be developed." Ayub has stated many times that the system of democracy which eventually emerges in Pakistan must develop from the smallest units of society, that representatives must be elected from small primary social groups, and that elected assemblies should participate actively in carrying out development schemes. The mechanism created to carry out these aspirations involves four tiers of councils: union (one or several villages), *tehsil* or *thana* (groups of villages), district (groups of *tehsils*), and division (groups of districts). At the union level, a group of from one thousand to fifteen hundred adult voters are represented by one elected council member. Formerly a portion of union council members were appointed but since November, 1964, all members are elected. One of the members is elected chairman and becomes automatically a member of the council of the next tier.

Thus begins the system of indirect election upward formerly used in both China and Japan with the *pao-chia* and *tonari-gumi* as the base units. Membership of the *tehsil/thana* councils consists

of chairmen of the union councils and a like number of appointed
citizens. The district council has the most important functions; its
membership is appointed by government. At least half the non-
official members (amounting to one-quarter of the total membership) must be chosen from among chairmen of union councils.
The final tier, divisional council, is also an appointed body, 25 per
cent of whose non-official membership (or one-eighth of the total
membership) must be union council chairmen. At this level, half
the membership must be representatives of government departments functioning in the districts. Thus, the representation of
government increases with each tier. In towns, cities, and canton-
ments, the nomenclature is changed but the system remains
essentially the same. At the end of 1964, 8,344 union councils or
their equivalents were in operation in both provinces of Pakistan.
Nearly 70 per cent of those elected to the councils are literate;
most of them are between the ages of thirty-five and forty and
seem to come from the lower-middle and middle classes. Government places great hope in the development of this new leadership
which will eventually be represented in the upper tiers of the
system. Efforts have been made to increase the power and prestige
of the Basic Democracy units in many ways, including the granting of immunity from judicial action for remarks made by members in the course of meetings of councils and subordinate committees and subcommittees (President's Order No. 22 of 1962;
Basic Democracies [Second Amendment] Order, 1962, article
16[b][7]). The purpose of the system is to devolve as much
authority as possible on their local groups and to associate the
citizenry with the formal bureaucracy as closely as possible. The
effectiveness of such delegation depends in large measure on the
financial resources of the councils. Union and district councils are
allowed to levy various local taxes including a percentage of the
land revenue tax. Grants have been allocated by both the central
and provincial governments. Functions assigned to the councils
are usually described as administrative, developmental, service,
and constitutional. The administrative functions are largely those
of making public views known to government and co-ordinating
the activities within the area. It is the hope that councils will

eventually initiate development plans in their areas and provide services such as schools and roads. Judicial responsibilities are assigned to union councils by the Family Laws Ordinance (VIII of 1961) and by the Conciliation Courts Ordinance (XLIV of 1961). The question remains as to whether the new units will be more successful and responsible than the local bodies developed under British rule. The pattern of relations between the official bureaucracy, functioning in a tutorial way, and the councils—with a balance of power shifting gradually in favor of the councils— remains to be worked out. Since little empirical investigation of Basic Democracies has been carried on, the only conclusions which can be made with certainty are that the scheme has been carefully devised and that there are great expectations for its success. Further, it is clear that all other reforms initiated after 1960 have been articulated to the scheme which is regarded as the keystone of the arch of national reconstruction.

Early in 1961 the United States International Cooperation Administration terminated its support of the Village AID program, the term Village AID disappeared, and rural development became entirely incorporated in Basic Democracies. This evolution of rural development into various structural forms is still a continuing process. The *Report of the Food and Agriculture Commission* (Karachi, 1960) recommended, for example, that Village AID withdraw from the field of agricultural development and that the Basic Democracies Scheme be limited to developing a "grass-roots democracy" with no responsibility for agriculture. These agencies were to be replaced, for agricultural purposes, by two provincial agricultural corporations, each responsible for agricultural improvement within the respective province. Subsequently, this concept was enacted in the statutes creating the new corporations (West Pakistan Agricultural Development Corporation Ordinance, No. XXV of 1961, *Gazette of West Pakistan, Extraordinary,* September 20, 1961, pp. 2265–2306; the equivalent statute for the East Pakistan Agricultural Corporation is accessible in the *Dacca Gazette, Extraordinary,* October 16, 1961, pp. 1933–1972). The statutes assign broad powers to the corporations, including the power to declare "project areas" and virtually to control not only agricultural production, but transportation, communications, and the entire economy within that area. Thus, in theory at least, the rural development movement has been encompassed within the ambit of the corporate device with more sanctional powers to enforce it than even traditional district administration provided. In practice, however, the agricultural corporations have not functioned as they were planned, and the rural development movement remains suspended in the midst of shifting bureaucratic forms.

In 1964, only two project areas were being operated by the West Pakistan Agricultural Development Corporation. Neither of these involved a change from normal district administration to corporation control. One area was already under the Thal Development Authority which had been created as early as 1949. The TDA was simply absorbed by the corporation. The second project area consisted of the Ghulam Mohammad and the Gudu barrage, which were both colonization areas administered within regular divisions, to be sure, but under somewhat different rules. The East Pakistan ADC planned to open two project areas, the Chittagong Hill tracts and the Haor area of Sylhet, Mymensingh, and Comilla, but these had not yet been established in 1964. The West Pakistan Agricultural Development Corporation publishes a report entitled *Evaluation and Progress: Quarterly Report, Annual Number* (Lahore: West Pakistan Agricultural Development Corporation). The East Pakistan Corporation's report is called *At the Service of the Farmers: One Year of EPADC* (Dacca, 1962).

In East Pakistan, the rural development movement has assumed a form quite different from that contemplated for the agricultural corporations. Probably the most successful institutional mutation of rural development, it has captured the imagination of the United States Agency for International Development, and plans are being made to adapt the system to West Pakistan. The East Pakistan scheme, started in 1961, is called the Rural Works Programme of East Pakistan. It differs from previous arrangements in at least three ways. First, it concentrates on the construction of public works by mobilizing unemployed labor during slack agricultural seasons. Secondly, its implementation is carefully co-ordinated with the existing structure of Basic Democracies, yet the managerial discipline and technology of traditional bureaucracy is applied through careful supervision. Thirdly, the scheme is closely linked with the activities of the Academy for Rural Development at Comilla which assists in the preparation of plans and in supervision. The Comilla academy also develops its own research competence by using aspects of the program as source material for evaluation. The Rural Works Programme is described in Section IV of *Circular No. 44 (No. S.IV/WP-45/63)* issued on July 1, 1963, by A. M. S. Ahmad, secretary of the Basic Democracies and Local Government Department, Government of East Pakistan. This circular reflects the conjunction of the coercive role of bureaucracy with the voluntary role of rural groups. The first rural works program was a pilot project in one of the *thanas* of Comilla. This is the subject of *Reports on a Rural Public Works Programme in Comilla, Kotwali Thana—June, 1962,* published by the Academy for Rural Development at Comilla. A *Manual for Rural Public Works,* which the academy published in August, 1962, shows the detail and precision with which the program has been planned. The Comilla academy's *An Evaluation of the Rural Public Works Programme, East Pakistan, 1962–63* (Comilla, October, 1963), and the supplement of documents and questionnaires used in the evaluation and published in December, 1963, are major contributions to social science survey technique in Pakistan and suggest the adequacy of the program.

The literature on the community development concept on the subcontinent is vast, hence it is useful here to mention only three analytical essays, which also serve as introductions to the literature: Hugh Tinker, "Authority and Community in Village India," *Pacific Affairs,* XXXII (1959), 354–375; Richard L. Park, "Administrative Coordination and Economic Development in the Districts of India," and Hugh Tinker, "The Village in the Framework of Development," in Ralph Braibanti and Joseph Spengler (eds.), *Administration and Economic Development in India* (Durham, N. C., 1963). The general concept is dealt with in several United Nations publications, including *Public Administration Aspects of Community Development Programmes* (New York, 1959), and

Horace Belshaw and John B. Grant, *Report of the Mission on Community Organization and Development in South and Southeast Asia* (New York, 1953).

In Pakistan published material on community development exceeds that on other government activities and is marked by a quality of imagination, use of empirical data, and spirit of self-criticism which are refreshing. The most complete general analysis is Jack D. Mezirow, *Dynamics of Community Development* (New York, 1963). Mezirow was associated with the Village AID program for several years. One of the earliest studies is the pre-partition essay of H. S. M. Ishaque, *A B C of Rural Reconstruction* (Dacca: Government of East Pakistan Press, 1959). Although originally printed in 1945, the second edition was revised and brought up to date. A detailed description and analysis of Village AID is *Village AID—Five Year Plan* (Karachi: Government of Pakistan Press, 1956). Both Five Year Plans have chapters on the subject. The official publication, *Village AID: Some Articles and Reports* (Lahore, 1960) is invaluable not only because it includes the full text of the Sufi Report but because of several perceptive articles. Some of the best writing on the concept of community development has been done by the former chief administrator for village development in West Pakistan, Masihuzzaman, in *Community Development and Its Audience* (Lahore: West Pakistan Government Printing, 1960). An excellent journal published in Pakistan was the *Chaupal Quarterly*, sponsored by the National Development Organization of the central government. Reflecting the freshness and enthusiasm of the community development movement, it avoided the clichés and public relations overtones of most government publications. The first issue, which appeared in April, 1961, included a perceptive essay relevant to district administration: H. B. Minocher Homji, "Community Development and Local Government," pp. 21–50. Only one issue appeared, however, for the journal ceased publication when the Village AID program was merged with Basic Democracies and other government agencies.

The Ministry of National Reconstruction and Information is prolific in its issuance of materials on Basic Democracies, much of which is of a public relations nature. Of particular value for research is its *Annual Report on Basic Democracies, October 1959–October 1960* (Karachi: Bureau of National Reconstruction, n. d.) and *Scope and Functions of Basic Democracies and Their Contribution to Development* (Karachi: Government of Pakistan Press, 1961). A valuable compilation of legal powers accorded Basic Democracy units, relevant case law, and related legal information is the compilation *Law and Principles of Local Government: Basic Democracies,* edited by Afzal Mahmood and published in 1964 in Lahore by All-Pakistan Legal Decisions Company. This is printed in two separate volumes each about 500 pages for East and West Pakistan. Advertisements for Mahmood's commentary featured a letter of congratulations from President Ayub which attributes the genesis of the Basic Democracies Scheme to the President. "You probably know," the letter of June 18, 1964, states, "that I am the author of this idea and also for the production of the Basic Democracies Order. This institution is closest to my heart as I know that it will do an immense amount of good to the people."

A *Reader in Basic Democracies,* edited by S. M. Z. Rizvi and published by the West Pakistan Academy for Rural Development in Peshawar in 1961, is a useful compilation of essays by Pakistani and Americans. An earlier symposium which gives more attention to the problems of district administration is *Village AID in West Pakistan* (2nd ed.; Lahore: West Pakistan Government Printing Office, 1958). A very effective evaluation of the Village AID program is *Report of the All-Pakistan Seminar on Village Agricultural and Industrial Development Programme* (Dacca: National Development Organization, 1960). The academy in Peshawar has sponsored several studies, including S. M. Haider's *Case Studies in Community Development* (1960) and *Decision Making in Administration* (1962). The latter is an empirical study of how decisions were made by Village AID officials in Lahore and Peshawar divisions in 1960 and 1961. Inayatullah's *An Analysis of Functioning of Seven Union Councils in Peshawar Tehsil* (1961) and *Study of Union Council in Nowshera Tehsil and Study of Union Councils in Rawalpindi Division* (1961) are empirical studies which reveal a convergence of actual village leadership with union council membership. The studies also show that union councils have done very little of a developmental nature; their functions appear to have been limited to the settlement of local disputes. Another useful empirical study is Inayatullah, *Basic Democracies, District Administration and Development* (Peshawar: Academy for Rural Development, 1964). This is a study of two districts in which the author examines both the district councils, all six *tehsil* councils, and several union councils. The rather alarming lack of realization among villagers that Basic Democracies are an integral part of an electoral system for a national assembly is shown in the study prepared by the Social Sciences Research Centre, *A Study of Knowledge and Attitudes Towards Basic Democracies* (Lahore: Superintendent, Government Printing, West Pakistan, 1960).

In East Pakistan, A. T. R. Rahman's *Basic Democracies at the Grass Roots,* published by the Comilla academy in 1962, is a careful study of three union councils in Kotwali *thana.* An earlier study covering the entire province by an evaluation team from the academy at Comilla was mimeographed in 1961 and printed in 1963 as *An Analysis of the Working of Basic Democracy Institutions in East Pakistan.*

While it would be less than cautious to predict the organizational form which the rural development movement will ultimately assume, it may be said with certainty that the movement continues to generate uncommon enthusiasm and to command dedication of large numbers of officials. Its idealism is high, its dynamism strong. The spirit of the movement is almost completely detached from the colonial bureaucratic ethos of privilege, formalism, and secrecy. Its own spirit is one of scientific inquiry, open publication of results, and continuous improvement. This ideology has generated a significant amount of research based on ready access to materials. The rural development movement is thus one of the most hopeful—and certainly the most challenging—arenas for research in Pakistan.

Although the political process has been carried on since 1960 by the Basic Democracies Scheme, some historical perspective on the earlier difficulties of that process is valuable. Three excellent reports on these difficulties at provincial and district levels can serve (as did the Munir Report on the Punjab disturbances of 1953) as case studies of government and are of value for that reason. *Report on the Central Elections to the Punjab Legislative Assembly, 1950–51* (Lahore: Superintendent, Government Printing, Punjab, 1952) describes election procedure in detail and shows why the Punjab Assembly was dissolved. The full panorama of intrigue and corruption in local elections is described in A. M. Khan Leghari, *Report on the Sargodha District Board Elections, 1952–53* (Lahore: Superintendent, Government Printing, Punjab, 1955). The riotous incidents which took place in the East Pakistan Assembly, one of the factors which precipitated martial law, are the subject of *Report of the Enquiry into the Incidents that took place on 20th and 23rd September, 1958, in the Chamber and Premises of the East Pakistan Assembly by the Hon'ble Mr. Justice Asir of the High Court of Judicature in East Pakistan at Dacca*, which was published in the *Dacca Gazette, Extraordinary*, May 9, 1959. This incident was referred to in President Iskander Mirza's declaration of martial law on October 7, 1958, and by Major General Umrao Khan, martial law administrator of East Pakistan, in his October 9, 1958, broadcast. Umrao Khan referred to the incident as the "proverbial last straw on the camel's back."

Local government bodies, especially highly developed in Bengal, are analyzed in a report by S. D. Khan, *Note on Reorganization of Local Bodies in the Province* (Dacca: East Pakistan Government Press, 1957). Conflicting and overlapping responsibilities of orthodox bureaucracy, local government, and community development are explored in *Proceedings of the Seminar on Welfare Administration, 28th September–1st October* 1959 (Karachi: Government of Pakistan Press, 1960). Less valuable but still useful is *Proceedings of the Local Government Seminar, 1956)* (Lahore: Superintendent, Government Printing, West Pakistan, 1957), sponsored by the Social Welfare and Local Government Department of West Pakistan.

4

Administrative Reform

Bibliographic Data on Twenty-Eight Reform Efforts

Since independence in 1947 through 1964, efforts to reorganize the structure of government and to improve procedures of administration have been the subject of twenty-eight major reports totaling 3,621 pages and involving the participation of 146 commission members. These reports are listed in Table 2 following page 214. Eleven of these reports of about 1,809 pages were published during the period of martial law from October 7, 1958, to July 8, 1962. Thus about half the volume of administrative reports appeared within a quarter of Pakistan's existence. The dynamics of reform suggested by these data were reflected in the only major public policy statement made by President Ayub on reform doctrine on the occasion of the inauguration of the Pakistan Administrative Staff College in December, 1960.[1]

Table 3 analyzing the background of members of the twenty-eight administrative reorganization efforts, suggests some interesting conclusions. First, it is quite clear that the task of administrative reform has been predominantly a Pakistani effort, with minimal participation of foreign consultants. Of the twenty-eight reports, only seven were prepared by persons other than Pakistani. One of these was a brief survey compiled under the pressure of partition soon after independence by Sir Victor Turner, a British officer of the ICS who opted for Pakistan and who was then serving as secretary of finance. Two other British ICS officers, both holding positions in the Government of Pakistan, Sir Jeremy Raisman and Sir Terence Creagh-Coen, were responsible for two more reports. In the respect that these three officers were regular

[1] Full text is given in Appendix 3.

employees of the Government of Pakistan, they can be regarded as Pakistani rather than foreigners. Only four of the reports were prepared with help from outside the regular government establishment. The first of these was written by Rowland Egger, a political scientist from the University of Virginia whose survey was financed by the Ford Foundation. The second was by Bernard Gladieux, again a Ford Foundation consultant, who was engaged by the Planning Board. The third was an official, L. Parnwell from the British Treasury, engaged under the Colombo Plan. K. S. Jeffries, on loan from the O & M Division of the British Treasury, made a preliminary O & M survey in Pakistan in 1951. The influence of the Egger and Gladieux documents, however, was greater than the fact that they were only two of twenty-eight reports would imply. In effect, they served as a guide for the pattern of reform; subsequent surveys filled in the details of the format.

A second conclusion suggested by Table 3 is the predominant influence of two elite cadres, the Civil Service of Pakistan and the Audit and Accounts Service, in the evolution of reform doctrine. Nearly 60 per cent of the 146 persons serving on reform commissions were from these two cadres. The CSP cadre predominated with 53 per cent of the officers serving in reform efforts coming from that group. Some 84 per cent of the participants were government officials of various cadres. The nineteen politicians who served on such committees appear before martial law in 1958. After martial law, the participation by CSP officers increases, and the participation of politicians, like politics, disappears.

A third observation is that a few men apparently had greater influence than others. Akhter Husain was chairman of four important committees during the periods when he was financial commissioner (resettlement and colonies), Punjab; secretary of defense; and governor of West Pakistan. G. Ahmed was probably more influential than any single person of the group of 146. He served as chairman of two important committees, one of which, the Administrative Reorganisation Committee, was among the two or three most important of the twenty-eight reform efforts. Perhaps more important is the fact, unrevealed by Table 3, that G. Ahmed was chairman of the Planning Commission which led the efforts for administrative reform. N. A. Faruqui also served as chairman of three groups during his incumbency as cabinet secretary, the highest post in the civil service.

Fourthly, it should be noted that the two pay and service commissions were headed by Supreme Court judges, one a CSP member, but the other, Munir, a former practicing lawyer. Lastly, the establishments officer was connected with the reform efforts only by membership on some committees but not by chairmanship. The Establishment Division became a powerful agency in reform from 1960 on because it controlled training, which became the principal means of diffusing reform ideology, and because it embraced the O & M function, which became the chief vehicle for introducing reform practices. But the reform efforts transcended the limited confines of the Establishment Division and actually involved higher policy levels of government with a different perspective.

So far as is known, Table 2 is the only complete listing of these reports. Some of the earlier reports were not published and are no longer available; many of them were not announced in the official gazette; the authors of some are no longer actively associated with administration; still other reports have been forgotten. For these reasons, it seems to be of some historiographic utility to record as much publishing information as is available for each report.[2]

1. As early as August 21, 1947, only six days after Pakistan became an independent state, a reorganization committee headed by Sir Victor Turner, then finance secretary, was established by the cabinet. Asked to begin work on September 1 and to submit its recommendations two weeks later, its purpose was to advise on the staff strength for the seven ministries and the cabinet secretariat of the newly created central government. It submitted its report on time in a brief memorandum of eight pages. In those early days of the formation of Pakistan, the *Gazette of Pakistan*

---

[2] Descriptions of reports are numbered sequentially to correspond with numbering in Tables 2 and 3. Where no review or analysis of the report is given, the report has been made unavailable because of classification, has been declared lost in government files, is included in the Appendix of this volume, or has been discussed elsewhere in this essay.

was not yet being printed and the Turner Report is available only in typed form. Not intended as a long-range analysis but rather as an interim emergency measure, the Turner Report filled a critical need and has the distinction of being the first administrative survey in the history of Pakistan. The order for the writing of this report was made orally, and there is apparently no record of it or of the report.

2. The second committee was appointed by Government of Pakistan Resolution No. 1 P.C./48, February 9, 1948, published in the *Gazette of Pakistan,* February 13, 1948. This was the first Pakistan Pay Commission, headed by Chief Justice Mohammad Munir, with Muzaffar Hussain, CSP; Abdul Matin Chaudhury; and M. A. Mozaffer, AAS, as members. Its report, published in 1949 and 1950, has been discussed elsewhere in this essay.[3]

3. On March 8, 1948, the Constituent Assembly, acting in its legislative capacity, appointed a Committee to Review the Organisation, Structure and the Level of Expenditure of Ministries, Departments, and Offices of the Government of Pakistan. The appointment of this committee was not announced in the *Gazette* but may be found in the Constituent Assembly (Legislature), *Debates,* March 8, 1948, p. 362. The membership changed frequently[4] and its thirty-page *Report of the Committee to Review . . . Government of Pakistan,* No. 40 DSE–Economy 48–49 (Karachi: Inter-Services Press, 1948), was eventually released. Copies of the report cannot be found. This committee was reconstituted by a Ministry of Finance Resolution of May 18, 1949, but retained the same name. It released three reports: *Second Interim Report . . .* (Lahore: NWR Press, 1951), 130 pp.; *Third Interim Report . . .* (Karachi: Sind Government Press, 1953), 12 pp.; *Fourth Interim Report. . . .* No date or publishing information is available for the *Fourth Interim Report,* which is said to be 124 pages long. Copies of these reports do not appear to be available in Pakistan.

[3] See above, pp. 134–135.
[4] See Constituent Assembly (Legislature), *Debates,* March 11, 1948, p. 484; *ibid.,* May 20, 1948, p. 704.

4. Akhter Husain, CSP, was the author of the *Report on the Reorganisation of Karachi Administration*, work on which was started January 13, 1951. There was no notification in the *Gazette* relating to this report. It was published as an 86-page document in Karachi by Inter-services Press, under date of March 16, 1951.

5. The brief eight-page *Report of Financial Enquiry Regarding Allocation of Revenues* was printed in Karachi by the Government of Pakistan Press in 1952. It was written by Sir Jeremy Raisman with H. A. C. Gill of the British Treasury and D. G. Layton, Bank of England, as advisers. The report, to examine central and provincial allocation of revenues, was authorized on December 12, 1951, but no notice appeared in the *Gazette*. The report is no longer available.

6. The first survey of O & M work was a 24-page report, *Development of Organisation and Methods Work in the Government*, published by the Government of Pakistan Press in January, 1952. There was no notification in the *Gazette* of the authorization for this survey, which was undertaken by K. S. Jeffries in November, 1951. Jeffries was on loan from the British Treasury. This report is significant because it marks the beginning of O & M work in Pakistan.

7. A cabinet resolution of May 14, 1953, appointed a committee headed by Akhter Husain, then financial commissioner, Punjab, and consisting of all central government secretaries and the chief secretaries of provincial governments, to study the morale of the public services. The work of the committee appeared as *Report of the Committee Set Up by Government to Examine the Question of Raising the Morale of the Services* (Karachi: Government of Pakistan Press, 1954), 57 pp. Classified as confidential, it is not available.

8. An effort to reorganize the central secretariat was made by the Administrative Enquiry Committee, appointed by Resolution No. 54(15) Cord./53, March 31, 1953, announced in the *Gazette of Pakistan*, April 3, 1953, p. 85. The committee consisted of T. B. Creagh-Coen, CSP, establishment secretary; Mumtaz Hasan, AAS, secretary of finance; and Sir Eric Franklin, CSP, joint secretary of

establishments. Its 114-page report was published in 1953 in Karachi by the Government of Pakistan Press.

9. In 1953 the Ford Foundation sponsored a study by Rowland Egger, who prepared a 134-page report for the prime minister: *The Improvement of Public Administration in Pakistan* (Karachi: Inter-Services Press, 1953). Although it was no more critical of Pakistan government than its Indian counterpart, the Appleby Report, was of Indian government, the mood of Pakistan's bureaucracy was unfavorable to reform, and it is only in recent years that the Egger Report has come to be accepted as something more than a contentious document. Until recently the Egger Report was almost impossible to obtain, but a revised portion was published in *Public Administration* (London), XXXIX (1961), 149–173, with a headnote indicating that it had been made public in 1960. Its release by a martial law government after suppression by previous governments is noteworthy. The Egger Report covers the whole spectrum of government reform and makes strategic use of earlier reports on Indian administration. It is distinguished also by the fact that although written by an American, it exhibits understanding of British government and of Whitehall organization particularly. Relying partly on Sir Richard Tottenham's report of 1946, Egger distinguishes between the British administrative system and that which developed on the subcontinent. This distinction is of contemporary significance because much resistance to administrative reform in Pakistan is based on the erroneous assumption that Pakistan's administrative system is essentially the same as Whitehall and is therefore not understood by Americans. Egger proposed changes in ministerial and departmental organization, such as the functional grouping of activities within a small number of ministries and the separate organization of commercial activities in the form of corporate entities.

The report deals with the secretariat system which divides work into (*a*) policy-making carried on by secretaries to government who collectively constitute the secretariat, and (*b*) line activities which are organized as departments attached to the secretariat. He cautions against creating a separate ministry for general staff functions and suggests a reassembling of co-ordinating activities in the Ministry of Finance and in the cabinet secretariat. The head of the public services should be the cabinet secretary. Subsequent functional allocation of responsibilities among ministries should be made by a cabinet committee. Egger emphasized continuing need for reorganizing the machinery of government, encouraged the strengthening of the O & M unit, which had already been established, and urged creation of a high-level committee on management improvement. The Egger Report was not limited to advocacy of good secretariat organization and an efficient civil service alone. It warned that "grass-roots" influences are important and that the real dilemma is "centralization versus localization of the processes of administrative decision." In this respect, it characterized the government as being over-centralized, over-coordinated, under-supervised and under-propelled.

In a cogent analysis of the failure to delegate adequately, Egger suggests a compromise between the classic prototype of the "itinerant" generalist staffing top managerial posts and technical managers in developmental operations. To effect this compromise he proposed the building of strong functional departments whose heads would be permanent general managers on a parity with secretaries. Within such departments maximum delegation should be practiced. The present secretariat should be reorganized as a ministerial general staff, not in the line of command but advising and doing general staff work. In such a reorganization each ministry would have a counselor, program officer, and general administrative officer, and the formal organization into secretariats would disappear. Financial management should include a program-based budget and a changed concept of the role of budget examiners in the Finance Ministry. Egger also urged increasing the strength of the public service commissions so that they might truly be the "watch dogs" of the civil service, opening the competitive examination for the higher civil services to those beyond the limit of twenty-four years of age, and eventually unifying the various services. He urged disavowal of the comment in the first Pay Commission Report that pay scales should not be prescribed to attract all the best intellect in the country; he also proposed creation of a staff college and public administration institute. The report cautions against the growth of community development programs too heavy and complex for the administrative machinery to handle, and it suggests three viable alternatives for the Village AID program: that it be placed either in the Ministry of Agriculture or Ministry of Social Welfare, or that it be abandoned altogether.

It is tacit tribute to the soundness of many of Egger's recommendations that in the twelve years since they were submitted, many of them have been put into effect. The major recommendations not favorably acted upon were his suggestions regarding secretariat structure and public service commissions. This is not to say that the report was acted upon as an integral whole; many of its proposals, in fact, were resisted for several years. The Egger Report identified administrative deficiencies so fundamental that eventually they were to be discovered by other administrative analyses. In this respect, the Egger Report unwittingly served as an effective irritant stimulating innovation rather than a master plan acted upon as a massive reform operation. This mode of stimulating social change is one of the most effective in certain circumstances, for it permits adaptation of change to the needs of the indigenous situation. In this way innovation emerges in acculturated form and from a genesis too diffuse to be easily identified.

10. East Pakistan established the Secretariat Reorganization Committee by East Bengal Government Order No. 892(61) GA, March 4, 1954, for which there was no *Gazette* announcement. The committee, headed by S. N. Bakar, CSP, consisted of S. G. Kabir, J. S. Trainor, CSP, and co-opted the services of A. A. Shah, CSP. Its 53-page report was published as *Report of the Secretariat Reorganisation Committee, March–April 1954* (Dacca: East Bengal Government Press, May 6, 1954).

11. When the Sind, Baluchistan, the Northwest Frontier Province, and the Punjab were united into the single province of West Pakistan in 1955, a Council for the Administration of West Pakistan was established by Governor-General's Order No. 8 of 1954 dated December 22, 1954, published in *Gazette of West Pakistan, Extraordinary*, December 18, 1954, pp. 2333–2334. The council's recommendations appear in three separately published docu-

ments totalling nearly five hundred pages. These reports are models of administrative analysis, and should be carefully studied by anyone interested in provincial government. The council was made up of ten well-known leaders from all the provinces to be integrated; the chairman was Mushtaq Ahmad Gurmani, governor of the Punjab. Four subcommittees, very much like task forces of the first Hoover Commission in the United States, were established under various chairmen who were not members of the council. These subcommittees dealt with (1) administrative organization, (2) integration of services, (3) law, and (4) integration and reorganization of police services. The council's seventy-one recommendations dealt with several controversial matters, e.g., it advised continuing the secretariat as a policy-making unit distinct from executive departments, although the First Five Year Plan and the Egger Report had urged that the secretariat system be abolished. The council recommendation that the powers of division commissioners be increased (in this instance agreeing with the Five Year Plan) is in contrast to the Rowlands recommendations for Bengal that commissioners' divisions be abolished. Common training for provincial civil services and Civil Service of Pakistan probationers was recommended, but as of 1964 it had not been implemented. The major report, incorporating the recommendations of the four subcommittees is: *Report of the Council for Administration of West Pakistan* (Lahore: Government of West Pakistan Press, February, 1955). Two of the subcommittee reports were separately published: *Report of the West Pakistan Administrative Organisation Committee* (Lahore: Government of West Pakistan Press, February, 1955) and *Report of the West Pakistan Integration of Services Cadres Committee* (Lahore: Government of West Pakistan Press, February, 1955). Each of these reports were printed in only five hundred copies and are now difficult to find.

12. The second major report by a foreign consultant was written for the Planning Commission by Bernard L. Gladieux of the Ford Foundation. It was submitted to the board in typescript in May, 1955, under the title *Report of Reorganization of Pakistan Government for National Development*. This comprehensive,

hard-hitting report was incorporated almost in its entirety as Chapter VII, "Public Administration," *First Five Year Plan— 1955–60* (Karachi, December, 1957).

13. A report which perhaps unwittingly reflects the caste structure of the bureaucratic apparatus is *Report of the Secretariat Assistants' Enquiry Committee—1957.* This committee was appointed by East Pakistan Government Resolution No. 3972-F, May 30, 1956, but was not announced in the *Gazette.* Secretariat assistants occupy positions between minor clerks and office superintendents. The committee, appointed in response to appeals that promotional possibilities be enhanced, made no affirmative recommendations.

14. No information is available concerning the substance of the *Interim Report of the Committee Appointed to Consider the Question of Financial Control over Defense Expenditures* (Karachi: Inter-services Press, 1956). Akhter Husain, CSP, then defense secretary, was chairman. Other members were the finance secretary, chief of staff, GHQ, and military financial adviser.

15. When the 1956 Constitution established a federal system of government with schedules of central, provincial, and concurrent powers, it was necessary to correlate the pattern of administration to it. This became the responsibility of the Federal Reorganisation Committee, appointed by Cabinet Resolution No. 54(13) 56-Coord., whose report was in the *Gazette of Pakistan, Extraordinary,* July 31, 1956, p. 1356. The short report of forty-eight pages has not been released by the government.

16. The second Economy Committee appointed by the legislature in 1957, announced in *Gazette of Pakistan,* May 17, 1957, p. 202, was the second and last effort by the legislature to report on administration of the executive branch. The report, which appeared in March, 1958,[5] during a time of severe instability in government and less than nine months before the declaration of martial law, was an abortive effort. Apart from historical interest derived from this fact, the report is worth attention on grounds of intrinsic merit; it is not only forthright in tone but specific in its denunciation of waste in government. The second report of the Economy Committee was printed in two separate volumes, di-

[5] See extract from the report in Appendix 6.

vided into three parts: *Report of the Economy Committee Appointed to Review the Expenditure of Central Government and Suggest Economies,* Parts I and II (Karachi: Government of Pakistan Press, 1957), 100 pp.; Part III (1958), 78 pp. Justice A. S. M. Akram was chairman of the group of four legislators and one civil servant. In the finance minister's budget speech of 1957–1958, the committee was charged with the task of determining if the expansion of government activities were "disproportionately high in relation to the total resources available." In following this mandate, the Economy Committee's work was the only effort at administrative reform which was oriented primarily toward economy rather than efficiency. The report attributed the lack of success of the earlier *Administrative Enquiry Committee Report* and the *Federal Reorganization Committee Report* to absence of a government strong enough to enforce its will on the ministries. But even in the second report of the Economy Committee reliance was placed on the rectifying effect of personal example of austerity by officials. A list of examples of ostentation included the use of private railway cars by ministers, chartered planes by officials, posting of police guards at officials' homes, and maintenance of official cars (the report stated nine were kept at the President's house). The committee felt strongly that government officials sent abroad should not be allowed to draw their full salaries. This it regarded as an unnecessary drain on foreign exchange reserves and allowed such officials to purchase prohibited luxury items denied to others by import restrictions. In support of this contention, it was said that thirty-four cars were imported into Karachi alone in the first half of 1957 and that some officers imported two cars in one month. It deplored the practice of allowing government servants to draw leave pay in foreign currency and was concerned about lavish furnishings in government offices and official telephones in residences. The committee, commenting on administrative practices leading to inefficiency and waste, indorsed the recommendation of the (Turner) Reorganisation Committee of 1947 which had urged that responsible officers deal immediately with a file instead of having notes made by assistants. It suggested a more even distribution of work load among offices and urged the relocation of offices into convenient functional groups. The committee felt that too much foreign exchange was being used for delegations sent to international conferences, and that foreign travel when made by officials on leave should be by tourist class. Finally, in its general survey, the committee felt that retirement of government servants at age fifty-five was unrealistic and wasteful in the face of shortage of experienced executive skill. In sum, these general comments of the committee are a recital of the administrative disorder faced by the nation a few months before the declaration of martial law seemed to corroborate the description. The Economy Committee's report is a valuable historical document, for while evidence exists to show the misdeeds of politicians (in the form of court cases and a white paper issued by government), little can be found to corroborate the general statements of administrative disorder made by the press and, after martial law, by the President. To be sure, the dismissal of some civil servants after martial law suggests the existence of lack of probity, but the screening procedure records are not available for study and the details of disorder are therefore lacking. The Economy Committee's report is the only such "documentary" allegation available.

The *Report of the Second Economy Committee* is one of the best in Pakistan's literature of administration. It reflects acute awareness and understanding of the conceptual problems of administration, yet it is firmly based on empirical data. It is well written, cogently organized, and is one of the few administrative studies which is interesting to read. It carefully considers and integrates findings of previous inquiries into its own analysis. As the only major committee appointed by the legislature, it manifests a degree of candor in criticizing the bureaucracy which no subsequent committee of government officials has matched. Finally, it is a vain plea for moderation and austerity during the last year before martial law when these values were submerged. It is an important historical record of the kind of legislative supervision which is possible given a committee of responsibility and insight. The high quality of this report sheds doubt on the common allegation of the bureaucracy that Pakistan before martial law lacked political responsibility and legislative competence.

17. In 1957 East Pakistan, under terms of the Colombo Plan, secured the services of L. Parnwell, of the Organization and Methods Division of the United Kingdom Treasury. The result was the report, *Organisation and Methods in the East Pakistan Government* (Dacca: East Pakistan Government Press, 1958), a masterpiece of lucid organizational analysis, which regarded the secretariat system with its separation of policy and executive functions as the root of the troubles of provincial administration.

18. The most comprehensive administrative reform effort and the first undertaken under the aegis of martial law was the work of the Administrative Reorganisation Committee, appointed by Cabinet Division Resolution No. Cord. (1)-8/101/58, published in the *Gazette of Pakistan, Extraordinary,* December 12, 1958, pp. 2595–2596. The commission consisted of G. Ahmed, then chairman of the Planning Board, later ambassador to the United States, chairman; N. A. Faruqui, cabinet secretary; H. A. Majid, finance secretary; Hamid Ali, health and social welfare secretary; M. Ayub, director of the Pakistan Industrial Development Corporation; James Hardy, establishment secretary; and Mumtaz Hasan, a member of the Planning Board. S. S. Haider, who was in charge of the O & M Wing of the Establishment Division, which was subsequently to implement the recommendations, was secretary. The work of this commission, made up of the highest-ranking members of the bureaucracy, is a landmark in the nation's administrative history. Its importance lies not only in the scope and the substance of the report, but also in the manner of its public release, for it was the first major report issued by the executive branch which was not made unavailable to the public. Presented to the President on January 19, 1961, its substance was announced to the public in a long press release by its chairman in January, 1961.[6] In June, 1963, the full report was printed, without classification, in one thousand copies by the Efficiency, O & M Wing and was widely distributed. The Ahmed Report is the only one of the twenty-eight which also includes summaries of cabinet deliberations and ultimate cabinet decisions on each major recommendation. The perennial problem of relations between the

[6] See full text of press release in Appendix 8.

policy-making secretariat and the operating subordinate departments was dealt with by preserving the traditional system but
delegating power within it. The ministries were to be limited
to policy-making and the departments were to have increased
executive powers.

One of the key problems in administration has been that of the
subordination of technically trained officials to the generalist CSP
officers who had traditionally been secretaries in ministries. Such
subordination fomented animosity between CSP officers and technical experts. The commission introduced from pre-partition
Indian experience the device of the economic pool—a small cadre
of experienced administrators drawn from all superior services.
Members of this pool will fill senior executive posts in certain
ministries, especially Finance, Commerce, and Industries. The
principle, although not the mechanism, has been extended also to
the Ministry of Education and the Health Division of the Ministry
of Health and Social Welfare. This will remove five important
secretaryships from the exclusive domain of the CSP, and, with
the rise of government corporations and authorities staffed largely
by technical persons, the participation of CSP officers in the total
range of high-level policy direction will be proportionately reduced. The commission also urged a regrouping of transportation
responsibilities into a centralized Transport Ministry. Positions of
commercial and press attachés were to be filled by members of the
Foreign Service, and the organization of the Foreign Affairs and
Commonwealth Relations Ministry and its missions abroad were
to be simplified. Perhaps the most important conceptual achievement of the committee was its recognition of the continuous need
for administrative reorganization. To survey such needs, a standing Organization Committee was established and the Organization and Methods Wing strengthened.

One of the most important major reforms made in administration was the "section officers' scheme," which the press often
described as an American institution, but which, in reality owes its
conceptual origin to the Tottenham Report of 1945,[7] and was
suggested by the Turner Report of 1947 and the 1957 Economy
Committee. The section officers' scheme was introduced in August,

[7] See above, pp. 110–111.

1959 for the secretariat of the central government but had been devised earlier in the secretariat of the Government of West Pakistan. The objective of the system is to devolve the authority to make decisions on certain cases to a middle-management group known as section officers. The effect has been to reduce the number of steps in handling cases and to bring a decision-making officer in closer contact with the pertinent empirical data and his immediate staff. Apart from the increase in efficiency and speed in resolving issues, the system has served to change somewhat the climate of human relations within the bureaucracy which has been characterized by a high degree of rigidity and stratification. The scheme was the subject of an important High Court judgment [8] in which a writ of mandamus was sought by a group of section officers who maintained that they should not be examined by the Central Public Service Commission after their selection as section officers. The judgment is valuable to students of administration particularly because it includes a description of the section officers' scheme and the text of pertinent regulations.

19. Although a substantial background of analysis for further reform was available during martial law, there was no comprehensive study of the organization of both provinces. To remedy this deficiency, the central government appointed the Provincial Administration Commission, under the chairmanship of Akhter Husain, then governor of West Pakistan (announced in *Gazette of Pakistan, Extraordinary*, February 12, 1959, p. 210). The resultant *Report of the Provincial Administration Commission* (Lahore: West Pakistan Government Printing, 1960) is the first complete study of all levels of administration below the national government. Although the full text of the report has not been released by the Government of Pakistan, and is therefore not available for research purposes, a detailed synopsis of the report was issued as a 22-page mimeographed press release, "Handout, Revolutionary Change in Provincial Administrative Structure" (Rawalpindi: Government of Pakistan, June 29, 1960).[9] The report is also important because it is the first effort to deal with the local

[8] The Abdul Latif Sethi case is important for several other reasons. Further discussion may be found above, pp. 125–126.
[9] An extract from this release is included in Appendix 7.

government of both provinces in a co-ordinated fashion. The task force research technique first used in the Gurmani Report for West Pakistan was again used in a systematic, elaborate, and useful way. There were only three members of the commission, but three subcommittees, with a total membership of ten officials, were established in East Pakistan, and six subcommittees with twenty members were appointed in West Pakistan. In addition, six officials in East Pakistan and three in West Pakistan served as consultants. The conventional methods of interview of officials and non-officials (some 785 in all), touring, and analyzing answers to a questionnaire were also used. But the active, systematic involvement of thirty officials organized as task forces was a departure from the workways of most such efforts of the past. The principal substantive recommendation was the redefinition of boundaries of districts and divisions in both provinces. The commission sought to strengthen the power of division and district heads, to whom more authority was to be delegated by the provincial government. It also suggested delegation of some powers to councils created under the Basic Democracies Scheme in 1959.

In budgetary and financial reforms, the commission deferred to the Administrative Reorganisation Committee which dealt with these issues comprehensively. The need for continuous training of government officials was recognized. Traditional district administration was upheld as basically sound; the division commissioner was to become a more effective co-ordinator and district office staffs were to be increased. The question of relations between the police and district magistrate was firmly handled. The traditional role of the district magistrate as head of criminal administration in the district was reaffirmed, and the superintendent of police was declared subordinate to him.

20. Ranking with the (G. Ahmed) Administrative Reorganisation Committee in importance is the Pay and Service Commission appointed by Ministry of Finance Resolution No. 2524—Admn. 111/59, published in the *Gazette of Pakistan, Extraordinary*, August 31, 1959, pp. 1461–1462. The commission submitted its findings to the President on June 1, 1962, but the report was not

released to the public as of early 1965. The terms of reference of the second (Cornelius) Pay and Service Commission were considerably broader than those of the earlier 1948 (Munir) Pay Commission. It was directed, among other things, "to review the structure and organisation of and sources and methods of recruitment relating to civilian services and establishments of all grades under the control of the Central Government . . . and to suggest measures designed to secure the maximum efficiency and economy in administration." Rarely has the report of a commission been awaited with such lively interest, partly because of the reputation for fairness and courage of Chief Justice Cornelius, but more because Cornelius' publicly expressed opinion that the whole structure of recruitment needed to be made more egalitarian encouraged the assumption that this view was reflected in the report. It was further assumed that the report proposed abolishing the CSP cadre and opening key positions in government to members of other services. Since the Cornelius Report remains classified and unreleased, its recommendations cannot be analyzed. Hints as to its contents can be gleaned from various public statements. For example, the comment by Finance Minister M. Shoaib in 1961 that the recommendations may be "revolutionary in nature" [10] seemed to corroborate assumptions made by the public concerning the radical nature of the proposals. Failure to present the report to the National Assembly for its deliberation provoked persistent queries by members, in the course of which the public's view of the contents of the report was suggested. Qamarul Ahsan stated that it "envisages a basic change in the structure" of the public services, and Mabubul Huq asserted that it recommended unification of services. [11] Persistent questioning designed to force release of the report to the National Assembly was unsuccessful. [12]

In April, 1964, President Ayub clarified somewhat the status of the Pay and Service Commission's Report, and in so doing, suggested the nature of its proposals. He stated that government had

[10] *Pakistan Times,* August 3, 1961, p. 10.
[11] National Assembly of Pakistan, *Debates,* December 5, 1962, p. 413, and April 13, 1963, p. 1807.
[12] See, for example, *ibid.,* March 12, 1963, pp. 196–199.

put into effect the recommendations reducing the disparity in pay scales, but that "no radical change should be made in [the] existing structure" of the civil services. Stating that the commission had recommended "radical changes involving a complete redesigning of the existing scheme and organisation of public services," he concluded that national development "required continuity in the functions and organisation of the public services, which have grown with time and become familiar to the people." Such continuity should be maintained and "nothing should be done which might involve the risk of disrupting the administrative fabric." [13] The implication of this statement seems to be that the executive branch acted unilaterally on its recommendations, and that it would not necessarily be referred to the National Assembly.

Another clue as to the report's contents may be implied from publicly expressed views of Chief Justice Cornelius on the structure of bureaucracy in a democratic state. Cornelius has in no way indicated that these views are incorporated in the report, although this is a common assumption in Pakistan. In the thousands of pages which have been compiled on aspects of administrative reform, little has been said of the theoretical relationship of such reform to the deeper meanings of constitutional democracy. Cornelius is alone in expressing unequivocally the need to articulate change in terms of political philosophy. His views were fully presented in an address before the Rotary Club of Lahore on September 1, 1961.[14] He struck at what he regarded as one of the basic defects in the bureaucracy of Pakistan, namely, the denial of opportunity for personal growth by a rigidly caste-structured and compartmentalized public service system. He deplored the tendency to assume that an inferior cannot rise above a certain level.

---

[13] Broadcast from Rawalpindi, April 21, 1964, and published in Government of Pakistan, *Speeches and Statements, Field Marshal Mohammad Ayub Khan* (Karachi, 1964), VI, 188. This same view was expressed in the National Assembly by the parliamentary secretary for finance who, in response to questioning, said that recommendations relating to change in service structure would not be implemented. In the same session, the parliamentary secretary said "now we have come to a stage where we will be able to make the report public. It will be done very soon and we are expediting it" (National Assembly of Pakistan, session of August 6, 1964, as reported in *Dawn*, August 7, 1964, p. 6). *Debates* for this session have not yet been published.

[14] Full text is given in Appendix 12.

He also noted that in a system in which there is opportunity for the release of initiative and energy, qualities of creativeness and unpredictable abilities are nurtured. This "realization of self through freedom" he related to basic principles guaranteed in the Objectives Resolution reflected in the 1956 Constitution. While acknowledging that grades and classifications are needed in any complex administrative system and that growth in freedom must proceed on uniform and rational lines, he asserted that "the rational test of equality for the determination of the status of two persons engaged in work of the same or equivalent character would appear to turn on the possession of necessary qualifications coupled with the capacity to produce results." While this may not seem like a remarkable statement to those acquainted with bureaucratic systems in which this has long been accepted as axiomatic, it is a landmark in the development of a theory of bureaucracy in Pakistan. The Cornelius statement was the first expression of such a view by a public figure in a position of eminence. Taken with the Cornelius proposals for the creation of administrative tribunals, this plea for the internal democratization of the bureaucracy constitutes a major constructive reform proposal which strikes deeply at fundamental legal, moral, and philosophical issues relating to bureaucracy. The degree to which this concept of internal democratization is incorporated in the report of the Cornelius Commission remains to be seen.

21. In this tabulation of episodic administrative reform efforts, inclusion of a report on agricultural administration by Charles M. Hardin warrants explanation. Like the Gladieux Report on administration for economic development,[15] the Hardin Report was never published as a separate document. It was a typed report submitted to the Food and Agriculture Commission. Hardin was engaged by the World Bank as a consultant to the Food and Agriculture Commission and spent three months in Pakistan preparing his report. A large part of the analysis was ultimately incorporated in the commission's report as Chapters VI and VII, which are an assessment of the adequacy of governmental ma-

[15] See above, pp. 221–222. The Food and Agriculture Commission Report is discussed below, pp. 324–326.

chinery to increase agricultural production. These chapters are among the best analyses of secretariat and local administration in print, largely because they deal with the traditional bureaucratic system and rural development administration in a co-ordinated way. The commission's final recommendations, discussed elsewhere in this essay, are controversial. They proposed the creation of two provincial agricultural corporations which would organize project areas in which all government activities would be co-ordinated for increased crop yield. This technique replaces the Village AID scheme and would, if implemented, seriously challenge the dominance of traditional district administration. It is probably the most revolutionary proposal for reform of local administration made in Pakistan. It suggests several research possibilities, such as (1) the reasons for not implementing the scheme as envisaged in the report, (2) the wisdom of using the corporate device as a substitute for traditional line government, (3) the adequacy of the corporate device to generate initiative in rural society, (4) the failure to use the corporate device for this purpose in East Pakistan and the substitution of the technique of the Rural Works Programme as the chief vehicle for rural development.

22. After the decision to remove the capital of Pakistan to Rawalpindi, it was necessary to change the administrative structure of Karachi. On July 1, 1961, Karachi ceased to be a federal territory and became one of twelve divisions in West Pakistan. G. Yazdani Malik was assigned to survey the changes in administration required by this merger. The result was *Report on the Merger of Karachi with West Pakistan* (Lahore: Superintendent, Government Printing, West Pakistan, September, 1961), a document of some fifty pages of text and seventy pages of valuable tabulations of allocation of authority and organization charts. This report is of value for at least two reasons: (1) it is a technically competent manpower and organizational survey of a large city government, and (2) there is a possibility that it may be used as a guide, if not a model, for the administrative organization of other major cities such as Lahore, Dacca, and Rawalpindi. Pakistan has not yet been faced with the problem of urbanization and hence

has not evolved a pattern of modern metropolitan administration. Cities continue to be administered as districts. The Yazdani Malik Report is the closest approximation to a metropolitan survey available in Pakistan.

23. The dominant motif in the reform reports issued after martial law (the G. Ahmed and Akhter Husain reports, numbers 18 and 19 in this survey) was decentralization of executive authority. The G. Ahmed Committee dealt with this at the central government level. While the Akhter Husain Commission concentrated on redefining the territorial boundaries of divisions and districts, it did not deal with the details of decentralization. This was the task of the Provincial Reorganization Committee, announced in a cabinet decision of August 4, 1961, but not, so far as can be determined, published in the *Gazette*. The committee was composed of the cabinet secretary, N. A. Faruqui, as chairman, Q. A. Huque, chief secretary, East Pakistan; M. M. Ahmad, additional chief secretary, West Pakistan; A. G. N. Kazi, finance secretary; David K. Power, additional chief secretary, East Pakistan; and M. A. Mozaffer of the Audit and Accounts Service. While this committee was deliberating, the provisions of the new 1962 Constitution became known. Hence the reports of this committee are the first to be correlated specifically to the provisions of the new Constitution. Recognizing the differences between the two provinces, the committee organized into two provincial subcommittees, each of which submitted a separate report: *Report of the Provincial Reorganization Committee—Part I—West Pakistan*, submitted December 27, 1961 (Lahore: Superintendent, Government Printing, 1961); *Report of the Provincial Reorganization Committee—Part II—East Pakistan*, submitted April 12, 1962 (Dacca: East Pakistan Government Press, 1962). The reports include organization charts for the structure of provincial government. They reaffirm the desirability of strengthening the authority of division and district administration and seek to integrate the role of Basic Democracy councils with traditional administration.

24. Even after the mode for decentralizing authority was specified by the G. Ahmed, Akhter Husain, and N. A. Faruqui committees, the issue of decentralizing government corporations

remained. To deal with this problem, the Committee on Decentralization of Institutions was appointed by Notice No. 2(3)-NGO/61, issued by the Cabinet Division of the President's Secretariat, November 4, 1961. No announcement appeared in the *Gazette*. N. A. Faruqui, the cabinet secretary, also headed this committee. Other members were H. A. Majid, finance secretary; Osman Ali, commerce secretary; Q. A. Huque, chief secretary, East Pakistan; S. M. Yusuf, representing West Pakistan; and S. I. Haque, industries secretary. The committee analyzed eight major government corporations, and four other agencies, i.e. Investment Promotion Bureau, Council of Scientific and Industrial Research, Central Technical Assistance Center, and the Planning Commission. The committee recommended that these agencies delegate as much power as possible to local provincial offices, but it did not suggest bifurcating any of the agencies into separate provincial entities. Disagreement within the committee on the question of dividing the Industrial Development Corporation into two separate provincial corporations was resolved by the central government in favor of two separate corporations. While the full text of this report has not been released, a summary was made available to the press and appeared in the *Pakistan Times*, March 21, 1962.

25. Decentralization of authority to the provinces requires reallocation of revenue to sustain new provincial activities. To deal with this problem, the central government appointed a Finance Commission on Allocation of Revenue to Central and Provincial Governments. The announcement was published in the *Gazette of Pakistan, Extraordinary*, December 19, 1961, pp. 1702c–1702d. Its 81-page report was submitted to the central government on January 27, 1962, but remains a classified report about which no information has been released.

26. A comittee on forms and procedures was appointed on January 26, 1962, to co-ordinate simplification of forms and procedures in the central and provincial governments. Headed by the secretary of the Establishment Division of the central government, the committee plans to submit no report. It is an advisory committee to the Efficiency, Organization, and Management Wing of the Establishment Division.

27. The most recent committee of major significance was appointed as the consequence of a decision made at the Governor's Conference in Dacca, February 1, 1962. Subsequently, Resolution No. 1/1/61-SOC, Establishment Division, dated February 20, 1962, at Karachi, authorized the committee and defined its terms of reference. No announcement was made in the *Gazette*. The committee consisted of Mohammad Shoaib, minister for economic co-ordination, chairman; G. Mueenuddin, establishment secretary; N. A. Faruqui, cabinet secretary; and Mumtaz Mirza, finance secretary. It was created to redefine the authority of ministries of the central government in accordance with the 1962 Constitution which no longer specified concurrent or provincial lists of powers. A summary of the 101-page *Report of the Standing Organisation Committee on the Reorganisation of the Functions and Structure of the Central Government in the Light of the New Constitution* (Rawalpindi: Efficiency, O & M Wing, Establishment Division, Central Army Press, GHQ, 1962) was released to the press on April 26, 1962. [16]

28. The last committee of this series of twenty-eight efforts in administrative reform was appointed by Cabinet Division Notification 105(3)/62 dated March 1, 1962, published in the *Gazette of Pakistan, Extraordinary*, March 1, 1962, p. 275c. The cabinet secretary, N. A. Faruqui, was appointed chairman. This group, designated Implementation Committee in Connection with the New Constitution, was expected to survey progress being made in reforms recommended by the Standing Organization Committee. It did not plan to submit a report.

Summary. At first glance, a summary of the accessibility of the substance of these reports is discouraging. Since the two reform efforts, listed as items 26 and 28 (Table 2) relating to forms and procedures and implementation of the new Constitution, will not submit reports, only twenty-six reports need be considered here. Ten of these reports (items 2, 9, 11, 12, 16, 18, 19, 21, 24, and 27 in Table 2) have been released for public inspection in some form. In some instances, the entire report is available; in other instances,

[16] For a reprint of this summary, see Appendix 9.

the report has not been released, but the official press release is either the complete text or an adequate summary of the text. These ten reports total 1,760 pages, or 48 per cent of the total page volume of all twenty-eight reports. In reality, the condition of accessibility is more favorable than such a computation suggests. First, it should be noted that most of the reports not available are no longer of great significance. In this category at least eight reports (items 1, 3, 4, 5, 6, 10, 13, and 14 in Table 2) can be placed. Many are not available, not for calculated reasons of secrecy, but simply because they were never printed. In two instances at least, (items 1 and 5 in Table 2) it appears that not even the typescript can be found. The unavailability of the remaining six is the consequence, not of deliberate government policy, but rather of inattention to historiographic matters in the early days of independence. Only eleven major reports (items 7, 8, 10, 13, 14, 15, 17, 20, 22, 23, and 25 in Table 2) totaling 1,381 pages, or 38 per cent of the total volume of twenty-eight reports, can be said to be unreleased probably because of official policy. And of these, only items 20, 23, and 25 (Table 2), totaling 819 pages or 22 per cent of the total volume, can be said to be of major significance to research.

Three important groups have established a precedent for substantive sophistication and public distribution: the first (Munir) Pay Commission (item 2, Table 2), the second (Akram) Economy Committee (item 16, Table 2), and the G. Ahmed Committee on Administrative Reorganisation (item 18, Table 2). They represent extrabureaucratic, legislative, and intrabureaucratic efforts, respectively. Perhaps each will in the future be used as a model for subsequent government reporting on administrative reform.

Rise of the Corporate Device

Expanded reliance on public, statutory corporations as an instrument of rapid development, like the procedural and structural reform efforts already discussed, is a major phenomenon in the development of bureaucracy. The First Five Year Plan, which considered the inadequacy of Pakistan's administrative apparatus as "the most serious single impediment to development," sug-

Table 4. *Condensed Data on Government Corporations, Authorities, and Boards (Arranged by date of establishment. Status as of July 30, 1964)*

Name of agency	Number of members	Date of establishment	Authorizing statute[a]	Ministry/department to which reports submitted[b]
Government of Pakistan				
1. Pakistan Refugees Rehabilitation Finance Corp.	9	April, 1948; reorganized, Jan., 1960	GPE, Jan. 25, 1960, 105–112	Finance
2. Pakistan Industrial Development Bank	11	Feb. 29, 1949; became bank, July 18, 1961	GPE, March 1, 1949, 137–149; GPE, July 29, 1961, 1167–1190	Finance
3. Security Printing Corp.	7	March 10, 1949	Agreement Feb. 1, 1949, with GOP, and de La Rue Co., Ltd.	Finance
4. National Bank of Pakistan	14	Nov. 9, 1949	GPE, Nov. 9, 1949, 735–749	Finance
5. House Building Finance Corp.	7	April 18, 1952	GPE, April 18, 1952, 557–573	Finance
6. Pakistan Insurance Corp.	9	May 8, 1952	GPE, May 8, 1952, 665–678	Communications
7. Pakistan International Airlines Corp.	9	Jan., 1955	GPE, Jan. 10, 1955, 83–92; GPE, Apr. 19, 1956, 801–809	Defense
8. Agricultural Development Bank (known as Agriculture Bank from establishment to 1961)	7	April 30, 1957; reconstituted, 1961	GPE, April 30, 1957, 1074–1089; GPE, Feb. 11, 1961, 649–664	Food and Agriculture
9. Pakistan Industrial Credit and Investment Corp.	16	Nov. 26, 1957	Not announced in Gazette	Industries
10. Capital Development Authority	3	June 27, 1960	GPE, June 27, 1960, 938c–939i	
11. Oil and Gas Development Corp.	3	Sept. 20, 1961	GPE, Sept. 20, 1961, 1486a, 1486k	Fuel, Power, and Natural Resources
12. Atomic Energy Commission	4	Dec. 11, 1959; amended May 19, 1961; reconstituted May 27, 1965	GP, Dec. 18, 1959, 564–565; GPE, May 29, 1965 *	Fuel, Power, and Natural Resources
13. National Shipping Corp.	9	Sept. 15, 1963	GPE, Sept. 18, 1963 *	
Government of East Pakistan				
14. Dacca Improvement Trust	9	Aug. 9, 1956	DG, Aug. 9, 1956 *	Works
15. East Pakistan Jute Marketing Corp.	3	June, 1957	DGE, May 7, 1957 *	Commerce, Labor, and Industry
16. East Pakistan Small and Cottage Industries Corp.	4	May 31, 1957	DGE, May 21, 1957, * EP Act XVII of 1957	Commerce, Labor, and Industry
17. East Pakistan Inland Water Transport Authority	3	Nov., 1958	DGE, Ord, LXXV of 1958 2517–2525; DGE, Jan. 19, 1959, 85–86; DGE, Jan. 30, 1959, 133–135; DGE, Feb. 1, 1959, 141–142	Works
18. East Pakistan Water & Power Development Authority	3	Jan. 1, 1959	DGE, Jan. 1, 1959, 1–3	Fuel, Power, and Natural Resources
19. Chittagong Development Authority	7	Sept., 1959	DGE, July 27, 1959, 945–977; GEPE, Feb. 22, 1964 *	Works
20. East Pakistan Forest Industries Development Corp.	4	Oct., 1959	DGE, Oct. 3, 1959, 1152–1157	Commerce, Labor, and Industry
21. East Pakistan Road Transport Corp.	5	Feb., 1961	DGE, Feb. 4, 1961, 317–330	Works
22. Film Development Corp.	5	May 21, 1957	DGE, May 21, 1957 *	Commerce, Labor, and Industry
23. Khulna Development Authority	12	Jan. 21, 1961	DGE, Jan. 21, 1961, 203–237	Chief Secretary
24. Agricultural Development Corp.	5	Oct. 16, 1961	DGE, Oct. 16, 1961, 1933–1972	Agriculture
25. East Pakistan Industrial Development Corp.[c]	3	July 1, 1962	GPE, June 4, 1962, 861e–861x	Industries
26. East Pakistan Shipping Corp.	5	March 7, 1964	GEPE, March 7, 1964, 321–338	Chief Secretary
27. East Pakistan Fisheries Development Corp.	6	March 25, 1964	GEPE, March 25, 1964, 354a–354i	Chief Secretary

[a] Key to abbreviations in this column:
GPE: *Gazette of Pakistan, Extraordinary*
DGE: *Dacca Gazette, Extraordinary,* called *Gazette of East Pakistan, Extraordinary, GEPE,* after 1963
GWPE: *Gazette of West Pakistan, Extraordinary*
GOP: Government of Pakistan
EP: East Pakistan
GP: *Gazette of Pakistan*
GWP: *Gazette of West Pakistan*
DG: *Dacca Gazette*

Since name of creating instrument is invariably the same as the name of the corporate entity, it is not repeated in this column. Place where text of instrument is available is given.

[b] Central government corporations report to ministries, provincial corporations to departments except when marked with # noted below.

[c] Two provincial industrial development corporations organized by dividing the Pakistan Industrial Development Corporation created April 19, 1950 (GP, April 7, 1950, Pt. V, 83–87). Dissolution accomplished by Ordinance No. XXVI of 1962 (GPE, June 4, 1962, 861a–861c).

* Pages not given.

					Railways and Communications
28. Karachi Port Trust	11	1886	Bombay Government Gazette, Feb. 8, 1887, Pt. I, 242		Railways and Communications
29. Karachi Electric Supply Corp. #	10	March 31, 1952	Managed by Pakistan Electric Agencies, Ltd., under Managing Agency Agreement, March 31, 1952		Fuel, Power, and Natural Resources
30. Road Transport Corp. (formerly Road Transport Board)	7	Oct. 12, 1957; reconstituted as corporation, May, 1963	Motor Vehicles Act, 1957; amended by West Pakistan Ordinance No. XI of 1963; GWP, May 16, 1963, 2175–2178		Railways and Communications
31. Karachi Development Authority #	5	Dec. 13, 1957	President's Order V, 1957, GP, Dec. 13, 1957, 534–562, GPE, Dec. 17, 1957, 2536		Works and Rehabilitation
32. West Pakistan Water & Power Development Authority	3	April 24, 1958	GWPE, April 24, 1958, 689–699		Fuel, Power, and Natural Resources
33. Karachi Road Transport Corp. #	6	May 18, 1959	GPE, Apr. 9, 1959, 535–545		Railways and Communications
34. Agricultural Development Corp. (absorbed powers of Thal Development Authority, Dec. 13, 1962)	5	Sept. 21, 1961	GWPE, Sept. 20, 1961, 2265–2306; GWPE, Dec. 13, 1962		Agriculture
35. West Pakistan Small Industries Corp.	5	May 5, 1962; retroactive to April 30, 1960	GWPE, April 16, 1960; GWPE, May 8, 1962		Industries
36. West Pakistan Industrial Development Corp.ᶜ	3	July 1, 1962	GPE, June 4, 1962, 861e–861x		Industries
Total members	**237**				

\# These were central government corporations prior to the merger of Karachi with West Pakistan in 1961 when the national capital was moved to Rawalpindi. As of 1964, these corporations still retained some features of central rather than provincial government entities. This accounts for reports shown as being submitted to the central government.

Sources: Statutes, Gazette notifications, annual reports, interviews, correspondence.

Table 5. *Professions of Members of Boards of Directors of 36 Central and Provincial Government Corporations, 1964 (Corporations listed in Table 4)*

	Central Governmentᵃ Domicile		Total of cols. A & B	Provincial Government		Total of cols. C, D, E	% Col. F of Grand total
Profession	West Pakistan A	East Pakistan B	C	West Pakistan D	East Pakistan E	F	G
Government official							
Technical, active	3	0	3	0	4	7	
Non-technical, active	24	3	27	17	25	69	
Technical, retired	1	0	1	0	1	2	
Non-technical, retired	4	0	4	3	2	9	
Police service	2	1	3	1	2	6	
Military, active	4	0	4	1	0	5	
Military, retired	2	0	2	4	5ᵇ	11	
Government corporation	4	0	4	0	1	5	
Total, Government Officials	44	4	48	26	40	114	48.3
Business	35	10	45	16	12	73	30.9
Railroad engineer	2	0	2	7	0	9	3.8
Politician	2	0	2	0	6	8	3.4
Foreign national	0	0	7	0	0	7	3.0
Engineer	0	0	0	0	6	6	2.5
Lawyer	0	0	0	1	4	5	2.1
Scientist	4	0	4	1	0	5	1.7
Academic administrator	0	1	1	0	1	2	.8
Landholder	0	0	0	0	1	1	.4
Woman	1	0	1	0	1	1	.4
Scholar	0	0	0	0	1	1	.4
Labor leader	0	0	0	0	1	1	.4
Editor	1	1	1	0	0	1	.4
Banker	0	0	0	0	1	1	.4
Religious leader	0	0	0	0	1	1	.4
Unknown	0	0	1	0	0	1	.4
Grand totals	87	17	112ᶜ	51	74	237	

Sources: Interviews and correspondence.

ᵃ Domicile is given only for members of central government corporations. It is assumed that members of provincial corporations come from the province in which the corporation operates.

ᵇ Military officers tabulated here are from West Pakistan although deputed to East Pakistan provincial corporations.

ᶜ One unknown and seven foreign nationals not included in domicile columns, hence this total of 112 is eight more than the domicile totals of 87 and 17.

gested the corporate device for implementing programs requiring a "commercial . . . or multi-purpose approach."[17] The Second Five Year Plan, although it warned against establishing too many corporations, praised their effectiveness.[18] Subsequent reports of major commissions of inquiry during martial law reflected this attitude of confidence in the corporate device.[19]

The research possibilities in the organization, operations, and relations of corporations to other agencies of government are numerous. Scarcely any research, even of the most basic kind, has been done. Table 4 is the first effort at classifying public corporations and identifying the authorizing statutes. Table 5 attempts to classify the occupational background of members of corporation boards of directors. Both of these tabulations may be useful first steps in encouraging research on corporations. The corporate device is of particular challenge in Pakistan because of expansion of its use beyond the usual contours of corporate activity. That expansion has occurred in the use of agricultural development corporations to co-ordinate all governmental activities in designated project areas to increase productivity.[20]

It appears to be appropriate to comment first on source materials available for research and then to suggest substantive topics of research feasibility.

The research materials available are limited and uneven in adequacy. Table 4 classifies corporate entities by the unit of government of which they are a part. The central government has fourteen corporate agencies; East Pakistan, fourteen; and West Pakistan, eight. Since the corporate agencies do not report to any single co-ordinating agency in the central or provincial governments, each agency must be dealt with separately. Research

---

[17] Government of Pakistan, *First Five Year Plan, 1955–60* (Karachi, 1958), pp. 100–101.

[18] Government of Pakistan, *Second Five Year Plan, 1960–65* (Karachi, June, 1960), p. 118.

[19] See, for example, Government of Pakistan, *Report of the Jute Enquiry Commission* (Karachi, 1960), p. 172; Government of Pakistan, *Report of the Credit Enquiry Commission* (Karachi, 1959), p. 187; Government of Pakistan, *Report of the Food and Agriculture Commission* (Karachi, 1960), pp. 212–248. See also above p. 218 ff. for discussion of the Egger Report, which also advocates use of government corporations.

[20] See above, p. 206 and below p. 324 for further discussion.

difficulties do not end here. Fewer than half of the corporate entities submit printed reports to any agency; the remainder are in mimeographed or typescript form or are not in existence. The corporation secretariat facilities in which records are kept vary greatly. The Pakistan Industrial Development in Karachi is probably the most sophisticated in this respect. It publishes its own management journal, sponsors courses in management development, and has a modern building and facilities of its own. The West Pakistan Water and Power Development Authority in Lahore also has modern administrative facilities.

The Economic Affairs Division of the central government published a 97-page survey of thirteen corporations of the central government, *Government Sponsored Corporations* (Karachi: Government of Pakistan Press, 1959), and the Finance Department of the Government of East Pakistan published a similar survey of forty-seven pages, *A Brochure on the Autonomous Bodies and Corporations Set Up by the Provincial Government* (Dacca: East Pakistan Government Press, 1960). Neither of these is complete, and the documentation does not include *Gazette* citations to statutes or information on reports. Somewhat more useful is a 117-page mimeographed study by Mohammad Uzair, "Government Sponsored Finance Corporations in Pakistan" (Karachi: Institute of Public and Business Administration, 1959). Uzair reviews the activities of nine finance corporations of the central government and compares them briefly with similar bodies in Japan and other countries. Several staff papers have been prepared by participants in various sessions or by visiting lecturers at the Administrative Staff College in Lahore. They are on file there, either typed or mimeographed. Among them are Mohammad Shafiq, "A Short Paper on the Co-ordination of West Pakistan's WAPDA's Functions with Other Government Departments and Agencies," Staff College Reading Paper No. 97; an address delivered at the Staff College in 1962 by Ghulam Ishaq entitled "The Public Corporation as an Organisation Device for Development in Pakistan." Also available is Hamid Akhtar Niazi, "The Thal Development Authority" (unpublished doctoral dissertation, Department of Political Science, University of the Panjab, 1957).

The National Institute of Public Administration in Dacca has released twelve relevant studies by staff members. These include: F. Rehman, "Development and Working of the Inland Water Transport Authority;" Salma Choudhry, "A Study of the East Pakistan Small and Cottage Industries Corporations;" M. Ramzan Ali, "System and Procedure Study of East Pakistan Small and Cottage Industries Corporation;" and others on the Khulna and Chittagong development authorities and the Forest Industries Corporation. In addition, the Dacca institute has issued some ten studies by participants in various courses. Both the staff and participant studies are available at the institute library but have not been widely disseminated.

The reporting system of the West Pakistan Water and Power Development Authority ([WP]WAPDA) is probably better than that of any government agency, either corporate or line, in Pakistan. The magnitude of (WP)WAPDA's operations makes it a major sub-bureaucracy, which in 1964 employed nearly 100 thousand persons. Even that figure, however, does not reveal the size of the operation, for it administers engineering contracts with several foreign firms involving several hundred foreign personnel, maintains permanent liaison with the International Bank for Reconstruction and Development, and is responsible for co-ordinating the work of the Indus Valley Replacement Water Works, involving a loan of $90 million in foreign currency. The (WP)WAPDA reports can be favorably compared with those of many major Western industrial concerns. There is interesting text, artistic use of line drawings and photographs, imaginative use of different colors and textures of paper, and artistic binding. The substance of the reports is as valuable as the format is sophisticated. In these respects they differ from the conventional reporting techniques of agencies of the old line bureaucracy. West Pakistan WAPDA has published four annual reports. The latest, *Annual Report of 1962–63,* is an outstanding example of government reporting premised on a sense of responsibility for informing the public. The *WAPDA Weekly,* published each Friday, combines the features of a house organ and official gazette, for it includes postings, transfers, and tender notices as well as news items. The first issue of the *WAPDA Directory,* which appeared in July, 1961, is again an outstanding example of clarity and precision, and the annual publication, *WAPDA Miscellany,* is a public relations document of uncommon sophistication and good taste. It is, in reality, an annual report of somewhat more than one hundred pages describing the activities of WAPDA. Its maps and charts are excellent, and it is a major source of engineering information, narrated in non-technical style, on the Indus Replacement Works. The WAPDA monthly journal, *Indus,* now in its fourth year of publication, reveals the same high literary and artistic quality. The cover of the June, 1961, issue of *Indus,* for example, was designed by A. J. Shemza, a well-known Pakistani painter. WAPDA's printing press in Lahore is the newest and most versatile in Pakistan.

The East Pakistan Water and Power Development Authority, (EP)WAPDA, is a smaller organization than (WP)WAPDA but it reflects the same new outlook in government reporting. Its annual report, published as *EPWAPDA Ensemble,* is similar in format to the *WAPDA Miscellany.*

The administrative behavior of both water and power development authorities will eventually have substantial impact on the attitudes and workways of the traditional bureaucracy. WAPDA represents a new style of government performance, unshackled by imperial bureaucratic traditions and conventional fiscal restrictions, and dominated by the ethos of the scientifically trained engineer. A sense of dedication, responsibility to the public, and relative administrative efficiency characterize its operations. It is, indeed, the first and only serious competition which the ICS-dominated line bureaucracy has had. Implicit in this competitive relationship is the difference between the empirically oriented, rationalist traditions of scientific organization and the literary-generalist ethos of an administration oriented toward law and order. Neither sphere of activity can long exist uninfluenced by the other, but it may be suggested that the permeative effect of the new corporations will be greater than that of the line bureaucracy.

The two industrial development corporations are also influential vehicles for the introduction of change in administration, although this is only a concomitant of their primary function, which is to stimulate and finance the organization of industries. West Pakistan

PIDC is concerned with management and operates an Institute of Personnel Training. Since 1960, the institute has published the *Pakistan Management Review,* a bimonthly of about fifty pages, the first such journal in Pakistan. Like WAPDA, PIDC has its own printing press in Karachi. Since 1955 it has published a monthly journal, *Forward,* which includes semi-popular articles on technical problems related to the activities of PIDC. The latest *Progress Report on P.I.D.C. Projects* (Karachi: PIDC, June, 1963) is a valuable means of ascertaining the scope of its activities.

Among a broad range of topics on which much research is needed are the following:

1. A careful inventory and classificatory scheme of all corporations and the collation of data concerning their authority, structure, census of employment, salary scale, and service rules.

2. Patterns of control and co-ordination of corporate activity with central and provincial secretariats and division and district administration. The extent of corporate autonomy and the conflict of such autonomy with line departments requires analysis.

3. The nature of fiscal control over the corporations and cost benefit analyses are needed. This looms as a serious problem since the establishment of legislatures in 1962. Both WAPDA and PIDC have been severely criticized, for example, in the West Pakistan Provincial Assembly.[21]

4. The relationship of the legislative process to the corporate process. Analysis of the nature and degree of both provincial and central legislative supervision of the corporate process is needed. If such supervision is required, such alternative means as legislative committee oversight merits exploration. Recently, for example, it was proposed that legislators be members of corporate boards of directors so that a degree of legislative co-ordination might be assured.[22]

5. It is significant to note the degree to which new managerial skills and an attitude of risk-taking are infused into the corporate device. The corporate enterprises have at least thirty-six full-time

[21] Provincial Assembly of West Pakistan, *Debates,* June 22, 1962, p. 22.
[22] Provincial Assembly of West Pakistan, *Debates,* July 3, 1962, pp. 18–40.

managerial posts and about 237 directorships on governing boards. Does the recruitment pattern to these positions suggest an infusion of (*a*) military skill, (*b*) private entrepreneurial skill, (*c*) traditional bureaucratic technology, (*d*) political experience, or (*e*) technical competence, such as engineering? Table 5 suggests that nearly half of the directorships are held by retired or active government officials, nearly a third by businessmen, about 6 per cent by engineers, and only 6 per cent by army officers. While Table 5 is valid for 1964, the construction of such a table for subsequent years would be helpful in plotting trends.

6. Closely related to the problem of infusion of new skills and attitudes is the relationship between the elite CSP cadre and the corporate device. The rise of powerful corporations may diminish the attraction of assignments in traditional district and secretariat administration. It appears axiomatic that the magnetic pull of bureaucratic position is in the direction of the locus of bureaucratic power and challenge. The controversial role of the Civil Service of Pakistan will be affected by the rise in prestige and power of government corporations whose empirical and scientific temper is essentially antagonistic to the classical-literary-generalist bias which dominates the ethos of the CSP. The CSP cadre might broaden its interests, incorporate within its generalist traditions advanced technical training (much like the management-engineer movement in Western countries), and claim executive posts of power within the corporations as its legitimate sphere of action. Or, the new status and rise in prestige of a class of technical and scientific executives, recruited from sources other than the traditional CSP, may operate to place a new technical elite in positions of power within the corporate entities. The CSP cadre has not moved into corporate management to any significant extent. In 1964, 19 of the total of 432 CSP officers (4.3 per cent) held full-time managerial or directing positions in corporate entities. This compares with 18 (4.4 per cent) in 1963 and 11 (2.8 per cent) in 1962. Of greater interest, however, is the nature of such CSP assignments. The two agricultural development corporations had four CSP officers in key places: the chairman of the East Pakistan ADC, the secretary of the West Pakistan ADC, and the directors of

two of the project areas of the West Pakistan ADC. Other similarly strategic positions held by CSP officers were chairman of West Pakistan WAPDA, member of East Pakistan WAPDA, and finance director of the National Shipping Corporation. From this tabulation, it cannot be said that the elite cadre dominates the new corporate bureaucracy. But it may be said that three of the four most important corporations (PIDC being the fourth) have CSP officers in strategic places.

7. Intensive studies of individual corporations are needed. Eventually, comparative studies of analogous corporations in the two provinces might be undertaken. Conceivably, comparative analysis of Pakistani corporations with those of other states might be feasible.

5

Legal Research

Legal research is of particular importance for the study of bureaucracy, not only for the usual reasons of the relationship of administrative law to bureaucratic action, but also because of characteristics of government especially prominent in Pakistan. The legal community takes pride in the fact that Article 2 of the 1962 Constitution declares that it is the inalienable right of every citizen to be treated in accordance with law. This provision is in addition to justiciable fundamental rights which are specified in detail by the first amendment. The constitutional eminence thus given law is symbolic of the eminence and pervasiveness of legal influence in the total society. First, there is a confluence of administrative and judicial power in local government where division commissioners and district officers are responsible for courts in their respective areas. There is no separation of executive and judicial functions in Pakistan despite the continuing demands of bar associations for such separation. For this reason, a significant part of the training and behavior of the elite cadre focuses on law. Secondly, a portion of the Civil Service of Pakistan is posted to the "judicial side" of the service. Transfer to judicial work is normally made early in the fifth year of a CSP officer's service, although such transfers may be made later in a career as well. In 1964, 6 per cent of the CSP cadre served in full-time, permanent judicial posts. Thirdly, members of the judiciary have played a major role in administrative reform. Chief Justice M. Munir headed the first Pay and Services Commission, 1949–1950; Chief Justice A. R. Cornelius was chairman of the second Pay and Service Commission of 1962. The interest of Cornelius in bureaucracy extends beyond the work of that commission as is indicated by his important statements on the functioning of the bureaucracy, some of which are in the appendices to this essay. Fourthly, the judiciary has been actively involved through the medium of the writ in dealing with internal problems of bureaucracy relating to civil service matters and in external problems relating to achieving due process in the exercise of administrative discretion. The extent of this involvement, probably greater in Pakistan than in any other developing state, is suggested in subsequent analysis and elsewhere.[1] Lastly, court judgments are indispensable case studies of administrative situations, rich in detail and illuminating in analysis. In the absence of other case materials they constitute the sole source of empirically derived descriptions of bureaucratic behavior.

Some of the impediments to research efficiency discussed elsewhere in this essay are absent in the pursuit of legal studies. The century-old tradition of justice pursued in full public view has resulted in an efficient, reliable system of public reporting of court decisions in constitutional, statutory, and administrative law. So far as published judgments are concerned, classification is no barrier to accessibility. A commendable degree of competition between commercial and official systems of reporting has resulted in a condition of speed and accuracy in publishing and efficiency in distribution which surpasses many other categories of public record issuance.

Nevertheless, there are difficulties. Research on the administration of justice is hampered by the absence of statistics on categories of cases for the entire judicial system. Copies of dockets and data showing time lags in decisions are difficult to obtain. There is some improvement in this matter as a consequence of the new practice of the Supreme Court and the high courts of releasing for publication in the journal section of *All-Pakistan Legal Decisions* a report on the disposition of cases, listed by category, after each session of the court. Uniform rosters and lists of judges and their qualifications are not available except in the provincial

---

[1] See the author's "Public Bureaucracy and Judiciary in Pakistan," in Joseph LaPalombara (ed.), *Bureaucracy and Political Development* (Princeton, 1963), pp. 360–441.

civil lists. Presumably, the registrar of each court keeps such data, but their availability for research not officially connected with the work of the court is necessarily limited to whatever arrangements can be made *ex gratia*. Research is also limited to published cases. Unpublished cases are usually available in typed or mimeographed form but usually in only one copy. Copies, however, can be made from the record on court premises. Lawyers' briefs, or "paperbooks," used in the course of trial are difficult to obtain, although they are now being printed and presumably may be somewhat more easily accessible. Below the Supreme Court and high courts, judgments are not published. Sometimes they are typed or mimeographed, but they cannot be easily obtained. The research apparatus of citator systems or a *corpus juris* have not been well developed. Reliance must be placed exclusively on an official decennial digest of Supreme Court decisions, two unofficial decennial and quinquennial digests, and the annual index of *All-Pakistan Legal Decisions,* which is indispensable.

Another possible impediment is the state of legal scholarship within the legal profession and within the academic community. Closely related to this is the stringency of the contempt law that may possibly affect scholarly work which states or implies criticism of courts and their judgments. In a sense, each of these impediments may be viewed as an advantage rather than a disadvantage, at least for the foreign researcher. As a consequence of the first, the entire research field is open to original inquiry. The second possible impediment challenges the researcher to observe that due caution, moderation, and sense of suspended judgment which should be hallmarks of scholarship in any case, but which the contempt law may make somewhat more urgent in Pakistan.

The Environment of Legal Scholarship

There are six law colleges in Pakistan, each affiliated with a major university. Of these, the law colleges of the University of the Panjab in Lahore and Dacca University in East Pakistan are probably the most highly developed. The work of none of the colleges compares favorably with adequate legal education in advanced Western nations. There are also some private, commercial colleges which conduct evening courses and whose standards are generally lower than those of the six university law colleges.

Law colleges are handicapped by the quality of students who seek law degrees and by the lack of professional interest of many of them. Typically, the best students attempt to enter one of the central superior civil services, and those in law college are often marking time between civil service examinations. Others enter law college because there is no alternative means of employment or activity. Since there are few full-time professors of law on the law faculties, the standard of instruction lacks the tone of professional scholarship. Those who teach law tend to be young lawyers without established practices who need the slight extra income earned by lecturing. Lectures tend to be anecdotal and are often based on chatting about cases the lawyer has in progress. There is little use of the case method in Pakistan's law schools, and the typical graduate will not have read judgments of the Supreme Court or the high courts of his own country.

This condition of legal education was recognized by the Law Reform Commission which made several remedial proposals. It suggested uniform degree requirements in all law colleges and a three-year course beyond the A.B. for a limited number of students whose admission into law schools would be restricted. It proposed the abolition of evening classes, revision of the examination system, and the appointment of at least three full-time teachers in each law college. Chief Justice Cornelius, alluding to the need for research and for legal journals, has proposed the establishment of honors schools of law and of Islamic jurisprudence to stimulate legal research.[2] Plans have already been made to establish a Law Research Institute in Karachi financed in part by private funds.

There is virtually no published research on Pakistani legal problems in Pakistan. The *Law Journal*, published as a quarterly at the University of the Panjab Law College, consists largely of

[2] A. R. Cornelius, "Role of Law in Present Challenging Times," PLD 1964 Journal, 9–13. In the same address Cornelius noted that "we have not in our country as yet reached the stage of producing learned legal journals to explain and project the justice of our Courts before the academic minds of our own and other countries as well. . . ."

anecdotal speeches and brief essays describing tours to the United States or similar matters. Occasionally, a research article will appear, but it seldom relates to Pakistani law. Several years ago considerable interest was shown in the establishment of a legal research center in Lahore under an independent board of trustees. The Asia Foundation provided funds for a library, and the Pakistan Legal Centre was established. Its principal activity is publication of the *Pakistan Bar Journal,* which has appeared since 1955 jointly under its auspices and those of the Pakistan Bar Association. The administrator of the center, Miss Rabia Sultana Qari, a barrister, maintains its headquarters in her home across the Mall from the High Court in Lahore. The *Journal* often publishes short articles of good quality, but they are almost invariably topics in international, British, or American law written by Pakistani lawyers who studied abroad.

The *All-Pakistan Legal Decisions* (PLD), primarily a commercial service, follows the established custom of the *All-India Reporter* (of which it is a descendant) in having a journal section for comments and research. The journal section had thirty-one pages in 1960, thirteen pages in 1961, fourteen pages in 1962, 116 pages in 1963, and 144 pages in 1964. The increase in 1963 and 1964 was due largely to the printing of several addresses by Chief Justice Cornelius. None of the articles in the journal can be characterized as a research piece in the tradition of American legal journals. The typical article on Pakistan law in the PLD journal, and other journals, consists almost entirely of extensive quotations from judgments and has little or no analysis or evaluation of issues.

There are several hopeful signs suggestive of improvement in research conditions. First, there is general recognition by the legal profession of the problem of legal education and research. The law colleges, especially those of the Panjab and Peshawar universities, are making strong efforts to raise their standards and to stimulate research. Libraries are slowly improving, and certainly publications are better now than a decade ago. But conditions remain unconducive to written legal analysis by professional scholars.

The legal community is probably the most powerful elite group, outside government service, in Pakistan. The total strength of legal practitioners and legally trained persons in the country (from which much of this elite's prestige is derived) is almost impossible to calculate from available data. Since the annual output of persons with law degrees can more easily be determined, it would appear convenient to begin an estimate of the size of the legal profession with a statement of this output of newly trained law graduates. Table 6 shows that the six university law colleges have awarded about 8,820 law degrees in the decade from 1954 to 1964. During the eight-year period 1954 to 1961 (the only years for which data on all university degrees are available), these six universities conferred a total of 30,356 degrees of all kinds.[3] During the same eight years, the same universities conferred 5,346 law degrees and 3,710 medical degrees. Hence law degrees constituted 17 per cent and medical degrees 12 per cent of the total number of degrees conferred from 1954 through 1961. The ratio of law degrees to total number of degrees has remained at about 17 per cent during this eight-year period. The average output of law degrees from 1961 on (as shown by Table 6) approximates one thousand each year, but since the total number of university degrees conferred for those years is not known, the ratio of law degrees to all degrees conferred cannot be determined. It is likely that the ratio has hovered around 17 per cent. To put these data in some perspective, it might be noted that in the United States of a total of 490,628 degrees of all kinds conferred in 1961, 9,514, or approximately 2 per cent were law degrees and 6,986, or approximately 1.5 per cent, were medical (M.D.) degrees.[4]

Statistics showing the numbers of legally trained persons employed in legal work have a reliability roughly comparable to the hierarchy of the profession, the least accuracy being found in the bottom ranks. Any estimate of the size of the legal community, therefore, should include a brief description of the organization of

[3] Data on total number of degrees are derived from correspondence with the Education Division, Pakistan Mission of the United States Agency for International Development, June, 1964.

[4] For the United States, data are taken from the United States Bureau of the Census, *Statistical Abstract of the United States for 1963*, 84th annual edition (Washington, 1963), p. 141.

Table 6. *Bachelor of Laws Degrees Granted 1954–1964*

University	1954	1955	1956	1957	1958	1959	1960	1961	1962	1963	1964 [a]	Total
Panjab	163	331	282	259	291	304	212	339	303	458	309	3,251
Karachi	105	193	148	187	153	175	160	250	412	399	280	2,462
Dacca	26	109	93	95	76	133	141	124	192	355	145	1,489
Peshawar	50	53	45	73	64	54	63	140	62	66	45	715
Sind	15	19	31	19	24	76	53	82	104	112	100	635
Rajshahi	—	—	34	23	21	7	14	37	53	61	18	268
Total	359	705	633	656	629	749	643	972	1,126	1,451	897	8,820 [b]

Sources: For 1954–1961: Inter-University Board of Pakistan, Letter, January 15, 1964. For 1961–1964: Correspondence with principals of law colleges, September and October, 1964.

[a] Does not include results of supplementary examinations held in May, 1964, not yet announced in December, 1964. Results of this examination will probably make 1964 total similar to that for 1963.

[b] This total would approximate 9,500 if an estimate of results of the May, 1964, examination (see note a) were added.

the profession. Graduates in law first become pleaders with the right to practice before district and sessions courts but not before the high courts or Supreme Court. In East Pakistan *munsifs,* who have the equivalent of a high school education, practice criminal law below the sessions court level. Advocates, the rank above that of pleader, practice before district and sessions courts and may be enrolled for practice before the high courts only after several years of practice and after being approved by a panel of High Court judges. Advocates may also appear before the Supreme Court after five years of practice and certification by the judges and chief justice of the High Court. The chief justice and judges of the Supreme Court may select from the roll of advocates "persons who are judged, by their knowledge, ability and experience, to be worthy" to be senior advocates.[5] At the pinnacle of prestige are the barristers who, before independence, usually studied in England at one of the Inns-of-Court. Barristers were distinguished from other legal practitioners by the privilege of practice before the High Court immediately upon completion of their training. Attorneys were not allowed to plead at trials before the Supreme Court and generally functioned as process servers and as residents at court for litigants. Some revisions of this organization were made in 1962, the principal one being that senior advocates of the Supreme Court are appointed not on the basis of seniority but for a distinguished legal record. The Supreme Court now designates some attorneys as senior attorneys with the privilege of pleading before the Supreme Court if they are associated with a legal firm. Legal firms have been allowed only since 1962. Senior attorneys must have at least seven years' practice and generally serve as assistants to senior advocates. At the top of the official hierarchy are members of the bench.

It is probable that there are approximately 18,000 persons trained in law in Pakistan. This figure is so tentative, however, that an explanation of how it was determined is in order. As Table 7 (items 9, 10) shows, beginning at the bottom of the hierarchy, there are about 12,599 legal practitioners of all categories practicing in subordinate and high courts in Pakistan; 7,289 are in West

---

[5] Supreme Court of Pakistan, *The Pakistan Supreme Court Rules, 1956* (Karachi, 1963), p. 5. These rules are amended up to June, 1963.

Table 7. *Estimated Number of Legally Trained Persons in Pakistan,*
1965

Classification	West Pakistan	East Pakistan	Total
1. Supreme Court judges	3	2	5
2. High court judges	29	15	46 [a]
3. District and sessions judges	64	43	107
4. Subordinate court judges and *Munsifs*	153	166	319
5. Law officers [b]	76	50	126
6. Executive officers (provincial service) with judicial powers	643	738	1,381
7. Executive officers (CSP) with judicial powers	114	65	179
8. Legal practitioners enrolled in supreme court [c]	533	169	702
9. Legal practitioners enrolled in high courts	3,132	649	3,781
10. Legal practitioners enrolled in subordinate courts	4,157	4,661	8,818
11. Legally trained persons not performing functions related to their training	711	1,000	2,311 [d]
Totals	9,615	7,558	17,775 [e]

[a] Includes two *ad hoc* judges not tabulated in provincial columns.
[b] Registrars, government prosecutors, pleaders, legal remembrancers.
[c] These figures can be further classified into 425 advocates and 108 attorneys for West Pakistan; 129 advocates and 40 attorneys for East Pakistan; total of 554 advocates and 148 attorneys.
[d] Estimated from *Census of West Pakistan Government Employees* (Lahore: Government of West Pakistan, 1963) which shows (pp. 34–35) 711 of 8,814 gazetted officers with law degrees in 1962. Assuming this proportion to be somewhat higher in the central government and in East Pakistan, I have estimated three hundred for the former and one thousand for the latter and have added three hundred for those outside government service. Six hundred in central government and outside government are not included in provincial columns.
[e] This figure is 602 more than the sum of provincial totals for reasons given in notes a and d. The figure has been rounded off to 18,000 in the text.
Sources: Correspondence and civil lists. Final results (except for item 11) prepared with help of Office of the Supreme Court of Pakistan, May, 1965, and the chief justice, East Pakistan High Court, June, 1965. Item 11 is an arbitrary estimate by the present author. Estimates of item 11 have ranged as high as ten thousand. My estimate of 2,311 is undoubtedly less than the real figure.

Pakistan and 5,310 are in East Pakistan. Of these, 649 are enrolled for practice before the East Pakistan High Court and 3,132 before the West Pakistan High Court.[6] The total number enrolled for practice before the Supreme Court is only 702,[7] or about 18 per

[6] Limitations of data are described in notes to Table 7.
[7] In 1962 the figure, taken from an untitled, unsigned article in PLD 1963 Journal, 104, which is based on data supplied by the Registrar of the Supreme Court, was 618. Thus, in two years, the number enrolled in the Supreme Court bar increased by eighty-four.

cent of those enrolled before the high courts, and about 5 per cent of the total enrolled for practice before any court. The sharply diminishing number at the top of the pyramid is an index of a marked difference in competence and skill between subordinate court practitioners and those in the superior courts. It is somewhat difficult also to estimate the number of officers involved in judicial work because of the variety of officers holding judicial powers. There are five judges on the Supreme Court, fifteen on the East Pakistan High Court, twenty-nine on the West Pakistan High Court, approximately one hundred district and sessions judges, and approximately three hundred lower judges, and *munsifs*, in the two provinces. In addition, each of the sixteen division commissioners and seventy-four district officers and their assistants have judicial powers in certain categories of cases. Probably, between fifteen hundred and two thousand persons are part of the judicial system. Using the figure two thousand (the actual figure in Table 7 being 2,037) and the figure 13,427 for legal practitioners who are not judges, the ratio of judges to legal practitioners is in the order of 1:7.

Outside the formal structure of legal practice are an unknown number of law graduates who have never practiced law. Although most of them are in government service, the civil lists do not always indicate the fact of legal training, hence the number in this group is a cruder estimate than those given above. I estimate this group at 2,311. This is based on the fact that 711 gazetted employees of the West Pakistan provincial government are known to have law degrees (note d, Table 7). It is assumed that a somewhat higher proportion will be found in the central government and in East Pakistan. Estimating one thousand with law degrees in the East Pakistan government and three hundred in the central government, we have a sub-total of 17,475. I have added to this total an additional three hundred for an estimate of those with law degrees, outside government employ. This makes a total of 17,775, which is rounded off to eighteen thousand. Since several sources in Pakistan insist that my estimate of 2,311 persons in item 11 of Table 2 is much too low, it is probable that the total of eighteen thousand is an underestimate. I am reluctant to increase it, however, without further clues as to limits. In any case, eighteen thousand is a base figure which can be improved by subsequent research.

Using eighteen thousand as the figure for persons with legal training, some suggestive tentative ratios can be constructed which might ultimately be compared with analogous ratios for Burma, Ceylon, Malaya, and India, all of which shared the common experience of British imperial rule. For example, assuming total public employment in Pakistan to be 995,000 the ratio of legally trained persons in all pursuits to the total number of government servants would be 1:55. Or, given (in 1965) a population of 99 million, the ratio of legally trained persons to population would be 1:5,500. These ratios can be compared to similar data for the United States which indicate 285,933 lawyers (both practicing and non-practicing) registered in 1960.[8] Using the official population estimate of 180 million for that year, the ratio of licensed practicing and non-practicing lawyers to total population in 1960 is thus about 1:630 for the United States. This comparison will be surprising to many who assumed that the ratio of "lawyers" to population is higher in many new states than in old states. In any case, these comparative data really have very little meaning and must be interpreted with the utmost caution. They clearly suggest that the per capita ratio of legally trained persons in Pakistan is much less than in the United States. On the other hand, it was shown earlier that the proportion of law degrees to total degrees is markedly higher in Pakistan than the United States. The significance of these comparisons is not clear. The vast difference between the legal needs of an industrial society and those of an agrarian economy, as well as the high status of alternative professions in the United States, should be considered in interpreting the data.

It is common to assume that developing states in the British imperial tradition have too many lawyers and that the consequent disproportionate emphasis on legal modes of thought is antithetical to the needs of development. This has been the view of President Ayub in Pakistan, although no measures have been taken to curtail the output of lawyers, which, it has been shown,

[8] U. S. Bureau of the Census, *Statistical Abstract . . . for 1963*, p. 162.

remains fairly constant. Ayub's view was summed up in an address before the Pakistan Lawyers Convention in Karachi on September 30, 1960, when he suggested that lawyers often gave assistance "in the fabrication of false evidence to support the case of their client." He added that the legal profession appeared to be over-staffed and that this, "apart from locking useful manpower unnec-essarily, creates cut-throat competition in the profession ushering in all sorts of abuses." [9] This condition is probably aggravated by the large number of lawyers. On the other hand, it can be argued that in Pakistan the very size of the legal group, strongly organized into bar associations and closely allied with equally strong courts, has not only been a major source for the diffusion and regeneration of Western norms generally, but by sheer weight of numbers has enabled the courts to remain strong and has impeded what some would regard as administrative lawlessness. It is not here sug-gested that size alone has made possible the power of the legal community in Pakistan. There are other factors contributing to this condition. An important one is the absence of effective competing elites such as business, artistic, professional, trade-union, eccle-siastical, political, agricultural, or educational interest groups. Some of these groups, such as the commercial, exist but are localized in Karachi or are not well organized. Others are rising in importance. But none can rival the elites of the civil and military bureaucracies and the legal community in prestige, effective power, and close identification with the ideology and techniques of modernization.

The legal community, while often antagonistic to government and constraining governmental behavior, is nevertheless closely identified normatively, and culturally, with the bureaucratic power elite. It is, in fact, this identification curiously coupled with antagonism which enhances the strength of the legal community. It derives popular support from its ostensible opposition to gov-ernment, and at the same time elicits bureaucratic support from its command of Western-oriented norms and techniques and com-mands the rather fearful attention of bureaucracy because of its

[9] Full text in Government of Pakistan, *Speeches and Statements of Field Marshal Mohammad Ayub Khan* (Karachi, 1961), III, 27.

support in the community at large. In the absence of other competing elites, it holds the field. Yet important though these factors are, it is doubtful if the legal community could be such an effective political force without the large number of persons within its ambit of influence.

The influence of legal practitioners is further strengthened by a network of relationships in rural areas and cities. A coterie of retainers such as *munshis, dalals, mukhtars,* clerks, and scribes are dependent on British legal proceedings for a livelihood and serve as linguistic and cultural mediators between lawyers and the vernacularized community at large.

Students in law colleges, who at any given time approximate fifteen thousand persons, must also be included as a source of strength for the legal community as an interest group. They are often as vocal and effective as agents of Western legal norms as law graduates. Indeed, considering their freedom as students to participate in anomic actions, they can and do fill an agitational role unavailable to their established colleagues.

Adding law students and retainers to the figure 18,000 we can estimate the larger community of law-oriented persons at roughly 33,000. It is true that those at the fringe of this larger community have only partial comprehension of the legal norms of Western jurisprudence. But at the core of the group stand persons of power and intellectual mastery of those norms, and they determine the style of the larger group. To society at large the internal stratifications of understanding are not visible; it regards the entire law-oriented group, core and fringe alike, as the vanguard of modernization. The persistent challenging of governmental policy during and after martial law was successful primarily because of the size of the legal community and its consequent network of influence throughout the country. In short, the legal community is of some magnitude and is a power with which to be reckoned. It has, *inter alia,* compelled the justiciability of fundamental rights, forced modification of the extension of the Frontier Crimes Regulation, and successfully agitated for amendment or abrogation of other restrictive enactments.

By and large, the judiciary, especially the Supreme Court and high courts, are highly respected and several important and influential judges such as Md. Munir, M. R. Kayani, Shabir Ahmed, M. Shahabuddin, S. A. Rahman, S. M. Murshed and A. R. Cornelius, have made contributions not only to legal thought but to other aspects of the nation's development. Legal erudition diminishes usually as the rank of the court becomes lower, but this is true of most judicial systems. Only one instance of a senior judge being debenched because of improbity has been noted since partition. This was the case of Syed Akhlaque Husain of the West Pakistan High Court, an able jurist, who was debenched for income tax evasion and falsification of expense accounts (*The State* v. *Mr. Justice Akhlaque Husain* [1957] 1 P.S.C.R. 231) and later suspended from practicing law as well (*In the matter of Akhlaque Husain* [1959] 2 P.S.C.R. 146). Although the bench is highly respected, some lawyers of considerable ability are reputed to have refused appointment to the bench because of what they regard as relatively low salary, early retirement age, inadequate retirement pension, and prohibition against legal practice after retirement. The salary of a Supreme Court judge is Rs. 5,100 a month and mandatory retirement is at age sixty-five; a High Court judge receives Rs. 4,000 a month and must retire at sixty years of age. These salaries compare favorably with civil service executive salaries (a full secretary receives Rs. 4,000 a month) but are lower than the income of a few very successful lawyers. Salaries are fixed by the Second Schedule of the 1962 Constitution, but the disqualification provision is found in Legal Practices (Disqualifications) Ordinance, 1964, published in the *Gazette of Pakistan, Extraordinary*, January 30, 1964. The Law Reform Commission recommended improving the pension scheme rather than changing the retirement age or the provision concerning disqualification from practice.

The legal profession in Pakistan is an influential, articulate group and indeed is probably the most important group in national politics. Many active political leaders such as Khan Abdul Qayyum Khan of the Northwest Frontier, S. H. Suhrawardy, Mahmud Ali Qasuri, and Mian Mumtaz Daultana were lawyers. Highly organized through regional bar associations and associations of members practicing before various courts, lawyers have in the past exerted substantial pressure on the government on behalf of such issues as fundamental rights, constitutional reform, and against extension of the Frontier Crimes Regulation. If perhaps they have a tendency to assume that the nation is in a more advanced state of political development than is actually the case, they are not unlike the intelligentsia in other developing countries who are suspended between the vision of a society based on the norms in which they are immersed and the realities of the social order. Be that as it may, the more distinguished lawyers are held in remarkably high regard by the public and by government. The legal profession as a group was opposed to the Constitution of 1962 and when Manzur Qadir was appointed chief justice of the West Pakistan High Court, several bar associations passed resolutions condemning the appointment, largely on grounds that he was the author of that Constitution.[10] Their earlier opposition to martial law and opposition to the 1962 Constitution and the form of government which evolved from it makes them the most powerful educated group in Pakistan. It is significant to note that many of the political leaders arrested in the sixties were lawyers. The arrest of Mahmud Ali Qasuri, who with others attempted to organize the National Freedom party as a coalition of several defunct groups, also revealed the interest of such distinguished lawyers as A. K. Brohi and Z. H. Lari as well as H. S. Suhrawardy, all of whom came to his support. Bar associations have been uncommonly vigorous in taking stands on political issues. The cohesion of the legal profession with its several thousand practicing members and the sense of identity of some thirty-one thousand persons trained in law or being trained have made the associations powerful institutions in articulating sentiments of the country. The network of followers of each legally trained person enhances the power of the legal community in villages as well as urban centers. Virtually all of the bar associations, including the two most important, the Lahore District Bar Association, and the West Pakistan High Court Bar Association, supported the Com-

[10] *Pakistan Times,* August 4, 1962, p. 1; August 7, 1962, p. 7; August 9, 1962, p. 5.

bined Opposition party's presidential candidate against President Ayub in the election of January 2, 1965.[11] The West Pakistan High Court Bar Association's support was virtually unanimous; there were only two dissenting votes of several thousand cast. Some of the most distinguished lawyers such as A. K. Brohi, Z. H. Lari, and Mahmud Ali Qasuri were active organizers of the Combined Opposition party. It is not surprising that the emphasis of the COP's manifesto [12] was on details of the concept of rule of law, such as the right of superior courts to review and revise administrative decisions and to issue writs to all citizens, and the separation of executive and judicial functions. The COP also stood for repeal of eight specific statutes, such as the Press and Publications Ordinance, Universities Ordinance, and Criminal Law (Amendment) Act which it deemed violated due process of law. So vociferous have bar associations been in their extra-courtroom political advocacy that they have been warned by otherwise sympathetic legal practitioners that they were assuming a role unbecoming their position. Thus, Khurshid Ahmed, minister of law in the central government, warned the associations during the election campaign that they were not political parties and could not organize like political parties.[13] Chief Justice Cornelius of the Supreme Court regards as inappropriate the public criticism through formal statements of laws which may ultimately be the subject of judicial scrutiny. In an address before the Karachi High Court Bar Association on June 5, 1964,[14] he said that he felt "some anxiety regarding the exact demarcation of the duties of lawyers in a political-legal complex such as that under which we live," and that he often felt regret when lawyers or bar associations openly criticized actions under statute law. "Even the private citizen," he continued, "hesitates to offer such criticism in fear of an action in contempt where on the face of the matter recourse to the courts seems plainly probable." He deplored the tendency of bar associa-

[11] For accounts of resolutions passed, see *Dawn*, October 5, 1964, p. 4; *ibid.*, October 15, 1964, p. 5.
[12] *Nine-Point Manifesto and Joint Declaration of the Combined Opposition Party* (Dacca, July 14, 1964).
[13] *Dawn*, October 8, 1964, p. 7.
[14] A. R. Cornelius, "Speech at Annual Dinner of High Court Bar Association," PLD, 1964 Journal, 107–112. Quotation at 110.

tions to pass resolutions disapproving laws which are likely to be brought before the courts. "In fact," said Cornelius, "I often suffer the apprehension that should a bar association pass a resolution condemning a political-legal action in such circumstances, the association and each of its members would find it difficult to discover a defence against a writ of contempt which an affected party might choose to take out." The predominant ethos of the legal profession appears to be that of political activity, concern for national political development, and preoccupation with trial advocacy rather than with theoretical legal research. Members of the legal fraternity feel keenly that the future of constitutional government in the nation rests with the legal profession. In this respect, they share with the civil and military bureaucracies the sense that they are the guardians of the polity of the state.

The judiciary, powerful, respected, sometimes feared, has preserved its integrity throughout martial law and has been perhaps the most stabilizing institution in the development of Pakistan. One of the outstanding characteristics of the whole legal-judicial system in Pakistan is the strong sense of corporate unity and *élan* between the courts and legal practitioners and between levels of courts. To some extent, this unity was enhanced by martial law and what was regarded as an executive effort to curtail judicial power and to limit fundamental freedoms. The very fact that lawyers and judges could not be divided against each other was important in the re-emergence of judicial review, justiciability of fundamental rights, and the writ jurisdiction. The high courts and the Supreme Court have been a cohesive group viewing major problems of doctrine in a similar way. The few classic instances of disagreement involved somewhat peripheral rather than fundamental questions. For example, in the Gurmani defamation case (*M. A. Gurmani* v. *Suleri et. al.,* PLD 1958 Lah. 747) Justice Shabir Ahmed made adverse remarks against Prime Minister Malik Feroze Khan Noon which were later ordered expunged from the record by the Supreme Court. Similarly, in the Snelson Case (*The State* v. *Sir Edward Snelson,* PLD 1961 Lah. 78), Shabir Ahmed imputed certain motives in the action of the attorney-general and this imputation was rejected by the Supreme

Court (*Sir Edward Snelson* v. *Judges of High Court of Pakistan,* PLD 1961 SC 237). In the recent case of the arrest of Mahmud Ali Qasuri, the chief justice of the High Court, Manzur Qadir, attached a political condition to the granting of bail which was struck down by the Supreme Court (*Mian Mahmud Ali Qasuri and others* v. *The State,* PLD 1963 SC 478). This intellectual compatibility is sometimes given more specific institutional form. For example, the Supreme Court co-opted three judges of the high courts, thus making a special bench of seven judges, to decide a major case affecting contract employees of government (*Khwaja Ghulam Sarwar* v. *Pakistan,* PLD 1962 SC 142). In such a major issue as the ruling of the East Pakistan High Court that cabinet ministers could not also serve as members of the legislature, the Supreme Court not only concurred but elaborated the doctrines of presidential government and judicial review in a significant way (*Fazlul Quader Chowdhry* v. *Md. Abdul Haque,* PLD 1963 SC 486). Even in such matters as overruling the High Court on the issuance of writs, twelve instances of which are discussed below, the courts did not disagree as to the authority to use writs, but merely on interpretation of a particular set of circumstances surrounding each instance of writ issuance. The absence of serious division on crucial juridical concepts accounts in large measure for the success of the courts in maintaining a rule of law against, at some periods, very great odds.

Contempt of Courts Power

Ironically, the very power and prestige of the judiciary, essential as it is in a new state, might be regarded as a source of discouragement in the pursuit of legal research. The power and prestige of the judiciary derives in part from the stringent law of contempt and its equally stringent interpretation and enforcement by the courts. Many able lawyers in Pakistan state that they are reluctant to comment analytically on judicial decisions for fear of being found in contempt of court. They assert that this is the reason for research being focused on foreign law, which is "safer," and for the few studies of Pakistan law being limited to extensive quotation from decisions with no commentary. To some extent this may be merely a rationalization for the absence of scholarly analysis of law in Pakistan. It is also probably true that the concept of "critical research" does not have the same connotation of meticulous, balanced, impersonal, and, above all, responsible research as can be found in American law. Passions run high in verbal altercations in Pakistan, and it might be felt not inappropriate to use intemperate, irresponsible language or to venture to make patently subjective judgments on a judge's erudition or ability. In any case, the power of each of the courts to determine if contempt has been committed and the correlative power to debar a lawyer from practicing before it is not taken lightly by some legal practitioners of Pakistan.

The basic law on contempt, the Contempt of Courts Act (XII of 1926) now incorporated in the 1962 Constitution as Article 123, has been interpreted by the courts in several important judgments. One of the earliest contempt cases decided after independence was *Haq* v. *The Honourable Judges of the High Court of Judicature at Lahore* (1953) F.C.R. 206, in which a lawyer, in addressing to the Supreme Court an appeal from a High Court decision, stated as a ground for appeal that the "remarks of the Honourable Judges betray a lack of the knowledge of elementary principles bearing on the administration of criminal justice." The Federal (Supreme) Court felt that the range of accepted legal expression was sufficient without belittling judges and that while it is one thing to point out an error in a judgment, it is quite another "to apply a damaging label to the Judge or Judges whose error is the sole matter requiring attention." The federal court, noting that the criticism made by the advocate was necessary in this instance, did not uphold the High Court's suspension. The publisher of a newspaper, which allegedly made a "technical error" of reporting that certain contempt proceedings "had been dropped in view of the qualified apology tendered by the contemner, while in fact the court had reserved orders," was found guilty of falsely guiding the public mind as to results of a case so as to embarrass the judge in his function. It was further held that intention or malice were not necessary attributes of contempt (*Abdus Salam* v. *The State* [1958] 1 P.S.C.R. 427). That allegations against a judge may be true or that they may be made in a legal application for transfer of a case are not sufficient reasons to justify scandalizing the judiciary (*Israr Hussain* v. *The Crown* [1951] 2 F.C.R. 7). The court trying contempt charges against itself may "follow the procedure it consider[s] . . . suitable," since the Criminal Procedure Code is not applicable to contempt proceedings (*Abdur Rashid* v. *The Crown* [1954] 2 F.C.R. 177).

The celebrated Snelson case dealt with the problem of contempt of court in High Court and Supreme Court judgments totaling some 140 pages (*State* v. *Sir Edward Snelson,* PLD 1961 Lah. 78; *Sir Edward Snelson* v. *Judges of the High Court of West Pakistan,* PLD 1961 SC 237). Sir Edward, secretary of the Ministry of Law and the most senior pre-independence British ICS officer remaining in Pakistan, talked informally to government officials participating in an administrative training program in Rawalpindi. His talk, dealing with the transitional Constitution of 1958, was published by the Secretariat Training Institute and circulated to government officers including High Court judges. By "transitional constitution," Sir Edward meant a series of instruments under which the nation was governed under martial law. They included the Proclamation of Martial Law, the Laws (Continuance in Force) Order, 1958, and four other instruments. The judges took the view that certain remarks made in the talk appeared to be contemptuous and charged Sir Edward with violation of the Contempt of Courts Act. These remarks dealt with the issue of the writ petition. Sir Edward said, in part:

9. Between 1956 and 1958, the High Courts had used the language of the 1956 Constitution, with its reference to orders and directions in the nature of writs—to claim a jurisdiction to interfere with the Government itself without reference to the strictly defined frontiers of the prerogative writs. . . . The Law Ministry has had to appeal a large number of times to the Supreme Court to have the position properly established, and has succeeded in every appeal but one. All this has cost a great deal of money, and to try to put the situation right without having to spend more money on more appeals a clause was inserted in the Order we are discussing giving the High Courts the power to issue the named "writs" (not "orders or directions" and so on, but writs) of *mandamus* and the rest. This was to indicate as politely as possible,

that a writ was a writ, confined to known limits, and the limits could not be exceeded. I must confess that, even with this civility, we have not entirely succeeded even yet, but this clause on the one side, and some very severe observations by the Supreme Court on the other, have at least had the effect of indicating that after all there are limits and that the limits must be observed. The great thing, in any orderly system of Government (and without orderliness there is chaos) is that every organ of the Government should be best adapted to the work it has to do and should know what that work is and what its own frontiers are. This avoids duplication. It avoids friction. It prevents usurpation of function and consequent uncertainty, with all the public confusion and private misery that it can lead to. . . .

10. . . . Perhaps you would have wished me to say something about the services, seeing that what was originally a single paragraph, Article 6, has now been increased to a further six paragraphs, some modifying the terms and conditions of service already guaranteed—but not all: one of the additions establishes the power to grant extensions of service, a power which was denied by the High Court. We have never been able to understand the judgment: We would, of course, have appealed against it, and I have no doubt we should have succeeded, but there was no time—a certain loan from abroad was made conditional upon the continued retention of certain people, and since the High Court had denied the power to retain, and we could not wait for the months an appeal would take, the existence of the power was formally asserted in an explanation. . . .

In pre-trial questioning by certain of the High Court judges, Snelson asserted that he "had written the Talk in the midst of pressing official pre-occupations and that if he had had more time he might have used different language" but that "nothing in the language he had used was meant in any way to ridicule or be derogatory to the High Courts" (*State* v. *Sir Edward Snelson,* PLD 1961 Lah. at 98 and 99). In this conversation Snelson "admitted that in paragraph 9 of the Talk he had intended to say that writs could not issue to Government." The High Court unanimously found Snelson guilty of contempt on the basis of the remarks in paragraphs 9 and 10. The court maintained (*a*) that Snelson indicated that it did not have the power to issue writs, which, in fact, it had, (*b*) that Snelson impugned the court by suggesting a usurpation of executive functions, (*c*) that the tone of the talk was offensive, particularly in the comment that govern-

ment "could not understand" a High Court decision. The Supreme
Court unanimously upheld the decision. Chief Justice Cornelius
made this comment:

[The] words "as politely as possible" are used ironically,
and . . . they carry the implication of the use of courtesy where none
was justified. . . . At the same time, a hope of greater success is
expressed which is based upon the wording of the amended clause and
"some very severe observations by the Supreme Court" which it is said
have had "the effect of indicating that after all there are limits and that
the limits must be observed." The existence of limits is very often
anathema to a judicial body charged with the function of interpreting
written words conveying powers to itself. The reminder of actual
corrections by a superior appellate authority adds a sting which could
not have been lost upon the audience of section officers.

At the time of Snelson's talk, the Supreme Court had overruled
the High Court of West Pakistan in at least twelve judgments
involving the use of writs. The Supreme Court's view of the use of
the writ appeared to be somewhat more restrained than that of the
High Court. Snelson did not mention these judgments nor did he
quote the language of the Supreme Court in disagreeing with the
High Court. The language of the Supreme Court in these twelve
cases may illustrate the range of permissible expression not involving contempt. It should be made clear, however, that this language is that of the Supreme Court commenting on the High
Court's judgments. The moderate tone suggests the need for even
greater moderation on the part of a researcher not a member of the
bench. Cornelius, who was later to become chief justice, wrote six
of the twelve judgments. The first of these deals with an issue
which had been raised by Snelson in his talk, namely, the construction by the High Court of the term "directions, orders or
writs" to mean more than writs. Under this construction the High
Court had ordered payment of salary. Cornelius overruled the
High Court on the ground that the power to issue directions and
orders did not exceed the confines of the power to issue writs.
Since writs could not be used to enforce payment of salary, neither
could directions or orders. "It represents," said the chief justice, "a
diversion of the due and orderly administration of the law into a
new and (we say so with proper respect) an improper course,

which cannot be supported, and must not be allowed to become a precedent for the future" (*State of Pakistan* v. *Mehrajuddin* [1959] 1 P.S.C.R. 34). This is the very issue to which Snelson referred. Although he had rather loosely summarized the view of the Supreme Court, his mode of expression lacked scholarly precision and circumspection. In the earliest relevant case, Amiruddin Ahmad said that the High Court made an order "without taking into consideration all the factors relevant to the case . . . [and it] had no jurisdiction to interfere by means of a writ" (*Central Board of Revenue* v. *Asad Ahmad Khan* [1959] 2 P.S.C.R. 215). In another case he stated that "the learned Judges considered that the first decision was taken properly and in the light of the facts; it would appear that this decision is plainly incorrect" (*Province of West Pakistan* v. *Akram Wasti* [1959] 2 P.S.C.R. 285). In a significant case overruling a High Court verdict that prospects of promotion were a "condition of service" which cannot be changed by the government, Cornelius held that "it seems to us impossible in the face of the wording of this proviso to support the conclusion reached by the learned Judges, which has the effect of overriding a power necessarily invested in the Government" (*Government of West Pakistan* v. *Fateh Ullah Khan* [1959] 2 P.S.C.R. 215). On at least two occasions the Supreme Court disagreed with a value judgment of the High Court which had ruled that a certain officer was entitled to promotion. Cornelius wrote, "consequently the order issued by the learned Judges was, speaking with respect, wholly inappropriate to a man of his type" (*Government of West Pakistan* v. *Fida Muhammad Khan* [1959] 2 P.S.C.R. 187). Similarly, Cornelius later said "in our opinion the learned Judges of the High Court, in issuing the writ here under appeal did not place the correct interpretation upon the order" (*Province of East Pakistan* v. *Md. Abdu Miah* [1959] 1 P.S.C.R. 259). On another occasion, the Supreme Court did not sustain a High Court order of writ because of inordinate delay in the applicant's prayer and because of other special circumstances (*Lahore Central Cooperative Bank Ltd.* v. *Saif Ullah Shah* [1959] 1 P.S.C.R. 164). Justice S. A. Rahman, writing two of the twelve opinions used such language as "the High Court seems to have erroneously assumed" (*Pakistan v. Hasan Ali Jafari and another* [1960] 1 P.S.C.R. 26), and "the direction to order payment of arrears of salary was misconceived and must be set aside" (*Government of West Pakistan v. Fazal-e-Haq Mussarratt* [1960] 1 P.S.C.R. 124). In another case, Chief Justice Md. Munir wrote that the view taken by the High Court was "wholly unsustainable" and that the High Court was "plainly wrong in the view . . ." (*Pakistan v. Hikmat Hussain* [1958] 2 P.S.C.R. 257). Munir, noting that the relief granted by the High Court was different from the one requested, referred to the "error in proceedings" of the High Court as being fundamental (*Pakistan v. Ali Afzal* [1959] 2 P.S.C.R. 160). Finally, former Chief Justice Md. Shahabuddin stated, "one would have expected a fuller consideration of the language of the rule in question in the judgement of the High Court. . . . They have, however, relied on observations in two cases which no doubt appear to support their conclusion but are clearly in the nature of *obiter dicta*" (*Pakistan v. Liaquat Ali Khan* [1958] 2 P.S.C.R. 234).

Perhaps Snelson intended to say no more than the Supreme Court said in these twelve judgments. Clearly, he erred in suggesting that the courts could not issue writs against the government, for this has never been the law. Nor has the Supreme Court ever denied the authority of the high courts to issue writs. It has, however, differed with the high courts in specific circumstances surrounding the issue of writs and on at least these twelve occasions has reversed the lower court's verdict.

In the view of the judiciary then, it was not the mere reference to the Supreme Court's overruling of several High Court decisions, but imprecision of language, tone, incorrect facts, and suggestion of judicial usurpation which led to Snelson's conviction. This observation appears to be supported by the late Chief Justice M. R. Kayani's comments in correspondence with the present author,[15] in which he stated, "To say that the High Court had a different view of the writ jurisdiction from the Supreme Court would not scandalize or ridicule either court. There would be no

---

[15] Cited in n. 21 below.

contempt in saying the High Court or the Supreme Court view was more reasoned, etc. It should be treated as legal criticism." It appears to have been corroborated more recently by remarks of Chief Justice Cornelius made in the course of a lecture at the Civil Service Academy, Lahore, April 25, 1964:

What provided some slight basis for the view expressed in the [Snelson] lecture was that a number of Writs issued by the High Courts had been recalled on reexamination of the matter in the Supreme Court. But it was clear that the criticism was misguided and misdirected and that the language employed was of a lowering type which the High Court could not be expected to tolerate, if it was to retain its position in the organisation and functioning of the State.[16]

It is noteworthy that both courts were unanimous in the Snelson decision, that distinguished lawyers such as Mahmud Ali Qasuri, who appeared in the case as *amicus curiae*, supported the decision, and that it was praised in the press, the *Pakistan Times*, for example, stating that "fresh lustre" had been imparted to the judiciary and the "country's prestige in the outside world has been enhanced." [17] The case suggests quite clearly the consummate delicacy and caution which might be required in legal research. To the American scholar, this might present a challenge because the tradition of legal scholarship is more openly critical in the United States, and the law of contempt of courts, as Justice Shabir Ahmed noted in the High Court judgment in the Snelson case, is also less stringent in the United States.

The seriousness of contempt is further indicated by the fact that the High Court judge, Shabir Ahmed, who found Sir Edward Snelson guilty of contempt of court in 1960, was, after retirement and while practicing as an advocate, found guilty of contempt of the very High Court of which he had been a judge. Shabir Ahmed had issued a statement supporting the validity of a ruling by the chief justice of the High Court attaching a condition to the bail bond of a defendant. The statement was published in the *Pakistan*

[16] Full text is accessible in Appendix 14.
[17] *Pakistan Times*, May 7, 1961, p. 6.

Times, and both the newspaper and the retired justice were found in contempt on the ground that the matter commented on was still under consideration by the court. Strict interpretation of the usual status of legal practitioners who are certified to practice before the courts as being officers of the court with the responsibility of assisting the court in obtaining justice may also affect research by Pakistani scholars. Just how far an officer of the court may go in criticizing or disagreeing with decisions of that court or with the line of reasoning even in activities outside the courtroom may not be clear to legal scholarship.

To determine attitudes toward scholarly legal criticism, the present author discussed this issue extensively with the late Chief Justice M. R. Kayani of the West Pakistan High Court, and present Chief Justice A. R. Cornelius of the Supreme Court of Pakistan. In an effort to elicit guidelines for acceptable scholarly criticism, the author submitted to each judge extracts or reprints of representative legal scholarship in the United States. One of these was a long quotation from the annual review of legal developments in the United States published in the *American Political Science Review*.[18] Fellman in this review used such expressions as "Considering . . . the expansiveness of his colleagues, Justice Black's opinion for the Court was unusually brief, and on the crucial constitutional issue almost peremptory. . . . The Chief Justice reviewed rather discursively and uncritically. . . . The Court has at long last come to grips. . . . Justice Jackson's dissenting opinion sounded more like a concurring opinion." The second sample was an article on the relations of lower courts to the United States Supreme Court.[19] The third was the text of a theoretical essay on the nature of the judicial decision,[20] in which the author called for a reappraisal of the judicial process which he regarded as essentially a trial by combat between counsel for opposing interests.

The specific reactions of Chief Justice Kayani to these samples

---

[18] David Fellman, "Constitutional Law in 1951–1952," *American Political Science Review*, XLVII (1953), 126–171.
[19] Walter F. Murphy, "Lower Court Checks on Supreme Court Power," *ibid.*, LIII (1959), 1017–1032.
[20] Carl B. Swisher, "The Supreme Court and the Moment of Truth," *ibid.*, LIV (1960), 879–887.

are noteworthy.[21] With respect to Fellman's review, Kayani said:

The words "expansiveness of his colleagues," "unusually brief," "peremptory," "rather discursively and uncritically" used in relation to the Judge in the first passage are the only words which will attract attention. In Pakistan, phrases and words less blunt would be used, but no action [for contempt] would be suggested even against the use of these words. In the second passage, the words "at long last came to grips" and "sounded more like a concurring opinion" would be of the same class, but would not be actionable.

Regarding Murphy's analysis of the capacity of lower courts to check Supreme Court power, Kayani asserted that this substantive analysis would not be made since lower courts in Pakistan could not evade an order of the Supreme Court or High Court. Of Swisher's article, Kayani said, "This is a criticism of the method of working in a Court, and would be most welcome in Pakistan. The only objectionable passage occurs in part IV, where a judge is described as possibly getting illumination 'from conversation with his law clerk or gossip with his secretary.'" In a general statement, the High Court chief justice said:

The law of contempt applies if the manner of criticism is contemptuous, that is to say, it lowers the Court in the eyes of others. So far as the criticism of judgments goes the law is now stated in Article 123(2)(b) of the new [1962] Constitution. A person commits contempt if he scandalises the Court or otherwise does anything which tends to bring the Court or a Judge of the Court into hatred, ridicule or contempt. This is an easily understandable definition, and if a legal critic merely states that an argument used by a Judge is wrong and gives reasons for it, good or bad, I do not see how he can use the law of contempt as a pretext for the lack of a critical faculty. Of course I can understand that, since there has been no legal criticism in Pakistan so far, Judges will for some time be sensitive to an adverse discussion of their judgments. But whatever be the private feelings of a Judge on such occasions, they will never have the temerity of taking action in a body unless the criticism is scandalising.

[21] Comments of Chief Justices M. R. Kayani and A. R. Cornelius discussed, quoted, and reproduced here are published with their permission and were written on June 21, 1962, with their understanding that they would be published. It is not unexpected that the possible effect of the contempt of court law would be viewed somewhat differently from the perspectives of the bench and of the researcher. Obviously my own analysis is from the point of view of the latter. Chief Justice Cornelius after reading this chapter commented in a letter of December 12, 1964, "We do not understand it [the contempt jurisdiction] as operating *in terrorem* quite to the extent that your text might suggest."

But it must be made clear—and it is widely known—that the law of contempt in Pakistan is based on the English law and that it is more rigid than the American law. This, in my opinion, is wholesome, because criticism in Pakistan is not so advanced as to steer clear of lapses into the personality of a Judge.

In dealing with this issue, Chief Justice A. R. Cornelius did not comment for publication on the specific examples discussed. He summarized his view in the following statement authorized for publication:

I have never entertained the apprehension that the Superior Courts in Pakistan were intolerant of reasoned analysis and criticism of their judgments. The field for academic examination and exposition of the principles underlying these judgments, and for critical appraisement of the decisions reached, in relation to earlier cases in Pakistan or elsewhere is entirely open. Judges and Lawyers alike would indeed welcome review of the development of law through the Courts, by detached and well-informed observers.

Thus, in legal research the scholar must function within the conditions of responsibility, temperateness, and maturity prevailing in the whole society. The extensive quotations in the foregoing analysis suggest the channels for criticism which might not be contemptuous. It is not yet clear if an independent scholar would be allowed to say of the High Court what the Supreme Court said in the twelve cases cited, i.e., it was "plainly incorrect," had "no jurisdiction to interfere," its direction was "misconceived," its view "wholly unsustainable," and that it had "error in proceedings." It is clear that the utmost tact, precision of language, and discretion are essential. Sir Edward Snelson was neither clear nor accurate in his review of the writ petition, and the combination of absence of clarity, indiscreet language, and a tone of facetiousness led to his conviction. The challenge thus presented to research is immense. For whatever reasons, it has not yet been taken up by Pakistani legal scholarship. The standards of research and the limits of legal criticism will be determined by the milieu of Pakistan and especially by the courts' assessment of the conflicting demands of order and freedom. The political context is one of unstable equilibrium, the tradition of disciplined, responsible criticism is weak, the sensitivities consequent to imperial rule are acute. Transcending all of these is a strong and proud judiciary, which regards its integrity as a mainstay of order and is intent on preserving that integrity. Perhaps the dictum quoted by the Supreme Court as a guide for comment on the judiciary is equally relevant to legal research: "If there must be an excess, let it be an excess of gentleness." [22]

Documentary Sources

During the period of martial law from October 7, 1958, to June 8, 1962, all legislative bodies were suspended, hence there was no daily record of proceedings of the National Assembly and the two provincial assemblies. Publication resumed on June 8, 1962, when the legislatures reconvened. The proceedings of the new National Assembly are now known as *National Assembly Debates, Official Report*. A separate issue appears for each day of the session. The *Debates* are well edited, competently printed, and fairly well indexed on the front cover. One difficulty, however, is the fact that only 350 copies are printed. Since there are at least twenty libraries in Pakistan and thirty libraries in foreign countries which should get copies, as well as 156 legislators and one hundred government officials who need them in their work, this stock may not be adequate. The time lapse between date of the session and date of printing is about ten months, which makes contemporary research difficult. The same comments are pertinent to the debates of the two provincial assemblies, except that the debates of the Provincial Assembly of East Pakistan are not printed in separate pamphlets for each session. Instead, the proceedings of several sessions are combined in one publication usually about five hundred pages in length. In an effort to reduce the gap between the session and publication of proceedings, the secretary of the West Pakistan Assembly is having the printing done by several commercial publishers instead of exclusively by the West Pakistan Government Press. This will speed publication considerably.

One of the problems consequent to partition and reorganization

[22] *Haq* v. *The Honourable Judges of the High Court of Judicature at Lahore* (1953) F.C.R. 206.

is that of knowing what laws are currently valid. While the Ministry of Law publication, *Unrepealed Acts and Ordinances of the Central Government,* has been published through Volume XII to include 1954, there is a time lag in publication. Of particular utility is the Central Laws (Statute Reform) Ordinance, 1960, which lists in appended schedules the current legal status of laws of the central government and of West Pakistan from 1834 to 1949. This is published in the official reporting service, *Pakistan Law Reports—West Pakistan,* September, 1960.

The Ministry of Law of the central government publishes annual compilations of laws, the latest being *A Collection of Central Acts and Ordinances* for the year 1954, but there is a time lag of several years. The Law Ministry has also published a twelve-volume compilation, *Unrepealed Central Acts, 1844 to 1954.* The most convenient and useful sources of new laws are the leading commercial reporting system for court decisions, the *All-Pakistan Legal Decisions,* and the analogous commercial and official government reporting systems for the two provinces. These are described below. Laws, ordinances, and rules are published in the central and provincial gazettes, and separate copies of such enactments are available within a few days of issuance at the government presses and such commercial agencies as *All-Pakistan Legal Decisions* in Lahore, Pakistan Law House in Karachi, and Obaidullah, of *Dacca Law Reports* in Dacca. Especially useful are "Bare Acts," i.e., separate acts published in pamphlet form by PLD and available almost immediately after enactment. Although all government publications list an extensive network of authorized sales agents which are book stores scattered throughout the nation, these agents rarely have government publications available and are not inclined to attempt to procure them energetically.

Statutory law passed by the National Assembly and the two provincial assemblies, ordinances and laws issued by the President and governors both before and after martial law, can be found in several sources. Copies of many of these are available from the central and provincial government presses. Since each law is listed separately, the catalogues of the three government presses are themselves a fairly complex index of statutory law. The primary official source for acts of the National Assembly, as specified by Rule 80 of the *Rules of Procedure and Conduct of Business in the National Assembly of Pakistan,* is the *Gazette of Pakistan,* which has already been described as an important source of notification of assignments of officials, appointments of officials, and texts of laws and reports.[23] It serves as an organ of both the executive departments and the legislature and as the legal instrument which actuates operation of ordinances, laws, rules, and all other legislative actions published in it. All three gazettes are used in the same manner, hence all are indispensable sources of legislative and executive matters. A dramatic instance of the importance of the *Gazette* fulfilling the function of statutory activation is found in an important judgment of the High Court of West Pakistan (*Abul A'la Maudoodi* v. *Government of West Pakistan,* PLD 1964 Kar. 478) involving dissolution of the influential orthodox Muslim group, Jamaat-e-Islami. The Governor of West Pakistan had extended the application of the Criminal Law (Amendment) Act to the whole of the province, and under authority of this law he immediately declared the Jamaat to be an unlawful association. Notice of extension of the law and of declaring the Jamaat unlawful appeared in the same issue of the *Gazette* on the same day that the government sealed the Jamaat's headquarters. One of the issues in the case was whether the two actions were properly publicized. The court upheld earlier judgments that an act becomes operative when published in the *Gazette,* a requirement specified in the West Pakistan General Clauses Act (VI of 1956), although it differed with earlier judgments which had specified that a reasonable opportunity to see the *Gazette* be given the affected party. The court held the actions to be operative instantly upon publication of the *Gazette* and relied on a definition from Webster stating "publish" to mean causing to print or issue from a press. In the court's view no element of distribution, dissemination, or reading of the material was involved. The works manager of the West Pakistan Government Press testified that the two notices were published within an hour after the press opened at 7:30 A.M. The court accordingly ruled that extension of the act

[23] See above, pp. 143–144 ff.

became operative at 8:30 A.M., and declaration of the Jamaat as unlawful became operative at the same time since it followed the extension notice both in numbering and in location in the *Gazette*. The precise time of printing was at issue because the Jamaat's offices were sealed at 4:00 A.M.—four and a half hours before publication of the notices. The High Court, upholding the government's action, dismissed this fact as a mere "irregularity." The judgment was upheld by the Supreme Court of Pakistan (Criminal Appeal No. 43 of 1964 and Civil Appeal No. 19-D of 1964, decided on September 25, 1964). It is the first case in which the act of printing a notice in the *Gazette* figures so prominently, and it is the most recent reaffirmation of the *Gazette* as a crucial legal instrument.

The official government series reporting Supreme Court and High Court cases consists of three separate publications. The *Pakistan Supreme Court Reports,* which, prior to March 23, 1956, was called *Federal Court Reports,* is the official reporting medium for the Supreme Court. These reports are carefully printed and are distinguished by meticulously edited headnotes which are invariably checked by the judge writing the judgment and often prepared by the editor of the reports. The time lag between date of judgment and publication has been reduced to somewhat less than two months. Only a small proportion of cases decided by the courts are published in the reports. A careful survey of previous unpublished decisions was made to determine if important constitutional principles were involved. Such decisions, together with those already published, are included in a new decennial digest, the first issue of which, covering the 1950–1959 period, appeared in October, 1961: Dr. Nasim Hasan Shah (ed.), *The Pakistan Supreme Court Digest, Decennial Digest* (1950–1959) (Karachi: Government of Pakistan Press, 1961). This 383-page digest is of considerable research utility. It follows the same headnote system used in the Supreme Court reports and is a well-edited summary of about seven hundred cases. The work of reporting and research in the Supreme Court has been accelerated by the personal interest of Chief Justice A. R. Cornelius and the registrar, A. A. Mirza. The survey of unpublished decisions is continuing, and it is possible that the publication of additional digests will result. In the meantime, a commercially published digest of Supreme Court decisions is of considerable utility: Sheikh Shaukat Mahmood (ed.), *The Supreme Court Digest 1950–June 1964* (Lahore: Pakistan Law Times Publication, 1964). Mahmood's digest is carefully written and is highly regarded by judges of the Supreme Court.

Each province publishes a reporter series corresponding to the *Supreme Court Reports,* but there is not, as yet, an official digest for the high courts. The provincial series are called, respectively, *Pakistan Law Reports—West Pakistan* and *Pakistan Law Reports—Dacca Series.* These are somewhat more comprehensive than the national series, since they include many Supreme Court as well as High Court decisions, and often print the texts of central and provincial statutes and administrative rules in a second part to each monthly volume. While these publications are the official government sources on case law and statutes and are accurately and well printed, there is a time lag of a year or more between the judgment and publication. Both of the official provincial series have adequate annual indexes and digests of cases.

Because of the delay in printing the official series, lawyers rely more on several equivalent commercial reporting systems. The most useful of these is the series known as *All-Pakistan Legal Decisions,* published in Lahore by a corporation of the same name at the Punjab Educational Press. The PLD, as they are cited, appear monthly and include judgments of both high courts, the Supreme Court, and the Board of Revenue. The reporting is relatively current; judgments rendered as recently as a month before often appear in the printed monthly volume. PLD publishes nearly twice the number of cases as do the three official series. An incidental advantage of PLD is the advertisements, which inform the reader of the most recent law publications. PLD also publishes a *Quinquennial Digest* of civil, criminal, and revenue cases, the latest issue being for the 1957–1961 period, and a *Decennial Digest,* the last issue of which covered 1947–1956. Two specialized reporting systems, both published by All-

Pakistan Legal Decisions, are *All-Pakistan Tax Decisions* (PTD) and *Pakistan Labour Cases* (PLC), both of which publish ordinances, rules, and notifications relating, respectively, to tax and labor law. All of these reporting systems publish the texts of statutes and ordinances. PLD does not publish all materials on East Pakistan, although some items appear intermittently. The publishing work of All-Pakistan Legal Decisions is a noteworthy episode in the history of Pakistan. Without the speedy, efficient, and imaginative work of this concern, research would be far more difficult. PLD was founded by Malik Mir Muhammad, who served as an apprentice in the Punjab Government Press before partition and later established a private printing firm. At partition, he founded PLD as an equivalent to the *All-India Reporter* (AIR). The work is carried on by his son, Malik Mohd. Saeed. The counterpart of PLD in East Pakistan is the commercial publisher, Obaidul Huq Chowdhury in Dacca, who publishes the *Dacca Law Reports* which promptly reports criminal and civil judgments of the High Court of East Pakistan and most of the judgments of the Supreme Court and the West Pakistan High Court. Obaidul Huq Chowdhury also edits and publishes the *Up-To-Date Civil Reference* (1st ed.; Dacca: Dacca Law Reports Office, 1960), which is useful because it covers the period 1947–1960 and is arranged by statute as well as by the usual civil law headings. Another valuable compilation is Kazi Muhammad Ashraf, *Legal Topics* (Lahore: Mahmood and Co., 1961), a digest of cases decided by the privy council, supreme courts, and high courts of Pakistan and India from 1798 to 1961. The Pakistan Law House in Karachi publishes annual compilations of laws, the latest being *Collection of 1960 Central Acts and Ordinances*. Since much of the work of the district officer has been judicial, knowledge of criminal and civil procedure is necessary for an understanding of district administration. The leading compilations, published by All-Pakistan Legal Decisions, are *Code of Civil Procedure, 1961; Code of Criminal Procedure, 1960;* and *Pakistan Penal Code, 1960,* all three of which are edited by M. M. Hasan Nizami and C. Fazal-i-Haq.

The authorized mode of citing these reporting systems is as follows:

I. Official Government Reporting Series

    A. *Federal Court Reports* and its successor (starting on March 23, 1956), *Pakistan Supreme Court Reports:* (Year of judgment), volume number (if any) in arabic numbers, abbreviation of series, first page of judgment.

        Example: (1954) 2 F.C.R. 105
                  (1958) 1 P.S.C.R. 432

    B. *Pakistan Law Reports* (West Pakistan Series): Abbreviation of series (year of judgment), volume number, bench abbreviation, first page of judgment.

        Example: P.L.R. (1957) 2 Lah. 635

    C. *Pakistan Law Reports* (Dacca Series): Abbreviation of series (year of judgment), volume number (if any; Dacca series seldom has multiple volumes), bench abbreviation, first page of judgment.

        Example: P.L.R. (1964) 1 Dacca 302

II. Commercial Reporting Series

    A. *All-Pakistan Legal Decisions* (authorized by government): Abbreviation of series, year of judgment, name of court or bench abbreviation for one of six benches of West Pakistan High Court or Board of Revenue, first page of judgment.

        Example: PLD 1964 SC 537
                 PLD 1964 Lah. 77

    Tax Decisions and Labour Cases series are cited as follows:

                1963 PTD 1
                1963 PTD (Trib) 1
                1963 PLC 1

    B. *Dacca Law Reports:*
    Volume number, abbreviation of series (year of judgment), first page of judgment.

        Example: 2 DLR (1964) 190

III. Authorized abbreviations for courts and benches:

SC	Supreme Court of Pakistan
Dacca	East Pakistan High Court of Judicature
	(also called High Court of East Pakistan)

Lah. or W.P.	High Court of West Pakistan
Azad J & K	High Court of Azad Jammu and Kashmir
Kar.	Karachi bench of High Court of West Pakistan
Pesh.	Peshawar bench of High Court of West Pakistan
B.J.	Bahawalpur circuit of High Court of West Pakistan (Baghdad-ul-Jadid is the capital of Bahawalpur, which before 1947 was a princely state.)
Quetta	Quetta circuit of High Court of West Pakistan (Quetta is principal city in former Baluchistan States Union.)
W.P. (Rev.)	Board of Revenue, West Pakistan

In Pakistani constitutional law there are no case books as are known in other countries. Four of the most important cases, however, have been analyzed by Sir Ivor Jennings in the 75-page introduction to his *Constitutional Problems in Pakistan* (Cambridge, 1957). The remainder of the book consists of the text of the judgments in these cases which relate to the governor-general's power of assent and its bearing on the constitutionality of government in Pakistan. A standard commentary on the 1956 Constitution is Volume VIII by Alan Gledhill in the series edited by George W. Keeton, *The British Commonwealth: The Development of Its Laws and Constitution* (London, 1957). A. K. Brohi's *Fundamental Law of Pakistan* (Karachi: Din Muhammadi Press, 1958) is the longest and perhaps the best-printed book published in Pakistan. It is both an analysis of the 1956 Constitution and a prodigious effort to integrate much comparative jurisprudence and political theory with Pakistan's constitutional development. It contains a valuable appendix of documents such as the Constitution and the Indian Independence Act. A revised edition of Brohi's book, based on the 1962 Constitution, appeared in 1964. Like the first edition, it is more than a commentary on constitutional law; it is essentially a study in comparative political theory and jurisprudence. Another authoritative, critical commentary on the 1962 Constitution is *Constitutional and Organic Law of Pakistan* (Lahore: All-Pakistan Legal Decisions, 1965), written by former Chief Justice M. Munir. The author also served as minister of law and parliamentary affairs and is highly regarded by the legal profession for his critical scholarship. Copies of the 1962 Constitution are available in pamphlet form at the sales depot of the manager of Central Government Publications in Karachi.

Legal Issues Relevant to Bureaucracy

a. The 1956 Constitution and martial law. The proclamation of martial law on October 7, 1958, abrogated the 1956 Constitution, dismissed the central and provincial cabinets and assemblies, and abolished political parties. Although the *tabula rasa* thus created made possible a totally new juridical and administrative system, this did not eventuate. Three days after proclamation of martial law, the President issued the Laws (Continuance in Force) Order, 1958, which declared that the nation was to be governed "as nearly as may be in accordance with the late Constitution." In effect, all laws were to continue in force unless specifically abrogated.

After the assumption of the presidency by General Mohammad Ayub Khan, the position of chief martial law administrator converged with that of president. The country was divided into three zones, each commanded by a military officer designated as zonal martial law administrator. In each zone, the chief secretary was designated as deputy martial law administrator, and zones were subdivided into sectors commanded by subordinate officers. The legal instrument for the assumption of martial law was the proclamation, subsidiary to which were three categories of instruments: regulations, orders, and ordinances. The distinction between these categories is significant and figured prominently in at least three cases: *Khuhro v. Pakistan*, PLD 1960 SC 237; *Iftikhar-ud-Din v. Muhammad Sarfraz*, PLD 1961 SC 585; and *Mohammad Afzal v. Commissioner, Lahore Division*, PLD 1963 SC 401. Since no definitions of these categories are to be found anywhere in martial law enactments, the distinctions must be derived by inference from previous practice and by judicial construction in these three decisions. It is clear that the proclamation of October 7, 1958, is the paramount instrument whose legitimacy was validated by the Supreme Court in several decisions starting with the

Dosso case, discussed later in this section. Martial law authority assumed both legislative and executive powers and established a hierarchy of instruments analogous to the two hierarchies which had previously existed. Immediately below the paramount instrument (proclamation) were regulations, which the Supreme Court in the Afzal case said were meant to describe laws of a general nature made by martial law authorities. Nearly one hundred regulations were issued during the martial law period. Martial law orders determined the manner in which the principles and policies of the regulations were to be carried out. Fewer than fifty such orders were issued by President Ayub as chief martial law administrator, and about one hundred were issued by the zonal administrators. The Iftikhar-ud-Din judgment held that in promulgating regulations and orders, the President exercised his "super-constitutional" powers assumed by the coup d'état. On the other hand, the issuance of ordinances promulgated by the President was in the exercise of his constitutional powers derived from the ordinance-making power of the 1956 Constitution, by which the nation was to be governed as nearly as possible. President's Order (Post-Proclamation) No. 1 of 1958 (Laws [Continuance in Force] Order) clearly removed from judicial scrutiny the proclamation, orders made in pursuance of the proclamation, martial law orders, martial law regulations, and orders of military courts.

An occasion for the courts to comment on martial law arose only six days after the proclamation of October 7, 1958, in *The State* v. *Dosso and another* (1958) 2 P.S.C.R. 180, in which four criminal appeals were grouped together for judgment. Under the Frontier Crimes Regulation, the deputy commissioner of Sibi referred a case of murder to a special *jirga* (council of elders) who found the respondents guilty. The respondents then applied for writs contending that the relevant provisions of the Frontier Crimes Regulation were void since they were repugnant to Article 5 (equal protection of the laws) of the 1956 Constitution. The High Court found the Frontier Crimes Regulation repugnant to Article 5, and the state appealed to the Supreme Court. The Supreme Court overruled the High Court, Chief Justice Munir reasoning that the Constitution itself, of which Article 5 was a part, had been abrogated, hence the Frontier Crimes Regulation could not be repugnant to an abrogated norm. Further, he maintained, the Frontier Crimes Regulation was revalidated by Article 1 of the Laws (Continuance in Force) Order. In arriving at this judgment, Munir found it necessary to "appraise the existing constitutional position in the light of the juristic principles which determine the validity or otherwise of law-creating organs in modern states." Relying largely on Hans Kelsen's *General Theory of Law and State* (Anders Wedberg, trans., Cambridge, Mass., 1945), he concluded that a "victorious revolution or a successful *coup d'Etat* is an internationally recognized legal method of changing a Constitution," and that such a revolution becomes a new law-creating organ. This view of the legitimacy of the 1958 coup d'état has not been departed from by the judiciary. In a later celebrated case in which an Indian army officer was convicted of espionage, the legitimacy of martial law was upheld by Justice Murshed and the judgment was later sustained by the Supreme Court (*Bhattacharya* v. *the State*, PLD 1963 Dacca 422). But there remained the further obstacle of dealing with fundamental rights, which as part of the Constitution were presumably abrogated. Do fundamental rights transcend national law-making authority? Munir reasoned that such rights are so fundamental that they cannot be taken away by law. Since under martial law there is no restriction on the President's law-making power, then there is no such thing as a fundamental right. As to the provision of the Laws (Continuance in Force) Order that Pakistan shall be governed as nearly as may be in accordance with the late Constitution, he reasoned that this applied to structure and form and not to laws which had been abrogated. This unanimous judgment was concurred in by Justices Shahabuddin, Amiruddin Ahmad, and Cornelius, but the latter, dissenting from the line of reasoning, wrote a separate opinion in which he was less certain than Munir that fundamental rights derive their validity solely from the Constitution. He then implied that certain rights are derived *de natura*. "A number of these rights," he reasoned, "are essential human rights which inherently belong to every citizen of a country governed in a civilized mode, and speaking with great respect, it seems to me that the view pressed before us by the learned Attorney General involves a danger of denial of these elementary rights, at a time when they were expressly assured by writing in the fundamental law of the country merely because that writing is no longer in force."

Cornelius developed further this line of reasoning as to the origin of fundamental rights in *Province of East Pakistan* v. *Md. Mehdi Ali Khan* (1959) 2 P.S.C.R. 1. Munir, affirming that the decision in the Dosso case was a right one, added that since "the present legal system derives its authority from the success of the October Revolution, and if the authority in whom, under the new regime, unfettered legislative powers vest, annuls or alters the law declared by the Supreme Court, the superseding law has supremacy over and prevails against the original law as declared by the Supreme Court." While Munir thus reinforced the view he advanced in Dosso's case, Cornelius appeared more certain of the validity of his Dosso "dissent." He attached greater significance to the words "shall be governed," which he described as mandatory in tone and effect. He asserted that martial law may be necessary in a peaceful country to reconstitute, in the light of past experience and future needs, the mode of exercising power in the state. In such a case there is no need for alteration of the processes of government, except the machinery of popular representation. Yet to establish a new sovereignty, it is necessary to demolish the foundation of the old; hence, the Constitution is abrogated. But this does not mean that it ceases to operate as a source of positive law. Cornelius then advanced a new theory of the meaning of Article 2(1) ("shall be governed in accordance . . ."), a theory which is probably the most significant piece of legal reasoning resulting from the martial law cases. Article 2(1) is merely an assurance carrying no legal sanctions; it is not an obligation assumed as a matter of law. It is as immune from the legal process as martial law itself. But this immunity is possible only because Article 2(1) has been subsumed into the martial law. Fundamental rights have a force not related to the Constitution but derived from martial law. Thus, Cornelius did not push further the natural law origins of rights which he seemed to invoke by implication in the Dosso "dissent." Instead, he cloaked the words "shall be governed" with the highest importance and gave them immunity because they were subsumed in martial law. Since he included fundamental rights as part of the provisions of the Constitution according to whose provisions the country shall be governed, these rights "have lost the operation which was conferred upon them" by the Constitution, and are "valid to the extent assured by Article 2(1)."

b. The 1962 Constitution. The Constitution of 1962, the promulgation of which ended martial law, presents several challenges to subsequent research which can only be alluded to here. Continuity of polity is provided by Article 225, which continues in force all martial law orders except four which are specified, and which repeals all martial law regulations except five which are listed. The major change affecting administration lies in the devolution of powers to the provincial governments in a pattern which departs significantly from earlier structural arrangements. The central, concurrent, and provincial lists of powers which the 1956 Constitution inherited from the Government of India Act are replaced by a list of forty-nine central government powers. These powers include defense, foreign affairs, inter-provincial and foreign trade and commerce, insurance, posts, telecommunications, and tourism. All other powers are presumed to be reserved to the provinces, except when the central government under Article 131 declares a subject as requiring central government legislation. Thus, the allocation of powers is somewhat like that found in the United States, although the terms "enumerated" and "reserved" are not specifically mentioned. Judicial construction has begun to resolve some of the ambiguities in the new structure, but it is likely that much more clarification will be required before a firm pattern emerges. A leading case, *Manzoor Ahmad v. Commissioner, Lahore Division,* PLD 1964 Lah. 194, declares unequivocally that the distribution of powers rests on a basis totally different from the 1956 Constitution and the antecedent Government of India Act. The authority given by Article 131 to the central government specifies that it has power to enact legislation when the national interest requires it in relation to security, economic and financial stability, planning, co-ordination, or achievement of uniformity in different parts of the nation. In the Manzoor Ahmad decision, the court implied that this central power to legislate for uniformity must be declared in advance. Since the central government did not declare criminal law to be of such interest, criminal law was held to be a provincial power. This doctrine of prior declaration of interest or pre-emption has great potential for modifying the pattern of central and provincial powers. The provinces, by virtue of the residual doctrine, have powers over such matters as agriculture, education, commerce, industry, land and inland water transportation, law and order, and water and power development.

When the central government has declared a subject to be within the national interest, as it did with respect to industrial disputes on the ground of uniformity of law, there is apparently no question as to the supremacy of the central legislation. Such, at least, was the ruling in *Chittagong Mercantile Employees' Association* v. *Chairman, Industrial Court of East Pakistan*, PLD 1963 Dacca 856. It remains to be seen what will happen if the central government declares within the ambit of "national interest" a residual subject already legislated on by the province. A progressively more comprehensive view of what is in the "national interest" may produce the same effect as judicial construction of the commerce clause did in American constitutional development. There are, of course, other modes by which the central government can assert its authority, but the political realities of the two disparate provinces and the prevailing temper of the nation seem to indicate a significant devolution of power to the provinces as is reflected in the Manzoor Ahmad decision. In accordance with the new pattern of distribution of powers, several central government corporations have been reorganized into two provincial corporations, and there has been a quickening of the administrative impulse in provincial governments.

A second major departure from the 1956 Constitution lies in the fact that the apparatus of government is now presidential rather than parliamentary. This was not clear from the 1962 Constitution itself, for although the president is ultimately responsible for executing state policy, the delicately balanced allocation of power among three branches of government was lacking and the legislatures have been organized on the pattern of parliamentary systems. Ministers, for example, usually attended sessions and answered questions during the question period. The use of parliamentary secretaries and the absence of strong legislative committees with substantive expertness and staff capable of focusing on relevant legislation contributed further to the ambivalence. It was, however, the relationship of cabinet ministers to the National Assembly which precipitated what may be characterized as the most momentous court decision in the history of the law of Pakistan, a decision which halted the progression toward greater ambiguity and established the structure of government as being clearly presidential. The 1962 Constitution unambiguously provided in Article 104 that a legislator who might be appointed a minister, or to any other "office of profit in the service of Pakistan," could no longer be a member of the assembly. This provision suggested a presidential system. Article 224 of the Constitution permitted the President to make adaptations "for the purpose of removing difficulties" impeding the implementation of the Constitution. He was granted this power for three months. Pursuant to this authority, President Ayub issued an order (Removal of Difficulties [Appointments of Ministers] Order, 1962) allowing ministers appointed from the assembly to retain their seats as legislators. According to a statement in the National Assembly by A. K. M. Fazlul Quader Chowdhury (who was subsequently elected speaker), the President issued this order because East Pakistan members of the National Assembly refused to accept appointments as ministers unless they could also retain their seats in the assembly (National Assembly of Pakistan, *Debates*, June 19, 1962, p. 145). An appeal was made to the High Court of East Pakistan challenging the validity of the President's order. The result was a momentous decision by Justice Murshed, upheld by a unanimous judgment of the Supreme Court (*Mohd. Abdul Haque v. Fazlul Quader Chowdhry*, PLD 1963 Dacca 669; *Fazlul Quader Chowdhry* v. *Mohd. Abdul Haque*, PLD 1963 SC 486). The courts reasoned that to allow ministers to serve in the assembly was to alter the nature of the Constitution itself. The Constitution was intended to bring into operation a presidential system of government in which the executive was to be completely separated from the legislature. But the President's amendment would have changed that system to "an anomalous Parliamentary form." This would not have been mere "adaptation" of a technical nature, which was the intent of the Removal of Difficulties Article, but a major change which could be made only by the normal amending process. In declaring the President's order null and void, the Supreme Court decision unequivocally established the principle of the inherent prerogative of the courts to interpret the Constitution and to review legislation for its constitutionality. This power of judicial review had been in doubt because Article 133 specified that only the legislature could decide if it had the power to make a law under the Constitution. After a comprehensive examination of this provision, Justice Murshed concluded that this article was intended to apply only to that section of the Constitution dealing with the distribution of powers between the center and the provinces. This view was concurred in by the Supreme Court, and a somewhat different ground justifying judicial review was suggested by Justice Rahman in his assertion that the power of judicial review must exist and that there can be no absolute prohibition against judicial scrutiny of legislation. *Marbury* v. *Madison* was cited by Justice Fazle-Akbar, and indeed the Fazlul Quader Chowdhry case is already as much a landmark in constitutional development as the equivalent American decision which preceded it 160 years earlier. The doctrine of judicial review was expanded further in the public liberties case involving government's action prohibiting the Jamaat-e-Islami, an orthodox Muslim organization, from functioning (Supreme Court of Pakistan, *Criminal Appeal No. 43 of 1964 and Civil Appeal No. 19-D of 1964*, decided on 25 September 1964). Considering the constitutionality of the 1908 law under which the Jamaat was banned, Chief Justice Cornelius reaffirmed the right of judicial review of legislative acts and set forth principles guiding judicial review of executive action.

The 1962 Constitution included a chapter called "Principles of

Law Making and of Policy" in which sixteen principles of law making, including the usual freedoms (e.g., speech, association, religion) were listed. Unlike the 1956 Constitution, they were not called "fundamental rights" and they were not justiciable. Since the non-justiciability of these freedoms was perhaps the most unpopular provision of the Constitution, it was not surprising that the first amendment passed by the National Assembly restored the earlier term "fundamental rights" and provided for their enforcement by the courts (Constitution [First Amendment] Act, 1963, published in *Gazette of Pakistan, Extraordinary,* January 16, 1964). Certain freedoms were added to the new list. The right which has direct bearing on the administrative system is No. VII, "Discrimination in Services." This prohibits discrimination based on race, caste, religion, sex, residence, or place of birth in making appointments to the public service. To permit the attainment of parity, particularly with reference to Bengali representation, posts may be reserved for a fifteen-year period to secure adequate representation of "persons belonging to any class or area." Thus, the question of parity in the services with regard to status and justiciability has been restored to the position it had in the 1956 Constitution.

Principles of policy in the 1962 Constitution have not been amended. They remain as directive canons but are not enforceable in the courts. Only three of these principles are relevant to administration: that administrative offices be provided in places convenient to the public, that disparity in remuneration in the public services be reduced, and that parity between the provinces in all spheres of central government power be achieved.

The most important constitional provision directly relevant to the public service is Part VIII, Articles 174 to 190, on the services of Pakistan. Chapter 1 of Part VIII consists of five articles relating to terms and conditions of service which are much more specifically described than they were in the Constitution of 1956. The effect may be to take away some of the jurisdiction of the high courts through the writ petition in matters regarding internal bureaucratic grievances. Although this limitation is not specifically mentioned in Part VIII dealing with service matters, it is implied when this part, particularly Articles 174–179, is read with Article 98(3)(a)(b), relating to the jurisdiction of the high courts. Thus, a civil servant who has a grievance regarding a service matter cannot appeal to the court for redress unless that matter is based on a term or condition of service specified in the Constitution. The terms and conditions of service are clearly specified, but there is no mention of such issues as seniority and other matters, which in the past have been the source of most of the litigation. It would appear, therefore, that most of the issues about which civil servants went to court in the past cannot now be appealed to the courts. It is possible, however, that subsequent judicial construction may modify this situation. One of the conditions of service is remuneration. It is conceivable that the word "remuneration" might be construed to include such matters as seniority and tenure simply because remuneration is contingent in part on seniority. Such a construction might serve to restore the position of seeking redress of grievance from the judiciary. But this is speculation. No decisions have yet been made by the courts on such service matters under the 1962 Constitution.

c. Corruption. The problem of corruption in government has not been systematically studied, nor have government reports been issued on the subject. That it was fairly widespread in the administrative system has been generally acknowledged. Chief Justice Cornelius' address on this subject [24] and a talk by Chaudhury Mohamad Ali, given at the University of the Panjab, March 8, 1963, are general analyses. Mohamad Ali, secretary-general immediately after partition, helped establish the central government and is one of the most distinguished of Pakistan's civil servants. His talk, "Corruption as an Impediment to Economic Development," was given at the department of public administration at the university. Ralph Braibanti's "Reflections on Bureaucratic Corruption," published in the British journal, *Public Administration,* XL (1962), 357–372, is based largely on experience in Pakistan. Few cases on corruption have reached the judiciary, hence the details of corrupt government operations are not as

[24] See Appendix 10.

readily available as, let us say, disarticulation in the administrative system. Of the few relevant cases, the most revealing is *Bashir Saigol* v. *The State*, PLD 1964 Lah. 148. This judgment establishes the principle that a police officer serving in the Anti-Corruption Establishment retains powers of an officer serving in the regular police force. More important for present purposes is the illuminating description of alleged collusion between a major textile industrialist and government officials in income tax matters. Another highly instructive decision which might serve as a case study is *Saeed Ahmed* v. *The State*, PLD 1964 SC 266, in which an attempt to bribe an inspector investigating alleged corruption is described in detail.

The bureaucracy of Pakistan inherited the mantle of protection which was given the Indian Civil Service under British rule. While this protection was necessary to preserve the independence of the civil service and to shield it from extreme political pressures and the web of reciprocal obligations which characterized Indian life, it made removal from service a difficult, though by no means unheard of, feat. The controlling principles were laid down in a case decided by the Privy Council in 1948, *High Commissioner for India and High Commissioner for Pakistan* v. *I. M. Lall*, 75 I.A. 225 (1948). These principles held that termination of services at the pleasure of the government was limited by certain conditions. These conditions, elaborated by substantial procedural safeguards against capricious removal, were embodied in section 96-B of the Government of India Act, 1919, in sections 240–243 and 276 of the Government of India Act 1935, and were revalidated by Article 181 of the 1956 Constitution of Pakistan. The procedures for removal were detailed in Civil Services (Classification, Control and Appeal) Rules (CCA Rules) which had been enacted by the Government of India in 1930 and which were controlling in Pakistan until 1959. Under the CCA Rules, an elaborate process for removal was prescribed. This process was further amplified by a substantial body of case law. The procedural niceties included the requirement of two stages of inquiry. The first was to determine the nature of the punishment to be proposed, and the defendant was informed in writing of the grounds on which action was to be taken. He was afforded adequate opportunity to defend himself in writing, and an oral inquiry could be held at his request. After the provisional determination as to punishment, the defendant was once again asked to show cause as to why it should not be taken. He could then appeal at various levels to the secretary of state in council or, after 1947, to the president of Pakistan. Charges of corruption were to be tried in the regular civil courts. Charges of inefficiency could not be upheld unless supported by entries in the defendant's performance record. Only commission of a corrupt act was actionable; there was no such ground as "reputation for corruption." Article 188(2) of the Constitution of 1956, read with Article 22 which guaranteed the use of writs as a fundamental right, was the principal means of obtaining judicial review.

This pattern was changed in 1959. Faced with the problem of quickly and vigorously screening out corrupt officials without vitiating the effectiveness of remedial action by attenuated litigation, the martial law government thought it essential to change the means of removing officials without doing gross violence to accepted notions of due process of law. The result was a change in removal procedures which came to be labeled "screening." The screening of central government officials, because it involved officers of high rank and of the CSP cadre, attracted the greatest attention. This was temporary, emergency, martial law screening carried out under the Public Scrutiny Ordinance and Public Conduct (Scrutiny) Rules, both newly enacted in 1959.[25] The emergency screening under the Public Scrutiny Ordinance seemed to remove any disciplinary action taken thereunder from judicial review. It was assumed at the time that litigation resulting from

[25] Text in *Gazette of Pakistan, Extraordinary,* January 24, 1959, pp. 109–116. The ordinance and rules were enacted under section 6(3) of President's Order (Post Proclamation) No. 1 of 1958 (Laws [Continuance in Force] Order). A source of confusion and serious error in analyzing the emergency martial law screening lies in the fact that the same issue of the *Gazette* includes the Government Servants (Discipline and Efficiency) Rules, 1959, which were originally intended to supplement the Public Scrutiny Ordinance and Public Conduct (Scrutiny) Rules. In fact, the 1959 rules were amended to come into force on such day as the President might appoint (see Cabinet Division Notification No. SRO 88, February 2, 1959, *Gazette of Pakistan,* March 2, 1959, p. 283). Since the President did not put these rules in force, the Public Scrutiny Ordinance and Public Conduct (Scrutiny) Rules governed the screening of civil servants from January 24, 1959, to January 19, 1960. (The writer is indebted to the President's Office for clarification of this point.)

appeals in the writ jurisdiction would be eliminated, although this authority to oust the jurisdiction of the courts was later questioned by the judiciary. Another change from the CCA Rules of 1930 was the introduction of "reputation of being corrupt" as ground for action. The new Public Scrutiny Ordinance did not explicitly guarantee to the defendant the right to confront and cross-examine witnesses, and it specified that the accused appear before a scrutinizing committee alone, "with no friend, adviser, or legal practitioner" with him. Screening was done by some forty-nine committees whose findings were recommended to the President or other appointing authority for action. Membership of committees was announced in *Gazette of Pakistan, Extraordinary,* January 28, 1959, pp. 125–159. These committees were, for the most part, made up of respected members of the civil service; many were known especially for their judicious temperament, although there is a touch of irony in the fact that two members of departmental committees were themselves later screened out.

The President announced the results of screening in a Nathia-gali message on June 27, 1959, and the names of those screened were published the same day (*Gazette of Pakistan, Extraordinary,* June 27, 1959, pp. 1117–1120). While the announcement was received with some shock by the higher bureaucracy whose security of position had been undisturbed since partition, the effects upon analysis do not appear either harsh or drastic. A total of 1,662 employees of the central government were penalized by screening procedures. Press headlines and coffeehouse gossip notwithstanding, this does not mean that 1,662 civil servants were actually separated from the service. On the contrary, only a relatively small number of officials were released. Table 8 below summarizes the screening of both central and provincial govern-ment employees. Only 49 per cent of the central government employees and 69 per cent of central and provincial civil servants penalized were separated from the service. Of the central govern-ment officers screened, only seventy-five were class I officers, but it is difficult to determine how many of these were policy-making executives. Although the CSP cadre was deeply affected emotion-ally by the screening, statistically they were not badly scathed.

Table 8. *Results of Initial Screening in 1959 and 1960 of Central and Provincial Government Servants*

Penalty [a]	Central Government				West Pakistan all classes	East Pakistan all classes	Grand total all classes
	Class 1	Class 2	Class 3	Total			
1. Dismissal	4	14	110	128	214	254	596
2. Removal	0	0	0	0	242	60	302
3. Compulsory retirement	71	68	547	686	0	877	1,563
4. Reduction in rank	8	31	163	202			202
5. Special report	25	88	362	475			475
6. Reduction in increment	2	5	0	7	88 [b]	152 [b]	247
7. Warning	27	14	121	162			162
8. Displeasure	1	1	0	2			2
Total	138	221	1,303	1,662	544	1,343	3,549

[a] Eight penalties listed here are those defined by the central government. See note b below.

[b] Provincial governments did not use central government penalties 4 through 8, hence one figure is reported for all categories of penalties numbered 4 through 8.

Sources: Compiled from Government of Pakistan, Press Information Department, Handout E, No. 3012, July 2, 1952; *Gazette of Pakistan, Extraordinary,* June 27, 1959, pp. 1117–1120; interviews with officials of the Home Department of the Government of West Pakistan and of the Services and General Administration Department of the Government of East Pakistan in 1959, 1960, and 1961.

Out of a total strength of 323 officers in 1959, only twelve (or 3.7 per cent) were screened. All of these were ordered into compulsory retirement, a penalty which permitted retention of full pension benefits. Ten of the twelve CSP officers had been members of the Indian Civil Service who opted for Pakistan. The most senior had nineteen years' service and the most junior three years' service at the time of partition.

Nevertheless, few bothered to analyze the statistics carefully and the shock effect on the government service generally was marked. Security of position had traditionally been one of the advantages of government service, and there were few alternate employment openings in the essentially agrarian economy of the nation. These social conditions coupled with sensational rather than sober, analytical reporting, account for the unnerving effect of the martial law screening of 1958 and early 1959 on the bureaucracy.

What little articulate criticism there was of the screening procedures was directed principally against (1) the use of "reputation for corruption" as a ground for penalty, and (2) the removal of review of the penalty from jurisdiction of the courts. Those who defended the former provision assert that the Public Conduct Scrutiny Rules provided some guidance for an empirical determination of such "reputation," principally analysis of income sources. The use of this ground was further defended by the government on the basis that guilty action would have been impossible to determine in an administrative climate which, prior to 1958, was highly unstable and characterized by an impenetrable network of intrigue and vindictiveness. Moreover, it was asserted that the judicial temperament of the screening committees mitigated against arbitrary action. Finally, it was noted that "reputation for corruption" was used as a ground for action in only eleven cases of eighty-two class I officers penalized and was used scarcely at all in the cases of lower-ranking officers. The first open expression of criticism came from Z. H. Lari, president of the Karachi Bar Association, who deplored the absence of judicial review.[26] The response of the government was expressed by the foreign minister, Manzur Qadir, a distinguished lawyer who said, in part:

With reference to the screening process, you have advocated an appeal to a tribunal presided over by a High Court Judge. As a permanent measure, the setting up of an administrative tribunal of the kind envisaged by you is a step which has a great deal to recommend it. The need of the moment, however, is to ensure as quickly as possible that the work of the Government is not only done honestly and efficiently but also that it is done in such a way as to inspire the confidence of the people and to rehabilitate genuine respect for the functionaries.

All possible care consistent with bringing this process to a speedy end is being taken. In the matter of dealing with those not to be retained in the service, humanitarian considerations are being allowed to prevail. A process of check and recheck of these cases has been undertaken. To err is human. The best one can do is eliminate as far as possible, dishonest and interested judgment. The procedure adopted, it is hoped, will achieve this to an appreciable degree. No doubt the step

[26] Reported first in *The Statesman* (New Delhi), May 4, 1959, p. 5, and later in *Dawn* (Karachi), May 6, 1959, p. 4.

recommended by you would ensure it to a great degree. It is felt, however, that the delay involved in a further appeal will more than offset the advantage gained.[27]

There is no way of determining in a scientific manner the nature of the screening process employed since records of the screening hearings have not been released. Shortly after the screening was completed, the case of Zafrul Ahsan, who protested his screening,[28] was decided by the High Court of West Pakistan and reviewed by the Supreme Court. The Supreme Court judgment is especially important because it describes the mode by which the defendant was notified and the procedure of his hearing. This description remains the only available published means of ascertaining the details of the hearing process. Beyond this item of ancillary interest, however, the Zafrul Ahsan case is of immense legal significance because the judiciary therein renders opinion on the martial law provision which ousted its jurisdiction in screening cases. Zafrul Ahsan, a former ICS officer of twenty-two years' service at the time he was screened out, was general manager of Pakistan International Airlines. He petitioned the High Court for a writ nullifying his retirement order. The petition was rejected on the ground that a remedy might have been sought administratively rather than at law (*Zafar-ul-Ahsan* v. *Republic of Pakistan*, PLD 1959 Lah. 879). The Supreme Court upheld the finding of the High Court that the action of the screening committee was immune from judicial review (*Zafar Ahsan* v. *Republic of Pakistan* [1960] 1 P.S.C.R. 41). The Supreme Court, however, did not agree that its jurisdiction was ousted in all instances, even when the law so specified. Only when certain conditions were met would its ouster be complete. The court listed five such conditions: (1) the authority should have been constituted as required

[27] Text of address by Manzur Qadir to Karachi Bar Association as reported in *Dawn*, May 3, 1959, p. 1.
[28] The jurisdiction of the courts to call in question the actions of a screening committee was barred by Section 10 of the Public Conduct (Scrutiny) Ordinance. To eliminate conflict between this ordinance and section 6 of President's Order (Post-Proclamation) No. 1 of 1958, Laws (Continuance in Force) Order, 1958, which provided for continuance of civil servants in office, the substance of the Public (Scrutiny) Ordinance was incorporated into President's Order No. 1 by Laws (Continuance in Force) (Amendment) Order, 1958 (*Gazette of Pakistan, Extraordinary*, March 10, 1959, p. 327–328).

by the statute, (2) the person proceeded against should be subject to the jurisdiction of the authority, (3) the ground on which action is taken should be within the grounds stated by the statute, (4) the order made should be such as could have been made under the statute, and (5) the proceedings should not be in *mala fide* and the statute not be used as a cloak to cover an act which in fact was not taken though it purports to have been taken under the statute. In the Zafrul Ahsan case, the Supreme Court found that all five requirements were met and hence it had no jurisdiction to question the order. In several subsequent cases, the reasoning of the Zafrul Ahsan case was upheld. In the Muhammad Zaman Khan case (*Muhammad Zaman Khan* v. *M. B. Nishat and others,* PLD 1962 SC 22; see also *Muhammad Ali* v. *Commissioner, Lahore Division,* PLD 1960 Lah. 641), the Supreme Court upheld a High Court judgment which invalidated an action of a screening committee of the Rawalpindi Cantonment Board. This committee had recommended the removal of four schoolteachers for inefficiency and misconduct, and the teachers were dismissed the day after they submitted their show-cause explanations. The High Court noted that this interval did not meet the requirement of the Public Conduct Scrutiny Rules that fifteen days be allowed between the show-cause notice and final action by the appointing authority. The court held that the scrutiny rules were an essential part of the ordinance, hence the fifteen-day interval provided by Rules 6 and 7 had the same force as the ordinance. The court found that the fourth requirement was not met, i.e., that an essential part of the procedure envisaged by the ordinance was not complied with and that therefore its jurisdiction was not ousted. Accordingly it dismissed the appeal of the government, thus overturning the screening action. In a subsequent case which attracted wide attention, the High Court of West Pakistan accepted a writ petition, thus declaring illegal the action of a screening committee on the ground that the Transport Board acted *ultra vires* in both convening the screening committee and hearing the appeal from its decision (*Syed Anwar Ali Shah and another* v. *West Pakistan Road Transport Board* [Writ No. 305, 1960, Hearing, November 13, 1961]). This violated the first of the five conditions specified in the Zafrul Ahsan case. In both of these cases, it is clear that the High Court and the Supreme Court refused to accept the ousting of their jurisdiction except under judicially defined circumstances and in "accordance with a long line of decisions in England" (*Zafrul Ahsan* v. *Republic of Pakistan* [1960] 1 P.S.C.R. 41, at 51). This reasoning was subsequently upheld in *Pahlomal-Motiram* v. *Chief Land Commissioner*, PLD 1961 Kar. 384, in *Gulab Din* v. *A. T. Shaukat*, PLD 1961 Lah. 952, and in *Muhammad Zaman Khan* v. *M. B. Nishat and others*, PLD 1962 SC 22.

The martial law screening procedures did not escape the attention of the Law Reform Commission of 1959, although its comments were limited to the tentative proposal of substituting for the screening system the Board of Inquiry system used in Ceylon. It is noteworthy that while the Law Reform Commission report and its dissenting minutes spoke out unequivocally on certain issues (notably separation of executive and judicial functions), they did not condemn the emergency screening procedures.[29]

Emergency screening under the Public Scrutiny Ordinance and Public Conduct (Scrutiny) Rules was replaced on January 19, 1960, by the Government Servants (Efficiency and Discipline) Rules 1960. They superseded Part XII of the Civil Services (Classification, Control and Appeal) Rules, 1930, which were in effect until January 24, 1959. These establish one procedure for cases of subversion and another for cases of inefficiency, misconduct, and corruption. In subversion cases, the inquiry committee consists of three secretaries to government and no consultation with the Central Public Service Commission is required. In other cases, initial inquiry may be made by a single officer, who must follow procedural safeguards similar to those of the CCA Rules of 1930. Appeal to the appointing authority is allowed and the advice of the Central Public Service Commission must be considered before final action is taken. The new rules do not have the category "reputation for corruption" as grounds for penalty. A new ground, however, is that an official "may reasonably be considered cor-

[29] Government of Pakistan, *Report of the Law Reform Commission, 1958–59* (Karachi: Government of Pakistan Press, 1959), pp. 57–59.

rupt" because he has resources disproportionate to his known income or lives beyond his ostensible means.

Concern for integrity in administration is also manifested in the work of anti-corruption agencies, found in the central and provincial governments. In the central government, the Anti-Corruption Agency has existed since 1941 but was reorganized as part of the Special Police Establishment in 1948. The activities of these agencies differ from the screening processes described above in that they deal largely with crimes cognizable in the criminal code such as embezzlement, bribery, black marketing, and misappropriation of funds, and not with questions of inefficiency, misconduct, or suspicion of corruption. The Anti-Corruption Agency has special investigative powers and may initiate investigations or be invited by departments to conduct investigations. The central government agency concerns itself primarily with central government employees, and the two provincial agencies with provincial civil servants. The Special Police Establishment of the central government is an organization of more than 450 employees with branches in each provincial capital, in the state bank, in the national capital, and in Peshawar, Quetta, and Chittagong. Its annual reports, submitted to the Ministry of the Interior, are not in printed form. In 1959 and 1960 the Special Police Establishment investigated 1,277 and 1,557 cases, respectively. In 1960, 723 cases were sent to the courts and 68 per cent of the cases resulted in conviction. In the same year the SPE estimated that it saved the government some Rs. 2.25 million in recoveries, fines, forfeitures, and money which would have been lost without timely action.

The provinces have given increased emphasis to anti-corruption activities and increased the authority of their anti-corruption departments by giving the director the powers of an inspector general of police.[30]

It is of significance to subsequent research that the government maintains an attitude of candor and open publicity concerning matters of corruption. Statistics of the anti-corruption units are published in the press, public seminars on corruption are spon-

[30] West Pakistan Anti-Corruption Establishment Ordinance, 1961, September 8, 1961; East Pakistan Anti-Corruption Establishment Ordinance, 1961.

sored by the Bureau of National Reconstruction, and a serious effort is made to enlist the aid of the public in identifying and reducing corruption in public service. None of the reports of any of these agencies is published except in press release form. A convenient compilation of relevant ordinances and rules was published in 1962 by the Pakistan Publishing House in Karachi under the title, *Manual of Anti-Corruption Laws in Pakistan,* edited by Zafar Yusuf.

d. The writ and judicial review of administrative action. All significant legal issues relating to administration are closely related to the instrumentality known as the writ, the use of which is by far the most compelling intellectual problem in the law of Pakistan. In this book, the writ jurisdiction has been discussed in context of education [31] and in analysis of the case of Sir Edward Snelson as it dealt peripherally with the Official Secrets Act [32] and, more fundamentally, with the Contempt of Courts Act.[33] Since the writ jurisdiction has been analyzed elsewhere in considerable detail,[34] only a brief survey is needed here. The writs referred to are the five well-known extraordinary remedies for redress of grievance against a governmental action: mandamus, quo warranto, prohibition, certiorari, and habeas corpus. In the relations between administration and the courts, only the first four of these writs are commonly used. A convenient survey of the concept and development of writs can be found in the judgment of Chief Justice Cornelius in *The State of Pakistan* v. *Mehrajuddin* (1959) 1 P.S.C.R. 34; a less technical analysis is found in Cornelius' address, "Writ Jurisdiction of Superior Courts." [35]

Writs were regarded in undivided India as one of the principal means of expanding Indian liberties and came to be equated with the preservation of liberty itself. In 1954, the Constituent Assembly of Pakistan passed an amendment to the Government of India

[31] See above, p. 35 ff.
[32] See above, p. 58 ff.
[33] See above, p. 236 ff.
[34] See the author's, "Public Bureaucracy and Judiciary in Pakistan," in La Palombara, (ed.), *Bureaucracy and Political Development.* The text above is a synopsis of pp. 418–440 with added analysis of developments from 1962 through 1965.
[35] See Appendix 14.

Act, 1935, enacting section 223-A of that act which gave to all high courts the power to issue "writs including writs in the nature of" the named writs to any person or authority (Constituent Assembly, *Debates*, July 6, 1954, p. 189). The scope of the writ jurisdiction, implied by the words, "in the nature of," was perhaps not fully appreciated by the High Court until 1955 (Syed Akhlaque Husain, "Writ Jurisdiction of Superior Courts in Pakistan," PLD 1958, Journal, 3). In any event, reliance on that expression was not necessary, for the 1956 Constitution expanded the writ jurisdiction more explicitly. Article 22 guaranteed the right to petition the Supreme Court for enforcement of fundamental rights conferred by the Constitution and gave the Supreme Court the power to issue directions, orders, or writs for enforcing fundamental rights. Article 163 further empowered the Supreme Court to issue directions, orders, decrees, or writs as necessary to do complete justice in any cause or matter pending before it. But the widest jurisdiction was given to the high courts which were empowered by Article 170 to issue directions, orders, or writs not only for the enforcement of fundamental rights but for any other purpose. The limitation imposed by Article 163 on the Supreme Court, that the order relate to a cause or matter before it, was not placed on the High Court jurisdiction. It is probably for this reason that the term "writ jurisdiction" is commonly thought of as applying primarily to High Court jurisdiction. What might have been an expansive interpretation of the terms "directions and orders" was contained by the judgment in the Mehrajuddin case, which maintained that the power to issue directions and orders was not in excess of or beyond the confines of the power to issue the five specified writs. Even earlier, the Supreme Court had ruled that the words "directions and orders" did not confer power to issue orders except with respect to those aspects of executive acts which are clearly judicial in nature.[36] The use of the writ to seek action against government became one of the most conspicuous features of Pakistani government. Under martial law, it was thought that the jurisdiction of the courts might be curtailed by three different means. First, the writ

[36] *Tariq Transport Company v. Sargodha Bhera Bus Service* (1958) 2 P.S.C.R. 71.

jurisdiction of the courts was thought to have been curtailed by omission of the power to issue "orders and directions" and of the words "to any government." Secondly, many acts which were martial law instruments included provisions prohibiting the issuance of writs to certain martial law authorities. The courts interpreted this prohibition as being applicable only to the chief martial law administrator (President Ayub) and not to his subordinates (*Gulab Din* v. *A. T. Shaukat*, PLD 1961 Lah. 952), and only to "Orders" spelled with a capital *O*, not to lesser instruments (*Khuhro* v. *Pakistan*, PLD 1960 SC 237; *Iftikhar-ud-Din* v. *Muhammad Sarfraz*, PLD 1961 SC 585). Further, the courts refused to accept the ousting of their jurisdiction except under judicially defined circumstances and "in accordance with a long line of decisions in England" (*Zafrul Ahsan* v. *Republic of Pakistan* [1960] 1 P.S.C.R. 41). Thirdly, when writs were sought in behalf of fundamental rights in matters not related to specific martial law legislation, their validity seemed in the same doubt as the existence of fundamental rights. These had been declared abrogated by martial law (*The State* v. *Dosso and another* [1958] 2 P.S.C.R. 180; *Province of East Pakistan* v. *Md. Mehdi Ali Khan* [1959] 2 P.S.C.R. 1; *Iftikhar-ud-Din* v. *Muhammad Sarfraz*, PLD 1961 SC 585).

The Constitution of 1962 and subsequent judicial construction of its provisions placed the writ jurisdiction in a somewhat stronger position in most respects. Article 98 defines the substance of writs without using their Latin designations. Any doubt that the powers granted by Article 98 were not intended to be equivalent to the writ jurisdiction appeared to be dispelled by Chief Justice Cornelius, who in discussing the status of writs under the 1962 Constitution stated that "it is difficult to suppose that earlier precedents will lose their value as guidance." [37] Less than a year after the new Constitution was made effective, a full bench of five judges of the West Pakistan High Court handed down the first major interpretation of the new writ power (*Mehboob Ali Malik* v. *Province of West Pakistan*, PLD 1963, Lah. 575). That power is

[37] A. R. Cornelius, "The Writ Jursidiction of Superior Courts," full text in Appendix 14.

strengthened by the fact that it is now Article 2 of the Constitution proper which can be invoked when a grievance by government is alleged. This article declares that it is an inalienable right to enjoy the protection of law and to be treated in accordance with law. Further, no action detrimental to "life, liberty, body, reputation, or property" of any person can be taken except in accordance with law. The significance of Article 2 lies in the fact that it is part of the Constitution proper, rather than part of the ten fundamental rights enumerated in the first amendment. It was thereby possible to seek redress of grievance from the day the Constitution went into effect. Without this transcendent, all-embracing provision, the right to seek redress would have depended on the existence of enumerated fundamental rights in the first amendment which was passed by the National Assembly in December, 1963, and made effective by presidential assent on January 10, 1964.

In the Mehboob Ali decision, Chief Justice Manzur Qadir clearly set forth guidelines for the judiciary in utilizing the remedy of the writ. The judgment stated that the use of certiorari has been enlarged because it is now available as a remedy for "all orders passed in excess of lawful authority, whether by judicial, quasi-judicial or non-judicial functionaries." Under the former Constitution, it was available only in relation to judicial and quasi-judicial actions. On the other hand, Manzur Qadir interprets the new writ jurisdiction as being somewhat curtailed by the constitutional requirement that it can be used only if there is no other adequate remedy. Setting forth a series of propositions by which such adequacy can be determined, he concluded that adequate relief must be requisite to the need created by the grievance. This interpretation of the writ jurisdiction was subsequently concurred in by the East Pakistan High Court in *Chittagong Engineering and Electrical Supply Co. Ltd.* v. *Income Tax Officer, Companies Circle IV*, PLD 1965 Dacca 11. A different line of reasoning in a subsequent decision appears to have linked up the defined rights of Article 98 of the 1962 Constitution with the writs of the 1956 Constitution. In *Maulvi Farid Ahmad* v. *Government of West Pakistan*, PLD 1965 Lah. 135, Justice Sardar Muhammad Iqbal referred to habeas corpus as a "high prerogative right" and as "one of the most fundamental rights known to the Constitution," in the exercise of which there is no limitation. The implication of this statement may be to cloak at least one writ with the same juridical eminence attained under the 1956 Constitution by transfer of the term "prerogative" from "writs" to analogous "rights" under the 1962 Constitution.

The range of substantive issues arising through the medium of the writ is wide; only a few of the more important issues are outlined below.

The first issue for research is the problem of judicial scrutiny of administrative actions affecting the public outside the sphere of bureaucracy. This is the same problem which has faced older Western constitutional systems and has been dealt with in the United States by the Federal Administrative Procedure Act of 1946 and related statutes. Several judgments suggest the range of legal-bureaucratic issues involved. It is clear that a consistent effort has been made to evolve a formula of judicial review presumably by restricting the court to defined channels of restraint. One of the earliest major decisions (*Muhammad Saeed* v. *Election Petitions Tribunal,* PLD 1957 SC 91) included a ruling by Chief Justice Munir that the court would not review a finding of fact, even when erroneous, unless the mode of ascertaining fact is outside the spirit and intent of the statute. This doctrine established a relatively expansionist interpretation of the court's role which has been a characteristic of the doctrine of judicial review of administrative action in Pakistan. The most important decision is that of the *Tariq Transport Company* v. *Sargodha Bhera Bus Service* (1958) 2 P.S.C.R. 71. An application for certiorari was made to review a decision of the Regional Transport Authority (RTA) which granted a route to a bus company without adequate announcement or proper hearing of the affected parties. The High Court had granted the writ which nullified the RTA's action. An appeal was made to the Supreme Court which resulted in a classic decision by Chief Justice Munir, which placed the standards of administrative law, in one respect at least, within the ambit of British and American practice. The Tariq Transport Company case clearly establishes that all administrative remedies must first be exhausted before appeal to the courts and that even then, appeal must be against an action which is clearly judicial, not executive, in nature. Whether the action is judicial is to be ascertained only by the nature of the process by which the executive is empowered to arrive at the decision. The important doctrine of judicial self-restraint is laid down in Munir's statement that expertise in modern states is such that the court cannot substitute its judgment for that of the administration.

In *Messrs. Faridsons Ltd. and another* v. *Government of Pakistan* (1962) 1 P.S.C.R. 1, it was held that the court had the power to insure that good procedure, such as a hearing, should precede withdrawal of a license, even when the statute did not prescribe such procedure. The court's jurisdiction in such a case was determined by the fact that the administrative action was quasi-judicial in function. This judgment suggests that the role of the judiciary in Pakistan is somewhat different than in other Commonwealth states in Asia. The Pakistan ruling departs, for example, from the regnant doctrine in Ceylon which is that the court will not compel an administrator to act judicially unless the statute so specifies (*Nakkuda Ali* v. *M. F. de S. Jayaratne* [1950] Privy Council 102). The Faridsons judgment declared that the Nakkuda Ali doctrine "goes too far in restricting the power of the superior courts to control actions of the executive under statutes which plainly import the performance of a quasi-judicial act." Further definition of the limits of administrative discretion was given in the judgment of *Ikram Bus Service* v. *Board of Revenue*, PLD 1963 SC 564, in which it was held that administrative agencies in deciding on applications for permits could not introduce considerations or criteria extraneous to the intent of the statute under which they functioned.

In some of these judgments the classic issue of fact versus law, or the impact of procedural niceties on substantive value determination, is dealt with. Much litigation involving administrative decisions as to evacuee property, land reforms, fixing of rents and granting of licenses emerges within this ambit. An illustration of the difficulty in applying the fact-value dichotomy is in the case of *Ata Ullah Malik* v. *Custodian, Evacuee Property*, PLD 1964 SC

236, in which three judges agreed that the court could not substitute its judgment for that of the administrator since it was convinced that he had functioned within the spirit and intention of the Evacuee Property Law. The remaining two judges, after a detailed description of the process by which the decision was reached, concluded that the spirit and provisions of the law were not followed in several respects. Even if there had been agreement as to unjust process, it is likely that the case would have been returned to the administrative agency for a new decision in accordance with law, since this principle was established in *Azmat Ali* v. *Chief Settlement and Rehabilitation Commissioner,* PLD 1964 SC 260. One of the most important decisions relating to administrative discretion is the case of *Ghulam Zamin* v. *A. B. Khondkar* 16 DLR (1964) 486, decided by the East Pakistan High Court. Citing largely American precedent, Chief Justice S. M. Murshed ruled that the power to regulate by license is a legisative power which can be delegated to the executive branch only when the legislature has set policy guidelines within which executive discretion must flow. The extension of this doctrine of legislative definition and guidance of executive implementation will do much to move the operation of governmental power more clearly into the limits of a presidential system in which the areas of executive and legislative responsibilities are more clearly defined.

While the foregoing survey deals with the external actions of bureaucracy, i.e., the actions of government over citizens, there is a second dimension which deals with redress of grievances within the bureaucracy. This involves "service matters," complaints of civil servants regarding promotion, discipline, severance from service, and related matters. In these issues the courts, in the absence of Whitley councils, employee unions, effective public service commissions, and an effective internal mechanism, have played a major role. The conditions under which the courts review administrative action in these issues have been somewhat different than in "external" matters. There has been disagreement, not on principle, but on the evaluation of circumstances surrounding the decision, as the twelve cases analyzed earlier in the Snelson matter demonstrates. Both the high courts and the Supreme Court have been reluctant to act in many instances involving internal griev- ance but have felt compelled to in the interests of "natural justice." In a sense, the courts have actively infused the bureaucracy with their own norms of due process.

Since many of the principal cases dealing with internal service matters have already been mentioned in relation to the Snelson contempt case, only a few outstanding judgments will be analyzed here. A major case involved twenty police officers who held temporary posts and were dismissed without the procedural re- quirements of the civil service rules: *Noorul Hassan* v. *Federation of Pakistan* (1956) P.S.C.R. 128. Chief Justice Munir held that a temporary incumbent could be dismissed without a hearing, but a majority of the court held that a hearing was required even for temporary employees. Subsequently, this protection was extended to employees engaged on contract for specified terms (*Khwaja Ghulam Sarwar* v. *Pakistan*, PLD 1962 SC 142). The determi- nation of seniority and promotion has sometimes led the court to analyze the administrative structure of operating departments as it did in *Mohammad Ali Akhtar* v. *Pakistan*, PLD 1963 Kar. 381. Closely allied with the issue of preventing removal from service except in accordance with due process of law is the problem of payment of arrears of salary to an official, who, having been removed illegally, was reinstated by court order. Until 1964, the courts held that the executive could not be ordered to pay such arrears. Payment of salary was regarded as the "bounty of the crown," and the court could only hope that the executive would pay such arrears *ex gratia*. But the executive defaulted in many instances and the courts deplored this condition of inhumaneness and irresponsibility (*State of Pakistan* v. *Mehrajuddin* [1959] 1 P.S.C.R. 34; *Government of West Pakistan* v. *Fazal-e-Haq Mussar- ratt* [1960] 1 P.S.C.R. 124). The situation went to the extreme of a government department disobeying an order of the governor to pay arrears. Without departing from the principle that the court could not order payment, the court in this instance ordered compliance with the governor's order (*Rehmatullah* v. *Province of West Pakistan*, PLD 1963 Baghdad-ul-Jadid 19). Earlier Chief

Justice Kayani held that the Supreme Court had already suggested a departure from the "bounty of the crown" doctrine in *Pakistan v. Muhammad Hayat,* PLD 1962 SC 28, by ruling that it could compel government to pay salary at a certain rate. Kayani's interpretation was never brought to the Supreme Court. Ultimately, the question was resolved for litigation involving arrears averaging no more than Rs. 200 a month simply by construing the terms of the Payment of Wages Act, 1936, to cover government employment. Thus, government can be compelled to pay arrears averaging no more than Rs. 200 a month under terms of this act. This decision, *Divisional Superintendent, Northwest Railroad v. Muhammad Sharif,* PLD 1963 SC 340, does not reverse the "bounty of the crown" principle, nor does it even mention it. It remains to be seen if the principle will be extended to arrears in greater amounts.

The burden which the judiciary has assumed in internal and external issues relating to the bureaucracy has led to proposals of other modes of judicial control over administration. The principal mode suggested has been the establishment of a system of administrative tribunals patterned after the French structure. Chief Justice Cornelius has been the major proponent of this scheme, which he first suggested in an address at the 1959 convocation of the Lahore College of Law. He expanded his views in a subsequent address before the Rotary Club of Lahore in 1960, in which he related bureaucratic probity to the existence of administrative tribunals.[38] His fullest analysis of the problem was in another address to the All-Pakistan Lawyers Association in 1960 [39] and in an obiter dictum in *Faridsons Ltd. and Friederike Ltd. v. Government of Pakistan* (1962) 1 P.S.C.R. 1. Chaudhury Mohamad Ali, distinguished former prime minister, supported the proposal for administrative tribunals in his answers to Question No. 27 of the questionnaire of the Constitution Commission.[40] Apart from this the proposal has not received widespread support. It was rejected by the Law Reform Commission which favored instead

[38] Text in Appendix 10.
[39] Text in Appendix 11.
[40] Text of Mohamad Ali's answers in *Pakistan Times,* June 13, 1960, pp. 8.

modifications of procedure and of statutory law which would make redress of administrative grievance easier to achieve within the traditional bounds of the writ jurisdiction.

Readiness to involve the judiciary in administrative matters by appealing for review of administrative action is indicated by the extent of litigation relating to Basic Democracies. The Basic Democracies Scheme became effective October 27, 1959, yet through June, 1964, twenty-four High Court decisions and four Supreme Court judgments were published. It may be assumed that a much larger number of appeals to these courts were rejected and that a greater volume of such cases reached district and sessions courts. A formula limiting the contours of judicial review of such administrative action is slowly evolving. No clear limitations such as those set by Munir in the Tariq Transport and Mohammad Saeed judgments are yet in evidence, nor has there been a transfer of the Munir formularies from the review of administrative discretion to the realm of Basic Democracies. The character of action is not quite analogous, for Basic Democracies involves both political and formal bureaucratic participation. Hence, the formulary deemed suitable for review of exclusively bureaucratic action may not be found suitable to the mixed character of Basic Democracies. In any event, the conceptual aspects of the role of the judiciary in this matter have not yet been dealt with. The jurisdiction of the courts, except in removal of elected councilors, is clearly established by Article 86 of the Basic Democracies Order and is not challenged in any of the cases. Because of this exception, the determination of who is "elected" and who is "official" is crucial. This was the issue in *Manzur-ul-Haq* v. *Controlling Authority*, PLD 1963 SC 652, in which it was also held that a show-cause process preceding removal of councilors was discretionary. Most of the cases involve definition of terms rather than procedural questions. In *Mahmudal Haque* v. *Controlling Authority, S.D.O. (North) Chittagong*, PLD 1963 SC 233, the most important of these cases, Cornelius ruled that the court could not compel an elected councilor to be restored to his position when he had been disqualified because he was a government official. Subsequently, the Supreme Court ruled that the term "business" in the Basic Democracies Order included election of the chairman (*Mohd. Nawaz Khan* v. *Ghulam Farid,* PLD 1963 SC 623). The contours of judicial review of administrative action within the ambit of Basic Democracies are only beginning to evolve into a definitive form.

6

Commissions of Inquiry under Martial Law

The existence of a martial law government for nearly four years and the consequent moratorium on legislative and political activity necessarily changed the source of national policy. In a static social system a martial law government might be merely a holding action, maintaining paramountcy of power and preserving the status quo. The martial law regime in Pakistan, however, was marked by considerable ideological ferment characterized by a comprehensive scheme of change across the entire spectrum of political and social life. It is not likely that the ideological source for such plans would be found exclusively within the military establishment. In fact, much of the edifice of reform, whether by design or fortuitously, was the consequence of the combined deliberations of thirty-three major commissions of inquiry involving the active participation of 280 persons who were either government officials, non-official experts, or leading citizens. The published results of their deliberations total some five thousand printed pages.

As a consequence, almost every major innovation in policy during the martial law period, except for Basic Democracies and foreign policy, has emerged from a consensual process of sorts. This is not to say that this corporate deliberation was the creative genius of martial law reforms or that it was a substitute for a sovereign legislative process embodied in mature constitutional systems. The commissions owed their very existence to the will of the President, in whom all legislative power was vested, and their recommendations were merely advisory. It is clear that often commissions seemed to corroborate policy judgments previously made known by the President. But it is equally clear that the

President did not always act in consonance with the recommendations of the commissions. The reports of the Constitution Commission, the Press Commission, and the Law Reform Commission are the most conspicuous instances of such divergence. Nevertheless, it is also true that most of the recommendations of most of the commissions were enacted into legislation. There emerges from this experience one of the most significant uses in modern times of a corporate device for the formulation of state policy under a martial law regime. The commission reports were discussed in detail by the President and his cabinet meeting with the two provincial governors. Cabinet subcommittees were often appointed to review the reports and to advise on their implementation. This co-ordinative process was the responsibility of the Cabinet Secretariat of the President's Office. The deliberations of the cabinet and government, together with recommended actions were usually printed, but necessarily as classified documents not available to the public or to researchers. Therefore, it is almost impossible to ascertain with precision the extent to which the thousands of detailed recommendations made by the thirty-three commissions were favorably acted upon by the President's group. Some suggestions were acted upon administratively by oral orders; others were dealt with by a variety of instruments such as rules, regulations, ordinances, orders, and statutes. It appears to be the consensus of those in crucial policy posts in government that action was taken on most of the commissions' reports. In most cases, government concurred in the recommendations. Publicly announced non-concurrence was primarily on such issues as the Constitution, separation of judicial and executive functions, and franchise.

Table 9 lists relevant data for all thirty-three commissions of inquiry. In general, the commissions followed the practice established under British rule of issuing questionnaires and interviewing key witnesses. Typically, each report explains the procedure by which decisions were reached. Appendices usually include the questionnaire and lists of witnesses. With a few exceptions, the reports of the commissions do justice to the long tradition of governmental inquiry started under British rule. Certainly the reports of the Food and Agriculture Commission, Film Fact Finding Committee, the commissions on jute and textiles, and the four reports on administration are skilful, comprehensive analyses which can be favorably compared to similar reports in older constitutional systems.

Not all of these commission reports are directly relevant to problems of administration, although they all deal with issues ultimately under the control of the public bureaucracy. The four commissions dealing specifically with administrative reorganization, provincial administration, pay and services, provincial reorganization (items 9, 13, 18, and 30 in Table 9) have been discussed elsewhere in this essay and are therefore not considered here.[1] Their inclusion at earlier points in the essay was based on considerations of substantive relevance rather than on classificatory uniformity. In reality, all four commissions were important sources for determining national policy under martial law and should be thought of as part of the group of thirty-three martial law commissions of inquiry.

The reports of several commissions are classified or have not yet been released by government, hence cannot be discussed here. They are merely listed in Table 9 with a brief description of format. Included in this category are reports of the nine commissions on maritime affairs, pay and service, federal capital, company law, eradication of social evils, manpower, power, allocation of revenue, and taxation and tariff (items 7, 18, 19, 20, 27, 28, 29, 31, and 33 in Table 9). The reports of the five commissions dealing with Quetta-Kalat laws, press, law reform, education, and food and agriculture (items 1, 2, 8, 10, and 16 in Table 9) have been discussed in other contexts throughout this essay, hence further discussion at this point will be limited. Not all of the remaining fourteen commission reports are crucially relevant to administration, but each is briefly discussed in this chapter.

Since these thirty-three commissions are crucial as sources of national policy, their structure, composition, and mode of operation are questions of importance. Table 10 reveals several facts as

[1] See above, pp. 218, 222, 225–231.

Table 9. *Summary of Data on Commissions of Inquiry under Martial Law*
(Listed by date of appointment)

Name of commission and chairman	Number of members	Date appointed	Date report signed	Number of printed pages	Days' duration
1. Quetta-Kalat Laws Commission (Sheikh Abdul Hamid)[a]	2	Oct., 1957	Aug. 14, 1958	44	300
2. Press Commission (H. B. Tayabji)[b]	6	Sept. 5, 1958	March 25, 1959	138	201
3. Commission on Marriage and Family Laws (Mian Abdul Rashid)[a]	7	Aug. 4, 1955	June 20, 1956	234	321
4. Taxation Enquiry Committee (Abdul Qadir)[c]	7 #	July 4, 1957	July 8, 1960	845	860[d]
5. Sugar Commission (M. A. Husain)	10	Sept. 30, 1957	July 19, 1959	78	657
6. West Pakistan Land Reforms Commission (Akhter Husain) ##	7	Oct. 31, 1958	Jan. 20, 1959	74	81
7. Maritime Commission (Rear Admiral A. R. Khan)	5	Nov. 19, 1958	April, 1959	93	147
8. Law Reform Commission (S. A. Rahman)	9 #	Nov. 23, 1958	Aug. 27, 1959	145	277
9. Administrative Reorganization Committee (G. Ahmed)[o]	7 #	Dec. 12, 1958	Jan. 29, 1961	359	779
10. Commission on National Education (S. M. Sharif)	11 #	Dec. 30, 1958	Aug. 26, 1959	360	239
11. Special Commission for the Location of the Capital (Maj. Gen. A. M. Yahya Khan)	10	Jan. 21, 1959	July 15, 1960	45	541
12. Scientific Commission (A. K. Khan)	14	Jan. 30, 1959	July 5, 1960	102	522
13. Provincial Administration Commission[o] (Akhter Husain) ##	3 #	Feb. 12, 1959	Feb. 16, 1960	237	369
14. Credit Enquiry Commission (Abdul Qadir)	8 #	Feb. 24, 1959	Sept. 8, 1959	218	196
15. Jute Enquiry Commission (Zakir Husain)	13	June 8, 1959	Dec. 13, 1960	319	553
16. Food and Agriculture Commission (M. Amir Mohammad Khan)	9	July 11, 1959	Nov. 29, 1960	582	507
17. Textile Enquiry Commission (Nazir Ahmad)	6 #	Aug. 1, 1959	March 31, 1960	190	242
18. Pay and Service Commission (Chief Justice A. R. Cornelius)[o]	11 #	Aug. 31, 1959	June 1, 1962	300	1,004
19. Federal Capital Commission (Maj. Gen. A. M. Yahya Khan)	4 #	Sept. 7, 1959	June, 1960	Unknown	271
20. Company Law Commission (S. S. Pirzada)[e]	5 #	Oct. 13, 1959 / Feb. 4, 1961 (reconstituted)	Dec. 9, 1961	300	788
21. Medical Reforms Commission (Col. M. K. Afridi)	11 #	Nov. 24, 1959	April 20, 1960	140	148
22. Police Commission (Sir George Constantine)	5 #	Dec. 31, 1959	May 17, 1961	122	503
23. Constitution Commission (Md. Shahabuddin)	11 #	Feb. 17, 1960	May 6, 1961	178	444
24. Prices Commission (I. I. Chundrigar)	12	Feb. 24, 1960	June 21, 1960	157	118
25. Culture, Art, Sports, and Youth Movement Committee (H. Rahman)	14	Feb. 9, 1960	Sept. 14, 1960	36	218
26. Film Fact Finding Committee (N. M. Khan)	10	March 10, 1960	April 19, 1961	410	405
27. Eradication of Social Evils Commission (A. B. A. Haleem)	10	Jan. 13, 1961	June 18, 1964	102	1,252
28. Surplus Manpower Commission (Maj. Gen. Fazal Muqueem)	8	Feb. 3, 1961	July 7, 1961	95	154
29. Power Commission (Dr. I. H. Usmani)	16	May 12, 1961	Aug. 8, 1963	289	818
30. Provincial Reorganization Committee[o] (N. A. Faruqui)[f]	6	Aug. 4, 1961		197	128
31. Finance Commission [on Allocation of Revenues to Central and Provincial Governments][o] (Hafiz Majid)			Part I (West Pakistan) Dec. 15, 1961; Part II (East Pakistan) April 12, 1962	241	251
32. Franchise Commission (Akhter Husain)[f] ##	10 / 5	Dec. 11, 1961 / Aug. 4, 1962	Jan. 27, 1962 / Aug. 16, 1963	81 / 74	47 / 377
33. Commission on Taxation and Tariff (Abdul Qadir)[f]	8	March 31, 1964	Not yet submitted		
Totals	280			6,785	13,590

[a] Although this commission was appointed before martial law and its report was submitted before the Martial Law Proclamation of October 7, 1958, it is included in this tabulation because the issues dealt with were a substantial part of martial law policy.

[b] Press Commission was originally constituted under chairmanship of K. Zaman, September 28, 1954, with twelve members. Later it was reconstituted as shown above.

[c] First chairman was Zahid Husain.

[d] This figure does not include 240-day lapse after death of Zahid Husain, first chairman, until commission started to function under new chairman.

[e] First chairman was I. I. Chundrigar. Reconstituted after his death as shown above.

[f] These commissions were appointed after the end of martial law, but are included because of their important recommendations on the mode of elections basic to the new post-martial law parliamentary government and on the total tax structure.

[o] Also included in Table 2 on Reports of Major Inquiries in Administration.

# Indicates a non-member secretary of commission; otherwise secretary is a member.

The chairman of commissions listed as items 6, 13, and 32 is the same person although his name is variously spelled in the three reports. In some instances the spelling in the signature at the end of the report is different from the spelling in the terms of reference at the beginning. I have arbitrarily made these spellings uniform in this table and in the text.

Sources: Published reports, interviews, and correspondence.

Table 10. *Professions and Provinces of Domicile of Members of Central Government Commissions of Inquiry (Based on membership of 33 commissions listed in Table 9)*

Profession	West Pakistan	East Pakistan	Total	Percentage of total
Civil service				
Non-technical, active	68	12	80	28.6
Non-technical, retired	15	5	20	7.1
Technical, active	12	3	15	5.4
Technical, retired	2	1	3	1.1
Total, Civil Service	97	21	118	42.1
Military officers				
Active	14	1	15	5.4
Retired	3	0	3	1.1
Total, Military	17	1	18	6.4
Judicial				
Supreme Court, active	3	0	3	1.1
Supreme Court, retired	1	0	1	0.4
High Court, active	5	2	7	2.5
High Court, retired	2	1	3	1.1
Sessions Court, retired	2	0	2	0.7
Total, Judicial	13	3	16	5.7
Government corporation	14	6	20	7.1
Lawyer	6	9	15	5.4
Professional scholar	6	8	14	5.0
Academic administrator	3	8	11	3.9
Business	8	3	11	3.9
Interest representative	3	7	10	3.6
Scientist	9	1	10	3.6
Woman	5	2	7	2.5
Foreign national[a]	—	—	6	2.1
Landholder	4	2	6	2.1
Politician	3	1	4	1.4
Governor	3	1	4	1.4
Cabinet minister	3	0	3	1.1
Plant manager	0	2	2	.7
Religious leader	2	0	2	.7
Accountant	2	0	2	.7
Physician	1	0	1	.4
Total	199	75	280[b]	100.0
Percentage	71.1	26.8		
CSP officers				
Active	43	3	46	
Retired	5	1	6	
Total	48	4	52	

[a] This category includes only members of commissions, not consultants or advisers. Foreign nationals in the employ of the Government of Pakistan are not included.
[b] Total 280 is sum of 199, 75, and six foreign nationals. Percentages do not add to 100 because the six foreign nationals (2.1 per cent) are not included in provincial percentages.
Source: Interviews and correspondence, *Gazette* notifications, statutes.

to composition which are noteworthy. The Bengali–West Pakistan disparity, analyzed earlier in this essay,[2] is reflected in the fact that somewhat less than 25 per cent of the total membership of these commissions came from East Pakistan. It is strikingly evident that foreign nationals played a minimal role since only 2.1 per cent of commission members were non-Pakistani. It is not surprising that, if military officers, judges, and corporation directors are included, some 60 per cent of the membership was drawn from within the bureaucracy, and nearly half (fifty-two) of these were members of the elite CSP cadre. Military officers were only slightly represented (6.4 per cent), and most of these were on a few highly specialized commissions. Judges, lawyers, and professional scholars were about equally represented (5 per cent in each category). Politicians (1.4 per cent) were hardly represented at all. These data, however, must be interpreted with caution. First, the representation of various interests in society was by no means evenly distributed among the thirty-three commissions. On the contrary, each professional group was concentrated in particular commissions dealing with that group's interest. The 5 per cent representation of lawyers is concentrated almost entirely on the Law Reform Commission, physicians are found on the Medical Reforms Commission, and scholars and academic administrators are almost exclusively on the Education Commission. Secondly, it should be noted that these commissions functioned in a climate of martial law which, while orderly and stable, was not a climate conducive to open disagreement with what was thought to be the official views of the President. Notwithstanding this, there were some spectacular departures from the President's views. Nevertheless, this method of formulating national policy does not assume the free interplay of political forces found in a sovereign legislative process. Finally, the quality of representativeness, and hence perhaps the content of ideas presented, may have been affected by the fact that commission members were appointed by the President. It is clear that commission membership was predominantly that of government officials on active duty performing generalist

[2] See above, pp. 44–55.

functions. Certainly the commissions on administrative reform were composed almost entirely of such officials. Yet generalist bureaucrats had little to do with other technical, reform efforts, each of which was dominated by relevant technical specialists. Association of politicians, religious leaders, and non-professional business leaders with the reform efforts was minimal. These three groups were represented only to the extent of 6 per cent and were concentrated in the commissions on company law, land reform, and marriage and family laws. Viewed from the point of view of technique for formulating national policy, Pakistan had a series of discrete occupational entities, submitting reports based on the needs of each discrete segment. Presumably a synthesis was to be achieved by the President's cabinet and the Cabinet Secretariat of the President's Office. In fact, a surprising degree of harmony, at least in concept if not in implementation, was achieved as a new polity of government was forged from the issues raised by the commission reports.

The first report [3] included under martial law commissions is the *Report on Quetta-Kalat Judicial System—1958* (Lahore: West Pakistan Government Press, 1958) (item 1, Table 9) by the Quetta-Kalat Laws Commission, headed by former Justice Sheikh Abdul Hamid, later principal of the Law College of the University of Peshawar. Since the report has already been mentioned in the context of tribal problems,[4] it need not be discussed at length here. Of all thirty-three reports, the Quetta-Kalat Laws Report is the least known, and since only fifty copies were printed is the least widely distributed. Strictly speaking, the commission should not be classified as a martial law commission since it was appointed and submitted its report before the coup d'état of 1958. But the report is of significance because it raises the issue of tribal law in the Northwest Frontier and the suitability of British criminal law which subsequently became an important facet of martial law ideology. Although it ostensibly deals with only the two districts of Quetta and Kalat in Baluchistan, the conceptual issues dealt

[3] Since not all the reports of commissions of martial law inquiry listed in Table 9 are summarized in this chapter, serial numbering of reports to correspond with numbering in Table 9 is not feasible.
[4] See above, p. 195.

with relate to the entire Northwest Frontier. Significantly, the point of view of its two members, Sheikh Hamid and Kazi Ghazanfar Hussain, favoring extension of British law and abolition of tribal law, is diametrically opposed to the policy later adopted by martial law. This fact adds to the importance of the report as a document.

The report of the Commission on Marriage and Family Laws (item 3, Table 9) aroused such sharp difference of opinion between orthodox and "modernist" Muslims that it was almost forgotten until, resuscitated by the martial law regime, it was enacted into law in 1961. The report of the commission, published in the *Gazette of Pakistan, Extraordinary,* June 20, 1956, pp. 1197–1232, and August 30, 1956, pp. 1505–1604, is a document which facilitates understanding of the difference in point of view of the "modernist" and "traditionalist" interpreters of Islam. A long dissent by Maulana Ihtishamul-Huq, reflecting the latter point of view, is given in the report. Further elaboration of this point is found in a volume of critical essays by orthodox Muslims, Khurshid Ahmad (ed.), *Marriage Commission Report X-Rayed* (Karachi, November, 1959), p. 315. It is not appropriate in this essay to discuss this issue; the relevant aspect of the report is the fact that the enactment into law of some of the commission's majority recommendations does affect administration, particularly at the local level. The enactment is known as the Muslim Family Laws Ordinance (VIII of 1961). Each province enacted corresponding laws called West Pakistan Rules under Muslim Family Laws Ordinance, 1961, and East Pakistan Muslim Family Law Rules, 1961. The new ordinance vests authority in the union councils, created as part of the Basic Democracies Scheme. The union council must keep marriage records and may issue licenses to marriage (*nikah*) registrars. Applications for second marriages are passed on by an arbitration council, consisting of the chairman of the union council and a representative of each interested party; appeal from this decision may be made to the district officer. Dissolution of the marriage is similarly effected only through the arbitration council. Thus the ordinance fits into the pattern of local government envisaged under the Basic Democracies Scheme, a pattern which places greater responsibility on union councils and transfers some responsibility from the district officer.

The *Report of the Press Commission* (Karachi: Government of Pakistan Press, March, 1959) (item 2, Table 9), also created before martial law, encountered serious difficulties. Originally constituted in 1954 of eleven members, most of whom were from the press, the commission was unable to function because of differences among the members. It was reconstituted in 1958 with seven members, none of whom were from the press. Most of the report deals with the working conditions and pay of journalists, distribution of newsprint, and financial organization of newspapers. There are recommendations with respect to freedom of the press, which call for a balance between freedom responsibly exercised and the security of the state. The report was prepared during a period of great anxiety felt by the government toward the *Pakistan Times* and other publications of Progressive Papers, Ltd., which were later sold under government order and were the subject of a series of cases in the High Court and Supreme Court.[5] The suspicion that the *Pakistan Times* may have been supported by foreign sources was reflected (without direct reference) in the commission's recommendation that newspapers list their sources of support. In a chapter on liaison between government and the press, the commission suggested that while liaison was satisfactory in the national and provincial capitals, it was inadequate in *mofussil* towns. It criticized the inadequacy of press handouts and suggested more frequent press conferences and the employment of a greater number of working journalists in government public relations agencies. The press ordinances, imposing a greater measure of control over the press than the Press Commission suggested, were promulgated as a sequel to the commission's report. Another consequence generally well received by the press was an ordinance regulating hours and conditions of work for journalists.[6]

A fourth pre-martial law commission, the Taxation Enquiry Committee, met with unexpected delay. Because of the death of

[5] See above, p. 80 ff.

[6] See above, p. 83 ff., for comment on press ordinances. See also Working Journalists (Conditions of Service) Ordinance XVI of 1960, published in *Gazette of Pakistan, Extraordinary*, April 27, 1960.

its chairman, there was a lapse of 240 days during which the commission did not function. Appointed in July, 1957, it submitted two interim reports in 1957, and issued its final report in two volumes early in 1960 (item 4, Table 9). The two interim reports, *Taxation Enquiry Committee Interim Report (Central Taxation)* (Karachi: Government of Pakistan Press, January 15, 1959), and *Taxation Enquiry Committee, Interim Report (Provincial Taxation)* (Karachi: Government Printing Office, May 28, 1959), make more than one hundred recommendations. The basic land revenue system is regarded by the commission as worthy of retention with only minor changes. The major issue of relevance to administration is the articulation of the commission's recommendations with the local government evolved under the Basic Democracies Scheme. The report establishes a tax base for the various units of local government sufficient to sustain the new activities assigned.

The *Report of the Pakistan Sugar Commission, 1957–59* (Karachi: Government of Pakistan Press, 1960) (item 5, Table 9) is an important technical document on one of the most important of Pakistan's crops. There is little in it of direct relevance to administration, however, except its suggestion that the organization for technological research be improved.

Among the most far-reaching changes undertaken under martial law were the land reforms of West Pakistan. Although the actual reform was accomplished by promulgation of a martial law regulation (West Pakistan Land Reforms Regulation, No. 64, 1959, published in *Gazette of Pakistan, Extraordinary*, March 3, 1959), it was preceded by a three-month study by a commission of seven members headed by Akhter Husain, a distinguished former ICS officer who was then provincial governor. The result of this study is the *Report of the Land Reforms Commission for West Pakistan* (Lahore: West Pakistan Government Press, 1959). The commission's recommendations included limiting ownership by one person to five hundred acres of irrigated land or one thousand acres of unirrigated land. Land in excess was to be repossessed by the government for compensation in bonds redeemable in twenty-five years and bearing 3 per cent interest. The ensuing legislation is of significance to administration because of the powers accorded to the Land Commission in interpreting the legislation.

The Report of the Law Reform Commission, 1958–59 (Karachi: Government of Pakistan Press, 1959) (item 8, Table 9) is not one of the longest or most analytical of reports of the martial law commissions. The seven-member commission, headed by Justice S. A. Rahman, made several significant recommendations, not all of which were accepted by the government. The commission's recommendation for separation of the executive and judicial functions and the vesting of all control of subordinate courts in the high courts was not approved by the government. Its recommendations relating to the writ jurisdiction were accepted. A wide range of recommendations dealing with matters of detail in legal procedure and with legal education were adopted or are in process of being implemented.

Ultimately, the proposals in the *Report of the Commission on National Education* (Karachi: Government of Pakistan Press, 1960) (item 10, Table 9) will affect attitudes toward government and of government servants. Its advocacy of work programs for students to enhance the dignity of labor and its strong suggestions for the recognition of native talent are significant egalitarian tendencies which may ultimately be reflected in government service. The role of education in revising the prevailing view of government as the initiator of action and the source of change was recognized by the commission. The attitude of the government servant must also change, the report states, and there must be recognition of his role in serving the public. His satisfaction should come not from a sense of power but from the pride of doing his work fairly, honestly, and efficiently. The vexing complex of educational problems described earlier in this essay have been dealt with by a program of general reform.[7] The commission does not deal directly with the absence of unremitting discipline and hard work in university life. It appears to rely on general social reform to change these conditions. The problem of the external

[7] See above, p. 14 ff. For an official statement of the extent to which the recommendations of this commission have been implemented, see National Assembly of Pakistan, *Debates, Official Report*, March 9, 1963, pp. 62–63.

examination is recognized, but the commission is not willing to depart from it completely, for it recognizes that teachers' "preferences, favouritism, laziness or plain incompetence" are still factors which must be considered. Hence, it suggests that 25 per cent of the total grade in each paper (course) be determined from internal, periodic examinations administered by the teacher. The report also pays much attention to the psychological problems of the developing adolescent and urges athletics, student activities, and close student-faculty relations as means of overcoming these difficulties. The commission's report devotes a chapter to the "dignity of labour" for university students. This appreciation of manual work is to be accomplished in summer work camps or community projects, and for younger students it is to be achieved by cleaning the school premises. These are unquestionably valuable ends in a society which has looked with disdain on manual work. The report does not mention training for the public service. No reasons for this omission are given. It may be guessed that, heretofore, university graduates aspired primarily to government service, hence the need was to redress the balance away from government service. In any event, the report does not consider the continuing need for associating the universities with government and particularly with research on government as a logical extension of the belief that government must not be the exclusive preserve of a few. Acceptance by the university of a responsibility for challenging the monopoly on government expertness held by civil servants and for undertaking to improve the practice of government by research and courses in administration and public policy is not raised specifically by the report. Its significance to the development of government administration in Pakistan, therefore, while important, is generalized and remote, rather than specific and immediate. A department of public administration was established at the University of the Panjab in Lahore in 1962 under aegis of the United States Agency for International Development under contract with the University of Southern California. Although this clearly recognized the responsibility of higher education for public service training, this recognition derived from sources other than the commission's report.

The decision to remove the national capital from Karachi to a new city, Islamabad, on the Potwar plateau near Rawalpindi, was made after extensive study by the Commission for the Location of the Federal Capital. Headed by Major General A. M. Yahya Khan, chief of the general staff, the commission organized nine subcommittees. Dr. C. A. Doxiadis, Greek architect and city planner, was appointed its adviser. Its *Report on the Location of the Federal Capital* (Karachi: Government of Pakistan Press, 1959) was not released to the public, but its principal provisions were released to the press on July 15, 1959. The commission considered many factors, among them geography. It concluded, after an array of statistics, that only Quetta, the Kithar Range, and Potwar had agreeable climates which were free from waterlogging and earthquakes, and had subsoil structures adequate to support a large city. One part of the report dealing with aesthetic considerations merits the attention of urban planners:

Planned towns tend to grow like beehives, soulless; inspired by the architectural impulse of a single generation. Their rigidity of layout and design create a sterile environment lacking the emotional impulse to engender creative thought. It enforces mediocrity which is an easy prey to the onset of decay. To neutralize rigidity in planning, an undulating landscape is preferable to a flat, unbroken terrain.

The commission rejected Karachi as not meeting enough of the criteria it had posed, but it felt that it would continue to flourish as a great port and commercial center. The commission projected a capital city of from eighty to one hundred square miles, including parks. Around this would be a wide belt of productive farming land. It found the Potwar area to be adequate in water, food, fuel, and power sources and felt that construction material could be the marble readily available near Peshawar and Nowshera. Communications are already well developed in northern Pakistan, and Potwar, adjacent to Rawalpindi, is also within convenient distance of other major cities such as Lahore and Peshawar.

Accepting the recommendations of the Commission on the Federal Capital, the President appointed the Federal Capital Commission, headed by Major General Yahya Khan (*Gazette of Pakistan, Extraordinary*, September 7, 1959, pp. 1507–1509). Doxiades Associates were appointed consultants, and fourteen committees were organized to make plans for Islamabad. Several reports were prepared by Doxiades Associates and the commission. The reports are technical and are not generally available. The commission subsequently became the Capital Development Authority (*Gazette of Pakistan,* June 27, 1960, pp. 938c–939r), with a membership of three government officials headed by W. A. Shaikh, CSP.

It is somewhat unfortunate that greater publicity has not been given to the plans for Islamabad, which represent implementation of Doxiades' concept of the dynapolis. It promises to be one of the world's great planned cities. The best public source of information about the plans is a special anniversary issue (June, 1961) of the technical journal, *Engineering Forum,* with which students of government would ordinarily have little contact. Published in Karachi since 1958, *Engineering Forum* is a well-designed, well-edited journal for engineers. The anniversary issue includes several articles on the master plan, with illustrations of designs and models of buildings. Especially instructive is an essay by C. A. Doxiades in which the theoretical concepts underlying the "dynapolis" are developed.

A key problem in the development of Pakistan has been the attitude of disdain toward technical and scientific training which has characterized a bureaucracy long dominated by a classical, generalist tradition. This has been manifested in the subordinate roles which technical and scientific personnel play in the bureaucracy and by the exodus from the country of a large number of technically trained men who have felt that the situation in Pakistan was hostile to the satisfactory pursuit of their specialty. The more basic problem lay in organizing resources for scientific research so that science might be harnessed for the rapid development of the nation. These problems were dealt with in the *Report of the Scientific Commission of Pakistan* (Karachi: Government of Pakistan Press, 1960) in an incisive and skilful manner. After a brief introduction describing the Muslim scientific heritage and the reasons for its decline in recent history, the report surveys existing private and governmental facilities for scientific research.

The report is limited to the natural sciences and does not touch on the problem of the social sciences at all. The commission urges the rapid development of scientific research in universities and deplores the administrative control over research in government departments. It is in this context that one of the commission's most significant recommendations is made, namely, that a separate scientific service be created on a level of esteem with the Civil Service of Pakistan. This strikes at a fundamental problem in the channeling of scientific talent into effective work, for each year several well-trained scientists enter the Civil Service of Pakistan only because no other activity has comparable prestige. The commission describes the scientific problems of the nation as being those of food, irrigation and power, mineral resources, and public health, and proposes the establishment of five separate research councils to deal with research directed to these problems. Better organization of research for defense and more effective utilization of research results in all fields are urged. But it is the problem of the status of scientists to which the commission returns in a separate chapter of detailed suggestions. In an appendix the report lists by name some eighty trained Pakistani scientists who have remained abroad because of government's neglect in giving to scientific professions status comparable to those of the other services. To achieve this status, it proposes that the five research councils employ the largest number of scientists to be recruited in a separate service. Reflecting awareness that the Pay Commission will deal with salary structure, but fearful that the issue of scientists' pay may not receive adequate attention, the commission makes specific recommendations as to pay and promotion policies. The commission's recommendations have been accepted by the cabinet and when implemented may alter somewhat the monopoly on prestige which the Civil Service of Pakistan has until now enjoyed.

The *Credit Enquiry Commission Report* (Karachi: Government of Pakistan Press, September 8, 1959) is a survey of particular merit which has some bearing on administration in the districts. The commission discusses the possibility of organizing credit in villages within a multipurpose co-operative society but concludes that the administrative problems involved may be beyond the competence of local management committees. It urges simple one-purpose societies and suggests that the changes proposed in East Pakistan leading to multipurpose societies be reconsidered. Acknowledging a general weakening of the co-operative movement which was formerly an important aspect of rural life, the commission urges that bold measures be taken to strengthen co-operatives. This can be done by assigning to them such responsibilities as the procurement of food grains for government and by treating non-payment of co-operative society dues as land revenue arrears. The effect of such recommendations politically would be in the direction of pluralization of power within the districts and this would affect traditional district administration, probably for the better. Although the co-operative movement has been generally strengthened as a result of this report, its significance remains somewhat eclipsed by the rural works program in East Pakistan and agricultural development corporation plans in West Pakistan.

The *Report of the Jute Enquiry Commission* (Karachi: Ministry of Commerce, 1960) is one of the most comprehensive and sophisticated reports in the martial law series. It includes elaborate statistical appendices and extensive technical analysis of jute production, which is the major industry in East Pakistan. One of the most helpful features of the report is the summary of its 107 recommendations with the action of government on each item. Only this report and that of the Administrative Reorganisation Committee include such information. The commission recommends continuing government supervision and regulation of the jute industry but suggests several ways of improving such government control.

A report comparable to the jute report in quality of analysis and format is that of the Textile Enquiry Commission (Karachi: Ministry of Industries, 1960) whose fifty-four recommendations concern the cotton textile industry of West Pakistan. The commission suggested continued government supervision, but it called for the establishment of work committees in mills to deal with conditions of work and for greater activity on the part of the millowners for technical advances in the industry.

Certainly the longest and in many ways the most comprehensive and most competent of all thirty-three martial law surveys is the *Report of the Food and Agriculture Commission* (Karachi: Manager of Publications, November, 1960). This report is crucially relevant to administrative problems on several counts. For some years, several approaches to rural reform have been put into effect in Pakistan: Village AID, Basic Democracies, strengthening of district administration, co-operative societies. These different structural responses have been advanced within such a short span of time that carefully designed plans for integrating these activities appeared to be badly needed. None of the literature on administration or community development nor the government commission reports on administrative reform seem to provide the framework for integration. The Food and Agriculture Commission is the only group which has faced this problem squarely and incisively and has proposed a plan to remedy the situation. In a carefully written sixty-two page chapter (VI), "The Tools for the Job," the commission describes the deficiencies in administrative organization and proposes ways to accomplish the national need for increased agricultural production. It contends that the attitude of government officials toward agriculture has too often been one of neglect and contempt and that the low status of technical men generally has prevented scientific agriculture from making an impact on governmental policy. Moreover, in the absence of a commercial sector to service agriculture, the whole responsibility has fallen on government, which has not devised new machinery but has allowed several departments to handle agricultural development in competition with other responsibilities. The commission then assesses the administrative capacity of each agency concerned with agriculture, starting with the agricultural departments of the provincial governments. It states that line officials in the field are poorly trained and have areas impossibly large to handle. The irrigation department merely supplies water and collects charges and does not have a sense of service to the farmer. The water and power development authorities have not paid adequate attention to the ways farmers have used water. The co-operative societies, once so vigorous and flourishing, the commission found, with the exception of those in the Punjab, "generally moribund." The Village Agricultural and Industrial Development Program was seen to be somewhat more satisfactory and even "impressive in the spirit they conveyed of social progress through participation and motivation." But, the commission continued, competition and overlapping with the functions of the agriculture departments mar Village AID work, and, more importantly, demonstrations, lectures, and encouragement are not sufficient to meet agricultural problems. What is needed is vastly improved organization with Village AID "being a forerunner . . . a motivator and . . . a point of contact where the additional patience and time can be applied which an action organisation lacks." The commission appreciated the need for participation which is the purpose of Basic Democracies, but asserted that the nation needs efficiency as much as participation.

The commission next comes to the agency of greatest interest to students of bureaucracy, namely, orthodox district administration which the report characterizes as the "district team approach." The report briefly describes the organization of the district and states that the deputy commissioner is overburdened and has no really effective control over the technical officers assigned in his district. Efforts to alleviate the administrative burden in the district are regarded as inadequate, and a new machinery of action is proposed. The agricultural service organization must be emancipated from the tight control of the deputy commissioner, and the only means by which this can be done, in the view of the commission, is by creating an agricultural development corporation in each province. These corporations will direct unified programs of agricultural development in project areas which will not necessarily be coterminous with districts. Conflicting relations with district administration and Basic Democracies would be resolved by prohibiting the former from interference and by the latter's withdrawal from actual execution of agricultural programs. The tone of the report conveys a vivid impression that the corporations must have freedom of operation and cannot be subordinated to the generalist administration of the district. The report manifests a commendable toughness in dealing with realities, eschews the obvious clichés found in many other reports, and makes bold, sweeping, yet specific proposals for change. Agricultural development corporations were organized in 1961 in consequence of this report and their authority to declare "project areas" and to initiate development plans in those areas is unusually wide.[8] If they assume the form envisaged by the commission, the pattern of administrative power in the districts may be substantially changed. The role of co-operative societies is important under the new scheme, since the registrar of co-operative societies is an ex officio member of the board of directors of the corporation, and the ordinance prescribes that certain activities can be carried on through the societies.

The Medical Reforms Commission was one of the two commissions (the other was the Food and Agriculture Commission) to include foreign experts as members. Two professors from the Universities of Liverpool and Birmingham were among the ten members headed by Col. M. K. Afridi, a physician who was then vice-chancellor of the University of Peshawar. The *Report of the Medical Reforms Commission* (Karachi: Government of Pakistan, Ministry of Health, Labour and Social Welfare, January, April, 1960) (item 21, Table 9) comprehensively covers the problems of national health, medical education, and research. It recommends a national health service to be administered by the central government rather than by Basic Democracies. The health service is to be administered by the Ministry of Health which guides policy but does not exercise authority in detail. The commission describes its philosophy of administration as being "based on peripheral autonomy under Central Government." In effect, the proposals call for an intensification of control over the existing system of state medicine.

The *Report of the Pakistan Police Commission, 1960–61* (Karachi: Government of Pakistan, Home Affairs Ministry, 1961) remains classified, but a digest of the recommendations accepted by the government was issued to the press and published in the

---

[8] See above, p. 207.

Pakistan Times, May 4, 1962. The approved recommendations related to improved work conditions, salaries, and training of police officers. Better public relations were to be achieved by providing for press rooms in police stations and by the police department's assumption of responsibilities for educating the public in such matters as traffic safety.

The *Report of the Constitution Commission—Pakistan—1961* (Karachi: Government of Pakistan Press, 1961) is the work of the major commission appointed to suggest the political system under which the state would function upon termination of martial law. The commission was composed of five members from each of the provinces and was headed by retired Supreme Court Justice Muhammad Shahabuddin. It was assisted by five honorary advisers, a research staff of three officers, and a small clerical force. The commission followed the traditional method of issuing questionnaires, interviewing leading citizens, collating the results of this public opinion sampling, and relating them to its recommendations. Some 6,269 completed questionnaires were received and 565 persons were interviewed. The report begins by analyzing the causes of failure of previous governments and extracts lessons from this analysis which should guide subsequent organization of the state. After concluding that the absence of disciplined parties, responsible politicians, and a disciplined society were the main causes of political failure, the commission strongly urged a representative form of government. After surveying the nature of parliamentary and presidential forms, it concluded that the presidential form would be more suitable for the nation. Considering next the question of distribution of powers within a federal system, the commission urged the adoption of the three lists of central, concurrent, and provincial powers which were features of the 1956 Constitution. It recommended a bicameral central legislature and universal suffrage by direct election rather than through the structure of Basic Democracies. A strong, independent judiciary with its powers in the writ jurisdiction was to be preserved. Fundamental rights were to be included in the Constitution and their justiciability assured. Finally, Islam was to be provided for by provisions for bringing the law into consonance with Islamic teaching. The Constitution Commission is the only major commission whose recommendations were not concurred in by the President. The Constitution of 1962 which emerged from the consequent discussions did not provide for three lists of powers, a bicameral legislature, direct elections, or enumerated justiciable fundamental rights.

The *Report of the Prices Commission* (Karachi: Government of Pakistan, Ministry of Finance, 1960) (item 24, Table 9) is a competently prepared economic survey of the commodity price structure. It makes no drastic proposals affecting bureaucracy. It assumes no government responsibility for price-fixing but suggests that the prices of essential commodities be controlled.

The briefest report in the martial law series is the 36-page *Report of the Committee on Culture, Art, Sports and Youth Movement* (Karachi: Ministry of Education, 1960). The commission assumes that government must stimulate and finance cultural activities without controlling them. Its proposals regarding sports and youth activity are similarly based on government initiative.

One of the longest and most comprehensive reports is the *Report of the Film Fact Finding Committee* (Karachi: Ministry of Industries, 1962) (item 26, Table 9). As an industry survey, it is probably the best thus far published in Pakistan. It includes an excellent review of the overlapping responsibilities of various government agencies exercising control over the film industry. This section of the report (pp. 21–27) is almost a case study in bureaucratic control of industry. The proposals to remedy the duplication are not as clearly set forth as the description of the situation.

The Franchise Commission (item 32, Table 9), which was appointed after martial law to devise an electoral system, is included in this series because the issue it deals with derives essentially from martial law ideology embodied in the 1962 Constitution and is a part of the edifice of government reform. The commission, headed by Akhter Husain, was composed of two High Court judges and two members of the National Assembly. The report includes a survey of the evolution of the electoral system in India and Pakistan. The commission unanimously recommended universal adult franchise and the direct election by the total electorate of members of national and provincial assemblies. The commission did not agree on the mode of electing the president. Three members recommended direct election by the total electorate. Akhter Husain and Hassan Ali, however, recommended indirect elections by an electoral college. Their dissenting note and the explanation of the majority view constitute a lucid analysis of the electoral problems of the nation. This report, like the report of the Commission on Marriage and Family Laws, appeared in the *Gazette of Pakistan, Extraordinary,* August 23, 1963, pp. 637a–637bt, rather than in a separate publication.

Summary

Almost every significant national problem has been the subject of a martial law commission of inquiry. These documents are more accessible than the reports of the twenty-eight administrative reform efforts, partly because they are more recent and partly because they involve major questions deemed to be of broader public interest than administrative problems. Of the thirty-three reports, ten (items 7, 18, 19, 20, 22, 27, 28, 29, 30, and 31 in Table 9) are classified so that they cannot be used. Reports so classified total 1,560 pages or 24 per cent of the total volume of 6,485 pages of reports of these commissions. However, if three reports are eliminated (items 18, 30, and 31 in Table 9) because they are reports on administration which have already been included in calculations for administrative reform reporting, we find only 731 pages, or 14 per cent, of 5,070 pages of martial law reporting classified so that the reports cannot be used. Some of these reports, such as those of the maritime, federal capital, and company law commissions (items 7, 19, and 20 in Table 9) deal with technical issues of rather narrow range. Only four important reports (items 22, 27, 28, and 29 in Table 9), totaling 608 pages or 11 per cent of reports of martial law commissions, excluding reports on administration, are not available because of classification.

7

Concluding Observations

An essay which is essentially a critique of bibliographical sources for research and of conditions and directions for research on bureaucracy does not yield conclusions which arise incontrovertibly from a cohesive argument. Nothing is sought to be proved or demonstrated here except that the documentation for research exists, that it has been arranged within this essay in a preliminary classificatory system, and that the issues for research are numerous and provocative. Yet there are observations suggested by the essay which might be made, more by way of extending analysis of issues raised than by way of arraying conclusions with a positive consequential relationship to the data.

Contextual Ambivalence of Scholarship

It is axiomatic that all segments of institutional behavior and attitudes bear an ecological relationship to the total social order in which they are implicated. In an earlier period of political science influenced by the method and language of natural science, this relationship was characterized as the "ecology" of government. More recently, under the influence of anthropological and psychological concepts of the social order and the network of synaptic relationships within it, it has been designated as "political culture." Awareness of the existence of this relationship is hardly new. Bacon, Montesquieu, and Bryce perceived and commented on it, and in our own time F. S. C. Northrop has redirected our attention to it in his analyses of the nexus between institutions and norms. It is, therefore, of no surprise to note that research as an institution (embodying process, attitudes, and behavior) reflects the idiosyncracies of the total social order just as surely as it is a part of it. Surveying the status of scholarship as a profession in Pakistan, it was stated earlier in this essay that research must be recognized as an autonomous process devoid of such value-laden considerations as nationalism, religious aggrandizement, international animosities, and intra-societal rivalries. This is the ideal in the development of a society moving toward the rational resolution of conflict. It is essential in a nation like Pakistan that the method and attitude of scientific inquiry, which means autonomy of process, permeate intellectual life. This autonomy may not resolve the ultimate issue of the relationship between value and fact which no social science in Western countries has yet resolved, but the greater need at this juncture in Pakistan's affairs is recognition of this distinction and the creation of institutional means to encourage it. The subsequent relationship between its methodological isolation and its evaluational congruence is a step in the nation's intellectual development which can come later.

The harsh truth which the researcher in Pakistan and in other developing states must accept is that the institutions of research and the profession of scholarship are not accepted as autonomous; on the contrary, they are enmeshed in a web of emotion and feeling. The expectations and values of American research can only rarely be fulfilled or applied in this social context. The immersion of research in the societal matrix creates physical impedances and emotional and intellectual limitations. In most instances these can be surmounted except when certain subjects, such as Islam or regionalism, are pursued in a manner offensive to deeply held views. The conduct of scholarship and the limits on research are determined by government, not by the scholar. Determination of these needs derives in part from the sense of responsibility in the total society and the demands of order as interpreted by the state exercising its inherent right to preserve itself. This relationship between the limits of scholarship and social context is clearly illustrated by the role of the judiciary, the press, and bureaucracy. It is not likely that the judiciary will relax its vigilance over criticism of its actions until the social order is stable enough to withstand attack and a sense of responsibility and moderation are diffused throughout society sufficiently to temper such criticism. Similarly, the degree of freedom accorded the press will depend on the same two factors of national stability and individual responsibility. It is probably true that in a precariously developing society there must be a delicately tooled articulation between the limits of freedom and the growth of responsibility. The nature of the formula contrived to achieve this articulation spells the difference between orderly yet dynamic development and tyranny.

It has been said that institutions are not likely to allow criticism of themselves so long as their own power in society is uncertain. Perhaps there is a relationship between their felt sense of security and the degree of criticism, hence of meaningful research, they allow or encourage. Yet such a relationship is bound to be influenced by the ideological conditions which have molded the traditions of the institution. Thus, even a judiciary which feels its power secure may be bound to some extent by its traditions regarding the contempt law. New institutions such as community development or the corporate device, though insecure in power, may be so strongly affected by the ideology which created them that they may generate rather than impede criticism. Further, if an institution has a messianic zeal for change, or regards its own status as capable of improvement by change, it is likely to facilitate criticism of the total social order and even of itself as a means of enhancing its influence in society. It is probable, then, that the role of specific institutions as facilitating or impeding agents of research is related to more than power status. The vitality of generating ideology and perceptions of improving the institutional role by change in the social order may be other factors whose interaction may be important. It is conceivable, for example, that the ideological disposition manifest in the judiciary's view of contempt will be modified by the changing nature of the judiciary's status in society or by its perception of its need for enhancing that role. The community development movement's response to its ideological commitments of empirical research and self-criticism may similarly be modified by its status and by a strategy for improving that status.

From these considerations there emerges the suggestion that

the facilitative and impeding qualities of various generants of research change as they interact. The pattern of such interaction
will affect the total research environment. Whatever the peculiar
segmental influences of particular institutions may be, the over-
riding determinant of the research environment will be the possibility that hysteria and bedevilment which lurk beneath the
surface may break through the thin veneer of self-confidence and
rationality which precariously covers a turbulent society. Whether
executive, judicial, and legislative agencies can themselves
maintain internal calm and moderation and can infuse the same
qualities in the larger society remains to be seen.

Determinants of Improvement in Research Environment

It is clear that the problems of research and of education as a
determinant of scholarship are not peculiar to Pakistan. The
impediments to research efficiency generally, and the deficiencies
of higher education and legal research, are similar to those found
in most new states [1] and in many old states as well.

While the segmental influences of specific institutions on research cannot be predicted, one impression stands out clearly,
namely, that change, indeed rapid change, in research environment is the order of the day in Pakistan. It may not be apparent to
the new researcher fresh from the technical efficiency of Western
libraries and from a culture long mature in the practice of secular
scholarship. But viewed in the perspective of a decade, the
changes are perceptible and some are spectacular. It is doubtful if
any emerging states have demonstrated such self-revealing awareness of research inadequacies and have attacked the problem on
so many fronts. Some of the deficiencies are being corrected by
comprehensive plans, others slowly disappear as small segments of
activity, being "tidied up" after the trauma of partition, begin to
be related to apparently more urgent developmental schemes. In
the first category is such activity as reform of the universities

[1] See, for example, Robert E. Ward and others, *Studying Politics Abroad: Field
Research in the Developing Areas* (Boston, 1964); T. H. Silcock, *Southeast Asian
University* (Durham, N. C., 1964); "Report on the Conference on South Asian
Law" held at the University of Chicago, May 31–June 1, 1963 (mimeographed);
David H. Bayley, *Public Liberties in the New States* (Chicago, 1964).

which derives from a comprehensive national plan for education and from individual university master plans articulated to it. In the second category of what might be called "incidental amelioration" is such an aid as a census of government employment, which emerged as part of a larger scheme but only when its relationship to budgeting, fiscal predictability, and bureaucratic staffing became evident.

The tradition of public record issuance which was one of the legacies of British rule has been continued in Pakistan not with completely unbroken continuity but with intermittent incidence and vigor. The first five years after independence were marked by an effort to reassemble the order of documentation which had been shattered by partition. Irregularities, inconsistencies, tardiness of issue, and secretiveness characterized this period. From 1952 through the next five years some gains continued, but these were almost entirely vitiated by the progressive deterioration in government from 1956 to the proclamation of martial law in 1958. From 1958 through 1965, improvement was accelerated even though martial law was in force during most of that period. The utility of research began to be recognized and was supported by government, and the ordering and accessibility of data demonstrably improved. Several reasons for this change may be conjectured.

1. The first of these appears paradoxical. Earlier in this essay, analysis of the roots of an intellectual tradition in Pakistan was ventured. It was maintained that because there was minimal confluence of religious scholarship with secular bureaucratic scholarship, whatever intellectuality was found in bureaucracy was derived from the more recent sources of British administrative ideology rather than from the venerable and ancient sources of Qur'anic scholarship. The result in bureaucracy has been an impatience with rumination and philosophical analysis. To be sure, the climate of scholarship may be thereby adversely affected. But there may also be an advantage in the short run. The bureaucratic mentality, impatient with philosophical rumination, seems to be disposed to a more pragmatic attention to the detail of ordering and classifying in the interests of efficiency and consist-

ency. Ideally, the pragmatic inclination to order should be conjoined with the philosophical disposition to question purpose and to relate order to universals. But it need not be the function of a bureaucracy to achieve this conjunction. In a system in which legislative, judicial, and executive sectors are functioning along with non-governmental institutions such as religion and education, the application of purpose to order may be achieved outside the bureaucratic realm. The bureaucracy is relatively neutral normatively. Therefore, it has less need of a normative disposition than does the judiciary, church, or university. If it has minimal normative responsibility, the absence of normative sense need not be bad, especially if such absence permits the development of an empirical disposition. This may be what is taking place within Pakistan's bureaucracy.

The bureaucracy appears not to have been a source of normative ideology. Such ideology has been generated primarily by the judiciary, seeking to infuse the total social order with concepts of "natural justice" as the use of writs amply demonstrates. By keeping viable the notion of fundamental rights during martial law and by urging equality of opportunity within bureaucracy, the judiciary has generated norms of ideology outside the conventional sphere of juridical action found in many older states. Ideological norms have emerged from martial law itself, as in the case of land reform, and are now beginning to come from the legislative process, as in the first constitutional amendment restoring fundamental rights and rendering them justiciable. But the bureaucracy itself has not been a significant source of ideology. While it participated in the work of martial law commissions of inquiry, that participation was predominantly in administrative reform. In the major ideological reforms of Basic Democracies and land reform, it participated not at all. Its contribution has been in process, implementation, and ordering of data. Insofar as this diverted energy from idle disputation as to ends to construction of efficient means, it conduced to attitudes sympathetic to research. To put it another way, the literary-generalist disposition of the ICS tradition was the dominant characteristic of the bureaucratic ethos. But it was never deeply rooted because it did not conjoin with a deeper current of philosophical disputation. Hence, it is giving way to an emergence of the Islamic legal disposition to order, classify, and render consistent, and to the earthy pragmatism of the Punjabi and the Pathan leading to action and efficiency. These dispositions have been stimulated by the dynamics of martial law and the accompanying impatience with debate and rumination. The action orientation of the military mind thus converged with the pragmatism of the bureaucracy and the legalism of Islam. This analysis, if valid at all, is relevant principally to the bureaucracy of the central government and of West Pakistan which are dominated by West Pakistani, mostly Punjabi and Pathan. In East Pakistan, the Bengali disposition for romantic idyllics and endless philosophical disputation are qualities which have actually delayed the rise of attitudes toward action and efficiency and hence impeded the evolution of a viable administrative system. Such a system will eventuate only when the earthiness of an F. L. Brayne triumphs over the poetics of a Tagore. This may be occurring by infusion of Punjabi and Pathan ideology in the bureaucracy through assignment of key non-Bengali executive talent (as happened in the Rural Works Programme and the community development activity), by a sense of competition between the two provinces, and by the impact of diffusion of new values of action through contact with foreign technical assistance.

2. There are other reasons for improvement in the environment of research. Probably the most important is the massive diffusion of Western administrative norms through the medium of American technical assistance. The pragmatic emphasis of these norms reinforced the pragmatic disposition which already existed. Such diffusion occurred in three different, apparently unconnected substantive programs, but the impact of their attitudinal consequences conjoined. The first of these programs was the ideology of the community development movement with its strong messianic impulse and its inclination to relate the findings of microscopic social analysis to broader ends. The ideology thus carried with it a technology of empirical research focused on a search for new, consultative, non-coercive means of encouraging initiative in village life. Its manifestation in the Village AID movement was the

closest to ideological revolution that Pakistan has come. The conversion of orthodox bureaucrats to the new technology and ideology of community development was marked, and the collapse of Village AID almost produced a minor bureaucratic revolt by these new devotees. This new attitude toward empirics and freedom of inquiry continues with vigor, even though under government auspices, and its effects are becoming diffused in the social order. The second influence is the corporate device with a different emphasis, i.e., scientific technology, especially engineering. Coupled with this is a strong sense of zeal that the application of this technology to problems of water and earth is the only means of preserving the state. Agents of these new ideologies derive strength from their antagonism to orthodox bureaucracy which they regard, with some justification, as ideologically inimicable and as a structural impediment to their own aspirations. Their confidence in themselves, their ideology, and their desire to be understood and appreciated are powerful generants of research, a spirit of inquiry, and a public diffusion of governmental information. The third strand is the technology and accompanying ideology implicit in administrative reform through training of officials. This technology carries with it implications of a changed relationship between bureaucracy and the public—a relationship characterized best by the old term "stewardship," or public responsibility.

Although these three strands by which new ideology is diffused in the system are different, their institutional manifestations are related and their consequences for developing a research environment converge. All three are alike in the sense that commitment to them tends to detach the agents thus committed from contrary indigenous ideologies and tends to relate them to sources of the new ideas. This changes configurations of power within the country and hastens the process of modernization. The speed of diffusion and the volume of new ideas fomented may be quite overwhelming. Under certain conditions, these factors alone, rather than the merit or inadequacy of doctrine, may impel social change which will improve research environment. A second common attribute of these three strands is that the technology and ideology which they purvey have been refined into doctrine and codified. This capsulization gives them an attractiveness and, at least initially, enhances the ease of diffusion. It is noteworthy that both the United Nations and the United States Agency for International Development have held international conferences and prepared rather elaborate handbooks on community development, the corporate device, and administrative reform. Codification of doctrine may tend to rigidify the process of diffusion by making accommodation and adaptation to the indigenous milieu more difficult, but this may be an advantage in forcing and sustaining new attitudes. A third common attribute is the impact of professionalization on the speed and strength of diffusion. Professionalization is accompanied by a sense of universal validity of doctrine, and this sense accelerates and forces diffusion, as, for example, the rapid spread of public health, public administration, and educational doctrine in underdeveloped states amply attests. Fourthly, there has arisen a new matrix for diffusion of ideas—the "institution," which not only initially generates but continues to radiate its ideology. Thus, the two rural development academies and the three national institutes of public administration and certain corporations, especially the industrial development and water and power entities, are significant sources for sustaining an environment conducive to research. The fact that they draw on financial resources from foreign technical assistance increases their diffusional capacity. The impact of this phenomenon of "institution-building" has not yet been adequately assessed.

3. Martial law and the transitional government which followed it through 1964, though repressive in many respects, also may have helped in improving the climate of research. That part of the essay dealing with thirty-three martial law commissions of inquiry has suggested this. But there are other observations to be made. Clearly, the martial law government was bent on refurbishing state polity and restoring a modified constitutional rule. Both by inclination and by force of circumstances, it could not forge the new polity by fiat. It not only needed a measure of public participation in the process, but it required a measure of public

approval. It was thereby compelled to place the public polity on the record and to communicate it to the larger society. This polity was forged by essentially a research process—although sometimes primitive—and the communicating of it, like the process itself, gave impetus to research. President Ayub was committed to the operational utility of research, particularly in law, social questions, administration, and the adjustment of Islamic ideology to modern needs. The overarching presence of martial law power compelled a condition, not of freedom of speech or inquiry, but of a degree of freedom for responsible utterance which did not attack certain sensitivities of the paramount authority. No impartial observer would conclude that the scope of liberty for criticism was as great in Pakistan as in older constitutional systems. For, while Rehman Sobhan went unpunished for advocating a separate regional economy for East Pakistan, the exercise of restraints over such persons and enterprises as Mahmud Ali Qasuri, Maulana Maudoodi, Maulvi Farid Ahmad, Abdul Ghaffar Khan, H. S. Suhrawardy, the *Pakistan Times*, *Outlook*, and others, albeit for alleged anti-state activities, are sufficiently sobering to cause concern that any research which departs from government views might not be deemed "anti-state." A distinction must be made between the attitude toward research carried on within a bureaucratically regulated context and the freedom to probe and criticize public issues. The former improved under martial law; the latter diminished. But further shrinkage of the sphere of larger public liberty was prevented by the judiciary in 1964 in two significant judgments. The Supreme Court struck down an attempt by the executive to ban the orthodox group, Jamaat-e-Islami, and Chief Justice Cornelius seemed to imply a view of a formula for balancing the need of order with the demands of liberty which leaned toward libertarianism.[2] The West Pakistan High Court overruled the action of government in the arrest of Maulvi Farid Ahmad for allegedly making public speeches prejudicial to public safety.[3] In so doing

[2] Supreme Court of Pakistan, Criminal Appeal No. 43 of 1964 and Civil Appeal No. 19-D of 1964, decided on September 25, 1964.
[3] *Maulvi Farid Ahmad* v. *Government of West Pakistan*, PLD 1965 Lah. 135.

the court expanded the concept of free speech and created juridical support for the vigorous campaign preceding the presidential election in January, 1965.

Despite these actions by the judiciary, there can be no illusions about restraints imposed by martial law or by ordinances promulgated after martial law. While the 1964–1965 election campaign included criticism of basic ideological issues, such as indirect elections, presidential government, and Basic Democracies, it does not necessarily follow that research within the ambit of bureaucratic control would be permitted if the conclusions seriously challenged the adequacy of these or other issues. The existence of such restraints appears to be premised on the notion that the degree of freedom prevailing in a given society must be balanced by the state's interpretation of its stability and by the sense of responsibility existing within it. What is involved is the classic problem of political theory, the achievement of balance between order and liberty, a balance which perhaps cannot be the same in a developing state as that constructed in Lockean thought. The implications of this dilemma for a developing state were expressed by President Ayub thus:

I hope, however, that till such time as the wisdom to distinguish between freedom and license does not become the character of the majority of our people, some provision on the lines of the already existing limitations will be introduced in the law to regulate the freedom of speech. I do not think that in the fast moving world of today we can afford the luxury of indulging in suicidal activities by bringing about instability in Government for the sake of satisfying some requirements of foreign theoreticians applicable to their own conditions.[4]

Considering this view of the requirements of stability and responsibility, there was a commendable degree of public revelation of national polity. By 1965 somewhat more than 75 per cent of the reports of commissions of inquiry were accessible, and roughly the same proportion of important reports on administration were made available.

4. The complex pattern of relations between Pakistan and

[4] Address at inauguration of Pakistan Lawyers' Convention, Karachi, September 30, 1960. Text in Government of Pakistan, *Speeches and Statements of Field Marshal Mohammad Ayub Khan* (Karachi, 1961), III, 30.

Western nations may serve to generate conditions favoring research. The dynamism of the modernization process in Pakistan is in marked contrast, for example, to the moribund conditions in Burma, Ceylon, and Malaya where there is little to regenerate beyond whatever quickly fading ideology remains from imperial rule. Massive assistance from the Colombo Plan, World Bank, United States Agency for International Development, Ford Foundation, and from many European countries; membership in SEATO, CENTO, and the Commonwealth; sustained American assistance through the Military Assistance Advisory Group; training of civil officers at Sandhurst, Fort Leavenworth, and Fort Bragg are but evidences of what may well be the largest and most complicated network of diffusing foreign ideas in all of Asia since the occupation of Japan. Such activity demands planning and forecasting which, in turn, beget research and analysis. Institutions for research are created and they generate their own ideologies. It is difficult to overestimate the force of such foreign associations which have compelled a fomentation of research activity useful for scholarship.

5. Every nation offers a unique blend of conditions and problems provocative of research effort. It is futile to claim that any single nation presents a greater challenge than another in this regard. It may be useful only to summarize at a somewhat different level of generalization the research issues which have already been analyzed, in some cases in considerable detail, throughout the essay. Pakistan remains essentially an administrative state whose legislative process is limited by a political process. This political process, by design, is slowed down to keep pace with what is thought to be a developing sense of responsibility. The device by which this deceleration is achieved is that of limited franchise exercised by indirect elections through the Basic Democracies apparatus. This may give way to direct elections and universal franchise as the Franchise Commission of 1963 recommended. The bureaucracy remains dominated by a small, cohesive group, moderately well-educated, foreign-trained, and somewhat detached from the wellsprings of indigenous culture. Although the bureaucracy is not necessarily the source of ideol-

ogy, its power in governing remains strong, unsullied by a vigorous local political process. In its external contours of power the bureaucracy appears to have remained unchanged since 1947, yet in reality its absorption and integration of new Western administrative ideology has been marked. It has controlled the rate and direction of change induced by such absorption, committed itself to modernization, and has increased its power by controlling training for secretariat, clerical, and community development functions, organization-methods analysis, and administrative reform. The increased power derived from these new functions supported by substantial American aid enables the bureaucracy not only to preserve itself but to proliferate its power and diffuse its own attitudes and ideology. The degree of similarity between administrative ideology thus diffused and standards codified in UN and USAID handbooks would make a significant study in transnational diffusion of ideas.

The power of bureaucracy is equalled only by the power of the judiciary which occupies a position of strength probably unparalleled in developing states. While a principal source of ideology, the judiciary has not blindly sought to supplant all aspects of indigenous juridical norms with its own British legal norms. It has significantly accommodated to tribal customs in the Northwest Frontier, and that accommodation has resulted in the gradual modernization of tribal justice rather than in its forced disappearance.

Although in its sense of generalism and in its corporate ethos, the higher bureaucracy remains decidedly elitist and introspective, in its technique it is being influenced by American doctrine. That the ideological radiation of such technique will change its elitist quality seems not unlikely. A presidential form of government modeled after the American system has been forged within a federal structure which has unitary features and certain qualities blended from indigenous elements. This amalgam has been fused by a martial law government which has not been tyrannical and which at times has been pushed (as in the cases of a presidential form and of fundamental rights) into directions it disliked. Though apparently powerless in these respects, the executive has

retained immense power over fundamental freedoms, thus compelling the outward manifestations of order. Its control of fiscal
and foreign policies has enabled it to sustain an infusion of Western technology and ideology which have profoundly influenced
the development of government since 1947. The society and the
state remain proud of their achievements and of Islam, keenly sensitive to criticism of certain values held dear, tolerant of sympathetic and responsible criticism, intolerant of irresponsible extrav-
aganza. The stability which exists, exists precariously. It is in this
context of conflicting influences, having available some but not all
sources, that research on problems of political and bureaucratic
transition in one of the most challenging political experiments of
the twentieth century must be carried on.

Appendix • 1 •

Quaid-i-Azam's Talk to Government Officials, April 14, 1948

[*Explanatory Note.* The words of a nation's founder are always significant parts of the national heritage. Speeches of the Quaid-i-Azam are accessible in *Quaid-i-Azam Mahomed Ali Jinnah: Speeches As Governor General 1947–1948* (Karachi: Pakistan Publications, n. d. [1962?]); Jamil-Ud-Din Ahmad (ed.), *Some Recent Speeches and Writings of Mr. Jinnah*, Vol. I, *1935–43*, Vol. II, *1943–46* (5th ed., Lahore: Shaikh Muhammad Ashraf, 1942, 1952); *Speeches of Quaid-i-Azam in the Constituent Assembly of Pakistan 1947–48* (Karachi: Governor General's Press and Publications, 1949). After leading the nation to independence, Quaid-i-Azam served as its first governor general for little more than a year preceding his death on September 11, 1948. One of his recorded addresses is the following informal talk given to government officials at Government House in Peshawar, April 14, 1948. Characteristically brief and pointed, the talk reflects the stern dedication to duty and detachment from partisan politics which marked his own eminent career.]

The reason why I wanted to meet you is that I wanted to say a few words to you who are occupying very important positions in the administration of Pakistan in this province.

The first thing that I want to tell you is that you should not be influenced by any political pressure, by any political party or individual politician. If you want to raise the prestige and greatness of Pakistan, you must not fall a victim to any pressure, but do your duty as servants of the people and the State, fearlessly and honestly. Services are the backbone of the State. Governments are formed, governments are defeated, prime ministers come and go, ministers come and go, but you stay on and, therefore, there is a very great responsibility placed on your shoulders. You should have no hand in supporting this political leader or that; this is not your business. Whoever be the prime minister or minister coming into power in the ordinary constitutional course your duty is not only to serve that government loyally and faithfully but, at the same time, fearlessly, maintaining your high reputation, your prestige, your honour and the integrity of your service. If you will start with that determination, you will make a great contribution to the building up of Pakistan of our conception and our dream into a glorious state and one of the greatest nations in the world.

While impressing this upon you on your side, I wish also to take the opportunity of impressing upon our leaders and politicians in the same way that if they ever try to interfere with you and bring political pressure to bear upon you—which leads to nothing but corruption, bribery and nepotism which is a horrible disease from which not only your province but others too are suffering—if they try and interfere with you in this way, I say, they are doing nothing but a disservice to Pakistan.

I hope that each one of you will understand his own sphere of duty and responsibility and act with others harmoniously and in complete co-operation, keeping in mind that each has to do his duty within the sphere to which he belongs. If you, on your side, start with this determination and enthusiasm I hope the other side will also realise what a terrible evil they are raising up and how it demoralises the services to try and influence this department or that department, this officer or that officer. If you will stick to your determination you will have done a great service to your nation. Putting pressure and influence on service people, I know, is a very common fault of politicians and those with influence in political parties. But I hope that you will now, from today, resolve and determine to act according to my humble advice that I am giving you.

Maybe some of you may fall victims for not satisfying the whims of ministers. I hope it does not happen, but you may even be put to trouble not because you are doing anything wrong but because you are doing right. Sacrifices have to be made and I appeal to you, if need be, to come forward and make the sacrifice and face the position of being put on the black list or being otherwise worried or troubled. If you will give me the opportunity of your sacrifices—some of you at least—believe me we will find a remedy for that very soon. I tell you that you will not remain on the black-list if you discharge your duties and responsibilities honestly, sincerely and loyally to the State. It is you who can give us the opportunity to create a powerful machinery which will give you a complete sense of security.

Everybody should realise that there is a fundamental and vital change of the entire government and the constitution under which we are working. You should try to create an atmosphere and work in such a spirit that everybody gets a fair deal and justice is done to everybody. And not merely should justice be done but people should feel that justice has been done to them. There may be some selfish people—and I know your class is no exception—who think of immediate advantages and work or act for better prospects and promotions and so on for themselves and, therefore, for the time being, they create difficulties and sometimes they describe themselves as lovers of their province and sometimes they start slogans about outsiders such as Punjabis, Sindhis or Pathans. All such things are a hindrance and an obstruction in the way of galvanising the people and welding them together as one great nation.

Appendix • 2 •

President Mohammad Ayub Khan's Message to the Services, June 27, 1959

[*Explanatory Note*. The coup d'état of August, 1958, by which General Mohammad Ayub Khan became chief martial law administrator and later president of Pakistan, created some apprehension among career civil servants. To some extent this was allayed by the fact that the structure of government was retained and the bureaucracy functioned much as before. Temporary emergency screening of civil servants, carried on during the first six months of 1959, again shook the confidence of the bureaucracy. (See above, pp. 289–299, for analysis of the 1959 emergency screening.) The following address by the President was meant to reassure the services when the results of this screening were made known. It is also one of President Ayub's few major statements setting forth his concepts of administration. President Ayub's major speeches given from October, 1958, through June, 1964, have been published in six volumes by the Government of Pakistan under the title, *Speeches and Statements of Field Marshal Mohammad Ayub Khan, President of Pakistan*.]

One of the objectives of the Revolution was the clearing up of the public life of Pakistan. So far as the Services are concerned, there were well-known complaints of corruption, misconduct (in the form of favouritism and nepotism) and the inefficiency of some of the Government servants. But the rules which then existed were so lax as to make it almost impossible to remove a public servant, for misconduct or inefficiency. My Government, therefore, felt duty bound to take powers to undertake the speedy screening of Government servants in order to weed out corrupt or inefficient persons or those guilty of favouritism or nepotism.

It was suggested to us that known corrupt or inefficient persons should be summarily dismissed. This we did not consider fair.

Instead, we gave everybody a chance to show cause, and to appeal to the appointing authority against the findings of the Screening Committee. A large number of cases were screened a second time by a Cabinet Committee consisting of the Foreign Minister, the Law Minister, the Minister of the Interior and the Finance Minister. There could not have been a more high-powered body or a better combination of judicial and administrative talent to have a second look at cases. In this respect, the screening was far more fair to the officers than the ordinary departmental inquiries.

The result of the screening will be found in the annexure to this statement. These are officers of All Pakistan Services and Class I Central Services. For Classes II and III of the Central Services, orders have been issued separately. The Provincial Governments have done their own screening and issued their own orders. I am sorry to see so many of our officers going out. Some of them are able and experienced. But we have had to part company with them in the larger public interest.

My Government has decided to be generous and to grant proportionate pension or gratuity to those who are being compulsorily retired. But if any of them is convicted later in a court of law for his misdeeds, the Government of Pakistan reserves the right to forfeit his pension in whole or in part.

This closes the emergent screening, but for the future more realistic rules are being framed which will enable speedy and effective disposal of disciplinary cases. Let us hope that there will not be any occasion to use them.

Since the Revolution, a large majority of public servants have given of their best and done a very good job. I should like to take this opportunity to thank them publicly for their sense of duty and patriotism and would ask them to continue in this path so as to bring about a better future for the people.

And I wish to reassure the Services that so long as they remain honest, fair and hard-working, they have nothing to fear. Their prospects are as secure as before. In fact, they will be better as the Services will not be subjected to the strains and stresses of the past. They will be dealt with on merits alone. My Government has set up a committee consisting of the past Cabinet Secretary and the Chief Secretaries of the Provincial Governments in order to recommend how merit in public service should be recognised so that those who work devotedly and honestly are not blocked by those who don't but happen to be senior.

As a general rule of conduct, my advice to the Services is—(1) to be honest, (2) work hard, and (3) be fair, and let us re-dedicate ourselves to the service of Pakistan and her people.

Pakistan Paindabad.

Address of President Mohammad Ayub Khan at Inauguration of Administrative Staff College, December 25, 1960

[*Explanatory Note*. The address reprinted here is the most important policy statement on administrative reform made by President Ayub. The Administrative Staff College was the first new training institution to be established as part of a comprehensive training program, and the President used the occasion of its inauguration for setting forth his ideas on administration. In this address, the President attempts to infuse a new dynamism into the administrative reform program which had languished before 1960. The address includes a strong statement deploring the "superior class of de-nationalized individuals" and urging a new attitude of service to society. This was the first occasion on which this concept of public service had been so forcefully advocated by the nation's martial law leadership.]

The inauguration of the Pakistan Administrative Staff College marks the birth of a new enterprise in which senior executives from the public services, public corporations and other private sectors will, for the first time, live in residence together to discuss and deliberate over the multiple problems with which we in Pakistan are faced today.

The idea to establish a college of this nature emerged out of the compelling need to give a static administration its dynamic dimension. The system of stereotype administration which we inherited was devised over a 100 years ago to suit the purpose of a colonial Power. Its fundamental emphasis was on the maintenance of law and order and one of the many ways in which this object was fulfilled was to create a superior class of somewhat de-nationalised individuals who could maintain proper distances and rule with awe and disdain under the cover of public service. It was a perfect system for the purpose for which it was intended, but the demands of an independent society are entirely different.

As you are no doubt aware, human society developed from the stage of cave-man to the family structure: from family structure to feudalism; from feudalism to capitalism; and from capitalism it has blossomed into diverse material channels like communism, socialism and the concept of a welfare state. In Pakistan we have not yet reached even the stage of capitalism. We have, therefore, to make a big jump and develop into a social welfare state which in fact is the inevitable demand of the ideology on the basis of which this country has come into being. The extent to which we can reach this target expeditiously is the real touch-stone of all our developmental programmes and administrative reforms.

With the growing involvement of Government in many new spheres of social life, the role of administrators—whether in civil service, business or industry—has to assume fresh techniques and attitudes. The old sense of rulership has to yield place to a new sense of service and this requires a high quality of leadership based on honesty, humility and a creative application of one's mind and heart. In this context, the essential prerequisites of a worthwhile administrator are a ceaseless urge to invent and organise new fields of development; ability to bridge the gulf between the Government and the people; and a genuine endeavour to stimulate the broad mass of our population and goad and guide them on the path of progress, enlightenment and responsibility.

This college is intended to cater for these paramount needs of the highest class of public and business executives. For the public executives it would be an occasion to assess the administrative techniques and evaluate the administrative measures in the light of international events, new advances in the social and physical sciences, experiences and experiments and above all, the aspirations of the people. The decision to provide these facilities for business executives is a healthy step as it would afford them an opportunity to look beyond their restricted and specialised spheres of commercial interests and to appreciate the true role of private sector in the field of national development. This experiment would bring together public and business executives and thus narrow the distances that exist at present in the approach and outlook of these sectors.

I have noted that in your syllabus the Principal has given you the opportunity to consider the attitudes of mind, the qualities, and the standards of behaviour required of men in positions of responsibility. Ethical and moral standards need to be set high if our country is to prosper and I cannot overemphasise the desirability of senior officers setting the highest possible examples for others in the maintenance of these standards.

I pin great faith in this enterprise as a means of developing the strength and quality of men who must play an increasing part in resolving our national problems and leading the country to the goals that we have set for ourselves. To those who have been privileged to join the first session of the college, I have to say that it is you who will lay the foundation-stones on which this college will rise. It is you who, by the spirit in which you tackle the work put before you by the Principal and his staff, by the confidence you build in each other, and by the discipline that you set for yourselves, will really cause this college to play its destined role. You set your standards high so that others may follow and build on secure foundations.

In the quiet and serene environments of this college, you will be free from the chores of the home (and worries from your wives, I hope), free from the telephones and the files and the decisions which are part of the daily round, free to devote yourselves to the work that is put before you and to re-think your own attitudes. So, take the fullest advantage of this opportunity and when you go out practise what you have learnt here.

Mr. Principal, I have followed with great interest the preparations and efforts that have gone into the establishment of this college. I have no doubt that this college will fulfil its object and shall grow from strength to strength. I wish you Godspeed.

Appendix • 4 •

Extracts from Speeches of Maulvi Farid Ahmad and Others before the National Assembly of Pakistan, February 15, 1957

[*Explanatory Note.* This extract from a speech by Maulvi Farid Ahmad is illustrative of attitudes toward parity in government and toward the role of the higher bureaucracy held by some groups in both provinces. Maulvi Farid Ahmad has been one of the most controversial and provocative members of the National Assembly. Born in Dhabir Chara village in Chittagong district, East Pakistan, in 1922, he received A.M. and LL.B. degrees from Dacca University. Entering politics, he was a member of the first National Assembly (from the proceedings of which this extract is taken) and was minister of labor in the Chundrigar cabinet. He was again elected to the National Assembly when it was reconvened after martial law in 1962 as a representative of the Chittagong NE 7 constituency. On September 13, 1964, he was placed under arrest under provisions of the West Pakistan Maintenance of Public Order Ordinance, 1960. He was released as a result of a judgment of the West Pakistan High Court (*Maulvi Farid Ahmad* v. *Government of West Pakistan*, PLD 1965 Lah. 135). The strong feelings reflected in the speech extracted below were characteristic of views held especially by Bengalis before martial law in 1958. Many of the disparities of which he complains have since been removed, and relations between the two provinces appear to have steadily improved, but the theme of "parity" continues to dominate much of the discussion in the post-martial law National Assembly. Maulvi Farid Ahmad's speech is important not necessarily as an accurate account of conditions but as an example of the intensity of feeling on the issues of parity and the higher civil service. Short speeches by other National Assembly members continuing the line of argument developed by Maulvi Farid Ahmad are included. This extract is from the *Parliamentary Debates—Official Report of the National Assembly of Pakistan, February 15, 1957,* pp. 426–431, 433–437. It is reproduced with the permission of the speaker of the National Assembly of Pakistan, A. K. M. Fazlul Quader Chowdhury, in a letter dated January 9, 1965, with the understanding that "the

Speaker of the National Assembly of Pakistan does not vouch for the correctness or otherwise of what was stated by Mr. Farid Ahmad." These speeches were published in the National Assembly *Debates* without being corrected by the assembly members who gave them. The editor of the *Debates* noted this fact in several footnotes which have been deleted from this appendix. Obvious misspellings have been corrected by the present author. A few seriously awkward constructions have been modified when it was felt that the meaning would not be changed. Such modifications have been enclosed in brackets by the present author. Changes made in capitalization are not indicated in the extracts that follow.]

MAULVI FARID AHMAD: Mr. Speaker: Sir, I will deal with the cut-motions in the order in which I have moved them. Sir, a few years after the achievement of Pakistan East and West relationship assumed great importance in view of the maladjustments and disparities that were being perpetuated in the matters of appointment in commercial, industrial and several other fields; so the matter has been agitating the mind of the people in both the wings and saner section of community. [The] saner section of the leadership, it seems, had to do all that was possible to prevent the voice of provincialism which raised its naked head a few years after the achievement of our independence. It is now a well-known fact that in the first Constituent Assembly that was constituted, East Pakistan had majority of members so far as the representation of East Pakistan was concerned and some of the ministers including the first Prime Minister, late lamented Mr. Liaquat Ali Khan, were elected out of the quota of East Pakistan. That speaks of the goodwill that existed between the people, [and] of the cordial relationship and the desire for unity between the two wings. But it seems, Sir, that even that did not prove satisfactory, and even those members whenever there was a recruitment in the cabinet and [an] outsider had to be brought in a seat had to be found and in some of the cases it came from East Pakistan. I am speaking all this not that I denounced that policy, but I am telling this because it speaks of the confidence that existed at that time, but as time went on the quota of other provinces had to be increased and vis-a-vis West Pakistan the proportion of East Pakistan was reduced in the

Constituent Assembly. Then coming to the time of the beginning of 1955 when our present Prime Minister was the law minister in the cabinet he propounded the theory of parity which was not acceptable to any political organization at that time except himself. In the teeth of bitter opposition the Prime Minister went round the country in East Pakistan and told the people that this was one method by which provincialism could cease and the East and West Pakistan tensions could be curbed down and that it would ultimately pave the way for greater national homogeneity and greater cohesion.

So, Sir, all that happened subsequently is a matter of recent history, and the other political parties in East Pakistan, forced by the exigencies of circumstances, had to accept the principle of parity, with the result that parity has been embodied as state policy of the Constitution of Pakistan. So, it must be remembered, Sir, that East Pakistan had to make tremendous sacrifices as regards the numerical superiority over West Pakistan. It is therefore an accepted fact that East Pakistan accepted that position. [Maybe] they were compelled by circumstances, in the hope that that way would ultimately reduce the East West tension and might bring both the wings closer together. But I want to know from the Prime Minister, as it is almost five months since he assumed this office, has parity been maintained during the course of this Assembly? I put a number of questions, to elicit information as to the manner in which recruitment and promotions in the government services have been made since the Constitution Day last year. In most of the cases the information was not collected. If that is so, it is a very sad commentary on the efficiency of the working of the administration, because similar question I also put during the Dacca Session of the National Assembly in October, 1956. So, how is it that th[is] information could not be compiled for the information of this House and as well as the nation? The answer that I have got is that the matter is under examination. It is now, Sir, eleven months since the Constitution Day, but I regret to say that no regard has been paid to the maintenance of parity in services, and I regret very much to announce on the floor of this House that it has not resulted in betterment of feelings between the two wings. After all, Sir, it was expected that the letter of the Constitution and the spirit of the Constitution will be honoured by one and all. There seems to be running a feeling in some interested quarters and I am very sorry to say that in most of the cases it is the Services. However might we may take pride in ourselves as the politicians, leaders of different parties, that we are responsible for running the administration of the country, unfortunately the truth is that except in limited matters the politicians have a little say. They might have decided a national policy but when it comes to execution, it is the permanent services that matter. The Prime Minister out of kindness may pass an order which is just and equitable and that will promote friendly and brotherly relations between the people, but what it comes to if the order is not implemented due to the political instability, due to the lack of organisation and several other deficiencies in our national life? Unfortunately this has been the case for the last five years. There has not been a continuity of policy due to frequent changes of Government. Ministry after ministry came and went, with the result that the ministries which came did not succeed in making appreciable changes in the administrative and executive policies of the government. Unfortunately the same policy, the same mentality is at work and who benefit by it? It has now assumed a fashionable name—provincialism. Whereas previously a man could be easily singled out for being unjust—and his activities laid bare before the public—now a very convenient phrase has been discovered. It is a big shelter—provincialism. I am not interested in my province but when it comes to appointing my own relations or granting import and export licenses or opening cinemas, I appoint my relations and say, because he is from our own province, therefore I have given these concessions, and when I am in danger of being detected, then I say because I belong to such and such province, this conspiracy has been hatched against me! This is how criminal offenders smuggle their relations and friends and the result is that government offices—not all of them—I do not accuse all officers because there are patriotic officers as well—have become corrupt and inefficient. There is a section of officers who are out to further their own end, to secure the interest of their relations either in appointments or in trade or in industry. So, this is what is happening.

Now, if parity is maintained, who is there to suffer? It is only the interested persons who want to continue corruption. It is these officials again either from our side or from this side that go out into the public and say that East Pakistan is either being finished for West Pakistan or in a particular manner! Nobody stands to lose if parity is maintained; nobody stands to lose if justice is done. Had matters being decided with the sole criterion of meting out justice, then the question of parity would not have agitated the mind of anybody. Our friends who are in the government from East Pakistan, were most vocal in maintaining that parity, not only in services but parity in all spheres of life, should be practised. That is what they said. But I am surprised to say that this has not been the case.

Now, let us take and consider one aspect of the problem of parity. I say, Sir, parity today, after it has been accepted with so much heart-burning, will definitely cement the bonds of friendship. Justice is the only common platform and it must be seen that justice is done. Therein lies the safety of Pakistan. The Prime Minister has himself sounded notes of warning that subversive forces are at work to wreck this state of ours. There is no doubt that there is discontent in the two sections. That is a great danger against which we must be careful. But unless parity is scrupulously maintained right from the beginning, there is no safety [for] Pakistan. A time may come when the anti-national forces will come to the forefront, and play their ignoble part [aimed] at the disintegration of the country. Justice must be done. I do not single out any province. I say if justice is not done, it is one more cause for embittering the relations between the two wings. Parity needs examination. If straightaway from today we are going to exercise or practise the policy of parity in the case of appointments alone it may take us one century, on a purely arithmetical calculation, to achieve that because a number of posts have been filled. There are few vacancies in the senior posts. Moreover, I understand and possess evidence that service rules have been changed from time to time only to suit the convenience of some particular persons. A post has been created because my relation had to be provided there. I would appeal to the Prime Minister to examine the rules that have been framed since partition—how the same rule has been changed from time to time to include or exclude certain persons; how it has been interpreted in different fashion, just to include somebody or to bring in somebody's favourite. After all we say that if we owe anything to the Britishers, in spite of all the legacies, it is the rule of law. It is the rule of law that sustains democratic institutions and it is that rule of law that can sustain us in this country in maintaining and establishing democratic traditions. Now, if you want the rule of law in other spheres of activities, how is it that you should give a good-bye to this rule of law here? Are our officers so immune or so powerful that at their sweet will they can frame rules in any manner they like? There should be after all some fundamental principles on which any sound administrative policy must be based. Now what is that fundamental basis or background on which our administrative structure is built? If we are merely to depend on the whims of officers, there is no safety for anybody. Now, to what it has led us? So, I appeal to the government to consider the proposition as to the manner in which they want to maintain parity. I give you specific illustrations. In the Ministry of Foreign Affairs, even after you have assumed office, very few appointments have been made. Now, Sir, in order to block the claim of East Pakistan a new theory has been invented that all recruitment must be stopped. I am not personally in favour of administrative expansion and so many posts being filled up by persons who do not even hold a diploma from a university. But persons are placed in technical positions even when they do not possess any technical qualifications. There are cases where one criterion is laid down which is efficiency, or merit before the departmental promotion committee. But when a fellow cannot get a job through that principle, another principle is enunciated, i.e., experience. We must have the same principle whether efficiency or experience or both. How much percentage for experience and how much percentage for efficiency should be decided? Rules cannot be made and altered so as to suit the convenience of any individual at any time. There are departments where East Pakistanis are grossly underrepresented. So something concrete must be done. Even now in East Pakistan agitation is going on on several fronts. There are elements who do not like that both the wings of this country should remain together. If you really want to prevent that disaster, because God forbid, if it ever happens, it will equally spell doom and disaster of both wings because we have chosen to stay together and we can never afford to stay separate; therein lies the salvation of this country and every governmental action and public utterance must be coordinated to that supreme paramount consideration. The fact that we have to live together and we have chosen to live together and we must live together should not be forgotten and those who are trying to stand in our way must be eliminated no matter how big they are. Now, Sir, this corruption, this provincialism, this favouritism has spread discontent not only between the two wings, it has spread discontent among the services. There are cases as became clear in reply to my question that a matriculate is now working as deputy secretary. A provincial service man who can become a commissioner is not even considered suitable because he is not somebody's favourite. Now in a particular wing, suppose West Pakistan, this kind of corrupt practice gives rise to discontent as it causes maladministration, shakes confidence of people who are serving and there is no inspiration for work and people think that they have sincerely tried to serve this country but the result is that favourites are promoted while honest people find doors of future promotion closed and even recognition of their work is not there. What inducement are you going to offer to work hard? What inducement you give to honest men before whose eyes the corrupt officials are rising and getting loans of 50,000 rupees from the Finance Corporation to build houses and realize advance rents without paying government dues? These people possess foreign passports and in case of emergency they can sweep out of this country. Compare the position of honest officers with these corrupt officials who have chances of buying cars every six months and selling them at greater price after one year's use. What do you think of poor honest officers who have to work so hard when even big officials are keeping huge amounts of foreign exchange in foreign banks in spite of rules and regulations of the State Bank and there is no inquiry against them. This is a deplorable state in this country and in administration. No Ministry, however powerful or popular, can function effectively until the root of the disease is diagnosed and justice done to all and parity is maintained and grievances removed. A man who had very little to do in the achievement of Pakistan, who might have served the Britishers for another 50 years or for generations if the country were not liberated, what right he has to claim extra weightage over the common man, over whose blood and sweat this independence has been achieved. Should they not be ashamed of themselves and what would have been their plight under the Government of India; what would have been their status under foreign rule; would they have ever thought of all the amenities, privileges and honours which they are now enjoying? Men from Services have adorned the highest positions in this country; people have not grudged this; people have been patient with every type of administration and politician; they have given a fair chance to everyone who held out certain amount of hope; still what [have] 10 years of independence brought us to? I demand of the Government that they should frame certain fundamental service rules, examine all cases of irregularities [and] examine the cases of all irregular appointments. For example, the Finance Minister the other day in reply to budget debate said that instead of 14 he had 10 Joint Secretaries. May I ask him and other concerned as to how many secretaries there were in the Government of India with a much bigger country, stretching from Arabian Sea to the Bay of Bengal; how many Joint Secretaries did they have? It is only because we have achieved Pakistan, that we have got liberty to increase our own emoluments and our privileges and create any number of posts and not for purpose of increasing efficiency. Now, the Minister for Finance was telling the House that he wants huge increase in expenditure on the revenue side of his ministry for purpose of taking effective measures to prevent smuggling. There are in his department papers where either police [have] detected huge cases of smuggling of maunds of gold but the Police officer has been transferred because at the most his rank was that of subinspector or inspector or deputy superintendent of police. Why does he need all this staff for? If he is prepared to come along with me I can show him and any member of the cabinet that huge amount of smuggling of gold is taking place. There are crores worth of commodities in Karachi market where there are the custom rules, where are the prevention of smuggling rules? Is this the efficiency of the administration that the government has achieved or wants to achieve? If this is so, then one of the two possibilities is correct. Either the government and administration is ineffective and powerless to stop smugglers or the smugglers are more efficient. Is there not sufficient machinery present in Federal Capital where there is the police force, defence force, secretaries and ministers and high officials and everybody else then how is it that these things still take place here in Karachi? Either this Government must have representatives of smugglers in the Government or they are afraid of smugglers. If the latter is the conclusion then hand over the administration to the smugglers because then the people would have the satisfaction of knowing that this is after all the Government of smugglers and they are trying their best under the circumstances to get the maximum profit for themselves.

The Assembly re-assembled at Half Past Three of the Clock, in the Afternoon, Mr. Speaker [Mr. Abdul Wahab Khan] *in the Chair.*

* * *

MR. FARID AHMAD (East Pakistan: Muslim): Sir, there is another aspect of the problem of which I want to make a passing reference and it is that in the cabinet secretariat and the establishment division there is an organization called Method and Organisation Division which had been created a few years back solely for the purpose of streamlining the organisation and advising the different Ministries for imparting works, eliminating delays and increasing efficiency. It is headed by a foreign expert and every month Government is spending nearly Rs. 25,000 on this organisation. But it has failed to justify its existence. It has got no power at all; its recommendations are not accepted by anybody. So I do not see what justification there is for spending this huge money for the purpose of doing no work.

A MEMBER: This assertion is not correct.

MR. FARID AHMAD: Sir, it was the old cabinet decision—and in the matters of appointment a formula was evolved—that 44 per cent of the appointments will be filled on the basis of provincial quota and 20 per cent of the appointments will be made on the basis of merit. Now, it has become necessary in view of the changed circumstances and constitutional provisions to amend the rule. But I do not understand why it was not possible for the Cabinet Secretariat to frame definite rules for this purpose. Certainly, the absence of these rules and the delay in framing these rules is telling adversely on the interest of East Pakistan. So the Prime Minister owes us an explanation on this score.

Then, Sir, my other motion is in respect of the policy of the Government in the matter of recruitment to C.S.P. The old Civil Service of India was supposed to be the steel frame of the British Empire though it was neither Indian nor Civil nor service in any sense.

A MEMBER: Do you mean the old I.C.S.?

MR. FARID AHMAD: Yes, I mean the old I.C.S. Of course, Sir, while saying this I do not minimise the very high standard of service, the very high standard of efficiency maintained by the Service in spite of so many other defects. The service had a name for itself for high integrity and efficiency and though not service to the people. They have also rendered valuable services in different spheres of life but such a service, namely, the Indian Civil Service was necessary from the point of view of the British imperialists who wanted to rule this country and wanted the people to be treated as slave people. Nobody can deny that it was the basic principle which operated in the minds of the members of the Indian Civil Service. Even though recruitments were made from this country at a progressive basis in order to take the people of this sub-continent into confidence but scrupulous care was taken to see that the members of the I.C.S. did not get mixed up with a native and they were made to feel, even though they were natives, that they were superior to natives. They belonged to the soil, yet they were taught to revolt against everything that belonged to the soil. That was the tradition of this Service. It might have been extremely efficient for a certain limited purpose. Therefore, Sir, the question which now arises is whether after the creation of Pakistan, such a background of mentality should be allowed to continue and flourish in this country. Certainly, the old I.C.S. believe in living in isolation, in working in their ivory tower detached from the people so that just on the mountain they could deliver a sermon as to what is right and what is wrong regarding the trivial affairs of the native people. Now, it was expected that this mentality, this outlook would change in a free country because the requirements of a free country are definitely of a different nature from the requirements of a ruling power. It is true, Sir, that when partition came about there was only a single representative of East Pakistan in the I.C.S. and efforts have been made from time to time to give increasing representation to the East Pakistani boys and officers already serving in different capacities in this cadre of service in Pakistan but to my mind the policy that has been followed is one of complete lack of planning and foresight. It is true that there was only a very poor representation of East Pakistan in the services but the service as such was not adequate to meet the requirements of the country. Naturally the services had to be expanded and in order to give some weightage or to associate East Pakistanis in the highest service of the land, certain promotions were made not by any sound principles but just because a demand has to be satisfied, five of them were recruited from the provincial service of the province just as were recruited from this side also. What is the policy that is being pursued with regard to the appointment in the Civil Service of Pakistan? About 20 to 25 appointments on an average are made every year. Are we to suppose that there is such abundance of talent in our country that while in the United India we could not produce on competitive basis an appreciate number in the Indian Civil Service, all of a sudden overall availability of talent in the country is on the increase?

In this connection I will be doing a definite injustice to the Members of the East Pakistan Civil Service if I do not point out the important thing which has been completely lost sight of in the matter of recruitment to the Civil Service of Pakistan. There was a time beginning from the Sepoy Mutiny of 1857 that the Bengalees, specially the Bengalee Muslims, were supposed to be just capable of doing nothing. They were excluded from the Army. They were not to be found in any responsible position and the Indian Muslims have left behind for us a vivid description of the days of 1873 with the result that no brilliant boy of East Pakistan could ever think of achieving any measures of success in the Indian Civil Service but this fact has been belied by the fact that students from this side of the different Universities belonging to the different Provinces did appear in the competitive I.C.S. Examination and they qualified themselves. When after partition for the first time in 1949 the examination was held a friend and colleague of mine from East Pakistan stood first in the Civil Service. That gives a complete lie to the theory that we lack in brain and efficiency. Two of my colleagues—we were serving in the same College as Lecturers of English—are in the Civil Service. That those persons who had previously competed in the Bengal Civil Service were equally competent but opportunities were not made available to them. Now, what is the policy that is being pursued? If you recruit on the presumption that talents are available in the country as plentifully as blackberries you will definitely spoil the integrity and efficiency of this service. Why not make some ad hoc appointments. Give some promotions from the Civil Service of East Pakistan. There are qualified persons who as compared with the members of the old Indian Civil Service could hold their heads high and look forward to achievements as administrators and as distinguished servicemen in the cause of the people. Certainly a change has come about. Now, what this policy of bundle recruitment will lead us to? These young officers in 20's and 25's who are being recruited will take nearly another 30 to 35 years, if you make the age of retirement as 60. They enter service at the age of 25. That means 35 years. After five years you shall be closing the doors of the Civil Service of Pakistan to all the competent boys of the land, no matter whether from East or from West. They shall have to knock the doors of commercial firms to get a job. So, time has come to take stock of the entire situation and it calls for an immediate revisions of the entire recruitment policy. It is the grievance which we made from this side of the House about the poor representations of East Pakistanis in different cadres specially in the senior service of Pakistan. Here is a particular case. As I have already told the House the very fact of a boy from East Pakistan coming at the top of the Civil Service of Pakistan is not just an accidental affair. The performance has been repeated in subsequent years. So, Sir, all of a sudden neither in the East nor in the West the brain has been sharpened due to independence. The same quality of men, the same quality of youth were also previously available in the East also. Only the point that was wanting was that they did not get a chance. Is it their fault that they happened to be recruited to the East Pakistan Civil Service in the year 1948, just by this margin of one year? Does it mean that in spite of all the brilliance you shall deprive these persons? So, Sir, I appeal to the Government to kindly turn their serious attention to this aspect of the problem. I was referring to the Civil Service that we have continued in the old tradition of the Indian Civil Service. Our Service has been formed and drawn up by the best talent in the country, yet what is the training that is imparted? Are they taught any background of our national movement, and the history of Islam and the history of India? They are being taught in the same old tradition of the British days to live in the D.C.'s bungalow in the Punjab and D.M.'s bungalow on the hill top in East Pakistan. They are inaccessible people. The fault is not theirs. The initial human material was quite good. I know quite a number of them. Even students have become C.S.P.'s. When they see me putting on sherwani they think me to be foolish.

SHEIKH MUJIBUR RAHMAN (East Pakistan: Muslim): Particularly the beard.

MR. FARID AHMAD: Yes, anything and everything which has anything to do with Islam or Muslims. Is it that you are going to train your own people to hate your own system, to hate your own civilisation and culture? Are you going to give to the country out of this manufacturing laboratory of the Civil Service Academy at Lahore some more anglicized officers? If you are really keen that a person should be taught to become an adapt in what dresses should be worn on what particular occasions, if you want to convert the youth of our country into connoisseurs of drinks and cocktails, then what the training would lead to? A friend of mine who is a member of the Civil Service was complaining to me that in spite of his getting about Rs. 1,000 a month he did not know how to meet his expenses. I said to my friend, "You have only one or two sons and a wife and you are not maintaining any large family. It is because of having been anglicized it is not honourable to continue relationship with the old type of people because they are of the old school and the old tradition." He said that he had to attend this party and that party and said that he had to make a dress for each which would cost him Rs. 300 to Rs. 350 at the big tailoring houses it may cost from Rs. 500 to Rs. 550 because the cost of sewing is more than the cost of the cloth; sometimes it is even more than twice as much. So, Sir, he has to keep a car and he has to purchase so many things. So, if you really want to bring up a band of old I.C.S. people stiff-necked with a bow-tie and who know how to bow and say "How do you do?" then bring some from England. They will be better people, with better integrity. Why not do that? So, Sir, this made policy must be revised. Our people should be made to feel that they are the sons of the soil. The C.S.P. is to serve the country. Members of the public, however, small or whatever might be their social status, the service should be made available to those persons. People should not be afraid on any score to approach them with their petty little grievances. After all the administration in many ways represents the leadership of this country. They are the basic structure of the society. Political society, political institutions, social relationship go on changing patterns but the Civil Service is a permanent factor in maintaining the stability of this country. That the service has deteriorated there is no denying the fact. There is no escape from that fact. So, Sir, the very fact that there are today allegations of corruption against the former members of the I.C.S. may be wrong, they may be true but the manner in which the allegations against the highest service in the land is on the increase shows that the people's confidence has shaken. Let me, Sir, remind the House what the

Quaid-i-Azam said, while addressing the gazetted officers at Dacca Government House. He advised them and very rightly so: "Do not rest content with merely doing justice to the people. Let the people feel that justice is being done unto them." So, this is very relevant so far as the integrity of the highest service in the land is concerned. It should not be presumed that I am indulging in whole sale condemnation of the Service. There are good people, very excellent people to serve the nation. But what is happening to them? They are getting progressively disillusioned because they have no recognition. Their number is dwindling year by year. Is there nothing that we can do at least to boost up the morale of the service? Let the honest men that are left behind give their best service to this land. Is it not our moral duty? Ask the people and you will find that people have no two opinions on the subject. They are one in this matter and this is time that the Civil Service itself should start seriously thinking, because, Sir, if you go on in this fashion just drifting with the current, a time may come when there will be no Government of this type who can sustain and maintain that big Civil Service. It is after all the scope of employment which is available to the brilliant boys of this country in the covenanted services and in the matter of emoluments. Other privileges and allowances, they are certainly much more than the privileges of the I.C.S. Certainly it is that which is attracting the best boys of the land to that service. Now, if this will go on, then we are going to undermine the very structure of this service. Then there will be no sustaining factor which will come in to fill that interregnum and interlude without one Ministry, when there is chaos and confusion. So, Sir, the Civil Service has a great responsibility and duty to perform.

Now, Sir, I will turn in brief to some other points of the cut-motions which I have brought. Now this matter of the extension of services in appropriate cases because the candidates in such cases are always found very suitable for they happen to be the relations of somebody or because somebody from the big bosses is interested in them. What is the net result of giving this kind of extension to services. It is blocking the progress, it is blocking the way of the junior officers to go up the ladder and take their legitimate right. It is depriving them of all the initiative of doing their best and putting and exerting themselves or straining themselves for improving the service conditions. By extending the service up to 58 years from 55, in certain instances, I think, the Government has created a very unhappy situation. They have taken an unhappy measure by which they have only given rise to a serious discontent in the lower cadres of service. I know what the typical argument from other side will be to defend their own policy, that they have put in a number of years, they have become more or less experts in their own line. Is this a sufficient answer? Certainly this is not the sufficient answer, Sir. When Pakistan came into being, there were very few experienced hands. So, if you wanted experienced hands why did you at all spare the British members of the Civil Service then, why did not you import some Hindus from India because there was a great dearth then? Everybody should get his legitimate right. It will not stop here, Sir, because once you give extension to a man for five years there are 10 others standing in the queue and then those who will come afterwards being recruited in the Service shall have to pay for it. So, this will be a continuous process of discontent that will run in the Service and you shall have to take a long time to get rid of it. It is an admitted fact that after all the bulk of the decisions, excepting the final one, is made at the lower level resulting in notings that are done and quite a fund of information is collected at the lower level. So, it is definitely going to have a very bad repercussion. It has already taken away all the stimulus and the incentive for honest and hard work. So, this policy must be stopped. There are still services available outside. After all government have spared persons of the ex-I.C.S. and members of the Audit and Accounts Service who preside over several boards and other semi and quasi-government organisations. If we can spare such big guns from the administration, why do not you retire them. If you still want experienced wisdom, then go on digging the graves of persons who have already died because the logical extension must be stopped. Another decision is to increase the age of superannuation, i.e., retirement from 55 to 58. I do not understand why a discrimination should be practised in the Services. Do you want to create a scheduled caste in the juniors amongst the Services? There should not be separate standards for different services. They should always remain the same. You should not give and go on extending these facilities of serving for some more years to other services. Why are you going to make that exception in the Civil Service of Pakistan? Is it merely because of the fact that they have the final say or control in the matter of determining the policies of the Government? Is it because that they are getting all the key administration posts in this country? Certainly, Sir, this has already given rise to a serious discontentment in the Services because once you agree to the extension of a principle in the case of 300 or 200 officers, certainly you have to look to the interests of other officers. It cannot, therefore, be said that simply they are better looked after, they require more facilities, they retain more energy to continue for another three years, while the members of other services do not possess. I do not speak for any personal motive whatsoever, I have no grudge against anybody, but conditions of service, as far as practicable, should be made uniform. Of course, there is a little difference between service to service so far as concessions, emoluments and salaries are concerned, but such things as retirement, pension rules, leave rules, these should be uniform. There should be certain basis so that decisions can be arrived at and whenever you go by rules there is no discontent; so that nobody can say that there has been a violation of rules. The uniformity in the applicability of rules if of great importance; the rules should not be such as may be interpreted in a particular way for a particular individual, as by such kinds of deviations, different applicability of rules in case of one service, in case of an individual or a group of individuals, is a very dangerous policy. It should not be allowed to continue in the greater interest of the country, as this has already created discontent amongst the Services. Now, Sir, we find that the rules have been relaxed in case of certain other services, such as Superintendents and also other cadres. As a matter of principle no exception should be made. There are persons for whom the rules are relaxed simply because they have made themselves indispensable, such persons take maximum advantage, they have so appropriated themselves that they think that nobody in the land knows about the subject excepting themselves and these people happen to control the administrative machinery of the Government. Therefore plea is advanced that they are indispensable and in their cases the sympathy of the Cabinet is always with them. This should not be the criterion so that you can proceed for extending the term of officers or relax it in some cases and you will not relax it in some cases. This is, Sir, an unfortunate state of affairs and I maintain and I will once more remind this House that, as I understand, the Government is now following a policy of retrenchment and I have come to know immediately after the conclusions of the morning session that four Assistants were recruited in the Ministry of Agriculture and three of them have been served with retrenchment notices. Those people came here in search of jobs for the last about 8 or 10 months, and only after two months' service they are being retrenched. This is the fruit of parity we are getting and we know where it has led us to. Somebody has to show the beacon light, someone has to take us out of this darkness.

MR. SPEAKER: Mr. Mohyuddin Lal Badshah please continue.

✿   ✿   ◢

[At this point, SYED MOHYUDDIN LAL BADSHAH addresses the assembly in Urdu. A half-page of discussion relating to the defense services is omitted. His comments on the CSP follow.—R.B.]

Sir, I want to draw the attention of this august House towards other Central Services as well. The distinction maintained between the P.C.S. and the C.S.P. is a source of worry to the personnel of our Provincial Service. I do not mean to suggest that the grades of the C.S.P. may be reduced. I simply want that instead of these two Services, namely, P.C.S. and C.S.P., there should be only one service with one cadre. The Central Government and the Provincial Governments should employ men belonging to that one service and should determine their seniority on the basis of the length of their service and their merit and not on the basis of their cadre. Of course, the P.C.S. officers too, will have to pass the same academic and competitive examinations as are prescribed for the C.S.P. officers. This scheme of one service will eliminate the possibility of a C.S.P. officer of only two years' service becoming senior to a P.C.S. officer of ten years' standing. The privileged position given to the members of the I.C.S. by the British Government was understandable as the Government was alien and imperialist. But now there seems to be no justification for such a distinction.

In other Government departments too, for instance the Income-tax Department and the Customs Department, there is a similar distribution between Class I and Class II officers. Class I officers supersede Class II officers in spite of being junior to them and this causes great disappointment and frustration. The Cabinet should appoint a Committee to solve this problem and the Committee should prepare a consolidated scheme for removing the cause of this disappointment and frustration.

MR. SPEAKER: Khan Jalaluddin Khan! Please move your cut-motions also!

MR. ZAHIRUDDIN (Minister for Education and Health): You may speak generally on the demand under the head "Cabinet."

MR. SPEAKER: You do not move your cut-motion?

KHAN MOHAMMAD JALALUDDIN KHAN (West Pakistan: Muslim): I am told so, so I do not![1]

Mr. Speaker, Sir, I shall not keep the House engaged for long. I deem it my proud privilege to say a few words about the poor and helpless Government servants, that is, Class IV and Class III employees, who are directly dependent on the Government. I would first like to draw the attention of our beloved Government towards the rehabilitation of Class IV employees. At present when an employee of this category dies or retires from service, his family is served with a notice of ejectment and evicted from the Government quarter after two months. I, therefore, request the authorities to provide shelter to these homeless beings who spend their lives in the service of the Government. They too deserve to be rehabilitated in our country like the refugees. It is indeed pitiable to see the family of a deceased Government servant, who was perhaps

---

[1] English translation of the speech in Urdu.

the only earning member of the family, being turned out of the quarter only sixty days after his death. So, I hope the Government would take this matter into consideration.

Secondly, I would draw the attention of the Government to the fact that with the meagre pay they receive, these employees cannot afford to undertake any journeys to see their relatives living at distant places or attend such important functions as marriage or funeral of their kith and kin. I would, therefore, suggest that if the Government is averse to paying them the fare in cash, it should issue Railway warrants to enable them to travel with their wives and children. In view of their low pay, they deserve this help in the form of Railway warrants.

Sir, if the Minister concerned goes out to look at the quarters provided to Class IV employees, he would find that the entire accommodation consists of a single room, 14 feet by 14 feet. The inconveniences that they have to put up with in living in these one-room quarters with their wives and children can be better imagined than described. I had referred to this matter last year and requested the Government to pay attention to the quarters allotted to the low-paid Government employees. I had also re-quested that the quarters in question should be supplied with electricity. Up to now arrangements for the supply of electricity have been made only in 20 per cent. of the total quarters while the remaining 80 per cent. lack this amenity. This work should be completed at an early date.

So far as medical aid is concerned, the Government has no doubt passed orders on paper for the reimbursement of the cost of medicines purchased by Government employees from the market. But in actual practice these orders are honoured more in breach than in observance, specially in the case of Class IV employees. Higher officers, however, get back the cost on such medicines on presentation of the bills. There are secret orders, directly or indirectly, ruling out Class IV employees from the purview of this concession. This is a clear injustice upon which I do not like to dwell at the moment. I have also said something about the necessity of bringing down the prices of wheat. This is not meant as mere propaganda. It is a genuine demand for improving the lot of poor people. I am a faithful servant of the people and to me their true representative is one who tries to avert any clash occurring between them and the Government and reminds the latter of its bounden duties. No one who tries to suppress the truth can deserve to be called their honest spokesman. It is extremely regrettable that big officers are allowed to monopolize all the rights and privileges to the total neglect of the low-paid government servants who simply pine for the ordinary amenities of life. To illustrate this point, I would compare the Government to living human body with the Class IV employees as its legs, Class III employees as its trunk, hands, eyes, ears, etc., and Class II and Class I officers as its brain. It would not look decent if the feet are left without socks. So, it is necessary that the Government should provide proper food and clothing to Class IV employees for that matter fulfil its duties in respect of all whether they are Government servants or private citizens.

Sir, I thank the Finance Minister for having gone out of his way to provide 30 lakhs of rupees in the Budget towards gratuity to be given to Class IV employees. I would here say that the mere word "fire," whether written or spoken, would not set anything aflame. We have actually to light a flame to create fire. So I would submit that no useful purpose would be served by merely making a provision for gratuity on paper. It is said that gratuity would be given to the survivors only after the death of a Class IV Government employee. But as I see it, the benefit given after death is no benefit at all. It would be better if these 30 lakhs of rupees are given to the employee in the shape of cash certificates in their lifetime or utilized in enhancing the present rate of dearness allowance admissible to them. This would provide some comfort to them and their children would pray for the stability of the Government. The prayers of the poor never go unanswered and God blesses the Government with security in response to the supplications of the humble and the helpless. The Government servants who are drawing up to Rs. 300 or even Rs. 500 a month, are finding it difficult to make both ends meet. They have to maintain their position and attend offices decently clad. But unprecedented dearness has made the matters worse for them and they obviously deserve some help in the form of increased dearness allowance. It would be damaging to the prestige of the Government if its employees are compelled to work in offices in a shabby dress. I am afraid the sum of Rs. 30 lakhs provided for the payment of gratuity to Class IV employees would stand lapsed on 31st March, 1958.

SYED AMJAD ALI (Minister for Finance): It would not lapse.[2]

KHAN MOHAMMAD JALALUDDIN KHAN: [3] I thank you. I have to make another submission which, I hope, you would not take as a complaint. Government employees should not be asked to work at the houses of officers in addition to carrying out their duties in offices. They are paid to discharge only official duties and not for doing private work at the residence of officers. To me it is sheer injustice to call upon these employees to attend to private work of the officers' bungalows and this practice should be stopped forthwith.

The Government had some time ago announced its decision to give a loan of Rs. 1,000 to each Class IV employee for housebuilding purposes. But the conditions imposed by the Government for granting this loan are too stringent to be easily fulfilled by the employees. They cannot furnish the required security. Moreover, the amount of loan fixed, namely, Rs. 1,000 is too meagre for the purpose in these days of soaring prices. I therefore, request the Government to make the terms and conditions of the advance easier. In addition to this, the Government should also undertake to build new quarters on its own account to solve the problem of accommodation facing Class IV employees.

As I have already said, Class IV and even Class III employees are hard put to it in these days of unbearable dearness. They have to pay bus fare, spend something on the education of their children and clothe themselves in keeping with their official status. The responsibility of running governmental machinery lies mostly on their shoulders, so they deserve some increase in dearness allowance in proportion to the rise in prices. Otherwise, they

[2] English translation of the interruption in Urdu.
[3] English translation of the speech in Urdu.

would not be able to maintain their position and do their best in carrying out their duties.

The Government has provided Class IV employees with free quarters and several allowances such as cycle allowance, etc. I thank the Government for this relief and at the same time request it to pay attention to the condition of Class III Government servants who are an important part of the administrative machinery. If these parts are neglected, the machine would not move smoothly. The Government should, therefore, keep these employees satisfied and increase their dearness allowance. The prices of the daily necessities of life, such as food, cloth, education, etc., have reached new heights.

Sir, I would appeal to the Finance Minister to enhance the rate of dearness allowance admissible to Class III employees to a reasonable extent so that they may live a comfortable life. I request him on my own and on behalf of the people at large to take up this matter because these employees are your own brethren and your prestige is bound up with theirs. Karachi is the Capital of the Islamic Republic of Pakistan where foreigners stay and pay frequent visits to Government offices. Class III employees should, therefore, be enabled to attend offices clad in decent suits. The foreigners would then be impressed by their "position" as becoming those who serve the Islamic Republic of Pakistan.

Sir, I had made certain suggestions last year. Some of these were accepted and the rest were thrown into the wastepaper basket. This is not proper. If you want to consult me, provided of course, you do not think it as detracting from your prestige, I am always prepared to offer my advice. God has asked us to consult our own conscience if we do not find others to seek advice from. God enhances the power and prestige of the country whose people have a high moral character.

MR. ABDUS SATTAR (East Pakistan: Muslim): [4] Mr. Speaker! Sir in rising to take part in the discussion with regard to the demand under the Cabinet, it is not my intention to take much time of the House, nor to enter into a detailed examination of all the activities

[4] English translation of the interruption in Bengali by editor of *Debates*.

of all the Ministries. But, Sir, there are certain matters which have been brought to the notice of this House by some of these cut-motions and I want to emphasize those. Sir, the first matter that I want to take up is the question of extension as well as the question of raising the age limit of superannuation. Sir, if you permit me, I shall presently show you that these matters are interconnected. Sir, I do not want to cast reflections on anybody, but I cannot help pointing out that during the last few years, there were a certain number of officers who strongly felt, perhaps honestly too, that this age limit of superannuation should be raised from 55 years to 58 years. Sir, in the beginning, I know there was opposition from the Provincial Government and, therefore, the matter could not be brought before the Cabinet and a decision taken. Now, Sir, on account of persistent demands and persuasions perhaps the Provincial Government ultimately agreed and I am really surprised to learn that a decision by the Central Cabinet has been taken in recent months. Sir, again I say I do not want to cast any reflection on any member of the Cabinet, but I am really surprised to see my friends coming as they do from Bengal, knowing the conditions of unemployment there, knowing the conditions of our educated young men roaming about in the streets, not only in the streets of Dacca and other district headquarters of East Bengal, but also in the streets of Karachi, should be a party to such a decision. . . .

Appendix • 5 •

Extract from Report of the First Pay Commission, 1949

[*Explanatory Note.* The report of the first Pay Commission is the first major administrative report appearing after independence. Headed by Muhammad Munir, who was the first chief justice of the Federal Court of Pakistan, the report includes a description of the organization of the public services and an analysis of pay scales and concepts of remuneration. The extract reproduced below deals with the issue of cultural bifurcation which is the root of much misunderstanding between the higher civil service and the masses. This extract treats the problem at a somewhat different level than the more emotional analysis of Maulvi Farid Ahmad in Appendix 4. The Civil Service of Pakistan (CSP) inherits the traditions and way of life of British ICS officers; it has a standard of living and, to some extent, values different from the vernacular, tradition-oriented values of society. This cultural disparity is reflected in the problem of remuneration which is dealt with in this extract taken from *Report of the Pakistan Pay Commission* (Karachi: Governor General's Press, 1949), I, 25–34. Other aspects of this report, listed as item 2, Table 2, are discussed in the text, on pages 133–135, 216.]

Standards of Remuneration

We are required by our terms of reference to report on the standards of remuneration that should apply in Pakistan in view of its financial resources. We have already dealt with Pakistan's financial and economic position in general and now proceed to consider the question of standards of remuneration.

2. The pay structure of Government officials in a modern State is not a mere conglomeration of ad hoc appointments and salaries but is invariably based on some broad and easily understood principle. Such structure is the result of several factors, more important of which are tradition, the form of Government, the State's outlook on life, the conception of the reciprocal rights and

obligations of the State and the individual, the relations of the ruler and the ruled and the economic and international position of the State. Thus while some States regulate the remuneration of their servants purely by the utility or competitive wage principle, others qualify this principle by providing for the various categories of their servants certain conventional social standards or proceed on the principle that the servant must give his best to the State and take what as a citizen of that State he should need. None of these standards can at present be exclusively adopted in Pakistan. The socialistic or quasi-socialistic standard must be rejected not only on the ground that divorced from an all round socialistic policy in the distribution of natural wealth it is unfair both to the tax payer and certain categories of State servants but also because, in the present politico-economic set up of Pakistan beyond which we cannot go, it is not practicable. The competitive wage principle is now regarded as a relic of the Ricardian theory and no modern State can accept or propound the doctrine that like a casual employer of labour it should pay as little as possible to its servants. Further, the competitive system can only work under conditions of free supply and demand and such conditions do not at present exist in Pakistan.

3. Our present salary structure in its main outlines is more than 60 years old and though recruitment to its lower and middle class services has been on the competitive principle, it will be incorrect to assert that that principle has been the governing factor of the entire service organisation. In fact no single principle can be said to have been followed in the past in the remuneration of our services and the present system is the outcome of so many varied factors that it is well nigh impossible to replace with one stroke of pen the whole system by an entirely independent organisation. The roots of the system are too deeply embedded in the past and the services have become so accustomed to its broad features that any violent departure from it is at present out of the question. The best thing to do at present, therefore, is to allow the present system to continue, prune it of its archaic and objectionable features and modify it here and there by a new principle.

4. All the higher services in our system were originally intended

to be recruited from the British who could only be induced to accept employment overseas by a salary much above what they could get at home. This remuneration for service in India was much above the standard for comparable material and a fortiori considerably above what it should have been if recruitment had been in India and from among Indians. Thus before every Public Service Commission that sat to inquire into the matter it seemed to be common ground that Indians could be recruited to the higher services on substantially lower salaries than Europeans, and it was chiefly due to political reasons that the standard of remuneration for Europeans and Indians recruited in England continued to be the same. The introduction of Provincial Services and the releasing of posts reserved for members of the Secretary of State's Services was an express recognition of the principle that Indians could be recruited on lower salaries for work which when done by Europeans carried higher remuneration. If, therefore, some other factors have not intervened which justify the maintenance of present salaries attaching to higher posts, the case for reduction of the salaries for such posts is unanswerable.

5. The only grounds that have been urged in support of the present salaries for superior services is the rise in prices and the increasing incidence of Income tax. The increase or decrease of Income-tax is dependent on factors which have nothing to do with the fixation of salaries. The rise in prices is certainly a relevant factor as real salaries depend upon the purchasing power of money. We have elsewhere discussed the rise of prices and since we are fixing our salaries on the assumption of a fall in prices for which we have given detailed reasons and are providing for dearness allowance during the transitory period, the present high level of prices is no reason for not revising and rationalizing the pay scales.

6. The standard of living on which considerable emphasis has been laid by the higher services is as foreign to us as the salary structure of which it is the result. While every State must aim at raising the standard of material comfort of its subjects, we cannot make a fetish of conventional standards of life or subscribe to the proposition that the State should prescribe or recognize standards

of living for its servants quite out of tune with the generally prevailing standards. With the departure of those who introduced these standards we must evolve a new outlook on life and adopt our own standards which rest on the realities and limitations of our national resources. We do not think it is a right policy for the State to offer such salaries to its servants as to attract the best available material. The correct place for our men of genius is in private enterprise and not in the humdrum career of public service where character and a desire to serve honestly for a living is more essential than outstanding intellect. We cannot, therefore, prescribe our pay scales with the object of attracting to public service all the best intellect in the country.

7. We have given our reasons for the reduction of salaries of the higher services. As against this we are quite clear that our outlook towards the low paid servants should change and that the State must do everything within its power to raise their standard of living. Our erstwhile foreign rulers were completely indifferent to the position of the low paid staff. Now that our affairs are in our own hands, our duty to the proletariat of low paid employees is clear and in suggesting our standards of remuneration for this class of employees we have done all that we could do at present for them consistent with the financial resources of the State and its obligations to the taxpayer.

8. We have been advised by the various Service Associations and Unions that in making our recommendations about the salary structure and salary scales we must follow the course suggested by the Indian Pay Commission before the Partition. The method adopted by that Commission in fixing the rates of remuneration for the various classes of public services was to ascertain the cost of living index which would be obtained when prices stabilize and to fix the pay scales for each class of service on that basis, making up the difference in certain cases during the transitory period by a system of dearness allowance. They purported to adopt the principle enunciated by the Islington Commission in determining the rates of remuneration of public servants and qualified it only by the proviso that in no case should the salary of a Government servant be below the subsistence level. Acting on the opinion of

some experts they thought that when prices stabilise they would give a cost of living index between 160 and 175, and on that assumption they fixed the basic scales of pay of the various classes of service. They considered that on the assumption that an average family consisted of three consumption units the living wage for the lowest paid employee should be Rs. 55 and for a clerk recruited from the middle class Rs. 90 at a cost of living index of 260 which was the prevailing index when they submitted their proposals. Accordingly, they fixed the initial basic salary of the former at Rs. 30 and that of the latter at Rs. 55 and supplemented these by Dearness Allowance of Rs. 25 and 35 respectively. The system of Dearness Allowances suggested by them was that its proportion to the basic salary should decrease as the salary rises or as the cost of living index falls. The allowance was to be admissible to the employees drawing basic salaries up to Rs. 1,000 and was to cease in the case of all employees when the cost of living index fell below 180. If the cost of living index went above 280, they suggested the adoption of a progressive course but did not make any suggestion in regard to the situation that might arise if the cost of living index fell below 160. Except for a few select posts they thought that the maximum salary of a Government servant should not exceed Rs. 2,000 per month and in between that figure and the minimum wage they suggested a variety of scales for the superior, subordinate and inferior services.

9. We have given careful consideration to the question whether we should adopt the method suggested by the Indian Pay Commission. The system of basing salaries on the assumption of a fixed price level and adjusting the difference consequent on the rise or fall of prices by a system of Dearness Allowance and cuts is open to some very serious objections. Apart from the position that when a person accepts employment in a public or private office, he contracts for the receipt of a money salary and is, therefore, expected to adjust his cost of living according to the rise or fall in the purchasing power of money, a system of Dearness Allowance reflecting in its occasional variations the precise changes in the purchasing power of money creates in the minds of the employee the belief that his contract with his employer is for real salary as

distinguished from money salary and that the slightest variation in
the purchasing power of money gives him a right to demand more
whenever and to the extent that such purchasing power falls. Thus
the system raises hopes and expectations and leads to actual
demands which Government may not be able to satisfy. Further, if
the purchasing power of money rises and the cost of living index
falls, the employee is not willing to accept the converse logical
result of the system, namely, a proportionate cut on his salary, to
whatever extent the financial position of Government be affected.
We think that the system of fixing the remuneration of public
servants which when measured in terms of money rises or falls
according to the variations in the purchasing power of money is
impracticable and has to be subjected to so many qualifications
that it is hardly worth while adopting it as a principle. We prefer
to follow the rule laid down by the Islington Commission that
Government should pay so much and so much only to its employees as is necessary to obtain recruits of the right stamp and to
maintain them in such a degree of comfort and dignity as would
shield them from temptation and keep them efficient for the term
of their service. The machinery of administration can be run only
if Government is able to obtain efficient and honest workers, and
this mainly, though not wholly, depends upon what they are likely
to get or make otherwise than in Government service as it cannot
be denied that the salaries of public servants must have some
relation with the prospects of remuneration outside Government
service. It is true that except in Law, Medicine, Education and
some branches of Engineering, Government is in the position of a
monopolist for the employment of educated youth to its services
and that an unqualified application of the competitive wage
theory would enable it to exploit its position as an employer and fix
rates of remuneration at a dangerously low level. That such a
result is possible became quite clear to us when we examined the
representatives of various Scientific and Technical Services of
Government on the range of avenues that were open to them
outside Government service. To negative this possibility the principle of competitive wage can be qualified by the rule that in no
case should Government pay to any class of its employees a salary

which is insufficient to maintain them. Subject to this qualification
we think the primary consideration governing the remuneration of
public servants should be that the remuneration offered must be
sufficient to attract the right type of men to Government service.
This should originally be the standard determining remuneration
of Government servants unless Government followed the policy
and has also the means of raising the standard of living of its
servants. In cases where the competitive wage principle is not
applicable because of the monopolistic position of Government,
several other factors, for instance, the investment in the education
and training of the employees, the standard of comfort which
Government considers to be reasonable for members of the different classes of its employees have got to be considered. If a person
who has spent considerable time and money in his education and
mental equipment cannot receive from Government sufficient
emoluments to maintain the standard of comfort which society
considers him to be entitled to, he is not likely to go straight in the
discharge of his public duties. Though a man with whom honesty
is an active principle in life will not deviate from that principle by
a slight decrease in his standard of living, and a man to whose
character honesty is completely foreign will not become honest
however high a salary Government might give him, the principle
holds good that, other things being equal, the man who is possessed of the means to maintain a reasonable standard of living
among his fellowmen is less likely to go astray than a person whose
salary is wholly insufficient to maintain him in that degree of
comfort which society considers to be reasonable for him. In our
opinion the broad test suggested by the Islington Commission for
recruitment to the public services still holds good and should
constitute the foundation of our recommendations. The Indian
Pay Commission thought that this principle needed qualification
by the condition that in no case should a man's pay be less than a
living wage. We do not think that the principle requires any
qualification, because the condition considered by the Indian Pay
Commission to be a qualification of the rule is to be found in the
rule itself. If a servant is not paid a living wage, he has an open
invitation to resort to illicit activities to enable him to live and if

the salary paid to him is not a living wage it cannot be said that it shields him from all temptations. If, therefore, shielding a public servant from temptation is a material factor to be considered in fixing his salary, the minimum amount that must be paid to him must be such as is sufficient to enable him to live. This is another way of saying that the minimum wage permissible under a Government system of remuneration must be a living wage for its least paid employees.

10. Living Wage.—Before the application of the theory of a living wage to the public services of Pakistan is discussed and its financial implications are pointed out, it is necessary to explain the theory itself and to draw attention to some of its broad aspects. The theory is closely connected with the question of food shortage and over-population in the world in general, and in each country to which it is sought to apply it has its limitations in these two factors and the national wealth of the country. On the assumption that it takes 2½ acres to support one person on a minimum diet, an assumption the correctness of which has been conclusively established by Dr. Hugh Bennett of the U. S. Soil Conservation Service, the present arable land of the globe could provide a minimum for 1,600,000,000 people which is less than the present population of the earth by 650,000,000. World population, however, goes on mounting, and since the beginning of the present century has increased by 700,000,000, two world wars, many famines and mortality by epidemic diseases notwithstanding. Writing in a recently published book, *Human Breeding and Survival,* Messrs. Guy Irving Burch, Director of the Population Reference Bureau of Washington and Elmer Pendell, Doctor of Philosophy at the Baldwin-Wallace College, Ohio, say "If suddenly India's death rate could be lowered to the level of the United States, India with her present birth rate could fill five earths, as full as ours, in a single century—China could do the same and it would not take the U.S.S.R. much longer."

On these premises, namely, food shortage and overpopulation, the conclusion is plain that a portion of the existing population must go without minimum diet and any increase in population without a corresponding increase in food production would increase the number of those without minimum diet.

11. The doctrine of living wage was first propounded by Ricardo in reference to the supply and demand of labour in industry and asserted that the price of labour depended on the subsistence of the labourer and that, therefore, wages tended to be equal to the amount of commodities necessary to feed and clothe a worker and his family which represented to society the cost of enabling the labourer to subsist and to perpetuate his race. In its purely economic aspect it invoked the cost of production theory to determine the price of labour in each industry, and rested on the Malthusian Law of population. But in the language of later Economists it implied that the supply of labour was infinitely elastic and that the supply always tended to increase indefinitely if the price offered for it rose above a certain level. If wages went above what was necessary to maintain the supply of labour, then workers would enlarge their families and the labour supply would increase, with the result that there would be competition in labour for employment bringing about a fall in the wages. Conversely, if wages, owing to the supply of labor, fell below the subsistence level, children would die off or never be born and this would result in a decreased labour supply in the next generation so that competition among the employers for employment of the available labour would again raise wages. In determining the subsistence level to which wages were supposed to adapt themselves, the exponents of this theory included in the subsistence wage not only bare physical necessities but also a modicum of comfort which by habit and custom the wage earner would stick to even if he had to reduce his expenditure on physical necessities.

12. While this theory of wages recognised short term periods in which the wage level might fall below the subsistence level, the claim for a living wage was founded on the principle that men and women must live and that the State or the employers should determine wages on a level which permitted the wage earners to carry on their work. An industry that does not pay its workers enough to enable them to maintain themselves is extracting more

vitality from its employees than it is giving them. It is, therefore, parasitic and either other sources are bearing the burden of supporting the workers or the workers themselves are making inroads upon their own strength. The two fundamental problems in the application of this theory are (1) how many persons is a worker supposed to support, and (2) what commodities and services are necessary to enable them to live. Social workers and budgetary students both in America and England have all been virtually united in declaring that each able-bodied male should receive enough to maintain a family of 5, consisting of father, mother, and 3 children all under 14, not because the average family does as a matter of fact consist of 5 persons but also because at least 3 children to a family are needed to provide for the perpetuation of the race. In fixing women's wages the standard commonly accepted is that of a single woman living away from home without dependents. The second main problem in giving precision to the idea of living wage is the determination of what commodities and services a family of 5 must have in order to live. It has been calculated by social research workers in America that each worker maintaining a family of 5 would require 17 dollars per week to maintain a subsistence—plus standard of living—a level according to which sufficient surplus is accumulated to enable the standard family to house itself, to purchase food with sufficient calories to meet the needs of the family and to buy cheap but neat clothing. The total national income in the United States at the time of these calculations was 71,000,000,000 dollars and if each labourer had been given the amount which was declared to be basically necessary, there would have been a surplus of 12,600,000,000 but if allowance had been made for differential wages, payment of interest, profits, and rents and 12 per cent. of the national income to be saved, the entire surplus would disappear, and it would be impracticable to pay the workers either under the existing economic system or under any other the sums which are commonly demanded for them by advocates of the living wage.

13. This being the position in the world's most economically advanced country, let us compare it with that in our own country.

In 1870, Dadabhoi Naroji calculated the annual per capita income in British India at Rs. 20. In 1913–14, Wadia and Joshi estimated that such income was about Rs. 44/5/6. Findlay Shiras' estimate brought the figure to Rs. 107 in 1920–21. Mr. Rao, who made an elaborate research in the matter, put down the national per capita income of India at Rs. 65 for the year 1931–32. Dr. Anwar Iqbal Qureshi, Deputy Economic Adviser to the Government of Pakistan, has, on a system of his own, estimated the national per capita income in Pakistan at Rs. 195, but as admitted by him this money income is less than the real income represented by Mr. Rao's figures. There has never been a regular census of production of the kind held by Mr. Flux in the United Kingdom in 1907 and no official or reliable calculation of national income is available. There can, however, be no question that the national income of Pakistan can bear no comparison to the national income of western industrial countries though if a comparison were made with India not much difference would be found between the two. The following table gives the average income per capita in India in 1945–46 and some other countries:

	Rs.
Undivided India	198
Provinces that now constitute the Indian Dominion	204
Australia	1,799
Canada	2,868
United Kingdom	2,355
U. S. A.	4,668

If the average annual income per capita of the whole of India before the partition was Rs. 198 and that of the Provinces that now constitute the Indian Union Rs. 204, it follows that such income for the Provinces that now constitute Pakistan is substantially less than Rs. 198.

14. The application of the living wage doctrine to the salaries of public servants raises some fundamental issues. In pressing the claim for a living wage the claimants are apt to lose sight of the fact that wages can only be paid out of the national income and that the lesser the national income the lower must be the wages. A claim for higher wages can be justified only where there has been

a corresponding increase in production and national income and a consequent addition to the public exchequer. In the case of Government employees the salaries are paid from the public exchequer and the incidence of a rise in the salaries must fall on the tax payer. If, therefore, an average Pakistan national is not contributing to national production more than Rs. 16 per month, can he demand and would the State be justified to give him, say Rs. 50 a month? Secondly, if the doctrine of living wage cannot be applied to wage earners in general, can Government employees demand its application to themselves? We are not called upon to discover an answer to these problems or to deal with the general economic repercussions that a liberal application of the living wage doctrine would cause. We have been referred to the public speeches of various spokesmen of the Pakistan Government including the Premier wherein the claim of the least paid employees of Government to a living wage was conceded and in the discussion that we had with the Finance Minister we were formally informed that Government accepted that claim as it was understood here and in India. We must, therefore, proceed on the assumption that the minimum wage that we may decide to fix must be a living wage. There are at present about 2 lacs of Central employees who will benefit by the acceptance of the living wage theory and an average increase, say of five rupees, in the remuneration of each such employee would involve an additional financial burden of Rs. 12,000,000 per year.

15. The next question is, how is a living wage to be determined? In the case of the remuneration of the least paid employees of Government it should be borne in mind that the financial position of Pakistan is completely irrelevant. If the principle is once recognised that a servant must receive and the State must pay what is necessary to maintain him, the claim cannot be negatived by the argument that the State is not in a position to pay, because that would negative the claim which has been held to be valid. The real question, therefore, that requires determination in this connection is that of the price level with reference to which the minimum salary must be fixed. As already pointed out the Indian Pay Commission fixed it with reference to the cost of living index

that would be obtained when prices stabilized after the present crisis has passed. Now the cost of living index is an extremely elusive figure and is never as exact as the figures that are employed to indicate a rise or fall in the cost of living. Though one may be quite certain that the cost of living has risen where the index has also risen and that the cost of living has fallen where the index registers a fall, it is impossible to say that the rise or fall in the actual cost of living has been in exact proportion to the rise or fall in the index. The method of indicating the rise or fall in the cost of living by employing the device of numerals is an attempt to measure the precise extent of a dynamic economic phenomenon which is incapable of being measured by the device employed. The accuracy of an index figure wholly depends upon the relevant family schedules remaining constant in quality and quantity. This, however, is never the case because, as prices vary, each class of employee goes on making alterations in the quality and quantity of the various items that were included in the basic family budget. Further, apart from the fact that an index is never an exact measure to indicate the rise or fall of the cost of living of a particular class, it is almost impossible to judge the probable figure at which the cost of living index would stand when prices stabilise after a crisis. It must be remembered that the price phenomenon of the present day world is governed by wholly different principles from those which governed prices quarter of a century ago. No modern State allows those factors which governed prices in the past to have unrestricted operation for any length of time, and in practice prices, if not of all the commodities, of several basic commodities are regulated by the State on high grounds of public policy. The doctrine of laissez faire and unhampered competition among producers is a story of the past, and it has become impossible for any one to predict with any degree of exactitude what the general price level or the prices of particular commodities would be a few years hence. The state of international trade of a country, its tariff policy, its mode of financing major development schemes, its currency regulations, its attitude towards infant industries, its general policy to encourage or discourage profits among competing tradesmen and producers, and above all the supply and demand of basic commodities are only some of the factors which go to determine the general price level in a country and one has got to be a prophet to predict with any degree of certainty the exact course that either the general price level or the price of a particular commodity would take in future. If the cost of living index has to be made the basis of the salaries of public servants, one must have a perfectly clear vision of the future and be able to say what the long range price level in future would be. Otherwise the salaries would vary from time to time, according to the method suggested by the Indian Pay Commission every six months, and the basic salaries would be entirely eclipsed by the dearness allowance which might increase out of all proportion to the basic salaries. If the principle of dearness allowance to compensate for the rise in prices is once recognised, there is no logical principle by which its operation can be confined only to certain classes of servants or to those in receipt of particular salaries and no valid reason for the rate at which it is allowed to decrease as salaries go up. In our view any system attempting to relate the salaries with the varying price level with any degree of accuracy is foredoomed to failure and we must discover some broader and less compli- cated method for fixing the salaries of public servants. That the system of varying the rates of remuneration according to varia- tions in the cost of living index is impracticable, is clear from the fact that the Government of India in the case of the least paid employees have not been able to implement the recommendation of the Indian Pay Commission that the rates of dearness allowance should be raised according to a certain scale as the cost of living index rose about 260.

16. Though we cannot take the cost of living index as the determining factor in the fixation of salaries, it is undeniable that rates of remuneration in order to be rational must have some broad connection with the purchasing power of money. Therefore, if pay scales have to be recommended, which may remain in force for a reasonable length of time without causing hardship to the em- ployees or financial difficulties to Government some kind of fore- cast of prices must be hazarded, otherwise there would be no basis for the superstructure. In fixing a living wage for the low and

middle class employees the most important factor to be borne in mind is not the general price level but the price index of the necessities and ordinary comforts of life. The most weighted item in the consumption schedule of these classes is food. This is an unalterable item and with minor adjustments tends to remain constant even in the acutest period. Next comes cloth but as compared with food it is a variable item as in times of financial stringency men reduce their expenditure on this item and purchase as little as possible. Nevertheless there is always a minimum requirement of this commodity also in each family and in determining a living wage provision must necessarily be made for it. We have already pointed out that Pakistan is a surplus country in food even at present, and with completion of the various irrigation schemes that are being worked out or executed with unabated zeal and vigour, the present surplus is bound to assume larger proportions. The prices of food-stuffs are, therefore likely to fall; but as in the present international position no predominantly agricultural country can allow the prices of its agricultural produce, particularly foodgrains, to fall indefinitely, we anticipate that some system of control of prices of foodstuffs will be introduced by Government with a view to preventing the prices to fall below a certain level. This level will be determined by the cost of production which will also include a reasonable margin of rent and profits or by what Government considers to be a reasonable standard of living for the farmer. Of course, the prices of imported goods which figure in the consumption schedule of an agriculturist will have to be considered in fixing the control prices of foodgrains. Such imports at present show a very high price level but it is reasonable to presume that as means of production are employed more and more in the production of consumer goods, the prices of imports will also fall. Even if, therefore, the prices of agricultural produce have to be determined by Government with reference to the price of imports we anticipate that in the normal times of which we are thinking the general price level of consumer goods will be somewhere between one-third and one-half of their present level. There would, therefore, be a corresponding fall in the price of wheat which will also affect the prices of other commodities and goods. Similarly the price of cloth will show a decline as more cloth is manufactured by the foreign countries for export or more textile mills and handlooms are set up in Pakistan. At present we are substantially subsidising the Indian textile industry because India, taking full and merciless advantage of our position, is charging us enormously high prices for cloth. This is a purely temporary state of affairs and cannot last for any appreciable length of time, as more and more foreign countries would gradually be willing to supply to us this commodity, and as time passes and we earn more foreign exchange on our exports of jute, cotton, hides and skins and wool, we will be finding it easier and easier to adjust our economy to our essential needs and setting up more and more textile mills. Though it is impossible to say for us, as assumed by the Indian Pay Commission, that within a few years the cost of living index would come down to a level between 160 and 175, we can reasonably presume that the price of cloth will decline to a much greater extent than the price of foodstuffs. Keeping these tendencies in view we consider that in a few years' time a basic salary of Rs. 25 as against the present basic salary of Rs. 14 in the case of the least paid employees and a salary of Rs. 50 in the case of the least paid clerk will be a reasonable monthly remuneration in Pakistan.

17. In determining what is reasonable remuneration for the least paid employees, it must be borne in mind that their salaries have got to be correlated with the income of others of the same social and economic standard. Most of the employees belonging to this class are illiterate and unskilled and have no notion of what the average income of an agricultural labourer whose work is undoubtedly more arduous than theirs is. The salaries of public servants can only be paid from what is taken by the State out of the total national production as revenue. It will not be right for those entrusted with the public funds of the country to make an exception in the case of employees of this class and pay them a salary out of all proportion to the average income of a man in same status of life as this would amount to taking something from a person who though engaged in work involving more discomfort and physical exertion has already less and giving it to another

whose work is comparatively easier. If any equalisation of the distribution of national wealth has got to be effected, it can only be done by the State under a carefully considered scheme and not by us as we can only proceed on the assumption that salaries of public servants have to be determined within limits of the present social and economic set up of the State.

Extract from Report of Second Economy Committee, 1957–1958

[*Explanatory Note*. The following extract appears on pages 1–10 of Part I of the *Report of the Economy Committee Appointed to Review the Expenditure of Central Government and Suggest Economies* (2 vols.; Karachi: Government of Pakistan Press, 1957, 1958). Parts I and II are in one volume published in 1957; Part III is in a second volume that appeared in 1958. This report is significant for several reasons. First, it reflects an awareness of principles of government and practices in other countries. Secondly, it is unusually comprehensive in coverage, yet specific in details. Thirdly, it is the only major legislative effort at administrative reform in the history of Pakistan, and its impressive quality suggests a high level of legislative competence in the 1957 National Assembly. Finally, the extract printed below is virtually the only documentary evidence suggesting the administrative conditions which prevailed immediately before martial law. As such, it is a corrective to the common impression created, often by administrators' allegations, that pre-martial law conditions were the consequence solely of legislative and political incompetence. This report is listed as item 16, Table 2, and is discussed further in the text, page 222 ff. The term *crore*, used several times in this extract, equals ten million. One *lakh* equals one hundred thousand. The value of the rupee is $0.21. Reproduction of this extract has been authorized by His Excellency, G. Ahmed, Pakistan ambassador to the United States, on January 26, 1965.]

The Economy Committee was set up in pursuance of the announcement made by the Finance Minister in paragraph 85 of his Budget Speech of 1957–58 which reads as follows:

This budget clearly brings to light the economic difficulties which the country is facing. The scope for further taxation is limited and we must turn our attention to the task of reducing expenditure, particularly expenditure which is of a non-productive character. I do not wish to suggest that such expenditure is without justification. Nevertheless, I feel that we must make a determined effort to reduce it to the essential minimum. The cost of general administration has, for instance, developed from about Rs. 8 crore in 1948–49 to nearly Rs. 17½ crore in the next year. While it is understandable that administrative expenditure may grow with the development of the economic and social life of the country and the expansion of the functions of government, it is for consideration whether it is not disproportionately high in relation to the total resources available. It is of vital importance to the economy of a developing country like ours that expenditure on administration is kept to the barest minimum and that resources are diverted to the productive and creative purposes of development to the maximum extent possible. The present position calls for a thorough examination of the non-productive field of Government expenditure and I propose that an Economy Committee be set up as early as possible consisting of members of this House and senior officers of Government. The work of this Committee will be of great importance as the economies that can be effected in our current expenditure will go to help the development effort of the country and to afford relief to the tax-payer.

We have quoted from the speech as we propose to revert to it later in our report.

2. The Government resolution (Appendix "A") constituting the Committee and announcing its personnel was published in the official gazette dated the 17th May, 1957. According to the resolution, the Economy Committee was required to review the expenditure of the Central Government and suggest economies. The set-up of the Committee is as follows:

1. Justice A. S. M. Akram   Chairman
2. Mr. M. A. Khuhro, M. P.   Member
3. Mr. Farid Ahmad, M. P.   Member
4. Choudhry Abdus Salam, M. P.   "
5. Mr. Muzaffar Ahmad, M. P.   "
6. Mr. M. A. Mozaffar, Joint Secretary, Finance   "
    Ministry

Mr. M. A. Mozaffar was designated as Secretary to the Committee.

3. The first meeting of the Committee was held on the 28th of May, 1957 to determine the procedure and to draw up a question-

naire. It was decided that the members should study the set-up of
the various Ministries and offices subordinate to them and examine the justification with reference to the resources available in
Pakistan.

4. The Committee invited the suggestions of the public for
effecting economies in Central Government expenditure, through
a press note issued on the 11th of June, 1957. Twenty-two
members of the public sent in their suggestions. The Jamaat-e-
Islami sent two of their representatives to appear before the
Committee.

5. In their approach to the problem the Committee were
guided by the following considerations:

 (i) Is the organization necessary?
 (ii) Has it fulfilled the purpose for which it was created?
 (iii) Would it be possible to achieve the same results by a smaller
   organization or by amalgamation with some other organization?

6. In order to assess the position the Committee called for the
necessary information from the various Ministries in respect of the
offices as well as the organizations under them. The Committee
decided that the information made available by the Ministries
concerned should be circulated to the members for their study
after which the Committee would examine the representatives of
the various Ministries. In spite of reminders the Ministries concerned took a long time to send the information. In some cases the
information furnished was incomplete. The facts and figures mentioned in the report are based on the information supplied by the
Ministries concerned or from those obtained from other Government sources.

7. We have been asked to submit the report in time to enable
Government to make use of our recommendations in the preparation of the next Budget. Therefore, in the short time available it
has not been possible for us to go into greater details particularly
in regard to question (iii) mentioned in paragraph 5, namely,
whether the same results could be achieved by a smaller organization or by amalgamation with some other organization. In this

connection we have certain suggestions to offer, but which we propose to set out at the end of the report.

8. During the course of our discussions with the representatives of various Ministries we noticed that not even a single Ministry had given proper consideration to the need for economy pointed out by the Finance Minister in his Budget Speech. They all argued that they were under-staffed which fact was responsible for inefficiency, arrears of work and other ills. Even the departments whose functions have been transferred to provinces were not prepared to surrender staff or effect economies. In their opinion, as a result of the new Constitution there has been an increase in work throughout. We also noticed a tendency to interpret (mis-interpret?) the provisions of the new Constitution as well as the Rules of Business in such a manner as could justify their claim not only for the retention of existing staff but also for augmenting it further. In some cases attempts have also been made to enlist the support of the Ministry of Law. We will revert to the subject later when we discuss the Ministries concerned. Our objective in referring to this matter at this place is to point out the extent of co-operation we received from the Ministries concerned in our effort to suggest economies. In this context we cannot help mentioning our apprehension that any attempt at economy will be resisted strongly by the administrative Ministries concerned and unless Government are strong enough, they may find it difficult to implement the recommendations in the report. Government's action on the various recommendations of the Economy Committee appointed earlier and which submitted the report after five years of deliberations has not been of much encouragement to us. We are also constrained to remark that the *Administrative Enquiry Committee Report* and the *Federal Reorganization Committee Report* have not met with better fate either. Another factor which has been very disconcerting to us is that while the Economy Committee was being constituted to effect economies Government decided to provide an air-conditioning unit to each of the Secretaries. These air-conditioners were imported during the Baghdad Pact meeting in Karachi and the intention was that after the meeting these sets would be made available on payment to hotels

which cater for the requirements of foreigners. If this intention had been carried out Government would have been saved the expenditure and at the same time the hotels would have earned foreign exchange in the shape of rents. Government decision to make these air-conditioning units available for use in the offices of various secretaries at a time when the need for economy was considered imperative naturally leads one to ask the question whether the administrative Ministries have at all taken heed of the warning which the Finance Minister gave in his Budget Speech. Incidentally an American Expert, Mr. Charles Abrams who came to Pakistan to advise Government in connection with the setting up of the Housing Authority, in his discussions with one of the members of the Committee said that his own office was not air-conditioned and he could not think of air-conditioning his own office before providing the same amenity to his subordinate staff. While it is not our intention at this stage to preach a leveling of the various grades in Government service in the matter of working conditions we do feel that there was absolutely no justification for the expenditure on air-conditioners particularly at a time when a fervent appeal was made for economy by the Finance Minister. It is hardly a consolation to say that the extra expenditure will be met from savings within the grants. This is not all. According to our information new posts have been created, some posts have even been upgraded and supplementary grants are being proposed to complete the picture.

9. We believe that Government will not be able to effect economies unless they are really serious about it and the best proof that they can give of their intention is by following an austerity programme in their official life. It is seldom realised that "every defect which a sultan approves of becomes a quality" [1] and people look up to the dignitaries of the State for a cue and shape their conduct accordingly. The display of luxury and show at the higher level creates an unhealthy desire for emulation, even in people who may not have the necessary means, with results too well-

[1] In the Economy Committee's report this quotation is given in Persian script, a transliteration of which is "Har aib ki sultan ba pasandad hunar ast." An English translation by Syed M. Haider has been inserted in the text above in lieu of the Persian.

known. It is bad enough in the days of prosperity but is worse in times when the nation is required to practise austerity.

10. Before we offer our comments on the set-up of the various Ministries and offices subordinate to them we would like to place before the Government certain general observations which concern all the Ministries and offices subordinate to them:

(*a*) We note that the Ministers and certain officials of Government are entitled to requisition, at the cost of Government, Railway Saloons. We suggest that this concession be withdrawn altogether.

(*b*) We also suggest that police guards should be withdrawn from the residences of the Ministers and other High officials. But if that be not practicable there should be an effective reduction in their number, particularly when they accompany the Ministers travelling by train. In our opinion a single guard, i.e., 1 & 3 should be adequate.

(*c*) A moderate scale of residential accommodation should be laid down by Government for Ministers and officials. Annual expenditure on their maintenance and repairs should not exceed 2% of the capital cost.

(*d*) We notice that a sum of Rs. 1 lakh was incurred on furnishings of the Ministers' residences during the year 1956–57 alone. We suggest that the monetary limits of furnishing should be so fixed as not to be out of tune with the economic conditions of the country in general.

(*e*) The Prime Minister and other Ministers should ordinarily travel by ordinary trains and planes.

(*f*) Government officials when travelling by air should travel in tourist class. If the members of the Parliament could be required to travel at government expense by tourist class, there is no reason why officers should not. The extra baggage allowed to be carried by air at government expense in the case of government servants sent abroad on delegations or on training should be abolished. Government should pay only for the carriage of government records.

(*g*) It is noted that almost all the previous Economy Committees suggested restricting the number and use of the staff cars. The various Ministries and their subordinate offices however continue to possess a large number of such cars; there are nine cars in the President's house, 22 cars in the Ministry of Information and its subordinate offices, 9 cars in the Customs House and six in the Ministry of Industries and the office of the DGS&D.

Even the relatively very small Ministry of Parliamentary Affairs has a staff car. These examples are only illustrative. On an average a staff car costs Rs. 8,000 per annum including depreciation, maintenance, repairs and pay and allowances of the driver. At present staff cars are seen all over the streets, in odd places including places of recreation. It is understood that the private use of staff cars was not permissible in 1948. Apparently these orders no longer hold the field. We feel that the restriction on the private use of staff cars should be reimposed. We also feel that senior officers drawing pay of Rs. 1,000 or above per mensem, should not be allowed the use of staff cars within a radius of five miles for which no T. A. is admissible. Further, we strongly recommend that instead of purchasing luxurious cars only jeeps should be purchased for use as staff cars. This would serve the purpose and eliminate their misuse to a large extent.

(h) Expenditure on entertainments should be drastically curtailed so as to be in keeping with the general economic conditions obtaining in the country. There is scope for reduction both on the scale as well as the occasions on which these parties are thrown. We feel that serving of liquor or wine should be completely banned in official parties or on ceremonial occasions.

(i) Meetings of the various committees are at present very often held in hill-stations during the summer resulting in avoidable expenditure. In future committees and conferences should be held at the Headquarters of Government, Central or Provincial.

(j) Government servants sent abroad on delegations or training should not be allowed to draw their full pay and allowances abroad. As Government pays them well (perhaps more than is justified) for meeting their expenditure, it should be sufficient if they are allowed to draw abroad only 50% of their pay subject to a maximum of Rs. 1,400. Incidentally the drawal of full pay and allowances abroad is not allowed by countries like India, Indonesia and Turkey and there is no reason why this should be allowed in Pakistan. Again, Government servants who draw their pay and allowances abroad and spend them there, are allowed a rebate in Income-Tax to the extent of Rs. 4,500. This provides the incentive for wasting foreign exchange, so badly needed by the country for the import of drugs, medicines and other essential goods. In Karachi alone as many as 34 cars were imported by Government servants in the first half of 1957, besides refrigerators, silver-ware, cooking range, radiograms, sanitary ware, tiles, etc. Some officers have even imported two cars in the same month. This shows the extent to which foreign exchange is lost to the country because of the special advantage which government officers enjoy. We recommend that the Income-Tax concession should in any case be withdrawn completely.

(*k*) At present Government servants are allowed to draw leave salary abroad. In some countries they are even given higher rates of leave salary under certain conditions provided for in the Fundamental Rules. These rules are a legacy of the past, of the time when Pakistan formed part of the British Empire, and are completely irrelevant in the present conditions. They place Government servants in a more advantageous position in the matter of obtaining foreign exchange vis-a-vis the public. We feel that these rules should be amended and Government servants placed on the same footing as any other private person in the matter of travel abroad. As far as is known to us no other country in the world practises this type of discrimination. Even India which inherited the same set of rules has already changed them to fit in with the changed conditions. We understand that the Ministry of Finance initiated a proposal to that effect even before action was taken by India. The proposal, however, could not go through because it was argued that a change in the rules would affect the vested rights of Government servants. The Fundamental Rules, were framed in days when there were no foreign exchange restrictions and we do not think any Pakistani Government servant should possess a vested right to draw his leave salary in foreign exchange. If he must go to Europe or the States for recreation or for recoupment of health he should be entitled to the same treatment as any other member of the public. We need not look to India for our inspiration but in this case, we would commend to Government the action taken by the Government of India in similar conditions. Apart from the savings in foreign exchange it will also reduce the work in the Missions.

(*l*) The Committee has noted with grave concern the increasing expenditure on contingencies. Some of the officers' rooms continue to be furnished lavishly, hardly in keeping with the essential needs for economy. In this connection we would reiterate the recommendations made by the first Economy Committee in the year 1948.

> The Committee suggests that except in the case of the Hon'ble Ministers and Secretaries no officer should be allowed the use of a carpet. Daris may be given to only Joint Secretaries. Costly tables and chairs should not in future be purchased. In any case the cost of a table

should not normally exceed Rs. 100 in the case of an officer of and below the rank of Deputy Secretary. Requirements of officers and staff should be reviewed and limited to the minimum absolutely necessary. Steel cabinets should not normally be provided to any officer below the rank of Secretary with the possible exception of Private Secretaries to the Hon'ble Ministers, whenever necessary steel or wooden almirahs which are cheaper may be provided.

(*m*) Transfers of Government servants involve invariably large expenditure particularly on transfers between the two zones and between Pakistan and foreign countries. Transfers should be made only in the interest of public service, and where large expenditure is involved as in the case of transfers between the two zones we would suggest that so long as the present emergency continues as far as practicable, these transfers should be deferred. This recommendation should apply with still greater force in cases involving transfers between Pakistan and other foreign countries. We are informed that a number of Seamen Welfare Officers who were transferred from Pakistan to the United Kingdom only last year are being replaced now by another set. The selection of persons sent out last year was approved by the then Minister of Labour himself. In order to avoid such situations in future we would suggest that Government servants posted abroad should not be transferred unless they had completed at least three years of their tenure in that country. Should a transfer become unavoidable, sanction of the Cabinet Secretariat should be obtained invariably before such transfer orders, resulting in large expenditure in foreign exchange, are issued by the administrative Ministry.

(*n*) The question of provision of residential telephones to Government servants was examined by the previous Economy Committee in 1951 and also by the Administrative Enquiry Committee in 1953, and orders were issued by Government restricting their provision to officers of the rank of Joint Secretaries and some Deputy Secretaries. The present position is that residential telephones have been provided to a large number of officers below the rank of Deputy Secretaries such as Assistant Secretaries, Personal Assistants, and Junior Officers of the Posts and Telegraphs and the Railways. We would suggest that residential telephones should not be provided to officers below the rank of Deputy Secretaries. In the case of officers of the Railways, the Posts and Telegraphs, the P.W.D. and similar other departments, required to attend to urgent repairs or maintenance, it should be sufficient to provide a residential telephone for the Head of the Department only and another for the office of the duty staff. The residential addresses of all the officers should be maintained in that office. In case of emergency, arrangements could always be made through the duty staff to send the message at the residence of the officer. This will enable Government to place at the disposal of the public hundreds of telephones and earn more revenue and at the same time meet partially the urgent demand of the public.

(*o*) The Re-organisation Committee set up in 1947 recommended that all incoming letters meant for a branch should be sent direct to the Branch officers who will put up to higher officers important receipts and the remaining receipts should either be disposed of by him finally or he should call for previous papers or should give specific instructions to office to examine and note on particular points. No noting should be done by office unless specifically asked to do so. When called upon to note, Assistants should be discouraged from writing long notes and paraphrasing the contents of the receipts. We endorse this recommendation which, if implemented, would eliminate delay and improve efficiency all round.

(*p*) In our review of the Secretariat set-up of the various Ministries we have noticed that some of the Branch officers have only one Section to deal with, some Deputy Secretaries have only one Branch officer to control and that some Joint Secretaries supervise the work of only one Deputy Secretary. We appreciate the fact that no hard and fast rule or yard-stick could be laid down but we cannot help reiterating here that an earlier Economy Committee had suggested that the claim for a post of Joint Secretary should not normally qualify unless there were 3 Deputy Secretaries' work to be controlled by him. Similarly a Deputy Secretary should control the work of at least 3 Branch officers and that a Branch officer should have under him at least 3 Sections in charge of Superintendents.

(*q*) We have noted with concern the growing tendency in Government offices for duplication of work. While we do not deny that "two heads are better than one," we cannot help pointing out that "too many cooks spoil the broth," and that is what Pakistan is suffering from. The fact that before a decision is taken a number of departments have to be consulted leads not seldom to inordinate delay. This also is responsible in no small measure for inefficiency, as no one officer can be held responsible if anything goes wrong.

(*r*) The all-round expansion of Government activities has resulted

in worsening of the position of office accommodation in Karachi. This hampers efficient working. Apart from congestion the
various branches of a Ministry not seldom are located in different and distant places. For example, the Ministry of Finance
has its branches in five different buildings spread over the city
and separated from one another by long distances. It is suggested that arrangements should be made for the provision of
office accommodation according to the standard laid down by
Government. Meanwhile, it should be possible by a careful
planning to ensure that the various branches of a particular
Ministry are all located in one building or at least in buildings
adjacent to each other.

(s) We are very much concerned to note the increasing expenditure on delegations sent to participate in International conferences. We have pointed this out also in our comments on the
set up and expenditure of the various Ministries. As the expenditure incurred on these delegations involves expenditure in
foreign exchange, Government should have taken note of the
recommendations of the previous Economy Committee of 1950
which recommended that delegations to such conferences need
be sent only where the matter of the conference was very important and materially affected the interests of the country.
Our impression like that of the previous Economy Committee
is that this primary consideration is more often than not ig-
nored, and participation in the conference is more often than
not with a view to gratifying personal inclinations of the members participating rather than the interests of the country. We
also recommend that the size of the delegations sent abroad
should be limited to the barest minimum absolutely necessary.
As far as possible, members of the delegations should be drawn
from the nearest Missions posted abroad suitably briefed for
the purpose by the Centre. In most of the International conferences we have noticed that only platitudes are talked out.
In such cases Government need not send any representative.
If, however, for political reasons, it is considered necessary that
Pakistan should be represented, an officer from the nearest
Pakistan Mission should be deputed to attend the conference.
It should also be noted that recently a delegation has been
sent abroad to the U.S.S.R. and the Eastern European coun-
tries for developing trade . . . with those countries and as
many as eight members were included in that delegation. The
Ministry of Commerce even deemed it necessary to send their
Secretary as well as their Joint Secretary on this errand.

(t) At present T. A. is admissible in every 2 years to Government servants who are posted in a zone other than the zone of their domicile. As the period of travel is reckoned as duty and not debited to their leave, most of them travel by ship. As Government servants are entitled to claim fares for the members of their families also, Government incur large expenditure on this account. In the Lee concession granted to Government servants of Asiatic domicile, passage benefits amounted to once in 7 years for the Government servant and his wife and only one passage for each child during his tenure of service. Boys over 12 were not entitled to any Lee concession benefit. We do not want to suggest exactly the same standard but we feel that in the present conditions the T. A. benefits should be reduced and granted once in 3 years instead of every 2 years and that Government servants during leave should travel at Government cost one class lower than that to which they are entitled while travelling on duty. We have suggested 3 years because normally a Government servant is posted for 3 years to the zone other than his own zone of domicile and T. A. during leave should be admissible only if he is required to stay longer than that period. We have also suggested that Government servants on leave should travel one class lower than the one to which they are entitled on the analogy of the rules obtaining in the Defence Department. Government servants if they like can still travel by the higher class by paying the difference. For travel between the two zones we suggest that Class I, Class II and Class III Government servants should only travel by the PIA on the Tourist Class, and by train between their place of duty and the air port and again between the air port and their home.

(u) There is an acute shortage of technical persons and the position is getting worse with the increased tempo of development. This is largely due to the rule which requires Government servants to retire at the age of 55 except in the case of the I.C.S. and the Ministerial Government servants in whose cases the age of superannuation is 60. We understand that in connection with a loan application, the World Bank made it a condition that Government should extend the age of retirement to 60 in the case of Railway employees as otherwise the shortage of technical persons would result in inefficiency and in that case the chances of the Railways being able to pay back in time the Bank's loan would recede. We have noticed that in other countries the age of retirement is very much higher. We also found that Government servants in most cases continue to remain efficient and fit both physically and mentally up to 65 years and even beyond that. The pension bill is rising. It has already in-

creased by 100%. In addition Government servants on retirement withdraw their G.P. Fund balances and commute their
pensions. The result is that on the one hand Government
is compelled to man the ever increasing technical posts by
persons hardly qualified by experience for the job and on
the other lose large sums of money in the shape of G.P. Fund
accumulation and the commuted value of pension at a time
when Government need all the money for its development requirements. We, therefore, strongly recommend that the age of
compulsory retirement should be raised to 60 in the case of
technical persons and to 58 in the case of nontechnical employees. Under the existing rules Government has the clear
right to retire any Government servant who has completed 25
years of service. Government should take recourse to these
rules freely and retire Government servants considered physically or mentally unfit even before they attain the age of fifty-
five. The present practice of giving extensions is objectionable
as it affects the right of others for promotion who may not get
similar extension. If, however, the age of retirement is raised
as recommended by us, every one will be placed in the same
position and there will be no cause for dissatisfaction or heart-
burning. Our recommendation is subject to the condition that
Government servants who do not want to continue in service
beyond the age of 55 should not be compelled to do so.

11. We have before us the Annual Report of the State Bank of
Pakistan for the year 1956–57. In spite of the fervent appeal made
by the State Bank from time to time to reduce Government
expenditure we find that during 1956–57 the net increase in the ad
hoc treasury bills created by Government was Rs. 70 crores against
Rs. 25 crores during the last year. The total outstanding of such
treasury bills amounted to Rs. 110 crores on 30th June, 1957 as
indicated below:

Amount outstanding at 1–7–1955	Rs.	15	crores
Created during 1955–56	Rs.	30	crores
	Rs.	45	crores
Cancelled during 1955–56	Rs.	5	crores
Outstanding at 30–6–1956	Rs.	40	"
Created during 1956–57	Rs.	95	"
Cancelled during 1956–57	Rs.	25	"
Outstanding at 30–6–1957	Rs.	110	"

The money supply which stood at about Rs. 260 crores in 1949 increased to Rs. 500 crores by the end of June, 1957. It is no consolation to note that the increase in money supply in the year 1956–57 (45 crores) compares favourably with the increase of Rs. 65 crores in the preceding year as during the year the balance of payment position was one of deficit and exercised restrictive influence on money supply to the tune of Rs. 21.71 crore. The Government sector, however, accounted for more than 90% of the increase in money supply. We are glad that the Governor, State Bank has again called for a sincere effort on the part of Government to reduce public expenditure. This is all the more necessary as Government expenditure in the past has shown a tendency to increase and which increase bears no relation to Government's own resources as will appear from the statement appended to this Chapter. It will appear from that statement that the collections under the principal heads of revenue which stood at Rs. 109 crore in 1950–51 increased to Rs. 127 crore in 1951–52 and dropped to Rs. 99 crore in 1957–58. The expenditure on collection charges on the other hand increased from Rs. 2.21 crore in 1950–51 and Rs. 2.50 crore in 1951–52, to Rs. 3.18 crore in 1957–58. Again the expenditure on General Administration which stood at Rs. 2.88 crore in 1950–51 has increased to Rs. 7.32 crore in 1957–58. The expenditure on Foreign Affairs has increased from Rs. 1.45 crore in 1950–51 to Rs. 3 crore in 1957–58. The expenditure on Civil Administration which stood at Rs. 17 crore in 1950–51 increased to Rs. 32 crore in 1957–58. We have mentioned these figures in the hope that the Departments of Government will appreciate the severe strain the economy of the country is being subjected to, largely as a result of the ever increasing Government expenditure without a corresponding increase in revenue receipts.

Official Press Release Summarizing Report of the
Provincial Administration Commission, 1960

[*Explanatory Note.* The *Report of the Provincial Administration Commission* (*1960*) (Lahore: Superintendent, Government Printing, February, 1960) was the first episodic effort to reorganize local government below the central level. Although modifications were subsequently made to articulate the structure to the new pattern of decentralization in the 1962 Constitution, most of the suggestions of this report have been incorporated into government reforms in contemporary Pakistan. This report is listed as item 19, Table 2, and is discussed in the text on pages 227–228. The extract below is derived exclusively from portions of the official press release.]

Rawalpindi, June 29, 1960

The Cabinet Division of the President's Secretariat today released details of the decisions of the Presidential Cabinet taken at a special meeting held in Murree on June 23 on the Provincial Administration Commission's Report first considered by a special Committee of Cabinet Ministers appointed last February.

A short summary of these decisions was released to the Press on June 23 soon after the Cabinet meeting.

SALIENT FEATURES

The foremost among the decisions is the rationalisation of the administrative machinery at all levels in the Provinces of East and West Pakistan. This revolutionary step taken by the present regime will stop the various departments of the provincial administration working in diverse directions and will ensure better coordination amongst them as also speedier action on the part of the administration. The new system has been so designed as to ensure that the development work, which is given the top-most priority by the present regime, is carried on smoothly and surely. The whole machinery of administration will now move together to attain the national objective of bringing greater prosperity to the people of Pakistan.

Another redeeming feature of the new system is that executive pockets have been created at provincial level as well as divisional and district levels wherein authority is rationally delegated to various agencies for the implementation of Government policies and decisions.

Developmental activities will receive great impetus under the new arrangements as the bulk of the development work has now been entrusted to the divisional councils and to the district councils which, in short, means that there has been a link-up between the basic democracies and the working of administration. All departments working in a divisional headquarter will be directly under the commissioner and will work in an atmosphere of better understanding of each others activities.

Perhaps the most outstanding decision on the Provincial Administration Commission's Report is provided in enabling the various councils to receive complaints of public grievances which will be dealt with by them expeditiously. Questions can be asked by B.D. members on these complaints on more or less the same system as is operative in legislative assemblies.

Provision has also been made for the introduction of village police under the union councils in three selected districts in each province. This police force will be appointed and paid for by the union councils. If this experiment proved successful it is intended to introduce municipal police on a higher level.

The units of administration have been so organised as to ensure a greater social homogenity in various regions.

As regards tribal areas it has been decided that commissioners of Peshawar and Dera Ismail Khan Divisions will be made responsible for the administration of the tribal areas adjoining their Divisions. Consequently these two Divisions have been reconstituted. A new Karachi Division is to be constituted consisting of a new extended Karachi District and the Las Bela District of Kalat Division.

Following are details of various cabinet decisions:

UNITS OF ADMINISTRATION

[A long section dealing with division of the two provinces into divisions and districts was included in the press release but is omitted from this extract.—R.B.]

THE PATTERN OF ADMINISTRATION

The following are the requirements of an effective administrative set up in the provinces:

1. (*a*) a vertical distribution of authority in a straight line of command running from the Governor through the Directorates to the Divisional and District officers; and (*b*) a horizontal coordination of governmental activities at the appropriate levels.

2. There should be clear-cut distribution of line of authority so that the roles of the Secretariat and directorates are clearly demarcated. The Secretariat should be concerned with the formulation of policies and the directorates with their implementation.

There should be maximum decentralization all along the line by delegation of legal, executive, administrative, and financial powers. Existing delegations are inadequate. Every department should work out a comprehensive scheme of delegation under the relevant laws and rules.

3. Unnecessary administrative tiers should be eliminated.

(1) The Government should ensure that heads of directorates or other officers should not issue any instructions abridging or assuming authority conferred on subordinate officers by Governments. The delegated authority may be circumscribed only under special circumstance and in specific cases after obtaining the permission of the delegating authority. This should be done only in exceptional cases when the difficulties of the situation cannot be resolved in any other way.

(2) The abuse of delegated authority by individual officers should not be made an occasion for withdrawal of the delegation. In

such cases, disciplinary action should be taken against the officer concerned.

(3) Bonafide mistakes made by subordinate officers in the exercise of authority should call for the guidance and advice of senior officers rather than for punishment.

(4) In order to discourage the lower officers from shirking responsibilities, higher officers should discourage the submission to them the cases for which the necessary authority exists at lower levels. Higher officers should not ordinarily call for reports in respect of matters which are within the competence of their subordinates.

The present independent and disconnected activities of government in the field have led to a serious situation and there is urgent need of coordinating governmental activities at district/divisional level. This coordination should be secured through the district/divisional councils of which the Deputy Commissioner/Commissioner will be ex-officio chairman as contemplated under the Basic Democracies Order. In order to make the Commissioners/District Officers effective coordinators and supervisors of governmental activities in their areas the following should be done:

(1) Departmental schemes should be coordinated through divisional and district councils.

(2) The jurisdiction of various departments in the field should conform to the civil divisions/districts except in a few departments where it is not feasible.

(3) Divisional Commissioners and district officers should be declared as the heads of administration within their jurisdiction and this position should be made known unambiguously to all departments. They should not however interfere in the technical aspects of a programme or the internal administration of the departments. However, *the staff of agricultural department of a district should work under the directions of the Deputy Commissioner in respect of all matters relating to the increase in food production.*

(4) It should be the responsibility of the divisional/district/departmental/officers to consult the commissioner/district officer in all important matters affecting the welfare of the people.

(5) Divisional commissioner/District Officer should have the authority to call for a report direct from any regional/divisional or district level officer (as the case may be), having jurisdiction in their areas. The commissioner should, in addition, have the

power to call for the relevant files and papers and order the taking of a particular action. If he considers necessary, he may also report the matter to the government, recommending action.

(6) The Divisional commissioner should have the power to require the divisional or regional officers of any department having jurisdiction in his division to inquire into the conduct of any of his subordinates and to report the result of enquiry to the Commissioner.

(7) The recommendations of the commissioner in respect of transfer or posting of any particular officer of divisional or regional rank serving in his division should not be disregarded except with the approval of the Governor.

(8) The divisional commissioner/district officers should record remarks as a matter of course in the confidential report of a divisional/district level officers of all departments on the following points:

(a) integrity;
(b) cooperation with other department;
(c) relations with the public, and
(d) interest shown in development.

These remarks should be given due weight by the government and should form part of the permanent record of the officer concerned.

REORGANIZATION OF DEPARTMENTS

The activities of the provincial governments should be categorised as follows:

Category A

This category should consist of subjects in which decentralisation should be largely feasible. But the provincial headquarters should retain policy functions as well as such operational control as may be necessary. Directorates should be retained but on a reduced scale and their field units re-adjusted to conform to civil divisions. As a matter of principle all those activities of the government which concern the common man should be decentralised to the divisions and even to the districts. The directorates along with the heads of directorates, as distinct from the secretariat, should continue for the purpose of supervision and for advising the government in policy matters.

The category A should include:

(1) Village AID and Basic Democracies
(2) Social Welfare
(3) Cooperation
(4) Labour
(5) Protection of Wild Animals and Birds
(6) Education
(7) Medical and Public Health
(8) Agriculture
(9) Animal Husbandry
(10) Fisheries
(11) Building and Roads
(12) Revenue and
(13) Police (Law and Order)

The extent of decentralization which should be ordered in respect of Village AID, Basic Democracies, Social Welfare, Cooperation, Labour, Protection of Wild Animals and Birds should be worked out by the provincial governments on the basis of the principle enunciated above.

Category B

This category should consist of subjects in which operational control from the Provincial headquarters will be necessary and the Directorates with their field units will be retained substantially in their present form.

The category B should include the following subjects:

(1) Judiciary, Magistracy and Jails
(2) Irrigation and Power
(3) Industries
(4) Food
(5) Forests
(6) Excise and Taxation
(7) Govt. Publicity.

Regional Transport Authority

The Provincial Governments should take measures to abolish route permits or restrictions on public vehicles and report to the Cabinet the measures taken to secure the object. The Government of West Pakistan should denationalise their road transport as far as possible and disinvest the capital which could be used for such development schemes in the Province for which private capital was not forthcoming. The road transport in big cities should, however, continue to be run by Government unless it could be handed over to sound corporations.

In East Pakistan, the subject of road transport should be transferred from the Home Department to Works, Housing and Settlement Department.

Police

(*a*) The DIG [Deputy Inspector-General] should continue to have the same relationship with the Commission as obtains at present.

(*b*) The Divisional Commissioner should have the authority to invite the attention of the Inspector General of Police to any defects in the Police administration or the conduct of any police officer serving in his division; and

(*c*) The Divisional Commissioner should be able to call for any reports or papers from the Deputy Inspector General of Police or the District Magistrate regarding the position of crime in any district of his division and issue such lawful directions as he may consider necessary.

Anti-Corruption

1. In East Pakistan the district anti-corruption staff should be made completely independent of the regular police department. This segregation should be secured immediately.

2. Anti-corruption directorates in both provinces should be normally headed by a senior officer and should function directly under the Chief Secretary.

Law Officers of Government

In East Pakistan, the post of Inspector-General of Registration under the Judicial department be abolished and the work redistributed in due course.

Financial Administration and Control

The three questions regarding budget, expenditure sanction, and accounts and audit have also been dealt with comprehensively in the report of the Administrative Reorganisation Committee. In accordance with the directive of the Cabinet the Provincial Governments have already been asked to revise their existing financial systems in the light of the decisions taken on the report of the Administrative Reorganisation Committee. An implementation Committee had also been created with which were associated the Chief Secretaries of the Provincial Governments.

These recommendations should be accepted in so far as they do not come in conflict with the decisions of the Cabinet taken on the report of the Administrative Reorganisation Committee. If there is a conflict between a recommendation and that of a decision already taken on the recommendations of the Administrative Reorganisation Committee, the decision of the Cabinet shall prevail. In case the Provincial Government wish to press their proposals they may submit a summary to the Governors' Conference. Other recommendations on this subject which have not been dealt with by the Administrative Reorganisation Committee and are peculiar to the Provincial administration, should be implemented by the Provincial Governments after obtaining concurrence of the Ministry of Finance. In case of disagreement, the Provincial Governments may raise the matter in the Governors' Conference, if they do desire.

PUBLIC SERVICES

Recruitment

(1) Recruitment to the Provincial class I, class II and unclassified gazetted services should continue to be made by the Provincial Government except in the case of class II officers who should be appointed by Heads of Directorates in consultation with the Public Service Commission.

(2) Recruitment to subordinate services should be made as follows:

(*a*) A divisional selection board be constituted for conducting recruitment to subordinate services within
the division except in respect of those subordinate
services recruitment to which is at present made at
the district level.

(*b*) A Provincial Selection Board should be constituted
to conduct recruitment to subordinate services for
Provincial Secretariat.

In both cases (*a*) and (*b*) above no reference shall be
made to the Public Service Commission.

Promotion

(1) There should be a clear demarcation between promotion
posts and selection posts.

(2) Appointment to selection posts should be made through
Selection Board from amongst the best officers within the zone of
selection according to the prescribed procedure. Seniority should
be considered only when the officers concerned are practically of
the same standard of merit.

(3) Appointment to promotion posts should be made on the
basis of seniority subject to fitness.

As in the case of CSP and certain other central and provincial
services, comprehensive training followed by elaborate tests
during the probationary period should be held so that the unfit are
eliminated at that stage.

(4) Promotion to selection grade should be made on the basis
of seniority subject to fitness.

(5) For promotion from non-gazetted to gazetted services and
from class II to class I service, selection should be made on the
basis of merit from amongst those qualified for promotion with
particular reference to their fitness for higher responsibilities.

(6) In respect of promotion posts within non-gazetted and
class II gazetted services, 10% of the vacancies should be reserved
for exceptional merit to form a "merit quota" in the services. Rules
should be framed to ensure that merit quota is not abused. There
should be certain minimum conditions which should be fulfilled
before an official becomes eligible for selection against the posts
reserved for the merit quota.

(7) The proposal that the PCS should be treated as members of the CSP on substantive appointment to listed posts should be referred to the Pay and Service Commission.

(8) Government servants should be carefully graded in their annual confidential reports with regard to their suitability for promotion. The provincial governments should adopt the new annual confidential report form which has been introduced by the Establishment Division.

(9) The Public Service Commission should be consulted in all cases of promotion to such posts initial appointment to which would have been made in consultation with the Public Service Commission. The Public Service Commission should also be consulted in respect of promotion to selection grade of a gazetted post.

All other cases of promotions should be handled by the Divisional Selection Board and the Provincial Selection Board as decided above except where the district level officers are competent to order promotion.

Transfer

(1) Members of the Provincial Services and officers of the Provincial class I and class II services should be transferable within the entire province but class II officers should normally be assigned to the Divisions to serve for longer periods.

(2) Divisional and District Officers should not ordinarily be transferred before completing a minimum period of 3 years in their posts. Those districts or divisional headquarters which are regarded as unattractive postings should be made attractive by giving additional allowances and by providing more amenities to the officers concerned.

(3) Regional and Divisional heads of departments including Commissioners should have the authority to transfer any officer subordinate to them within their jurisdiction except Deputy Commissioners and Superintendents of Police who should be transferred under orders of the Provincial Government. In respect of SDOs and SDPOs the Divisional Commissioners and the DIG's (as the case may be) should have the power to transfer the officers concerned within their jurisdiction but only under exceptional

circumstances and in consultation with the Provincial Government.

Discipline

(1) Heads of Directorates, if not the appointing authority, should have the power to take disciplinary action against any Class II officer serving under them and may impose punishment except those of reduction, removal, compulsory retirement, or dismissal.

(2) Divisional departmental officers including Commissioners should be empowered to initiate disciplinary action against any of their subordinates, including provincial Class I officers in which case prior concurrence of the appropriate authority should be taken. In the case of Class II officers these powers should include the authority to suspend pending enquiry and of imposing any of the following penalties in accordance with the prescribed procedure:

(a) censure;
(b) stoppage at an efficiency bar for a period of three years; and
(c) stoppage of increment for a period not exceeding three years.

In case of officers belonging to All Pakistan Services serving in a Province, the disciplinary control would be exercised by the central government.

(3) In respect of orders in disciplinary cases passed by provincial governments, consultation with the Public Service Commission should be necessary except in the case of suspension pending enquiry.

In respect of disciplinary orders passed by authority subordinate to the provincial government, consultation with the Public Service Commission should not ordinarily be necessary regarding:

(a) any original or appellate disciplinary order in respect of non-gazetted employees; and
(b) an order imposing the penalties of censure, and withholding of increment or stoppage at efficiency bar for a period not exceeding three years.

(4) Pre-integration personnel in West Pakistan should be subject to the same disciplinary control as other government servants and necessary constitutional and legal amendments should be made for this purpose.

(5) Subject to work load, wholetime enquiry officers assisted by counsel should be appointed in the Divisions to ensure prompt completion of enquiries against government servants of all departments. In such enquiries, the responsibility of making out a case against a government servant and the furnishing of material and evidence, shall rest entirely with the department concerned.

Training

The Provincial O&M units should be made really effective. A scheme for training of lower staff should be worked out by each department and should be undertaken in consultation with the O&M unit.

(2) (*a*) CSP and PCS officers should, after some years of service, undergo refresher courses in the work of nation-building departments.

(*b*) The activities of Development Departments should be adequately reflected in the courses of study in the CSP Academy and other training institutes. The CSP probationers should be required to prepare development plans for certain areas after having been provided with the requisite data. These plans should be compared with the plans prepared by departments concerned for the development of those areas. This comparison would help the probationers in appreciating the practical problems of development.

(3) (*a*) All technical departments should establish suitable inservice training arrangements for their officers both in the probationary period and in later years.

(*b*) Officers should be encouraged to undertake specialised courses of training not only in respect of purely technical subjects but also in subjects relating to industrial, economic and social welfare fields on study leave or other suitable basis.

(4) Steps should be taken to supply modern books particularly on development to the district and divisional libraries. In order to save expenditure, books could be lent by rotation to district and divisional headquarters from a central library in the provincial headquarters.

(5) Existing training facilities in Village-AID Academies and other similar institutes should be utilised for officers of other departments as well.

(6) All officials likely to be appointed as Superintendents in various government offices should undergo a course of training in office procedures and work methods. O&M unit should go round the districts and hold courses of study for the Superintendents and others concerned.

EFFECTS OF TERRITORIAL CHANGES ON SUBORDINATE SERVICE CADRES

(1) The cadres of various officials may be fixed in accordance with the new Divisional and District jurisdictions.

(2) Seniority on integration should be determined on the basis of the date of continuous appointment to a grade, provided that the existing seniority *inter se* of the officials concerned remains undisturbed.

(3) The provincial governments should acquire legal powers, if necessary, for giving effect to (1) and (2) above.

REVENUE ADMINISTRATION

Land Assessment

System of fluctuating assessment of land revenue on the basis of soil classification and bifurcation of composite charge into land revenue and water rate should be adopted. The complaints that the yield figures in Hyderabad and Khairpur divisions are not realistic and that the block system is not fair should be examined by the Government of West Pakistan.

2. Collection should not be entrusted to the same agency as is

responsible for maintenance of accounts. The provincial governments should examine whether the land revenue can be collected through the Union Councils. But, if it was considered unpracticable the collection should be made through Lambardari agency, which should be strengthened where it already exists and established where it does not exist. It should also be examined whether the collection fee was adequate. Where feasible, payment of land revenue should also be allowed through money-order.

Preparation, Maintenance and Access to Revenue Records

(*a*) Pattern of land records under the Punjab system should be progressively adopted in all areas.

(*b*) Proper maintenance of land records through careful observance of existing comprehensive instructions should be ensured.

(*c*) For the convenience of the public, copies of all revenue records should be made available also at headquarters of tehsil/taluka. Copies of permanent records should also be kept in the Union Council office.

Reorganisation of Revenue Set Up

(*a*) Boards of Revenue should be: (1) the executive head of the revenue administration exercising general superintendence and control over all revenue officers;

(2) the supervisory agency for proper and adequate training of revenue staff at all levels;

(3) the chief adviser to government for formulation of policies on land revenue, land management, agrarian and colonization matters;

(4) an expert body for making of rules and prescribing of uniform standards for governing and regulating the disposal of revenue matters and the powers and duties of revenue officers.

(5) the highest revenue court with appellate and revisionary jurisdiction and exercising same control and supervision over the working of the subordinate revenue courts as the High Court exercises in respect of civil and criminal courts.

These duties should be clearly stated in the legislation governing the Board of Revenue.

Commissioners of Divisions

(1) Divisional Commissioners should be made more effective executive heads of revenue administration in their divisions and should be given considerably more powers for disposal of revenue work both judicial and administrative under various laws and rules.

(2) Additional Commissioners be appointed in each Division (except where not needed) for revenue appellate work and to provide other relief to Commissioners;

(3) Commissioners should undertake systematic touring and inspect at least one Tehsil/Taluka in each district in a year.

Collectors

(1) Collectors should be delegated larger powers in matters affecting daily life of the people, particularly in relief measures during calamities and grant of taccavi etc.;

(2) Staff assistance be provided to Collectors by appointment of Additional Collectors/Additional Deputy Commissioners in heavy districts and Revenue Assistants/Deputy Collectors in others;

(3) Collectors be given authority to delegate powers to subdivisional Officers/Additional Collectors and Revenue Assistants for appointment and removal of patwaris, and other establishment matters;

(4) Regular inspections should be undertaken by Collector, and every Tehsil/Taluka in the district should be inspected by him at least once a year.

(5) Collectors should personally scrutinize tour diaries of subordinate officers and give more attention to work of harvest inspections.

Sub-divisions

(1) Sub-division should be made an effective unit for revenue administration and SDOs should exercise most of the statutory

and some administrative powers of the Collectors within their jurisdiction.

(2) Sub-divisional Officers should have their headquarters within the sub-Division.

(3) Sub-divisional officers should inspect every Tehsil or Taluka in their charge once a year and undertake regular harvest inspections.

Revenue Officers at Tehsil, Taluka and Lower Levels

(1) Existing strength of Patwaris/Tapedars fixed a long time ago should be suitably increased in the light of the present increased volume of work;

(2) disparity in the size of the halqas of supervisory Tapedars/Field Qanungos should be reduced;

(3) rules requiring Patwaris and other revenue staff to reside within their jurisdiction should be strictly enforced;

(4) Present practice of frequent summoning of revenue field staff to Tehsil or district headquarters should be resorted to only occasionally in cases of special importance or urgency. Whenever this has to be done it should be reported to the next higher authority along with reasons.

TRAINING PROGRAMMES AND FACILITIES

Existing training is defective and facilities are inadequate. Practical aspect in training should receive more attention and training institutes should be established for different levels of revenue officers. Important key revenue posts like that of Collector should not be held by any official who has not passed a special promotion examination.

Inspection and Touring

Touring should be systematic and extensive with sufficient advance notice to the people of the area to enable them to bring matters to the notice of the touring officer. Camp halts should be of longer duration and tour diaries should be maintained and should receive proper attention of higher authorities.

Procedure of Revenue Courts

(1) Procedure of revenue courts should not be governed by elaborate provisions of Civil Procedure Code, but should be simpler and more expeditious. Justice should, however, be ensured.

(2) Revenue cases of administrative nature, like Lambardari appeals, Tawan (fine) cases should end at District Divisional level and should not come up before the Board of Revenue;

(3) an appeal or revision should lie to the Board of Revenue on questions of law only;

(4) in order to save expense to litigants, a court deciding a case should also be permitted to receive an appeal/revision which may be preferred by an appellant against its order; and

(5) as far as possible, appeals should be heard at Divisional headquarters by the Board and at District headquarters by Commissioners and in camp by other revenue officers.

A committee of experts drawn from both the provinces should be constituted by the Ministry of Food & Agriculture to recommend to the Government a common nomenclature for units of revenue administration and revenue officers, which should be adopted throughout the whole of Pakistan.

EAST PAKISTAN

The Government of East Pakistan should adopt, as far as possible, the system of revenue administration prevailing in West Pakistan.

Explanation

The idea behind this decision is that regular settlement should take place in East Pakistan for two purposes:

(a) Keeping of up to date permanent land records,
(b) For assessment of land revenue on the basis of average production and prices,
(c) So far there was no officer below the Collector to do revenue work. This work was being done by the Zamindar under the Permanent Settlement arrangement.

The West Pakistan system introduced in East Pakistan will rationalize the revenue work and in this manner Government will be able to be constantly in touch with the public.

DISTRICT ADMINISTRATION

(1) The main duties of the district officer are to be:

(*a*) Development and coordination of governmental activities.
(*b*) Revenue.
(*c*) Law and order.

LAW AND ORDER

The Cabinet decided to adopt the following instructions prepared by the Government of West Pakistan:

1. The District Magistrate is the head of the criminal administration in the District.

He is primarily responsible for the good order of the District and the efficient working of the Police. As such, the Superintendent of Police is subordinate to him.

The Police force is the instrument provided by Government to enable the District Magistrate to enforce his authority and fulfill his responsibility for the maintenance of Law and Order. The Police force in a District is, therefore, placed by Law under the general control and direction of the District Magistrate who is responsible that it carries out its duties in such a manner that effective protection is afforded to the public against lawlessness and disorder.

2. The Superintendent of Police is the Executive Head of the District Police Force and is responsible for all matters concerning its administration internal economy and management and for its efficiency and discipline.

He is responsible, subject to the control and direction of the District Magistrate, for the proper performance by officers subordinate to him of all preventive and executive duties.

3. The administration of the Police force is vested in the Superintendent of Police, but he is expected to place himself and his Force at the disposal of the District Magistrate as an effective instrument in the maintenance of Law and Order.

4. The District Magistrate has no authority to interfere in the internal organization and discipline of the Police force, but it is his duty to bring to the notice of the Superintendent of Police all cases in which the conduct and qualifications of a Police Officer affect the general administration of his District.

In all that affects the relations between the Police and the public or the keeping of the public peace, the District Magistrate must be consulted and his orders complied with.

5. The District Magistrate shall exercise constant supervision over the prevention and detection of crime for the proper conduct of which he is ultimately responsible. An important part of his duties is to inspect the Police Stations of his district at regular intervals. It is not necessary for him to examine the details of the working of the department, but he should give special attention to:

(i) the general diary and the manner in which it is written up;
(ii) the recording of vital statistics;
(iii) the proper working of the Arms Act;
(iv) the general state of crime in the police station area and any reasons for its increase or decrease;
(v) whether the Sub-Inspector appears to have a proper knowledge of his duties, whether he is in touch with the respectable inhabitants of his charge, has acquired local knowledge, and takes an interest in his work;
(vi) whether the police station officials appear to be working properly and have a proper knowledge, of their duties and the neighborhood;
(vii) whether the police station has been regularly and properly inspected.

6. The District Magistrate, in the exercise of his power or control, shall abstain from any action which is likely to weaken the authority of the Superintendent or to deprive him of responsibility. For this reason, he shall avoid, as far as possible, the issue of an executive order unless he has consulted the Superintendent.

7. All orders of the District Magistrate relating to the Police except those passed in his judicial capacity shall be addressed to the Superintendent or in the event of his absence from the headquarters to the officer-in-charge during his absence. The Superintendent, as the local head of the Police under the District Magistrate, is bound to carry out his orders except in regard to the internal economy, organisation and discipline and matters of a purely departmental nature.

8. Should any difference of opinion on any question relating to the Police administration arise between the Superintendent and the District Magistrate, it is the duty of the Superintendent to carry out the District Magistrate's instructions. The Magistrate shall in such cases forthwith refer the matter to the Commissioner and the Superintendent shall similarly make a reference to his Deputy Inspector General. The Commissioner and the Deputy Inspector General shall consult together

and, if possible, arrive at an agreed decision. If they are unable to agree, the matter shall be referred to the Provincial Government through the Inspector General.

9. No circular or general order dealing with questions of Law or procedure other than purely departmental matters may be issued by a Superintendent until it has been approved by the District Magistrate.

10. As in the case of the district level officers, the District Magistrate will make his observation on the Superintendent of Police in respect of the following items relating to his work and conduct:

(i) Integrity

(ii) Cooperation with other Departments

(iii) Relations with the public

(iv) Maintenance of law and order

11. (*a*) All postings, removals and transfers of officers-in-charge of police stations within the District shall be made by the Superintendent with the approval of the District Magistrate.

(*b*) If the District Magistrate observes in any Police officer of or below the rank of Inspector marked incompetence or unfitness for the locality in which he is stationed, or unfitness for his particular duties, he may draw the attention of the Superintendent to the fact and request him to consider the advisability of transferring him to another locality or to other duties. He shall, however, bear in mind that not only are transfers detrimental to police work, but the officer transferred may do as badly or even worse in another place. Unsatisfactory work is as a rule met by punishment and a transfer should not be recommended unless it is likely to improve the criminal administration of the District as a whole.

(*c*) If the Magistrate observes in any police officer above the rank of Inspector any incompetence or unfitness, he may communicate with the Inspector General who after paying careful attention to the views of the District Magistrate, shall determine what measures should be taken and shall inform the Magistrate of the action which he takes in the matter.

12. (*a*) The Superintendent shall remain in constant personal communication with the District Magistrate whenever possible, and consult him on all important matters. It is incumbent on him to afford the District Magistrate all possible assistance in the criminal administration of the district, and in such matters he shall, as far as possible, accede to his wishes. Should any question arise on which they do not agree, the District Magistrate shall give the Superintendent written orders and the Superintendent will carry them out; but the District

Magistrate shall refer the point under dispute, if the Superintendent so desires, to the Deputy Inspector-General when the matter will be settled as laid down in PRB 15(e).

(b) The Superintendent shall keep the District Magistrate fully informed of all matters coming to his knowledge affecting the peace of the district, and when he is on tour the Police officer-in-charge of headquarters shall send direct to the District Magistrate all important information which would not reach him soon enough through the Superintendent.

(c) Whenever he is about to leave the Station, the Superintendent shall report his intention to the Magistrate, specifying as far as possible, the places at which he may be found from day to day; and the Magistrate, for reasons to be recorded by him, may require the Superintendent to remain at headquarters.

13. Correspondence between District Magistrates and Superintendents shall be carried on by means of unofficial notes or memoranda. The original file shall be sent for action, when possible, and formal letters shall on no account be written.

ASSISTANCE FOR DISTRICT OFFICERS

(1) The question of giving more staff assistance to district officers should be examined by the provincial governments.

(2) In view of the fact that permanent needs should be catered for on a permanent basis, temporary staff in the districts engaged on work of permanent nature should be placed on permanent footing in the interests of better administration.

(3) Efficient administration at district and divisional levels will be facilitated by strengthening the administration lower down. The sub-divisional system should be strengthened and extended to areas where it does not exist at present. This will relieve the District Officer of a great amount of routine work and will provide a good training ground for young officers before being given independent charge of a district.

We recommend that:

1. Existing tehsils in West Pakistan should be merged and formed into at least two sub-divisions per district according to a phased programme of three years.

2. To make sub-divisional officers effective, they should be given adequate powers and their headquarters located within their sub-divisions.

3. The sub-divisional officer should exercise more or less the same authority over the senior most police officer in the sub-division as is exercised by the district magistrate over the superintendent of Police.

VILLAGE POLICE

The following scheme for the introduction of village police in East Pakistan and West Pakistan should be given a trial.

Where there is no village police at present, the position is that the nearest police is available at the Thana or police out-post. Because of the increasing calls on the time of the ordinary police, they are unable to visit the villages on patrol or even on the commission of a crime, in time. Besides, with the introduction of the Basic Democracies, certain functions may have to be performed by them in which the assistance of a village policeman will be necessary.

It was proposed that in each village there should be one or more policemen depending upon the size of the village, the extent of local crime or other factors. He should be recruited locally and given suitable remuneration.

There were two suggestions as to the method of appointment of the village policeman. The first one was that he should be appointed by the Sub-Divisional Magistrate (or the District Magistrate) on the recommendation of the officer in charge of the police station for that area. He should be instructed in his duties and controlled administratively by the officer in charge of the police station. He should carry out his duties under the over-all direction and control of the local thana. He should also carry out such duties as may be entrusted to him under the Basic Democracies order by the local union council.

The other suggestion was that the village policeman should be appointed by the local union council and paid by it. He would carry out his duties under the directions of the Chairman of the union council. But he would be instructed in his police duties and trained by the district police.

Both the suggestions should be given a trial in three selected districts of East Pakistan as well as West Pakistan. All merits and demerits of the alternative schemes suggested above should be reported to the Government of Pakistan in the Ministry of Interior after 6 months.

ORGANIZATION AND METHODS

(i) The O&M units in the two provinces should be strengthened and placed under the charge of a specially trained senior officer.

(ii) O&M Units should undertake regular assignments in various departments according to an annual programme. They should bring out annual reports which should be circulated.

(iii) Departmental heads and other senior officers dealing with administrative and establishment matters should be given instructions in O&M.

(iv) Definite organisational improvements effected by departmental heads or other officers should receive favourable notice of government.

(v) Each O&M Unit should maintain a library of books on Public Administration and periodically issue a digest to the departments. This digest should consist of two parts. One part should contain our own thinking on the problems of public administration etc. and the other should contain summaries of the books and reports written by foreign experts on the subject.

REDUCTION OF PAPER WORK

(1) A general review should be undertaken to eliminate unnecessary statistical returns and statements in each department.

(2) All statistical forms and returns should be compiled in a book form after examining the necessity of keeping them. New statistical forms and returns should not be prescribed without consultation with the provincial Bureau of Statistics.

(3) Inter-departmental correspondence should be reduced by setting up working parties for disposal of cases through discussion. The course on how to conduct meetings which has been initiated by the Establishment Division should also be arranged by the provincial governments.

(4) The orders of government, should be obtained, as far as

possible, on the files of the Directorates without starting fresh files.

EXTENSION OF SECTION OFFICERS SCHEME

The Section Officers scheme should be extended to the Commissioners' office as well as to the Directorates.

INSPECTION AND TOURING

(1) Tours should be properly planned and advance notice given to the people of the area. They should be of sufficient duration and a minimum number of nights to be spent out of headquarters should be prescribed by all departments for their inspecting officers. The night halts should be enforced rigorously. In cases where no reasonable ground existed for not completing the prescribed number of night halts outside the headquarters, T.A. for the month should not be allowed.

(2) Regular forms of inspection should be prescribed in all departments and tour diaries should be kept.

(3) Touring on horse-back should be encouraged by grant of adequate Horse Allowance. The Travelling Allowance rules should also be rationalised to make travelling allowance commensurate with expenditure incurred on tours. Police horses, if available in a district, should be used by touring officers in order to save expenditure.

(4) Pools of government vehicles should be maintained in each district and Division under the Deputy Commissioner/Commissioner for touring requirements of all divisional and district officers.

(5) Out of the existing pool of aircraft of the provincial government, a small aircraft should be provided for touring officers of the Quetta and Kalat Divisions.

(6) (a) More rest houses should be built and maintenance of existing ones improved. (b) Each union council should have a building of its own in which one room should be reserved for the touring officers. All touring officers should be allowed to use Thana inspection rooms.

(7) Provincial governments should, in order to reduce unnec-

essary expenditure, consider the abolition of maintaining of tents in the district and divisional headquarters.

DISCRETIONARY GRANTS

Each Commissioner and Deputy Commissioner should be given a discretionary grant of Rs. 2,000 and Rs. 1,000 respectively to enable them to meet the minor local requirements.

BOARDS OF GOVERNORS

Important educational institutions in the province should be administered through semi-autonomous Boards of Governors.

UNIFORMITY OF NOMENCLATURE

(i) All executive departments should be known as Directorates.
(ii) The head of district administration should be uniformly known as Deputy Commissioner.
(iii) The designation of Commissioner should not be attached to posts of Executive Heads, who should be called Directors; nor should it apply to Secretariat posts.

TREATMENT OF THE PUBLIC

(1) The necessity for consideration and sympathy towards the people should be impressed on all public servants and emphasised in their training programmes. Serious notice should be taken of proved failure to show proper courtesy to the public.

(2) Every communication received from the public should be acknowledged and the person concerned informed of the action taken on it.

(3) Municipal Committees particularly in bigger towns, should set up centres of information and guidance for the citizens.

(4) Suitable accommodation should be provided in or near government offices for the convenience of the public.

(5) Complaints arising in Thana/Tehsil, District or division should be placed before the respective council by the representatives of the areas concerned. The chairman of the Tehsil, district divisional councils should ensure disposal of the complaints within a specified period. Action taken should be reported to the Council in their normal meetings.

Appendix • 8 •

Official Press Release Summarizing Report of the Administrative Reorganisation Committee, 1961

[*Explanatory Note.* The *Report of the Administrative Reorganisation Committee* (Karachi: Efficiency and O & M Wing, 1963) was originally released only by the press notification reproduced below. The committee was headed by G. Ahmed, present ambassador to the United States, who as chairman of the Planning Commission was intimately involved with the administrative reforms suggested in the two Five Year Plans. The recommendations of this committee reflect concepts of modern administrative technology which had been introduced into Pakistan administrative thought as early as 1953 in the Egger Report. The Ahmed Committee Report, although comprehensive in its design for reform, is not ideologically revolutionary. It is premised on retention of an elite cadre and discrete entities of services and on the separation of policy and operating functions in secretariat and departmental structure. This report is listed as item 18 of Table 2 and is discussed in the text on pages 225–227.]

January 26, 1961

Following is the text of Mr. G. Ahmed's statement:

The work of the Administrative Reorganisation Committee is practically over, and most of the recommendations submitted by it have been accepted by the Government. These recommendations, when implemented, will lead to great decentralisation of administrative responsibility, better distribution of Governmental business and substantial economy in expenditure. The full impact of the administrative reforms already introduced, and those to be introduced may not be immediately visible, but the changes and improvements recommended by the Committee are intended to streamline the administration and to eliminate the rigidity of long-established administrative practices, which do not accord with present-day conditions.

Three recommendations of the Administrative Reorganisation Committee, which have already been implemented, may well be regarded as the most important contribution made by the Committee to administrative concepts. The first recommendation relates to the system of budgeting and financial control, which has been radically revised. The Budget will henceforth serve as an instrument of continuous planning, and the administrative Ministers will exercise full control over their expenditures within the Budgetary limits. The intervention of the Ministry of Finance has been reduced to the minimum, and the spending authorities have been entrusted with direct responsibility for the effective and prudent administration of appropriated funds. The new system makes a decisive break with the past, and is designed primarily to expedite the implementation of development programmes.

The second recommendation, also of a fundamental nature, relates to the introduction of the Section Officers Scheme in the Central Secretariat. The main purpose of the scheme is to improve the decision-making machinery so as to ensure expeditious and efficient disposal of Government business. A whole hierarchy of subordinate officials, with much power to delay but no power to decide, has been abolished. The Section Officer combines in himself the tasks hitherto performed by a host of clerks, Superintendents, Assistant Secretaries and under-Secretaries, and is expected to take decisions. All important work in the Secretariat is initiated and dealt with at the Officers' level. The extension of this scheme to some of the attached departments, which lend themselves to its application, is under consideration.

The third recommendation relates to the delegation of increased administrative and financial powers to heads of attached departments. The relationship between Ministries and the attached departments has been the subject of a prolonged controversy. In the past, the activities of attached departments have been hampered in a varying degree, by restricted administrative and financial powers or by undue interference from the Secretariat, mostly at lower levels. Increasingly, the responsibility for the furtherance of the economic and social development of the country must rest on the executive departments, and it is, therefore, imperative that adequate administrative and financial powers should be delegated to the heads of departments to enable them to perform their functions efficiently and expeditiously. The delegation of powers recommended by the Administrative Reorganisation Committee, has been accepted by the Government. They will need continuous study. The heads of departments will be primarily responsible for the technical soundness of their proposals, and entitled to submit cases direct to the Secretaries and Joint-Secretaries of their Ministries. Heads of departments with ex-officio status of Joint-Secretary may report direct to the Minister.

The Government has also accepted the principle that Ministries should confine themselves to the formulation of policy, and executive functions should be left to the attached departments and subordinate offices.

As a result of the transfer of executive functions and the delegation of increased powers, and because of a sizeable reduction in the clerical and Class IV staff following the introduction of the Section Officers Scheme, the size of the Central Secretariat is now much smaller. The total strength of all Ministries and Divisions which increased from 4,500 in 1953 to 7,500 in 1958 has, as a result of the recommendations of the Administrative Reorganisation Committee, been reduced to about 6,000. This reduction of 20 per cent in the size of the Secretariat in a single year is perhaps unprecedented.

Modern administration demands greater specialisation. The Committee made a number of recommendations to secure a greater degree of specialisation in various fields; the most important recommendation relates to the constitution of the economic pool. The principle underlying this recommendation is not new, but its extension to cover the Ministries of Finance, Commerce as well as Industries is new. In view of the increasingly specialised character of work in these Ministries, it is necessary that an expert cadre should be built up of officers, drawn from the various services, who will acquire an intimate knowledge of the working of the economic policies of the Government through comprehensive initial training and long experience in the economic Ministries and continue to work in this field throughout their careers.

Another recommendation of the Committee, also accepted by the Government, is an entirely new departure. The Ministry of Education and the Health Division of the Ministry of Health and Social Welfare will be manned exclusively by technical officers. The gradual abolition of generalist staff will convert these Ministries into purely technical organisations dealing with their respective specialised functions. The shift from the generalist to the specialist approach, illustrated by these recommendations, is in accord with the need to adjust the administrative machinery progressively to the complex and multiple activities which engage a modern Government. Other recommendations made by the Committee relate to reorientation of the training of civil servants so as to enable them to meet the demands of a dynamic development administration.

An important change resulting from the Committee's recommendations is the centralisation in one Ministry of the responsibility of developing all the different means of transportation. Previously, the subject of shipping was dealt with by the Ministry of Commerce and the subject of civil aviation by the Ministry of Defence. The Ministry of Railway and Communications was responsible only for railways, road transport and ports. With the transfer of shipping from the Ministry of Commerce and the transfer of civil aviation from the Ministry of Defence, the Ministry of Railways and Communication would become a full-fledged transport Ministry and would be in a better position to ensure the speedy development of all transportation in a co-ordinated manner. The transfer of civil aviation from the Ministry of Defence will not affect the present integration of civil aviation with the Pakistan Air Force, and the existing arrangements under which civil aviation shares with the Pakistan Air Force all airport maintenance and personnel facilities will continue.

The Department of Shipping Control, and the Department of Lighthouses and Light-ships has also been merged with the Mercantile Marine Department. The new department would be known as the Shipping and Mercantile Marine Department. Other measures recommended for streamlining the administrative machinery to secure a more efficient performance of Governmental functions include the creation of the Investment Promotion Bureau and Bureau of Mineral Resources. Previously, prospective investors had to approach a number of Ministries and departments, and go through a lengthy procedure to secure the required permission and necessary facilities for setting up new industries. The establishment of the Investment Promotion Bureau has simplified the procedure and provided a single agency for disseminating information, encouraging investment, granting permission and securing facilities.

The creation of the Bureau of Mineral Resources has fulfilled an urgent need for self-contained machinery for the stimulation of coordinated mineral development in Pakistan.

In the Karachi area, which has already been taken over by the Governor of West Pakistan, the Central Government continued to maintain a number of institutions. The Government has now decided on the Committee's recommendation that except institutions engaged in scientific research, the responsibility for which rests with the Central Government and pilot projects which are not fully developed, all the remaining institutions should be transferred to the control of the Governor, West Pakistan, in his capacity as Agent to the President. The organisations and institutions thus transferred include the Karachi Development Authority; the Central Government College for Women; the Central Government College for Men; the Central Skin and Social Hygiene Centre, Karachi; the Maternity and Child Welfare Centre, Karachi; the T. B. Control and Training Centre, Karachi; the Civil Defence Training School, Karachi; the Poultry Experiment Station, Landhi; the Pakistan Animal Husbandry Research Institute, Melir and the Karachi Fish Harbour. The Karachi Road Transport Corporation will be transferred after a period of one year. Some of these institutions have counterparts in East and West Pakistan, which are also being transferred to the respective Provincial Governments. In keeping with the principle of maximum decentralisation of administration, the Government has already transferred the purchase work for the Provinces from the Department of Supply and Development to the respective Provincial Governments. The Government has also decided to transfer the responsibility for the administration of labour laws and for labour welfare, other than that work arising from the Mines and Dock Labour Acts, to the Provincial Governments. The Employment Exchanges and labour training centres, at present maintained by the Central Ministry of Labour, will also be transferred to the Provincial Governments as soon as these institutions have been fully developed and organised.

The most important recommendation of the Committee, which the Cabinet has accepted, relates to the expansion of the scope of the responsibilities of the Pakistan Foreign Service. In future, in addition to diplomatic and consular functions, the officers of the Pakistan Foreign Service will also perform the duties and functions of Commercial and Press Attache. Special training arrangements will be made for PFS officers in commercial and public relations work. The existing incumbents of the posts of Commercial and Press Attaches will be considered for absorption in the Pakistan Foreign Service, in consultation with the Federal Public Service Commission. The Government has also approved a number of proposals for reorganising the Ministry of Foreign Affairs and Commonwealth Relations and the Pakistan missions abroad. These proposals, when implemented, will streamline the structure of the Ministry and the missions and, at the same time, achieve substantial reduction in expenditure.

Although the main object of the proposals formulated by the Administrative Reorganisation Committee was to streamline the organisational machinery of the Government and to improve its procedures, it is estimated that the recommendations made by the Committee will also yield financial savings of about Rs. 1 crore a year, and thus help to achieve the objective of the Government to secure maximum economy in non-development expenditure.

All Ministries dealing with economic and social development have been directed by the Government to constitute small planning cells. These cells will draw up detailed programmes for achieving the targets of the second Five-Year Plan, assess

concretely the man-power and training requirements of the programmes and determine in advance the needs for material and
equipment to be procured to implement the programmes.

The work relating to administrative reorganisation and the
improvement of procedures is not something which can be finalised once for all, at any given time. To be effective and successful,
it has to be a continuous activity because the circumstances
change and the organisation and procedures have to be adjusted
accordingly. Recognising the need for effective standing arrangements to ensure that the organisations and procedures of the Central Government are kept under continuous review, the Government has constituted a Standing Organisation Committee, to
advise on all organisational and procedural problems and to
process, whenever necessary, the recommendations made by the
Efficiency and O. and M. Wing for improving the organisation and
procedures of Ministries and departments. The Standing Organisation Committee would consist of the Cabinet Secretary as Chairman, the Finance Secretary and the Establishment Secretary as
Members and the Joint Secretary, O & M, as Member/Secretary.

Official Press Release on Report of the Committee on Organisation of the Functions and Structure of the Central Government in the Light of the New Constitution, April 26, 1962

[*Explanatory Note.* The report of this committee, headed by Mohammad Shoaib, minister for economic co-ordination, and listed as item 27 in Table 2, deals specifically with articulating the administrative structure of the bureaucracy to the new configuration emerging from the 1962 Constitution. The 1962 Constitution departed from the earlier format of distribution of powers between central and provincial governments by prescribing greater devolution of authority to the provinces. This extract is taken entirely from the official press release. The report appeared as *Report of the Standing Organisation Committee on the Reorganisation of the Functions and Structure of the Central Government in the Light of the New Constitution* (Rawalpindi: Central Army Press, April, 1962). It is further discussed in the text on page 235.]

Following is the text of an official hand-out issued here today on the reorganisation of the administrative set-up in the country.

The President appointed a committee consisting of Mr. Mohammad Shoaib, Minister for Economic Co-ordination, Mr. Mueenuddin, Establishment Secretary, Mr. N. A. Faruqui, Cabinet Secretary, and Mr. Mumtaz Mirza, Finance Secretary, to consider the changes that should be made in the organisation and functions of the Central Government as a result of the transfer of subjects from the Centre to the Provinces under the new Constitution.

The committee held discussions with the Secretaries of the Ministries of the Central Government and with the Chief Secretaries and some other officers of the Provinces. It also consulted the Deputy Chairman, Planning Commission and the Railway Board.

The committee's report came up for consideration in the Cabinet meeting held yesterday. The President was in the chair. Others present were the Governor of West Pakistan, Central Ministers in station, Mr. Ghulam Faruque and Secretaries of the Ministries concerned. The Cabinet accepted the recommendations of the committee with minor changes.

Role of Central Government

Extracts from the committee's report are reproduced below:

The first task which the committee set for itself, was to define the role of the Central Government under the new Constitution. The new Constitution provides only a central list of subjects: There is no concurrent or Provincial list and, therefore, the subjects not included in the third schedule of the Constitution are ipso facto the responsibility of the Provincial Governments.

The National Assembly, however, has the power under Article 13(2) of the Constitution to make laws with respect to any matter not enumerated in the third schedule. Where the national interest of Pakistan in relation to (*a*) the security of Pakistan, including the economic and financial stability of Pakistan; (*b*) planning or co-ordination; or (*c*) the achievement of uniformity in respect of any matter in different parts of Pakistan so requires, it has also the power to make laws.

(I) Under item 2 of the third schedule with regard to (*a*) relations and dealings of all kinds with other countries; (*b*) international organisations, and bodies, and the implementation of their decision; (*c*) The Making and implementation of treaties, conventions and agreements with other countries; and

(II) Under item 6, concerning "national economic planning and national economic co-ordination."

Centre's Intervention in Provincial Matters

The Central Government is also competent to intervene in Provincial matters in the following manner:

(I) The President can issue a directive to the Governor of a Province, who in the performance of his functions, is subject to the directions of the President under Article 66(2) of the Constitution.

(II) The President can issue a proclamation of emergency under Article 30(1) if he is satisfied that a grave emergency exists: (*a*) In which Pakistan or any part of Pakistan is (or is in imminent danger of being) threatened by war or external aggression; or (*b*) In which the security or economic life of Pakistan is threatened by internal disturbances beyond the power of a Provincial Government to control.

(III) The Central Government under Article 135(B) of the Constitution can assume executive authority if so provided by a law under Article 131(2) even in matters falling within the purview of the Provincial Governments.

The Committee, therefore, considers that in order to discharge its responsibilities satisfactorily, the Central Government has in all matters:

(*a*) To keep in close touch with broad policy and planning on a national scale; (*b*) to secure co-ordinations and (*c*) to deal with international aspects even of such matters as fall wholly within the Provincial sphere.

Small Administrative Units

As a natural corollary of the above it would be necessary to maintain appropriate but small administrative units in the Central Government to deal with education, health, food and agriculture, labour, social welfare, railways, industries, and fuel and power. These administrative units should: (I) perform duties in connection with international aspects of these subjects.

(II) look after the "Central agencies and the Central institutions for the promotion of special studies and special research" which is a Central responsibility under item 30 of the third schedule; and

(II) keep in touch with the conduct of affairs in the Provinces in their respective fields, especially in regard to broad policy and planning, in order to assess the need for Central legislation or Presidential intervention.

While conceding the need for such units, the committee is, however, of the view that every possible measure should be adopted to ensure that the functions of these units do not tend to extend in the executive and operational fields which should remain the exclusive domain of the Provincial Governments.

In proposing a reorganisation of the functions and departments of the Central Government, the committee has, therefore, applied the principle that the Central Government should have an effective role to play in national co-ordination and planning in the case of those subjects which have an important bearing on the social and economic development of the country even though they may fall within the purview of the provinces. The Central Government should also deal with international aspects of these subjects, including negotiations with foreign countries and foreign aid-giving agencies. It should however be insured that in the guise of this role, the Ministries or divisions of the Central Government do not encroach upon the legitimate field of activity of the Provincial Governments and they should in no circumstances be allowed to undertake operational functions in the provincial sphere of responsibility unless they are specifically authorised under the provisions of Article 135. Even in the field of planning, the Central Ministries should only apply broad policy scrutiny of the Provincial schemes from a national angle and should refrain from undertaking detailed technical examination.

New Centre-Provinces Relationship

During the course of their discussion with the Secretaries to the Central Government, the committee took the opportunity of explaining to them the role of the Central Government under Articles 13(2); and 135 and the philosophy of the new relationship between the Centre and the Provinces. In particular, it emphasised that although the presidential form of Government envisaged a strong Central Government, this did not mean that the Centre should extend its authority to the provinces in areas which were clearly the Provincial responsibility. The shift in the Constitution towards the decentralisation should be translated into practice and the Centre should only control broad national policy and not enter into executive and operational fields. The committee, therefore, has aimed at an administrative framework which should maintain in essence the strong character of the

Central Government but only by vesting the Centre with broad policy functions, as opposed to operational or executive functions which must remain the sole responsibility of the Provincial Governments.

Suitable Machinery for Planning

In view of the responsibility of the Central Government in terms of item 6 of the third schedule relating to "national economic planning and national economic co-ordination" and Article 13(2) of the Constitution, the committee considered in consultation with the Deputy Chairman of the Planning Commission and the Secretary and Director-General of the Progressing wing of the Planning Commission the question of providing a suitable machinery for planning, progressing and implementation of development schemes.

At present there is the Economic Council and the Economic Committee of the Cabinet to deal with economic problems and to sanction development projects. The other forum for discussing economic problems, in addition to the Cabinet, is the Governors' conference.

The Economic Council, headed by the President, consists of the Governors of the Provinces, the Ministers of the Central Government incharge of the principal development Ministries, the Deputy Chairman of the Planning Commission and the Chairman of the PIDC and East and West WAPDAs.

Functions of Economic Council

Its functions are:

(i) To review the over-all economic position of the country and to formulate economic policies. (ii) To approve the five-year plans and the annual development programmes. (iii) To sanction development schemes including those falling under the five-year plans and the annual development programmes; and (iv) To review the progress made in the implementation of plans and programmes mentioned above, and to ensure that balanced economic development of all parts of the country is achieved.

The Economic Committee of the Cabinet is responsible to take day-to-day decisions on economic problems, supervise the implementation of economic policies and to sanction development schemes pending their submission to the Economic Council.

The committee considers it necessary to review the existing machinery of the Government for dealing with economic matters and to evolve a new set-up in conformity with the provisions of the Constitution.

Abolition of Economic Committee Recommended

The committee recommends that the Economic Committee of the Cabinet should be abolished and the present Economic Council should, with appropriate changes, be reconstituted as the National Economic Council in accordance with Article 145 of the Constitution. The National Economic Council should include the Finance Ministers of the Provincial Governments also.

As the National Economic Council would not be able to meet frequently, the committee considers it expedient to provide a suitable machinery for the disposal of current business and recommends that two committees should be appointed to assume the existing responsibilities of the Economic Committee of the Cabinet—one for sanctioning development schemes and the other for the co-ordination of economic policies.

Composition of Committee

The Committee recommends that the committee for the co-ordination of economic policies should consist of the following: Deputy Chairman, Planning Commission—Chairman; Secretary, Finance—Member; Secretary, Commerce—Member; Secretary, Industries—Member; Secretary, Economic Affairs—Member; Secretary, Food and Agriculture—Member.

The committee considers that it would be desirable to co-opt a Secretary having experience in East Pakistan problems in case none of the members of the committee is acquainted with the special problems of that Wing.

The committee of the National Economic Council for sanctioning development schemes may be known as the Executive Committee of the National Economic Council and its composition should be as under:

Finance Minister, Central Government—Chairman; Governor, West Pakistan or a Minister nominated by him—Member; Governor, East Pakistan or a Minister nominated by him—Member; Deputy Chairman, Planning Commission—Member; Finance Minister, East Pakistan—Member; Finance Minister, West Pakistan—Member.

The Committee should meet at least once every quarter at Lahore and Dacca and any three members should form the quorum.

The Committee also considered the question whether the functions pertaining to economic co-ordination and planning relating to subjects which constitute the specific responsibility of the provinces should be lodged in the Planning Commission or be performed by the Administrative Units to be maintained at the Centre to deal with the national and international aspects of those subjects. The Committee feels, and the Deputy Chairman, Planning Commission agree with this view, that apart from being administratively undesirable, it would be difficult for the Commission to assume total responsibility for these subjects. It would also make the Commission too unwieldy an organisation and distract them from their planning work.

The Committee is, therefore, of the view that the functions of economic co-ordination and planning in these subjects should be the responsibility of the Administrative Units at the Centre, but their responsibility should not be exercised in a manner that would result in divesting the Provincial Governments of their initial responsibility in the respective fields.

According to existing practice, the development schemes of the Provincial Governments in respect of industries, fuel and power, food, agriculture, health, labour, social welfare, and education, are scrutinised by the Central Ministries before being presented to the Central Development Working Party. Since the Provincial Governments are primarily responsible for these subjects under the Constitution, the schemes for provincial projects should be formu-

lated by the Provincial Governments and submitted direct to the
Central Development Working Party. The Administrative Units
concerned of the Central Government should be represented in
the Central Development Working Party at the highest possible
level. The Central Government should not, however, undertake a
detailed scrutiny of these projects.

Planning Cell

The Committee in this context considered the question of
providing planning cells in the Ministries and Divisions on the
pattern suggested in the existing Government orders which visu-
alise a cell in each Ministry, composed of one professionally
qualified economist and two or more technically trained officers. It
recommends that in the case of such Ministries or Divisions as
would be dealing with subjects wholly provincial in nature there
should be no need for providing a planning machinery as the
Central Ministries and Divisions would be responsible only for a
broad examination of the scheme in the national perspective. In
the case of Central projects, the planning cells should be lodged in
the technical departments themselves which are primarily and
essentially responsible for planning in their own sectors. For
example, in the C & T Division the Director-General, Ports and
Shipping should constitute a planning cell for the development of
ports and shipping, and in the Ministry of Industries, the Development Wing should be the planning cell for the development of
industries, etc. The Ministries responsible for projects concerning
more than one sector of development, may have a co-ordinating
cell, if necessary, for the purpose of integrating and co-ordinating
plans of various sectors from a broader angle of national development but not for purposes of technical scrutiny.

The Committee reviewed, in consultation with the Deputy
Chairman, Planning Commission, the Director-General, Progressive Wing and the Chief Adviser, Planning Commission, the
organisational set-up of the Planning Commission with special
reference to the Progressing Wing (formerly known as the Project
Division).

The Committee was informed that the Progressing Wing was

created with the specific purpose of providing a high-powered agency to secure speedy implementation of projects by eliminating administrative bottlenecks and other factors which retarded their progress. The second important function assigned to this wing pertained to the evaluation of projects.

The Committee noted that it had not been possible for the Progressing Wing to achieve any substantial results on the implementation side because of certain inherent difficulties in the situation itself arising from possible resentment on the part of operating agencies against outside interferences. In so far as the evaluation work was concerned, there too a good deal had yet to be achieved.

Implementation

The Chief Adviser, Planning Commission made a point that it was desirable to have a machinery for expediting implementation of projects and for tackling situations when progress was visibly retarded owing to red-tapism or other difficulties which required immediate remedial measures. He, however, conceded that it was a difficult role for any organisation to play as the agencies responsible for accomplishing the task never welcomed such interference.

The Committee considers that the role of the Progressing Wing, particularly in the light of the new Constitution does not fit in very well with the general pattern of decentralisation especially insofar as the implementation part of work is concerned. The inspection work on the implementation side of the Provincial projects would have to be abandoned in any case in respect of the Provincial projects which are the responsibility of the Provincial Governments. The Committee, therefore, agrees with the Deputy Chairman, Planning Commission and his Chief Adviser and recommends that the Progressing Wing of the Planning Commission should be abolished and the sections of the Planning Commission dealing with specific sectors should be appropriately strengthened to enable them to undertake appraisal and evaluation work. The Committee feels that if the evaluation and progressing of projects were done by those responsible for planning, the quality and standard of planning would improve. To co-ordinate the evaluation of projects of various sectors of the plan as a whole, an evaluation section should be formed in the Commission. This arrangement would help in establishing a proper co-relationship between planning and progressing and also provide for the work to be done in a more co-ordinated fashion.

The Committee, however, strongly recommends that the Provincial Governments should keep a very close watch on the implementation of projects through the Additional Chief Secretaries Incharge of Planning and Development.

House Committees

The Committee took note of the fact that important transitional problems would have to be faced and solved after the National and Provincial Assemblies come into being. The Committee recommends that the following Committees should be formed as early as possible both at the Centre and in the Provinces:

(1) Budget and Appropriations Committee,

(2) Public Accounts Committee;

(3) Standing Finance Committee for capital items; and

(4) Standing Committees for the respective legislatures for various divisions and departments.

The Committee recommends that at the Centre the following Standing Committees of the Legislature should be formed:

(*a*) Industries and Natural Resources and Commerce Divisions.

(*b*) Food and Agriculture, Rehabilitation and Works, Health, Labour and Social Welfare, and Education Divisions.

(*c*) Planning and Economic Affairs Divisions.

(*d*) External Affairs Division.

(*e*) Communications Division.

The Senior Officers of the Ministries of the Central Government and the departments in the Provinces should be associated with these Committees as members. The Standing Committees of the Legislature may be consulted by the divisions and departments concerned on legislative measures proposed to be sponsored by them and also in other matters where their advice may be useful.

For a more critical examination of legislative proposals in the legislature itself, Select Committees would of course be formed for specific items of legislation.

Ministers and Parliamentary Secretaries

The Committee feels that there is need also for the framing of new roles of Ministers and Parliamentary Secretaries and specifying their precise functions and extent of responsibilities. In view of the change in the administrative arrangements that would come into force under the Constitution the Committee holds the view that the Ministers should be concerned only with policy and not with day-to-day administration and Secretaries should deal only with Parliamentary affairs and perform "public relations" functions on behalf of their Ministers and should not be concerned with the Secretariat work. The Committee recommends that both the Central and Provincial Governments should draft appropriate rules on these lines for incorporation in the revised rules of business.

The revised rules of business for the Central Government should also cover the provisions of Articles 131(2) of the Constitution in order to define the extent of responsibility of the Ministries of the Central Government under this Article.

Secretaries and Departments

The Committee considered the question whether the Technical Head of a department should submit his cases directly to the Minister or whether the files should pass through the Secretary or the Joint Secretary. It feels that in view of the following consideration, Secretariat security regarding policy and financial implications is a necessary step and should not be discarded:

(i) The Head of a Technical Department may be able to ensure the technical soundness of the scheme but the remaining aspects of it can be examined appropriately only in the Secretariat which is properly equipped to deal in a co-ordinated fashion with all aspects of the proposals.

(ii) The efficiency of an executive department essentially depends on the effective performance of the normal operational duties in the field by its Head. If the Head of a department is employed on Secretariat work or a department to tender advice to a Minister as one of his normal functions, this is bound to affect adversely the efficiency and effectiveness of the department as he will have very little time left to attend to his field functions.

(iii) The Secretariat Security provides the necessary objectivity essential for dealing with personnel cases which cannot be effectively ensured if left to the Head of the department who is to be influenced by departmental prejudices developed over the years.

(iv) The Secretariat as a repository of conventions and precedents is in a better position to ensure that all relevant documents and papers are furnished to decision-making authority, a condition which it has been observed, technical department is often unable to fulfil.

(v) The departmental Head is generally not in a position to devote full time to international negotiations for loans or otherwise or to give due consideration to national and international implications.

The Committee, however, recommends that;

(i) The proposal of a Head of a Department should not be scrutinised at a level lower than that of a Deputy Secretary;

(ii) There should be no scrutiny of the technical aspects of the case in the Secretariat;

(iii) There should be no bar on the technicians being appointed to Secretariat posts. In some cases it may even be desirable to post a technician in preference to a generalist, and

(iv) The Heads of Department could be allowed direct access to the Ministers in cases of disagreement or might in some instances be given ex-officio Secretariat status.

Provincial Government Secretaries

Another aspect which the Committee considered as relevant to the question of reorganisation was the status of Secretaries to Provincial Governments. At present the Secretaries to Provincial Governments are equated with Deputy Secretaries and, in some cases, with Joint Secretaries to the Central Government. The

Committee considers that the Provincial Secretaries holding important charges, e.g. Finance, Industries, Planning and Development, Establishment, etc., should enjoy higher status than at present for the following reasons:

(*a*) The responsibilities of Provincial Secretaries have increased considerably, particularly after the integration of the former Provinces of West Pakistan into One Unit. They will be required to shoulder still greater responsibilities under the new Constitution with the withdrawal of Central jurisdiction from some of the important fields of Administration.

(*b*) The Provincial Secretaries are required to advise the Governor and to supervise in their own spheres, the work of Divisional Commissioners who are equal in status to Joint Secretaries to the Central Government.

(*c*) The Heads of Executive Departments generally being very senior officers, it is necessary that the Provincial Secretaries who scrutinise their work should be of appropriate seniority.

(*d*) The inter-change of officers between the Central and Provincial Governments at higher levels becomes extremely difficult with a very limited number of comparable posts in the Provincial Governments. As a result most of the senior officers spend a major part of their service in the Central Government. This position is likely to be aggravated further with the age of superannuation having been advanced to 60. In the interest of efficient administration in the Provinces it is necessary that the services of senior officers should be shared equally by the Central and Provincial Governments.

This question was considered in consultation with the Chief Secretaries of the Provincial Governments and it was decided that the Provincial Reorganisation Committee should be asked to determine the status of the Secretaries to the Provincial Governments in accordance with the importance of the department concerned. The status of Secretaries to Provincial Governments should not, however, be lower than that of a Deputy Secretary and higher than that of a Joint Secretary to the Central Government. Every effort should be made to fill these posts with officers of requisite seniority but if a post has to be filled by a junior officer, he should be given the pay and allowances admissible under the rules.

Post of Chief Secretary to Continue

The Committee also examined in consultation with the Chief Secretaries of the Provincial Governments the question whether the post of Chief Secretary should continue in the light of the changed circumstances. The Chief Secretaries explained that the pattern of administration in the Provincial Governments was different from the Central Government where the Secretaries to Provincial Government being of varying seniority a tradition had been built up for them to look up to Chief Secretaries for advice whenever necessary. The Provincial Governments had also more managerial functions and responsibilities as compared to the Central Government and these required effective co-ordination in the day-to-day work of administration which could be achieved only at the level of the Chief Secretary. The Committee came to the conclusion that since the balance of advantage lay in favour of the existing arrangements, the post of Chief Secretary in the Provinces should continue, but the functions of the Chief Secretary should be properly spelt out and their relations with the Governor, the Ministers and Secretaries and departments clearly defined.

There should be one or two Additional Chief Secretaries in each Province, for establishment and planning and development work to assist the Chief Secretaries.

Personnel Administration

The Committee took note of the fact that various All-Pakistan Services were at present being administered by different Ministries. This resulted in varying standards being followed in matters of recruitment, promotion, transfers and discipline. The system was also uneconomical as a number of Ministries had to maintain separate establishment cells. The departmental prejudices and influences also sometimes reacted unfairly on the personal prospects of individual officers in the Provinces . . . . There was a strong feeling that the "likes" and "dislikes" developed by departmental officers were not conducive to impartial and equitable treatment in personnel matters.

The Committee considers that in order to ensure uniformity of standards and greater objectivity in personnel management, all establishment work pertaining to All-Pakistan Services should be centralised in the Establishment Division and its counterparts in the Provinces.

The Committee further recommends that the existing system of personnel management should be reviewed and revitalised after the recommendations of the Pay and Service Commission have been submitted to Government.

Provincial Government

The Committee feels that as the Provincial Governments have not been used to the Ministerial system of Government for nearly three years and a half, it would be necessary for them to prepare themselves to switch over to the new system under the Constitution and to reorganise and regroup their departments according to the number of Ministers and Parliamentary Secretaries that would be justified by the size of the Provincial Administrative machinery. The Chief Secretaries of the Provincial Governments should submit their proposals to their respective Governors to enable them to reorganise the administrative set up of the Provinces before the Provincial Assemblies went into session. In their reorganisation scheme, the Provincial Governments should take special care that proper and adequate machinery is set up for the administration of the subjects that would be transferred to them from the Central Government in order to avoid any serious dislocation of work.

Transfer of Staff

The Committee also feels that it is necessary in the interest of the continuity and smooth take-over of the work by the Provincial Governments that the staff engaged on the work in the Central Government should be transferred along with the work. This will not present any difficulty in cases where *en bloc* transfer of Institutions, Departments or offices has been recommended. But in those cases where only partial transfer of functions or offices to the Provincial Government is envisaged some difficulty arises.

Even in these cases it is recommended that the Ministries of the Central Government should negotiate with their counterparts in the provinces for securing employment of staff that may be rendered surplus.

The Committee also recommends that it should be stipulated that the recruitment by Provincial Governments to those categories of posts for which surplus staff of the Central Government would be available should be made from amongst the surplus staff. The above arrangements should be made a *sine qua non* of any financial assistance that may be given by the Central Government to the Provincial Governments for undertaking new and additional functions. The position about the absorption of the Central Government staff in the Provincial Governments should be periodically reviewed to ensure implementation of this recommendation.

The Committee considers it important that the machinery for co-ordination and transitional arrangements consequential to the changes proposed by the Committee in this report should be evolved as early as possible in order to facilitate the process of transfer of some of the functions and offices of the Central Government to the Provincial Governments. The Committee therefore, recommends that the Ministries concerned should get into touch immediately with their counterparts in the provinces to work out details of the transfer of functions and offices, on the basis of the recommendations of the Committee. The question of transfer or duplication of files, where necessary, should also be examined from now on with a view to assessing the work involved and making necessary arrangements for their transfer at the appropriate time.

Reorganisation of Ministries

The Committee examined the functions of the Ministries and Divisions of the Central Government other than:

(*a*) The President's Secretariat, comprising the Cabinet and Establishment Divisions, and

(*b*) The Ministries of External Affairs, Defence and Finance, which were not affected by the provisions of the Constitution.

It interviewed the Secretaries of the various Ministries held

discussions with the Chief Secretaries of the Provincial Governments to determine the functions to be retained by the Central
Government under the Constitution. The functions of Ministries
and Divisions dealing with subjects, which under the Constitution
were essentially the responsibility of the Provincial Governments,
namely, Food and Agriculture, Health, Labour and Social Welfare, Industries, and Fuel, Power and Natural Resources, were
scrutinised in great detail with a view to transferring to Provincial
Governments the functions which belonged to them in accordance
with the provisions of the Constitution.

The Committee did not find time to examine the staff position of
the Ministries and Departments in the light of the Recommendations made in this report. It is, therefore, recommended that
Efficiency and O and M Wing should conduct a survey on the basis of the changes proposed—particularly in the Attached Departments and subordinate offices of the Ministries of Education,
Health, Labour and Social Welfare, Food and Agriculture, Industries and Fuel, Power and Natural Resources—and submit its staff
reports and recommendations for reorganisation of these offices if
any, as far as possible before the 1st July, 1962.

Reorganisation of the Central Government

The Committee after having determined the functions and
organisations of the existing Ministries and Divisions in the light of
the Constitution considered the organisational pattern of the
Central Government. It recommends that the organisational structure of the Central Government should be as follows:

There should be a President's Secretariat which should consist
of the following Divisions:

  (i) Cabinet Division.
 (ii) Establishment Division.
(iii) Planning Division.
 (iv) Economic Affairs Divisions, and (Planning Commission).
  (v) States and Frontier Regions Divisions.

In addition to the President's Secretariat, there should be the
following Ministries:

(i) Ministry of Defence.
(ii) Ministry of External Affairs.
(iii) Ministry of Finance.
(iv) Ministry of Commerce.
(v) Ministry of Home and Kashmir Affairs (including (1) Home Affairs Division and (2) Kashmir Affairs Division).
(vi) Ministry of Industries, and Natural Resources (including (1) Industries Division and (2) Natural Resources Division).
(vii) Ministry of Communications.
(viii) Ministry of Health, Labour and Social Welfare (including (1) Health Division and (2) Labour and Social Welfare Division).
(ix) Ministry of Education and Information (including (1) Education Division and (2) Broadcasting Division).
(x) Ministry of Law and Parliamentary Affairs (including (1) Law Division and (2) Parliamentary Affairs Division).
(xi) Ministry of Agriculture and Works (including (1) Food and Agriculture Division and (2) Rehabilitation and Works Division).

There would thus be 22 Divisions as follows:

1. Cabinet Division.
2. Establishment Division.
3. Planning Division.
4. Economic Affairs Division.
5. States and Frontier Regions Division.
6. Defence Division.
7. External Affairs Division.
8. Finance Division.
9. Commerce Division.
10. Home Affairs Division.
11. Kashmir Affairs Division.
12. Industries Division.
13. Natural Resources Division.
14. Communications Division.
15. Health Division.
16. Labour and Social Welfare Division.
17. Education Division.
18. Information and Broadcasting Division.
19. Law Division.
20. Parliamentary Affairs Division.
21. Food and Agriculture Division.
22. Rehabilitation and Works Division.

The Committee recommends that depending on the importance of the work, a division should be placed under the charge of a Secretary or a Joint Secretary, but in a Ministry with more than one division, the Secretary may even control a division through a Deputy Secretary. The Committee further recommends that:

(a) The President may have one or two special assistants with the rank and emoluments not higher than those of Cabinet Ministers.

(b) There should be a Special Secretary in the Ministry of Finance for implementation of the recommendations of the Pay and Service Commission.

(c) The Ministry of Information and Education should be under the overall charge of one Secretary. This arrangement should, however, be made after the expiry of the contract of the present Secretary of Education who is particularly implementing the Government decisions on the report of the Education Reforms Commission. Until then, the Ministry of Information and Education should have two Secretaries, one Incharge of Information and Broadcasting Division, and the other Incharge of the Education Division.

(d) A Joint Secretary, Information and Broadcasting Division, should be located at Dacca and should be responsible for the publicity of the Central Government in that Wing;

(e) The Establishment Committee of the Cabinet should go into session immediately after the regrouping of Ministries and Divisions is approved by Cabinet in order to select Secretaries. This should be finalised as early as possible by the Establishment Secretary in consultation with the Selection Board.

(f) The Committee recommends that the Standing Organisation Committee consisting of the Establishment Secretary, the Cabinet and the Finance Secretary, should act as the Implementation Committee to ensure that Cabinet decisions on the recommendations made in this report are expeditiously implemented.

The Committee feels that in translating the spirit of the Constitution which laid special stress on rapid economic development of the country any scheme of reorganisation should be accompanied by effective financial devices to achieve the goal set by the

Constitution. In this connection, the Committee has considered the report prepared by the Efficiency and O. and M. Wing after review of the new financial procedure and recommends it for separate consideration by the Finance Ministry and other concerned at an early date.

Summary of Recommendations

It would be necessary to maintain appropriate but small administrative units in the Central Government to deal with Education, Health, Food and Agriculture, Labour, Social Welfare, Railways, Industries and Fuel and Power.

The Central Ministries Divisions should not encroach upon the legitimate field of activity of the Provincial Governments or undertake operational functions in those spheres. Even in the field of planning, the Central Ministries Divisions should only apply broad police scrutiny from a national angle to the provincial schemes and should refrain from undertaking detailed technical examination.

The Economic Committee of the Cabinet should be abolished and the present Economic Council should with appropriate changes, be reconstituted by the National Economic Council in accordance with Article 145 of the Constitution. The National Economic Council should include the Finance Ministers of the Provincial Government also.

Two Committees should be appointed to assume the existing responsibilities of the Economic Committee of the Cabinet—one for sanctioning Development Schemes and the other for the co-ordination of economic policies.

The Committee for the co-ordination of economic policies should consist of the following:

Deputy Chairman Planning Commission (Chairman); Secretary, Finance; Secretary, Commerce; Secretary, Industries; Secretary, Food and Agriculture (Members).

It would be desirable to co-opt a Secretary having experience of East Pakistan problems in case none of the members of the Committee is acquainted with the special problems of that Wing.

The Committee of the National Economic Council for sanctioning development schemes should be known as the Executive Committee of the National Economic Council and its composition should be: Finance Minister, Central Government (Chairman); Governor, West Pakistan or a Minister nominated by him; Governor, East Pakistan or a Minister nominated by him; Deputy Chairman, Planning Commission; Finance Minister, East Pakistan; and Finance Minister, West Pakistan (Members).

The Committee should meet at least once every quarter at Lahore and Dacca and any three members should form the quorum.

The Provincial Governments should submit their projects direct to the Central Development Working Party but the administrative unit concerned of the Central Government should be represented in the Central Development Working Party, at the highest possible level. The Central Government should not, however, undertake a detailed scrutiny of these projects.

(i) In the case of Ministries Divisions dealing with the subjects wholly Provincial in nature, no planning cell should be provided as they would be responsible for broad examination of the schemes in the national perspective;

(ii) In the case of Central Projects, the planning cell should be lodged in the Technical Departments themselves, which are primarily and essentially responsible for planning in their own sectors, and

(iii) Ministries and Divisions responsible for projects concerning more than one sector of development may have a co-ordinating cell, of necessity, for the purpose of integrating and coordinating plans of various sectors from a broader angle of national development but not for purposes of technical scrutiny.

(i) The Progressing Wing of the Planning Commission should be abolished;

(ii) The various sections of the Planning Commission dealing with specific sectors should be appropriately strengthened to enable them to undertake appraisal and evaluation work;

(iii) To co-ordinate the evaluation of projects of various sectors of the Plan as a whole, an evaluation section should be formed in the Planning Commission, and

(iv) The Provincial Governments should keep a very close watch on the implementation of projects through Additional Chief Secretaries incharge of Planning and Development.

The following House Committees should be formed as early as possible both at the Centre and in the Provinces:

(1) Budget and Appropriation Committee;

(2) Public Accounts Committee;

(3) Standing Finance Committee for Capital Items, and

(4) Standing Committees of the respective legislatures for various Divisions and Departments.

At the Centre the following Standing Committees of the legislature should be formed: (*a*) Industries and Natural Resources and Commerce Divisions; (*b*) Food and Agriculture, Rehabilitation and Works, Health Labour and Social Welfare, and Education Division; (*c*) Planning and Economic Affairs Division; (*d*) External Affairs Division, and (*e*) Communications Division.

The senior officers of the Ministries of the Central Government and the Departments in the Provinces should be associated with these Committees as members. The Standing Committees of the legislature may be consulted by the Divisions and Departments concerned on legislative measures proposed to be sponsored by them and also in other matters where their advice may be useful. For a more critical examination of legislative proposals in the legislature itself, Select Committees would of course be formed for specific items of legislation.

The Ministers should be concerned only with policy and not with day-to-day administration, and Parliamentary Secretaries should deal only with Parliamentary Affairs and perform "public relations" functions on behalf of their Ministers and should not be concerned with the Secretariat work. Both the Central and Provincial Governments should draft appropriate rules on these lines for incorporation in the revised rules of business.

Responsibilities

The revised rules of business for the Central Government should also cover the provisions of Article 131(2) of the Constitution in order to define the extent of responsibility of the Ministries of the Central Government under this Article.

(i) The proposal of a Head of a department should not be scrutinised in the Administrative Ministry at a level lower than that of a Deputy Secretary.

(ii) There should be no scrutiny of the technical aspects of the case in the Secretariat.

(iii) There should be no bar on the technicians being appointed to Secretariat posts. In some cases it may even be desirable to post a technician in preference to a generalist.

(iv) The Heads of department should be allowed direct access to the Ministers in cases of disagreement or might in some instances be given ex-officio Secretariat status.

The Provincial Reorganisation Committee should determine the status of the Secretaries to the Provincial Governments in accordance with the importance of the department concerned. The status of Secretaries to Provincial Governments should not however, be lower than that of a Deputy Secretary and higher than that of a Joint Secretary to the Central Government. Every effort should be made to fill those posts with officers of requisite seniority but if a post has to be filled by a junior officer, he should be given the pay and allowance admissible under the rules.

The post of Chief Secretary in the Province should continue, but the functions of the Chief Secretary should be properly spelt out and their relations with the Governor, the Ministers and Secretaries of Departments clearly defined. There should be one or two Additional Chief Secretaries in each Province for Establishment, and Planning and Development work to assist the Chief Secretaries.

All Establishment work pertaining to All-Pakistan Services should be centralised in the Establishment Division and its counterparts in the Provinces.

Personnel Management

The existing system of personnel management should be reviewed and revitalised after the recommendations of the Pay and Services Commission have been submitted to Government.

The Provincial Governments should reorganise and group their departments according to the number of Ministers and Parliamentary Secretaries that would be justified by the size of the Provincial administrative machinery. In their reorganisation scheme, the Provincial Governments should take special care that proper and adequate machinery is set up for the Administration of the subjects that would be transferred to them from the Central Government in order to avoid any serious dislocation of work.

It is necessary in the interest of the continuity and smooth take over of the work by the Provincial Governments that the staff engaged on the work in the Central Government should be transferred along with the work. This will not present any difficulty in cases where "en bloc" transfer of institutions, departments or offices has been recommended. But in those cases where only partial transfer of functions or offices to the Provincial Governments is envisaged some difficulties may arise. Even in those cases it is recommended the Ministries of the Central Government should negotiate with their counterparts in the Provinces for securing employment of staff that may be rendered surplus. It should be stipulated that recruitment by Provincial Governments to those categories of posts for which surplus staff of the Central Government would be available, should be made a "sine qua non" of any financial assistance that may be given by the Central Government to Provincial Government for undertaking new and additional functions. The position about the absorption of the Central Government staff in the Provincial Governments should be periodically reviewed to ensure implementation of this recommendation.

The Ministries concerned should get in touch immediately with their counterparts in the Provinces to work out details of the transfer of function and offices on the basis of the recommendations of the Committee. The question of transfer or duplication of files, where necessary, should also be examined from now on with a view to assessing the work involved and making necessary arrangements for their transfer at the appropriate time.

The Efficiency and O and M Wing should conduct a survey on the basis of the changes proposed—particularly in the attached departments and subordinate offices of the Ministries of Education, Health, Labour and Social Welfare, Food and Agriculture,

Industries and Fuel, Power and Natural Resources—and submit its staff review reports and recommendations for reorganisation of these offices, if any, as soon as possible before July 1, 1962.

Organisational Structure

The organisational structure of the Central Government should be as follows:

There should be a President's Secretariat which should consist of the following Divisions:

(i) Cabinet Division.
(ii) Establishment Division.
(iii) Planning Division (Planning Commission).
(iv) Economic Affairs Division.
(v) States and Frontier Regions Division.

In addition to the President's Secretariat, there should be the the following Ministries:

(i) Ministry of Defence.
(ii) Ministry of External Affairs.
(iii) Ministry of Finance.
(iv) Ministry of Commerce.
(v) Ministry of Home and Kashmir Affairs. Including (1) Home Affairs Division and (2) Kashmir Affairs Division.
(vi) Ministry of Industries and Natural Resources. Including (1) Industries, Division and (2) Natural Resources Division.
(vii) Ministry of Communications.
(viii) Ministry of Health, Labour and Social Welfare. Including (1) Health Division and (2) Labour and Social Welfare Division.
(ix) Ministry of Education and Information. Including (1) Education Division and (2) Information and Broadcasting Division.
(x) Ministry of Law and Parliamentary Affairs. Including (1) Law Division and (2) Parliamentary Affairs Division.
(xi) Ministry of Agriculture and Works. Including (1) Food and Agriculture Division and (2) Rehabilitation and Works Division.

The President may have one or two special assistants with the rank and emoluments not higher than those of the Cabinet Ministers.

There should be a Special Secretary in the Ministry of Finance for implementation of the recommendations of the Pay and Service Commission.

The Ministry of Information and Education should be under the overall charge of one Secretary. This arrangement should, however, be made after the expiry of the contract of the present Secretary of Education who is particularly implementing the Government's decision on the Report of the Education Reforms Commission, until the Ministry of Education and Information should have two Secretaries, one Incharge of the Information and Broadcasting Division, and the other Incharge of the Education Division.

A Joint Secretary, Information Division, should be located at Dacca.

The Establishment Committee of the Cabinet should go into session immediately after the above regrouping of Ministries and Divisions is approved by Cabinet in order to select Secretaries for the reorganised Ministries and Division. The selection and appointment of Joint Secretaries should be finalised as early as possible by the Establishment Secretary in consultation with the Selection Board.

The Standing Organisation Committee consisting of the Establishment Secretary, the Cabinet Secretary and the Finance Secretary should act as the Implementation Committee to ensure that Cabinet decisions on the recommendations made in this report are expeditiously implemented.

The suggestions made by the Efficiency and O. and M. Wing for the improvement of the new system of financial control are commended for separate consideration by the Finance Ministry and others concerned at an early date.

Detailed recommendations for the Reorganisation of the Ministries and Divisions and their attached departments and subordinate offices are contained in an annexure.

Address of Chief Justice A. R. Cornelius on Corruption, August 12, 1960

[*Explanatory Note.* Chief Justice A. R. Cornelius of the Pakistan Supreme Court is a former officer of the Indian Civil Service (now a member of the Civil Service of Pakistan) who has long been interested in administrative problems. In various court judgments and in some ten major public statements, he has developed a philosophy of administration which, taken as a whole, constitutes the most systematic administrative doctrine which has yet emerged in the ideology of Pakistan. In this address, he urges consideration of the French system of administrative tribunals as a means of controlling corruption. Developing a concept of "vertical combination," he implies that the aloofness of senior officers did not conduce to greater probity but actually encouraged subordinates who were not in collusion with their superiors to dishonestly implicate their superiors. The screening of ICS officers to which the chief justice refers is the same screening referred to by President Ayub in Appendix 2 and analyzed in the text on pages 291–299. This address was given at a meeting of the Rotary Club in Lahore, August 12, 1960.]

I deem it a privilege to be allowed this opportunity to address this distinguished gathering. Some of you probably feel that the subject which I have chosen for my address is too large in scope to be suitably dealt with in the course of a dinner meeting. I freely concede that that is the case and that moreover it is a subject which bristles with a great many difficulties not only of a practical nature, but also in relation to policies which vary from time to time. Accordingly, I have attempted to confine this talk to one or two aspects of the matter only, and even on those matters, to say as little as is decently possible. I may say that apart from the legal and judicial aspects, my acquaintance with what I may call the widespread fabric of corruption is extremely slight.

Briefly, one may define corruption among public servants as the acceptance or demand of consideration from a member of the public for doing or omitting to do some act which lies within the powers of the particular public servant. Generally, it may be said that whenever a public servant has it in his power to expedite or delay the decision of a case and, again, whenever it is placed within his complete discretion to decide a case in one way or in another way whatever the circumstances, the occasion at once arises for the person affected in the case to feel or to be made to feel that he can gain an advantage by becoming a source of gratification to the officer.

Corruption there has always been even in Governments of the most primitive kind. In recent years, however, and particularly with the growing control exercised by Governments in regard to distribution of goods and services and facilities which are all essential to the life of the community, occasions of this kind have been greatly multiplied. The difficulties in the way of proving acts of corruption are very well known and I shall not dwell on them. In addition, there are the well-recognised difficulties in the way of proving an act of corruption to the satisfaction of a court, if that court is governed by the strict rules of evidence which are designed in our country to provide every facility for an accused person to take benefit of all doubts and of lacunae or gaps in the evidence, even though they may be created by himself.

But what may be difficult for a court need not necessarily have the same obstructive effect for an honest authority working within the department to investigate and prove. That is the really strong argument in favour of administrative tribunals.

The system of administrative tribunals exists and is operated in a thorough-going fashion at all levels of the public service in France. These tribunals are composed of public servants sitting with others who are men of position or distinction in public life with a mature experience of affairs all drawn from a large council known as the *Conseil d'État*. Where a court would be guided as much by what is brought on the record as by what it thinks is kept out of the record, the administrative tribunal, applying more elastic principles of evidence and enjoying the advantage through

actual knowledge of the conditions and maturity of experience of
affairs, does not need to exercise the same discrimination and
selectiveness in receiving evidence, and otherwise becoming acquainted with all the facts and circumstances of the case. Accordingly, it is placed in a much better position than is a court to
determine the rights and wrongs of the matter, and the general
result is as it might be expected to be, namely, that the decisions of
these tribunals in France are known to give general satisfaction
both to public servants, as well as to members of the public whose
grievances they are charged to redress.

Recently, a certain amount of attention has been given in our
country as well to the possibility of introducing a system of
administrative tribunals here. Since the suggestion involves a
serious departure from the British practice, which the people are
so thoroughly accustomed to and which they regard as the only
possible system, there has so far not grown any real strength of
public opinion in favour of introducing these tribunals. One
important commission whose report was published some considerable time ago expressed the opinion that to introduce these
tribunals at present would be inopportune. My feeling is that if the
working of these tribunals in the country of their origin, namely,
France, were examined with sympathy and a keen eye to the
modifications necessary for securing the same benefits in the
different conditions prevailing in Pakistan, it might be found
possible to alter that view. I need not go into the question any
further, but I would like to register my opinion that introduction
of administrative tribunals with the necessary powers would provide a strong agency for suppression of corruption among public
servants, at the instance of the members of the public who have
suffered injury at the hands of such public servants.

In the absence of administrative tribunals, it is necessary for us
to make the best use we can of the existing means of redress,
namely, either through Government agencies or through the court.
I am sure that all of you like myself would rather avoid coming to
a conclusion that the Government is not a safe agent to whom the
discovery and punishments of acts of corruption by its servants
can be entrusted with full confidence. But, admittedly, the body of

public servants graded one above the other constitutes a very important part of the Government itself. In the formation of opinion at the highest level of Government, these public servants play almost a decisive part at certain times and, in certain climates, the entire Government is controlled and operated by public servants.

In those circumstances, if uncontrolled power be given to any section of the administration to deal with corruption in that section, the only hope of success would lie in the absence of community of interest between the different grades of officers who compose that department. In one respect, of course, if the department is an integrated whole, there must always be community of interest among all the public servants who compose it, whatever their grade may be. Merely in order that it should run smoothly, it is necessary that they should work together. But if it be supposed that the canker of corruption has entered deep into the operation of this department, one might say that the control could yet be exercised if at any of the higher levels, the officers are free of corruption. In the case of certain departments it has been possible at certain times in the past to make such a supposition. In the case of my own Service, the Indian Civil Service, the condition of lack of combination between them and the public servants working under them was the maintenance of a very clear distinction between the status enjoyed by members of the Service and those public servants belonging to other services.

Many of you will at once ask how then it happens that so many members of the old I.C.S. were got rid of by the method of screening last year. To that the reply which I think can be given in all sincerity is that it was mainly because there was no vertical combination between them and their subordinates that evidence was forthcoming against those I.C.S. officers who had allowed themselves to depart from the highest principles in the discharge of their duties. And if you ask for a further, although indirect, proof in support of my view, you might consider that the casualty rate in a number of other departments, where the possibility of vertical combination in the practice of corruption was not excluded by any obstructive factor, was in fact very low. With reference to two or three great departments, their officers are able to declare proudly that the casualty rate was in fact nil. Several of these departments are money-earning and money-spending departments on a very large scale.

I have spoken of vertical combination and I trust that all of you understand what I mean by that expression. I will try now as briefly as possible to examine the law upon the subject with a view to showing whether or not it encourages this kind of malpractice to the detriment of the public interest, and the maintenance of corruption at its present level. Some of you may be aware that in this country the Government retains it in its power to allow public servants to be prosecuted or not by the method of sanction. Until early in the year 1947, there was but a single provision in the law on the point and that was in the Criminal Procedure Code, where section 197 laid down that if a judge or a magistrate or any public servant of the higher classes, namely, those who could not be removed from their office except by an order of the Central Government or a Provincial Government, was accused of any criminal offence "alleged to have been committed by him while acting or purporting to act in the discharge of his official duty," the prosecution should not proceed without the sanction of the proper Government. You can at once see the purpose of this provision. Judges and magistrates and public servants of the highest classes are invested with powers and duties, but actions by them outside those powers or outside the scope of those duties, which have the effect of injuring a member of the public, are conceivable.

The sanction then concedes that an injured subject should be able to proceed against any judge or magistrate or higher public official who caused injury to him by some action outside his power or duty. The Criminal Procedure Code left it to the courts to decide when any charge was brought before them whether the action was outside such powers or duties. At the same time it was possible to conceive of actions which could be thought to be within the scope of the officer's duties, and yet to be in excess of his precise powers. The frequent case is of an officer who becoming enraged on finding a violation of some law which he is appointed to enforce, goes to the length of abusing and even striking a member of the public with whom he is dealing in the discharge of his duties. It is possible of course that an officer may equally go to excess in dealing with his subordinates. In such cases one may well assume that the intention being to discharge the duty, where the injury was not very great, the Government could use its full administrative control to punish the officer adequately, and also to compensate the sufferer. But, as I have said already where this condition was not satisfied the sufferer was at liberty to raise the matter before the court and have it decided in the ordinary way. In fact it is one of the most important liberties allowed to a subject in a country with a liberal form of Government that he is free at all times to take his grievances before a proper court. No Government of a country enjoying a liberal constitution would wish at any time to be in the position of being blamed for stifling a prosecution.

That was the condition up to 1947, in which year the Prevention of Corruption Act was passed, which was later supported in 1948 and subsequent years by other instruments. These new laws deal expressly with bribery in all its forms and, in addition, with embezzlement of public money and with acts of cheating, forgery and falsification of accounts by public servants.

As to embezzlement and the other three offences I have mentioned one may say that since these take place entirely inside the framework of the operations of the Government, it is proper that the investigation and punishment of these offences should be made the exclusive duty of the Government, so that the Government might have complete discretion whether or not they will bring the case to a court rather than to punish the official at fault within their disciplinary power over him. The new laws indeed prescribe that no prosecution for the offences of embezzlement, cheating, forgery and falsification of accounts by public servants shall be commenced or continued without the sanction of the appropriate Government. In addition, these offences are to be investigated by a special police staff and to be tried by special judges.

But what may be more easily open to question is the provision which has been added that all offences of bribery by public servants in all its forms shall fall within the same rule, namely, that the Government sanction is necessary for a prosecution, that the investigation shall be by the Special Police and the trial shall be before a special judge. The condition of the matter lying entirely within the operation of the Government does not obtain in this case since bribery is never as between public servants but is between a member of the public and a public servant making a perverted use of his function and power. Such an abuse of power causing direct injury to a member of the public is a crime if there be a demand of acceptance of illegal gratification. No one would suppose for a minute that such a duty is intended to lie within the field of operations of any department and, therefore, there might be thought to be a departure from principle in giving the Government an uncontrolled and unguided discretion to decide whether or not such offence shall be placed before the Court.

In other words, the existence in the present law of a power in the Government to sanction a prosecution or refuse sanction for an alleged act of bribery by the public servants might, in certain aspect, be regarded as a naked power to stifle a prosecution. The right vested in the member of the public to take his grievance before a court is thus taken away in a respect which is of the gravest importance to the public interest.

It is here that the danger of vertical combination inside a department becomes so clearly apparent. If the power of granting sanction were ordered to be exercised by some officer or some group of officers not directly connected with the working of the department, this danger of vertical combination might perhaps be avoided, yet, at the same time, the violation of the fundamental right of seeking redress before the courts would remain.

I do not wish to suggest that the new laws have not been made with sufficient circumspection or that their purpose is not that of providing in good faith a system by which the disease of corruption may be fully and effectively eradicated. What I am attempting to stress is that for the purpose of bringing the evil to light, full consideration may perhaps have not been given to the important circumstance that the member of the public who suffers should be at liberty to take his matters before a court and to attempt to establish it there in case the governmental machinery is not available to him. That is to say, in a case where the Government declines to proceed further with a complaint of corruption or a report of a reputation of corruption of an individual or even of general corruption in a department, the machinery should be provided by which the injured subject should be enabled to raise the matter and to attempt to establish his grievance by such means as are within his powers.

An administrative tribunal might serve this purpose admirably but it is not my purpose at present to make a full or a close examination of the available ways and means. The whole problem is pretty well within the cognisance of all responsible authorities, and that has been indeed the case for a very considerable time. My concern is at present merely to point out that the law as it operates at present is open to criticism on the ground that it debars citizens from the exercise of a fundamental right to ventilate their grievances before competent authorities and that it also carries the powers of the Government to a point at which the danger of stifling prosecutions is clearly apparent.

Address of Chief Justice A. R. Cornelius on
Administrative Tribunals, October 1, 1960

[*Explanatory Note.* In the address reproduced below, delivered at the All-Pakistan Lawyers' Convention in Karachi, October 1, 1960, Chief Justice Cornelius elaborates further his advocacy of a system of administrative tribunals similar to the French model. In the talk reproduced in Appendix 10, he viewed such tribunals as a means of preventing corruption; here he regards them as suitable means for redress of internal bureaucratic grievance and of external bureaucratic action. He refers to the two leading judgments in the Noorul Hassan and Tariq Transport cases, which are analyzed in the text on pages 303 and 306.]

It is probably true to say that throughout the period since the Partition thinking minds in Pakistan have applied themselves to the difficult and important questions of the most suitable political and administrative organisations for the special conditions of the country.

At certain times, it is true, the general deterioration had reached such a pitch as to react, even upon the most vigorous minds, so as to produce a feeling of apathy. But in recent years, the conditions have been such as to induce once again the belief that the search for better schemes of things in every branch of the public life could perhaps be profitably pursued.

My purpose today is to refer once again to a subject upon which I have spoken briefly once or twice already, namely, the question whether a well-tried system of justice and law, compendiously described as *droit administratif*, which is established in France and some other European countries, might not with advantage be pondered over for possible adoption in our own country.

On this occasion, I propose to refer this learned assembly to a few recent cases before the Supreme Court with which all of you are no doubt completely familiar. The first is the well-known case of Noorul Hassan [*Noorul Hassan and others* v. *The Federation of Pakistan* (1956) P.S.C.R. 128] decided in 1956 upon appeal by a number of police officers of Karachi who had been dismissed by a peremptory order on the ground that their work had been found unsatisfactory.

The case engaged the full attention of the Full Bench of the Supreme Court for no less than nine days, and each of the Judges delivered a separate judgment.

In the course of the leading judgment, the Chief Justice, Mr. Justice Muhammad Munir, had occasion to make certain observations which I think you will find of interest in the present discussion. The question which the learned Chief Justice placed before himself was as to the right of the Government to dismiss a public servant under the terms of his contract, viewed against the mandatory provisions of Sub-section (3) of Section 240 of the Government of India Act.

He observed [pp. 150–151 of the Noorul Hassan decision] that termination of services would not:

> amount to removal or dismissal where the services of Government servants have been dispensed with in accordance with the terms of his employment, whether those terms are to be found in the rules or the order of his appointment or his contract of service. Suppose, for example, a person is employed for a year to a post which is either a permanent post or which has been sanctioned for a period of five years, one of the conditions of his employment being that his services may be terminated on one month's notice. Before the expiry of the year the servant misbehaves or the authority competent to terminate his services believes that he has misbehaved and without any inquiry into the matter he is given a month's notice of discharge. In such a case, it cannot possibly be contended that because the reason for the termination of his services was suspected misbehaviour, the order terminating his services was illegal or wrongful and that he had a right to come to a court of law for reinstatement or for compensation.

Then the learned Chief Justice went on to say:

As long as the action to dispense with the services of an employee is in accordance with the terms on which he was employed, it is wholly immaterial whether the reason for the termination was misbehaviour or some other reason. And the position does not differ even if in the order terminating the service it is expressly stated or hinted that the employee's service has not come up to a certain standard. . . .

The learned Chief Justice then opined [p. 151] that:

A contrary view would in all such cases enable the employee to prove by evidence *aliunde* that though the order terminating his services did not state that he had been guilty of misbehaviour or had been found unfit, that was the real reason for the termination of his services, and that, therefore, the order having been passed without giving him an opportunity to show cause against the termination of his services, the termination was illegal and therefore actionable.

I did not find it necessary to deal with this particular question in my judgment in the case, but, I remember clearly that the authorities cited showed how much attention had been attracted by this problem in at least one of the High Courts in Pakistan, and in a number of the Superior Courts in India where also the Government of India Act had been the constitutional instrument for a great number of years.

Quite clearly, two views could be taken and a sustained argument to produce the contrary result from that appearing in the quotations I have read from the judgment of the learned Chief Justice could be presented. The matter in issue was of extreme importance. The retention or otherwise in service of an officer or officers in so important a department as the Police, actually concerns the public interest.

A person could undoubtedly, in all conscience, hold the view that the opinion of the Government must prevail, since it could not be compelled by any outside authority to entrust its powers for the enforcement of law and order to a person or persons in whom it had ceased to place any trust. Its duty to the public would oblige the Government acting honestly, to withdraw the powers which had been delegated to these officers for the purpose of maintaining law and order, once it was found that they were unfit to possess and exercise those powers.

On the other side, the question might have been placed as one of legal rights, i.e., the legal right in law to hold a particular office unless and until the holder was deprived of it by due process. Strong though this argument might be or might be made to appear to be, in the last analysis one could say that a legal right to an office in an individual could not transcend the public interest which was involved in the bona fide and efficient exercise of the powers vested in the office. The problem on the one hand was a legal problem and, on the other, was very closely connected with the functions of the administration.

It is not surprising to find that such a problem has received consideration at the hands of the French *Conseil d'Etat* which is the administrative court at the apex of the hierarchy of such tribunals in France. As recently as the years 1947 and 1950 cases have occurred where public servants were retired on pension for disciplinary reasons. This action was taken under a statute which gave power to a new Government in France in quite absolute terms to retire public servants on pension after fifteen years' service. When the cases came before the *Conseil d'Etat* they held that to exercise the power of compulsory retirement in order to secure disciplinary ends was a *detournement de procedure*, that is to say, the misuse or malversation of procedural power, because disciplinary action against such servants was subjected to many safeguards devised in their interests.

I have selected this example and dwelt on it at some length especially in order to indicate that although the *Conseil d'Etat* is a body composed of public servants, yet the common charge made against it that it cannot be trusted to do justice as between the administration and the subject or any public servant is quite without foundation.

In these cases, the *Conseil d'Etat* took a view of the matter which any Court, however strong its attitudes, could only take with hesitation and could never take with confidence that it would not be acting to the serious detriment of the administration thereby.

Situated as it is, in a country like ours, the judiciary may well on occasions be found reluctant to embark on a course of open conflict with the executive in matters affecting the stability of the country or the strength and safety of the administration in its most important aspects. That attitude need not necessarily be the result of pusillanimity as so many suppose, or of time-serving as many believe. It could well be understood as being inspired by a desire for the over-all integrity and health of the body politic. Head-on collisions between any two of the three great limbs of State are apt to shake its very foundations. Moreover it is often said that in administrative matters, the judiciary should not interfere in such a way as to find itself in a position of having to exercise a discretion which has been vested by law in the executive, since in effect that would amount to usurping the functions of the executive.

These are some of the considerations which Courts might well place before themselves in approaching questions of the kind we are here considering. But the *Conseil d'Etat* was faced with no such difficulties. It is a body whose jurisdiction has in the 160 years of its life been securely established as covering every aspect of the internal administrative field. Any Government or official act which is fairly within public powers may be brought before it and no Minister of authority objects to a judgment being passed upon his action by the *Conseil d'Etat*. Ministers and authorities regularly appear and offer to justify their acts in the confidence that the *Conseil d'Etat* being composed of selected public servants of high integrity and ability, knows the necessities of the administration of which it has a thorough understanding and will not interfere with any executive authority any more than is consistent with the due performance of his functions.

It is not content with mere formality or legality, although it places the highest value upon correctness of form. It sets great stress upon the requirements of reason, and especially it battles against "organised injustice." What it acts upon is that portion of the field of administrative power which lies in the discretion of statutory authorities. To an increasing extent, discretionary powers must of necessity in the conditions of the modern State be vested in executive authorities.

The next case [*Tariq Transportation Company* v. *Sargodha Bhera Bus Service and others* (1958) 2 P.S.C.R. 71] from the Supreme Court to which I propose to refer was decided in the year 1958, and arose out of certain proceedings of the Regional Transport Authority (RTA) of Lahore whereby some stage carriage permits were granted to transport companies. A writ petition having been moved in the High Court by one of these companies which had objected to the grant of permits to another company to operate buses on the same route.

The High Court granted the writ prayed for, and quashed all the proceedings of the RTA. The case coming up on appeal before the Supreme Court was heard for no less than six days and there had been a lengthy hearing in the High Court as well. The unanimous view of the Judges in the Supreme Court, reached after lengthy examination of relevant cases in the English jurisdiction, before the Privy Council, and in India, was that the grant of such licences at a hearing as provided by the relevant statute could not be regarded as a quasi-judicial proceeding and therefore, a writ of certiorari which had been granted must be recalled.

If an account be taken of the time and the effort which has been spent by parties in Courts in England and in other countries like our own where the principles which are followed in England, are accepted and acted upon, in obtaining orders of this negative kind, the total would be found to be impressive to the point of being disheartening.

In each of these cases no doubt whatsoever could be entertained that there was a substantial matter in issue. An executive authority had acted in its discretion in such a way as to cause material injury to the party which sought redress. The circumstances of the exercise of the executive power were in each case of considerable complexity, and the courts were undoubtedly well advised to avoid interfering with the action, as to the surrounding circumstances, an essential nature of which they could not be as well informed as the executive.

It is axiomatic that the executive knows and the judiciary does not know the necessities of the administration and the judiciary, therefore, cannot interfere within the discretionary field strictly reserved to the executive without running the risk of having to undertake the performance of important executive duties itself.

In the Tariq Transport Company case, the RTA whose actions came under inquiry was under no obligation in the particular case to give its reasons when it granted a permit, or when it rejected a representation by a person opposing the grant of a permit.

It had been argued that since an appeal was competent against an order of this kind, it was incumbent upon the RTA to give its reasons.

In the judgment which I myself wrote in the case I find myself saying that I did not consider this ground a sufficient one for holding that reasons should have been given, and I also said that "where the record itself did not afford sufficient reasons upon which the appeal could be decided, the appellate authority could always obtain from the RTA a statement upon which its action was based."

I find that the *Conseil d'Etat* among its "Rules of Due Administration" has laid down that all administrative acts must be supported by reasons, even though the statute should be given. The argument that is adopted is that in judging an allegation of excess of powers, it is necessary to appreciate both the negative prohibitions of the law as well as its positive requirements, and this cannot be done unless the administration furnishes the grounds upon which it exercised its discretion.

If such a function were entrusted to the courts here, the principle enunciated by the *Conseil d'Etat* would undoubtedly be found to be most valuable. But the courts are debarred from such an exercise, and the precedents which we follow have gone to the length of avoiding entry into a field which, on the words of the statute, might be thought to be very suitable for judicial review.

I refer on this point to the case of Nakkuda Ali [*Nakkuda Ali* v. *M. F. de S. Jayaratne*, PLD 1950 Privy Council 102] before the Privy Council in 1949, where the question arose whether the action of a Controller in withdrawing a licence which had been issued to Nakkuda Ali to act as a dealer was amendable to the writ of certiorari. The law in the case was not as favourable to the executive as in the case of the Tariq Transport Company. The powers of the Controller to cancel the licence was to be exercised only when he had "reasonable grounds to believe" that the holder was unfit to be allowed to continue as a dealer.

A great many persons, with ample justification, would think that by the introduction of the word "reasonable" adjacently to the word "grounds" there was more than a hint that judicial supervision was competent, but the Privy Council rejected the suggestion of a judicial act. They did so upon the ground that in cancelling the licence the Controller was not determining a question or adjudicating upon a right. His action was to be regarded as exclusively executive action, to withdraw a "privilege" because he had reasonable grounds to believe that the holder was unfit to enjoy it. The mere injunction to act on "reasonable grounds" did not convert the course of action into a judicial process.

Now, it may be true that no fundamental right is involved in a function performed under a licence, yet the case was one of deprivation of a valuable right, which could only be ordered on reasonable grounds, and therefore, the elements of a judicial process clearly appear. In the English jurisdiction, however, the character of a judicial process has been denied to such an act, upon a process of argument favouring its placement entirely within executive discretion.

And, as all those present must already be aware, that is not the farthest reach to which the principle of deference to the executive has been extended in the English jurisdiction. The extreme case up to the present is the well-known case of Liversidge [*Liversidge v. Anderson* (1942) A.C. 206] which came before the House of Lords in 1942.

The action in question was that of the Home Secretary in the British Government and was taken under a Regulation which enabled him to order the detention of a person in the following circumstances, namely, that he had "reasonable cause to believe any person to be of hostile origin or associations or to have been reasonably concerned in acts prejudicial to the public safety or the defence of the realm or in preparation or instigation of such acts, and that by reason thereof it is necessary to exercise control over him."

Here, it was not a matter merely of "reasonable cause," but even the grounds were specified with particularly, and each of them was of a concrete nature, susceptible of proof or disproof. The arguments in favour of holding the Minister's act to be of judicial nature have been stated with great thoroughness in the dissenting judgment of Lord Askin, and I do not need to reproduce them before you. The courts had nothing to go upon beyond the bare statement of the Home Secretary that he had reasonable cause to believe that Liversidge was possessing one or more of the characters specified in the Regulation.

Those specifications themselves have the effect of limiting discretion vested in the authority, yet it was held by the House of Lords that the Home Secretary was entitled to refuse to give any particulars as to his reasons. Putting it in general terms, the liberty of a subject was denied protection on the mere statement that the Home Secretary believed himself to have reasonable cause to believe that Liversidge should be deprived of his liberty.

Each of those cases would have received a wholly different treatment had it arisen in France. In the Tariq Transport Company case there would have been none of the enormous waste of time and effort expended to reach ultimately the conclusion that the High Court had no jurisdiction in the case because the executive act was not made subject to a judicial process.

The *Conseil d'Etat* cares nothing about whether the act is administrative, judicial or quasi-judicial. It is sufficient that the act should be of an administrative nature performed in the exercise of public powers by a public authority, and even if the act be within the purely discretionary field the *Conseil d'Etat* will inquire into it and discover the reasons which led to the grant of a franchise to one person and the refusal of a similar franchise to another person.

They have then the power to enforce what is in their view the substantial justice of the case, either by quashing the order and directing that it should be made once again in accordance with the principles which the *Conseil d'Etat* itself lays down, or that the party which has suffered loss in consequence of the act should be compensated in money.

There can be no doubt that in such a case as the Tariq Transport Company case very large and valuable interests were involved.

The attempt to have the action of the RTA inquired into would not have been made and sustained, with so much trouble and expense, if that action had not resulted in loss to one party and gain to the other, both being applicants for a franchise before the Authority.

Similar interests were undoubtedly involved in the large number of precedent cases from many countries, where the most acute reasoning and the most ample learning were devoted to no better end, than a judicial declaration of *non possumus* from which no party could conceivably derive any satisfaction. But, in all these cases, the executive authorities were no doubt left with a feeling of deep satisfaction that once again they had staved off the attack upon the citadel of their discretionary powers.

It may sound like a contradiction in terms to say that control can ever be applied to the exercise of discretionary powers. That is indeed the attitude which has consistently been maintained by the courts in the English Jurisdiction.

> In a number of leading cases it has been held that where the legislature has given unfettered discretion to any authority to act in given circumstances, there it is not for the court to indicate its opinion how or when such a discretionary power should be exercised, for that would be to legislate.

But, it is precisely in the field of discretionary power that executive authorities need the utmost guidance. It is in that region that acts may be performed which on the surface have all the appearance of legality and are true to form, but in fact conceal an exercise of power tinged with the grossest partiality.

It is to be said, with regret, that in these modern days with democratic Governments in power, where to the possible partialities of officials are added the politically inspired and other partialities which afflict Ministers, the danger of such abuse of power is very great. Under the present conditions, it is only when the abuse is carried to the extent of a public scandal that it ever comes to light.

Alternatively, there may be a case of an individual who regardless of the risks and dangers which he runs may choose to fight out his case against the opposition of the authorities to a point where he can attract the sympathy of the highest in the land, or of the public at large. But it is almost certain that the amelioration cannot come through the intervention of the courts acting within their limitations and in their proper spheres.

> A court is required by its very function to be blind to all that is not properly placed before it, and where discretion has been exercised with partiality, it may be taken for granted that the authorities have been careful to conceal everything that may serve as proof of their true purpose. That can only be ascertained by diligent inquiry with the aid of enormous administrative experience and by the use of powers of inquiry amounting to inquisition, which far transcend those admissible to courts in our jurisdiction.

Take the simple case of distribution of relief blankets after some local disaster. Somehow, with the best of intentions on the part of the authorities entrusted with the distribution, the blankets find their way to those among the sufferers from whom the powers that be have received or hope to receive the greatest measure of support.

Take the matter a little higher, and consider the case of the disparities between the grants of foreign exchange made to persons who wish to go abroad for the same or similar purposes. There are great inequalities and I have heard a High Court Judge arguing that such matters should be brought within the writ jurisdiction. But I ask myself—how can a Judge hold an inquiry into such a matter in the face of the power of the executive to withhold all official documents on the ground of privilege? And even if the documents were all there, how would a Judge be capable of estimating the expected supply of foreign exchange over a certain period and how could he gain an adequate grasp of all the requirements so as to be able to distribute that supply among the applicants in the public interest, that is to say, to the greatest advantage of the public at large?

The strength of the executive in the discretionary field lies in this, namely, that it knows the necessities of the administration and is seized of the large question of the overall public interest. If the acts of the executive in discretion are to be scrutinised, it is obvious that this can only be done appropriately and adequately by an administrative authority of greater experience armed with all the necessary powers to the point of inquisition.

In the Tariq Transport Company case which I have mentioned, an appeal to a higher official authority was yet possible when the writ was moved in the High Court. That may or may not serve as an indication of the degree of confidence felt by the parties in the possibility of a real reconsideration of all the circumstances of the case in such an appeal. But if there had been a revising authority with the powers and status of the *Conseil d'Etat* no hesitation need be felt that the case would have been brought before them for a judicial inquiry and a decision which would be both just to the private parties as well as consistent with the requirements of the administration.

The basic idea of administrative tribunal is that it is perfectly possible to carry on the administration safely and efficiently, without encroaching upon the rights of any individual, and without dealing otherwise than equally with all individual subjects. That in my opinion, is the true foundation for the establishment of the principle of "equality before the law."

> I venture also to say that the courts of our country do not and cannot afford a true guarantee to the individual, of equality before the law, in the face of the daily increasing scope and complexity of interference by public authorities with the lives and activities of the subjects, under the authority of statutory powers.

Recently I had occasion to observe that a method similar to that of the administrative tribunal probably offered the best chance of exercise of control over corruption in the public administration. Experience of cases of corruption which come up before the courts indicates that the present machinery is effective only to bring up isolated and unimportant cases, and that it is ill-adapted to expose anything in the nature of organised corruption.

In the absence of a proper means of exposure and investigation, the result at present found must continue, namely, that here and there by the method of the trap, some under-brained official might perhaps be caught. And where there is a danger that a whole system may thereby be exposed I have an uneasy feeling that undesirable result can be only too easily prevented by the exercise of the uncontrolled power of the superior executive to withhold sanction to prosecution. The citadel of organised corruption might thus be thought to be the prevention of corruption act. For the investigation and eradication of organised corruption, such as may be inter-twined with all the processes of a particular department, it is necessary to have a high administrative authority exercising inquisitorial powers, and imbued with a desire to maintain probity in the administration.

With all the determination in the world, no purely judicial court can attempt to produce such a result. It lacks the necessary minimum knowledge to follow the ramifications of administrative action and it does not possess the powers necessary for conducting an inquisition. Such powers are possessed by the *Conseil d'Etat* and it has shown itself to be capable through possession of the necessary mature experience of administrative processes, and a single-minded desire to maintain the purity of the administration, of bringing evils of every kind to the surface and properly dealing with them.

Can such tribunals be established in this country also? The question is a large one, and the immediate reaction of most people will be a negative one, based upon the consideration that what is suitable for France is not necessarily suitable for a country whose administration through the years of British rule has followed other principles and other traditions.

To this I consider that a proper answer may be that undoubtedly the wholesale transplantation of the system of administrative tribunals to this country entails the possibility that it will be a misfit. In France itself, the system which was established by that great administrator, Napoleon the First, and which has proved worthy of its founder, has been in active operation since the year 1799. It has grown up within, and is an essential part of the administrative machinery of France. But I consider that if it be borne in mind that France is also a country governed under statutes like ours we may be able to discover the true principle upon which is founded the success of the system, and that a similar system could perhaps successfully be introduced into this country, provided the central principles were borne in mind and respected.

The *Conseil d'Etat* in France has developed within the executive and is a part of the executive. It is composed of senior officials selected for their high general and administrative ability. Now, the executive of a country is composed of officials each exercising independently and within his limited sphere, powers derived from the Constitution or from a statute. However limited or defined these powers may be they yet in all cases will leave scope for the official to exercise his discretion i.e., whether to act or not, and if to act, then how to act? In that sense, every statutorily authorised official is a power in himself. All others at his level in the same department and the superior hierarchy exercising other and sometimes higher powers, form a compact group, carrying within themselves the full powers vested in the department. Within the limits of that department, this ordered array of powers bears a fairly close resemblance to a principality. Every department places value upon its *esprit de corps* which is regarded as essential for efficiency in the operation of the department for the public benefit. But the sense of unity can operate in other ways as well, according to the climate, and a common interest of a material nature is a very powerful cementing force.

Putting these elements together, it is not difficult to see that where deterioration has set in, it will need some authority equipped with very high powers, and charged with inquisitorial functions, to arrest the process and restore healthy conditions within the department. It is much the same as the case of a prince or State in the international field. The only external law which an independent international unit recognises is a law which it accepts for itself as applicable to itself, and the enforcement of such law must be by an international authority composed of other States of equal status. It is only where a State has suffered defeat in war that any law can be imposed upon it without its consent.

Viewing a department or a statutory authority in this light, it seems to me fairly obvious that nothing but another statutory authority of equal or superior status can bring down the law upon the erring department or authority. As I have already observed a court constituted as are the Courts in our country is not well fitted to enforce the law upon statutory authorities, except in regard to their visible duties, namely, the express requirements of the law under which they act. Those requirements are only too easily met, but it is in the discretionary field that the actions of the executive are most often found to require scrutiny and if possible corrections.

It is greatly to the credit and advantage of France that the country has been able to build up a system of administrative tribunals before which all official authorities and even the Government itself acting through Ministers can be arraigned for their acts, even though such acts have been performed in the field of pure discretion. The investigations carried out by the *Conseil d'Etat* are permitted, and the decisions of the *Conseil d'Etat* are respected and accepted and carried out because it is recognised that although its function is of a critical and judicial nature, yet that function is performed with real and intimate knowledge of all the processes underlying official acts forever.

Its processes from start to finish are imbued with the desire to maintain purity within the administration. So high is the authority which the *Conseil d'Etat* has acquired for itself in the century and a half of its existence that it has gone to the length of laying a restraint upon the powers which may be exercised by a "caretaker" Ministry, notwithstanding the availability of legal authority for the exercise. It is difficult to conceive of an administrative authority exercising higher power than this, in a corrective fashion.

I end, as I began, with the remark that the time may possibly be ripe for careful consideration of the question whether a system of administrative tribunals would not in our country also meet a need of a real, and even pressing kind. Believing that this assembly of lawyers is inspired with the feeling that purity and probity in the administration are one of the highest of desirable ends, I leave the suggestion to you for proper consideration and for such action as your association may deem proper.

Address of Chief Justice A. R. Cornelius on Equality of Opportunity in Public Service, September 1, 1961

[*Explanatory Note*. In this address before the Rotary Club of Lahore on September 1, 1961, Chief Justice Cornelius formulates the only theoretical basis for bureaucratic organization to emerge from Pakistan sources. He suggests that the internal structure of bureaucracy should be in consonance with the philosophy of government embodied in the Objectives Resolution and in the preamble of the 1956 Constitution. Implicit in his comments is criticism of the closed cadre system which prevents officers of cadres other than the CSP from rising to positions equal to their talents. His espousal of the concept that bureaucracy is itself a social organism which must provide internal means of personal development is consistent with socio-bureaucratic concepts found in older constitutional systems. Because this address is the first effort to relate structural organization to a philosophy of democracy it is a significant development in the evolution of administrative theory in Pakistan.]

As an honorary Rotarian I bow my head in acknowledgement of the great motto of Rotary—"Service before Self." These three words are simple in themselves but there is no doubt that the meaning of the phrase is a complex one, which could vary from person to person. For instance there are persons whose needs are met out of private means which they do not need to administer themselves. If such persons engage in activities of a nature useful to their fellowmen, such as charitable or social activities, one may assume in their favour that they do so "without strings attached." One might assume that they derive from it no personal advantage. Yet, it is an undoubted fact that by such service the doer gains development of important skills which might previously have been latent in his own character.

Inside every person, over and above those capacities and abilities which his activities indicate, there lie other potentialities which only require favourable circumstances to make themselves apparent. Activities undertaken for no personal economic purpose constitute a form of self-expression which has the power to bring out a number of such latent talents. In other words, such persons may derive something of greater value than mere material gain through such charitable or social activities of the purest nature. They could be taking steps towards the goal of the realisation of the self.

I gather that among members of Rotary an appreciable number are, like myself, employed in the public service. It is interesting to examine the meaning of the Rotary motto to this category of persons. I do not doubt that even for persons whose whole time is, by the conditions of their employment, to be devoted to the service of the Government, it is possible to find the leisure and the attention which is necessary to be of substantial service to their fellow men in a field outside that of their employment.

But today, I would like to take a different problem for my subject, namely, the question of "service through self" with particular reference to public service. You will appreciate that when I say "through self" I do not mean it in the extreme sense of utter selfishness. What I have in mind is the realisation of the self through and by means of the service of the public. You will appreciate that the realisation of self is a very noble and one might even say, a necessary motive animating the activities of every intelligent human being. For the past year or so I have been enjoying an unusual opportunity of studying the public administration of Pakistan in a number of important aspects. It is natural that the question should pose itself—is one taking into account that for each person who is employed in this vast machine of the Government, the work which he does is probably his sole avenue of self-realisation? Is it possible by taking thought to provide that throughout the enormous complexity of departments and cadres, through the medley of classifications and regulations, the scope for self-realisation for each person should, other things being equal, be equalised? It has been borne in upon me that the answer is not to be found in mere enumerations or classifications or modification of remuneration. It is much more simply to be ascertained by bearing in mind what is the national objective or idea of the State. By idea, of course, I do not mean the mere concept of the organisation known as the State. I use the word in the sense of ideology. There was a time when the whole existence of the State was a mere extension of the personality of the Prince, and the governmental agency existed purely to assert his uncontrolled power and authority, but that was comparatively long ago.

It is now 200 years since the French philosopher Rousseau said that the State was a "moral person" and that the sovereignty which it enjoyed was manifested in the form of a "general will" of the people thereof. The idea of the general will is not one of universal acceptance, nor can it be said to be very commonly understood. People find it easier to grasp the sovereignty of a majority, even if it be by a single vote or voice. In one of the simpler aspects, the general will of a people who are constituted as a nation, is a matter of historical determinism, that is to say those urges and ideals common to the entire population which have developed as a result of the influence upon their character of the external and internal factors which have determined their lives. The general will is like a principle operating among and underneath the whole mass of activities of the population of the country. In the formation of this principle, as well as in its manifestation, the directive and regulatory activities of the governmental agencies play a very large part. Yet, the general will is, in itself, essentially free, to the extent that the external conditions permit. It is in that sense only that one can comprehend Rousseau's famous declaration that "man is born free and everywhere we see him in chains." His conception of the freedom of the general will was sufficiently profound to enable him to declare that "whosoever affects to be the master of men is himself the greatest slave." And, as to the purpose and rationale of authority, it was he who formulated the imperishable ideal for all liberal governments, namely that "the State is the realisation of freedom."

Today, it is only in a few countries that those who acknowledge these ideas refer to the originator for the relevant scripture. These matters are now usually written into the constitutions of countries. As I have said before in attempting to draw some kind of principle which gives true life to the public service of the country, an important factor is to find in that principle true scope for the self-realisation of the individual public servant. At first sight it appears that one is catering for mere gratification, or self-aggrandisement, and the familiar picture comes to mind of public servants jockeying for promotion and the highest appointments. As it happens, the field is too fully occupied by rules and regulations to permit of any such unbridled ambition being successfully pursued. Here and there persons may be found in every government, however well-ordered it might be, who cherish and sometimes even achieve such ambitions. But these are mere freaks and there are always chinks in every armour. The problem is to find an integrated purpose by submission to which each individual public servant, working in his own sphere according to the rules and requirements of his office, may be conscious of gaining through faithful service a sense of added stature as a human being according to the highest principles and in the highest interests of the country which he is serving.

By great good fortune, there is such a purpose clearly formulated in words of high import and for this precise object, namely, for the guidance of public servants in Pakistan. I refer to the Objectives Resolution passed by the Constituent Assembly more than ten years ago, which forms today the preamble of the operative constitutional instrument of Pakistan, namely, the constitution which was abrogated in October 1958. Many of you perhaps think that by that abrogation the constitution became a dead letter. That is a totally incorrect impression, for one of the first acts of the new regime was to declare by a formal legal instrument of the highest validity that the country would continue to be governed in accordance with that constitution, subject only to express orders and regulations issued by the supreme authority. I am not aware that in any particular to which I shall have occasion to refer today the supreme authority in the country has issued any express instrument to override the high purposes expressed in that Resolution.

The Objectives Resolution is, in its every word and phrase, worthy of the deep and respectful consideration of every citizen of Pakistan. Among a number of directives of the most profound importance, it lays down that the principles of freedom and equality are to be fully observed by the Government, and that such "fundamental rights" as equality of status and of opportunity are to be guaranteed. It is true that by a solemn pronouncement of the court over which I have today the honour to preside, the fundamental rights have been held to be no longer in force, but I trust that no one will conclude therefrom that such a thing as equality of status and equality of opportunity does not exist in Pakistan, or that it is not a primary duty of the Government to ensure that the principles of freedom and equality, which incorporate such rights as the right of equality of status and equality of opportunity are fully observed. For, without attempting to minimise the importance of legal sanctions in support of the rights mentioned above, I think it can be said with confidence that the duty resting upon the Government in consequence of the pronouncement that the country will be governed in accordance with the late constitution, includes a duty to see that the principles of freedom and equality are fully observed.

I do not propose here to touch upon the general question of how the Government should ensure the due observance of these principles with respect to the population at large. What I have in mind is to examine the application of these principles to the public service in its various gradations. The need is to satisfy at the same time the requirements of the public servant both as an individual and as a public servant on the one hand, and the requirements of the public service as well as of the basic ideology of the State on the other. And first let me consider what are the requirements of the public servant as an individual.

Naturally, one cannot think in terms of the peculiar desires and ambitions of every single public servant. One must treat them as a class. In all civilised countries, the category of public servants has gained recognition as a separate body, and the rights which public servants as a class ordinarily claim for themselves are very well formulated.

There is firstly the right to be paid while serving and the right to a pension or post-service relief in some form at the termination of active service. There is generally a claim to security of tenure. There is a right also claimed to be subjected to discipline by special authorities and through a special process. And finally, what is of importance to my subject, all over the world the public servants claim a right to a career within the service. These are rights which they ordinarily claim as a condition of their being true to their oath or their undertaking of office to be diligent and strive to the utmost of their ability to satisfy the requirements of their office, to obey their superiors, to observe official secrecy and not to seek material advantage from any other source than the salary which is paid to them. In fairly recent years, public servants have begun to claim, and in certain countries have actually succeeded in obtaining, a number of additional rights which had earlier been conceded in favour of citizens in private employment. Thus, in a number of countries, public servants are entitled to form their own unions on the pattern of the trade unions which had for many years existed in the industrial field for the protection of the rights of industrial employees. It was natural that public servants should be slow to seek this right. Being subject to immediate authority themselves and forming a part of the organised authority of the State, it was only proper that they should be slow to take up techniques which might visibly detract from the absolute authority of the State. In a great many countries, the tradition of the public service went back to a period of absolute rule. The reluctance of public servants with that kind of tradition to gain strength against their own government by combination among themselves was therefore natural. But the example of industrial employees was one which public servants, at any rate those engaged in labour administration, could not fail to observe with interest. It has been followed, in varying degrees, in every country with an organised administration. In a number of European countries the process has gone so far that it is possible to say that the public servants have now gained most of the characteristics of a profession. The recruitment of the new public servants is in the hands of the new public servants. Disciplinary action is confined to domestic tribunals composed of public servants. The conditions of service and the terms thereof are settled by the authorities in consultation with representative groups of public servants. Questions of promotion are similarly decided and all matters of discipline are dealt with in the same way. The dangers involved in over-emphasising such privileges are apparent, but it is not my purpose to go into that matter here. The gradual development of a drive towards the attainment of autonomy by public servants as a class is a phenomenon worthy of careful examination.

Public servants have been slow to taste the benefits of freedom, even when it became a recognised principle of the State. It was only in the course of conferring the benefits of freedom through the agencies of government upon the population that it appears to have come back to them that they also were entitled to some say in matters affecting their own welfare as a body. For the most part the steps they have taken to gain that measure of freedom were suited to their position. Within the body which they themselves manned and to a large extent controlled, they sought to entrust their liberties to representatives selected from among their own number. They have mostly preferred the method which in the circumstances was the most agreeable and efficient, namely, the presentation of their point of view in the form of consultative advice.

It does not take a long argument to show that a State which holds out a promise of growth in freedom to its population must also pay attention to the provision of similar growth to that body of persons who form the governmental agency. It is through that agency that the benefits of freedom are to be disseminated among the people. No person who feels himself shackled can conceivably have the right mental attitude towards the conferment of greater liberty upon persons placed under his own control. I may give the instance of the operation of ships in mediaeval times. The propulsion of certain ships was by galley slaves who were confined in the lowest quarters mostly below water level. The persons who exercised direct authority over the galley slaves lived in a middle deck, above which they had no prospect of rising just as the galley slaves had no prospect of ever rising to the middle deck. The superior direction was in the hands of a privileged group living on the top deck under the control of the captain of the ship. It is quite obvious that the gospel of liberty could not possibly under those conditions be preached to the galley slaves, nor could any advancement of their liberties be afforded to them through the agency of the occupants of the middle deck who were themselves strictly confined in their rights and liberties. Similarly, when a government assumes as its objective the enlargement of freedom generally among its citizens, it cannot *ex hypothesi* ignore the necessity of providing such freedom, of the appropriate kind, to the agency through which that noble objective is to be attained.

One cannot of course mean that each public servant should be free to act as he pleases in the sphere of his work. In fact, all public servants live and work under very tight sets of rules and regulations which determine their actions to a very great extent. The kind of freedom which I have in mind is, as I said at the outset, freedom to develop the self within the limits of one's duty as a public servant to the maximum of the talent with which one is endowed.

Under systems which are inspired entirely by traditional ideas, it is common to find a tendency to minimise the scope of self-development that ought to be permitted to an employee. There is a strong tendency to say about an inferior that he cannot possibly rise above a certain level. Under modern conditions, and particularly in the new world, the discovery has been made that the capacity for self-development in the individual, provided he is given the necessary scope and opportunity, is far higher than was previously imagined. It is found that the common man is by no means common in the sense that he possesses individual characteristics to a remarkable degree. Each man embodies in himself the experience and the developed thought of centuries, and it is therefore necessary to treat him as being much older than his actual age. It is found that every individual has one or more extraordinary qualities and characteristics which only appear and develop if he is allowed a chance to show and cultivate them. Finally, it is universally found that each person possesses a capacity for growth, of which the counterpart is a profound hope of an improved future for himself. In the United States where for some three centuries persons have been migrating from Europe in order to build up a new and freer life for themselves, it has been found that to bring out some of the most remarkable qualities of creativeness in an otherwise ordinary looking person it is needful only to place before him a chance to better his lot. In such a field of free enterprise there is continuous growth in improvement since the creativeness of the citizens in every field of activity can always find room for improvement in every new situation. The concern of the persons at the helm of affairs in modern civilised countries is to provide for the fullest release of the initiative and the energy of each individual employee towards constant personal growth and self-development. That is the sense in which I understand the process of the realisation of the self through freedom.

Where the constitution of the State requires that it should fully observe the principle of freedom, I conceive that one very important direction in which effort has to be made is towards providing conditions favouring the fullest release of the energies and creative abilities of public servants in the service of the State. It is in this aspect that the principles of equality of status and equality of opportunity become of great importance. The first of these principles does not mean that all employees should be given equal status inside the public service. There must be classifications, and there must be grades. The need is to make these differentiations depend more and more upon, firstly, the nature of the service rendered, and secondly, the individual's capacity to render service of high quality. In other words, inferiority of initial status must not be permanent and insuperable where the necessary ability is perceptible. It does not rectify the matter from the viewpoint of freedom, that in a rare case, a capable subordinate may be raised out of his inferiority by catching the sympathetic eye of an influential superior. Growth in freedom must proceed on uniform and rational lines.

The rational test of equality for determination of the status of two persons engaged in work of the same or equivalent character would appear to turn on the possession of necessary qualifications coupled with the capacity to produce results. You may have a country which is rising out of poverty or which suffers from paucity of training institutions. It may therefore be under the necessity of employing under-qualified persons for functions usually requiring training of a higher standard. In some quarters, the tendency, in such circumstances, is to emphasise only the aspect of deficiency. Others ask why the fact that the work is being done should be overlooked and advance various grounds against the barrier of tradition. The resolution appears to lie in the practical application of a great principle enunciated by Napoleon Bonaparte, undoubtedly one of the most brilliant administrators the world has ever seen. Faced with the task of producing order and a disciplined people and government out of the chaos created by the French Revolution, he laid down as one main rule, that "the career should be open to the talents." Within these words lie the seeds of the two rights which in the way of freedom, public servants may rightly claim, that is to say, equality of status as well as equality of opportunity. The test of talent in Napoleon's time, when qualifications did not hold the same importance as today, was the capacity to get things done efficiently. When that was apparent in a person, the post belonged to him by that fact alone, and not, as previously, on the basis of privilege of birth or autocratic gift.

Since Napoleon's day, education and the acquisition of qualifications have been brought within the reach of great sections of the population in all civilised countries. Among the benefits conferred by modern Governments, one of the most important is that of universal and free primary education. Apart from the intrinsic value of education, the importance of making primary education universal and free, lies in the equalisation which it brings about in the opportunity for advancement laid before the entire body of the citizens. The talented child, whether from a humble or a wealthy home, is started on the road of self-improvement through knowledge. His further progress may be swift, if the means come to hand, or it may be retarded if he has to provide them for himself, but there is no doubt that, accidents apart, he will gain the career which his talents deserve. Something of the kind is in operation among the public servants of most civilised countries.

For the talented or ambitious worker who has the grit to acquire knowledge during his few hours of leisure from his work, instruction is made available through night classes in technical and other schools, and through correspondence courses. An advanced civil service organisation has cells for advice on career planning and provides for in-service training so as to upgrade men who, for lack of means or other reasons, entered the public service at a lower level than their potentialities deserved. In the absence of any such system the rule of equality of opportunity cannot be said to be in practical operation in relation to employees, as well in the public service as in any other form of service.

The answer which I find to the question of the realisation of the self through service by a public servant may be put in a single sentence. Open out the career in the public service to the full and effective display of the talents, and provide at the same time for improvement of talent, as it appears, by training facilities inside and outside the departments. The constitutional requirements of freedom, equality of status and equality of opportunity mean precisely this in relation to public servants. Too often they are left to stagnate in their appointments because they have reached the top of their grade, or because they do not possess prescribed qualifications although their ability to perform the duties of the higher posts to which they aspire is admitted. They suffer frustration through the desire for self-expression being suppressed, and to that extent, the standard of efficiency and the prospect of improvement in the work of government is diminished. The prospect of advancement in freedom and independence of the citizens whom they serve is proportionately reduced. The high ideals contained in the Objectives Resolution are dear to the hearts of all Pakistanis and come close to being an expression of the general will. Not least among the citizens in adherence to those ideals, in strength of spirit to achieve them are the public servants of Pakistan. To be sure, there are occupational diseases to be found among them, the most notable being the disease of corruption, but those are susceptible of cure, through positive methods of control. But the disease of apathy through frustration goes deeper still. I think it is possible to find a remedy for it in adherence to certain clear principles contained in the Objectives Resolution.

Appendix • 13 •

Address of Chief Justice A. R. Cornelius on Public Administration and the Law, November 30, 1963

[*Explanatory Note*. In this address, Cornelius develops a facet of public service responsibility somewhat different from the institutional restraints implicit in his earlier advocacy of administrative tribunals (see Appendix 11). Here, the chief justice emphasizes that the Confucian ideal of virtue and good conscience are essential for sound administration but insufficient unless combined with institutional restraints. These restraints are embodied in the Constitution and are applied to administration by judicial review of administrative action. Cornelius thus relates the ancient concept of rule by personal virtue with the theory of a check on personal virtue by encouraging a continuing dialogue between administrators and clientele and by subjecting administrative action to judicial review. This address was delivered at the Third Advanced Management Course of the National Institute of Public Administration, Karachi, November 30, 1963.]

I would like to start by saying how much I appreciate this opportunity to be present here in this Institute this morning. It is always interesting to a person of my age to receive views from his juniors and particularly from those who are engaged in preparing or improving themselves for the purpose of better management of the affairs of the country. I will try to give you today my idea of the condition in which the principles and attitudes governing the problem of management are found to exist in the minds of our people and of those who are placed over them at the present time.

Traditions die hard among Eastern people, but equally the stresses of modern life are in irresistible operation. There is thus a certain mixture of the old streams with the new or perhaps it would be more true to say that the two streams are running side by side because they are fundamentally very different from each other and a mixture between them seems impossible to imagine. As has happened in the West, where two centuries or so back, ideas of Government were not very different from what they are today in our country, so here, the conditions brought about by an enormous increase in the population, unimaginable extension of all economic activities, and the injection at long last of the principles of "liberty, equality and fraternity" which broke upon the world in explosive form at the close of the eighteenth century, should take their effect. It is on account of these and many other compelling factors that certain practices have grown up in the West, which we are now busy importing into our body politic, and for the same reason, namely, to ensure good order in the lives of the people. But I ought really to begin at the beginning.

I propose to set out the traditional views regarding management in the words of the Chinese sage Confucius. I do not have to describe him in detail. He was born in the middle of the sixth century before Christ, and, as was possible in those days, he practised as a philosopher. Also, as was not uncommon at that time, he achieved positions of ministership, by virtue of his philosophical distinction, in a number of States and was thus in a good position to portray the objectives of Government in his age as well as the special qualities of the rulers in contradistinction with those of the ruled. Confucius had an almost over-whelming interest in Government. He once said "were any prince to employ me, in a twelve-month something could be done, but in three years the work could be completed." His own experience belied this expectation, for it appears that with the exception of a single stay of some length at the age of about 55, most of his time was spent in wandering from one State to another and between whiles in running an academy of his own. Confucius described the essentials of good Government as being sufficient food for the people, sufficient forces, and finally the confidence of the people, and when asked in what order he would dispense with these, he placed first the forces, secondly the food, and thirdly the confidence, without which as he rightly said it was impossible for a people to stand at all. Asked about governmental action, he said, it should be "in advance of the people." Asked what was the test of a good Government he replied "the near are happy and the distant attracted." One readily sees that he was speaking of a China divided into small princedoms with fluid boundaries, so that aggrandisement was possible even through good Government. Confucius was a great believer in personal rule. In a striking analect he said:

> When good Government prevails in the empire, civil ordinances and punitive expeditions issue from the emperor. When good Government fails in the empire, civil ordinances and punitive expeditions issue from the nobles. When they issue from a noble, it is rare if the empire be not lost within ten generations. When they issue from a noble's minister, it is rare if the empire be not lost within five generations. But when a minister's minister holds command in the kingdom, it is rare if it be not lost within three generations. When there is good Government in the empire, its policy is not in the hands of ministers.

In this proposition, he was clearly building up a pyramid of power, placing the highest potentiality for good at the apex, in the person of the emperor. As he goes down the pyramid he finds the men less and less capable of holding the empire together. You can see how clearly this is the contrary of the condition we find in modern democratic countries, where power is to be derived directly from the people by those who put themselves forward for the function of leadership.

Confucius has many injunctions for rulers. Thus, "if a ruler is himself upright, his people will do their duty without orders; but if he himself be not upright, although he may order they will not obey." In another place he says:

> When a ruler loves good manners, his people will not let themselves be disrespectful; when a ruler loves justice, his people will not let themselves be unsubmissive; when a ruler loves good faith, his people will not venture to be insincere; and if he be like this, then people will come from every quarter carrying their children strapped on their backs;—what does he want with learning agriculture?

To a prince who questioned him as to Government, Confucius replied: "If your aspirations are for good, the people will be good.

The moral character of those in high position is the breeze, the character of those below is the grass. When the grass has the breeze upon it, it assuredly bends." To which, we may add that it would probably bend in any case. Again, asserting the force of good qualities in a prince acting in aid of his authority, he says: "Is a prince able to rule his country with courtesy and deference; then what difficulty will he have? And if he cannot rule his country with courtesy and deference, what use are the forms of courtesy to him?" Certainly, in such a case he would be required to use instruments of greater power than mere courtesy and deference. Confucius was capable of returning a very firm answer even to a prince. One of them asked him whether there was any single phrase through which a country may be ruined, and he quoted to him the popular saying: "I should have no gratification in being a prince, unless none opposed my commands." He went on to say that if the commands were good and no one opposed them, then surely all would be well, but if they were not good and there was no one to oppose them, might not one expect that single phrase to ruin his country? Among his adages is one containing an advice to a minister as to his duty towards his prince. He said: "Never deceive him, and then you may boldly withstand him." That advice, followed in his own case, probably led to Confucius having to find so many new masters so often. When asked why he went from failure to failure, he gave the answer: "Did right rule prevail in the world, I should not be taking part in reforming it."

In his times as in our own, the rule was carried on through public servants, and throughout the analects we find injunctions by Confucius to the public servants which should strike an echo in our minds as well. He said for example: "When those in high position are found of orderly behavior, service from the people is easily commanded.

"Men of noble mind," he said, "seek to achieve the good in others—not their evil" while the little-minded man is the reverse. The good public servant should put duty first and success thereafter; he should attack his own failings first instead of those of others. "A man," he said, "who puts himself right will have no difficulty in the public service; but if he does not, how will he put others right." Here, one perceives very clearly that in Confucius' times as in our own times, almost up to the period of the Partition, the duty of the public servant was conceived to be to "put the citizens right," as if they were erring children. The conception of a public service provided for the regulation of the proper activities of the citizens was nowhere in the picture.

In Confucius' view, in order to merit the title of a public servant, it was necessary that in his personal conduct, a person should have sensibility to dishonour, and wherever he may be sent, he would be sure not to disgrace his prince's commission. One can see here the pattern of the British *Raj*, operated through an hierarchy of British civil servants, with which we were so familiar until some 16 years ago. All of us are aware what extreme care these administrators showed to avoid any departure from the highest standards in their personal conduct. We know how quickly any of them who were found at fault appreciably in this respect, were required to leave the service. The monolithic structure of the public service, in regard to which an analect has been quoted above, appears very clearly in the British administration. The administrator in India felt himself to be in the place of the Emperor of India, or as it happened to be in the palmy days of the I.C.S. in the place of the Queen Empress. He fully realised that by any dishonourable act he would bring dishonour upon the whole structure of which he was a part, as well as upon the person at the apex of it, namely, the Emperor or the Empress of India, because in that structure was an image of the British *Raj* and only by such dishonour could it be destroyed. I remember how sad a day it was for that image when the first of a long series of departmental enquiries into disgraceful acts by Indians in the I.C.S. were commenced. It clearly foreboded the onset of a new order of things.

When asked what was dishonour in a public servant, Confucius replied: "When his country is well-governed to be thinking only of pay, and when his country is ill-governed to be thinking only of pay—that is dishonour for a public servant." Perhaps, today, when salaries are admittedly inadequate, we should add to the word "pay" the supplements of "T.A. and D.A." He condemned servility in public servants in no uncertain terms, speaking of them, and of the danger which they represented to the public interest in the following terms: "Before obtaining their position, they are in anxiety to obtain it, and when they have it, they are anxious lest they lose it; and if men are in anxiety about losing their position, there is no length to which they will not go." To which may be added another pithy saying: "Actual address and an insinuating demeanour seldom accompany virtue."

Confucius is commonly regarded as having succeeded in outlining the qualities of the "superior persons." The analects are full of pithy sayings on the subject, such as the "noble person is easy to serve, but difficult to please; the inferior person is hard to serve, but easy to please"; "the well-bred are dignified but not pompous; the ill-bred are pompous, but not dignified." Does not that call to mind a picture of one Judge in full robes at a ceremony looking at another and either thinking or saying "he, of course, is merely pompous but *I* am dignified."

Confucius provides a great many tests of what constitutes the difference between the superior person and the inferior. The superior knows what is right, but the inferior knows what is likely to pay; the superior thinks of his character, the inferior of his position; the man of honour desires justice, the inferior man favour. One can easily see that these tests as applied between equals can be the foundation of a wide-spread system of snobbery. Even the honourable man needs means of subsistence; values his position, has a need to make requests. If he succeeds in these matters, it is a question of opinion whether he did so because he knew what was right, or because he was thinking only of his character, or in making request based it on pure justice, or whether he allowed some baser motives to influence his conduct.

But what is of importance is that the superior persons are those who gain that position in the eye of those above and in that case they acquire a certain authority. Confucius was once asked "Do men of the nobler class detest others?" and he immediately replied "They do detest others" and proceeded to give examples. There is visible in that outlook a settled cynicism as to inborn or inherent power among some to rule over others, and this is clearly the basis of class rule and the caste distinctions which have been so strong a feature of the ancient order of things all over the world. It was from that condition that the protagonists of the French Revolution undertook to free the whole world when they announced and propagated their doctrine of "liberty, equality, fraternity." It is probably true that when rule is reserved to a very small number of persons, somewhere in the chain of authority, passing down to the common person, and possibly in more than one place, the feature of snobbery provides a powerful agency for maintaining the necessary gradations.

Perhaps at this point I might digress to tell you a little story of the old I.C.S. A young British Officer in the Punjab Commission was suddenly appointed to be the British Government's Trade Agent at a place called Gangtok on the Hindustan-Tibet road. Knowing nothing about the conditions there, he moved among some senior civilians in Simla and met a person by the name of Mackworth-Young, then a Secretary to the Government of India, who in his young days had occupied the post at Gangtok. Mackworth-Young readily obliged with the information sought from him and added some advice as to how the young officer should deal with the locals in order to be successful. "One thing" he said, "which stood me in good stead was that my father had been Lt. Governor of the Punjab. Whenever I was in difficulty I used to bring that up." Whereupon the young civilian replied "What an excellent idea, I must try that trick myself," although his father had never been in India at all. That kind of thing still prevails and it is not uncommon to meet officers who will tell you of the positions occupied by their fathers and grandfathers and how useful they have found this circumstance, in quickly gaining authority over the people.

Confucius' theory of Government is one of personal power exercised by an ideal emperor through ideal public servants, bending the people to the imperial will by gentle methods, if possible, but bending them in any case, for the people are "to be set right." For this it is important that those who are placed above the people, and those in the ladder right up to the emperor, should be there by reason of their "superiority," and should maintain their positions by being opposed to any suggestion of possible equality between themselves and those in the inferior grades. That is the exact contrary of rule by law. Confucius made no secret of this, for in one of his analects he has clearly said:

> If you govern the people by laws, and keep them in order by penalties, they will avoid the penalties and lose their sense of shame. But if you govern them by moral excellence and keep them in order by your dutiful conduct, they will retain their sense of shame, and also live up to this standard.

Clearly, what Confucius insists upon is that in order to make the rule effective, each offender should be found out and visibly punished so as to ensure right conduct among the whole people. Implicit in this is that public punishment is necessary in order to maintain power. It is not enough that the man should know right from wrong. One is reminded of the couplet in Omar Khayyam: "Geeram ke ze-man dar guzarani ba-karam; Zeen sharm ke deedee ke che kardam che kunam" [In the original speech this appears in Persian script. The accepted translation of this quatrain is "I verily believe that Thou wilt generously pardon me on account of my shame that Thou hast seen what I have done, —*but* what can I do?" (*The Ruba'iyat of Omar Khayyám*, A Facsimile of the Ms. in the Bodleian Library, translated and edited by Edward Herron Allen [London, 1898], p. 227, ms. 55, verse 109.)]

It is of course a mistake to attribute everything evil to the ideas of the past, which have been swept away by the tide of events. Not that the ideas of Confucius have been totally swept away. I feel no doubt that many of the quotations from him which I have reproduced, have found a sympathetic ear among my listeners and probably many of you can produce equivalent adages, which are current in Urdu and other local languages, to match those of Confucius.

But at the same time we cannot ignore that today we do not live under personal rule and the concomitants of that rule, that is to say the personal and ethical agencies by which it was operated are no longer valid. I may remind you that the preamble of the Constitution which the President gave to the country in March 1962, declares that the will of the people of Pakistan is that the State should exercise its power and authority through representatives chosen by the people, and that the principles of democracy, freedom, equality, tolerance and social justice as enunciated by Islam should be fully observed in Pakistan. By Article 2 of the Constitution, it is declared to be the inalienable right of every citizen "to enjoy the protection of the law and to be treated in accordance with law and only in accordance with law." The laws are to be made in accordance with the principles of law-making, the second of which lays down in comprehensive terms that all citizens shall be equal before the law. The conception of rule under law was of course introduced into the country by the British during the latter part of their long rule. This was provided side by side with a strong paternalistic administration of which the principal features are scarcely to be distinguished from the ideas of Confucius. It was indeed found by the British Administrators as a remarkable element of the character of the people whom they governed, that they were devoted to litigation. Perhaps this impression was gained in contrast with the lives which these officers themselves lived or were familiar with in their own country, for in England as well, litigation is pretty rampant, and there would be a great deal more, but for the agency of solicitors in settling matters outside Court. But the phenomenon could well be explained also by the attractiveness to the people of India of a system operating upon their lives which was *not* dependent upon the caprices or whims of any person, however exalted, but was based upon settled law and ascertained principles. The British rulers of course withheld the writ jurisdiction from the Indian Courts, although it had been in operation in their own country for some seven centuries for the purpose of controlling the exercise of public power by public authorities including public servants. It is natural that this power should not have been given to the Indian Courts at a time when all executive power was exercised by British personnel. In England, it was exercised over the public authorities in the name of the King, but in India, most such authorities practically represented the King, to whom no writs could issue. Administrative powers over the population continued to be exercised on the basis of Confucian paternalism, namely, through local rulers of careful upbringing and education, whose qualities for the exercise of rule had been duly tested and who were given practically uncontrolled power to "put the people right," if possible by example and deference and courtesy, but if that would not do, then by all means. Against such paternalistic exercise of administrative power, no writs were conceivable.

I do not propose to speak on the subject of these writs further, but would like to suggest to the gentlemen attending this course that it would be a useful study for them to collect and read the published judgments of the Courts in Pakistan on the subject of these writs, along with the Supreme Court judgments. They would find much to interest and instruct them on this important subject, which is closely connected with the functions which they are being trained to exercise, in a number of judgments by the late Mr. Justice Kayani. The law on the subject is continuously being shaped by these judgments and it is of interest not only to those in the public service, but also to those who are engaged in managing considerable bodies of workers.

The writ jurisdiction operates to ensure equality before law and there can be no question but that for its proper operation, it is necessary that there should be a formulation of principles applicable to the control of all sizeable organizations working within the body politic, as well as their personnel. No longer can these matters be left to the discretion of a single person or a small group of persons merely by virtue of their authority, and however ideal in point of character and ability, he or they might be, there is a clear line of distinction between what is required today and what was enough for Confucius. In the sixth century before Christ it was enough to ensure competent Government of a principality that the ruler should be a man highly cultivated, intelligent, shrewd, cynical, a person who could successfully be "all things to all men," and such were also his agents and administrators in a smaller way. Today, the administrator is expected to observe the rule of equality and to be the *same to all men*. In our country it is only a few dignitaries at the highest level who are required to take an oath upon assumption of office that they will exercise their powers and discharge their functions "without fear, or favour, affection or ill-will," and that they "will do right to all manner of people according to law." But in fact, that is the precise duty which lies upon every person who has a position whether in the public service or in a public or private corporation or other institution, requiring the exercise of powers over others. That duty cannot be discharged unless the power vested in such persons is guided by principles laid down to cover the infinite variety of cases that may come up.

Here then, it begins to appear fairly clear that every administrator whether great or small is bound, by the dictates of the Constitution to follow certain principles in exercising his power, in relation to the circumstances appearing before him. These functions thus assume a judicial aspect and today every administrator in every sphere is fortunate that he may find those principles laid down in a great number of published books on the law relating to practically every human activity in a civilized State. You will find in these books that the practice is increasing of providing within the administrative complex for matters to be taken up for decision, according to their size and importance in the manner usual for the Courts, that is to say after notice to all interests and after hearing all interested parties. You may compare, for instance, the working of the Road Transport Board today with what was the case prior to the Motor Vehicles Act of 1939, when the grant of licences was within the uncontrolled power of the Deputy Commissioners.

It is practically universal also in all civilized countries to allow judicial review when fault is found with the administrative action. In certain countries, this judicial process is applied by a cell within the executive described as an administrative Tribunal. In other countries the grievances are allowed to be ventilated in Courts. By such means from case to case, principles are laid down not only as to the action to be taken under the law or the regulation involved, but also as to the procedure to be followed. The Courts have a long history behind them and the tradition which they have observed throughout is one of fairness. It can be confidently assumed that where the Courts give their attention to matters arising out of the administrative sphere which call for correction, they will incline in the direction of ensuring fair dispensation of benefits, fair application of remedies, fairness in imposition of penalties, and generally fairness in "putting people right."

Address of Chief Justice A. R. Cornelius on the Writ
Jurisdiction, April 25, 1964

[*Explanatory Note.* Use of the writ jurisdiction, analyzed in the text on pages 299–309, is the most important legal issue in Pakistan. It survived a stormy period of martial law and the new Constitution of 1962. Chief Justice Cornelius, addressing probationers of the CSP cadre at the Civil Service Academy in Lahore on April 25, 1964, reviews the concept of the writs and explains their legal position under the 1962 Constitution. His address summarizes a voluminous body of case law on writs and illustrates the high regard which the judiciary has for the writs in modern Pakistan.]

I have been asked to speak today on the subject of the writ jurisdiction of the High Courts and the Supreme Court. The Supreme Court under the new Constitution only deals with writs in appeal from the judgments of the High Courts. Under the old Constitution for the purpose of asserting fundamental rights, there was a direct writ available in the Supreme Court, and I believe one or two attempts were made to invoke that jurisdiction but without success. The formulation of fundamental rights being totally new in Pakistan, the Court preferred, since it could only give final decisions, that there should be in the first place an examination of the case by a High Court. Today, of course, no writ can be moved directly in the Supreme Court but from every order in a writ case by the High Court an appeal lies to the Supreme Court. Where the matter in dispute requires interpretation of the Constitution, say the question whether or not a fundamental right has been denied, the appeal would lie as of right. Otherwise, it would be by special leave, and I would say that unless the matter is already concluded by a final decision of the Supreme Court, leave would ordinarily be granted.

Now to speak more generally on the subject, I might start by giving you a brief account of the origin and development of the writs. The writ is a peremptory order issued by a Superior Court, *i.e.*, one of the Courts of the King as understood in the British jurisdiction. It is an order of the highest authority and efficacy and is so because it is being issued in the Sovereign power of the King. The practice and procedure of the writs commenced in the first century of the Norman Rule in England. As you are aware, the rule of England passed from the hands of the Anglo-Saxons to those of the foreign conqueror, William, who defeated the English King Harold in 1066. England had a rather weak Government which had been unable for a period of years to avoid inroads by the Vikings of Northern Europe. It was the weakness of the indigenous Government which invited the Norman invasion but that did not make the invaders necessarily welcome among the natives and it may well be imagined that it required political and administrative devices of great intricacy for the Normans with their small army to extend their power effectively over the rest of the country. Under Henry II, one of the most astute kings in the history of Monarchy, no device was left untried. One which is relevant to the present subject was the establishment of Royal Courts presided over by the King and in his absence by the Courtiers. The country was for judicial purposes under three different kinds of Courts. There were the local Council Courts known as Shire Courts and there were the Courts of the great nobles. There were also the ecclesiastical Courts which dealt generally with the questions falling under Canon Law and in a limited way with ordinary litigation. It became necessary for the establishment of the King's Supreme power that the judicial arm should be stretched over the whole country. The indigenous system could not be replaced at once owing to the King not having the necessary number of clerks and Judges. Yet the principle was accepted that through the agencies of law and order, the rule of the conqueror should be effectively established in every corner of the realm. It was for this purpose that the writ was devised by the King's legal advisers who were mostly ecclesiastics. A writ was invented which when issued to any Court in the realm had the effect of withdrawing the case to be tried in the King's own Court. Any local Court which resisted the writ incurred the Sovereign's displeasure. You can well imagine how effective this scheme was and how quickly it became a vested interest among the lawyers and the Courtiers surrounding the King. To withdraw the cases from the local Courts and have them decided in London was to the great benefit of the lawyers and at that time also the Judges, for they were then paid by fees. It worked also mightily to the political advantage of the King. That is not to say that it was without benefit to the people as well. Uniform application of laws through judgments duly recorded became the rule, and justice began to be administered in a way previously unknown. It became possible for the Central Courts to give guidance through their judgments to the local Courts regarding the proper procedure to be followed in different cases. Since the Judges were appointed and dismissed by the King, and the times were uncertain, as Norman rule had not yet been accepted in the country, one may be sure that a great many judgments delivered in the King's Courts were designed to produce political advantage to the King. But the facility of both sides being represented through learned lawyers ensured that by and large, since both parties were heard, the eventual decision would be in accordance with reason and the law, so far as it had been formulated in that early period. The judicial process operated, as it always does, to produce all-round benefit.

That was a formative period when all the agencies of the administration, both Central as well as local, were being regularised, that is to say, reduced to rule. England like most of Europe has always been a country where a great deal of administrative responsibility for civil arrangements at local levels has been carried on by local representatives and notables of the locality. A necessary feature of such Government is decision in council, so that you find boroughs with their elected Council and Mayor and County Councils and so forth in many other branches of the administration. It is perhaps from this period that the practice of issuing Royal charters to provide a basis of authority for such administrative activities was begun. The essence of the system lay firstly in due and proper elections to representative office, and secondly in the provision of officers to carry out the orders of the elected representatives under proper delegation. Proper instruments, that is to say, sets of rules or small constitutions were devised for each of these bodies and of course the delegation to their officers was also in writing. It was necessary that the Central Government should retain corrective power in respect of all the subordinate jurisdictions in the field of local administration as well as in the judicial sphere. Here again the centralised justice maintained by the King provided suitable writs to control such actions. There was a writ of *mandamus* which is simply an order to an authority in the realm, below the sovereign authority, requiring it to do that which the law obliged and which it had failed to do. In the course of time, as the laws became more detailed and were furnished with enumeration of specific requirements for the taking of such action as they authorised, it became possible for the superior Courts to lay down elaborate principles to guide the exercise of such power and eventually, to lay down the principle that when all the requirements of the law were satisfied in a given case, the executive authority would be under obligation to take action authorised by the law, in other words that the executive authority would be left with no discretion to avoid taking such action in appropriate cases. *Mandamus* was also used for the purpose of obliging the conferment or restoration of office. Thus, if a person had been duly elected to a particular representative office, but for local or personal reasons was being prevented from occupying that office the King's Courts would issue a *mandamus* requiring that such person should be allowed to take his seat, and equally in the case of a public office. A person might have been appointed to be the clerk of a borough or even to be the sexton, that is to say, the bell-ringer and grave digger of a parish, and if he was not allowed to assume his office, he could obtain a *mandamus*. If he were deprived of his office unlawfully or otherwise than in accordance with correct procedure he could obtain restoration by *mandamus*.

The range over which this power was exercised covers practically the entire field of autonomous and representative local Government and even included such limited authorities as universities.

All jurisdiction being matter of provision in writing, in order that discipline might be maintained over the entire field of administration, the King's Courts devised the writ of Prohibition, to prevent excess of jurisdiction. Where power existed which had not been exercised, *mandamus* would apply. Where the power exercised was in excess of the jurisdiction, prohibition could issue. As you can see this was a most valuable writ to ensure the harmonious exercise of all jurisdictions, for the healthy functioning of all subordinate administrative bodies.

Again, as a corollary to the recognition of the representative and appointive officers under law, a power was required enabling scrutiny of the basis upon which such offices were occupied. In the absence of such a central power there was the obvious danger of usurpation of office by powerful local interests, of which the result could only be confusion and possible dissolution of the local administrative arrangements. A special writ was devised to meet this need, which goes under the name of *quo-warranto*, that is to say, it poses the question by what warrant or authority the respondent holds or claims a particular office. Though rarely employed, it was a very great aid in a troubled period in subjugating unruly elements among those who had been ousted from power by the foreign conquerors. The celebrated Pakistan case of Tamizuddin Khan [*Federation of Pakistan and others* v. *Moulvi Tamizuddin Khan* (1955) 1 F.C.R. 155] fell under this writ.

As time went on, in respect of every jurisdiction, procedures were laid down by which the exercise of authority in different fields was to be governed. It is an essential of justice and of the due exercise of public power over the citizen that it should follow a procedure which is consonant with the proper ascertainment of rights and claims, and with the requirements of natural justice, one of which is that each of the conflicting parties should be allowed a hearing and an equal opportunity of representing its case. This is described as the rule of "due process." There were numerous subordinate jurisdictions, some judicial and others only *quasi*-judicial, which were governed by such rules and, where there were no rules, were required to follow the principles of natural justice. To ensure that the procedure was followed in letter and spirit, the writ of *certiorari* was devised which enabled the King's Court to require any subordinate judicial or *quasi*-judicial body to certify to the King's Court the proceedings which it had taken in a particular case. The King's Court had the power to scrutinise the case and if there had been a substantial departure from a prescribed rule or a rule of natural justice, there was power to quash either the whole proceedings or a part of the proceeding, as well as the order which had been made, and to issue a direction as to the proper manner in which the case should be dealt with. The Court would not decide the case itself, for that would be usurpation of power, but would only correct any departure from correct procedural requirements.

These are the main writs which have survived to this day in respect of subordinate authorities, judicial and executive. There were many others in English judicial history which have fallen out of use in the course of years. But there was one important writ besides, namely the writ of *habeas corpus* which quite simply enabled the King's Court to examine the grounds of detention of any person held in custody in a place within the realm and if the detention was illegal to direct release of the detenu. From the earliest times it has operated strongly against the tendency of strong or corrupt local authorities to abuse the power of imprisonment to gain personal or political ends. In our own times, it is very frequently invoked in the Courts.

Although at the time when the British began to conquer India, these writs were already in regular use in the English Courts, they were never brought into general use in India. One can understand the reason. Executive power was held absolutely by the foreign rulers and was exercised for the most part through foreign personnel. As a necessary concomitant to foreign rule, it was not appropriate that writs should issue to these important agents, or to the Government. The Superior Courts appointed by the foreign rulers could not be allowed to control the agents of the foreign rule, who acted everywhere in the name of the Sovereign. Until the departure of the British rulers from India, it was only in the Presidency Towns of Madras, Calcutta and Bombay that the writ jurisdiction was enforced. There too it had been introduced only for British nationals living in those towns, but in the course of time it became impossible to deny the same relief to other citizens. It was not until after the Partition that both in India as well as in Pakistan the Constitution, namely, the Government of India Act, 1935, was amended so as to give the High Courts the powers of issuing these writs, that is to say, the Writs of *Mandamus,* Prohibition, *Certiorari* and *Quo-warranto. Habeas Corpus* has already been provided by a section in the Criminal Procedure Code, namely, section 491.

The true purpose of the four main writs other than *habeas corpus* is thus to maintain discipline in the administrative and judicial or *quasi*-judicial spheres. Each one of them operates to control the exercise of public power over the citizens. Even in British times, when interference by the High Court was limited to cases of detention, a number of cases arose where interference by High Court with orders of detention issued by the Government led to serious conflict and even to determination of relations between the Executive and the judiciary. This was particularly so during periods of war and as is well known, the pressure from the people for self-government was greatly enhanced with the commencement of the Second World War and was maintained until Independence was finally granted. That was a period of great tension between the Government on the one hand and the judiciary and the politicians on the other and finally even between the Government and the people as a whole. It is difficult to imagine how greatly that tension would have been increased had other writs besides that of *habeas corpus* been available to the people during that anxious time. There is no doubt that a great many things were done during that period on the ground of necessity of War or political disturbance, which the Courts would have found little difficulty in setting aside had the writs been available. There is equally no doubt that such action would have led to extreme exacerbation of relations between the administration and the judicial authorities, to the great detriment of the country.

Something of the kind, though of course on a much lower plane, has actually been observed since the introduction of writ jurisdiction in our own country. In fact, one result of the celebrated case of *Tamizuddin Khan* was that the writ jurisdiction was lost to the Courts and it was only restored by a constitutional amendment much later. In the recent period of Martial Law which the country went through, the writs were made available only in a very limited field, but with a recent amendment of the Constitution, they are now available to the maximum extent.

This necessarily leads to enlargement of the responsibility of the Courts to protect the constitutional rights of citizens both against each other as well as against possibly irregular or excessive exercise of public power. It is certain that the Courts will not hesitate to act where they find that their duty is clear. But I may be permitted to express regret for the unavoidable result that in a number of cases such action is liable to lead to the development of serious misunderstanding between the Executive Departments and the higher judiciary. Not so long ago another celebrated case brought this matter into sharp focus. I refer to the case of Sir Edward Snelson [*Sir Edward Snelson* v. *Judges of High Court of West Pakistan* (1961) 1 P.S.C.R. 193], then Law Secretary of the Central Government who was convicted of contempt of the High Court, and the conviction was maintained in appeal by the Supreme Court. The fault there found was that in a speech addressed to a group of subordinate officials in the Central Secretariat he had made observations concerning the exercise of the writ jurisdiction by the High Court which were found to be derogatory to the dignity of that Court. The burden of his lecture in the offending part was that the High Courts had, despite all efforts to advise them correctly in this respect, chosen to interfere with the structure and working of the Executive. There had been a number of Writs issued by the High Court in service matters and other such cases and these were represented as being an unwarranted excursion into the reserved field of Executive power. Having myself sat on the case, I can say that the opinion so expressed was vitiated by the incorrect assumption that the body of persons constituting the public service is itself the State. What provided some slight basis for the view expressed in the lecture was that a number of Writs issued by the High Courts had been recalled on re-examination of the matter in the Supreme Court. But it was clear that the criticism was misguided and misdirected and that the language employed was of a lowering type which the High Court could not be expected to tolerate, if it was to retain its position in the organisation and functioning of the State.

I have said before and I may say briefly here that an equally effective method of correction of the exercise of the public power, which is moreover free of all danger of bringing into conflict two of the major organs of the State, is that of the administrative Tribunal which is in vogue in France, in most of the Continental countries and in many countries of the Middle East, as well as in all ex-French colonies. The system includes a hierarchy of Tribunals headed by the Council of State or *Conseil d'État* as it is called in France. These Tribunals are staffed not by Judges but by the most experienced public servants who have been withdrawn from their particular departments and permanently absorbed into these Tribunals. All cases where the exercise of public power over citizens has given rise to complaint are referable to these Tribunals in the simplest form and at the smallest cost. The burden upon the complainant of establishing his case is reduced to the minimum by the practice of these Tribunals, which are equipped with their own machinery of enquiry, and in the course of time have gained the power to procure all relevant information from the administrative departments. Being themselves fully experienced in the technique and the difficulties of the administration, the members of these Tribunals can place themselves in the position of the official concerned to appreciate the nature and the quality of his acts. They are familiar also with the laws, rules and regulations, and how they are to be interpreted for their due application. Having themselves been in contact with the public, they can appreciate also the position of the complainant and they are thus very well placed to provide a solution for each question arising before them, and to give wise direction as to the proper attitude and action in the case, without giving offence in any direction. Being strictly a judicial body within the executive sphere, they can be trusted to exercise their powers consistently with all the requirements of the executive and, in the course of the centuries since Napoleon first laid down a proper organisation for these Tribunals, they have developed a reputation for acting always with a due sense of justice for the citizens as well. Having myself sat in the Superior Courts of this country for a considerable number of years, I can say that it is no pleasure to a Judge to be obliged to criticise a governmental action at any level, but a Judge is a servant and agent for enforcement of the rule of law, and he cannot deny his function. Nothing can be further from the truth than the criticism sometimes heard when an important case of this kind has been decided in a Superior Court, that the judiciary is operating as a State within the State.

Now in Pakistan we have Article 98, and the ancient names of the Writs have been eliminated from the Constitution, although the categories distinguish themselves easily under those names, and they will always be used with their specific meanings in judgments. In Article 98 the true content of each of the major Writs has been set out in the long form of words. The object probably was to attain certainty as to the limits within which the Courts may act. Previously, in each case, the Courts referred to precedents from England, the United States, India and several other countries to determine whether they had power to interfere in the case before them. It is perhaps supposed that this may not be necessary now that the powers are stated not by label, but by full expression. However it is to be remembered that the superior Courts have the power and duty of interpreting the words of the Constitution and it is difficult to suppose that earlier precedents will lose their value as guidance. In the new Article there are verbal changes in respect of the availability of the writ to public servants, for the protection of their rights in the public service. It is possible that some of you may have a special interest in the matter, but since it is quite likely that the relevant provisions will come up for interpretation in one or more cases before the Supreme Court, it is desirable that I should avoid saying anything here regarding the possible interpretation of the words used.

As you are all aware the Constitution has held out in plain words a full promise to every person in Pakistan that he will be governed in accordance with the Constitution and the law. There can be no more clear pronouncement that the rule of law is to prevail in every sphere of the public administration and public life. You, who have been selected to occupy in due course, important positions in the public administration, are charged with the duty of implementing this constitutional dictate, through your actions, and to ensure that it is equally observed in their actions by all your subordinates. Over the greatest part of the field of administration, guidance is now to be found in Statutes and in rules and regulations which are daily becoming more intricate. The final interpretation of what is meant in a particular case by the words of a Statute is of course reserved to the Courts, but the effort of the law-makers and of the Legislative Assemblies is always to use language which is clear in its meaning. They generally adopt terms already in use, which have usually undergone interpretation by the Superior Courts. In a difficult case, of course, it would be necessary to make some research into the law as laid down by those Courts, before action is taken, but for the most part an executive officer does not require such aid. But he does need to see the law before he acts and here I may perhaps share with you the advice which was given to me by the second Deputy Commissioner under whom I had the privilege of being trained. This was Mr. Jenkins who later became Sir Evan Jenkins, and at the close of his very distinguished career became Governor of the then Punjab. The advice which he gave to his Assistant Commissioners was that in every case which came before them under a new Statute which they had not previously studied they must not be content to look at the section which had been cited but must read through the entire law as well as the statement of Objects and Reasons, to get full understanding of its purpose and how it would apply to the particular case. It meant that if one was looking at a land revenue case one had to go through the entire Punjab Land Revenue Act which runs into over a hundred sections, and equally so with the Tenancy Act and many other Acts. But it certainly developed the capacity to understand the objectives of the Act and the machinery provided, so that the action one took was not upon a few words contained in a section, but was in line with the true intent of the Legislature as applicable to the particular case. It developed also capacity for attempting to make sets of rules and even later on to draft a law and that too is a function which may perhaps be entrusted to some of the ablest among yourselves. I regret that legislative training is not more regularly given to all officers in the superior service, particularly those directly concerned with the administration of public affairs under Statutes. To understand now a law is made, how rules are made thereunder, to grasp the significance of the substantive provisions and the technical terms employed these are great aids towards extension of the mental grasp over the whole administrative responsibility which is covered by that law. It is also of value to officers entrusted with the administration of departments under laws to study the main principles of statutory interpretation. Throughout the life of a superior administrator, he will be called upon to interpret and apply law. These principles are by no means intricate and the subject is of absorbing interest to anyone who has an interest in law and legal matters. There was perhaps a time when a man could be a highly efficient administrator without carrying any great burden of legal knowledge but today that is not possible. Any attempt to impose administrative authority by a person who is ignorant of the law governing the matter would involve the risk of violating the Second Article of the Constitution, that which places the whole country under the rule of law.

Address of Chief Justice A. R. Cornelius on the Relation of Political Theory to Administration, January 23, 1965

[*Explanatory Note.* In this address, Chief Justice Cornelius combines several strands of thought to which he had given attention in scattered judgments and commentaries. After defining the nature and function of society, the state, and community (following Jacques Maritain), he emphasizes that the liberties to which man is entitled as embodied in the ten fundamental rights in the first amendment to the 1962 Constitution, though adopted from other constitutions, yet can be shown to derive from Islamic values. These religious values must create the conditions for the attainment of liberty and must activate religious conscience in the exercise of political and executive power. Public administrators share with the judiciary the responsibility of infusing the work of government with such religiously derived ethical values. He thus suggests an ideological underpinning for bureaucratic efficiency and seeks its roots in Islam. This address was given at the National Institute of Public Administration in Karachi on January 23, 1965.]

I would like to say that I greatly appreciate the invitation to address the trainees at this session. I am aware that I do not qualify to give them advice such as will help them in the handling of situations, or in meeting exigencies and emergencies that may arise in the performance of their duties. It has never fallen to me to practise that art, nor have I received from my seniors at any stage, much advice on these lines. I remember a British deputy commissioner under whom I served once telling me that in a situation which involved legal complexities, but required immediate decision, it often paid to affect a certain stupidity, that is to say, insensitiveness to arguments presented. I never had occasion to try out that advice. The same officer at a later stage, when I had gone over to the judicial side, gave me some advice about how to dispose of insolvency cases wholesale, on some technical ground, which he had been able to spot, and thus to lighten the burden. That advice too I never tried, because it seemed clear that when justice was sought, justice had to be done. It was hardly right to treat suppliants for justice as nuisances to be brushed out of the way, however tedious and irritating their cases or their behavior. Between those who bring their conflicts to the courts, and the courts themselves, there was direct mutuality of obligation. It slowly grew upon me that the assurance of justice in such affairs was an essential element in the stability and success of an administration, and that the image of such an assurance can be dissipated even by a single action of denial or negligence in the dispensation of justice. To maintain that assurance is a necessary condition for the advancement of the human community from a state of savagery, in which power and caprice are synonymous, to the condition of general responsibility which is civilization. So, if it is guidance in *ad hoc* techniques for the maintenance of personal authority which you seek, you will not find it from a judge, who is an instrument for the elucidation and implementation of principles. Nor can a judge enliven his discourse with fruity anecdotes about successes he has achieved in getting the better of those with whom he has had to deal. So you will forgive me if what I say has a quality of dryness. It is never found that the seed has the same outward attractiveness as the plant, much less the flower or the fruit out of which it develops.

On the last occasion when I spoke at this Institute, I treated of the character of paternalistic administration using the Analects of Confucius as representative of the best rules devised for establishing that form of government. I pointed out that twenty-five centuries after Confucius, governments now exist rather to promote "fraternalism," that is, to ensure equality and equality of opportunity among the population. I touched briefly on the requirements of our Constitution to indicate that if in the words of Confucius, the objective be simply to "put the people right" that purpose could now only be served, and much more efficiently than in earlier times, by recourse to the judicial method in the conduct of affairs so far as possible. I mentioned also that in certain countries, of which today I might name the United States of America, there are now statutes requiring that administrative procedures should include the judicial process at all necessary stages. At one time I thought that I might today talk to you about the provisions contained in the Federal Administrative Procedure Act of the United States, but later I reflected that Confucius had said very wisely that "he who does not hold the office does not discuss the policy," and I thought better of it. In any case that statute can easily be made available to you for study, as an accepted norm of administrative practice in an advanced state.

At best, of course, judicial process is only a means to an end, so I decided to place before you in a general way, a short and necessarily superficial analysis of what one important end of administration, in the light of our present Constitution, might be. I thought that it might later be useful for the trainees, in their work within the different spheres or pockets of administration to which they belong, to hear my views on this subject. I have spoken of "community" and "policy." These and concepts such as "state," "nation," "body politic," and "political society" are of great currency today. I would like to begin by attempting to give a meaning to some of these expressions. Nothing that I say is at all original. These matters have been examined by a great many learned persons for many centuries.

A "community" as I understand it is a thing of natural growth. It carries a biological sense. In a large sense, going beyond mere blood-ties, a "community" is built round a central group of equals who enjoy somewhat superior rights, with accompanying ancillary groups necessary for making provision for them all. An ancestrally owned village together with its serving groups may be an example. They are held together by a consensus as to the "common good," which is not concerned merely with material things. It contains besides the sense of providing the material needs, including security, consciousness of ancient and beneficial customs, laws and freedoms, of institutions, of tradition and inherited culture, of the distinction between right and wrong, and what is fine and what is base in human character; it contains also the civic conscience in the sense of mutual obligation which is the seed of political consciousness. Appreciation of such a consensus as to the "common good" among the people to be administered, is of primary importance to a good administrator. What is true of a community is equally true, but in an enlarged sense, of a nation, which, in one aspect, is a community composed of smaller communities. Here material interests and their interplay have to be dealt with and managed over the entire territory. Reconciliation of the needs, spiritual, social and material of all the included communities is a prime consideration. All these communities which have been woven together into a nation, are united by incorporeal forces of great power, among which are included awareness of past history and tradition and of cultural and religious ties. Consciousness of greatness acquired from sharing the size and importance of the nation: high hopes for the future in the nation's march in the international community. Collectively, and apart from the material and organizational aspects, these factors may be described as the national "mystique." It is an indefinable feeling of sharing in that which is great in visible aspects, and noble in those which are none the less estimable because they are intangible.

The "community" is differentiated from a "society" by the fact that a society belongs more markedly to the cerebral sphere, and is to be appreciated in an intellectual sense. As of communities so of societies there may be and are a great many in every nation. But just as a nation can be described as a greater community, so it also qualifies to be described as a great society, that is, a political society or body politic. Within that political society, there is to be found in every duly administered state, a smaller society which is the "state," that is the administrative agency which by entrustment, concerns itself with the advancement of the "common good" of all the included communities, as well as of the whole nation regarded as a community, through the recognised administrative processes. The entire people form the political society, with the "state" at its head operating in both political and administrative aspects.

You are all aware that the organization of the "state" in different nations has assumed different forms according to the consensus developed within the political society or body politic of each nation as to the entrustment, or where there has been no entrustment, the exercise, of the public power by the administrative agency. In Pakistan ever since its inception, what has been accepted is the democratic form, which represents, in the long march of history, the culminating point of perfection so far achieved in the fulfilment of the character of the people, through its overall organization, for the advancement of the "common good." The body politic as a society is generally pluralist in character, that is to say it is not homogeneous throughout its fabric, but is composed of communities showing recognized difference from each other. Our political society contains a great many such communities, and its organization has necessarily to take account of this quality, namely pluralism.

At the same time, in a modern democracy, it is accepted that in respect of rights and duties, this society is an aggregate of individuals, and therefore in all material respects, the individual is entitled to individual treatment under law. The justification for law as a technique in human affairs is, as to a great part, derived from, and bound up with this conception. This right to individual treatment is the case no matter how strong may be the bonds of race or religion, which bind a person within his particular community. His inclusion within that community is biological in character. In the body politic, he belongs as of right and choice, and through personal as well as general consciousness that as a human being, he is entitled to certain freedoms, and is under the corresponding obligations, to the country as well as to all other citizens.

These aspects of political obligation are formulated in the governing instrument of the body politic of the Pakistan Nation, namely, the Constitution, in the shape of Fundamental Rights of which the text is easily available. The Fundamental Rights ensure, by provision in detail, the right to life and liberty, to freedom of contract as to personal services, to freedom of assembly and association, to freedom of speech, freedom in regard to trade, business or profession, freedom to own and enjoy property, freedom in respect of religion, language, script and culture, the right to equality before the law, to equal opportunity of entry into the public service, and to enjoy public facilities and finally, freedom from the curse of untouchability, which was known only in pre-partition India. By providing assurance of these rights to every person, the political society of Pakistan gains the quality of being personalist in character.

Finally, a point which in importance transcends all the rest, the political society of Pakistan is "theocentric"—a term to be firmly distinguished from the epithet "theocratic" which certain persons who ought to have known better, have chosen to apply in a politically derogatory sense to our country. When the Constitution in its preamble accepts that sovereignty vests "in Almighty Allah alone" and that the authority of the people is a sacred trust from the Almighty, when it declares that Pakistan is to be "a democratic State based on Islamic principles of social justice" and that "the principles of democracy, freedom, equality, tolerance and social justice, as enunciated by Islam" are to prevail, it speaks with a clarity which should have stilled any such doubts. There is no entrustment of rule in Pakistan to the agencies of religion to be spelt out of those words. In truth, they are operative to make all of us, citizens of Pakistan, irrespective of our personal religion, followers of Islam in the sphere of political obligation. They have effect to bind us by the religious conscience in all our activities as members of the political society. In other words, within the rational order of humanity, where it deals with the concrete aspects of human affairs and sets them in the direction of the public good, there is introduced a restraint against evil and excess, which is found in no other Constitution. It is the restraint of religious conscience, in the field of ethical behavior, on the secular side.

The sovereignty of the Almighty, which the Constitution, an essentially political instrument, acknowledges also imparts a juridical concept. Likewise, the public power or "the authority exercisable by the people," "democracy," "social justice" and all the Fundamental Rights are concepts of a political character. By the expression "theocentric" which I have employed, I mean that the political society which the Constitution envisages is one which is built round the idea of one God, and that the will of God is to prevail among the people, through their political organization in the way of democracy, for the advancement of their "common good" as a nation. All agencies within that organization are to operate with a sense of profound responsibility to the Almighty for the discharge of their respective trusts. Under that major obligation, they are to act so as to ensure social justice, freedom, equality, tolerance and all the other entitlements and franchises now formulated in the Fundamental Rights but as enunciated by the religion of Islam. Like the call to prayer which resounds five times a day through the length and breadth of Pakistan, the call of the Constitution to the political society of Pakistan enjoins its members, and in particular all those who operate that society, to "hasten to the good, hasten to the true"; to cleave to that which is true and honest and of good report.

It seems regrettable that so far we in Pakistan have accepted the formulation of the Fundamental Rights as being derived exclusively from earlier enunciations in other Constitutions, mainly that of the United States of America. I feel no doubt that the basic principle underlying each of these Fundamental Rights can be shown to derive from the dictates contained in the Holy Scriptures of Islam, and that in course of time men of learning will be found who will expound on this aspect of our Constitution, and show convincingly that this is so. Even though the differences between Islamic ethical values, and the values which are built into the Fundamental Rights of other constitutions, are probably confined to matters of small detail, yet the members of the body politic of Pakistan are entitled to the confidence and comfort of knowing that they are following the lights of their own State religion.

I have said already that the State in its true conception is composed of that part of the political society, which is the agency, by entrustment, for the implementation of the meaning and principles of the written requirements of the Constitution in order to secure the "common good" of the entire people. This trust is to be discharged through the processes of administration. All the administrative agencies within the body politic, however high or low they may be, are thus included within the concept of the state. In a special sense, their operation under law is a part of the constitutional law of the country. They operate in a sphere which represents the most active conflict of forces between personal interests, small and large, on the true development of which the advancement of the nation and the "common good" is based, and on the other hand, the duty of maintenance of the general freedoms and rights. The most apparent signs occur when there is conflict between government and the governed, but there are such conflicts prevailing in the entire sphere of human relations, which require continuous treatment by administrative process, for their proper regulation. In all such cases, the public power is to be exercised and it has to be exercised so as to satisfy the citizen that he is being dealt with in conformance with his ideas of liberty, fair dealing and good administration.

The citizen can only hold those ideas subject to the over-riding principles laid down in the Constitution which I have endeavoured to place before you. You, who are to exercise administrative power, that is to say, power within the body politic, will do so as part of the administrative complex which is the state. It is immaterial whether you are a public servant or employed in a private or public corporation or company. The exercise of power in relation to your fellow-citizens, under the disciplines of law and rules, makes you an element in the machinery of the administration of the affairs of the country. Upon you will fall this duty to satisfy the citizens as well as the particular constitutional obligation which it falls to you to discharge. It is possible, I think, to say that the task of reconciliation will not be difficult. The very powerful agency of religion is there in support to secure the approval of the citizens, provided you are meeting the constitutional requirements in full, since these requirements are based upon the dictates of holy religion. I might quote here a saying of the great political philosopher of Islam, Imam El-Ghazali, who said, "Religion and administration are twins, one of which cannot do without the other." That statement is entirely true with reference to political society, under the Constitution of Pakistan. You, as components of the administrative complex which is the State, will have to provide by your actions for the advancement of democracy, freedom, equality, tolerance and the other Fundamental Rights, not merely in their secular sense, but as these norms are understood and elucidated, in terms of the ethical principles of Islam. That imports a duty to inquire in respect of each of these matters, or at least generally with reference to the larger concept of social justice, in which they are all included, what indeed are the relevant dictates of Islam as contained in the Scriptures. That inquiry should provide for you an avenue of study, which I feel sure many of you will undertake with devotion and even joy. It will be a rewarding study, for if anything can give greater satisfaction to an administrator than to understand the highest principles and standards which govern him, it is the knowledge that he has fulfilled his responsibility in accordance with those principles and standards. I have endeavoured to show you that the Constitution of Pakistan sets standards and lays down principles, which you are under obligation to follow, which are at the highest level conceivable to man, and, in my belief, higher than the corresponding obligation upon your counterparts working under any other Constitution. I pray that you may all achieve success in your careers, and that your success will be earned by ardent effort to rise to the full height of your function.

Glossary

The historical development of many of the terms explained here can be found in such sources as four studies by Bernard S. Cohn, (1) "From Indian Status to British Contract," *Journal of Economic History*, XXI (1961), 613–628; (2) "The Initial British Impact on India, A Case Study of the Benares Region," *The Journal of Asian Studies*, XIX (1960), 418–431; (3) "The British in Benares: A Nineteenth Century Colonial Society," *Comparative Studies in Society and History*, IV (1962), 169–199; (4) "Some Notes on Law and Change in North India," *Economic Development and Cultural Change*, VIII (1959), 79–93; and in (5) Muhammad Basheer Ahmad, *The Administration of Justice in Medieval India* (reprinted in Karachi, 1951, from Aligarh, 1941); (6) H. H. Wilson, *A Glossary of Judicial and Revenue Terms* (London, 1855); (7) Henry Yule and A. C. Burnwell, *Hobson-Jobson: A Glossary of Colloquial Anglo-Indian Words*. . . , edited by William Crooke (new ed.; London, 1903).

Lengthier descriptions of administrative procedure and organization in which duties of various officials are defined can be found in the two manuals by Sir James M. Douie, (8) *Punjab Settlement Manual* (Lahore, 1961); (9) *Punjab Land Administration Manual* (Lahore, 1960). Also useful is (10) *District Office Manual*, Punjab (Lahore, 1960).

Contemporary usage in Pakistan is emphasized in this glossary. No effort is made to trace the development of these terms, though this would be an exercise of considerable fascination. When, in the interests of clarity, it seems helpful to refer to earlier usage, such reference is made. When further reference to sources, especially those listed above, is indicated, such sources are cited by the author's (or first author's) last name followed by a number corresponding to the item number given above. Such citation does not mean that the definition here given is derived from that source; it merely suggests that earlier usage can be found in the cited source.

allama. A Persian Muslim title meaning "Great Learned," indicating a scholar of the highest Qur'anic learning who is also well versed in secular and Western knowledge. In modern Pakistan the term, used as a form of address, commands greater prestige than such titles as *maulvi, maulana, mullah,* or *imam.* The term *imam,* however, if derived from the Middle East or if used by a Middle East Muslim, may be equal to or higher than the term *allama.* In Pakistan this form of address has been accorded only a few scholars such as Allama Sir Mohammed Iqbal, Allama Mashriki, and Allama Alla-ud-Din Siddiqi.

babu. Originally a term of respect or title used more in Bengal than elsewhere and more commonly (though not exclusively) among Hindus than among Muslims. While the term connotes a status roughly equivalent to that of *maulvi* (in fact, the two terms were used as equivalents on the printed character rolls of the East Pakistan Civil Service), the two terms are otherwise not comparable. *Babu* connotes a government clerk who speaks, reads, and writes English, whereas *maulvi* connotes Qur'anic rather than English learning. The term, *babu,* now has a pejorative connotation, suggesting the outlook of a petty government functionary; hence, "babu-mentality." Before independence, the title "Mr." was reserved for British and Indian officers of the ICS or men with comparable status, and the term *babu* was used to refer to office clerks considerably below officer class. *Babu* is no longer used as an official title, having been replaced by the title "Mr." in many instances, thus upsetting the rigid distinctions of pre-partition days.

chaudhry. The term has various meanings, all suggestive of a town or village person of some local importance: usually a landholder, in some areas ranking higher than a *zamindar,* and in other areas somewhat below a *zamindar* (see Cohn, 4, p. 87). In the Punjab, *chaudhry* was the title accorded a "rural notable" to whom the government had given an *inam,* i.e., a cash grant or a gift of tax-free land as remuneration for service to government (see Douie, 9, p. 38).

chaukidar. Watchman or guard employed by either a private or public agency. In cities and towns, *chaukidars,* armed with a *lathi,* a whistle, and often a shotgun, are privately employed to guard homes and office buildings. In villages, the *chaukidar* is a semi-official constable.

dalal. Also commonly called "tout." The *dalal* is an intermediary between a *vakil* and potential clients. In rural areas and cities alike, the *dalal* encourages litigation wherever he senses the beginnings of an altercation. The *dalal* is not officially recognized by the courts, and some courts have signs "No Touts Allowed" prominently displayed. The *dalal* nevertheless seems to be an indispensable agent, in part because he is a cultural and linguistic go-between for the legal practitioner who practices Western law and a potential clientele which knows neither English nor Western law.

gymkhana. Refers to a clubhouse, the social equivalent of the country club in the United States. Facilities for sports, dining, and other social activities are provided by the *gymkhana*. Before independence the *gymkhanas* of major cities like Lahore and Karachi were reserved exclusively for British officers. Now, they are clubs largely for well-to-do Pakistani and cater to a society which is Western-oriented, somewhat secular in its religious orientation, and thereby separated from the masses.

jirga. A council of tribal elders, typically five in number, assembled to decide certain types of criminal cases, especially those involving blood feuds. Found exclusively in the area of the former Northwest Frontier Province in West Pakistan, the *jirga* was officially recognized by the Frontier Crimes Regulation of 1901 and continues to be widely used as an institution of justice.

kanungo. A local administrative official who supervises the crop inspection work of several *patwaris*. Each *tehsil* has an office *kanungo* who is the *tehsildar's* land-records clerk and who keeps statistical land records for the *tehsil*. He in turn is supervised by the district (*sadar*) *kanungo* (see 10, p. 5). Field *kanungos* are on tour most of the time checking on the work of the *patwaris* of several circles.

karakuli topi. A fur or simulated fur hat worn especially by Muslims in West Pakistan. *Topi* is the generic word for hat. *Karakuli* refers to astrakhan, or, as it is now rendered in English, caracul fur, the wool of very young or stillborn lambs from Central Asia. This fur, or a cloth made to resemble it, is one of several materials used to make a cap known in Pakistan as the "Jinnah cap" after the nation's founder who usually wore one.

lal kitab. The literal meaning is red book. It refers to a book, invariably with a red cover, used in local administration. The *lal kitab* contains consolidated statistics about a single village. Entries are made in a vernacular rather than in English.

lathi. A sturdy staff of bamboo, about five feet long and from one to two inches in diameter. Often one or both ends are weighted with lead. It is used by policemen and *chaukidars* both as a club and as a fence-like barrier to push back crowds. The term *"lathi*-charge," meaning an attack by police using the *lathi,* is commonly used in the press and in official publications.

madrasa. Muslim religious school at primary, elementary, and less frequently at secondary levels. Instruction is almost entirely in Islamic subjects. The report of the Commission on National Education suggested that the curricula of these schools was excessively narrow and that they should "adapt their curriculum to the requirements of our complex society and present Islam in a way acceptable to the national mind" (p. 279). In West Pakistan such schools, fewer in number than in East Pakistan, are called *maktab.* They function mostly at the primary level, the *dar-ul-ulum* being the school educating up to the high school level.

maulana. The title accorded a Muslim teacher or scholar learned in the Qur'an, Muslim law, and literature. In prestige this title is below *allama* and usually is above *maulvi* in distinction. A *maulana* is customarily addressed as *Maulana sahib* or by his full name following the title.

maulvi. A Muslim title accorded a religious man usually knowledge-able in the Qur'an, but usually not of the same level of learning as a *maulana.* A *maulvi* usually has memorized the Qur'an but knows less about Muslim law, philosophy, and theology than a *maulana.* It is used, as is *maulana,* as a term of address.

mofussil. Refers to rural areas, the provinces or outcountry as distinct from the city or large town. In a district the whole area except the district headquarters and towns of comparable size is referred to as the *mofussil.*

mukhtar. An authorized agent or attorney, especially in criminal matters. *Mukhtars* are found almost exclusively in East Pakistan. They are not trained at the LL.B. level. Of *mukhtars* the report of the Law Reform Commission said: "this class has provided a cheap system of legal advice for litigants in subordinate courts. However, the number of students taking up a regular LL.B. course has increased sufficiently to obviate the necessity of retaining an inferior class of lawyers in the field of practice" (p. 121).

mukhtiarkar. A local official sometimes belonging to the provincial civil service cadre, found exclusively in the Sind of West Pakistan. He performs mainly administrative duties in a *taluka* connected with the collection of revenue. Some *mukhtiarkars* are given powers of class II magistrates and perform quasi-judicial functions relating to land revenue. The Civil List for West Pakistan shows some seventy *mukhtiarkars* in the Sind. The position is equivalent to that of *tehsildar* found elsewhere in West Pakistan.

mullah. A generic term indicating a class of men who perform Muslim religious duties, particularly in villages. *Mullah,* unlike such related terms as *maulana, maulvi,* and *allama,* is seldom used as a title of address. Sometimes a *mullah* is addressed as *maulvi sahib.* Usually he is a person whose Islamic learning is limited to having memorized the Qur'an and being able to recite it. *Mullahs* usually wield considerable influence over the attitudes and behavior of villages. Yule (7, p. 579) reports that the term was used "for a man who reads the Korān in a house for 40 days, after a death. When oaths are administered on the Korān, the servitor who held the book was called *Mullā Korāni.*" The *mullah* is regarded by Western-oriented Pakistani as being an iconoclastic, uneducated person who stands in the way of the enlightened progress of Islam. By the villagers he is often regarded as the final authority in religious and temporal matters.

munshi. Derived from the Persian *insha,* meaning essay, the term refers to someone especially concerned with drafting letters, petitions, or briefs. A *munshi* is a superior "petitions-writer" whose skill goes beyond mere copying and extends to originality, literary style, and, in legal practice, to the rudiments of research in law. Successful advocates, or *vakils,* who maintain an office staff employ one or more *munshis* who serve as legal research assistants and writers of briefs. Often an advocate is accompanied in the courtroom by one or more *munshis* who look up references as he argues the case and generally assist him in the proceeding. In some areas, such as the former princely state of Bahawalpur, *munshi* is a particularly honorific term among persons associated with the practice of law, and *vakils* who are especially esteemed are addressed also as *munshi,* e.g., Munshi Abdul Kabir Vakil. A more common use of the term *munshi* among foreigners is as a title given a tutor in Urdu, Hindi, or some other vernacular. In the text of this book, however, the term is used to refer to a legal assistant.

munsif. A Persian term, the first use of which is reported for 1793. Originally engaged as low-ranking civil judges trying petty revenue cases including those between a landholder and tenant (see Ahmad, 5, p. 130), *munsifs* are now found almost exclusively in East Pakistan where they are officers in the judicial branch of the provincial civil service. The East Pakistan Civil List for 1961–1962 lists 166 *munsifs,* all with LL.B. degrees. *Munsifs* are regarded as subordinate judges for civil cases. The Law Reform Commission recommended that they be redesignated as class II civil judges with power to try civil cases involving amounts up to Rs. 5,000.

nikah. A ceremony associated with the signing of a contract between a Muslim male and Muslim female leading to permanent conjugal life. Although commonly regarded as a marriage, this ceremony is essentially a civil contract witnessed and certified by Muslim religious leaders, such as *maulanas, maulvis,* or *mullahs.* Negotiations relating to the amount of dower and maintenance are usually conducted by *vakils* engaged by the two contracting parties. The person who registers the marriage is called *nikah-khwan;* the registration certificate is called *nikah-nama. Nikah* figured prominently in the controversy between orthodox Muslims and secular-oriented Muslims in discussions leading to the *Report of the Commission on Marriage and Family Laws* released in 1956. The majority held that *nikah* could be registered by a civil official; a dissenting view, shared by most orthodox Muslims, held that *nikah* should be performed only by a spiritual leader or teacher. The Muslim Family Laws Ordinance VIII of 1961, passed in consequence of the commission's report, provides for *nikah* being performed by those learned in Arabic and in Muslim marriage law. The administrative arrangements involved in *nikah* registration figured prominently in a well-known case decided by both the High Court of West Pakistan and the Supreme Court: *Syed Ali Nawaz Shah Gardezi* v. *Lt. Col. Muhammad Yusuf Khan,* PLD 1962 Lah. 558; *Syed Ali Nawaz Gardezi* v. *Lt. Col. Muhammad Yusuf Khan,* PLD 1962 SC 465.

panchayat. A council of five village elders used to settle minor local disputes and, to some extent, to decide local administrative matters. It is an important term in India, where the rural development movement is denominated *panchayati raj.* The term is no longer widely used in Pakistan, having been replaced in both provinces by the term union council. *Panchayats* organized within Hindu castes for the adjudication of caste matters still exist in Hindu villages in East Pakistan and in the Sind (see Cohn, 1, p. 617).

patwari. A local revenue official employed on a full-time basis for a circle of villages. Such circles are formed on the basis of population and *khasra* numbers. In densely populated areas a *patwari* may have only one village in his circle, but usually he has four or five. A group of perhaps as many as twenty *patwaris* are supervised by a field *kanungo.* The *patwari* is responsible for maintaining a record of crops grown at every harvest, keeping the record of land rights up to date, and preparing statistical records based on crop inspection, record of mutations, and record of right. The *patwari* is required to keep a diary, or *roznamcha,* and a workbook on such matters as relations of landowners and tenants (see Douie, 9, pp. 98 ff., 125–135, 162–163).

purdah. From the Persian *parda,* meaning curtain, *purdah* refers to the practice of concealment of women by various means, ranging in completeness from wearing a *burkah,* which conceals the entire person, to wearing a thin veil over the lower face. It is common to refer to a woman as being "in purdah." The term "purdah lady" is also common, being often used in court judgments in which such matters are discussed. There are varying degrees of strictness in the practice of *purdah,* ranging from village practice in the Northwest Frontier where a woman seldom ventures beyond her home or village and is always in *burkah* to more relaxed practice in Lahore, Karachi, and elsewhere where an unveiled woman, while not seen alone, ventures out in a group or in the company of her husband or father. There are some women in larger cities who do not practice *purdah* in any form.

sherwani. An outer coat worn by men, it reaches below the knees, has a high collar, and is close-fitting. It may be made of various materials and come in different colors, or even in patterned worsted or homespun. It was commonly worn by Mr. Jinnah with the *karakuli topi;* hence, both are considered "national dress" and are often prescribed for state functions. The *sherwani* was worn especially by Muslims of the Lucknow area and increased in popularity with the migration of refugees to Pakistan from that area. It quickly became associated with Pakistani nationalism. Black (and in summer, white) *sherwani* are considered the protocol equivalent of evening dress (either black or white tie) and are worn by some Pakistani at appropriate state and diplomatic functions. The wearing of the *sherwani* is not, however, limited to any class in society; it can be seen in varying degrees of elegance among all but the lowest classes, and in various fabrics for informal day wear as well as for formal evening attire. It is prescribed dress for students at the University of Peshawar and is not uncommon in Dacca during the cold season. It has almost disappeared from use in large cities except for occasions such as marriage festivals or patriotic celebrations. It is, however, worn as standard daily attire by the governor of West Pakistan and by some tribal *maliks* and *sardars* in the Northwest Frontier area.

tapedar. An administrative official in the Sind who has duties almost identical to those of the *patwari* in the Punjab. In addition to certain duties relating to revenue administration, the *tapedar* now has some duties in colonization and land reform matters. The *tapedar* has jurisdiction over a circle of villages, i.e., an administrative grouping below the level of *taluka.* Hence, several *tapedars* come under the supervision of a single *talukdar.*

tehsil. An administrative subdivision of a district, principally a revenue unit embracing a number of villages, sometimes as many as seven hundred. Usually there are from three to six *tehsils* in a district. The chief administrative officer for revenue work is the *tehsildar* who is assisted by one or several *naib-tehsildars.* In the Sind, the equivalent of the *tehsil* is *taluka* and its chief official is the *talukdar* (see Cohn, 2, p. 422, and 3, pp. 190–191; Douie, 9, p. 97). In East Pakistan neither *tehsil* nor *taluka* is the term used. There the unit immediately below the district is the subdivision, of which there are an average of three per district. These subdivisions are further divided into *thanas.*

thana. An administrative entity in East Pakistan below the subdivision. Formerly the *thanas* were primarily police stations, but they are now important units for other administrative responsibilities. In West Pakistan, *thana* is a police jurisdiction headed by a subinspector of police locally known as *thanedar.* In West Pakistan the *thana* often overlaps the revenue area, *tehsil.*

vakil. A Persian term widely used to refer to a legal practitioner allowed to practice in courts at the *tehsil* and district levels. *Vakils* conduct cases before the courts of district judges, *tehsildars,* district magistrates, and others at similar levels, while legal practitioners practicing before the High Court and the Supreme Court are known generically as "advocates." Yet advocates are often addressed *"vakil sahib"* since this is a generic term for law practitioner (see Cohn, 1, p. 626; Ahmad, 5, p. 163).

wallah. An adjectival affixed to the end of words and denoting doer, agent, practitioner, vendor, thus: *lukri-wallah*—a wood vendor; *pan-wallah*—vendor of betel leaves; *garhi-wallah*—driver of a cart. Hence, the title of G. O. Trevelyan's *The Competition Wallah* (London, 1864), meaning an ICS officer who entered service by competitive examination. *Wallah* is commonly found as the last part of names of families near Bombay, especially Parsi families. Sometimes it is added to the English designation of an occupation and both become the family name. Thus: Sodawaterwallah. See, for example, a Pakistan Supreme Court case, *Abdul Hamid* v. *Abbas Bhai Abdul Hussain Sodawaterwalla,* (1962) 1 P.S.C.R. 86.

waqf (auqaf). Muslim religious properties including mosques and holy places or "land dedicated for religious, pious or charitable purpose." The plural of *waqf* is *auqaf.* A substantial body of case law relating to the administration of these properties has developed.

Such administration is an important activity of the provincial governments which have secretariat departments for *auqaf* usually headed by experienced civil officers rather than by religious leaders. This supervision of *auqaf* by government is one of the few areas in Pakistan in which government supervision of religious matters is found.

zamindar. A landholder who pays revenue to the government, such revenue being usually collected by the *lambardar* who deposits the money in the district treasury. The meaning of *zamindar* varies with tenancy laws in different parts of Pakistan. In some parts it indicates merely a person who cultivates his own land. In some areas of West Pakistan, *zamindars* are powerful feudal landlords in effective control of several villages. Before the land reforms of 1958, some *zamindars* had estates of several hundreds of square miles. Since the land reforms, however, tracts owned by one person have been restricted to five hundred acres of irrigated land or one thousand acres of unirrigated land.

Index